S0-BDQ-479

THE BLUE GUIDES

Countries **Austria**
Belgium and Luxembourg
Channel Islands
China
Corsica
Crete
Cyprus
Czechoslovakia
Denmark
Egypt
England
France
France: Burgundy
Western Germany
Greece
Holland
Hungary
Ireland
Northern Italy
Southern Italy
Malta and Gozo
Morocco
Portugal
Scotland
Sicily
Spain
Switzerland
Turkey: the Aegean and Mediterranean Coasts
Wales
Yugoslavia

Cities **Athens and Environs**
Barcelona
Boston and Cambridge
Florence
Istanbul
Jerusalem
London
Moscow and Leningrad
New York
Oxford and Cambridge
Paris and Versailles
Rome and Environs
Venice

Themes **Churches and Chapels of Northern England**
Churches and Chapels of Southern England
Gardens of England
Literary Britain and Ireland
Museums and Galleries of London
Victorian Architecture in Britain

Dolbardarn Castle by Richard Wilson (National Gallery of Wales)

BLUE GUIDE

WALES

John Tomes

A & C Black
London

W W Norton
New York

Seventh edition 1990
Reprinted with corrections 1992

Published by A & C Black (Publishers) Limited
35 Bedford Row, London, WC1R 4JH

© A & C Black (Publishers) Limited 1990

Published in the United States of America by
WW Norton & Company, Incorporated
500 Fifth Avenue, New York, NY 10110

Published simultaneously in Canada by
Penguin Books Canada Limited
2801 John Street, Markham, Ontario LR3 1B4

ISBN   0–7136–3153–8

A CIP catalogue record for this book
is available from the British Library.

ISBN   0–393–30688–7   USA

Maps and plans by Doug London.

Educated at Oxford, where he gained his degree in Modern Languages, and after careers in the Royal Air Force and the aero-engine
industry, **John Tomes** was invited to update the Blue Guides to
Greece and Sicily. Subsequently, he became author of Blue Guides
Scotland, Wales, Belgium and Luxembourg and *Holland*, a group
which he has now seen through several editions. A number of his
short stories have been published and broadcast, and his other travel
books include the *Shell Book of Exploring Britain* (A & C Black), of
which he is co-author with the late Garry Hogg.

Typeset by CRB Typesetting Services, Ely, Cambs.

Printed and bound in Great Britain by
BPCC Hazells Ltd
Member of BPCC Ltd

PREFACE

Easily accessible, and long and confidently established as a holiday choice, the Principality of Wales—as more fully outlined in the Introduction to Wales below—invites with rich and often astonishing variety.

Previously published as 'Blue Guide Wales and the Marches', this new edition is now, and deservedly, devoted solely to Wales. For the Marches—the bordering English counties with their lush countryside and historic cities such as Chester, Shrewsbury and Hereford—see 'Blue Guide England'.

Comments and Suggestions. A continually evolving guide such as this (with this edition, approaching its 70th year) profits immensely from the contributions of its users. Comments, corrections and suggestions—whether on fact, on layout and style, on content, or the result of personal discovery—will always be welcome.

Acknowledgements are due first to all who have contributed to the distinguished reputation of this Guide since the publication of its first edition in 1922. For this Seventh Edition, the author and editor are grateful to the staffs of the headquarters and many information centres of the Wales Tourist Board, as also to the information officers of several other organisations, notably Welsh Historic Monuments (CADW), the National Trust, the Countryside Commission, the three National Parks, the Forestry Commission and the Nature Conservancy Council. Districts, cities, towns, museums and sites of all kinds have also been ready with information and advice, particular appreciation being due to Mr Hywel Rees (Head of Publications and Publicity) for suggesting a text that would do justice to Cardiff's National Museum of Wales during a period of major change and refurbishment; as also to Mrs Jane Pearson, Director, Merthyr Tydfil Heritage Trust. On a personal note the author would like to record the very real contribution made by his wife, as map reader, typist and perceptive critic.

Background sources. The author wishes to mention the following as having been particularly valuable for reference and background: 'Encyclopaedia Britannica'. 'Dictionary of National Biography'. 'The Mabinogion', translated by Gwyn Jones and Thomas Jones (Dent, Everyman's Library). 'The Shell Book of Exploring Britain', by Garry Hogg and John Tomes (A & C Black). Several publications of the Wales Tourist Board, notably 'North Wales', 'Mid Wales', 'South Wales', and 'A Glimpse of the Past'. 'The Penguin Guide to Prehistoric England and Wales', by James Dyer (Penguin Books). 'Castles and Historic Places' and other publications by CADW (Welsh Historic Monuments). Several HMSO publications, amongst these 'Snowdonia National Park', edited by G. Rhys Edwards for the Countryside Commission; 'Snowdonia Forest Park Guide', edited by Herbert L. Edlin, Forestry Commission; 'Ancient Monuments of Anglesey', by O.E. Craster. 'The National Parks of Wales', by Margaret Davies (Cardiff Naturalists' Society). 'Pembrokeshire Coast National Park' (Dyfed County Council). 'Isle of Anglesey Official Guide', compiled and designed by Robert Williams and Jenny Steele (R.E. Jones and Bros., for Isle of Anglesey Tourist Association). 'A Guide to Gower' (Gower Society). National Trust publications, especially 'Plas Newydd', 'Penrhyn Castle', 'Powis Castle' and 'Erddig'. 'History of the French Invasion of Fishguard', by Pamela Horn (Preseli Printers).

For permission to reproduce the illustrations in the guide the publishers would like to thank Mr Anthony Kersting, the National Museum of Wales and Blaenavon Ironworks.

A NOTE ON BLUE GUIDES

The Blue Guide series began in 1918 when Muirhead Guide-Books Limited published 'Blue Guide London and its Environs'. Finlay and James Muirhead already had extensive experience of guide-book publishing: before the First World War they had been the editors of the English editions of the German Baedekers, and by 1915 they had acquired the copyright of most of the famous 'Red' Handbooks from John Murray.

An agreement made with the French publishing house Hachette et Cie in 1917 led to the translation of Muirhead's London Guide, which became the first 'Guide Bleu'—Hachette had previously published the blue-covered 'Guides Joanne'. Subsequently, Hachette's 'Guide Bleu Paris et ses Environs' was adapted and published in London by Muirhead. The collaboration between the two publishing houses continued until 1933.

In 1931 Ernest Benn Limited took over the Blue Guides, appointing Russell Muirhead, Finlay Muirhead's son, editor in 1934. The Muirheads' connection with Blue Guides ended in 1963 when Stuart Rossiter, who had been working on the Guides since 1954, became house editor, revising and compiling several of the books himself.

The Blue Guides are now published by A & C Black, who acquired Ernest Benn in 1984, so continuing the tradition of guide-book publishing which began in 1826 with 'Black's Economical Tourist of Scotland'. The Blue Guide series continues to grow: there are now more than 40 titles in print with revised editions appearing regularly and many new Blue Guides in preparation.

'Blue Guides' is a registered trade mark.

CONTENTS

MAPS AND PLANS

NOTES ON USING THIS GUIDE

'Blue Guide Wales' is in two parts. The first provides *Background and Practical Information*, the subjects covered being listed in the Contents. Intending visitors with no firm plans as to where to tour may be helped by the section headed Introduction to Wales, which outlines the main features of the country, as also by the section describing the Counties and the National Parks. The second part of the book comprises detailed descriptions along 46 *Routes* which criss-cross virtually all Wales (see Plan of Routes on p 66). Since Routes not infrequently cross or run close to one another, it is advisable to be aware of places lying either side of the road being travelled; use of the comprehensive *Index* will then ensure that places within easy reach, but described under other Routes, are not missed.

History, Antiquities and People. Throughout any tour of Wales prehistory and history always accompany the traveller, usually in the visible form of man's activity, ranging from ancient burial mounds and earthworks through ruined abbeys and castles to more recent and intact sites. Both for background interest, as also to avoid repetition, the first part of this book includes an outline *History of Wales*; and, for the same reasons, there are also *Biographical Notes* indentifying selected people who are not covered in any detail in the History or Routes texts.

Distances. The preamble to each Route (other than those devoted to individual towns) states its total distance. Both in the preambles and texts, italicised distances are those between points along the basic Route, i.e. each italicised distance is the distance from the previous one. Other distances (e.g. along diversions) are in Roman print. For obvious reasons distances can only be approximate.

Maps. The map on pp 12–13 shows Wales as a whole, but is not of course intended to take the place of motorists' maps. Of such there is a wide choice, from which four may be mentioned. Michelin Sheet 403 (1:400,000; approx 6m to an inch) covers on a single face all SW Britain including all Wales; Ordnance Survey Routemaster Sheet 7 (1:250,000. 1 inch to 4m), also on a single face, includes all Wales, the Marches counties and some distance farther east; the Automobile Association's Wales Road Map (approx 3m to an inch) provides similar cover but on two faces; and a similar area is covered to a scale of 1:250,000 or 4m to an inch on a single face by a map published by Estate Publications (in association with the Wales Tourist Board), this map clearly and usefully overprinted to show in red most sites of tourist interest. Additionally, for detailed exploration, most visitors will probably choose the relevant Ordnance Survey Landranger maps (1:50,000. 1m. to 1¼ inches).

Opening Times. For a variety of reasons few sites, official or private, are willing to commit themselves for even a year ahead. Therefore, rather than offer information which may well be misleading, this Guide provides a telephone contact for all sites with formal opening arrangements, these numbers usually being that of the site itself but in some cases that of the nearest Tourist Information. *Welsh Historic Monuments* (WHM, or CADW) publish a Standard Opening Time, this being 15 March–15 October: Monday–Saturday, 09.30 to 18.30. Sunday, 14.00 to 18.30. 16 October–14 March: Monday–Saturday, 09.30 to 16.00. Sunday, 14.00 to 16.00. Closed 24–26 December, 1 January. Nevertheless several of the more important sites are likely to be open Sunday mornings in summer, while some less important sites are closed all winter. For all WHM sites the telephone number given (0222–465511) is that of the central information facility in Cardiff. For *National Trust* (NT) properties, information may also be requested from the Regional Offices (see p 55).

There remain a large number of other sites, some of which do not admit visitors (no adm.), some of which allow informal entry, while many others may be viewed only from outside. The local form will usually be clear enough, but the warning must be given that many sites are ruins and the fact that access is possible does not necessarily mean that it is safe.

Tourist Information Offices will also of course provide information on Opening Times. While for local sites this will normally be accurate, for sites farther afield local offices reasonably enough have to refer to whatever publications they may have, and experience is that these may well be out of date.

No firm ruling can be given regarding public holiday opening, but the trend is increasingly towards opening.

A number of *Churches* feature in this Guide. Sadly, due to modern vandalism, churches will increasingly be found to be locked. In some cases the name and whereabouts of the key holder is on the door or adjacent noticeboard; more often, initiative and perseverance will be required to gain entry.

Tourist Information Offices are operated by various levels of the tourist industry; from Wales Tourist Board down through Counties, Districts, National Parks, Cities and Towns. The entry *Inf.* after the name of a town advises that there are manned Tourist Information facilities. Addresses are given only in the cases of selected larger towns. Many offices, which are sometimes temporary caravans, tend to move around and also to be closed from roughly end September to Easter. There are usually clear signs.

Telephone Numbers. Britain's telephone system is being modernised to digital switching, resulting in four-figure area codes followed by six-figure numbers. This process seems likely to extend over some years, during which numbers not conforming to the above pattern will change. For some time after change—generally until the publication of a new directory—a recorded announcement will give the new number. If nevertheless in difficulty, callers should dial Directory Inquiries on 192.

Asterisks draw attention to places of special attraction or interest.

Abbreviations. In addition to generally accepted and self-explanatory abbreviations, the following occur:

FC	= Forestry Commission
HMSO	= Her Majesty's Stationary Office
MP	= Member of Parliament
NC	= Nature Conservancy
	(from 1991, Countryside Council for Wales = CCW)
NNR	= National Nature Reserve
NT	= National Trust
RNLI	= Royal National Lifeboat Institution
RSPB	= Royal Society for the Protection of Birds
VC	= Victoria Cross
WHM	= Welsh Historic Monuments

BACKGROUND INFORMATION

Introduction to Wales

Nothing could be more mistaken than to regard Wales simply as a westward extension of England. Wales has a long and colourful history of its own, large parts of the land in the past enjoying prolonged periods of independence; most of the true Welsh can claim their own ethnic origin, Brythonic Celt rather than Anglo-Saxon; and the separateness of the country's identity, the very real sense of a national homogeneity, will quickly impress itself on the visitor as soon as he crosses the border and encounters tongue-twisting Welsh names and signs, hears the distinctive and musical Welsh accent and appreciates the still widespread and natural use of the Welsh language.

In shape Wales is roughly a rectangle (some 160m from N to S, and some 50m from W to E), from which Anglesey and the Lleyn project at the NW and Pembroke at the SW, between curving the huge crescent of Cardigan Bay. The greater part of the country is hilly or mountainous, the principal ranges or massifs being magnificent Snowdonia and Cader Idris to the NW, with the more modest Clwdian and Berwyn hills to the NE; the succession of the Rheidol Forest, Plynlimon and Towy Forest stretching N to S behind the coast between the Dyfi estuary and the valley of the Towy at Llandovery; and, across the SE, the mountains of Brecon Beacons National Park, with, to their S, the high ground (once that of the South Wales coalfield) which is broken by the series of once largely industrialised valleys which slice in from the busy coast. The border lands are mainly undulating, pastoral country, varied here and there by upland moor, a description which applies also to much of the SW, to the NE immediately behind the string of coastal resorts, and to Anglesey and much of the Lleyn. Other scenic features of Wales are the many lovely river valleys (Wye, Conwy, Teifi, Towy); lakes and reservoirs, frequently in moorland or afforested settings; and some spectacular cliff scenery, especially in the south west. Indeed, apart from the resort areas with their holiday camps and caravan sites and the industrial SE, there are few parts of Wales which cannot claim to be scenic, and few also which do not offer almost limitless opportunities for walking.

But, leading attraction though it is, there is a lot more to Wales than its scenery, and a list of just some of the other things the country has to offer could include the wide choice of holiday resorts strung around an ever-changing coast; a wealth of remarkable prehistoric and Dark Ages sites, the former especially notable in Anglesey and scattered across Presely, the latter mainly the hillfort settlements which seem to crown just about every significant hilltop in Wales; several of the largest, most imposing and most historic castles in Europe; religious establishments, ranging from abbeys—which, though today only skeletal ruins, still spur the imagination to conjure up both the monastic simplicity and the liturgical pomp of the Middle Ages—through historic, still active cathedrals, to a wealth of interesting churches, some solidly Victorian, many others humble, tiny and primitive; great mansions, splendidly decorated and furnished and many owned by the National Trust; the famous little railways of Wales; museums and art galleries, from Cardiff's superb National Museum of Wales to modest but invariably interesting local collections; choirs, legend, weaving and much else.

The Counties and National Parks of Wales

Since the local government reorganisation of 1974 Wales has comprised eight counties in place of the historic previous thirteen. The main features of the counties are outlined below, reference also being made to the former counties which have been embraced, most of these becoming, in whole or in part, administrative districts of the new counties. The present county and district names, and in very general terms the areas they cover, reflect early Welsh principalities and lordships.

CLWYD (County town, **Mold**. Former counties of **Flintshire** and most of **Denbighshire**) occupies the NE corner of Wales. Flintshire, although the smallest of the former counties of Wales, once ranked fifth in population because of the industrialisation arising from the varied mineral wealth both here and in neighbouring Denbighshire. Geologically Clwyd is thus of considerable interest since nearly all formations between the Lower Silurian and Triassic are represented (*Geological Museum of North Wales* at Bwlchgwyn). Of the county's five districts, that of Glyndwr recalls that this area was the home of Owen Glendower.

Within Clwyd are the part-industrialised estuary of the Dee; Wales's NE coast, with its string of popular resorts, holiday camps and caravan parks; the Vale of Clwyd, with to its E the Clwydian Hills and to its W the bleak upland of Mynydd Hiraethog with Clocaenog Forest below; the Vale of Llangollen (river Dee); and most of the range of the Berwyns. Among places of particular interest are *Chirk, Flint, Rhuddlan* and *Denbigh* castles, the first still occupied, the others massive Edwardian ruins; the ruined abbeys of *Valle Crucis* and *Basingwerk*; the mansion of *Erddig* (Wrexham); the cathedral of *St. Asaph*; and *Llyn Brenig* (on Mynydd Hiraethog) with its varied attractions. Churches, particularly in what was Denbighshire, are characterised by their parallel naves.

GWYNEDD (County town, **Caernarfon**. Former counties of **Anglesey, Caernarfonshire, Merioneth**, and part of **Denbighshire**) fills the NW of Wales, its inland boundaries running E of the Vale of Conwy and to the S generally following the course of the Dyfi to its mouth. The county includes the whole of *Snowdonia National Park*, the most scenic and probably the most visited area of Wales. Other, if gentler, scenic parts of the county are the Lleyn, with its mixture of mountain and pastoral land and choice of resorts, and the pleasant Vale of Conwy, lying just outside the National Park.

Anglesey is described as Rte 11. The former county of Caernarfon is now roughly divided into the districts of Dwyfor (Lleyn) and Arfon (SE of Menai Strait and including the Pass of Llanberis and most of Snowdon), while the district of Aberconwy straddles the length of the

Conwy. Merioneth, now the district of Meirionnydd and forming the
S part of Gwynedd, was the Mervinia of the Romans and derives its
name from Meirion, a grandson of the 5C Prince Cunedda.

Gwynedd is full of places of interest. On **Anglesey** are many
prehistoric sites, notably *Bryn Celli Ddu* burial chamber, the hut
circles on *Holyhead Island*, and the Iron Age village of *Din Lligwy*;
Plas Newydd, with works by Rex Whistler, the magnificent Menai
Strait home of the marquesses of Anglesey; and the great ruin of
Beaumaris Castle overlooking the N end of the strait. The resort of
Llandudno, with *Great Orme's Head*, is in the district of **Aberconwy**,
as is also *Conwy*, with its castle and town walls. In the district of
Arfon, *Bangor*, with its cathedral, and the mansion of *Penrhyn
Castle*, are at the N end of the Menai Strait, while at the S end is
Caernarfon, with castle and town walls and Roman *Segontium*. The
Iron Age hillfort-village of *Tre'r Ceiri* and *Criccieth Castle* are both in
the district of **Dwyfor** (Lleyn), while across the bay historic *Harlech
Castle* stands high above the coast of **Meirionnydd**. In Meirionnydd
too are the interesting *Tanygrisiau* (pumped-storage) *Power Station*
near Blaenau Ffestiniog, and, between Dinas Mawddwy and Bala,
Bwlch-y-Groes (1790ft), the highest point on any motor road in
Wales. Gwynedd is known also for its huge and mostly disused *Slate
Quarries;* two near Blaenau Ffestiniog are open to visitors, and the
Welsh Slate Museum is at Llanberis. Most of the *Little Railways* are
also in Gwynedd (Snowdon, Llanberis Lake, Ffestiniog, Talyllyn,
Fairbourne, Bala Lake and West Highland).

POWYS (County town, **Llandrindod Wells**. Former counties of
Montgomeryshire, **Radnorshire** and **Breconshire**) lies entirely
inland to the E of Gwynedd's district of Meirionnydd and the county
of Dyfed. The county's N boundary is with Clwyd, its E with England,
and its S with the counties of Gwent, Mid Glamorgan, and West
Glamorgan, this last boundary being roughly the line followed by Rte
31 between Brecon Beacons National Park and the uplands of what
was once the South Wales coalfield.

The former counties now form Powys's three districts, and it is
convenient to describe the county under these. **Montgomery**, in the
N and roughly matching the ancient principality of Powys
(*Powysland Museum* at Welshpool), is named after Roger de
Montgomery, the Norman who subjugated these lands in c 1090.
Scenically the district is generally hilly, one of the most attractive
places being Lake Vyrnwy in its wooded setting and with its
mountain approaches from the direction of Bala. Another wild and
attractive area is to the NW of Llanidloes, with Hafren Forest (below
Plynlimon and source of the Severn and Wye) and the Mountain
Road across to the valley of the Dyfi. The main place of interest is the
mansion of *Powis Castle* (Welshpool). The *Welshpool and Llanfair
Railway* also attracts many visitors.—**Radnor**, the central district,
created by Henry VIII from the lands of the Lords Marcher and
almost entirely English-speaking, perhaps traces its name to the
Anglo-Saxon 'radenore' meaning 'land of hill tracks'. The district
includes the high moorland of Radnor Forest and, in the NW near
Rhayader, the beautiful Elan Valley reservoirs. One of the loveliest
stretches of the Wye provides the district's border between Rhayader
and Hay-on-Wye. The scanty remains of *Cwmhir Abbey* are worth
visiting for their pastoral setting and as possibly the resting place of
Llewelyn the Last. Also of interest are *Old Radnor Church*, and
Llandrindod Wells Museum, with finds from the nearby Roman fort
of *Castell Collen*.—**Brecknock**, the southern of the three districts of

Powys, is named from Brychan, a local prince of the 5C, and was earlier known as Brycheiniog. In the 11C the district was conquered by the Norman Bernard of Newmarch. Mountainous and hilly, Brecknock is largely made up of *Brecon Beacons National Park*, while in the far NW of the district the uplands of Irfon and Towy forests provide another remote and scenic area. The city of *Brecon* has a historic cathedral, the outstanding Brecknock Museum, and (3m. away) the Roman fort of *Y Gaer*, still with much of its stonework. *Tretower*, N of Crickhowell, has a fine medieval manor house alongside a ruined castle with a circular tower, and in the SW corner of the district *Dan-yr-Ogof* caves are much visited.

DYFED (County town, **Carmarthen**. Former counties of **Cardiganshire, Carmarthenshire** and **Pembrokeshire**) is a large county which administers all the south west. The long coastline starts at the estuary of the Dyfi on Cardigan Bay, swings round the rugged Pembroke peninsula, and finishes at the estuary of the Loughor at the E end of Carmarthen Bay. Because of the county's size it is convenient to describe it under the headings of the districts or groups of districts which make up the former counties. **Ceredigion** (Cardigan), with a coastline extending from the Dyfi to the Teifi estuary, is the N district of Dyfed. Though largely agricultural, the district has the mountainous area of Plynlimon (with the scenic road past Nant-y-Moch reservoirs) at the north. Also in the N is the Vale of Rheidol, up which the small *Vale of Rheidol Railway* runs from Aberystwyth to Devil's Bridge. The district's principal town is *Aberystwyth*, with a castle, the National Library of Wales, and the Ceredigion Museum. The ruins of the important abbey of *Strata Florida* are to the S of Devil's Bridge, and those of the lesser abbey of *St. Dogmaels* are near Cardigan town.—The districts of **Carmarthen** (W), **Dinefwr** (NE), and **Llanelli** (SE) represent the former county of Carmarthen. Carmarthen was the chief centre of the Rebecca Riots in 1843–44 and the county's story is illustrated in the *County Museum* at Abergwili (Carmarthen). Places of interest in the Carmarthen district include the *Museum of the Woollen Industry* and *Llanstephan Castle*, while *Kidwelly Castle* is the main site in Llanelli. The district of Dinefwr offers the Roman *Dolaucothi Goldmines* at Pumpsaint; and ruined *Talley Abbey* and *Dryslwyn, Dynevor* and *Carreg Cennen* castles, all near Llandeilo.—The districts of **Presely** and **South Pembrokeshire** make up what was the county of Pembrokeshire, noted for its coastal scenery, all now within *Pembrokeshire Coast National Park*. Pembrokeshire was a part of the Demetia of the ancient chronicles, so called from the local tribe. There was extensive Flemish settlement in 1107 and South Pembrokeshire is sometimes called 'Little England beyond Wales'. A line drawn roughly E and W through Narberth and Haverfordwest divides the Welsh-speaking population on the N from the English-speaking descendants of the Flemings on the south. Presely and South Pembrokeshire include a large number of places of outstanding tourist interest, among these being the large ruined castles of *Cilgerran, Llawhaden, Carew, Manorbier,* and *Pembroke; St. David's*, with its historic cathedral and ruined bishop's palace; the attractive ruins of *Lamphey Bishop's Palace*; the *Presely Hills* rich in prehistoric sites; little *St. Govan's Chapel* clinging to its cliff; and the great anchorage of *Milford Haven* with its oil tankers and terminals.

The earldom of Pembroke was created in 1138, Gilbert de Clare, popularly known as Strongbow, being the first holder of the title and first of a long line of nobles who were amongst the most powerful and rapacious of the Lords Marcher. Families holding the title included the Marshals, De Valences, Hastings, and Tudors, one of these last being Jasper, uncle to Henry VII. In 1138 the Pembroke lands, mainly S of Milford Haven, became a county palatine (independent of the national system of administration), the earls maintaining their local rights of sovereignty until the palatinate was abolished in 1536.

The former county of **Glamorganshire** is now the three counties of West, Mid, and South Glamorgan.

WEST GLAMORGAN (County town, **Swansea**) includes the Gower, with caves, popular beaches, important nature reserves, some prehistoric sites (notably *Parc le Breos*), and the ruined castles of *Oystermouth* and *Weobley*. Also of interest in the county are *Neath Abbey; Margam Park* and *Abbey; Port Talbot*, with its deep-water harbour and steelworks; and, leading NE from Port Talbot, the *Cwm Afan Scenic Route* with the *Welsh Miners' Museum*.

MID GLAMORGAN (County offices, **Cardiff**) is the county of The Valleys (see Rte 37), slicing into the barren mountains of the N part of the county. *Caerphilly Castle*, the largest and one of the most imposing ruins in Wales, is passed on the approach to Rhymney Valley. In the county's very different coastal zone either side of the Ogmore estuary are *Ogmore Castle* and *Ewenny Priory*, while the extensive remains of *Coity Castle* are to the NE of the fast expanding industrial town of *Bridgend*, itself with a castle.

SOUTH GLAMORGAN (County offices, **Cardiff**) is made up of Cardiff and its environs (see Rte 36) and to the W the largely rural Vale of Glamorgan. Sites here include prehistoric *Tinkinswood Cairn*, *Turner House Art Gallery* at Penarth, and the church at *Llantwit Major*.

GWENT (County town, **Cwmbran**), forming the SE corner of Wales, was formerly **Monmouthshire**, lands which, though strongly Welsh in character, were removed from the jurisdiction of the Lords Marcher by Henry VIII and included among the English counties. Ecclesiastically though, Monmouthshire remained part of Wales, to which it returned under the local government reorganisation of 1974. Today's name of Gwent, originally applying only to the region between the Usk and the Wye, derives from Venta Silurum (*Caerwent*), the Romano-Welsh town between Chepstow and Newport, the extensive remains of which are one of Gwent's more important sites. *Caerleon*, N of Newport, is another important Roman site. *Newport* is visited for its cathedral and for its good museum with finds from Caerleon and Caerwent as well as more recent local material. Topographically Gwent divides roughly into three N–S strips. To the W are the mountains into which cut the industrialised Ebbw and Sirhowy valleys (Rte 37E). In the centre, either side of the Usk, the country is undulating and agricultural, though to the N of Abergavenny it rises to become the S part of the Black Mountains; within this central strip the main sites are (N to S) *Llanthony Priory*, and *Grosmont, Skenfrith, White* and *Raglan* castles. The E border of the county is the beautiful wooded Lower Wye Valley. Here *Monmouth* has a unique 13C fortified bridge and a local history centre; *Tintern Abbey* is one of the most visited sites in Wales; and impressively sited *Chepstow Castle* stands high above the river.

SNOWDONIA NATIONAL PARK (*Inf.* Snowdonia National Park Office, Penrhyndeudraeth, Gwynedd, LL48 6LS. Tel: 0766-770274.— Information Centres at Aberdyfi, Bala, *Betws-y-Coed, Blaenau Ffestiniog, Dolgellau, Harlech and Llanberis). The largest (845 square miles) and scenically most splendid of Wales's three parks, Snowdonia stretches from Conwy in the N to Aberdyfi in the S, averages some 25m in breadth, and between Tremadog Bay and Aberdyfi includes a long and varied coastline. Although named for its highest and best-known mountain group, Snowdon is in fact only one part of a park which embraces several ranges, with 15 peaks over 3000ft, as well as wide tracts of forest and moorland. The various areas merge into one another but can be identified (roughly from N to S) as the *Carneddau Range* (Rtes 1C, 6B, 9); *Gwydir Forest* (Rtes 6B, 6C, 7); *Snowdon* (Rte 7, 8, 9, 10); *Moelwyns and Siabod Range* (Rte 7); *Arenig Range* (Rtes 15, 16); *Rhinog Range* (Rte 17); *Coed-y-Brenin* (Rte 16); the twin *Arans* (Rte 20); *Cader Idris* (Rte 21).

BRECON BEACONS NATIONAL PARK (*Inf.* Brecon Beacons National Park, 7 Glamorgan Street, Brecon, LD3 7DP.—Information Centres at Abergavenny, Llandovery, the Mountain Centre and Garwnant Forest Centre). Brecon Beacons National Park covers 519 square miles forming a rectangle some 45m long from W to E (Llandeilo to Abergavenny) and an average of some 15m from N to south. The greater part of the park is above 1000ft (with several heights over 2000ft) and the whole area, especially Brecon Beacons and the Black Mountains, is very popular with walkers and pony trekkers. Scenery apart, the park is known for its several important prehistoric sites, for Roman remains at Y Gaer near Brecon (Rte 26A) and at Y Pigwn near Trecastle (Rte 27) and for the great 13C castle of Carreg Cennen (Rte 24). Although the park is named for its principal mountain group, the Brecon Beacons are in fact only a small part of the whole which conveniently divides into the following five distinct areas (from W to E): *Black Mountain* (Rtes 24, 27, 33); *Fforest Fawr* (Rtes 26B, 33); *Brecon Beacons* (Rtes 26B); *Black Mountains* (Rtes 25A, 32); *Monmouthshire and Brecon Canal* (Rte 30B).

PEMBROKESHIRE COAST NATIONAL PARK (*Inf.* Pembrokeshire Coast National Park, County Offices, Haverfordwest, Dyfed, SA61 1QZ. Information Centres at Broadhaven, Haverfordwest, Kilgetty, Newport, Pembroke, St. David's, Saundersfoot). Pembrokeshire Coast National Park embraces some 225 square miles around the coast and, in the N, spreads some 10m inland to include the Presely Hills. Rtes 42 to 46 all traverse parts of the park, which conveniently divides into four sections. The *Coast*, most of it with grand cliff scenery, is traced by a Coastal Path of 180m between the estuary of the Teifi in the N and Amroth on Carmarthen Bay in the south. *Islands* include the monastic island of Caldey off Tenby, and also St. Margaret's, Skokholm, Skomer, Grassholm and Ramsey, all nature reserves. The *Preseley Hills* are noted for their prehistoric remains and as the source for some of the stones of Stonehenge. *Daugleddau* is the tidal estuary of the Western and Eastern Cleddau rivers.

Aspects of Wales

Bards. The bardic tradition is purely Celtic and in some aspects seems to have been associated with the Druids. Later—as prophets, exhortators, and as the guardians and tellers of tales—the bards filled the gap left by the Roman extermination of the Druids, playing a semi-political role in encouraging local pride and enjoying positions of honour at princely courts, where, needless to say, flattery of the prince and his line was an essential skill. As early as the 6C Gildas censures Maelgwn Gwynedd for being over-influenced by bardic flattery. Hywel Dda's codified legal system (10C) shows that by this date there had developed three grades of bard. Chief bards (who won their positions through competition, were awarded a chair of honour, and received a harp as symbol of office) ranked as senior officials. A chief bard's field of poetry, however, was limited to the lord and his family, God, and the saints. The second grade provided for the household what the chief bard did for the princely family, and was given more latitude of subject, in particular being allowed to sing of love and nature. The third grade (loosely called Minstrels) embraced a whole range of popular entertainers, restricted only in that they might not trespass on the metres or subjects of the upper grades. This third grade is important not least because it was they who told the popular tales which later found written form as the 'Mabinogion'.

The above system survived into late medieval times, when the patronage of the princes began to be superseded by that of the gentry, and bards, no longer court officials, made regular circuits of patrons' halls. At the same time popular entertainers scarcely ranking as bards wandered around on unofficial begging circuits and, though at the time despised, were nonetheless important for their influence on folk poetry. At the Caerwys eisteddfodau of 1523 and 1568, in an attempt to safeguard professional standards, a system was introduced by which apprentices progressed through three grades and were licensed to make a circuit of the halls of the gentry. Anybody unlicensed yet seeking patronage was officially classified as a vagabond.

Despite the above, however, the bardic system went into decline and the 17C saw the rise of poets independent of patronage and, more important, freed from ancient conservative poetic tradition.

Today's bardic system (with the *Gorsedd;* or Assembly, or Council), in some respects based on dubious foundations, was introduced in 1792 by Edward Williams (Iolo Morganwg), a self-taught scholar whose passion was ancient manuscripts bearing on Welsh history. His lead was followed up by enthusiasts who organised local eisteddfodau. In modern Wales a bard is a poet whose qualities have been recognised at an eisteddfod, and the Gorsedd has a defined role which includes the safeguarding of bardic custom and ceremony as well as much of the responsibility for the administration of the National Eisteddfod.

Choirs. As long ago as the 12C Giraldus was writing of the Welsh love of music and of their gift for singing in harmony. However, the development of today's choirs, although of course rooted in this national gift, dates from the early 19C when the Industrial Revolution brought crowded living conditions in the valleys, a boost for nonconformity, and the spread of chapels which became the focus of social life. Music was needed for the services, song schools were formed (music now being more easily taught by the newly invented tonic-solfa method), and from these roots grew the choirs. Today many choirs welcome visitors at their rehearsals, information on some of these being included in some Routes texts.

Coracles, made of intertwined laths of willow and hazel to a design which has changed little since the Iron Age, may occasionally be seen on the rivers Teifi, especially between Cenarth and Cilgerran, and Towy near Carmarthen. Those on the latter, the waters of which are calm, are light and oval in shape; those on the Teifi, however, with its turbulent eddies, narrow at the waist and lie deeper in the water.

Crafts. There does not appear to be any significant craft which is peculiar to Wales. Nevertheless many skills are traditional (for example the carving of love-spoons, the traditional Welsh courting gift up to about the 17C), and craft studios, workshops and retail outlets will be found in most parts of the country, among the products being textiles and fabrics; woodwork; slate and stonework, slate sculpture being a particularly attractive souvenir of a craft which reached its peak in association with the huge quarries of the 19C; jewellery, with craftsmen using local stones, and designs which reflect Celtic tradition; pottery, Port Meirion being perhaps the best known; and wrought-ironwork, a tradition dating back to the firedog of the 1C BC found at Capel Garmon and which reached a peak with the 18C work of the Davies brothers.

An **Eisteddfod** (plural, eisteddfodau) originally meant simply a meeting of bards, whether in poetic competition or simply to discuss professional problems. Although bards had for centuries won their positions through competition, the first recorded bardic contest is that of 1176 convened at Cardigan by Rhys ap Gruffydd. This, though the word eisteddfod was not used, had many eisteddfodic features, notably the fact that the festival was proclaimed a year and a day in advance, this being considered, as it still is today, essential to the achievement of high standards. The prizes, for both poetry and music, were miniature silver chairs, symbols of the chairs of honour of the chief bards. In 1450 the term eisteddfod was used for a festival at Carmarthen, important for having been the occasion when metrical rules were codified which even today apply to the principal or Chair Poem of the National Eisteddfod. Later important eisteddfodau were those of 1523 and 1568 at Caerwys when the licensing of bards was introduced.

During the 16 to 18C both bards and eisteddfodau sank to a local and largely impromptu level.

The conception of an eisteddfod as a major public occasion dates from the Corwen eisteddfod of 1789, an occasion which (under the patronage of the Gwyneddigion, a society of London Welshmen) marked both the start of a series of successful eisteddfodau and also a return to the custom of proclaiming the festival a year and a day in advance. Similar eisteddfodau flourished in the 19C, one noteworthy development being the inclusion of choral competitions as a result of the development of the chapel choirs.

The *National Eisteddfod of Wales* was established between 1861–80 as a means of achieving worthy national standards, of safeguarding the Welsh language, and of promoting Welsh culture. The governing body is the Court of the National Eisteddfod of Wales, and the festival is held alternately in North and South Wales annually during the first week of August. The National Eisteddfod (with details of the now wide-ranging competitions) is proclaimed by the Gorsedd at least a year and a day in advance, normally at a traditional ceremony within a Gorsedd Circle of Stones (itself laid out to a ritual pattern), the rites being to the accompaniment of harp music. These circles of stones will be found in many places at which the National Eisteddfod has been proclaimed.—For the *International Eisteddfod*, see Rte 13, Llangollen.

The Flag (Red Dragon). The origin of Wales's flag, a red dragon on a green and white field, is lost in legend but may derive from Roman custom, a dragon having been the emblem of the cohort. In post-Roman times and legend warriors sometimes became known as 'dragons'. Arthur's father was Uther Pendragon, the 'chief dragon', and legend tells that he had a vision of a fiery dragon, interpreted by his seers as a sign that he would mount the throne. Legend (see below) tells too of the struggle between the red dragon of Wales and the white dragon of England, foretelling the victory of the former, a tradition that was fostered by the bards and made true by Henry Tudor whose standard was a red dragon. As Henry VII he incorporated the Welsh dragon in the Royal arms, where it remained until James I displaced it in favour of the Scottish unicorn. In 1901, however, the red dragon was officially recognised as the Royal badge of Wales, and in 1959 the Queen commanded that the red dragon on its green and white field should be the Welsh flag.—The *Leek*, the national emblem, may well have been introduced into Britain by the Romans. Of many theories as to why it became the Welsh emblem the most popular is that in some ancient battle the Welsh wore leeks in their caps as an identification; the battle was won and thus the leek remained in favour.

Industrial Archaeology (see also Mining). In the SE, Wales is still an industrial country, but today's activities are essentially limited and local compared to the proliferation of the past which included the huge slateworks of Snowdonia; the copper, gold, silver and lead mines of northern and central Wales; the iron-making of Bersham near Wrexham; the many mills, and the ubiquitous woollen and textiles industry; and, above all perhaps, the explosive developments in coal, iron, tinplate and steel, with the accompanying network of railways and canals, which during the 18C and 19C transformed the southern valleys.

Many causes—new processes and materials; foreign competition; a move to the ports; the exhaustion or flooding of mines; the replacement of coal by oil—led to an often rapid decline which left in its wake a desert of abandoned sites ranging from individual kilns to entire mines and factories. Today, though, and increasingly, the best of these sites are being identified, recorded, and in many cases restored, converted to museums or otherwise opened as tourist attractions. Industrial Archaeology is, though, something of a specialist field or acquired taste and one which the layman—confronted perhaps with no more than rusting ironwork half-buried in undergrowth—may well find disappointing. Principal sites are of course mentioned in this Guide's Routes, but the specialist visitor should use the WTB's publication 'A Glimpse of the Past' which outlines industrial trails and details some 200 sites, at the same time providing much background information.

Legend. Most of the legends of Wales spring from the 'Mabinogion', the creation of the bards of the Dark Ages, freely using material from their own imaginations, from romanticised historical or quasi-historical figures (e.g. Arthur and Macsen Wledig, the latter the Roman Magnus Maximus), and from folk tales and characters coeval perhaps with the earliest Celts. The earliest known written forms of the stories are in the 'White Book of Rhydderch' (1300–25; National Library of Wales) and the 'Red Book of Hergest' (1375–1425; Jesus College, Oxford). The 'Mabinogion' was translated by Lady Charlotte Guest, wife of a Merthyr Tydfil ironmaster, in 1838, but the engaging stories, with their improbable heroes but many easily identified place names, are now available in modern and very readable form in the translation (1948; with an admirable interpretive introduction) by Gwyn Jones and Thomas Jones (Everyman's Library).

The hero Arthur figures prominently in the 'Mabinogion' and thus in Welsh legend. He slew a giant and was mortally wounded on Snowdon, and a number of burial chambers, older than Arthur by around 2000 years, bear his name. On the Presely Hills standing stones commemorate two of Arthur's sons, killed by a great boar.

Vortigern and Merlin are two other characters associated in legend with Wales, and since the legend refers to much visited places (Carmarthen and Dinas Emrys) and also relates to the Welsh Dragon flag, it is told below.

Vortigern, King of Britain during the 5C, invited the Saxons Hengist and Horsa to help him against the Picts and Scots, rewarding them with land. But Hengist and Horsa were not satisfied, and soon the British were at war with the Saxons, Vortigern having to flee both the Saxons and his own angry people. Reaching Wales, he was told by his wizards that he must build himself a strong tower, and after much searching Vortigern chose Dinas Emrys. However, every time his masons started to build, the foundations were swallowed by the earth, whereupon the wizards said that Vortigern must find a youth born of no earthly father, kill him, and sprinkle his blood on the mortar. Messengers were sent far and wide, until one, reaching Carmarthen, overheard a dispute between two youths, Dinabutius and Merlin, in which the former mocked Merlin for never having had a father. Brought to Vortigern and questioned, the mother (a king's daughter) admitted that a spirit in the shape of a man had lain with her, thereafter disappearing and leaving her pregnant. Merlin however mocked the wizards, telling Vortigern that his tower kept falling down because there was a pool below, the home of two sleeping dragons, one red and one white. Digging proved Merlin right, and when the awoken dragons started to fight and the red dragon killed the white dragon, Merlin interpreted this as the eventual victory of Wales over England. This theme became a favourite with the bards, leading to the adoption of the Red Dragon as the emblem of Wales and the realisation of the prophecy through the accession of Henry VII.

Little Trains, narrow gauge, increasingly steam-drawn and in most cases tracing their (often horse-drawn) origins to the industrial needs of the 19C, have well repaid their rescuers' enthusiasm by today ranking among Wales's most popular tourist attractions. See also WTB publication 'A Glimpse of the Past' which provides much background and technical detail.

Mining in Wales, once a vigorous national feature, has since the early years of this century experienced a steady and even dramatic decline, the reasons including exhaustion, alternative materials, foreign competition and lack of demand (see WTB publication 'A Glimpse of the Past'). *Gold* was known in Wales in prehistoric times, but it was the Romans who started serious mining. Between then and the present day frequent ventures have been launched, but although gold is extracted the return has never justified continuing operations. There are a number of places where old workings can be explored, by far the best being the Roman and later Dolaucothi mines near Pumpsaint.—*Copper* was mined in Anglesey from Roman times until the late 19C, the opencast scars on bleak Parys Mountain remaining as reminders of this prosperous past. The copper mines around Snowdon carried on until about 1916, the remains of some of their buildings today being a feature of the Miners' Trail up the mountain.—*Lead* was mined in several places, notably on the plateau between Trefriw and Betws-y-Coed where between 1838 and the First World War there were as many as 19 mines, some producing over 2000 tons a year until defeated by competition from richer American deposits. Among other disused lead mines are those which rise beside the mountain road between Devil's Bridge and Rhayader.—*Slate* has been quarried and mined since the time of the

Romans, but operations are now on a much diminished scale compared to the peak period of the late 19C. The principal survivor, still the largest opencast site in the world, is the Penrhyn quarry near Bethesda. Slate quarrying and mining has left scars which, though ugly, can at the same time because of their sheer size be awe-inspiring. Today some of these huge gashes into the mountains have been converted into imaginative tourist attractions (notably above Blaenau Ffestiniog), while the great disused quarries at Llanberis are the site of one of the world's largest pumped-storage power stations.—*Coal* is still mined, but on a very small scale compared to the past.

Welsh Mountain Sheep, the native breed of the Welsh uplands, are one of the hardiest and most productive breeds in Britain. The sheep are small and normally white, though black and brown fleeces occur. The fleece is light in weight but of good quality, and Welsh lamb is renowned. Variants of the breed are Black Welsh Mountain and Badger-faced Welsh Mountain, the latter being rare and thought to be descendants of the original breed before the introduction of improvements.—Among other Welsh sheep, all named after their place of origin, are Beulah Speckle Face; Lleyn; Llanwenog, with brown hornless heads; and Kerry Hills, also hornless and with black spots on faces and legs.

Welsh Black Cattle will be seen in many parts of Wales, and since 1966 have been increasingly exported, especially to countries where their hardiness is much valued. The breed has existed in Wales since pre-Roman times, but in its modern form derives from two strains, the compact Anglesey and the larger Pembrokeshire (Castlemartin). Though good milk providers and sucklers, Welsh Black are primarily beef cattle.

Woollen Industry. The Welsh woollen industry, known to have been well established before the Normans arrived, is perhaps the oldest such in Europe. By the 15C, if not considerably earlier, cloth fairs were a familiar feature of Wales and the Borders, and the 15–18C saw a steady climb to prosperity until by the end of the 18C production of cloth had reached such a level as to be largely dependent on exports. Knitting was an important allied activity, particularly in Merioneth where, according to Pennant, the women had learnt to knit as soon as they could talk. Stockings, gloves, and woollen caps (known as Welsh wigs) were among the popular articles offered to coach travellers and bought also by middlemen for resale in London and elsewhere in England.

In Wales spinning and weaving were essentially home crafts, side activities to farming and other occupations. However, because of the difference in cost between a spinning wheel and a loom, a separation developed between cottagers spinning yarn and the more prosperous owners of looms to whom they sold it. These latter were frequently farmers, who insisted that their employees be as skilled at the loom as in the fields and in many cases found their cloth-selling to be more profitable than farming. All this ended with the Industrial Revolution, Wales showing herself loath to give up the traditional ways and slow to adopt machinery. The decline which then set in lasted through to the late 1960s when an upsurge in tourism brought with it a demand for traditional Welsh work, a demand which is now being met by a reborn and increasingly prosperous industry which is successfully adapting traditional designs to modern requirements.

History of Wales

Prehistory
(BC)

Much of Wales was under ice during the Ice Ages (until approximately 20–25,000 years ago) and man first made his way here as the
glaciers retreated. The earliest trace is a skeleton found in Paviland
Caves (Gower), radio-carbon dating placing this in the 19th millennium BC. Other evidence of man's early presence is provided by
remains found in the limestone caves of the NE, and perhaps also by
shell heaps, though these are of unknown age.

The ice was replaced by swampy valleys and pine forests, these
features and the local lack of flint confining man to open upland or to
the coast. During the third millennium (Neolithic, or New Stone Age)
there was a general drift of peoples northwards following the
European coast, this drift embracing Wales and bringing primitive
agriculture, domesticated animals, and, later on, the first visible
structures made by man. Around 1800 BC, at the dawn of the Bronze
Age, these early people seem to have been joined in the S and N by
others who crossed the North Sea and drifted westwards; these are
sometimes called the Beaker People, known for their round barrows
and pottery and probably also responsible for many standing stones.

Other than hillforts the **Prehistoric Monuments** of Wales belong to the New
Stone and Bronze Ages. There is a great deal of overlapping in both time and
place, but roughly the monuments divide as below.
    Burial Chambers or *Long Cairns* (2500 BC or earlier). Used for communal
burials, these were megalithic structures, i.e. made of massive stones covered
by a mound. Few signs of mounds survive, what remains now usually being the
chamber capstone, frequently still resting on its uprights. In this Guide the term
'burial chamber' is normally used. Some maps and local names, however, may
refer to these sites either as 'cromlechs' (curved stones), a term first used in the
16C, or as 'dolmens' (Breton for 'table stone'), a term invented by an 18C French
archaeologist.
    Standing Stones (c 1800 BC) may have served a variety of purposes, including
deity symbols, memorials, and boundary or route markers. They are sometimes
called 'menhirs' (long stones).
    Round Barrows (c 1800 BC) are associated with the Beaker People who gave
their dead individual burial.
    Stone Circles and *Alignments* (1800–500 BC) probably marked places at
which the people met for both ritual and secular purposes.
    In the Dark Ages (roughly the period between the Roman departure and the
Norman arrival) prehistoric sites were frequently associated with Arthur and
other heroes, and were also protected under ancient law.

During the later Bronze Age (say 400–100 BC) there was continuing
westward drift from the continent, now of men armed with metal
weapons, by some authorities considered to be the first Celts.

Celts is the generic name for the ancient peoples who inhabited central Europe.
During the last five centuries BC these people embarked on an expansion
which took them into France, Spain, and Italy, down the Danube into the
Balkans, and (by 300 BC) into Greece and Asia Minor, where later those who
held on became the Galatians. Two sets of Celts, the Goidels and the Brythons
(Britons), reached the British Isles. The Goidels crossed in the 4C BC directly to
Ireland, and may also have been the metal-weaponed people who came to
Wales; if these latter were Goidels, then their speech, later to become the Gaelic
of Ireland and Scotland, took no permanent root in Wales either now or as the
result of their invasions after the Roman withdrawal (see below). Rather later
the Brythons crossed the Channel and spread through England and Wales.—
Druidism was the Celtic religion up to the time of the Romans, the

Druids themselves being not only priests but, more importantly, teachers, administrators, and judges exercising an authority which, backed by religion, crossed the many tribal boundaries. Druidism accepted many gods, preached immortality through rebirth, and sometimes practised human sacrifice. In Wales, Druidism was strongest in Anglesey.

It was thus the Brythonic Celts who in the Bronze–Iron Age centuries immediately preceding the Roman invasion provided the main influx into Wales (as also Cornwall and Cumbria) and whose language became Welsh. These were the people who penetrated the valleys, made a start with land clearance, developed farming, and began to live in villages. And it was these people who, now and later, built the drystone, wood, and earthwork hillforts (often referred to as British Camps), the remains of which are such a feature of the Borders and Welsh landscapes. At the same time, up on the moors, the earlier people and their ways lingered on.

Roman Period
(AD 61 to early 5C)

Suetonius Paulinus attacked northern Wales and Anglesey in 61, and between 74 and 78 Frontinus crushed much of the S (the Silures and the Demetae). In 78 Agricola arrived in Britain (he stayed some 7 years), at once subduing the Ordovices in central Wales and also completing the conquest of the NW and Anglesey where the Druids were exterminated. Wales was held throughout the centuries of the Roman occupation of Britain, but, except to a limited extent along the S coast, always as a military zone controlled by legions based on Deva (Chester) in the N and on Isca (Caerleon) in the south. From these places roads penetrated westwards to stations such as Segontium (Caernarfon) and Maridunum (Carmarthen), with smaller forts even farther west. In the E the linking road ran through Viroconium (Wroxeter) and Castra Magna (Kentchester). In the W the N to S link was Sarn Helen (perhaps from the Welsh 'sarn heolen', a paved causeway) which ran from Caerhun through Tomen-y-Mur and Llania, beyond the latter bearing W for Maridunum and E and S for Y Gaer (Brecon) and Nidum (Neath).

Thus Wales was never fully Romanised, its inhabitants continuing to follow a more or less independent existence in and around their hillforts. The Silures, transferred from their hillfort capital to Venta Silurum (Caerwent), were the exception. In the Borders Roman remains include walls and an amphitheatre at Chester, and the fine site of Vironconium. In Wales the outstanding sites are the amphitheatre at Caerleon, the extensive walls of Caerwent, and clearly defined forts such as Y Gaer near Brecon and Castell Collen near Llandrindod Wells.

Irish, Anglo-Saxons, and Norsemen
(Dark Ages. Early 5C to 1066)

The Romans were withdrawing early in the 5C and as their grip loosened the Welsh coast became open to the attacks of Irish (Goidelic) pirates, on their heels coming settlers in large numbers who established themselves particularly in what are now north-west Gwynedd (with Anglesey), and in the Pembroke peninsula. It is generally accepted that Goidelic became the language in these areas until the 7C, and it is known that there was an Irish dynasty of kings in the SW from the late 3C to the early 10C. Thus Wales became divided between the native Brythons and the Goidel invaders, the struggle between the two and the more or less simultaneous introduction and spread of Christianity now becoming the two main features of Welsh history.

The struggle between the Brythons and the Goidels, though obscure in its details, eventually resulted in complete victory for the former who, under the leadership of the northerner *Cunedda*, probably a romanised Northumbrian, forced the Goidels out of northern Wales, Cunedda's descendants becoming the rulers and establishing their headquarters at Deganwy on the Conwy estuary. The most notable of these descendants was *Maelgwn Gwynedd* (Maglocunus, died 547), known from the writings of his contemporary, the monk and chronicler Gildas, who while describing Maelgwn's court as licentious at the same time suggests that he was a Christian, at one time even eager to exchange his position as prince for that of a monk. Despite their defeat and absorption it was the Irish who brought Christianity to Wales, actively spreading the Faith and thus leaving their permanent legacy. These missionaries, named 'sancti' by Gildas (a word which soon became 'saint'), generally led the lives of hermits and often became known for their healing powers; hence the Holy Wells found throughout Wales, many of which date back to this time. One saint was Dewi, or David, later adopted as patron of Wales. Such was the influence of these saints that they before long achieved a status equal to that of the local lord, and it became the custom that the latter should grant the holy man a piece of land as a sacred enclosure ('llan'). In 546 St. Dubricius (or Dyfrig), Bishop of all Wales, divided his see into three, appointing Deiniol to Gwynedd, Padarn to central Wales and Teilo to the south.

Wales is rich in Early Christian monuments, such as inscribed stones, grave-slabs, and crosses, dating from the 5C onwards. Many bear interesting Latin inscriptions; others bear Ogham characters, the oldest written form of Goidelic and thus of Gaelic (the writing takes the form of strokes or notches along a base line). The oldest known example of written Brythonic is a stone of c 650 in Tywyn church.

Towards the end of the 6C the Brythons had to face the onslaught of new invaders, the pagan Anglo-Saxon tribes who had swept across southern Britain, and there now started a struggle which would continue with little respite until Henry Tudor ascended the English throne as Henry VII some nine hundred years later.

The hero Arthur, if he ever existed at all, appears to date from about this time. Traditionally he was born at Tintagel in Cornwall, the son of Uther Pendragon and Ygrayne, and would have been a Christian chieftain (but not a king) who, as a military leader, perhaps serving Ambrosius, a chief with Roman blood seeking to restore Roman law and order, led the Brythons against the Saxons. He is credited with victory at Mount Badon (?Liddingstone, near Swindon) and may have died in battle, reputedly being buried at Glastonbury. Arthur's association with Wales, as opposed to with the Brythons generally, is largely a matter of bardic legend.

In 577, after a victory at Deorham near Bath, the invaders reached the Bristol Channel, and in 613 Ethelfrid, the Anglian king of Northumbria, defeated an army of Brythons near Chester. It was these two battles which geographically determined the Wales of today. The first cut off the Brythonic people of what is now known as the English West Country, and the second those of today's Cumbria.

For the first time contained within their own frontiers, the still free Brythons of the mountainous west now began to call themselves 'Cymry' (fellow-countrymen) and the land 'Cymru' (whence Cambria). The name Wales derives from the Anglo-Saxon 'wealas' meaning 'foreigners'. The Brythons' hopes of reunion were finally shattered in 634 when Cadwaladr ap Cadfan, who had penetrated far to the E, was defeated S of the Tyne, this enabling the Angles (or English as they would be called) to consolidate up to the foothills of the Welsh mountains. Only eight years later the Christian Oswald of Northumbria was killed by the pagan Penda of Mercia at Oswestry, thus opening the way for the rise of that warlike people who inhabited England's Midlands and had their capital at Tamworth. In c 784 Offa, the greatest of all the Mercian kings, constructed the long dyke which bears his name.

Offa's Dyke, built more as a line of demarcation than as a fortification, runs from the coast near Prestatyn southwards across the neck of Wales to Chepstow. Thus substantially the dyke still marks the border, the place names to the E being English and those to the W largely Welsh. Many sections of the dyke are still clearly visible and a waymarked path follows its 167m length.—**Wats Dyke**, possibly the work of the earlier Mercian king Aethelbald (716–57), is a shorter dyke (38m) running E of Offa's Dyke between the Dee estuary and Oswestry.

By the middle of the 8C the Mercians became Christian, and it was also at about this time that the Welsh (Celtic) Church first submitted to the practices and ritual which later resulted in the absorption of the Celtic Church by the Roman; an important date was 768 when the Welsh accepted the Roman Easter, the date of which had long been a major cause of dispute between Augustinian and Welsh authorities.

Throughout the 9 and 10C Wales suffered under the savage raids of the Norse pirates (Vikings), who made their way round the N of Scotland, settling there, in Ireland, and on the Isle of Man. That they did not to any lasting extent colonise Wales was due in large part to *Rhodri Mawr* (Roderick the Great of Gwynedd, died 879), who became ruler of all Wales except the extreme SE and SW, and also to the activities of Alfred the Great on whom the Welsh had to rely after Rhodri's death. The Norse presence survives in place names, particularly in Pembrokeshire, and in the intricately carved designs on stone monuments of the time. Rhodri Mawr's line continued as two branches, in the N and in the S, his best known descendant being his grandson *Hywel Dda* (Hywel the Good, died 950), a member of the southern branch. Through marriage Hywel added Dyfed to his lands, and through force Gwynedd, but he is best remembered for the great assembly he convened at Whitland which succeeded in codifying the tribal customs of the various parts of Wales into a single legal system which remained in force until the arrival of Edward I. Meanwhile the Norse raids continued, St. David's being sacked as late as 1088.

Although Hywel Dda's legal code survived, the political unity he had given to much of the country did not, and until just before the Norman invasion Wales became four distinct principalities, with borders more or less definitely fixed. Gwynedd was the dominant power in the north. To the S of Gwynedd was Powys, corresponding roughly to the modern county but including also parts of Meirionnydd and Salop. This principality's ruling families, though often disunited, frequently sided with the English and continued to exert a powerful influence in the Marches until well into the Middle Ages. In the S and SW ruled the princes of Deheubarth, comprising the earlier principalities of Dyfed (SW), Ceredigion (Cardigan), Ystrad Tywi (the Vale of Towy and Gower), and Brycheiniog (Brecon). Occupying the SE was the principality of Morgannwg (Glamorgan), which included the former principalities of Glwysing and Gwent. These Welsh princes continued to divide the country and quarrel for supremacy until just before the Norman Conquest when *Gruffydd ap Llewelyn* (1039–63), an adventurer not of any royal house, succeeded in uniting the Welsh people and threatening the border. He was finally defeated and killed by Earl Harold Godwinson who, as King Harold, was to lose his own life three years later at Hastings.

Despite the splintering into principalities, the internal strife and the fighting with the English, it would be wrong to picture the Welsh scene of the time simply as one of disorder. Wales still enjoyed Hywel Dda's legal code, with a defined system of administration. Each principality was divided into a number of cantrefs, roughly synonymous with the Anglo-Saxon hundred, and each cantref comprised several cymydau (commotes), each of these subdividing into trefs. There were no towns and scarcely any villages in Wales at this time, these trefs being no more than groups of farmsteads, each the property of a particular family. Each cantref was ruled by a lord, answerable to the prince. Status within the cantref depended upon birth, and certain distinct classes were recognised: royalty, noblemen, freemen, unfree persons, and slaves. The relations of these classes were legally defined, and courts existed for the redress of wrongs. Descendants of a common ancestor to the ninth degree, known as cenedl (kindred), were automatically bound together in a common, self-governing unit, and the law of gavelkind was observed, i.e. at the death of a father his land was divided equally among his sons, the division being made by the eldest and the choice starting from the youngest. This arrangement held good until the time of Henry VIII.

From the Normans to Edward I
(1066 to 1272)

Welsh Lords	English Kings
Rhys ap Tedwr (Tudor) died 1093	William I (the Conqueror)
Gruffydd ap Cynan died 1137	1066–87
Gruffydd ap Ryhys died 1137	William II (Rufus) 1087–1100
Madoc ap Maredydd died 1160	Henry I 1100–35
Owain Gwynedd died 1170	Stephen 1135–54
Rhys ap Gruffydd	Henry II 1154–89
(Lord Rhys) died 1197	Richard I 1189–99
Llewelyn ap Iorwerth	John 1199–1216
(the Great) died 1240	Henry III 1216–72
Llewelyn ap Gruffydd	Edward I 1272–1307
(the Last) died 1282	

One of the results of the activities of Gruffydd ap Llewelyn was that the Normans, after William the Conqueror's victory at Hastings in 1066, regarded Wales as a danger. William, whose commitments elsewhere prevented him from giving Wales his personal attention, established three Marcher Lordships under earls of Chester, Shrewsbury, and Hereford. He encouraged these earls to extend their territories westwards at the expense of the Welsh, and to bring the Welsh leaders under Norman vassalage. The earls pursued the policy with vigour, but though some definite results were achieved (by 1098 Hugo d'Avranches, or Hugh Lupus, Earl of Chester, had virtually conquered Anglesey), the main objective of subjugating the entire peninsula was not realised.

Motte-and-bailey Castles were a Norman introduction, first appearing on the English side of the border c 1055 when Edward the Confessor invited Norman knights to help him resist the inroads of the Welsh under Gruffydd ap Llewelyn. Old Radnor is one which dates from this time. After 1066 and the establishment of the Marcher Lordships such castles proliferated. The standard castle was a ditch (moat), usually dry, surrounding an earth mound (motte), the rim of which bore a palisade protecting an inner tower, or keep. (The basic word 'moat', or 'mote', or 'motte', came to be used loosely both for the ditch and for what had been heaped out of it). Annexed to the tower (sometimes within the main defence, sometimes extending outwards and with some defence of its own) was a flat area known as the bailey, used for all those activities which could not be contained within the tower, e.g. stabling. Remains of large numbers of these castles are found in Wales, although in many cases only the motte and ditches are obvious, the bailey not being readily recognised. Only in the 12C were these primitive castles succeeded by stone keeps (later becoming full castles), often, when strength and space allowed, standing on the early mottes.

About 1081 *Gruffydd Ap Cynan* (died 1137) came over from Ireland, whither his father had fled, to claim his patrimony in Gwynedd which he succeeded in freeing from Hugh Lupus. At about the same time *Rhys ap Tewdwr* (died 1093), a descendant of Hywel Dda, returned from exile in Brittany to claim his lands in Deheubarth. Supported by Gruffydd ap Cynan he defeated his rivals, his rights were recognised by William I, and there followed twelve years of peace. At his death, however, his son *Gruffydd ap Rhys* (died 1137) had to face the full weight of the Normans who now swept into the south. Gwent was overrun by William FitzOsbern, Earl of Hereford; Glwysing by Robert FitzHamon of Gloucester; Brycheiniog fell to Bernard of Newmarch, and Dyfed and Ceredigion to the house of Montgomery. Farther N, however, Roger de Montgomery, Earl of Shrewsbury, made little progress, and thus Powys and Gwynedd, still independent, became separated from the rest of Wales.

William II made expeditions into Wales in 1095 and 1097, penetrating as far as Meirionnydd, but by the time of his death in 1100 the Normans, especially in the S, were tending to contract marriages with the leading Welsh families, some of these Welsh-Norman lords even playing with ideas of independence. One such was Robert of Belesme, son of Roger de Montgomery, who tried to establish a western kingdom with Shrewsbury as his capital, but his plans were frustrated by the accession of Henry I, who was successful not only in checking both his own rebel barons and the Welsh but also in consolidating Norman gains. He also planted Flemish colonies in the Pembroke and Gower peninsulas, where their descendants still remain, speaking English and with traditions different to those of their Welsh neighbours.

The accession of Stephen (1135) and the consequent civil war in England gave the Welsh an opportunity from which they profited, everywhere taking up arms and recovering much of their territory. *Owain Gwynedd* (died 1170) and his brother Cadwaladr, the sons of Gruffydd ap Cynan, had obtained control in Gwynedd and now harried the northern Marches, seizing the border fortress of Mold; Powys was united under *Madoc ap Maredydd* (died 1160), who took the castle of Oswestry. But Henry II acceded in 1154, soon turning his attention to Wales where he defeated Owain Gwynedd in 1157 and, in 1163, *Rhys ap Gruffydd* (Lord Rhys; died 1197), the able and energetic son of Gruffydd ap Rhys. However, these two princes rallied their armies, and, supported by Owain Cyfeiliog, Prince of Powys, and other leaders, in 1165 forced Henry to withdraw. After this his troubles with Becket occupied Henry's attention, and Rhys ap Gruffydd was able to extend his sway over South Wales so effectively that Henry, while on his way to Ireland in 1171, met and acknowledged him.

With varying fortune Rhys ap Gruffydd remained in power in the S until his death in 1197, and the Wales of this time has been vividly recorded by Giraldus Cambrensis (Gerald of Barry; died c 1223), the son of a Norman settler in Dyfed, who became a noted scholar and churchman. In 1188 he made a tour in the train of Archbishop Baldwin who was seeking recruits for the crusades (died 1190 in the Holy Land, professing himself appalled at the excesses of the crusaders he had recruited), and he recorded his reflections in two works 'Itinerary through Wales' and 'Description of Wales'. His picture is of a frugal and poor people living in simple huts, yet bred to arms and having a bold individuality and courage. They seem to have been a pastoral people, with little inclination to trade. Of particular interest, and of course still true today, is the report that the Welsh had a love of poetry and music, including a natural gift for singing in harmony.

Castles. It was Henry II who introduced stone keeps into England, as successors to the motte-and-bailey castles, and during the later 12C these began to appear also in Wales. One of the first, and still surviving, was that at Dolwyddelan.

Religious Houses. The 12C also saw the development in Wales of the Norman monastic system. The monastery in pre-Norman Wales had been of the usual Celtic type, with an abbot and a community of monks occupying individual cells. Such monasteries had however already begun to decline as far back as the 8C, and the Normans dissolved the surviving houses in favour of their own type. The Benedictine Order was the first to be introduced into Wales, houses being established at Brecon (late 11C), St. Dogmaels (1118), and Ewenny (1141). The Savigniac Order founded abbeys at Neath (1130) and Basingwerk (1131), but in 1141 this Order was merged with the Cistercian, because of its charity and simplicity by far the most popular in Wales. The first Cistercian houses were on the border at Tintern (1131) and in the heart of the country at Whitland (1140). From these, others were colonised (some under the patronage of native princes) at Cwmhir (1143), Margam (1147), Strata Florida (1164), Strata Marcella (c 1170), Aberconwy (1186), Cymmer (1199), and Valle Crucis (1199). The Cistercians, of whom Rhys ap Gruffydd was a liberal patron, came to own large tracts of land and their farming methods had a marked influence on the native agriculture; indeed their successful sheep rearing set a pattern which persists today. The Premonstratensians established themselves at Talley (before 1197), and the Augustinians later at Penmon.

After the death of Owain Gwynedd in 1170, the power of Gwynedd was weakened by a struggle for supremacy among his sons. In the S, though the agreement between Rhys ap Gruffydd and Henry II stood until the latter's death in 1189, the absence of Richard I on crusades was the signal for disorder. Rhys ap Gruffydd reduced many of the Norman castles, but his desperate struggle to keep his independence was cut short by his death in 1197.

In 1194 *Llewelyn ap Iorwerth* (died 1240), grandson of Owain Gwynedd and later styled Llewelyn the Great, became Prince of Gwynedd. He was to become the most powerful ruler in Wales since the Norman invasion. First he had to overcome the rivalry of Gruffydd ap Gwenwynwyn (died 1216), a prince of southern Powys who, departing from the normal pro-English policy of his house, attempted to lead a national revival. Llewelyn succeeded in taking over the whole of Powys, the result being that under his rule all North Wales enjoyed almost complete independence. In 1204 he married Joan, a natural daughter of King John, but despite this in 1211 he had to face an attack by his father-in-law, who himself held lands in the Marches and feared Llewelyn's growing power. After this experience Llewelyn sided with the English barons and obtained rights for Wales under Magna Carta. In the same year he invaded South Wales, making himself overlord of the feeble successors of Rhys ap Gruffydd and forcing the Normans to surrender many castles. It was not only militarily and territorially that Wales prospered under Llewelyn; he was also a patron of the bards, he encouraged the study of the Welsh laws, and he gave generously to the monastic orders. In 1238 he entered the monastery of Aberconwy, where he died two years later.

Despite all he had achieved, and although he had his son Dafydd (died 1246) recognised as ruler in Wales by the lesser princes, Llewelyn the Great had given Wales only a superficial unity. There was no central government; province was divided from province, commote from commote; and the system of gavelkind, with its continual division of property, was a constant weakness. Such unity as there was died with Dafydd. But only for ten years, for in 1255 *Llewelyn ap Gruffydd* (Llewelyn the Last), grandson of Llewelyn the Great, overcame his brothers and began a campaign designed to clear the English out of Gwynedd and to establish his own authority throughout Wales. His opportunity was that of his grandfather, the strife between the English king and the barons, and Llewelyn was soon close to his objectives; the English were thrown back from Gwynedd, and Llewelyn, demanding the homage of the other chieftains, proclaimed himself Prince of Wales, a title which was recognised by Henry III in 1267 under the Treaty of Montgomery.

Edward I. The Conquest of Wales
(1272 to 1307)

Only five years after the Treaty of Montgomery Edward I became king; his declared intention was to control his barons and to deal with unruly Wales and Scotland. Llewelyn the Last, seemingly unaware of the changed spirit in England, refused to pay homage and in 1277 Edward launched his attack and, by establishing a series of fortresses backed by the new weapon of sea-power, forced Llewelyn (Treaty of Conwy) to pay homage in London and to give up virtually everything except a part of Gwynedd reaching from the Conwy to the Dyfi and his now empty title. In 1282 Llewelyn's brother Dafydd rose against Edward, and Llewelyn, eager for revenge, joined him. Edward's response was shattering. He pushed through Gwynedd, extending his line of fortresses; took Anglesey, the granary of Wales; forced Llewelyn back into the fastnesses of Snowdon, whence he retreated southwards to be killed in a skirmish at Cilmeri; and finally disposed of the Welsh 'dynasty' by executing Dafydd. With these events—until the arrival of Owen Glendower on the scene a hundred years later—all serious hopes of establishing an independent Wales were ended.

Edward remained in Wales for about three years to secure his position and establish the direct rule of the English Crown. He issued the Statute of Rhuddlan (1284; sometimes called the Statute of Wales), which provided for the government of the conquered principality; he divided Llewelyn's small remaining patrimony of western Gwynedd into the shires (counties) of Anglesey, Caernarfon, and Merioneth; he created the county of Flint as a buffer for that of Chester; he reorganised the administration of the provinces of Cardigan and Ystrad Tywi (Carmarthen); he suppressed the Welsh code of laws stemming from that of Hywel Dda, imposing instead the English system; finally, he embarked on a massive programme of castle construction, in the shadow of some of their walls creating 'English boroughs'.

Castles. The motte-and-bailey castle had been followed in the 12C by the stone keep. Now, a hundred years later, Edward built in Wales huge concentric fortresses of a type previously developed on the Continent and in the Near East, much of the work being in the hands of James of St. George, an engineer whom Edward had brought back from France on his return from the last crusade. Detail depended on the site, but ideally the concentric castle consisted of two baileys or wards, square in shape and enclosed by strong buttressed walls. The inner ward, which contained the domestic buildings, was normally placed well within the outer, the whole being reinforced whenever possible by a moat. The castle was entered across a drawbridge and through an immensely strong gatehouse, which often also served as keep; if there could be a seaward protection, and perhaps a dock, so much the better. Edward completed castles at Flint, Rhuddlan, Builth, and Aberystwyth; he also built large new fortresses at Conwy, Caernarfon, Beaumaris, and Harlech, below these establishing 'English boroughs'; finally he took over and strengthened castles already built by the Welsh at Criccieth, Bere, Dolbadarn, Ewloe and elsewhere. Other castles built by the Lords Marcher (Denbigh, Caerphilly etc.) were to a similar pattern to the King's, although that at Caerphilly actually preceded the royal castles in date.

English Boroughs, the nearest approach to anything like a town hitherto seen in Wales, were founded below the walls of the castles mentioned above and also of some of the castles taken over from the Welsh. They were granted charters, often before the castles themselves were complete, and English traders, who were expected also to form part of the garrison, were encouraged to settle, to the exclusion of the native Welsh, usually compensated with land in other districts. Each town, protected by walls, was laid out on a regular plan, with wide streets at right angles and a central market place. As the Welsh were forbidden to trade in places other than these markets, the boroughs inevitably became the administrative centres for the regions surrounding them. Other similar ('royal') boroughs were later established at Newborough (Anglesey), Bala, and Pwllheli.

Efficient and orderly though Edward's measures may seem, it was no part of his plan to knit Wales into a unified nation. The largely self-governing lordships of Denbigh and Montgomery and those in southern Wales were left undisturbed, partly as a reward for their help in overcoming Llewelyn and partly no doubt because by this time the border lords had become so powerful that interference would have been both impolitic and difficult. Indeed the system of lordships was extended, so that others of Edward's helpers could have their share of the spoils. These included many Welsh lords who had had no wish to support Llewelyn; Powys and Deheubarth were amongst those who sided with Edward, and several leading families willingly provided him with administrators. The result was that much of Wales remained, as before, under the rule of numerous petty barons and outside the jurisdiction of the central courts in London.

Edward's measures inevitably led to rebellions, though none was effective and the last (by Madog ap Llewelyn) petered out in 1294. However he remained well aware that he had to continue to guard against revolt as much by his own barons as by the Welsh, the two by now not always distinguishable, and in 1301, in a move designed both to gain Welsh sympathy and to confront the barons with a royal Welsh authority, he revived the title of Prince of Wales, conferring this on his son, born at Caernarfon in 1284. Edward I died in 1307.

Wales appeared to settle down and apart from minor rebellions during the reign of Edward II the 14C was a peaceful one, the country becoming more prosperous and ports such as Rhuddlan, Beaumaris and Haverfordwest developing into trading centres. It was also the century in which Welsh poetry rose to perhaps its greatest heights with the work of Dafydd ap Gwilym, described by Borrow, who translated some of his poems, as the Horace of Wales. With the death of the strong Edward III, however, the Lords Marcher

Edward II to Henry Tudor (Henry VII)
(1307 to 1485)

Welsh Lords	English Kings	
	Edward II 1307–27	
	Edward III 1327–77	*Plantagenets*
	Richard II 1377–99	
Owain Glyndwr (Owen Glendower) died c 1416		
	Henry IV 1399–1413	
	Henry V 1413–22	*Lancastrians*
	Henry VI 1422–61	
	Edward IV 1461–83	
	Edward V 1483	*Yorkists*
	Richard III 1483–85	
Harri Tewdwr (Henry Tudor)	Henry VII (Harri Tewdwr) 1485–1509	

Note: Henry VI, deposed in 1461, was murdered in 1471. Edward V, with his brother one of the boy 'princes in the tower', was declared illegitimate by Richard III and murdered; he was never crowned.

again began to stir and the royal officials became increasingly rapacious. Revolt was in the air and came to a head in the person of *Owen Glendower* (Owain Glyndwr; died 1416), an enigmatic figure who has been both lauded as a popular national hero and condemned as a bloodthirsty tyrant seeking his own aggrandisement.

As a descendant of the princes of northern Powys, and also, through his mother, as a representative of the royal line of Deheubarth, Glendower had claims to be regarded as a rightful Prince of Wales. Nevertheless he had been a courtier in London, had fought under the banner of Richard II, and had made no protest on the accession of Henry IV, so his revolt in 1400, sparked off by Henry's refusal of redress when Lord Grey of Ruthin seized some Glendower land, came as a surprise. Raising his standard on the Dee, Glendower soon laid waste the English settlements in north east Wales, and what started as perhaps an act of personal pique became an excuse for Wales to unleash its resentment against the English and initiated a bitter struggle that lasted for nearly fourteen years and devastated much of Wales and the Marches.

At first Glendower had the advantage of facing a king who was insecure in his position (Henry was holding prisoner the young Earl of March, nephew of the powerful Marcher landowner Sir Edmund Mortimer and, as direct descendant of Edward III, a threat to the throne). Furthermore Henry underestimated the Welshman's personal qualities and the strength of the national sentiment to which, as a member of two princely houses, he could appeal. An early and important success was the battle at Pilleth; not only did Glendower for the first time decisively defeat a royal army and thus establish himself as a national leader, but here he also captured Sir Edmund Mortimer. Mortimer's position was of course equivocal, and it was not therefore surprising that he sided with Glendower, sealing the alliance by marrying one of Glendower's daughters.

Glendower was declared Prince of Wales and he held parliaments at Machynlleth, Dolgellau and Harlech. He sought alliances with the Scots and Irish, and to secure French support he concluded a treaty with Charles VI for the provision of troops; he even entered into negotiations with the Pope at Avignon. He appointed bishops, issued pardons under his Great Seal, and mapped out a statesmanlike policy, demanding the independence of the Welsh Church from Canterbury and proposing the establishment of two Welsh universities. He also formed an alliance with the powerful Duke of Northumberland and his son Hotspur, at the start disastrous as, while Glendower was engaged in the S, Hotspur, coming to his aid, was intercepted by the royal forces near Shrewsbury and killed (1403). Later, in 1405, Glendower, Northumberland and Mortimer signed the Tripartite Indenture by which England and Wales were to be divided among the three.

Glendower exercised great military skill, and, though Henry made at least five expeditions against him, not one of them came within sight of crushing the revolt. Despite this, in the end Glendower failed. The French assistance proved insufficient, and, as the position of the House of Lancaster grew less precarious (Henry held the heir to the Scottish throne, and Northumberland was crushed in 1408), the King became able to turn his attention to Wales. Glendower had pressed into England as far as Worcester, but was thrown back by Prince Henry (later Henry V); in 1408 the prince took Aberystwyth and soon afterwards he captured Harlech, Glendower then being forced into outlawry. After 1412 he disappeared from the scene and died four years later in an unknown hiding-place. (In 1413 and again in 1415 Henry V offered a pardon, but Glendower never responded.)

Wales was exhausted. Politically the country finished the long revolt virtually where it had started; still partly under English law, still partly ruled by barons. Economically the consequences were disastrous. The lords of the manor lost their rents and services, their houses and farm buildings had been destroyed and their lands neglected; Welshmen generally suffered heavy penalties, were barred from public life, and had every possible disadvantage heaped upon them. Nevertheless the people had experienced a new upsurge of national feeling, and the old idea preached by the bards, that a prince of Brythonic blood should rule in Britain, was still kept alive. Despite repression and a huge burden of fines and debts, the national spirit remained uncrushed, expressing itself by a flourishing of the arts, particularly in the field of literature; poets and prose writers abounded, old manuscripts were transcribed for the first time, and the intricate canons of Welsh verse were reduced to their final form.

The Wars of the Roses brought new unrest to Wales, years of strife which would, however, have a triumphant conclusion.

The **Wars of the Roses**, fought with great brutality by both sides, were between the house of Lancaster (red rose), whose representative, the simple Henry VI, was on the throne (though it was his wife, the indomitable Margaret of Anjou, who counted), and the Yorkists (white rose). The Yorkist claimant was Edward Mortimer Duke of York, great grandson of Edward III. The wars lasted from 1455 (first battle of St. Albans) until 1485 (accession of Henry VII). In December 1460, at Wakefield, the Yorkists were defeated and the Duke of York killed; but in February 1461 his son Edward won a victory at what is now called Mortimer's Cross, soon entering London, dethroning Henry VI, and assuming the Crown. Although vicious fighting continued (Margaret was captured, and Henry VI's son Edward, Prince of Wales, was killed at Tewkesbury in 1471) the Yorkists remained on the throne until Richard III was defeated by Henry Tudor at Bosworth in 1485, the latter then becoming Henry VII.

So far as Wales was concerned York was represented by Edward IV, a Mortimer and as such chief of a family which by marriage and attainder had absorbed many of the Marcher lordships. Lancaster however held sway, not only by virtue of Henry VI's royal castles and Welsh estates, but also because of the backing of the Tewdwrs (Tudors), an old-established family whose prestige was on the ascendant. Owen ap Maredydd ap Tewdwr, an Anglesey landowner (executed by the Yorkists after Mortimer's Cross), had married Catherine of Valois, widow of Henry V, and his sons Edmund and Jasper had been created earls of Richmond and Pembroke. Edmund, who had married Margaret Beaufort, a descendant of John of Gaunt, died before the birth of their son Henry Tudor (Earl of Richmond). Between the ages of five and twelve this boy survived the seven-year-long siege of Harlech, but after Tewkesbury in 1471 he had to flee to exile in Brittany, because the death at Tewkesbury of Henry VI's son now made him the main claimant to the throne. His uncle Jasper proved a loyal and valuable supporter, and it was to a great extent due to his efforts that in 1485 Henry Tudor returned from exile, landing at Milford Haven on 7 August. On 21 August he won the Battle of Bosworth Field, Richard III was killed, and Henry became Henry VII. If for England Bosworth Field marked the final triumph of Lancaster over York, for the Welsh it meant the fulfilment of an ancient prophecy, and the fact that a Welshman (a Briton) now occupied the throne.

The Tudors

(Henry VII, 1485–1509, Henry VIII, 1509–47, Edward VI, 1547–53. Mary I, 1553–58. Elizabeth I, 1558–1603)

Two important acts were passed during the reign of Henry VIII. The Act of Union (1535) removed the privileges of the Lords Marcher, converting their lands into shires, and decreed that Welsh shires and boroughs should return members to the English parliament. The Act for Certain Ordinances (1542) reconstituted the Council of Wales and the Marches, first established by Edward IV, and enacted that courts of justice should sit twice a year in every county; at the same time all Welsh laws which were at variance with the laws of England were declared void, this including the damaging system of gavelkind which now gave way to primogeniture. Thus Wales now officially enjoyed the same liberties as across the border, and the ruling classes found new careers open to them in England. Welshmen entered the army and navy and the learned professions, making names for themselves in Church and State. Indeed in many ways the Tudor years, and especially the reign of Elizabeth I, were, outside the country, the most brilliant in Welsh history, one noteworthy example of Welsh initiative in England being the foundation in 1571 of Jesus College, Oxford, by Hugh Price, treasurer of St. David's.

Within Wales though the picture was greyer. For the upper class of country squires the Tudor succession might mean a break with the past and the abandonment of native traditions in favour of English custom. But the peasantry remained poor and Wales predominantly pastoral. The two principal exports remained cattle and cloth, and scarcely any effort was made to exploit the great mineral wealth of the country. The Dissolution of the Monasteries, though in Wales none of these was very wealthy, also brought the disruption of a cultural tradition, learning having been very largely under the care of the monks. Tithes and church lands too passed into the hands of laymen, usually the local gentry, the country clergy thus being reduced to an unbefitting state of poverty.

The Dissolution apart, the Reformation created remarkably little disturbance in Wales. Some of the finest scholars fled to the Continent, but others equally brilliant were content to accept the new religion, and the main stream of native Welsh history now began to assume a largely religious and educational character. In the years 1567 to 1588 three works, as remarkable for what they were as for what they achieved both for religion and for establishing a classical written Welsh, were written in Wales, though published in London. Richard Davies, Bishop of St. David's and a leading spirit behind the moves for a national Church policy, worked together with his friend William Salesbury of Llanrwst, generally credited with being author of the first book printed in Welsh in c 1545, the result of their joint labours at Abergwili being the publication in 1567 of Welsh versions of the Book of Common Prayer and of the New Testament. The translation of the Book of Common Prayer was mainly the work of Davies, while that of the New Testament (except for some epistles translated by Davies, and the Book of Revelation, contributed by Thomas Huet, precentor of St. David's) was by Salesbury. Then in 1588, after eight years of work, William Morgan, vicar of Llanrhaeadr-ym-Mochnant and later Bishop of Llandaff and St. Asaph, saw his translation of the entire Bible issued by the royal press and distributed throughout the parishes of Wales; it would later be replaced in the reign of James I by the Authorised Version, translated by Bishop Parry of St. Asaph, helped by Dr John Davies of Mallwyd, the first real Welsh lexicographer.

The Stuarts and the Commonwealth
(James I, 1603–25. Charles I, 1625–49. Commonwealth, 1649–60. Charles II, 1660–85. James II, 1685–88. William III and Mary II, 1688–94. William III, 1694–1702. Anne, 1702–14)

With the accession of the Stuarts the special favour enjoyed in England by Welshmen came to an end. In addition the Council of Wales and the Marches, for long a guardian of Welsh interests and an anchor for law and order, now declined in importance until it became little more than an intermediary between the local courts and the King's Council in London. It was abolished in 1689. Nevertheless the tradition of loyalty to the Crown continued under the early Stuarts, and the development of Puritanism in England at the start of the 17C was little felt in Wales. As a result Wales was predominantly Royalist during the Civil War.

Wales and the Marches suffered relatively little from the fighting. After raising his standard at Nottingham in August 1642, Charles I moved to Shrewsbury which he used as a base for recruiting and where he was soon joined by Prince Rupert. In South Wales Lord Hertford was in arms, but moved to Oxford as soon as Charles went there. In April 1643 the Parliamentarian Sir William Waller took Hereford, but soon had to retire back east. In 1645, after the decisive Royalist defeat at Naseby in June, the King and Rupert retired to South Wales to try to raise more infantry. They had little success, and when in August Rupert was defeated and surrendered at Bristol, Charles moved northwards; there was some skirmishing at Chester, then Charles, defeated at nearby Rowton Moor, withdrew temporarily to Denbigh. Chester held out for the King until starved into surrender by February 1646, Denbigh until August, and Harlech until March 1647. Except for Raglan, which did not surrender until August 1646, South Wales was overrun by the Parliamentarians by the end of 1645. What is sometimes called the Second Civil War (1648) started in Wales in March 1648 when Colonel Poyer, Parliamentarian governor of Pembroke, openly declared for the King with most of South Wales rising in support. But the rising was defeated in May at St. Fagans, near Cardiff, and by 11 July Pembroke Castle had been battered into submission.

As has been noted, Puritanism had been slow to develop in Wales. Nevertheless the roots were there. In 1588 John Penry of Brecon sent two appeals to parliament urging a Puritan policy for Wales, while later Rhys Pritchard (1579–1644) of Llandovery became celebrated for his Puritan preaching and writing. William Wroth (died 1642), another Puritan, in 1639 founded a community at Llanfaches, this now generally being accepted as the first dissenting chapel in Wales. The Civil War intervened, but with its close Cromwell, doubtless mindful of Welsh Royalist loyalties, was not slow to act. Within a month of the King's execution in 1649 he passed an Act for the Better Propagation and Preaching of the Gospel in Wales, which gave his 70 commissioners almost unlimited control over Welsh Church affairs. As a result huge numbers of incumbents were dismissed (330 out of 520 in St. David's and Llandaff alone), their place being taken by carefully selected itinerant preachers. Not until the Restoration and the Act of Uniformity (1662) were the ejected clergy restored, several Puritans in their turn losing their positions.

The Eighteenth Century. Methodism and Education
(George I, 1714–27. George II, 1727–60. George III, 1760–1820)

Daniel Defoe, passing through Wales in 1722, described a scene of calm and apparent content. He found the Welsh gentry 'civil, hospitable, and kind'; all that 'they valued themselves much upon their antiquity' and 'had preserved their families entire for many ages'; rural life, and the trade in cloth and cattle, was still carried on in the old way. But this calm was to a great extent illusory; beneath the surface was gathering the storm that broke over Wales in the shape of the Methodist Revival, a movement which, together with the closely allied educational movement, was to alter the life and thought of the Welsh people, which created new organisations, evolved new habits, and brought about a wholly changed social atmosphere.

It was the continued disregard of the problems of Wales both by the Welsh gentry and the English parliament that led inevitably to the great rupture in the Established Church, conservative, pro-English, and indifferent or even opposed to the particular needs of Wales. Directed from England, it was becoming increasingly out of touch with the people; all the bishops were English (no Welshman was elected to a Welsh see between the reign of Anne and 1870), and the majority were also non-resident, regarding the Welsh sees, without exception poor, merely as stepping stones to more remunerative positions; plurality was rampant, and such country clergy as did attend to their parishes were hampered by poverty and unfitted by education to administer to the spiritual needs of the people.

In such fertile ground the seeds of dissent were sown, at first unwittingly by men whose real concern was the education of a people the mass of whom at the opening of the century was illiterate.

An early example was Stephen Hughes (1623–88), an ejected Puritan minister who published religious literature in Welsh. Later came Sir John Philipps of Picton (died 1736), a wealthy Pembrokeshire landowner and one of the founders of the Society for the Promotion of Christian Knowledge, who issued devotional books and founded schools in which children were encouraged to read in their own language. Most influential of all perhaps was Griffith Jones (1683–1761), rector of Llanddowror, who, helped both by Sir John Philipps and Mrs Bridget Bevan of Laugharne, organised a system of itinerant teachers; so successful was Jones that by the date of his death nearly a third of the entire population of Wales could read the Bible.

Thus a basis of popular education was provided upon which the Nonconformist movement could at last develop. The first Nonconformist chapel had been founded (by William Wroth) as long before as 1639, and the Quakers (Society of Friends), Baptists, and Independents had all opened chapels in the 17C, but teaching, falling on illiterate and ignorant ground, had made little impression. Now all was changed, and for the first time since the Reformation an appeal could be made to the people themselves. There were a number of able and eloquent Methodists ready to seize this opportunity. One was Hywel Harris (1713–73) who at Trefecca in 1752 founded an institution for dissenters on a communal system similar to that of the Moravians; it survives today as a museum. Others were Daniel Rowlands (1713–90), curate of Llangeitho, who soon became one of the most popular preachers in Wales; William Williams (1717–91) of Pantycelyn, whose hymns have become part of Welsh literature; and Peter Williams (1722–96), who made a name as a Welsh Bible commentator. Towards the close of the century Methodism began to spread through North Wales, a leading influence here being Thomas Charles (1755–1814) of Bala, one of the founders of the British and Foreign Bible Society.

At first the Methodists attempted to work within the framework of the Established Church—they had no intention of forming a separate denomination—but their departures from conventional discipline and the opposition this aroused among the bishops (all, it should be remembered, English) finally led to schism in 1811 when an independent, dissenting communion, known as the Calvinistic Methodists, was founded. The communion's adherents were mainly drawn from the farming and labouring classes, while the gentry remained faithful to the Established Church. After the death of John Wesley (1703–91), who generally had kept aloof from Wales, the Wesleyan Methodists began to infiltrate, and at the same time the Baptists and Independents increased their influence. But the Calvinistic Methodist Church remained independent, and is today usually known as the Presbyterian Church of Wales.

The 18C was also not without its cultural advances. The Morris brothers of Anglesey became widely known as men of letters and patrons of the arts. Lewis (1701–65) was a poet and scholar; Richard (1703–79) was also a patron of the arts, while William (1705–63) was founder in 1751 of the Cymmrodorion Society to encourage Welsh literature, science, and art. Goronwy Owen (1723–69), son of a tinker and also born in Anglesey, was inspired by Lewis Morris and became leader of a group of poets writing in a classical style still alive today. Other important events of the century were the eisteddfod at Corwen in 1789 which marked the rebirth of such festivals, and the introduction by Edward Williams, in 1792, of what has become today's bardic tradition. At the same time, and given impetus by the growth in coach travel, cultivated Englishmen began to take a discerning interest in Welsh scenery and antiquities.

The Nineteenth and Twentieth Centuries

(George IV, 1820–30. William IV, 1830–37. Victoria, 1837–1901. Edward VII, 1901–10. George V, 1910–36. Edward VIII, 1936. George VI, 1836–52. Elizabeth II.)

The developments of the 19 and 20C can conveniently be recorded under headings.

Industry (see also the opening paragraphs of Rte 37). The Industrial Revolution had already exploded in South Wales by the later years of the 18C, its stimulus being the combination of iron ore and coal, the attendant metal industries, and the convenient ports. Over only a few years small market towns such as Merthyr Tydfil, Newport, and Cardiff became centres of industry, quiet valleys were torn apart for iron and coal, and a network of railways began to spread across the country, including I.K. Brunel's Great Western which by 1845 had reached Treffgarne, only 10m short of Fishguard. Such a change in a short time, while bringing prosperity to some, brought grinding hardship to the majority and with this came social unrest, the two best known occasions being the Chartist Riots of 1839 and the Rebecca Riots of 1843.

Chartist Riots. Largely as a result of the inadequate Reform Bill of 1832, a 'People's Charter' was drawn up in 1837 by the London Workingmen's Association, the charter's six points being equal electoral areas; universal suffrage; payment of MPs; no property qualification for voters; vote by ballot; and annual parliaments. This movement for social equality spread rapidly over much of Britain, the Welsh miners being among the most militant groups. A petition signed by over 1¼ million people was rejected by parliament in July 1839, and in November rioting broke out in Lancashire, Yorkshire, and Wales, where an attack on Newport was led by the ex-mayor John Frost. The operation was poorly planned, the Chartists walked into a trap, and Frost and other leaders were sentenced to death, this sentence later being reduced to transportation. In 1842 another petition, this time with nearly 3½ million signatures, was rejected. Chartism then went into decline, this being accelerated when the repeal of the Corn Laws in 1846 much bettered the lot of the working classes.

The **Rebecca Riots** were confined to South Wales. Though caused by the same economic circumstances as the Chartist troubles, the riots were in the first instance directed against tollgate charges (which hampered the small itinerant traders) and took their name from Genesis XXIV 60 'And they blessed Rebekah and said unto her, thou art our sister, be thou the mother of thousands of millions, and let thy seed possess the gate of those which hate them'. The rioters, often disguised as women and led by group leaders called 'Rebeccas', destroyed tollgates and their houses, and then, encouraged by success, demanded redress of other grievances. The disorders were quelled, but in South Wales tollgates disappeared.

In Wales, and especially in the South, the industrial upsurge did not last. The demand for better quality ore for improved and more specialised steel manufacturing processes, the depression, two world wars, the appearance of cheap imported coal as also the replacement of coal by oil (on nationalisation in 1945 there were 212 pits in Wales; by 1989 there were 11), and the drop in world demand for steel and slate, all combined to bring about an accelerating decline. But by the early 1980s the lessons of over-dependence on confined sectors of industry were already fast being learnt and diversification and trading estates were increasingly becoming the pattern. The momentum gathered and the decade saw explosive change as much in attitudes as in industrial scope. The traditional picture of cloth caps, miners, chapels, choirs (though, thankfully, the chapels and choirs still flourish) and entrenched attitudes in a setting of gaunt, belching machinery in gloomy valleys has vanished, its place taken by vigorous initiative, bold expansion, clean modern factories and an increasingly pragmatic approach to industrial relations. Already by 1988—and perhaps as sound an industrial indicator as any—Wales was host to the highest concentration of Japanese companies in Britain.

Politics. The conservative attitude of the Methodists, who felt interference with the supposed Divine Will to be sinful, and also of the older Dissenters who although maintaining the Whig tradition of liberty were disinclined to bring about reform through force, did not at first favour the rise of a representative political party. But the Industrial Revolution meant that the reign of the landowning classes, who had long monopolised parliamentary representation, was at an end, and at length a new party arose, the Liberal Party, which expressed the aspirations of a rising middle class whose wealth was based on industry. In the General Election of 1868 Wales returned 22 Liberal members out of a total of 30, and less than half a century later it would be a Welsh Liberal, David Lloyd George, who would lead the British in the First World War. Not long after the birth of the Liberals, the working classes too began slowly to find political expression, and the first Labour MP in Britain was returned for Merthyr Tydfil in 1900.

In recent years many factors, not the least being the hardships caused by the reorientation of industry, led to increased pressure for more control of local affairs. Plaid Cymru, the Welsh National Party, won seats in parliament; Cardiff was granted capital status in 1955; the Welsh flag was given royal approval in 1959; the post of Secretary of State for Wales was raised to cabinet rank in 1964; and during the 1970s devolution in some form was, if briefly, a leading issue.

Culture and Education. The cultural advances of the 18C, with the rebirth of eisteddfodau after the Corwen festival of 1789, have already been noted. The 19C saw the founding of the annual National Eisteddfod. The desire for national expression also entered the field of education. The first institution of university rank was established at Aberystwyth in 1872, this being followed by university colleges at Bangor and Cardiff (1883). In 1893 these were combined to form the University of Wales, to which a fourth college, at Swansea, was added in 1920, while in 1971 St. David's College, Lampeter, became constituent.

Today there are seven constituent colleges (Cardiff comprising three, though mergers are planned) and the whole university technological emphasis is changing, with, for instance, 'sunrise' industries departments displacing traditional departments, increasingly close collaboration with industry, and the creation of college Science Parks.

Charters for the establishment of a National Museum and a National Library were granted in 1907, and these institutions—at, respectively, Cardiff (but now with branches throughout Wales) and Aberystwyth—rank among the culturally most valued and influential in Wales.

Religion. In the sphere of orthodox religion there had been from the mid 19C a movement to break away from the domination of the Church of England, but it was not until 1920 that an Act for the

Disestablishment of the Church in Wales was passed, and the four Welsh dioceses of St. Asaph, Bangor, Llandaff and St. David's were combined into an independent and self-governing body, though still in communion with the Church of England. Its archbishop has no fixed see. A new diocese of Newport and Monmouth was formed in 1921 (St. Woolos Church at Newport became a full cathedral in 1949), and another of Swansea and Brecon in 1923.

Conservation and the Countryside have become increasingly important themes during the present century, and especially so since the last war. Snowdonia, Brecon Beacons and Pembrokeshire Coast National Parks were all designated during the 1950s, Country Parks now abound, and there is impressive and continuing evidence of the rehabilitation of The Valleys.

Biographical Notes

These notes identify and elaborate on selected personalities about whom users may like to know more. Well known names are not generally included, nor are people who are sufficiently identified in the History or Routes texts.

Agricola, Gnaeus Julius (37–93). Roman general and governor of Britain, where he spent some seven years, conquering North Wales and Anglesey and southern Scotland. His daughter married the historian Tacitus. May have died of poisoning.

Baldwin (died 1190). Archbishop of Canterbury. His visit to Wales in 1187 was the first ever by an archbishop. In 1188 he toured Wales with Giraldus (then archdeacon of St. David's) preaching the Third Crusade. Professing himself appalled by the excesses of the crusaders, he died on reaching the Holy Land.

Bolingbroke, Henry (1367–1413) = Henry IV (1399). Son of John of Gaunt by Blanche of Lancaster. For several years he travelled and fought as an adventurer, but when on John of Gaunt's death in 1399 Richard II confiscated the estates of Lancaster Bolingbroke landed in Yorkshire and was joined by the Percys and other barons. Richard II, absent in Ireland and unpopular because of his arbitrary taxation, lost all support and soon surrendered at Flint. Richard died the following year, probably as the result of hardships of winter imprisonment rather than by murder as told by Shakespeare.

Borrow, George (1803–81). Philologist and linguist (he even translated the New Testament into Manchu). Travelled widely, acting as agent for the British and Foreign Bible Society. While in St. Petersburg he published 'Targum', a series of translations from 30 languages and dialects. He became something of a tramp, wandering the roads of England and Wales, in the latter context being known for his 'Wild Wales' (1862), a description of a tour he made with his stepdaughter. Very interested in gypsies, who provided material for several works.

Bradshaw, John (1602–59). Born at Presteigne. Lord President of the Parliamentary Commission which brought Charles I to trial, Bradshaw's signature headed the list of these who signed the death warrant. He refused to let the King speak in his own defence. Later he pronounced sentence of death on many Royalists.

Brunel, Isambard Kingdom (1806–59). Engineer, mainly of docks, railways and steamships. In 1833 Brunel was appointed engineer of the projected Great Western Railway, one of his early proposals being that the railway should be prolonged by a steamship ('Great Western', 1838) from Bristol to New York. He also designed the 'Great Britain' (1845) and the 'Great Eastern' (1859). Brunel's associations with Wales include the south coast railway and initial work on the docks at Milford Haven. His father (Sir Marc Isambard, 1769–1849), a refugee from revolutionary France, was also a distinguished engineer and inventor.

Burges, William (1827–81). Architect and decorator. His monuments in Wales are Cardiff Castle and Castell Coch. He is also associated with Salisbury chapter house, Brisbane and Cork cathedrals, and the College of Hartford, Conn.

Burne-Jones, Sir Edward (1833–98). Painter and designer. In 1862 Burne-Jones, William Morris, and D.G. Rossetti started a successful applied arts business. Burne-Jones most made his mark as a designer, and stained glass windows made from his designs are widespread.

Bute, 3rd Marquess. John Patrick Crichton Stuart (1847–1900). Inherited from his father the 2nd Marquess (first builder of Cardiff docks) huge estates in Scotland and in and around Cardiff. In 1868 he became a Roman Catholic, an incident which may have suggested to Disraeli the plot for his novel 'Lothair'. The 3rd Marquess published several erudite works, largely on religious topics. In Wales he is best known for commissioning the work by Burges on Cardiff Castle and Castell Coch.

Caractacus, or Caradog or Caratacus, was the British chief of the Catuvellauni tribe, and son of Cunobelinus, chief of the Trinobantes. He led the resistance against the Romans in 43–47, and after defeat at Wallingford on the Thames retreated into Wales, where a number of hillforts bear his name. He was finally defeated in 51 by Ostorious Scapula, most probably at the Caer Caradoc either near Church Stretton or between Clun and Knighton. He and his family were taken to Rome, where the emperor Claudius allowed them to live.

Caröe, William Douglas (1857–1938). Architect. Son of the Danish consul in Liverpool. Caröe's work was largely ecclesiastical, and he was consulting architect to several cathedrals (including Canterbury and Durham) and also to Malvern, Romsey, and Tewkesbury abbeys. In Wales he is known for his fine work at Brecon.

Clive, Robert (1725–74). Founder of the British empire in India. Went to Madras as a clerk in the East India Company, but soon made a name in the fighting which marked the Anglo-French struggle for India. His defence of Arcot prompted Pitt to call him a 'heaven-sent general', and there followed his campaign against Suraj-ud-Dowlah (notorious for the Black Hole of Calcutta) which ended with Clive's victory at Plassey. In 1760 Clive returned to England, was made Baron Clive (Irish peerage) and became MP for Shrewsbury. Back in India in 1765–67 he pushed through many reforms and left Britain supreme. On his return to England attempts by jealous enemies to impeach him largely misfired, but nevertheless, in ill health and depressed at being treated 'like a sheep-stealer', he took his own life. His son Edward, Governor of Madras, acquired Powis Castle (now home of an important Clive of India Museum) by marriage and became Earl of Powis.

Cobbe, Frances Power (1822–1904). Social writer and worker, and suffragist. Contributed to newspapers and reviews on such topics as vivisection (of which she was a strong opponent), destitution, women's rights, and divorce. Of her many works may be mentioned

'The Duties of Women' (1881) and her autobiography (1894). Buried at Llanelltyd.

Dafydd ap Gwilym (c 1340–c 1400). Poet and chief bard, described by Borrow, who translated some of his verses, as the Horace of Wales. Wrote nature poems, usually in the 'cywydd' form, a short ode with each line having the same number of syllables. Probably born at Broginin near Aberystwyth, he is said to have eloped with a princess of Anglesey. He may be buried at Talley.

Davies, John (c 1570–1644). Welsh lexicographer. Rector of Mallwyd (1604). Assisted Parry with his Welsh bible of 1620. His own major work was 'Antiquae Linguae Britannicae Dictionarium Duplex' (1632), in Welsh-Latin and Latin-Welsh parts.

Dyer, John (1700–58). Welsh poet born at Aberglasney, which district he describes in his 'Grongar Hill'. His longest work is 'The Fleece', an epic in blank verse coverng the subject of wool from the sheep through to the cloth trade.

Edward II (1284–1327). Irresponsible son of Edward I. Born at Caernarfon Castle and made Prince of Wales in 1301. Acceded in 1307. Probably homosexual. Notorious for his favourites and their influence over him. The first was Piers Gaveston, murdered by the barons in 1312. In 1308 Edward married Isabella of France. In 1314 he was ignominiously defeated by the Scots under Bruce at Bannockburn. In 1318 the Despensers (father and son, both Hugh) became Edward's favourites and effectively ruled England until 1326. In that year Isabella led a revolt against Edward, who found himself deserted. In Glamorgan he took refuge in the Despensers' Caerphilly Castle, but Isabella followed and, after an attempt to escape by sea from Chepstow, Edward was forced back into Cardiff. He and the younger Despenser were taken at Llantrisant Castle, both Despensers then being put to death while Edward was murdered the following year.

Evans, Christmas (1766–1838). Orphan son of a cobbler he became a Baptist minister because the Presbyterians demanded an academic standard he did not have. After a period in the Lleyn, he was in Anglesey for over 30 years, becoming the centre of the Baptist movement and attracting huge crowds to his oratorical and emotional sermons.

Evans, Petty Officer. See under Scott, Robert Falcon.

Gaveston, Piers (died 1312). Son of a Gascon knight. Favourite of Edward II. Twice banished on the insistance of the barons, he each time was called back and was finally executed by his enemies.

Geoffrey of Monmouth (died 1154). 'Historian' and churchman. Nephew of a bishop of Llandaff. Born at Monmouth, where he may also have been a monk. His best known work is his 'Historia Britonum' (c 1139), claiming to be a translation from a Celtic source but today generally accepted as Geoffrey's own work and to be a mixture of ancient tradition, pure fiction, and only to a very small extent fact. Whatever it was, it gained for its author a name for erudition and the appointments of Archdeacon of Llandaff (c 1140) and Bishop of St. Asaph (1151). He may also be the author of a 'Vita Merlini' (a life of Merlin) in Latin verse. The 'Historia Britonum' laid the written foundations of the Arthurian legend, and was widely accepted as history until as late as the 17C. It provided Shakespeare with the story of King Lear.

Germanus, Saint (?378–448). Bishop of Auxerre (418), of which he was a native. In 429 the British bishops asked the help of their colleagues in Gaul in their struggle against the Pelagian heresy.

Germanus and Lupus of Troyes were sent to Britain, one event during their visit being the Alleluia Victory near Mold. In 447 he again came to Britain, this time with Severus of Treves; a combination of miracles and vigorous preaching soon led to the decline of Pelagianism. Germanus was for some time in Wales, becoming the subject of several legends, amongst these that he cursed Vortigern for incest. He lives on in several place names.

Gibson, John (1790–1866). Sculptor, born at Conwy. First made his name in Rome, where he was befriended by Canova. Best known for his bas-reliefs, and as the first British sculptor to use colour.

Gildas (c 516–570). Probably a monk, the earliest British historian. His main work was 'Gildae Sapientis de excidio et conquestu Britanniae', comprising a preface, a history, and an epistle. The history, which is cursory, reviews the history of Britain from the arrival of the Romans until the author's own time; the epistle is largely a condemnation of the vices of his countrymen.

Giraldus Cambrensis (c 1146–1223). Nobleman, churchman, scholar, and historian. Born at Manorbier of mixed Welsh-Norman parentage, then studied in Paris until 1172. Archdeacon of Brecon (1175) and of St. David's (1180). Accompanied Prince John to Ireland and wrote a history of the conquest. In 1188 he accompanied Archbishop Baldwin through Wales preaching the Third Crusade, as a result of this writing his 'Itinerarium Cambrense' which gives a picture of Wales of the time. In 1198 he was proposed for the bishopric of St. Davids, but Rome did not approve. His friendship with such men as Innocent III, Richard I, John, Stephen Langton and others provided valuable background for his writings.

Gower, Bishop Henry (died 1347). Member of a noble English-speaking Gower family. Best known for his benefactions and as an architect, in the latter capacity being the originator of an attractive and unusual local form of Decorated Gothic. In 1322–23 he was chancellor of Oxford University.

Heber, Reginald (1783–1826). Bishop and hymn writer. 1812, Prebendary of St Asaph. 1823, Bishop of Calcutta, Heber dying in India three years later. Among his hymns are 'Holy, Holy, Holy, Lord God Almighty' and 'From Greenland's Icy Mountains'. In 1822 he edited the works of Jeremy Taylor.

Hemans, Mrs Felicia Dorothea (1783–1835). Poetess. Lived near St. Asaph before her separation from her husband. Worked together with Sir Walter Scott who wrote an epilogue for her play 'The Vespers of Palermo'. Probably her best known lines are 'The boy stood on the burning deck, Whence all but he had fled'.

Henry IV. See Bolingbroke.

Herbert of Cherbury, Lord Edward (1583–1648). Diplomat, soldier, and writer. Brother of the poet George Herbert. 1610, fought in the Netherlands for the Prince of Orange. 1617–24, Ambassador in Paris. 1624, created Baron Cherbury. 1644, surrendered Montgomery Castle to Parliament. His written works include religious philosophy, poems, and an autobiography.

Herbert, George (1593–1633). Poet. Brother of above. His poems, in Latin and English, are largely of a metaphysical religious nature, and he also wrote hymns. Ordained priest in 1630.

Hopper, Thomas (1776–1856). Architect. First made his name through alterations for the Prince Regent to London's Carlton House, after this becoming fashionable with the nobility and gentry. In Wales his monument is Penrhyn Castle. In London he was associated with the Royal Exchange, Houses of Parliament, and many other buildings.

Horton, Thomas (died 1649). Parliament's commander who (with Philip Jones) defeated Poyer and Laugharne at St. Fagans. Signed the King's death warrant. Died in Ireland, where he was accompanying Cromwell.

Hubert de Burgh (died 1243). Served Richard I, John, and Henry III, under the latter two being Chief Justiciar, the king's closest adviser. He reached the height of his power when in 1227 he declared Henry III to be of age, and when, as the result of four marriages, he had acquired extensive lands. But Henry, with ambitious military plans, became impatient at Hubert's caution and in 1232 stripped him of his post, honours, and lands, including White, Skenfrith, and Grosmont castles. In 1234 he regained some favour and his earldom, but the position of Justiciar declined in importance.

Isabella, Queen. See under Edward II.

Johnson, Dr Samuel (1709–94). Writer, lexicographer, and conversationalist. Best known for his 'Dictionary' which, though highly individual in its definitions, won fame as a dictionary that could be read with pleasure. He achieved a prolific output of miscellaneous writing (including his popular 'Lives of the Poets'), enjoyed a wide circle of friends, and became renowned for his brilliant conversation and pronouncements. His name is inseparably linked with that of his friend and biographer James Boswell. See also Thrale, Hester Lynch.

Jones, Inigo (1573–1651). Architect. His patron was the Earl of Arundel who sent him to Italy where he studied the style of Palladio. He was so successful in Venice that he was invited by Christian IV to Denmark where he designed the palaces of Rosenborg and Frederiksborg. Through the influence of Anne of Denmark, wife of James I, he became architect to the English court (1604) and Surveyor of Royal Buildings (1612). He held the same posts under Charles I but was heavily fined after the Civil War and died in penury.

Jones, Philip (c 1618–74). Born in Swansea, of which, as a Parliamentary supporter, he was made governor in 1645. In 1648, with Horton, he defeated Laugharne and Poyer at St. Fagans, afterwards being made governor of Cardiff Castle. Throughout the Commonwealth he was a trusted adviser to Cromwell, but somehow he survived the Restoration, keeping his estates and in 1664 even acquiring Penmarc and Fonmon castles.

Landor, Walter Savage (1775–1864). Poet, prose writer, and idealist with republican sympathies. In 1808 he went to Spain and at his own expense raised a troop to fight Napoleon, a venture which failed and cost Landor a lot of money but provided the material for one of his finest poems, 'Count Julian'. There followed the Llanthony Priory affair, after which Landor lived on and off in Italy. His first great poem was 'Gebir' (1798) and among his best prose works was his series of 'Imaginary Conversations' (1824–46).

Laugharne, Rowland (died after 1660). Home was at Laugharne. Successful Parliamentary commander in South Wales, taking Haverfordwest, Tenby, Carew, Cardigan, Picton, and Carmarthen. But Laugharne was dissatisfied with his rewards, complaining also that he had had no refund for personal moneys paid on Parliament's behalf and that for two years he had had to pay his soldiers out of his own pocket. He then joined Poyer's revolt, being defeated with him by Horton and Jones at St. Fagans. Laugharne, Poyer, and a Colonel Powell were sentenced to death, but Cromwell decided that only one should be executed, the choice being made by lot. Poyer was the loser.

Lloyd, William (1627–1717). Successively Bishop of St. Asaph, Lichfield and Coventry, and Worcester. Noted as an opponent of the Roman Catholic leanings of James II, he was one of the seven bishops tried for refusing to have the Declaration of Indulgence read in their dioceses.

Luxmoore, Charles (1794–1854). Helped by his father John Luxmoore, who was successively Bishop of Bristol, Hereford, and St. Asaph, Charles held at the same time the deanery of St. Asaph, the chancellorship of St. Asaph, the position of prebend of Hereford, and three rectories.

Magnus Maximus (died 387). Roman commander. While in Britain he was proclaimed emperor by disaffected local troops. After denuding Britain of troops he crossed to Gaul where he killed Gratian, co-emperor with Theodosius I. Theodosius then recognised Magnus as emperor in Gaul, Spain, and Britain. In 387 the ambitious Magnus crossed the Alps, but was defeated and beheaded. He passed into Welsh legend ('Mabinogion') under the name of Macsen Wledig.

Margaret of Beaufort (1443–1509). Countess of Richmond and Derby and mother of Henry VII. After the death of her husband, Edmund Tudor, she married in succession the son (died 1482) of the Duke of Buckingham, and Thomas Stanley, later Earl of Derby. Throughout his exile in Brittany she and Stanley were in constant communication with her son, Stanley doing much to help his cause. Margaret became known for her many foundations, these including Christ's and St. John's colleges at Cambridge, and chairs of Divinity at Oxford and Cambridge. In Wales she is associated with the chapel at Holywell.

Marten, Henry (1602–80). As an MP Marten was always outspoken against Charles I. Although he played no significant part in the Civil War, he was one of the King's judges and signed the death warrant. At the Restoration he was imprisoned in Chepstow Castle where he died 10 years later. Although a Puritan he kept a mistress, and while in Chepstow he published 'Henry Marten's Familiar Letters to his Lady of Delight'.

Merlin. Wizard of Arthurian romance who may possibly derive from an early bard. Traditionally he had a spirit father and a human mother (for this, as also for Merlin and Vortigern, see under Legend). An ancient 'Vita Merlini', which associates Merlin with Scottish legend, may be the work of Geoffrey of Monmouth. Geoffrey also collects the legends of Merlin and Arthur in his 'Historia Britonum'.

Morris, William (1834–96). Poet and artist. In 1862 Morris, Burne-Jones, Rossetti and others started an applied arts business. Stained glass windows and other decoration from his designs are often met in England and Wales, and in later years he became interested in printing, acquiring a private press. He founded the Society for the Protection of Ancient Buildings, largely because of his disapproval of the restoration work of Sir George Gilbert Scott.

Myddelton, Sir Hugh (died 1631). Engineer. Born near Denbigh. He is known for London's New River (1609–13), a 40m long aqueduct bringing water from springs near Ware in Hertfordshire to a reservoir at Clerk's Well (Clerkenwell).

Mytton, Thomas (c 1597–1656). Parliamentary leader and commander. Native of Halston, Salop. His many Civil War successes included the taking of Wem, Ellesmere, Oswestry, and Shrewsbury.

In 1645 he was appointed commander for North Wales, further successes including Ruthin, Caernarfon, Beaumaris, Conwy, Denbigh and Harlech.

Nash, John (1752–1835). Architect. Possibly born at Cardigan. Becoming fashionable with royalty and the nobility, his name is mainly associated with the part he played in the improvement of London (Regent Street, Regent's Park surrounds, reconstruction of Buckingham Palace).

Nash, Richard (1674–1762). Beau Nash, the dandy. Born at Swansea. In 1705 he became Master of Ceremonies at Bath, soon introducing sweeping reforms and making Bath England's leading centre of fashion.

Owen, Daniel (1836–95). Welsh novelist and short story writer, whose trade was that of tailor. A native of Mold (museum). Sometimes described as the Welsh Dickens, his writings are among the more important records of the era of the arrival of the railways and of the spread of religious revivalism.

Owen, Sir Hugh (1804–81). Born in Anglesey. Promotor of Welsh education, his main achievement being the establishment of the University College of Wales at Aberystwyth. He also played a large part in the reforms of the National Eisteddfod, and was concerned in the revival (1873) of the Society of Cymmrodorion which had died in 1843. Also did much philanthropic work (London-Welsh Charitable Aid Society. London Fever Hospital. National Temperance League). Knighted in 1881 for services to Welsh education.

Owen, Sir John (1600–66). Royalist commander. Born in Caernarfonshire. Knighted in 1644 by Charles I, at which time he was governor of Harlech. In 1648, at Caernarfon, he attemped a last uprising for Charles I but was defeated at Llandegai. He retired to Anglesey, where in 1659 he headed another uprising.

Owen, Robert (1771–1858). Social reformer born at Newtown (museum). He early made his name as an efficient yet humane cotton mill manager, and is most associated with the New Lanark mills in Scotland of which he became manager and part owner. Here, for a labour force of 2000 including 500 children, he built improved housing, opened a cost price store, and started the first infant school in Britain. Later (1825), impatient over government lack of support for his plans for industrial reform and for self-contained communities, he founded New Harmony in Indiana USA, but this failed and Owen lost most of his money. On his return to England he was accepted as the workers' leader and became much involved in the growth of trade unionism, as also in such fields as education and marriage law reform. His four sons all settled in America, the eldest sitting in Congress and achieving many social reforms. Buried at Newtown.

Patti, Adelina Juana Marina (1843–1919). American singer. She made her first appearance in 1859 in New York as Lucia in 'Lucia di Lammermoor'. Sang at Covent Garden in 1861, soon becoming world famous. Her marriage at Brecon in 1898, her third, was to the Swedish Baron Cederström. She bought her home at Craig-y-Nos in 1878.

Pelagius (c 360–c 420). British theologian who may have spent his early years at the monastery at Bangor-is-Coed. For the rest of his life he was in Rome, Africa, and Palestine. The main plank of his philosophy was the freedom of the human will, as opposed to the current official doctrine of original sin. His views were spread largely through the enthusiasm of his younger and bolder Italian friend

Coelestius. In 429 St. Germanus, Bishop of Auxerre, was sent to Britain to combat the heresy, which later was also a source of worry to St. David.

Pennant, Thomas (1726–98). Traveller, naturalist, and prolific writer. Native of Downing, near Holywell, his first publication (1750) was an account of an earthquake felt here. In 1767 he was elected a Fellow of the Royal Society, and in 1771 he published 'Synopsis of Quadrupeds'. He made tours of Scotland in 1769 and 1772, and, as a result, published 'Tour in Scotland' and 'Flora Scotica'. His 'Tour in Wales', written as the result of several journeys, was published in 1778. Amongst other works his 'British Zoology' and 'History of Quadrupeds' are classics of their time.

Philips, Katharine (1631–64), Poetess. She made her home (The Priory, Cardigan) a centre of a Society of Friendship, the members of which addressed one another by romantic names, she being Orinda, to which her admirers prefixed 'matchless'. It was she who pressed Jeremy Taylor to write his discourse on friendship.

Poyer, John (died 1649). In 1642, as mayor of Pembroke, he sided with Parliament. In 1648, alleging that Parliament had not repaid moneys he had disbursed on its behalf and that he had had to pay his soldiers out of his own pocket, he declared for the King and was joined by Laugharne who had similar grievances. The pair were defeated at St. Fagans and Cromwell battered Pembroke into surrender. In 1649 Poyer, Laugharne and a Colonel Powell were sentenced to death, but Cromwell decided that only one of the trio, to be chosen by lot, should die. Poyer lost, and was shot in London's Covent Garden.

Rees, Abraham (1743–1825). Encyclopaedist. Between 1778–88 he published a revised and expanded edition of Ephraim Chambers's 'Cyclopaedia' (shortened title), claiming to have added over 4400 new articles.

Repton, Humphry (1752–1818). Landscape gardener. Although a follower of 'Capability' Brown, he was far less rigid in his attitude, maintaining that the house must always be the principal factor in a design and that the gardens should be subordinate. Repton is known for his 'Red Books', these being reports in red covers giving details of each of his more important undertakings and including sketches showing what the effect would be as the trees reached maturity.

Richard II. See under Bolingbroke.

Richard, Henry (1812–88). Native of Tregaron. His lifelong theme was the need for arbitration in international disputes, these principles first being made public in a speech in London in 1845. From 1845–88 he was secretary of the Peace Society, as such attending a series of international conferences. He also did much for Wales, serving as MP for Merthyr and becoming known as the 'Member for Wales'.

Roberts, Samuel (1800–85). Social and political reformer, and leader of Nonconformist opinion. Advocate of free trade, franchise extension, Catholic emancipation, and temperance. He was also active in fighting for special railway routes through Wales. In 1827 he advocated a system of inland penny post, and in 1883 his efforts at general postal reform were recognised by an official testimonial and award. Between 1857–67 he was in America, with his brother Richard, preaching racial equality.

Rowlands, John. See Stanley, HM.

Savage, Richard (died 1743). Poet. He claimed to be the natural son of Richard Savage, 4th Earl Rivers, and of Lady Macclesfield, a claim rejected by the latter, by then Mrs Brett. However Savage black-mailed so successfully ('The Bastard' was published in 1728) that he was bought off with a pension from Mrs Brett's nephew, Viscount Tyrconnel. When, as the result of a quarrel, this pension was stopped, Savage was reduced to penury and his always faithful friend Pope gave him a small allowance and sent him to Swansea to escape his creditors. But impatient at the conditions imposed by Pope and others who had helped, Savage unwisely moved to Bristol where he died in the debtors' prison. As a writer he is best known as a satirist.

Scott, George Gilbert (1811–78). Architect. Among his achievements are the Martyrs' Memorial, Oxford (1840); the restoration of Ely Cathedral (1847), and later of Hereford, Lichfield, Salisbury, and Ripon cathedrals; several government buildings around Whitehall, these being the subject of much conflict between the Gothic and the Classical schools, the latter in the end winning; St. Pancras station and Hotel (1865); and the Albert Memorial (1872). The criticism was made that he remodelled rather than restored, and it is ironic that it was his work that to a great extent led to the founding (by William Morris) of the Society for the Protection of Ancient Buildings (1877).—His sons George (1839–1907) and J. Oldrid (1842–1913) and his grandson Giles (1880–1960) were all distinguished architects.

Scott, Robert Falcon (1868–1912). Leader of Antarctic expeditions in 1900–04 and 1909–12, on the latter occasion reaching the South Pole, only to find that he had been forestalled by Amundsen. He and his companions all died during the return sledge journey. His companions included Petty Officer Evans, whose home was Rhossili on Gower.

Shelley, Percy Bysshe (1792–1822), Poet. Shelley was in Wales on and off between 1811–13. The first occasion was a visit to his cousin Thomas Grove at Cwm Elan near Rhayader, after his expulsion from Oxford because of his pamphlet 'The Necessity of Atheism'. Soon after, he eloped with the schoolgirl Harriet Westbrook, marrying her in Scotland. In Wales the pair first stayed at Nant Gwyllt (April–June 1812) near Cwm Elan. Both places are now submerged below the Elan reservoirs. Later Shelley and Harriet moved to Tan-yr-Allt, scene of the Tremadog incident. After this they were briefly at Gwynfryn near Criccieth. In 1814 Shelley virtually deserted Harriet when he fell in love with Mary Godwin, and in 1817 Harriet drowned herself in London's Serpentine. Shelley then married Mary Godwin (as Mary Shelley, author of 'Frankenstein'), but in 1822 he too died by drowning in a storm at sea off Italy.

Siddal, Elizabeth (died 1862). Wife of D.G. Rossetti. A great beauty, who was painted by Holman Hunt and Millais and several times by Rossetti, who married her in 1860 when she was already dying of tuberculosis.

Simon de Montfort (c 1200–65). Born in France, youngest son of Simon IV de Montfort, leader of the Albigensian Crusade. Came to England in 1230, attached himself to Henry III, and was made Earl of Leicester. There followed constant quarrels with Henry, Simon on more than one occasion returning to France. When Henry accepted the crown of Sicily for his son and pledged England's credit to the Pope for the conquest of the island, Simon and the barons forced upon the King the Provisions of Oxford (1258), placing the government in the hands of a feudal oligarchy which strictly controlled expenditure. Henry submitted, but soon obtained papal absolution from his promises. In 1263 Simon led a rebellion, at Lewes defeating and capturing Henry and his son (the future Edward I). Simon then set up a parliamentary system, a feature of which was to be parliamentary control over the government. However Edward escaped from captivity in Hereford and soon defeated and killed Simon de Montfort at Evesham.

Stanhope, Lady Hester (1776–1839). Eldest child of the 3rd Earl of Stanhope and Lady Hester Pitt, she was niece of William Pitt. She was endowed with great energy and considerable business acumen, and from time to time acted as the statesman's private secretary. In 1810 she suddenly left England and settled on Mount Lebanon, where through a combination of sheer personality and careful fostering of the local belief that she had the gift of divination, she achieved a position of almost absolute authority over the Druse tribe.

Stanley, Sir Henry Morton (1841–1904). African explorer. Born John Rowlands at Denbigh, he was placed in St. Asaph workhouse at the age of six. Nine years later he ran away and sailed as a cabin boy to America where he was adopted by Henry Morton Stanley. During the American Civil War he served in the Confederate army, later travelling across America and becoming a recognised descriptive writer. After travels in Asia Minor and Tibet, and after being first with the news of the fall of Magdala in Abyssinia, he was commissioned by Gordon Bennet of the New York Herald to go to Africa to find David Livingstone. In this he succeeded in 1871. On his second African journey (1874–77), undertaken on behalf of Leopold II of Belgium, he traced the course of the Congo, remaining in what became the Congo State until 1884. On his third journey, a half political and half military expedition marked by appalling hardships, he discovered the Mountains of the Moon. He was knighted in 1899.

Steele, Sir Richard (1672–1729). Irish man of letters. Editor of the 'Gazette', the 'Tatler', and the 'Spectator', he achieved wide recognition through his many essays in the last two. Lived and died at Carmarthen.

Stephen, King (?1097–1154). Grandson of William I and nephew of Henry I. His reign was marked by civil war arising from the rival claim to the throne made by Matilda, daughter of Henry I and widow of the emperor Henry V. Although in 1126 Henry I compelled Stephen and the barons to recognise Matilda as his successor, on his death in 1135 Matilda was out of the country and the barons, unwilling to accept a woman sovereign, proclaimed Stephen. Civil war followed, during which Stephen was captured and Matilda ruled for a while as Lady of England. But Matilda's arrogance soon alienated her supporters, and after defeat at Winchester she had to release Stephen. Matilda retired to Normandy, and eventually Stephen recognised her son (the future Henry II) as his heir.

Stephenson, Robert (1803–59). Engineer. Surveyed the Stockton and Darlington railways. His monument in Wales is the Conwy tubular railway bridge. His similar bridge across Menai Strait was burnt in 1970.

Street, George Edmund (1824–81). Architect and architectural writer. His preference was the Gothic style and he specialised in ecclesiastical buildings. He also designed London's Law Courts, though the building was completed after his death by Blomfield and Street's son. Among his written works are 'The Brick and Marble Architecture of Northern Italy' and 'The Gothic Architecture of Spain'.

Taylor, Jeremy (1613–67). Divine, writer, and Royalist. As a Royalist he lost his rectorship of Uppingham and was later captured at Cardigan. After this he found refuge as private chaplain to Richard

Vaughan, 2nd Earl of Carbery, at the latter's mansion of Golden Grove near Llandeilo. Taylor's perhaps best known work is 'Golden Grove; or a Manuall of daily prayers and letanies' (1655). His 'Discours of the Nature, Offices, and Measures of Friendship' (1657) was written on the prompting of Katharine Philips ('matchless Orinda') of Cardigan. Taylor was imprisoned in 1654–55, a second time in 1655 at Chepstow, and in the Tower in 1657–58, on all occasions apparently because of his episcopal views rather than simply as a Royalist. At the Restoration he was made Bishop of Down, Connor and Dromore (in Ireland) and also Vice Chancellor of the University of Dublin. His second wife, Joanna Bridges, born at Mandinam, was said to have been a natural child of Charles I.

Telford, Thomas (1757–1834). Scottish civil engineer, specially known for his canals (Caledonian in Scotland), roads, and many still surviving bridges. In Wales his main achievements were what is now the A5 road, the Menai and Conwy bridges, and the Pont-y-Cysylltau aqueduct.

Thrale, Hester Lynch (1741–1821). Writer and social figure. Born near Pwllheli. Best known as the friend of Dr Johnson, a frequent resident of her house at Streatham, London, which became a regular meeting place for many distinguished people of the time. After her husband's death (he was a Southwark brewer) she married Gabriele Piozzi, an Italian musician, living at Brynbella near St. Asaph where Piozzi died. His widow then retired to Bath where she died soon after celebrating her 80th birthday with a ball for over 600 people. She wrote poems, essays, letters etc., and also much about Johnson, including 'Anecdotes of the late Samuel Johnson'.

Trevithick, Richard (1771–1833). Engineer and inventor. In 1801 his road locomotive became the first ever to pull a load of passengers by steam, and in 1804 he was active in Wales with tramroad steam locomotives. In 1808 he operated a circular railway at London's Euston Square. Later he built mining engines for Peru.

Vaughan, Henry (1622–95). Poet and mystic. Self-styled 'The Silurist' because the tribe of the Silures had inhabited the part of Wales in which he lived (Brecon area). A Royalist, he fought at Rowton Moor. As a poet he is known for his mystical view of nature and his works are thought to have influenced Wordsworth. Henry Vaughan's twin brother was Thomas, who gained some repute as an alchemist and poisoned himself with fumes of mercury.

Wesley, John (1703–91). Founder (with his brother Charles) of Methodism, which originated in meetings of a group of Oxford students. In Wesley's words the purpose of Methodism was to 'spread scriptural holiness over the land'; it was not to form a separate Church group. From 1735–38 he was in Georgia. Back in London he founded his Societies, and in 1743 he started his main itinerant work, travelling 5000 miles a year and preaching 15 sermons a week. Wesley is known too for his writings (hymns, philosophical works, and his 'Journal') and as a social reformer.

Whistler, Rex (1905–44). painter, decorator, and stage designer. Killed in action in Normandy while serving in the Welsh Guards. Among his works are the decorations in the restaurant of London's Tate Gallery (1926–27) and those at Plas Newydd (1937). He did stage designs for Covent Garden, Sadler's Wells, and C.B. Cochran revues.

Williams, John (1582–1650). Archbishop of York. Native of Conwy. During the Civil War he held Conwy for the King whom he afterwards joined at Oxford. Later, on discoverng that Sir John Owen, now at Conwy, had on the King's orders seized some property which had been entrusted to his care, Williams went over to Parliament and helped Mytton to take Conwy in 1646.

Williams, William Charles (died 1915). Able Seaman, V.C. Native of Chepstow (memorial). In the Dardanelles, while helping to move lighters to the shore, he stood firm under continuous fire holding on to a vital line until he was killed. Described by his commander as 'the bravest sailor I have ever met'.

Williams-Ellis, Sir Clough (1883–1978). Welsh architect and landscape designer, best known for his creation of Portmeirion. Won Military Cross during First World War. Chairman of Stevenage New Town Corporation. Knighted in 1972. His style is generally Classical and Georgian. A vigorous conservationist, he wrote several books.

Wilson, Richard (1714–82). Welsh-born landscape painter. An original member of the Royal Academy where he exhibited until 1780. His work was not appreciated until after his death and he lived in London in some poverty until his brother's death brought him a small property near Mold (Plas Colomendy).

Winde, William (died 1722). Architect. Born in Holland, son of a refugee Royalist, he came to England at the Restoration. He followed a military career (fighting at Sedgemoor) until 1688 when he changed to architecture. One of his buildings in London was Buckingham House (1705), later incorporated by John Nash into Buckingham Palace.

Wood, John (c 1705–54). Architect. Follower of the Palladian style. Best known for his work in Bath. In Wales he is known for his 'restoration' of Llandaff Cathedral by means of an Italianate temple, removed a few years later.

Wyatt, James (1746–1813). Architect, known as a reviver of Gothic. In 1776, appointed Surveyor of Westminster Abbey. He 'restored' several cathedrals, including rebuilding the nave of Hereford. His work earned him the title of the Destroyer from his contemporaries.

Yale, Elihu (1649–1721). Born near Boston, Mass. In 1672 he went to India, becoming governor of Madras. On his return to England he became known for the generosity with which he gave away the books, etc, he had collected. After being invited to help a struggling college in America, Yale sent off a cargo of books, pictures, etc., the sale of which raised so much that it was decided to give his name to the new college building at Newhaven. In 1745 the whole institution became Yale University. Buried at Wrexham, the family home.

PRACTICAL INFORMATION

So far as day-to-day practical matters are concerned—post, currency, banking and shopping hours, holidays and suchlike—practice in Wales is essentially the same as in England. The text below covers matters specifically Welsh.

Organisations

Wales Tourist Board (WTB). The Board operates information centres throughout Wales, several of which are open all year and all of which are open from Easter to September or October. Several centres provide an accommodation reservation service (see also Accommodation, below). The Board publishes a Tourist Map (see Notes on using this Guide, Maps) and a wide range of booklets and leaflets.

Head Office. Wales Tourist Board, Brunel House, 2 Fitzalan Road, Cardiff, CF2 1UY. Tel: 0222–499909.

North Wales Tourism Ltd, 77 Conway Road, Colwyn Bay, LL29 7LN. Tel: 0492–531731.

Mid Wales Tourism Ltd, Canolfan Owain Glyndwr, Machynlleth, SY20 8EE. Tel: 0654–702653.

Tourism South Wales Ltd, Pembroke House, Phoenix Way Enterprise Park, Swansea, SA7 9DB. Tel: 0792–781212.

London. British Travel Centre, 12 Regent Street, London. SW1Y 4PQ. Tel: 071–409–0969.

Outside Wales the Board is represented by the **British Tourist Authority** with offices worldwide: English-speaking countries include Australia, Canada, Ireland, New Zealand, South Africa and USA (Chicago, Dallas, Los Angeles and New York).

Welsh Historic Monuments (WHM or CADW), Brunel House, 2 Fitzalan Road, Cardiff, CF2 1UY. Tel: 0222–465511. Set up in 1984, WHM carries out the statutory responsibilities for protecting, conserving and opening to the public a growing number of ancient monuments and historic buildings. A membership scheme, 'Heritage in Wales', gives free access to all WHM (CADW) Welsh sites, and also reduced price access to sites in the care of similar English and Scottish organisations; membership cards, valid for one calendar year, from WHM or most sites. A series of illustrated guide books are available for most sites, and throughout the summer a full events programme is staged at major monuments.

Forestry Commission (FC), Victoria House, Victoria Terrace, Aberystwyth, SY23 2DQ. Tel: 0970–612367. Set up in 1919, the Forestry Commission is in evidence throughout most of Wales, an important part of its work being the provision of information and recreational facilities such as visitor centres, picnic sites, forest drives, forest trails and camping and caravan sites. Trails, of varying length (2m is about average), usually start from parking and picnic sites and make a round. For many trails leaflets are available, but not necessarily at the site itself (although 'honesty boxes' are increasingly being installed) and visitors planning to enjoy FC facilities are advised to start by going to the nearest information centre. Two leaflets (free)—Discover Forests North Wales, Discover Forests South Wales—can be obtained by postal application to the above address; these leaflets, with small maps, locate all forests and summarise walks and facilities. Also free—Camping and Caravan

Sites; Cabins and Holiday Houses; Conservation; Recreation in your Forests.

The Commission also issues a wide range of priced publications, a free catalogue of which can be obtained from the above address. These publications are available at leading booksellers and most FC information centres. The Commission's Forest Guides, containing a wealth of information and written in readable non-technical style, can be recommended.

The **National Trust** (NT) was founded in 1895 by a group of people who foresaw the threats arising from increasing population, spreading industry, and inadequate planning. The group's aim was to set up a body of private citizens willing to act as trustees for the nation in the acquisition and ownership of land and buildings worthy of permanent preservation. Only 12 years later, under the National Trust Act of 1907, Parliament gave the Trust the right to declare its land inalienable, this meaning that today the majority of the Trust's properties cannot be sold or compulsorily acquired. The Trust is in no way a government department, but a charity supported mainly by the subscriptions of its members and by the contributions of visitors to Trust properties. Members have free access to all properties including those of the National Trust for Scotland. In Wales the Trust owns or protects many, often extensive, areas of countryside, to most of which there is free public access. It also owns several small and large buildings, including a number of great houses, complete with their original decoration, furniture, and pictures.

The Trust may be joined at many of its properties, or by application to the Membership Department, PO Box 39, Bromley, BR1 1NH. Other addresses: *Headquarters:* 36 Queen Anne's Gate, London, SW1H 9AS. Tel: 071–222–9251. *North Wales* (Counties of Clwyd, Gwynedd and northern Powys): Trinity Square, Llandudno, LL30 2DE. Tel: 0492–860123. *South Wales* (Counties of Dyfed, Gwent, southern Powys and West Glamorgan): The King's Head, Bridge Street, Llandeilo, SA19 6BB. Tel: 0558–822800.

The **Countryside Council for Wales** (CCW), absorbing the functions of the former Nature Conservancy Council and the Countryside Commission, is accountable to the Secretary of State for Wales. In general terms the Council is charged with conserving the natural features and wildlife of Wales at the same time providing opportunities for public access and enjoyment. The Council also has specific responsibilities for National Parks, Areas of Outstanding Natural Beauty, Country Parks, Heritage Coasts, and Long Distance Routes (such responsibilities including designation; advice on planning and management; the development of paths, bridleways, picnic sites, car parks and suchlike) while also providing specialist advice to government departments, local authorities, voluntary organisations and interested individuals pursuing countryside management projects with or without grant aid.

One of the Council's statutory functions is the establishment, maintenance and management of Nature Reserves. Although generally responsible for such reserves, the Council does not necessarily own them, and in some cases leases them to, for example, local naturalists' trusts. A number of the more important reserves are mentioned in this Guide. For several such there is open or partially open access, but in other cases access is only by permit. For many reserves there are interpretive booklets and nature trail leaflets. These will sometimes be available at reserves or local information centres, but anyone wishing to visit reserves is advised to write first to the appropriate CCW regional office, i.e. *North Wales*: Hafod Elfyn, Ffordd Penrhos, Bangor, Gwynedd, LL57 2LQ. *Dyfed and Mid Wales*: Plas Gogerddan, Aberystwyth, Dyfed, SY23 3EE. *South Wales*: 44 The Parade, Roath, Cardiff, CF2 3UH. General information (including leaflets, posters, maps) from Countryside Council for Wales, Headquarters Offices, Plas Penrhos, Ffordd Penrhos, Bangor, Gwynedd, LL57 2LQ.

The **Welsh Development Agency**, set up in 1976, undertakes the inter-related functions of land reclamation, environmental improvements, the provision of industrial estates, and encouragement and financial backing for industry. To the visitor the Agency's work will be most apparent in the measures designed to treat the industrial scars of the past, especially in The Valleys (see beginning of Rte 37).

The **National Gardens Scheme** operates in England and Wales. It originated in 1927 (after the death of Queen Alexandra, who had done so much for nursing, particularly as patron of the Queen's Institute of District Nursing), many owners of gardens opening these to the public and charging a small fee which went to the Queen's Institute. Proceeds today go principally to nurses' general welfare, and a proportion to the National Trust to help in preserving gardens of national and historic importance. The Scheme publishes annually an illustrated guide of gardens open to visitors on certain days throughout the year. This can be bought, from about March onwards, from principal booksellers. The Scheme's address is 57 Lower Belgrave Street, London, SW1W 0LR. Tel: 071-730-0359.

Travel, Accommodation, Food and Drink

Weather and Season. In general the weather in Wales is much as in England—that is, changeable with only rare extremes of hot and cold—but because of the hilly geography Wales tends to get more rain. The NE coast has a reputation for being sheltered from rain, and the S and W coasts, especially Gower and Pembroke, for mildness and sunshine. Snow is never sufficient to guarantee winter sports.

The tourist season lasts from Easter to the end of September or October, although a number of sites which open at Easter close thereafter until a few weeks later. July and August are very crowded months and should be avoided by anybody wishing to visit the more popular areas; nevertheless even during these months it is possible to enjoy many out-of-the-way roads and districts. From most points of view May, June, and September are the best months for touring.

Road Travel. Within Wales there is only one motorway, this (M4) running roughly with the S coast. Other roads, the main ones increasingly trunk dual carriageway, are of general British Isles standard, but smaller roads in some areas are hilly and twisting. Main road passes such as Llanberis (1169ft. Rte 8A) or Bwlch Oerddrws (1178ft. Rte 20A) should present no problems, but the road across Bwlch-y-Groes (1790ft. Rte 20B) is in large part narrow and steep. Some of the remoter places mentioned in this book are accessible only by narrow lanes, not always suitable for large cars.

The principal road approaches to Wales are, in the *North*, A55 from Chester, running the breadth of the N of the country through Conwy to Bangor on the Menai Strait. Known as the North Wales

Expressway, this largely dual-carriageway road bypasses many towns and is making increasing use of tunnels, the latest being below the Conwy estuary. In the *Centre*, Telford's A5 from Shrewsbury serves Llangollen and Betws-y-Coed before crossing the Menai Strait for Anglesey and Holyhead; or, farther S, M50 from Tewkesbury becomes A40 at the Welsh border, thence continuing through Monmouth, Brecon and Carmarthen into the Pembroke peninsula. In the *South*, M4 from London crosses the Severn Bridge and then roughly parallels the S coast. Between the above there is a good choice of other roads.

Automobile Association, West and Wales Region, Fanum House, Park Row, Bristol, BS1 5LY. Tel: 0272–297272.

Automobile Association (Travel and Road conditions) Tel: 0222–394111.

Royal Automobile Club, 202 Newport Road, Cardiff, CF2 1YR. Tel: 0222–490959.

Express Coach Services to Wales from most major centres in England and Scotland are operated by National Express Ltd, Ensign Court, 4 Vicarage Road, Edgbaston, Birmingham, B15 3ES. Telephone enquiries to London (071–730–0202); or Bristol (0272–541022); or Cardiff (0222–344751 or 371331); or Swansea (0792–470820). Within Wales, coach services are operated by local companies.

Rail Travel. The main line for *North Wales* is from London (Euston), via Crewe and Chester, the line then following the N coast to cross the Menai Strait for Holyhead. Off this line there are branch services from Hawarden to Wrexham, and from Llandudno Junction to Betws-y-Coed and Blaenau Ffestiniog.—The main lines for *Central Wales* are from Shrewsbury, one heading more or less due W for Aberystwyth or Aberdyfi, linking to the scenic coastal line (Cambrian Coast Railway) which makes its leisurely way northwards around Cardigan Bay to Barmouth, Harlech, Porthmadog and Pwllheli; while the other line (from Craven Arms) meanders SW across the Heart of Wales (the name of the line) to Llanelli and Swansea.—The main line for *South Wales* is from London (Paddington) through the Severn Tunnel to Cardiff, Swansea and Fishguard. Off this line branch services include from Newport to Abergavenny and Hereford; from Newport and Cardiff up The Valleys; from Whitland to Pembroke Dock; and from Clarbeston Road to Haverfordwest and Milford Haven.

Accommodation. Hotel and other accommodation is of the range of standards to be found elsewhere throughout the British Isles, and establishments are listed, described and graded in the usual choice of general and specialised publications, these including WTB's annual and comprehensive 'Wales. Where to Stay'.

Accommodation of all kinds can be much in demand during the holiday season. Reservations can be made either by completing the special form provided in 'Wales. Where to Stay' and sending it to the appropriate North, Mid or South Wales regional company (see above), or, alternatively, through Holidays Wales Ltd, PO Box 40, Swansea SA1 1PX. Tel: 0792–645555.

Food and Drink *Food*. Welsh lamb is famous, and many visitors will also enjoy local salmon, trout (including sewin, a sea trout found only in Welsh waters) and seafood, as also local cheeses. There are, though, no really widely-known specialities. Nevertheless mention may be made of Laver Bread (bara lawr), misleadingly named since laver, or lawr, is a form of seaweed; traditional flat welshcakes; a fruit loaf known as bara brith (speckled bread); a shallow fruit cake called teisen lap; of cawl, a thick soup which includes meat, root vegetables and leeks; and of the cockles from Penclawdd, on the N shore of

Gower. Recently, too, there has been increasing interest in traditional Welsh recipes, many of which appear in the WTB publication 'A Taste of Wales'.

As regards *Drink*, there are Welsh whiskies and beers, and also, perhaps surprisingly, Welsh wines, with vineyards mainly in the Wye valley. And visitors travelling Rte 6B can sample the water of Trefriw Wells.—Licensing Hours vary from district to district but apart from Sundays are generally about 11.00 to 15.00 and 17.30 to 22.30. As to Sundays, Wales holds a referendum every seven years to decide whether local licensed premises should open or not. The trend seems to be clearly towards opening, and in any event, even in the few remaining dry districts, hotel residents can buy drinks for themselves and their guests.

Outdoor Pursuits

Walks and Climbs. Wales is a land rich in walks and climbs; so many and so varied that this Guide, while indicating the better-known areas, as also some key walks and climbs within them, can only touch the fringe of an activity which in its own right is the subject of a library of specialised maps and literature. Walks and climbs, both informal and WTB-listed and categorised (and there are over 600 of these), range from simple strolls along a river or canal bank to the ascent of mountains such as Snowdon or Cader Idris. Within this span there is also a wide spectrum. Some walks are simply walks, but most others are in one way or another specialist, e.g. nature trails; forest trails; archaeological trails, including industrial archaeology; walks or climbs tackling high, lonely or difficult terrain, demanding a prudent and planned approach and the use of special clothing or equipment; walks or climbs with, for the unwary or foolhardy, hazards such as hidden mine shafts, rusting machinery and even discarded explosive.

For the above reasons, visitors intending to enjoy anything beyond relatively simple local walking should first brief themselves. A basic publication is 'Wales Walking' (WTB). Divided into some 24 districts, each with a key map, the book suggests and outlines well over 600 walks, the entries in most cases including details on location, distance, the organisers, publications available and from whom, the grade of walk (i.e. family, energetic, fit enthusiasts), and the terrain (e.g. cliff, dune, woodland, special interest). Frequently—and especially in the case of nature, forest or special interest trails—there are guide leaflets or booklets. But unless the walk starts from close to an information or visitor centre, these guides will not necessarily be locally available. Serious walkers, and all with a particular interest, should therefore write for the literature required before leaving home. The principal providers, with their addresses, are listed in 'Wales Walking'.

Pony Trekking. Much of Wales is ideal country for pony trekking, a holiday activity which is becoming increasingly popular, whether simply for a half-day or for a week or longer. The Pony Trekking and Riding Society of Wales is concerned with the standards of centres, an approved list of which is contained in WTB's publication 'Pony Trekking and Riding in Wales'.

Beaches. With some 750m of varied coastline facing N, W and S, Wales can offer virtually every kind of beach and beach background, ranging from the sands of the popular resorts to remote open sweeps, hidden coves, and beaches below towering cliffs. WTB's three regional guides (North, Mid and South Wales) include special sections on beaches, with notes on their characteristics (sand, shingle, safety, facilities etc.).

Other Pursuits. WTB free Factsheets include Climbing; Cycling; Fishing; Golf; Inland Waterways; Sailing; Walking; Windsurfing; Horse Riding; Canoeing, Sub Aqua and Water-skiing; Shooting; Bird Watching and Nature Studies.

The Welsh Language

By V. *Eirwen Davies* BA and *Gwerfyl Moss* BA

The Welsh Language belongs to the Celtic branch of the Indo-European family. Goidelic developments of Celtic are Scottish Gaelic, Irish or Erse, and Manx; Brythonic developments are Welsh, Cornish and Breton. It seems probable that Welsh was already spoken in the 6C, at the time of the emigration to Brittany, and the earlier verse material found in Welsh may contain 6C elements, afterwards modified. A few glosses of the 9–11C are known, as also some poems which probably belong to the same period. The tales usually called 'Mabinogion' are known in 12 and 13C redactions, but there were certainly much earlier forms. The works of many of the bards of the 12C, with a few compositions even going back to perhaps the 9C, have been preserved, and from those times to this a vast amount of literature has been produced.

Welsh is phonetically written, each letter having one sound, except for Y which has two.

Consonants. Generally consonants are pronounced as in English, but *c* and *g* are always hard as in *cat* and *gun*, *ch* is pronounced as in the Scottish *loch*, *f* as *v*, *th* as in *sympathy*, *dd* as the *th* in *though*, *ff* as in *four*, and *ph* as in *phrase*. There is no real equivalent to the Welsh *ll* though the *tl* as in *Bentley* or *Pentland* is close; the true sound can be produced by placing the tip of the tongue against the front teeth and emitting the breath sharply without voice.

The consonants *j*, *k*, *v*, *x* and *z* are absent from Welsh. W and *i* can be both vowels and consonants, in the latter case corresponding to the *w* in *well* and the *y* in *yes*. Examples are *wedi* (after) and *iar* (hen).

Vowels. The vowels *a*, *e*, *i*, *o*, *w*, when long, are pronounced as the vowel sounds in *far*, *glare*, *meet*, *more* and *fool*; and when short as in *cat*, *get*, *pin*, *hot* and *took*. The vowel *u* is sounded as the Welsh long *i* in South Wales, but in North Wales it is more akin to the French *u* or German *ü*, both produced with rounded lips. In monosyllables (except as noted below) and final syllables y has the same sound as the Welsh *u* (known as clear sound), but the y heard in non-final syllables is pronounced as in English *sun* (known as obscure sound). Thus the Welsh word *Cymry* (the Welsh) embraces the two sounds and is pronounced as in English Kum-ree. Although monosyllables, the following y words are all pronounced as the *u* in the English *sun* ... y and yr (the), *fy* (my), *dy* (thy, your), *myn* (by), and some borrowings such as *syr* (sir) and *ffrynt* (front).

Diphthongs. *Ae, ai, aw, ew, iw, yw, wy, oe, oi,* and *ou* are pronounced by giving the two letters their individual proper sounds in fairly rapid succession, but tending to stress the first sound more than the second. *Ei, eu* and *ey* are pronounced as in the English *eye*, and *ow* as in the English *cowl*. Generally, in monosyllables (e.g. *pwy* = who, *mwy* = more), *wy* is produced by imitating the English *oo* with *ee*, but with some stress on the w. Sometimes the sounds of *wy* are distinguished by a circumflex. For instance, in gŵyr (knows) it is the w sound that is stressed, whereas in gwŷr (men) it is the clear-sound y.

Accent. The accent falls regularly on the penultimate syllable except in the case of contractions when it falls on the ultimate and is sometimes indicated by an acute accent (caniatáu = to permit) or by a circumflex (caniatâd = permission).

Mutations ('In the Celtic languages, a change of an initial consonant, depending on the character of the preceding word'—Shorter Oxford English Dictionary). Mutations occur, medially and radically, in many grammatical constructions. Depending, usually, on the preceding word, the initial consonants of the word that follows will sometimes change, and knowledge of these sound changes, or mutations, is essential to a proper understanding of Welsh (recommended grammar: 'Teach Yourself Living Welsh' by T.J. Rhys Jones, Hodder and Stoughton). Mutations often make it difficult for the layman even to derive a meaning from a dictionary since the Welsh word must be sought under its (to the uninitiated probably unknown) radical form rather than under the mutated form in which it is likely to be met. In the Glossary below, mutated forms are given for several words often forming part of place names.

Articles. There is no indefinite article in Welsh. The article is y, yr (before a vowel), 'r (after a vowel). For example, y *cartref* (the home), yr *afal* (the apple), o'r *tŷ* (from the house).

Genders. Welsh recognises only masculine and feminine; there is no neuter. There are no rules, other than that the names of trees are usually feminine.

Plurals. No rules. Plural terminations are *au, on, ion, i, ydd, oedd, edd, ed, od, ant, aint, er* and *yr*. Plurals may also be formed by internal vowel changes; for example, *bardd* (poet), plural *beirdd*, or *ffon* (stick), plural *ffyn*. Or by both internal vowel change and addition; for example *brawd* (brother), plural *brodyr*, or *cwch* (boat), plural *cychod*, or *gardd* (garden), plural *gerddi*. There are also occasions when endings are dropped in order to form plurals; for example *plentyn* (child), plural *plant*, or *mochyn* (pig), plural *moch*.

Adjectival Termination. The chief adjectival terminations are aid, aidd, ain, ig, as, inol, us, adwy, ys, llyd or lyd, gar.

Glossary

This Glossary is largely, though by no means exclusively, of words associated with place names.

pl = plural. sg. = singular. * = dropped; i.e. no sound. masc. = masculine. fem. = feminine. dim. = diminutive. OE = Old English. adj. = adjective. obs. = obsolete.

Aber, Mouth (of a river)
Adar. sg. *aderyn, ederyn*. Birds
Aden, Wing
Adwy, Gap. Pass
Ael, Brow. Headland
Aeron, Fruits
Afanc, Beaver. Monster
Afon, River
Alaw, Water lily (obs.). Tune
Allt, Wooded hill or cliff
Am, Around. About (in compounds)
Amlwg, Visible. Open. Obvious
Ap, Son of
Ar, Borderng on. Upon. High place
Aran, High place. Mountain
Arddu, Very black
Arian, Silver
Aur, Gold
Awst, August (month)

Mutations of B are F and M

Bach, Corner. Retreat. Small
Bala, Efflux of a river from a lake
Ban. pl *bannau*, Height. Mountain. Lofty
Banc, Bank. Hill
Banw, A sow
Bara, Bread
Barclod, Apron
Barwn, Baron
Bedd, Grave
Beddrod, Graveyard
Bedw, Birch tree
Bedwas, Birch grove. Place of birches
Benglog, Mutation of *Penglog* = Head
Berr (fem.), Short
Berw, Building
Betws, Bede-house; probably from Anglo-Saxon *bed* (prayer) and house
Blaen, Source. Point. Head of a valley
Boch, Cheek (part of the body)
Bod, Abode. Dwelling
Bon, Stem. Lower end
Bont, Bridge
Braich, Arm
Braith (fem.), Speckled
Bran. pl *brain*, Crow
Bras, Fat. Productive. Great
Bre, Hill
Brig, Summit
Brith (masc.), Speckled
Bro, Vale. Plain
Broch, Badger
Bron, Slope of a hill
Brwyn. sg. *brwynen*, Rushes

Brych, Speckled. Variegated
Bryn, Hill
Bu, Ox
Buarth, Cattle enclosure. Farmyard
Buwch. pl *buchod*, Cow
Bwch. pl *bychod*, Buck
Bwlch. pl *bylchau*, Pass. Defile
Bychan, Small
Byrr (masc.), Short

Mutations of C are G and Ch

Caban, Cabin
Cad, Host. Battle
Cadair. Cader, Chair. Seat. Stronghold
Cadarn. pl *cedyrn*, Mighty
Cadno. Cadnaw, Fox
Cae, Field
Caer, Fort. Thence, part of town name
Cafn. pl *cafnau*, Trough
Cail, Sheepfold or pen
Cain, Bright. Beautiful
Calan, New Year
Calch, Lime
Cam, Crooked or bent. Footstep or stride. Injury or wrong
Camlas, Canal
Canol, Middle. Centre
Cant, One hundred. Rim. Circle
Cantref, A Hundred (medieval division of land)
Capel, Chapel
Car, Kinsman. Friend
Carn, Cairn. Stone outcrop
Carnedd. pl *Carneddau, carneddi*, Cairn or stone outcrop. Mountain
Carreg. pl *cerrig*, Stone
Carrog, Stream. Brook
Cas, Castle
Caseg. pl *cesig*, Mare
Castell. pl *cestyll*, Castle
Cau, A hollow
Cawl, Soup
Cawr, Giant
Ceann, Head. Top
Ced, Gift
Cefn, Back. Ridge
Cegid, Hemlock
Cegin, Kitchen
Cei, Quay
Celli, Grove
Celyn or *Cellyn* (on some maps), Holly
Cemaes or *Cemais*, Bend (of coast or river)
Cerrig. sg. *carreg*, Stones
Cesail, Nook
Ceunant, Ravine

Chwech. Chwe, Six
Chwefror, February
Chwith, Left (directional)
Ci. pl *cwn*, Dog
Cil. pl. *ciliau*, Retreat. Nook. Church
Claf, Sick
Clafdy, Hospital
Clawdd. pl *cloddiau*, Ditch. Hedge
Cleddau. Cleddyf, Sword
Clegyr, Rocks. Stones
Cloch. pl *clychau*, Bell
Cloddfa, Pit
Clogwyn, Cliff. Crag
Clos, Close. Small field
Clun, Meadow
Clwyd, Gate. Perch
Clyd, Cosy
Clyder, Sheltered valley
Clywed, To hear (*Clywedog*, a common river name meaning the water that can be heard)
Cnicht (OE), Knight
Cob, Dyke
Coch, Red
Coed. sg. *coeden*, Trees. Forest. Woodland
Coes, Leg. Limb
Coetan, Quoit (often used for burial chambers)
Coll. pl *cyll*, Hazel
Coll. Colled, Loss. Slaughter
Cop. Copa, Summit
Cor, Choir. Cowhouse
Corn, Horn
Cornel, Corner
Cors. pl *corsydd*, Bog
Craig. pl *cregiau, creigiau, creigydd*, Rock
Crib. pl *cribau*, Ridge
Croen. pl *crwyn*, Skin
Croes, Cross. Crosswise
Croesffordd, Crossroads
Crog, Cross. Hanging or overhanging
Crom (fem.), Crooked. Bent
Cron (fem.), Round
Crud, Cradle
Crug. pl *crugiau*, Mound
Crwm (masc.), Crooked. Bent
Crwn (masc.), Round
Crwth, Type of musical instrument. Concave vessel
Crwyn. sg. *croen*, Skins
Crythor, Minstrel (player on the crwth)
Cul, Narrow
Cut. pl *cutiau, cwt, cytiau*, Hut
Cwm. pl *cymoedd, cymau*, Valley. Cirque
Cwn. sg. *ci*, Dogs
Cwrt, Court
Cwymp, Fall. Slope
Cwys, Furrow
Cyff, Stem. Trunk
Cyfyng, Narrow
Cymer. Cymmer, Confluence
Cymraeg, The Welsh Language
Cymru, Wales

Cymry, The Welsh
Cyngor. pl *cynghorion*, Advice
Cyngor. pl *cynghorau*, Council
Cyrn. sg. *corn*, Peaks
Cytiau. sg. *Cut*, Huts

Mutations of D are Dd and N

Dafad. pl *defaid*, Sheep
Dan, Under. Below
Dar. pl *deri*, Oak
Dau (masc.). *Deu* (in composition), Two
Deg, Ten. Also Mutation of *Teg* = Fair
Deheu. De, South. Right (directional)
Deheubarth, The southern part
Derw. sg. *derwen*, Oaks
Dewi, David
Diffwys, Precipice
Din. Dinas, Fortification. Thence, part of town name
Dir, Mutation of *Tir* = Land
Dol. pl *dolydd, dolau*, Meadow
Dor. pl *dorau*, Door
Dre, Mutation of *Tre* = Homestead
Drem, Mutation of *Trem* = Sight. View
Drud. pl *drudion*, Brave. Mighty
Drum, Ridge
Drwg, Bad. Evil
Drws. pl *drysau*, Pass. Door
Drys, Bramble
Du. Ddu. pl *duon*, Black
Dulas, Black-blue
Duw, God
Dwfr. Dwr. pl *dyfroedd*, Water
Dwy (fem), Two
Dwyf. Dwy, God
Dwyrain, East
Dwyran, Two parts
Dydd Llun, Monday
Dyyd Mawrth, Tuesday
Dydd Mercher, Wednesday
Dydd Iau, Thursday
Dydd Gwener, Friday
Dydd Sadwrn, Saturday
Dydd Sul, Sunday
Dyffryn. pl *dyffrynnoedd*, Valley
Dyfrydog, Unpleasant. Bad
Dyfyrm, To shorten. Curtail
Dyserth. Diserth, A retreat. A place apart
Dysgl, Dish
Dywarch, Mutation of *Tywarch* = Sod. Turf

Ebrill, April
Edwi, To fade. Wither
Efwr, Cow parsnip. Hogweed
Eglwys. pl *eglwysi, eglwysau, eglwysydd*, Church
Eifl, Two-pronged. Fork
Einion, Anvil
Eligug, Guillemot
Epynt, Horse-track. Bridleway
Erch, Pale colour. Terrible
Erw, Acre
Esgair, Long ridge. Escarpment
Ewenny. Ewenni, From Aventia, a Franco-Celtic goddess

Mutations of F arè B and M

Fach, Mutation of *Bach* = Small
Faen, Mutation of *Maen* = Stone. Boulder
Faes, Mutation of *Maes* = Field
Fair, Mutation of *Mair* = Mary
Fal. Fali, Valley
Fan, Mutation of *Ban* = Height. Mountain
Fawn, Mutation of *Mawn* = Peat
Fawr, Mutation of *Mawr* = Large. Great. Extensive
Fechan (fem), Small
Fedw, Mutation of *Bedw* = Birch tree
Felindre, Mutation of *Melin* = Mill
Ferched, Mutation of *Merched* = Women
Ffair, Fair
Ffin, Border. Limit
Fflur, Flowers. Blossom
Ffordd. pl *ffyrdd*, Road
Ffos. pl *ffosydd*, Ditch. Embankment
Ffraw, Rapid. Violent
Ffridd. Ffrith, Moorland. Meadows
Ffrwd. pl *ffrydiau*, Stream
Ffynnon, Well. Spring
Fihangel, Mutation of *Mihangel* = Michael
Foel, Mutation of *Moel* = Bare or rounded mountain
Forwyn, Mutation of *Morwyn* = Maiden
Fychan, Mutation of *Bychan* = Small
Fyrddin, Mutation of *Myrddin* = Merlin

Mutated forms of G are C, Ng, or (dropped)

Gadair, Mutation of *Cadair* = Chair. Stronghold
Gaer, Mutation of *Caer*, = Fort
Gafr. pl *geifr*, Goat
Gallt, Wooded hill or cliff
Gam, Mutation of *Cam* = Crooked. Footstep. Injury
Ganol, Mutation of *Canol* = Middle. Centre
Gardd, Garden
Garn, Mutation of *Carn* = Cairn. Outcrop
Garreg, Mutation of *Carreg* = Stone
Garth, Hill. Promontory
Gast, Bitch
Gau, False
Gawres, Mutation of *Cawres* = Giantess
Gefail. pl *gefeiliau*, Smithy
Gelli, Mutation of *Celli* = Grove
Gelyn, Enemy
Ger, Near. By
Gerig. Gerrig, Mutations of *Cerrig* = Stones
Glan, Edge. Brink. Shore
Glân, Clean
Glas, Blue. Also, in some uses, Green
Gleisiad, Young salmon
Glo, Coal
Gloddfa, Mutation of *Cloddfa* = Pit

Glyder, Mutation of *Clyder* = Sheltered valley
Glyn, Valley. Glen
Gobaith, Hope
Goch, Mutation of *Coch* = Red
Godre, Foot of a hill. Edge
Gogledd, North
Gogof, Cavern
Golau. Goleu, Light (illumination)
Gorffennaf, July
Gorllewin, West
Gors, Mutation of *Cors* = Bog
Gris. pl *grisiau*, Step
Gro, Gravel
Groes, Mutation of *Croes* = Cross
Grug, Heather
Gwaelod, Bottom
Gwair, Hay
Gwastad, Level area
Gwaun. pl *gweunydd*, Moorland. Downland
Gwen (fem.), White
Gwern, Alder. Damp meadow
Gwernog, Marshy
Gwig, Haven. Woodland
Gwr, Man. Husband
Gwrach, Witch
Gwrych, Shrubs. Hedge. Bristles
Gwryd, Fathom
Gwy, Water. River Wye
Gwỳdd, Trees
Gŵydd, Goose. Wild
Gwyddelod, The Irish
Gwyddfa, A wild place
Gwyllt, Wild. Savage
Gwyn, White
Gwynt, Wind
Gŵyr, Oblique. Slanting
Gwŷr, Men
Gwyrdd, Green
Gwyryddon. Gwyryfon, Maidens

Haf, Summer
Hafod, Summer residence
Hafren, The river Severn
Hebog, Hawk. Falcon
Heli, Brine
Helyg. Helig, Willows
Hen, Old
Hendre, Winter residence
Hengwm, Old valley
Henrhyd, Old ford
Heol, Paved road
Hir, Long. Tall. Tedious
Hiraeth, Longing
Hwylfa, Path. Entry
Hydd, Stag
Hydref, October
Hyll, Ugly

Ifan, Evan. John
Ionawr, January
Isel, is, isaf, Low, lower, lowest

Kil (Gaelic), Retreat. Church

L at the beginning of a word always signifies a mutation

Las, Mutation of *Glas* = Blue. Green
Llaeth, Milk
Llain, Blade. A stretch

Llaith, Damp. Wet. Disease
Llam, Leap
Llan, Enclosed place. Church. Hence a part of many place names
Llanerch, Clearing
Llanfair, Church of Mary
Llaw, Hand
Llawnt, Lawn
Llawr, Floor
Llech, Slate. Flagstone
Llechwedd, Slate slope
Lled, Width
Lleng, Legion
Llethr, Slope
Llew, Lion
Llidiart, Gate
Llif, Flood
Llith, Bait. Lesson
Llithrig, Slippery
Lliw, Colour
Lliwedd (obs.), Troop. Crowd. Nation
Llog, Interest payment. Part of a monastery
Llong, Ship. Damp (fem.)
Llwng, Damp (masc.)
Llwyd, Grey. Brown
Llwyn, Grove. Woodland
Llwynog, Fox
Llychau. sg. *llwch*, Lakes. Muddy marsh
Llydan, Wide
Llygad, Eye
Llyn. pl *llynnoedd*, *llynnau*, Lake
Llys, Place. Court. Enclosure
Llyw, Rudder. Ruler (a chief)
Llywarn. pl *llewyrn*, Fox

Mutation of M is F

Ma. In compounds *Fa*, Place. Plain
Mab. pl *meibion*, Son
Maen. pl *meini*, *main*, Stone. Boulder
Maes. pl *meysydd*, Field
Mai, May (month)
Mair, Mary
Mall, Rotten. Evil
Mam, Mother
Man, High place
March. pl *meirch*, Steed
Marian, Beach
Mawn, Peat
Mawr, Great. Big. Extensive
Mawrth, March (month)
Medi, September
Mehefin, June
Mei, Halfway. Centre
Meibion. sg. *mab*, Sons
Meirion. *Meirionydd*, Merioneth
Melin, Mill
Melyn, Yellow
Merch. pl *merched*, Woman. Daughter
Merthyr, Burial place of a saint
Mign, Bog
Mihangel, Michael
Mil, Thousand. Beast
Milwr. pl *milwyr*, Soldier
Min, Edge. Border

Moch. sg. *mochyn*, Pigs. Rapid (adj.)
Moel, Bare or rounded mountain
Môr, Sea
Morfa, Coastal marsh
Morwynion. sg. *morwyn*, Maidens
Mur, Wall
Murddyn, Ruin
Mwd, Mud
Mynach, Monk
Mynydd, Mountain
Myrddin, Merlin

Nadolig, Christmas
Nant. pl *naint*, *nentydd*, *nannau*, Valley. Stream
Naw, Nine
Neuadd, Hall
Newydd, New
Nos, Night

Ochr, Side. Slope
Od, Snow
Oer, Cold
Og, Harrow (agricultural)
Ogo. *Ogof*, Caves
Olau. *Oleu*, Mutation of *Goleu* = Light
Onn. pl *ynn*, Ash
Or, Border. Rim. Edge

Mutations of P are B, Mh, Ph

Pair, Cauldron
Pant, Hollow ground
Parc, Field. Park
Pasg, Easter
Pedwar, Four
Pell, Far
Pellaf, Farthest
Pen, Head. Top
Penglog, Head, Skull
Penmaen, Rocky headland
Pennant, Upper reaches or head of a valley
Pentre. *Pentref*, Village. Hamlet
Pig. dim *pigyn*, Point. Summit
Pili-pala, Butterfly
Pinc, Pink
Pistyll, Waterfall. Rapids
Plas, Hall. Mansion. Place
Plynlimon, Five chimneys
Poeth, Hot. Burnt
Pont. pl *pontydd*, Bridge
Porffor, Purple
Porth. pl *pyrth*, Landing place. Port
Pren, Tree. Timber
Pridd, Soil. Earth
Prys. *Prysg*, Shrubs
Pump, Five
Pwll, Pool

'r (after a vowel), The
Rhaeadr. *Rhaiadr*. *Rhayader* (English spelling), Waterfall
Rhagfyr, December
Rhan, Share. Part
Rhewyn, Pool. Gutter. Drain
Rhian. *Rhiain*, Maiden
Rhiniog. *Rhinog* (on some maps), Buttress
Rhiw. pl *rhiwiau*, Hill
Rhod, Circle. Wheel

Rhodwydd, Embankment. Earthwork
Rhos, Moorland. Rose
Rhudd, Red. Ruddy
Rhwth, Open. Glaring
Rhyd, Ford
Rhydd, Free
Rhyn, Headland

Saeth, Arrow
Saith, Seven
Sarn, Causeway
Sarthes (obs.), Reptile. Serpent
Sior, George
Skirrid, Anglicisation of
  Ysgyryd = Rugged
Stryt, Street
Sulgwyn, Whitsun
Sych, Dry

Mutations of T are D, Nh, Th

Tachwedd, November
Taf, Dark. Black
Tafarn, Tavern
Tal, Front. Forehead. End. Tall
Tan, Under. Beneath. Fire
Tarw. pl *teirw*, Bull
Teg, Fair. Comely
Teisen, Cake
Teledu, Television
Telyn, Harp
Telynor, Harpist
Teyrn, Monarch. King
Tir. pl *tiroedd*, Land
Tomen, Mound
Ton, Wave. Surface. Green
Torr, Flank
Traeth, Shore
Traffordd, Motorway
Trallwng, Muddy hollow (Welshpool)
Traws, Across
Tre. *Tref*, Habitation. Village
Trem, Sight. View
Tri, Three
Tro, Turn. Bend
Troed. pl *traed*, Foot
Tros, Over
Trothwy, Threshold
Trum, Ridge
Trwyn, Nose. Headland
Try, Very
Tryfan, Very high peak
Tryweryn, Very wet
Tud, People. Country
Twle. *Twlch*, Knoll
Twll, Hollow

Twm, Tom
Twmp, Tump
Twr. pl *tyrau, tyroedd*, Tower
Twrch, Pig. Boar
Twrch daear, Mole
Twt, Tidy. Neat
Ty. pl *tai*, House
Tyddyn, Farmstead
Tylwyth Teg, Fairies
Tyn, Small Farm
Tyrau. sg. *twr*, Towers
Tywarch. pl *tyweirch*, Sod. Turf
Tywyll, Dark
Tywyn, Shore

Uchel, uch, uchaf, High, higher,
  highest
Uchtryd, Upper ford
Udd, Lord
Un, One
Undeb, Union
Urdd, League. Society

Velindre (frequent but incorrect
  spelling of *Felindre*), Mill

Wastad, Mutation of
  Gwastad = Level area
Wen (fem.), White
Wern, Mutation of *Gwern* = Alder.
  Damp meadow
Wrach, Mutation of *Gwrach* = Witch
Wrth, Near. By
Wyn (masc.), White
Wyth, Eight

Y (before consonants), The
Ych. pl *ychen*, Ox
Yd, Corn
Ym (before m), In
Ymenyn, Butter
Yn, In
Yng (before C), In
Ynys, Island
yr (before vowels), The
Ysbyty. Yspytty (on some maps),
  Hospice
Ysgall. sg. *ysgallen*, Thistles
Ysgol, School
Ysgor, Rampart. Defence
Ysgubor, Barn
Ysgyryd, Rugged
Ystrad, Valley. Strath
Ystryd. pl *ystrydoedd*, Street
Ystum, Shape. Curve
Ystwyth, Pliable. Agile. Winding

1   Chester to Bangor

As far as Llandudno Junction, a short way E of Conwy, there is a choice of roads, one fringing the coast (Rte 1A), the other running a short way inland (Rte 1B). There are plenty of connecting roads, and in parts both Routes use A55, a fast road (North Wales Expressway) bypassing many places and, after Colwyn Bay, increasingly making use of tunnels to overcome the problems of the hill-backed coast.

As far as Conwy, the coast offers little that is scenic and indeed between Mostyn and Colwyn Bay the stretch is essentially one of popular resorts, caravan parks, holiday camps and, here and there, shoddy building. The inland road is both pleasanter scenically and more interesting; places lying between the two roads are included under this latter Route.

Conwy to Bangor—scenically more interesting along cliffs and with views across to Great Orme and Anglesey—is described as Rte 1C, while Llandudno and its environs are covered as a separate Route (Rte 2). The total distance from Chester to Bangor is some 60m.

Both routes (1A and 1B) start from **Chester** in England (see 'Blue Guide England').

A.   Coastal road to Conwy

A548 to Abergele. A55 to Conwy. Total distance 43m.—*13m.*
Flint.—*7m.* **Mostyn.**—*6m.* **Prestatyn.**—*3m.* **Rhyl.**—*4m.* **Abergele.**—
6m. **Colwyn Bay.**—*4m.* **Conwy.**

Chester (see 'Blue Guide England') is left by A548 which, running to the N of the Dee and soon entering Wales, traverses land reclaimed by the embanking of the river in 1752 and in 3m beyond the border turns S to cross the here canalised river at *Queensferry* where the royal ferry of the past has today been replaced by two bridges. *Connah's Quay*, just beyond, no longer a port of any significance, is said to derive its name from a local publican.

13m. **Flint** (15,000 inhab.), although now a modest enough small town, can boast two historical firsts; it was chosen as the site of the first of Edward I's Welsh fortresses, and the associated borough was the first in Wales to receive a charter (8 September 1284).

The remains of the once formidable *Castle* sprawl over a low rock platform beside the shore (WHM. Tel: 0222-465511).

History. Begun in 1277, and completed by James of St. George in about 1281, the castle was in 1312 the scene of the meeting between Edward II and his raffish favourite Piers Gaveston on the latter's return from exile in Flanders. Later, in 1399, it may have been here that Richard II met Bolingbroke (soon to be Henry IV), Richard then effectively becoming a prisoner. In Shakespeare's 'Richard II' the cringing king pleads 'What you will have, I'll give, and willing too; For do we must what force will have us do', whereupon, according to the chronicler Froissart, even Richard's favourite hound deserted him to fawn on the upstart. Two and a half centuries later, during the Civil War, Flint was held for Charles I by Sir Roger Mostyn until taken by General Mytton in 1647 and then slighted.

That the castle was once considerably larger than is immediately apparent today may be judged from the remains, on the S side, of an extensive outer ward, separated from the inner castle, as also from the borough, by moats. The main plan is roughly a square with a three-quarter drum-tower at each of three angles. At the SE angle, outside the main enclosure and separated from it by a moat, is a large circular tower which, with its own well, both served as a keep and commanded the entrance to the inner ward, the link to which was a rampart walk along a wall across the moat.

Beyond Flint the road continues parallel with the railway beside the *Sands of Dee*, at low tide a dreary expanse of sand and mud. Giraldus records that in 1188 he crossed the quicksands near Bagillt 'not without some degree of apprehension'; and in 1637 Edward King, Milton's Cambridge friend, was shipwrecked and drowned here, 'Lycidas' being the poet's contribution to a book of memorial verses.—*4m*. *Greenfield*, at the foot of Greenfield Valley Heritage Park, for which, as also for Basingwerk Abbey and Holywell, both just inland, see Rte 1B (park either here off A548 or, for Basingwerk, off B5121).—*3m*. **Mostyn**, though today little more than an industrial strip, can nevertheless claim touches of history. The manor of Mostyn was granted in 1295 to Edward I's architect James of St. George and he probably died there in 1308; it was from Mostyn Hall that the Earl of Richmond (the future Henry VII) escaped from the soldiers of Richard III by leaping from a window; and during the Civil War it was Sir Roger Mostyn who held Flint for Charles I.—*3m*. *Talacre*, to the N of which *Point of Ayr*, marking the SW end of the Dee estuary, is also a nature and bird reserve with dune, salt marsh and mud flat habitats.

3m. **Prestatyn** (*Inf.*) and, *3m* farther, **Rhyl** (*Inf.*) are virtually linked very popular holiday resorts with splendid beaches, holiday camps and all the facilities and lavish, extrovert entertainment to be expected. Prestatyn, at the N end of Offa's Dyke, is cut by the railway, the main town being to the S while the Promenade with its Central Beach entertainment complex and more modest amusement areas on Ffrich Beach (W) and Barkby Beach (E) is to the north. Rhyl, on the E side of the mouth of the river Clwyd, boasts a combined Parade and Marine Drive over two miles long, the outstanding features here being the Sun Centre and the tropical Royal Floral Hall and Butterfly Jungle. Rhyl Library in Church Street includes a museum of local maritime and tourism history.

Rhyl is left by Foryd Bridge spanning the river Clwyd (for Rhuddlan, St. Asaph and Bodelwyddan, all a short way S, see Rte 1B), to the S now being *Morfa Rhuddlan*, the marsh where in 795 the Welsh under Caradoc were routed by Offa of Mercia. Today the flanking road threads a succession of huge caravan sites and holiday camps.

4m. **Abergele** forms with *Pensarn*, 1m N on the coast, a joint resort, modest by comparison to such as Rhyl, Prestatyn and Colwyn Bay but popular with quieter and less demanding families content with a pebble beach which, however, reveals sand as the tide falls.—A55 is now joined, this road running below *Gwrych Castle* (Tel: 0745–825007), a flamboyant castellated folly of 1815, today sometimes the setting for jousting, to reach (*2m*) *Llandulas*, at the mouth of the Dulas, with a church designed by G.E. Street, and traditionally the place at which in 1399 the Earl of Northumberland betrayed Richard II into the hands of Bolingbroke. But it seems more likely that it was on Anglesey that, to quote David Hume, 'that nobleman, by treachery and false oath, made himself master of the King's person'. Beyond, the modern road sweeps past the small headland of Penmaen Rhos, a contrast to its 18C predecessor criticised by Dr Johnson as being so narrow and unprotected that few persons dared 'trust themselves upon their horses'.

4m. **Colwyn Bay** (*Inf.* Station Road. Tel: 0492–530478) is a large and straggling resort which has inexorably filled the gap between the former villages of Old Colwyn (E) and Llandrillo-yn-Rhos (W). The beach is served by some three miles of Promenade along the length of which will be found all the expected attractions, not least being the pier and Eirias Park with a Leisure Centre and many other features especially for children. Visitors are also welcome at rehearsals of the local male voice choir (Tel: 0492–515558). The very popular *Welsh Mountain Zoo* (Tel: 0492–532938), spread through attractive grounds on a wooded panoramic hill a mile SW of the town, is perhaps best known for its birds of prey and, weather permitting, their daily free-flying displays.—Colwyn Bay merges (NW) with *Rhos-on-Sea*, site of an abbey during the 12C and still preserving St. Trillo's Chapel, a humble small place of venerable if undetermined age built over an ancient holy well (below foreshore wall in W of the town; not visisble from a car but indicated by a plaque).

For (*2m*) **Llandudno Junction** and, *2m* farther, **Conwy**, as also for the Conwy estuary, see Rte 1B. For **Llandudno**, see Rte 2.

B.   Inland road to Conwy

A55 to Gorsedd. A5151 to Rhuddlan. A525 to St. Asaph. B5381 to Llandudno Junction. A55 to Conwy. Total distance 48m.—*7m.* **Hawarden.**—*11m.* **Holywell.**—*3m.* **Gorsedd.**—*6m.* **Dyserth.**—*2m.* **Rhuddlan.**—*2m.* **St. Asaph.**—*15m.* **Llandudno Junction.**—*2m.* **Conwy.**

Chester (see 'Blue Guide England') is left by Grosvenor Bridge, A483 and A55 for (*7m*) **Hawarden**, a small place which was for some 60 years the home of W.E. Gladstone (1809–98), the statesman, who in 1839 married the daughter of Sir Stephen Glynne whose family had acquired the Hawarden estate after the Civil War. *Hawarden Castle* (no adm.), Gladstone's home, was started in 1750 and enlarged and castellated by Sir Stephen Glynne in 1809. Although there is no admission to this new castle, there is access to the ruins in the park of the historically interesting *Old Castle* (Tel: 0244–531547). First a British fort, then in 1264 the scene of a meeting between Simon de Montfort and Llewelyn the Last, the earliest stone structure dates from about 1280 and was briefly held in 1282 by Llewelyn's son, Dafydd. There was considerable extension some 200 years later, but, after two Civil War sieges, the castle was slighted in 1646. Today, the chief remains are the circular keep and the hall, the whole within a double earthwork. In the town the parish *Church* has a window by Burne-Jones and also a Gladstone Memorial Chapel with marble effigies by W.B. Richmond of Gladstone and his wife, both of whom, however, are buried in Westminster Abbey. Adjacent to the church, *St. Deiniol's Residential Library* provides another link with Gladstone; founded here by him in 1895 for the encouragement of scriptural learning, the library houses large theological collections (Tel: 0244–532350).

2m. **Ewloe Castle**, the extensive ruins of a stronghold of Llewelyn the Great and Llewelyn the Last, has as its most interesting feature a well-preserved D-shaped tower of about 1210 in the centre of the upper ward; the rest of the building, including the circular W tower, dates from about 1257, two years after Llewelyn the Last began his campaign to drive out the English and establish his own authority throughout Wales.—At *(3m) Northop* the church, with an early 16C tower, is said to have been a foundation by Lady Margaret Beaufort.—*2m. Halkyn* with, to the W and roughly paralleling the road, the long ridge of Halkyn Mountain (943ft), much scarred by quarries and lead mines, the latter originally worked by the Romans whose Via Antonina from Deva (Chester) to Kanovium (Caerhun) is believed to have used this ridge. *Coleshill* (NE of A55, 2m short of Holywell) was where in 1156 Owain Gwynedd defeated Henry II.

4m. **Holywell** (Trefynnon. 11,000 inhab. *Inf.*) owes its name to its well which over perhaps 1000 years up to the Reformation—and continuing later—was a renowned objective of pilgrimage. The well is still here and, together with the adjacent St. Winefride's (or Beaufort) Chapel and the parish church, forms a part of a pleasant compact grouping below the main town on B5121, the road dropping down to the coast.

Legend and History. In the 7C St. Beuno built a chapel (probably on the site of today's parish church), and legend tells that, soon afterwards, Caradoc, a prince of Hawarden, visited here and attempted to rape Winefride, Beuno's niece. She fled towards the chapel, but failed to reach this sanctuary before the thwarted Caradoc slashed off her head. Where the head fell, there at once gushed a spring. Beuno, coming out of the chapel, replaced Winefride's head, the spring nevertheless continuing to flow and the lady living on to become an abbess and a saint whose remains were in 1138 entrusted to the abbey at Shrewsbury. Caradoc, however, was swallowed by the ground.

The well soon became a place of pilgrimage, healing (to quote from a 'Life of St. Winefride' published in 1485) 'al langours and sekenesses as well in men as in bestes'. Among royal pilgrims were Richard I in 1189; Henry V both before and after Agincourt, on the latter occasion reputedly travelling on foot from Shrewsbury; and James II in 1686, the Old Pretender being the result of his prayers for a son. From 1240 to 1537 the well was in the care of the Cistercians of nearby Basingwerk, and when in about 1490 it was decided to build a new chapel (perhaps the first one actually over the well) a principal benefactor was Margaret Beaufort. With the Reformation the well survived destruction, apparently because it was regarded as medicinal, but pilgrimages became dangerous (though not for the Catholic James II) until the advent of the more tolerant 18C. Today the well remains an important Catholic shrine.

St. Winefride's Well (Tel: 03526-62345. For services and pilgrimage information, write with stamped addressed envelope to the Presbytery, 15 Well Street, Holywell, CH8 7PL) was long an unfailing spring, but by 1917 mining in the hills above stopped the flow and water has since been chanelled from a reservoir. The spring is within a polygonal basin in what now forms the crypt of the chapel, adjacent being a medieval bath in which St. Beuno's Stone is supposed to be the stone on which Beuno sat while instructing Winefride. Custom is that pilgrims pass three times through the inner well (perhaps because of a prayer written by a 12C prior of Shrewsbury that pilgrims might have their wishes granted at least at the third time, but more likely deriving from the Celtic practice of triple immersion) and then kneel on St. Beuno's Stone to complete their devotions. The figure of St. Winefride dates from 1888.

St. Winefride's (Beaufort) Chapel (key from Well ticket office) is a notable example of Perpendicular architecture with a wealth of stone and wood carving, this including an external frieze of beasts, both real and mythical. The nearby *Church of St. James*, built in 1770, is last in a long succession on this site, starting perhaps with St. Beuno's original chapel and including possibly two medieval churches from the last of which a 15C tower survives.

Greenfield Valley Heritage Park (parking off B5121), the wooded valley linking Holywell with the ruins of Basingwerk Abbey, was in the 18 and 19C busy with newly-established industry, and today the course of the old railway provides a pleasant trail passing some modest industrial monuments and also Abbey Farm Museum and Visitor Centre (Tel: 0352–714172). The rather scanty ruins of *Basingwerk Abbey* sprawl over a pre-Norman fortified site. Founded in 1131 by Ranulph, Earl of Chester, as a house of the Savigniac Order, the abbey became Cistercian only a few years later (in 1147). At the Reformation the buildings were largely demolished and sold, the timber roof of the choir going to St. Mary-on-the-Hill at Chester, that of the refectory possibly to Cilcain, and stained glass to Llanasa and, possibly, Dyserth. Of the church, the few remains, effectively only some lower courses, are limited to the W and S walls, some pier bases and something of the transepts. Of the domestic buildings, there is rather more, the open space immediately to the S of the church representing the cloister, with (along the E side, from N to S) the sacristy, the chapter house with traces of the bench around the walls, the parlour, and the novices' lodging and warming house extending south. The large room to the W of the warming house was the refectory, with internal arcading on its W wall and traces of the hatch to the kitchen, though of this last, against the SW corner of the cloister, little remains other than the base of the fireplace against the S wall.

There are three other places of interest in or close to Holywell. *Holywell Textile Mills* (Tel: 0352–712022), adjacent to St. Winefride's Well, were first built in 1777, installed Wales's first wool-weaving power-loom in 1845, and were rebuilt in 1833 after a fire. The mills specialise in tweed made with wool from Jacob's sheep, with four horns and a spotted or striped coat. In contrast there is *Grange Cavern Military Museum* (Tel: 0352–713455), off A55 just W of Holywell, a huge cavern quarried during the 19C, used during the last war for bomb storage, and today displaying militaria from the 18C onwards, including a large collection of vehicles. Thirdly, there is *Pantasaph*, 2m W of Holywell, a Catholic community founded by the Earl and Countess of Denbigh in 1852. The complex includes the church, with the tomb of the Earl; a Franciscan friary; and a pilgrimage path (Tel: 0352–711053).

3m (from Holywell) *Gorsedd* where there is a choice of roads, the direct road to St. Asaph being A55 while this Route bears NW along A5151. Thomas Pennant (1726–98), whose 'Tours in Wales' was published in 1778, is buried at Whitford, a mile N of the road fork. From a crossroads reached 1½m after the Gorsedd fork a diversion may be made 1m N to see the *Maen Achwynfan*, a cross of the 10 or 11C, nearly 11ft high and one of the tallest of its type in Britain. The somewhat crude carving has not been interpreted and whether the cross commemorates a person or an event is not known.

For a short distance A5151 runs with the course of Offa's Dyke.— *4m. Trelawnyd*, sometimes called Newmarket, is known for a huge prehistoric cairn on Cop Hill (just N) and also for its male voice choir (Tel: 0745–591119), while at *Llanasa* (1½m NE of Trelawnd) the church has stained glass from Basingwerk.—*2m.* **Dyserth**, a small place at the foot of a limestone hill, offers a picturesque cascade and a church with a 15C Jesse window possibly from Basingwerk. On the hill, earthworks mark the site of a castle built by Henry III in 1241 but soon taken and destroyed (in 1263) by Llewelyn the Last, and, above, *Craig Fawr* is a National Trust property of geological and other interest. A main feature is a small disused quarry where the limestone bedrock is exposed, revealing shell and small marine animal fossils deposited some 300 million years ago when this place was a reef lapped by a shallow sea. *Bodrhyddan Hall* (Tel: 0745–590414), on A5151 just W of Dyserth, is a 17C manor house showing armour, furniture and portraits and with an arboretum in the grounds.

2m. **Rhuddlan** is a name notorious in Welsh history since it was from here in 1284 that Edward I issued his statute providing for the government of the conquered principality. Traditionally, the statute was enacted on the site now occupied by *Parliament House* in the main street (corner of Parliament Street) of today's small town, the wording of today's tablet misleadingly implying that the statute assured the rights and independence of Wales rather than that it laid down the terms of the country's subjugation. For some seven centuries, from the 10C up to the Civil War, Rhuddlan's story was that of its *Castle* (WHM. Tel: 0222-465511).

History. A primitive native fort of perhaps the 10C was succeeded by a motte-and-bailey of 1073, the builder being Robert of Rhuddlan, a kinsman of the Norman Hugh Lupus. Giraldus enjoyed hospitality here in 1188, apparently being impressed by the 'noble castle' traces of which survive today as Twt Hill (see below). In 1277 the victorious Edward I started work on today's castle, the architect being James of St. George and the castle Edward's second in Wales (Flint was the first). By 1282 Rhuddlan had been completed, as had also the task of diverting and canalising the river Clwyd, the mouth of which was previously two miles away. Edward was thus able to supply himself by sea and Rhuddlan continued to enjoy the status of port until about a century ago. In 1282 Edward's queen gave birth here to her daughter Elizabeth (later, wife of John I, Count of Holland); the year 1284 was that of the Statute of Rhuddlan and in 1292 the Dominican priory (see below) was founded.

Prior to the building of the castle Rhuddlan would have been no more than a settlement around the motte-and-bailey; now Edward created one of his boroughs, and it was from this that modern Rhuddlan developed. In 1399 Richard II was here, virtually the Earl of Northumberland's prisoner and on his way to meet Bolingbroke at Flint. The castle continued in use until the Civil War when it fell to General Mytton (July 1646); two years later it was slighted, thereafter for centuries serving as a ready source of building material.

The rectangular castle was designed on a concentric plan, a walled inner ward standing within and above an outer curtain of walls and towers, a design which enabled both outer and inner bowmen to shoot at the same time. The whole was guarded on the SW by the river, and on the other sides by a moat filled by tidal and river water. There were diagonal E and W gates, each protected by flanking towers, four levels high and with seven-sided rooms above a circular base. Around the outer ward perhaps the most interesting surviving feature is the dockgate and moat inlet at the angle nearest to the river.—*Twt Hill*, Robert of Rhuddlan's Norman motte, is 300 yards SE by a footpath which continues for about the same distance to *Abbey Farm*, incorporating some remains (S cloister) of the late 13C Dominican priory.

In the town the twin-nave church dates in part from the 13C; Edward I's daughter was christened here and some ancient grave-slabs are probably from the priory.

The river Clwyd is crossed, this Route then bearing S along A525 for (*2m*) **St. Asaph** (Llanelwy), astride a ridge between the Clwyd (E) and the Elwy (W), a small place (3000 inhab.) which by virtue of its cathedral ranks as a city. The *Cathedral* is small, too, in fact the smallest medieval one in Britain.

History. There is some evidence that St. Asaph may have been the site of the Roman station of Varae. More certain is that the town grew as the result of the founding of the cathedral in the 6C by St. Kentigern (also known as St. Mungo), his successor in 570 being Asaph, holder of an administrative post at the local monastery. At this time the place was known only by its Welsh name of Llanelwy (the holy enclosure beside the Elwy), the English name of St. Asaph not being recorded before 1100. There is no sure record of any bishops between Asaph and 1143, though the succession may well have been continuous. Among later bishops were Dr Morgan (1601–04), translator of the Bible into Welsh; William Lloyd (1680–92), one of the 'seven bishops' tried for refusing to have the Declaration of Indulgence read; and Samuel Horsley (1802–06), the opponent of Priestley in the Trinitarian controversy. John Luxmoore, father of the notorious pluralist Charles Luxmoore, held the see from 1815–30.

Giraldus thought little of the cathedral, describing it in 1188 'paupercula sedis Laneluensis ecclesia', and a century later, in 1282, it was destroyed by the English. Edward I then wished to rebuild at Rhuddlan, but Bishop Anian II (1268–93) insisted that the new cathedral be at St. Asaph and got his way, such was the power of the Church even against a conqueror such as Edward I. Today's building was therefore started by Bishop Anian II, and completed by his two successors. The woodwork was burnt in 1402, but the church was reroofed and restored by Bishop Redman (1471–96); the tower was rebuilt in 1715, after its destruction in a storm, and the choir was remodelled in c 1780. There was major restoration by Gilbert Scott in 1869–75, and further restoration in 1929–32. In 1920 Dr A.G. Edwards, bishop since 1889, was enthroned as the first archbishop of the newly constituted Church of Wales.

Outside stands a monument to Bishop Morgan, buried in the cathedral, and to his fellow translators of the Bible into Welsh.

Inside the cathedral the refurbished roof painting and gilding (1967) celebrate the investiture of Prince Charles as Prince of Wales. The Decorated Nave, begun in the 13C by Anian II, has 14C arcades with continuous mouldings and a 15C clerestory. In the South Aisle, the more interesting of the two, are a recumbent effigy of a bishop, almost certainly Anian II; the curious Greyhound Stone, bearing unexplained heraldic decoration; and tablets to Mrs Hemans (died 1835), the poetess, who lived for several years near St. Asaph, and to H.M. Stanley (died 1904) of African fame, who, as the youth John Rowlands, was an inmate of the St. Asaph workhouse. The Transepts are contemporary with the nave and something of Bishop Redman's 15C roof has survived. The South Transept now serves as a chantry chapel, the gift in 1957 of the Guild of All Souls; here there is an exquisite little 16C Spanish ivory Madonna, said to have come from an Armada galleon. The aisleless Choir was mostly rebuilt by Scott in the style of the 13C but also incorporates some genuine work of that period which escaped the English destruction of 1282. The stalls here date from the restoration by Bishop Redman, but the sedilia and the E window, with glass of 1968, are 14C (restored). The 18C bishop's throne stands over Bishop Morgan's tomb.

The cathedral's Chapter Treasury (shown on request, though normally not Sun.) is known for its collection of early bibles and prayer books. The collection includes copies of the first prayer book of Edward VI (1549), one of which belonged to Roger Ascham, the 16C scholar, and shows notes in his own hand; the first Welsh New Testament (1567); Bishop Morgan's Bible (1558), used at the investiture in 1969 of Prince Charles; the second and third editions of the Welsh Prayer Book (1586, 1599); and Middleton's and Prys's Metrical Psalms in Welsh (1603, 1621). Other curiosities here include the Triglot Dictionary (Welsh, Greek, Hebrew) of Dic Aberdaron (1780–1843; see also Rte 12, Aberdaron), who is buried here; prehistoric and Roman material; a copy of the newspaper 'Commonwealth Mercury' announcing the death of Oliver Cromwell; and a collection of Victorian autographs.

For St. Asaph to *Denbigh, Ruthin* and *Corwen,* see Rte 5.

This Route continues W along B5381, but a short diversion (2m NW) may be made along A55 to **Bodelwyddan**, with a 'marble' church and castle, the latter the focus of a major leisure, heritage and cultural complex. The *Church* was built in 1856–60 by Lady Willoughby de Broke as a memorial to her husband. The design of John Gibson, the arcades are of marble but the exterior is white limestone, while, inside, the font is by Hollings of Birmingham, the curious lectern by Kendal of Warwick, and the bust of Lady Willoughby by M. Noble. To the S of the choir are the graves of Canadian soldiers who died during the First World War at nearby Kinmel Park camp.

   **Bodelwyddan Castle (Tel: 0745–584060), essentially of the 19C but with roots reaching back to the 15C, was by 1982 in sorry condition after over 60 years' service as a girls' school. Imaginatively taken in hand by Clwyd County Council, determined to create a distinguished cultural focus in this area of Wales, the main part of Bodelwyddan (Williams Hall) was in July 1988 reborn as a sumptuous Victorian country mansion and splendid setting for important Victorian collections of fine and decorative art from the National Portrait Gallery, the Victoria and Albert Museum and the Royal Academy of Art.—Plans include further artistic ventures as also a County Museum and Heritage Centre.

History. The original 15C house here was owned by the Humphreys family (formerly of Anglesey), their successors during the later 17C being the Williams family, the 18 and 19C members of which from time to time extended and remodelled what soon became a mansion. Of Georgian aspect by the 18C, Bodelwyddan was in the early 19C not only further extended but also castellated, the principal architect being J.A. Hansom. The estate remained in the ownership of the family (which became Hay Williams) until 1920 when it became the girls' school (Lowther College) which, as noted above, closed in 1982. Rescued in 1983 by Clwyd County Council, the interior has been redesigned and decorated for its new role by Roderick Gradidge. Much of the furnishing and decoration belongs to the 19C house, while much else, but always compatible, is new design or furnishing brought in from elsewhere, notably, of course, the Victoria and Albert Museum as also the Clwyd County Council collection.—There is an admirable illustrated background guide, 'The National Portrait Gallery at Bodelwyddan Castle', with a foreword by John Hayes, Director of the National Portrait Gallery, and articles on the history of the castle by Peter Howell, on the design of the interiors by Roderick Gradidge, and on Victorian portraiture by Susan Foister.

The rooms visited are on two floors, linked by a Jacobean-style staircase which, with the staircase hall, represents the architectural core of Bodelwyddan. The ground floor rooms, together with the first floor Bedroom, are the historically decorated and furnished rooms and the home of the loans from the National Portrait Gallery, the Victorian and Albert Museum and the Royal Academy of Art. The remainder of the first floor is devoted more to museum-style displays and special exhibitions.

   Whenever possible the portraits are matched to the rooms in which they hang. Thus portraits of savants hang in the Library; those of women of the early 19C will be found in the Ladies Drawing Room decorated in late-Regency style; and the theme of the Billiard Room is sporting. Among the artists whose work may be seen here at Bodelwyddan are G.F. Watts (with a corridor specially designed for his important series of late 19C portraits), Ford Madox Brown, Margaret Carpenter, Hubert von Herkamer, W. Holman Hunt, Edwin Landseer, Thomas Lawrence, Edward Novello, John S. Sargent, David Wilkie, John Wood and A.J.S. Wortley. In the Drawing Room and Sculpture Gallery the emphasis is on John Gibson, others represented here being Thomas Woolner and Princess Louise.

On the first floor the Bedroom, mid Victorian in character, shows portraits of Queen Victoria's family. Elsewhere on this floor the exhibition themes are the Victorian Art World, Victorian Portraiture, Victorian Photography and the History of the National Portrait Gallery.

Other attractions at Bodelwyddan include woodland walks, formal gardens and children's play areas.

From Bodelwyddan A55 in 5m reaches Abergele on Rte 1A, on the way passing the village of *St. George* (Llan Sain Sior), by local repute the place where St. George slew the dragon.

B5381, the continuation of this Rte 1B, can be joined by a minor road leading S to Glascoed.

6m (from St. Asaph along B5381, here a Roman road) A548 is crossed, 2m S down which is *Llanfair Talhaiarn*, the burial place of John Jones ('Talhaiarn', 1810–69), a poet sometimes acclaimed as the Welsh Burns.—*3m*. *Dolwen*, 2m NW of which, in the church of *Llanelian-yn-Rhos*, is preserved the graveslab of Ednyfed Fechan, minister of Llewelyn the Great.—*6m*. **Llandudno Junction** (station for Conwy) where the Conwy Estuary is reached and this Route merges with Rte 1A. For the Vale of Conwy to the S, see Rte 6.

The **Conwy Estuary** (A55 tunnel bypassing Conwy) has long been known for its mussels, mentioned by Tacitus, praised in verse by Drayton and Spenser, and, together with other fishing (dabs in particular), still supporting an industry. *Deganwy* (Dinas Conwy, the fort on the Conwy), today a straggling small resort on the coastal road to Llandudno, once guarded the N shore and slight remains of the castle survive. Frequently mentioned in Welsh history, the castle is said to have been a favourite seat of Maelgwn Gwynedd as early as the 6C and it may have been here that he received Gildas who later wrote so maliciously about him and his licentious court. The first medieval castle was probably built soon after the Norman conquest, perhaps by Hugh Lupus, Earl of Chester, but today's ruins are those of a castle built by a successor Earl of Chester in 1211. Henry III was besieged here by the Welsh, and Deganwy was finally destroyed by Llewelyn the Last in 1263.

2m. ****Conwy** (3500 inhab. *Inf*. Castle Street. Tel: 0492–592248) lies beyond the Conwy river, here crossed by three adjacent bridges. The modern road bridge, opened in 1958, superseded Telford's graceful suspension bridge of 1826, still, however, open to pedestrians and cyclists and its toll house now a *Telford Exhibition* (NT. Tel: 0492–592246). The third bridge, carrying the railway, is a tubular one built in 1846–48 by Robert Stephenson.

With its splendid castle and contoured enceinte of high town walls complete with twenty-one towers, Conwy is the most dramatic and historic place along this northern Welsh coast. It is also a lively town, resort and yachting centre.

Early History. There would probably have been a primitive settlement around the Norman motte-and-bailey which stood on the site of today's castle, but Conwy's early history is more that of the Cistercian abbey of Aberconwy, founded in 1172 and completed 15 years later. In 1198 Llewelyn the Great

LLANDUDNO JUNCTION, COLWYN BAY

Conwy

C o n w y   E s t u a r y

Suspension Bridge

Road Bridge

Tubular Bridge

Chapel Tower

Kitchen Tower

King's Tower

Outer Ward

Castle

Prison Tower

CASTLE SQUARE

LLANRWST ROAD

Porth Bach

Landing Stage

Guildhall

Vicarage Gardens

Town Wall

QUAY

Porth Isaf

Town Hall

CASTLE STREET

Castle Hotel

St. Mary's

Porth-y-Felin

ROSE HILL STREET

LLANRWST ROAD

River Gyffin

LLANRWST ROAD

TYN-GROES, LLANRWST

MARINE WALK

Porth yr Aden

LOWER GATE STREET

BERRY STREET

Library

Aberconwy

CHURCH STREET

Visitor Centre

Llewelyn's Tower

SEA VIEW TER.

CROWN LANE

HIGH STREET

CHAPEL STREET

LANCASTER SQUARE

CHURCH STREET

TOWN DITCH ROAD

EGRYNE TER.

Plas Mawr

CHAPEL STREET

BANGOR ROAD

P.O.

ROSEMARY LANE

ROSE HILL STREET

UPPER GATE

Park

BANGOR ROAD

MOUNT PLEASANT

Porth Uchaf

WATKIN

Porth Ucha

100m
100yds

N

BANGOR   SYCHNANT PASS

granted a charter to the abbey, which later became renowned for its library; he became a monk here in 1238 and died here in 1240. In 1245 Henry III plundered the abbey, and in 1283 Edward I, requiring the site for his castle and borough, removed it to Maenan, the only traces surviving being parts of St. Mary's Church. From now on the history of Conwy becomes that of its castle.

Conwy Castle (WHM. Tel: 0222-465511), though smaller than some, is theatrically set and one of the most picturesque of Welsh fortresses. The ground plan is an irregular rectangle along an E–W axis, the curtain walls being 15ft thick and enfiladed externally by eight cylindrical towers of which the four on the E are crowned with smaller, circular turrets. A rampart walk is carried round the flattened inner face of the towers by corbelled-out galleries. Of the two wards the western is the larger and the castle proper, while the smaller ward beyond served essentially as a royal palace.

History. On the site of a Norman motte-and-bailey, the castle was begun by Edward I in 1283, the work being largely that of James of St. George, and

Conwy Castle, with Telford's suspension bridge on the left

completed a little over four years later, together with the associated borough which received a charter as early as 1284. In 1294 Edward was besieged here (nearly having to surrender through famine) during a Welsh uprising, the castle being in part garrisoned, in accordance with the terms of the charter, by the Anglo-Norman settlers who were the borough's first citizens. A century later, in 1399, Richard II sought refuge here on his return from his ill-timed visit to Ireland and just before his surrender to Bolingbroke (Henry IV) at Flint, and then, only two years later in 1401, Owen Glendower's supporters successfully seized both town and castle. During the Civil War the castle was first held for Charles I by Archbishop Williams of York, who was a native of Conwy, then later by Sir John Owen, but in 1646 it was taken for Parliament by General Mytton. It was finally dismantled in 1665.

The modern entrance is into a projecting barbican, formerly reached by a steep ramp and drawbridge, remains of the former and of its portcullis still being visible. Immediately S of this projecting barbican was a small fortified terrace and inner barbican from which the main gateway leads into the outer ward. The absence of a definite gatehouse is unusual in a castle of this date, some defensive compensation however being provided here by the exceptionally strong barbican and the abrupt right-angle turn immediately beneath the two towers.

The OUTER WARD encloses along its S side the Great Hall, its irregular shape dictated by that of the outer curtain wall. Rather unusually the wooden roof was supported by stone arches, one of which (restored) remains. The kitchens were, inconveniently, on the opposite side of the ward, below the Kitchen Tower, while on the E side, sunk in the solid rock, is the massive water tank, made necessary by the absence of a well. Here the INNER WARD or PALACE is entered, on the S side (first floor) being the King's Banqueting Hall, with his withdrawing room to the E and what was probably his bedchamber in the SE (King's Tower). The Queen's Hall occupied the first floor on the E side of the ward; on the same floor, opening out of the NE tower (Chapel Tower), a small oratory with a polygonal apse provides a welcome delicate touch. A gateway below the Queen's Hall leads to the EAST BARBICAN flanking the whole E end of the castle and possibly once doubling as garden for the queen; at its NE corner are the remains of the original watergate stairs.—Of the TOWERS the Kitchen Tower (Outer North N), the King's Tower (SE) and the Chapel Tower (NE) have already been mentioned. The other towers along the S side from E to W are Bakehouse Tower, with a large oven; the Prison Tower, with dungeon, and the South-West Tower. Along the N curtain, also from E to W, are the Stockhouse Tower, where criminals suffered in the stocks, the Kitchen Tower and the North-West Tower.

The *Town Walls*, some 1400 yards in circumference and contemporary with the castle, form with the castle one integral defence scheme, the borough growing in what was in effect an outflung ward of the castle. The walls are remarkable for their height (around 30ft), their 21 towers and the hilly area enclosed. From the castle an anticlockwise circuit follows the Quay of 1831 (along which will be found what claims to be the smallest house in Britain) to Porth Isaf (Lower Gate) at the foot of High Street, thence continuing to Porth-yr-Aden at the N corner; from here a spur, once ending in a tower, runs out to the water to protect the N entrance to the harbour. Continuing SW from Porth-yr-Aden the walls climb to their highest point to reach Porth Uchaf (Upper Gate), with its outer and inner barbicans the most elaborate of the three main gateways, and then descend generally E passing Llewelyn's Tower on their way to Porth-y-Felin (Mill Gate), set in an odd angle. This eastern entrance to the town would probably have been associated with a ferry across the river Gyffin. Beyond, the top of the wall carries no fewer than 12 conspicuous lavatories, two of them still roofed, said to have been reserved for the royal clerks.

Despite the importance of the castle, the borough's growth seems to have been slow. A mere 60 houses are recorded in Elizabethan times, and Pennant, writing in the 18C, remarks on the few inhabitants. Modern Conwy dates largely only from the arrival of the railway during the 19C.

From Castle Square, Rosehill Street, leading generally SW, soon reaches the *Conwy Valley Visitor Centre* (Tel: 0492–596288), the street here curving NW for Lancaster Square at the head of High Street along which are three places of interest. *Plas Mawr* (WHM. Tel: 0222–465511), the 'Great Mansion' built in 1577–80 by Robert Wynne of Gwydir and one of the finest examples in Britain of an Elizabethan town house, came to the Mostyn family in the 18C and was in 1991 given by Lord Mostyn to the nation. The main façade fronts Crown Lane, but the entrance is in High Street. Of particular interest are the elaborate plaster ceilings, copied from Gwydir Castle, and the chimneypieces.

St. Mary's Church, off the opposite side of High Street, occupies part of the site of the 12C Cistercian Abbey which was removed to Maenan by Edward I. When this happened the abbey church became the parish church of the new Edwardian borough and some interesting survivals are to be seen, the E and W buttresses and parts of the walls, particularly on the N side, all representing the original church while the striking if mutilated W doorway was probably that of the chapter house. But the bulk of the church grew over later centuries. To the 14C belong the lower stages of the tower, the S transept and the porches; to the 15C the upper tower, the rood screen (now without its loft though something of the stair can be seen), and the font at which John Williams, later Archbishop of York and defender of Conwy for Charles I, was christened (in the S aisle there is an effigy of Mary, his mother, who died in 1585). In the 16C the aisle roofs were raised, and in 1872 that of the nave as part of a restoration by Gilbert Scott. Connoisseurs of the curious will find on the choir floor the worn graveslab of one Nicholas Hookes (died 1637), the forty-first child of his father and himself father of twenty-one. The Parish Museum, in the church, is opened on request.

Aberconwy House (NT. Tel: 0492–592246), a stone and timber building (much restored) dating from the 14–16C, houses a Conwy Exhibition telling the borough's story from Roman times.

ENVIRONS OF CONWY. In summer, launches cruise the estuary and ascend the wooded and pastoral Vale of Conwy (see Rte 6. Tel: 0492–593484 or 592284).—*Conwy Mountain* (808ft), 1m W, has hut circles and traces of a hillfort around its summit. From here there are footpaths in most directions, including S to *Sychnant Pass* (550ft), the old road pass linking Conwy with Penmaenmawr.—*Gyffin*, 1/2m S off B5106, was the birthplace of Richard Davies, Bishop of St. David's and translator into Welsh (1567) of the Book of Common Prayer. The church has a 13C door and a painted barrel-ceiling (15–16C).

For Conwy to *Betws-y-Coed* and *Ffestiniog*, see Rte 6.

C.   Conwy to Bangor

A55. Total distance 16m.—*5m.* **Penmaenmawr.**—*3m.* **Llanfairfechan.**—*2m.* **Aber.**—*4m.* **Llandegai (Penrhyn).**—*2m.* **Bangor**.

Along this stretch, and despite tunnels, Rte 1 becomes scenically more striking, with views across Conwy Bay to Great Orme's Head and Anglesey, and, inland, high ground crossed by many paths.

Leaving Conwy the road rounds Conwy Mountain and there is a view across to Great Orme's Head before the curved tunnel (1932) below Penmaenbach Point (Little Stone Point) is reached. After the tunnel Puffin Island and Anglesey come into view.—*5m.* **Penmaenmawr**, spread up the hillside between Penmaenbach and Penmaenmawr (Large Stone Point), is a modest resort with a long sandy beach. For those with other interests there are many walks, one of which (the History Trail, 3 1/2m. Leaflet from local shops) visits Craig Lwyd, close to a prehistoric 'axe factory' discovered in 1919, and continues to the so-called Druids' Circle at about 1200ft on the NE slope of Moelfre (1922ft). The stones here are the remains of two prehistoric circles, long associated with the worship of two sinister goddesses, Andras and Ceridwen.

As today's motorist speeds past the quarry-scarred height of *Penmaenmawr* (1550ft; path), a thought may be spared for earlier travellers, many of whom preferred to use the sands at low tide. In 1685 Lord Clarendon found the path here impassable except on foot, and in 1774 Dr Johnson recorded his apprehension, even though in 1772 the bridlepath had been replaced by a road. Public houses then stood at either end of the 'pass' to encourage travellers at the start and calm them on safe arrival.

3m. **Llanfairfechan** is another pleasant modest resort, as popular for its beach as for the choice of walks exploring the high ground immediately above. For these walks there is a special local map, one walk (the History Trail, 5m) including the Aber to Kanovium Roman road, hut circles and, on the Bwlch-y-Ddeufaen (Pass of the Two Stones, 1403ft), two standing stones.—*2m.* **Aber**, set back from the sea and never a coast resort, is instead known as a centre from which to explore the upland behind, including, close to Aber, the beautiful *Coedydd Aber Glen* (nature reserve). Here a trail, about 3m long and in part steepish, ascends the valley to the Aber Falls (Rhaeadr Fawr), on the way passing a farmstead now serving as a Countryside Council for Wales information centre. The return may be by way of an alternative path through Forestry Commission plantations. Aber also has its place in history, the Mwd (motte) being the site of a motte-and-bailey built by Llewelyn the Great; it was here that Llewelyn the Last received and rejected Edward I's demand that he should acknowledge his sovereignty, a rejection which quickly led to Edward's subjection of Wales. Off the coast are the *Lavan Sands* (Traeth Lafan), across which, before the building of the Menai Bridge in 1819–26, travellers rode to find the ferry for Beaumaris, a bell in Aber church tolling to guide them in foggy weather. Welsh legend associates these sands, and indeed much of this coast, with drowned towns, splendid palaces and once lush meadows.

4m. **Llandegai** is the modern development of the model village built in the 19C for Lord Penrhyn's estate workers. The name derives from St. Tegai, said to have had a cell here in the 5C. The church (16C), perhaps on the site of the saint's cell, is of a cruciform type not common in Wales and is approached by an avenue of yews perhaps twice as old as the church itself; inside are monuments to Archbishop Williams of York (died 1650), defender of Conwy for Charles I, with his helmet and spurs hanging above, and (by Westmacott) to the first Baron and Lady Penrhyn. It was in this area, in 1648, that the Royalist Sir John Owen was defeated by a Parliamentary force under Colonel Thistleton.

Rte 9 is joined here, by the junction with A5 being the entrance to ***Penrhyn Castle** (NT. Tel: 0248–353084). Built by Thomas Hopper in 1827–37, Penrhyn is, both outside and inside, a huge complex of ostentatious Neo-Norman, well worth visiting both as such and for the splendid slate craftsmanship of the interior.

History. The estate, dating at least back to the time of Llewelyn the Great, in the 17C passed into the ownership of John Williams, Archbishop of York. Later, by marriage, it came in 1765 to Richard Pennant, who developed the Penrhyn slate quarries above Bethesda and was in 1783 created Baron Penrhyn of Penrhyn in the peerage of Ireland. His successor, through the female line, was George Dawkins, who assumed the name of Pennant and commissioned Thomas Hopper to rebuild on the site of the Neo-Gothic mansion he had inherited, the result being this astonishing castle. For all its medieval Norman exterior, the interior was thoroughly modern, boasting features such as hot air heating and water closets. Dawkins's successor, again through the female line and taking the name of Pennant (George Douglas Pennant), entertained Queen Victoria and the Prince Consort in 1859 and in 1866 was created Baron Penrhyn of

Llandegai. In 1949, on the death of the 4th Baron, the estate passed to his niece, Lady Janet Douglas Pennant, who in 1951 conveyed the castle and immediately surrounding grounds through the Treasury to the National Trust.

In the *Great Hall*, where the grilles in the floor are part of the original heating system, two features of particular note are the octagonal 'Norman' centre table and the Zodiac windows by Thomas Willement. The *Library*, with a billiard table mostly of slate, particularly well illustrates Hopper's richness of design in the carving on the walls, the plaster decoration in the arches, and the ribbed and bossed ceiling, while the *Drawing Room* emphasises the interior 'Norman' motif by the huge pillars of the window surrounds and the two large candelabra. By the door to the next room the spiral staircase is a survival from the 15C mansion. The sombre *Ebony Room* contains both genuine ebony furniture and, in the case of the arched surrounds of the fireplace and the doorways, plaster painted to match. It was in this appropriately gloomy setting that the coffin always rested before family funerals in the *Chapel*, otherwise the scene of daily compulsory services for the whole household, the family and guests occupying the balcony, and the staff, segregated by sexes, the pews.

The visitors' tour next moves to the keep in which the *King's Bed*, elaborately worked in brass and topped by a crown, was made for the visit of the Prince and Princess of Wales in 1894. The hangings of the bed, as also the wallpaper, were designed by William Morris, as is also the case with the *Slate Bed*, weighing nearly one ton. The *Dressing Room*, with wallpaper by Morris, contains a splendid wardrobe. From the keep the route returns along the gallery overlooking the Great Hall, passes the Chapel and reaches the *State Bedroom* where in 1859 Queen Victoria slept in the huge carved-oak bed designed by Hopper. The *Grand Staircase* has a plaster ceiling in the form of a fan vault with Norman motifs; in riotously carved slate the staircase absorbed ten years of work after the completion of the rest of the castle. In the *Dining Room*, with a fireplace, three sideboards and a curtain pole, all in polished slate, the original hand-painted decoration of the walls (c 1838) was only revealed in 1974 after the removal of the five coats of distemper which had covered it for perhaps 70 years. The *Breakfast Room* is notable for showing some of the Old Masters assembled by the 1st Baron Penrhyn, these include Rembrandt's portrait (1657) of Catrina Hoogstraet. Beyond is the *Domestic Area* where a tea room occupies the former Housekeeper's Room and the National Trust shop is in the kitchen.

The *Industrial Railway Museum* occupies the stable yard, here being models; railway equipment; tickets; several vintage engines, including the Fire Queen (1848) and Haydock (1879); a smart saloon coach (1896); and the original Llanfair PG platform sign. Also of outstanding interest are the collections of industrial prints and of examples of slate craftsmanship. In the stalls to the right of the stable yard entrance there is a *Doll Collection*, which has no connection with the castle but started with the presentation to the National Trust of a doll in Welsh costume. Spanning from the early 19C to the present day, the 1000 or so dolls are of worldwide provenance.

The *Grounds* include, near the car park, a Californian Big Tree planted by Queen Victoria in 1859, and a Turkey Oak planted by the Prince of Wales in 1894. The Walled Garden is terraced as three areas—the upper with formal beds; the middle with trees and shrubs, where something is in flower all year; the lower with a wild garden.

2m. **Bangor**, see Rte 3.

2   Llandudno and Environs

A.   Llandudno

LLANDUDNO (19,000 inhab., resident) is a large and distinguished resort which combines all the facilities (including, increasingly, those required by business conferences), cheerful attractions and high-grade entertainment (a highlight is the summer visit by the Welsh National Opera) which the modern visitor demands yet at the same time attracts older visitors and families by shunning the more strident forms which would detract from the town's underlying Victorian dignity and confident elegance. Straddling the neck of the Great Orme, a tourist attraction in its own right, the main town is on the NE side, its broad long promenade (2m) embracing the sweeping curve of Orme's (or Llandudno) Bay with its splendid sands.

Town Centre. Mostyn Street—Prince Edward Square—Gloddaeth Street.

Tourist Information. The main office is at 1 Chapel Street, within the angle formed by Mostyn Street and Gloddaeth Street (Tel: 0492–876413). Also, summer only, at the Arcadia Theatre, Promenade.

Town and Local Tours. Regular coach departures (Llandudno and Marine Drive Tour) from Prince Edward Square. Town Trail booklet. Local boats from the jetty opposite Prince Edward Square.

History. Llandudno finds its distant roots on Great Orme, home of prehistoric man, then of Romans who mined the copper, and later, in the 6C, chosen by St. Tudno as the site of the cell from which he preached; hence the town's name, meaning the Holy Enclosure of St. Tudno. In probably the 12C a church was built here, this later becoming the parish church. Until 1854 Llandudno remained no more than a village on the slope of Great Orme, but after this date, and due in considerable part to the initiative of the Mostyn family, a purpose-built resort rapidly took over the sand and marsh that backed the bay.

The heart of the town is a gently curving rectangle bounded on the N and the S by respectively the Promenade and St. Mary's Road, and on the E and W by Vaughan Street and the park of Happy Valley. Rather farther to the E (off Promenade, 500 yards E of Vaughan Street and adjacent to the Arcadia Theatre) stands the modern (1981) block of the *Canolfan Aberconwy Centre* (Tel: 0492–879771), a combined conference, exhibition and leisure complex.

Llandudno offers two museums and, at 12 Vaughan Street, the enterprising **Mostyn Art Gallery** (Tel: 0492–879201), recognised as one of the leading public art galleries of North Wales. Opened in 1979 in a building of 1901 designed for Lady Mostyn as an art gallery (which however closed in 1914), today's gallery mounts monthly exhibitions of past and contemporary fine and applied art, both British (especially Welsh) and foreign. Additionally there are arts films, lectures and workshop activities, while craft and book shops look after tourist needs.

The two museums are farther to the W, on and just off Gloddaeth Street which runs SW out of Prince Edward Square. **Charden House**, or **Llandudno Museum** (Tel: 0492–876517), at 17 Gloddaeth Street, caters for historical interests, the theme here, expressed through period rooms and other exhibitions, being the story of Llandudno and its district. But children, and adults with a sense of nostalgia, will make for the **Doll Museum and Model Railway** (Tel: 0492–876312) in Masonic Street off the N end of Gloddaeth Street. Here, in a mid 19C building, are over 1000 dolls from the past, together with bygones such as fans, exquisite lace and beadwork and much else, while in a separate room a model railway runs beside old tin plate and toys.

At the W end of the Promenade and at the foot of Great Orme, the **Pier** (Tel: 0492–876258) stretches 2296ft seaward, as popular with today's visitors who enjoy the bracing views and many traditional attractions as it was with the Victorians who built it. **Happy Valley**, immediately W of the base of the Pier, is a park with rock gardens, a children's playground and summer entertainment, here too being the station of the Great Orme cabin lift (see below). The wooded hill here is *Pen-y-Dinas*, with traces of a hillfort and hut circles and also a

stone known as St. Tudno's Cradle which must once have rocked and
may have been associated with prehistoric ritual.

Church Walks, the road running roughly SW from the base of the
Pier, passes the station of the Great Orme Tramway (see below) and,
beyond, the beautiful terraces of *Haulfre Gardens* with sweeping
views. Continuing SW, Church Walks merges with Abbey Road to
reach (1m from the Pier) Llandudno's WEST SHORE (also approached
by Gloddaeth Avenue, the extension of the street of the same name)
which, with dunes and a beach, offers a quieter alternative to the
main bay and also commands a view towards Snowdonia.

Below the West Parade there is a model yacht pond, to the N of this
being *Gogarth Abbey Hotel*, successor to a home of Dean Liddell,
often visited by Charles Dodgson (Lewis Carroll), whose walks here
with the dean's small daughter inspired 'Alice in Wonderland'. A
memorial by F.W. Forrester, portraying the White Rabbit, was
unveiled in 1933 by Lloyd George.

B.   Environs of Llandudno

GREAT ORME, much of which is a Country Park, is a limestone mass
rising sharply immediately NW of Llandudno. As noted in the town's
history above, this headland—with echoes of prehistoric (a burial
chamber), Roman and early Christian occupation—provides Llandudno with its early roots. A local booklet, 'Discovering the Great
Orme', explains in some detail the Orme's geology, flora and fauna;
and a leaflet guides around the summit nature trail.

The headland may be visited by boat (the best way to see the cliffs
and caves), by tramway, by cabin lift, by coach tour, by bus (to St.
Tudno's Church), on foot or by car. The *Great Orme Tramway* (from
Victoria Station, Church Walks. Tel: 0492–870870), in operation
since 1902, enjoys all the popularity of long tradition, while a
somewhat different ride is provided by the *Cabin Lift* (from Happy
Valley. Tel: 0492–877205), 1m in length and the longest cable-car
ride in Britain.

For motorists there are two approaches. One is the steep direct
road leading off Church Walks beside the Empire Hotel and more or
less following the course of the tramway. The other is the Marine
Drive (see below).

At the summit (679ft)—barren, open and as likely as not
windswept—are a Country Park Visitor Centre; an interesting Summit Rock Garden, the starting point of a nature trail (3½m); and a
café and shop. The views may embrace the mountains to the SW
(with Carnedd Llewelyn as the highest point), Anglesey and, in
exceptional circumstances, the mountains of Cumbria and the Isle of
Man.

Marine Drive (toll), opened in 1878 and some 5m long, makes an
anticlockwise circuit. The start is near Happy Valley, from where the
road gradually ascends, skirting the cliffs to reach Pen Trwyn, at
Orme's NE angle, thence bearing W to reach the diversion up to the
summit along which is St. Tudno's Church. As noted earlier, it was
here in the 6C that Tudno built the cell from which he preached.
Today's church is a humble, small place, the oldest part of which (N
wall, E of the porch) dates from the 12 or 13C, the remainder being
largely 15C. In 1839 the roof was destroyed in a storm, the church

then being abandoned until restored in 1855. Of note inside are 13C graveslabs, a 12 or 13C font, and, over the W door, a part of the medieval rood screen. Services, in the open weather permitting, Whitsun–mid Sept: Sun., 11.00. Bus from opposite the town hall.

Marine drive continues W to Great Orme's Head lighthouse at the N tip of the headland, then bears SW, passing above Llech Cave, said to have been used as a summer retreat by a 16C member of the Mostyn family, and then Hornsby Cave, named after a ship wrecked here in 1824. The old road (followed by the nature trail) comes in from the E, then, as Marine Drive rounds the W point, there is a fine view across Conwy Bay to Conwy Castle below its backdrop of mountains, while, more to the W, are Puffin Island and Anglesey. Now descending (through an area in which feral goats may be seen, descendants of a pair from the Windsor Royal Herd, released here in about 1900), Marine Drive runs above the ruins (no access) of a Bishop's Palace, probably built by Anian, Bishop of Bangor, in the late 13C on land given to him by Edward I as reward for baptising the royal son, soon proclaimed Prince of Wales; the palace was later destroyed by Owen Glendower. Marine Drive ends close to Gogarth Abbey Hotel (see last paragraph of Rte 2A).

EASTERN ENVIRONS OF LLANDUDNO. **Little Orme's Head**, the lime-stone headland at the E end of Llandudno's bay, boasts even finer and steeper cliffs (400ft in places) than Great Orme, and its summit (463ft; path) commands a wide view. A walk is also possible round the foot where there are several caves, in one of which, in 1587, there was found a secret Roman Catholic printing press, possibly the first press in Wales.

For *Deganwy*, on the S side of the peninsula, see Rte 1B. The castle here is said to have been a favourite of Maelgwn Gwynedd, said also to have died of plague in 547 in the church at *Llanrhos* (or Eglwys Rhos), a mile NE of Deganwy. Today's small church, in part 13C, contains an Early Christian inscribed stone (?6C) as also monuments to the Mostyn family, and, perhaps confirming the tradition about Maelgwn, the hill above the church bears his name.—*Bodysgallen Hall*, ½m SE of Llanrhos and now a distinguished hotel (Tel: 0492–584466), also has ancient associations, the name meaning Abode of Gallen and the site thought to have been the 5C home of a prince of that name. Although the hall is essentially 17C, the tower is in part 13C and may once have been an outpost of the castle at Deganwy.—*Gloddaeth Hall*, ½m NE of Llanrhos, was a seat of the Mostyns and also the last home of Archbishop Williams (died 1650) who held Conwy for Charles I.

3   Bangor

BANGOR (12,000 inhab.), the central part of which lies either side of a valley just S of and parallel to the Menai Strait, is of interest to the tourist largely for its cathedral and for Penrhyn Castle (see Rte 1C), 2m E of the city centre, while the University College of North Wales, prominent along the N slope of the valley, gives Bangor academic distinction.

City Centre. S side of the valley; Cathedral and High Street.

Tourist Information. Summer only. Theatr Gwynedd, Deiniol Road. Tel: 0248–352786.

History. Bangor owes its birth to St. Deiniol, a nobleman who founded a monastic community here in 525; the word Bangor derives from the wattle fence which surrounded St. Deiniol's primitive enclosure, 'bangori' still being used in parts of Wales to describe the plaiting of twigs in a hedge. Later, in 546, St. Dubricius (or Dyfrig), Bishop of All Wales, divided his large see into three, consecrating St. Deiniol as the bishop responsible for Gwynedd (St. Padarn got central Wales, and St. Teilo the south). Thenceforward for nearly 13 centuries Bangor's story is that of its bishopric (see below), significant change only coming with the commercial activities of the early 19C: in succession the opening of the Penrhyn quarries; the development of a port (Penrhyn); the construction of Telford's road (today's A5) in 1815–30 and of his Menai Strait suspension bridge in 1819–26; and the arrival in 1848 of the railway, with the building of Stephenson's tubular bridge two years later. Bangor was given formal municipal status in 1883, and the establishment in the following year of the University College of North Wales ensured that the city would be an educational as well as a commercial and ecclesiastical centre.

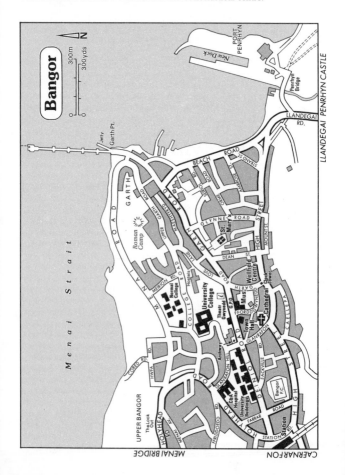

The broad Deiniol Road runs roughly E–W along the floor of the valley, the cathedral and main town being to the S while the University College dominates the N slope.

The unpretentious **Cathedral** is probably the oldest in Britain in continuous use as such.

History. The history of the see is virtually blank from St. Deiniol's time until 1071 when William II tried to force on it as bishop a Breton called Hervé; an unwelcome symbol of Norman power, he was in constant strife with his flock and soon departed. Between 1120–39 Bishop David, who is recorded as having ministered to the dying Gruffydd ap Cynan (died 1137), built the Norman cathedral, and it would have been here that Archbishop Baldwin preached the Crusade in 1188. In 1211, and again during the wars of Edward I, the cathedral was much damaged, but rebuilding was begun before 1291 by Bishop Anian I (1267–1305), who was responsible for a central tower (burnt c 1308), the Lady Chapel, and an enlarged S transept. Building continued through the Decorated period until c 1350, Bishop Anian II (1309–28) probably being responsible for the N transept and nave. Disaster came in 1402 when the cathedral was badly damaged by the followers of Owen Glendower, the ruins lying virtually untouched for nearly a century. Bishop Deane (1494–1500) largely rebuilt the choir, including the E window, and Bishop Skeffington (1509–34) added a nave clerestory and W tower. During the Civil War and the two centuries that followed, the cathedral again suffered damage and neglect. A bishop during this period was Hoadly (1715–21), whose sermon on the 'Nature of the Kingdom or Church of Christ' gave rise to a pamphleteering war known as the Bangorian Controversy (1717–21). Between 1868–84 Sir Gilbert Scott carried out a drastic but successful restoration. His plans envisaged a lofty central tower and spire, but subsidence made this impracticable and in 1967–71 the tower was battlemented at its present height and given its small cap spire.—Four bishops of Bangor became archbishops of Canterbury: Henry Deane (1501), Thomas Herring (1747), Matthew Hutton (1757), and John Moore (1783).

Points to be noticed around the EXTERIOR are a blocked window and plain buttress (both S wall of choir), the sole surviving visible evidence of the Norman cathedral; the inscription of 1532 over the W doorway recording the building of the tower; the unusually thin buttresses of the N aisle; and the late Decorated windows (?1350) of the aisles, the side walls of which survived the damage of 1402 by Owen Glendower. The transept ends were rebuilt by Scott to what are probably, from the indications afforded by fragments discovered in the 16C walls, the original designs. The fine buttresses on the end of the S transept, including the curious dwarf example in the middle, also escaped destruction in 1402. On the E of the S transept are traces of former chapels, probably demolished in the 15–16C and their stone used in the repair of the transept walls.

INTERIOR. On the right, on entering by the NW doorway, are various ancient stones, including the 14C slab of 'Eva, wife of Anwel'. The tiles on the floor are probably early 14C and were discovered under the floor of the choir during the 19C restoration. Here too are dog tongs, used to remove unruly dogs from the church; a 15C miserere; and some 16C Flemish wooden figures. On a nearby *Nave* pier hangs the *Mostyn Christ of 1518, thought to have been concealed by the Mostyn family at the Reformation; Christ, bound and wearing a crown of thorns, is seated on a rock. All the woodwork in the nave is modern. The nave altar frontal (1975), the main motif of which is the Celtic cross, is the design of Iris Martin and the work of Celtic Studios of Swansea. In the *South Transept* the arched tomb in the S wall was once thought to be that of Prince Owain Gwynedd (died 1170), originally buried before the high altar. However since the tomb is 13C, it is now thought that it may have been prepared for Bishop Anian I. As to where Owain Gwynedd lies, one account relates that, since he died under excommunication, his remains were secretly removed at the behest of Archbishop Baldwin and interred in the churchyard. Also in the S transept are a wallpainting (1955, Brian Thomas, two more of whose murals, depicting the six Welsh cathedrals and worthies of the Welsh Church from Dubricius to the first Archbishop of Wales, are at the cathedral's W end); a memorial to Edmond Prys (1544–1623), author of Welsh metrical psalms; and a tablet to Goronwy Owen (1723–69), the poet. In the *Choir* the stonework of the large Perp. windows in the E and S walls dates from 1494–1500; the glass is 19C. The stalls are 1868–79 and 1908, that of the Precentor bearing the arms of Gruffydd ap Cynan, and that of the Canon in Residence those of Owain Gwynedd; the bishop's throne is 1879; the reredos of 1881 was designed by J. Oldrid Scott.

The former close, just N of the cathedral, is now the *Bishop's Garden*, with a Biblical Garden. The S side of the path is planted with flowers and shrubs traditionally associated with the medieval Church, while on the N side, and planted chronologically according to mention, are examples of all trees, shrubs and plants mentioned in the Bible and able to survive the local climate. The *Town Hall*, between the garden and Deiniol Road, dates from the 16–17C with 18 and 19C additions to the N and east. Until 1899 it was the residence of the bishops.

The **Museum of Welsh Antiquities** (Tel: 0248–353368), housed in the Old Canonry (1862) in Ffordd Gwynedd in the town centre, contains primarily the collections of the University College, with also material from the former Bangor City Museum. Exhibits include prehistoric stone and bronze implements, and burial urns; Roman material; Early Christian and medieval graveslabs, and fine examples of medieval woodcarving; Welsh furniture of various periods; and Welsh costumes (mainly Victorian). There is also material on the Menai suspension and tubular bridges, including a brass model (1875) of the former. One room has been arranged as an old Welsh kitchen, and another contains relics of old Bangor.—*Oriel Bangor* (Art Gallery), run by the University College and also in the Old Canonry, holds 10 exhibitions a year of differing content (Tel: 0248–353368).

NORTH OF DEINIOL ROAD. On the corner of Deiniol Road and Glanrafon Hill stands the *North Wales Heroes' Memorial Archway* (1923, D.W. Thomas), which, with a number of bursaries tenable at the University College, commemorates the men of 'Gwynedd and Powis' who fell in the First World War. *Theatr Gwynedd*, farther E, is the county of Gwynedd's centre for live artistic entertainment, as also for films.

The main buildings of the **University College of North Wales** (Tel: 0248-351151) occupy a commanding position above the valley, and are approached via Glanrafon and College roads, or by the footpath from the memorial archway.

The College, founded in 1884, is one of the seven constituent colleges of the University of Wales (established in 1893), the other six being at Aberystwyth, Cardiff (3), Swansea, and Lampeter. There are faculties of Arts and Science, and departments ranging from Linguistics to Ocean Sciences. The original home of the College was a building previously known as the Penrhyn Arms Hotel (now demolished) near Port Penrhyn. Here William Smith O'Brien, the Irish patriot, died in 1864.

Views of Menai Strait and Anglesey can be enjoyed from the Look-Out on Menai Bridge Road and from Garth Point at the NE corner of the city.

For *Menai Strait* and its bridges, and *Anglesey*, see Rte 11. From Bangor to *Chester*, see Rte 1; to *Capel Curig*, see Rte 9; to *Caernarfon* and *Porthmadog*, see Rte 10.

4   Wrexham to Betws-y-Coed via Denbigh

A541 to Denbigh. A543 to Pentrefoelas. A5 to Betws-y-Coed. Total distance 46m.—*10m.* **Mold.**—*15m.* **Denbigh.**—*14m.* **Pentrefoelas.**—*7m.* **Betws-y-Coed.**

In large part high open moorland with mountain vistas.

Wrexham (40,000 inhab. *Inf.* Memorial Hall. Tel: 0978–357845), essentially an industrial centre, is best known to tourists, and especially Americans, for its *Church of St. Giles* with the grave of Elihu Yale (1648–1721), the benefactor of Yale University. The wrought-iron churchyard gates, of 1720 when they replaced a wooden lychgate, are by Robert and John Davies, and Elihu Yale's tomb (restored in 1968 by members of Yale University to mark the 250th anniversary of the benefaction) is in the churchyard W of the tower, a site chosen by Yale himself; the last two lines of the quaint rhymed epitaph are adapted from the funeral hymn to Ajax by James Shirley (1659).

Both the exterior and the interior of this church offer much else of interest, notably the richly decorated *Tower with its four graceful hexagonal turrets. Begun in 1506 the tower carries some medieval carvings, those of St. Giles, of which there are several, identifiable by his attributes of an arrow and a deer. The N porch (with, inside, a figure of St. Giles on the central ceiling boss) was restored by graduates of Yale in 1901 on the occasion of the bicentenary of their university, and—another Yale association—a stone on the tower replaces one removed and incorporated in a replica tower at the university. Inside the church, the lectern is of 1524, near it and the pulpit being the heads of the Earl of Derby and his (more celebrated) wife, Lady Margaret Beaufort, while nearby, over the choir arch, there are traces of a mural of the Last Judgement. In the North Aisle there are medieval carvings on the corbels; a monument by Louis Roubiliac to Mary Myddleton (died 1747) of Chirk; and in an adjacent window the words from the famous hymn 'From Greenland's Icy Mountains', written in 1819 by Reginald Heber, later Bishop of Calcutta, on the occasion of a missionary service held here while he was staying with his father-in-law, the vicar.

In Wrexham town the *Library Arts Centre* (Tel: 0978–261932), in Rhosddu Road, mounts a continuous programme of exhibitions, as also drama and musical events, while the *Borough (Wrexham Maelor) Heritage Centre* (Tel: 0978–290048), at 47–49 King Street, is an expanding museum of many aspects of regional history. *Acton Park*, in the N of the town, was the birthplace of the notorious Judge Jeffreys (1648–89), but the house was demolished in 1956.

For Wrexham to *Corwen*, via *Bwlchgwyn* (Geological Museum of North Wales) and places associated with the Yale family, see Rte 14; to *Chester*, see Rte 14.

ENVIRONS OF WREXHAM. **Bersham**, 2m W on B5099, was the home of the Davies brothers, masters of fine ironwork including the gates to Chirk park and Wrexham's Church of St. Giles. Today *Bersham Industrial Heritage Centre* (Tel: 0978–261529), on the site of the 18C ironworks, interprets the local industrial story, the emphasis being on the ironworks and its master John 'Iron Mad' Wilkinson, who became owner in 1762; amongst many other activities he bored cannon for use in the American War of Independence as also cylinders for Watt's steam engine. Among other features here there is material on the Davies brothers; there are several good models; the Centre is the focus of a long-term programme of excavation and restoration; and there are programmes of local industrial trail tours.

Bangor-is-y-Coed (Enclosure in the Wood), 4m SE of Wrexham by A525, also known as Bangor on Dee and with a picturesque 17C bridge sometimes attributed to Inigo Jones, may occupy the site of the Roman Bovium, though Holt, 6m to the N and known to have been the site of Roman pottery works, is a stronger claimant. Bangor was also the site of a monastic foundation of c 180 at which the heretic Pelagius is said to have lived (though not as a monk) during the 4C. The monastery was destroyed in 607 by Ethelfrid of Northumbria in the last great victory of Saxon heathendom over Celtic Christianity, 1200 monks being slain as the result of Ethelfrid's assertion that praying against him was as bad as fighting against him. Some survivors are said to have made their way to Bardsey. *Hanmer*, on A539 4m SE of Bangor-is-y-Coed, is where Owen Glendower and Margaret, daughter of Sir David Hanmer, are believed to have been married in the church that preceded the present Tudor one.

*Erddig (NT. Tel: 0978–355314), 2m S of Wrexham and standing within grounds of nearly 2000 acres, is a late 17C mansion with 18C additions. One of the National Trust's more important properties, a feature of particular interest is the complete range of outbuildings and domestic offices, equipped as they once were and including a remarkable collection of portraits of the staff. The main rooms, although rather cramped and gloomy, nevertheless contain outstandingly good 18C furniture. The gardens have been restored to their formal 18C plan.

History. The original house (the present central bays) was built between 1684–87 and soon turned out to be a financial disaster for the owner, Joshua Edisbury, High Sheriff of Denbighshire. Unable to meet his debts (one of those from whom he had borrowed was Elihu Yale), he fled to London before the house was even completed and died there c 1715. The following year John Meller, a London lawyer, acquired the property. To the original house Meller added two wings between 1721–24, and it was he too who collected the fine furniture which fills Erddig today. In this he was helped by his nephew Simon Yorke, to whom the property passed in 1733, remaining by direct line in the family (all called Simon or Philip) until given to the National Trust in 1973. Care for the staff was always a family tradition, one aspect of this being staff portraits, accompanied by verses by the various Philips and Simons. The first Philip completed (1774) new domestic offices to the S of the house. During the present century the house has suffered considerable damage from mining subsidence.

OUTBUILDINGS and DOMESTIC OFFICES. The *Estate Yard* is surrounded by buildings dating mainly from the early 19C and still in use today. These include joiner's workshop, sawpit, blacksmith's workshop, and wagon shed. The dovecot, just outside the yard, is early 18C. Off the *Limeyard* are the dog yard and the sawmill, the latter today containing an exhibition on the restoration of the house. In the *Outer Yard* the central enclosure was the midden where straw and dung from the stables was collected. The *Stableyard* was completed in 1774. Today it contains carriages, old cars, and bicycles. In an adjacent room is an introductory exhibition on the family and staff. The *Laundry Yard* and associated buildings was completed c 1773. Noteworthy are the stone-filled box mangle (possibly part of the original equipment) and the goffering irons used for crimping starched collars. The *Bakehouse* has scuffle ovens, from which the ashes were raked or scuffled before the dough was slid in. The *New Kitchen* with a Venetian window, is a particularly fine room, dating from 1772 when, possibly because of the danger of fire, the decision was taken to move the kitchen out of the main house. At this time it was completely detached, and the linking passage was not built until the 19C. In the basement passage hang photographs of the staff, one being a copy of a daguerrotype of 1852. The *Servants' Hall* contains Erddig's notable *Series of 18 and 19C portraits of the staff. The subjects range from John Meller's negro coachboy (early 18C; verses added c 1795) to portraits of 1830 of the carpenter, woodman and gardener. The principal artist of the series was John Walters of Denbigh.

FAMILY ROOMS. The Neo-Classical *Dining Room* (1826), the design of Thomas Hopper, was formerly the state bedroom and dressing room. It is hung with family portraits, among the artists being Gainsborough and Cotes. There is also a Still Life by Frans Snyders. Until 1770 the *Saloon* was two rooms, the N end being a smaller saloon and the S end a withdrawing room off the state bedroom and dressing room which now form the dining room. The early 18C furniture includes walnut chairs; a Boulle dressing table (c 1700); a plaster gilt side table; and gilt pier glasses (1723 and 1726). There is also porcelain and glass of the 16 to 18C. In the *Tapestry Room* the tapestry is early 18C Soho. The chairs, settee, and pier glass are also early 18C. In the *Chinese Room* are painted scenes, part Chinese and part English imitation, attractively illustrating ways of earning a living. The *Library* contains John Meller's legal library; also, added by Philip (died 1804), antiquarian books and copies of his own work of 1799, 'The Royal tribes of Wales'. The pictures in the *Entrance Hall* include three works by Kneller, one being of Judge Jeffreys. The hall also contains a collection of 18 and 19C musical instruments. In the *Drawing Room* the furniture includes armchairs and a settee, possibly of 1770 and by John Cobb, cabinet maker to the royal family. Among the pictures is a small landscape by Jan van Goyen.

BEDROOMS. In the *Red Bedroom* the ingenious lifting device of the bed may have been designed for the easier nursing of Anne Yorke, who died of consumption in 1770. The *Gallery* contains mother-of-pearl models (1765–80) made by Elizabeth Ratcliffe, daughter of a Chester clockmaker and companion to the then Mrs Yorke. The pictures include portraits of the royal family of Bohemia. Amongst the furniture are gilt pier tables with mother-of-pearl tops by Elizabeth Ratcliffe. In the *North Landing* there is a clock, signed by John Ratcliffe, father of Elizabeth. The bed in the *State Bedroom* is of 1720. Damaged by rain, leaking in as the result of subsidence, the bed was restored in 1968–70 by the Victoria and Albert Museum. The Chinese screen is thought to have been a gift (1682) from Elihu Yale. The *Blue Bedroom* has a bed dating from before 1726. The mezzotints are by Thomas Frye (1760–62).

Also to be seen are the *Chapel* (1721–4); the *Tribes' Room*, so called from Philip Yorke's book, now housing an exhibition of family documents; the *Butler's Pantry*, with 17 and 18C silver; and the *Family Museum*.

The **Erddig Visitor Centre** (Tel: 0978–264470), with a 17C barn and later 19C local farming machinery, houses an exhibition explaining the many changes experienced by the estate.

Wrexham is left by A541 for (5m) **Caergwrle**, once a Roman station occupied as an outpost of Deva (Chester) by the 20th Legion. The Castle, on a high ridge, vulnerable on one side only, this protected by a steep ditch, probably started as a Bronze Age hillfort (a particularly fine gold-decorated bowl of c 800 BC, now in the National Museum of Wales, was found here in 1820), but was built in more or less its present form—a simple polygonal enclosure with drum-towers at the angles—by Dafydd, brother of Llewelyn the Last. It was from here in 1282 that Dafydd launched the final and fatal Welsh rebellion against Edward I. Traces of *Wats Dyke*, which here generally followed the 400ft contour, can be found 1½m N beyond Hope, between A550 and the railway.—*Plas Teg* (Tel: 0352–771335), under 2m N of Caergwrle, is a mansion of 1610 showing decoration and furnishing spanning later centuries. There may be temporary exhibitions in the Long Gallery, and some exotic birds provide colour.—1m. Leeswood, where Leeswood Hall (1½m NW of the village) has iron gates of 1726 by the Davies brothers.

2m. **Mold** (8000 inhab. *Inf.* Town Hall. Tel: 0352–59331) is the pleasant, modest county town of Clwyd.

History. An important battle was fought near here in c 430 (see Maes Garmon below) but it was some 700 years later that Mold took root under the protection of the early Norman motte-and-bailey, now represented by Bailey Hill within the road fork at the upper end of High Street. This was probably built by Robert Montalt (Mont Haut), the town's name almost certainly being a corruption of this. In 1167 the castle was taken by Owain Gwynedd. In more modern history Mold is known as the birthplace and home of Daniel Owen (1836–95), who, while plying his trade as a tailor, at the same time achieved renown as a Welsh novelist and story writer. Sometimes described as the Welsh Dickens, his writings rank among the more important records of the era of the arrival of the railways and of the spread of religious revivalism.

Daniel Owen's statue stands in the open pedestrian area behind the town hall (or civic centre), alongside being the *Library* in one room of which there is a replica of Owen's tailor's shop with photographs, manuscripts and other memorabilia. The large mainly 15C *Church*, with a tower of 1773 and an apsidal choir added in 1856, is internally of interest mainly for its friezes of animals. There is also some good 15 and 16C glass while another, later, window remembers the landscape painter Richard Wilson (1714–82), who died near Mold and is buried in the churchyard near the N door. Mold is also known for *Theatr Clwyd* (Tel: 0352–56331), a leading North Wales entertainment complex of three theatres, a cinema and an art gallery.

Maes Garmon (the Field of Germanus; 1m NW of Mold on the Gwernaffield road) is traditionally the site of the 'Alleluia Victory' of 430, when the native Christians under Germanus, Bishop of Auxerre, who had been sent to Britain to fight the Pelagian heresy, decisively defeated the heathen Picts and Scots who, terror-stricken by the simultaneous cry of the Christians, fled without striking a blow. The site is marked by an obelisk of 1736 beside and above the road.

MOLD TO RUTHIN (A494. 11m. A pleasant drive over the Clwydian Hills). Beyond *Gwern-y-Mynydd* the road drops into the upper valley of the Alyn (Country Park; information centre and nature trail) at the Three Loggerheads Inn, with a sign, albeit showing only two loggerheads, painted by Richard Wilson who spent his last days at nearby Colomendy. At Tafarn-y-Gelyn (4m from Mold) the old road to Ruthin diverges to lead over *Bwlch Pen-Barras* (1100ft) whence the summit of *Moel Fammau* (1820ft. Country Park) can be reached; on the top is the stump of a tower erected in 1820 in honour of George III's jubilee, blown down in 1862 and restored in 1970. A494 continues to Llanferres, just beyond which B5430 leads SE to (2m) *Llanarmon* where the church (of St. Germanus) has two unequal naves divided by an 18C wooden arcade. Inside are the recumbent effigies of one Gruffydd ap Llewelyn ap Ynyr (late 13C and unusually well preserved) and of a vested priest; also a medieval bronze chandelier with a small statue of the Virgin. For **Ruthin**, see Rte 5.

Angel on the hammer-beam roof of Cilcain Church

A541 out of Mold in *2m* reaches *Rhyd-y-Mwyn*, 2m SW of which is *Cilcain* with a 14C church the chief features of which are the two unequal naves (the N and smaller of which serves as a vestry), a Norman font, and a hammer-beam roof reputed to have come from the refectory of Basingwerk Abbey, as may also have the 15C glass in the E window.—*7m*. **Caerwys**, to the N of the road, was, as its name suggests, a Roman station, later becoming a. village significant enough to receive a charter from Henry III. But the village is best known for its long association with the eisteddfod, the first of which is said to have been called here in 1100 by Gruffydd ap Cynan. There was another meeting here in 1523, and in 1568 Queen Elizabeth granted permission for the bards and minstrels of Wales to be called together 'in a competitive festival', this last occasion being

commemorated by a window in the church.—*3m*. **Bodfari**, just
beyond Offa's Dyke, is where the road leaves the hills for the Vale of
Clwyd. *Tremeirchion*, 2m N, has a 13C church housing a 14C tomb-
niche with the effigy of a vested priest, while in the chancel a tablet
commemorates Hester Lynch Piozzi (1741–1821), Dr Johnson's Mrs
Thrale, who lies here; she owned the estate of Brynbella just to the
south. St. Beuno's College, just N of Tremeirchion, is a Jesuit
seminary.

   3m. **Denbigh** (see Rte 5) from where A543 ascends steadily
through pleasant wooded country to reach open moor upland.—*5m*.
Bylchau—*2m*. *Llyn Bran* is a small lake S of the road. Here a smaller
road (B4501) branches SE, in just over a mile reaching ***Llyn Brenig**,
a large reservoir (opened in 1976 by the Prince of Wales) which in
conjunction with Lake Bala and Llyn Celyn regulates the flow of the
river Dee. More important for the visitor, the reservoir, with its
surrounds of pasture, forest and moor, provides an accessible yet
unspoilt large natural environment with a nature reserve, bird
sanctuary, picnic areas, fishing and sailing facilities, and walks
which include nature and archaeological trails, the latter visiting
sites which span from the Stone Age to a settlement of the 16C. The
Information Centre (Tel: 049082–463) tells the story of Brenig and
advises on the many recreational possibilities. *Alwen Reservoir*, 1m
SW of Llyn Brenig, was dug at the beginning of the century as a
water supply for Birkenhead. Some 3m long and attractively situated,
the reservoir offers car parking, picnic site and walks.

   Beyond the little Llyn Bran, A543 passes the *Sportsman's Arms*, the
highest inn in Wales, to reach summit level (1523ft) on the desolate
Mynydd Hiraethog with a sweeping mountain vista. Soon the little
Alwen stream is crossed, coming from Llyn Alwen (1251ft; 1m W)
and feeding Alwen Reservoir (see above).—*7m* (from Llyn Bran)
Pentrefoelas, see Rte 13.—*7m*. **Betws-y-Coed**, see Rte 6C.

5   Rhyl to Corwen

A525 to Ruthin. A494 to Corwen. Total distance 30m.—*2m*.
Rhuddlan.—*3m*. **St. Asaph**.—*6m*. **Denbigh**.—*7m*. **Ruthin**.—*12m*.
Corwen.

This Route ascends the pleasant VALE OF CLWYD, over 20m in length
and narrowing gradually from a width of 8m at the river's mouth to
4m at Denbigh, the river being insignificant compared to the width of
its valley. On the W the hills rise to the bleak high moorland of
Mynydd Hiraethog crossed by the road from Denbigh to Betws-
y-Coed (Rte 4). The E is marked by the more definite line of the
generally fertile Clwydian Hills, ending in the S at the mass of
Llantysilio and Eglwyseg mountains overlooking Llangollen and the
valley of the Dee. The hills are divided into short isolated ridges and
rounded summits by a series of passes, possibly ancient breaches
made by the sea. The highest point is Moel Fammau (1820ft), and
from Roman times the hills were a line of British resistance, many, if
not most, still bearing earthwork evidence.

   For **Rhyl**, see Rte 1A. For (*2m*) **Rhuddlan** and (*3m*) **St. Asaph**, see
Rte 1B.

   From St. Asaph the main road S is A525. An alternative is to take
B5381 westward out of the town, almost at once branching SW along

a minor road which in 3½m reaches *Cefn Caves* (summer only), unimpressive as caves but interesting for the fact that human and animal bones (bison, bear and suchlike) were found here. These caves are among a series of prehistoric settlements found on or near this ridge.

Approaching Denbigh, and just before the junction of A525 with A543 (Rte 4), the estate of *Plas Clough* off the W of A525 recalls Sir Richard Clough, associated with Sir Thomas Gresham in founding London's Royal Exchange in 1565. Just beyond, entering Denbigh and on the left, is *Denbigh Friary*, a Carmelite house founded in 1284 by Sir John Salusbury, a crusader, who was buried here in 1289. The friary was restored in 1954, the chief surviving association with the old friary being the somewhat later chapel.

6m. (from St. Asaph) **Denbigh** (8000 inhab.), with a historic castle, is an old borough on a hill overlooking the Vale of Clwyd from the west.

Natives. The town claims a number of distinguished natives, by far the best known being the explorer H.M. Stanley, born here in 1841 as John Rowlands. Others include Humphrey Lloyd (born 1568), antiquary and historian; Sir Hugh Myddelton (died 1631), the engineer, thought to have been born at Gwenynog (just SW) and to have been brought up, with his brother Thomas, later Lord Mayor of London, at Galch Hill, a short way SW of the castle; and Thomas Gee (born 1815), printer, publisher, Nonconformist preacher and leader of Welsh political thought.

Denbigh is mainly visited for its *Castle* (WHM. Tel: 0222-465511).

History. The first castle (on an unidentified site) was that of Dafydd, brother of Llewelyn the Last. Denbigh was a centre of resistance to Edward I, who, after his victory, entrusted the subjugation of this district to Henry de Lacy, Earl of Lincoln, who started to build the present castle in 1282, which, however, two years later in 1284, was taken and briefly held by the Welsh. De Lacy died in 1311 and the building work was continued and finished in 1322 by Thomas, Earl of Lancaster, the castle being modelled to some extent on the fortresses of Edward I, with the outer wall enclosing both castle and borough. The town was burnt in 1402 by Owen Glendower and again in 1468 by Jasper Tudor, after which the rebuilding was outside the walls. Queen Elizabeth gave the castle to Dudley, Earl of Leicester, who here entertained his sovereign in sumptuous fashion. In 1645 Charles I took refuge here after his defeat at Rowton Moor, and, after a siege of nearly 11 months, Denbigh was one of the last fortresses to surrender to Parliament, then suffering the usual fate of being slighted.

The plan of the castle is a single ward shaped as an irregular pentagon. Though much ruined it still has its impressive Gatehouse (the castle's principal feature) on the NE, the archway spanning the entrance passage bearing a mutilated statue, probably Edward I but possibly Henry de Lacy. The defensive system here is ingenious; a passage between two octagonal towers leads to a large central octagonal chamber, supported at the back by a somewhat smaller octagon, and the exit into the ward involves a turn to the right. Another interesting defensive feature is the Postern (rebuilt after the Welsh occupation of 1284) on the S side of the ward; it was defended by three rectangular turns, two drawbridges and an outer barbican, of which little survives. The postern tower, and the three towers to the W, originally formed part of the town walls, a section of which still extends E from the postern. To the W are the remains of the Mantlet, an additional defence work on the S and W sides. Within the ward the buildings are little more than foundations. Tradition has it that De Lacy's eldest son was drowned in the well.—There is an exhibition on the castle and on distinguished people associated with the town.

To the N of the castle entrance stands the tower of *St. Hilary's Church* (1334), the 'chapel within the walls', all that survives of a demolition of 1923, while just NE of this, in the grounds of Castle House, is the shell of *Leicester's Church*, a large building begun by Leicester in 1579, perhaps intended to supersede St. Asaph, but never completed. Also to be seen is the E portion of the *Town Walls*, begun when Denbigh was first taken from the Welsh in 1282 and greatly strengthened after the brief Welsh success here in 1284.

Eglwys Wen (or Whitchurch), a church rather over 1m E of the town centre, dates from the 15–16C and is of the typical local double-nave type. In the S choir is the alabaster Renaissance tomb of Sir John Salusbury (died 1578), descendant of the founder of Denbigh Friary; and in the N choir a brass remembers Richard Myddelton (died 1575), father of Sir Hugh, the engineer. There are also wall memorials to Humphrey Lloyd, the antiquary, and to Thomas Edwards ('Twm o'r Nant'; died 1810), bard and author of Welsh interludes, who is buried in the churchyard.

3m. **Llanrhaeadr**, where the *Church of St. Dyfnog* is worth a visit. Successor to one founded here in the 6C by the saint beside a holy well, the present church is mainly 15C though with a 13C tower. Grooves on the stones of the entrance archway are said to be due to arrow sharpening, recalling the days when the churchyard was used for archery practice. Inside the church there are two remarkable survivals; a Jesse Window of 1533, removed during the Civil War and buried until the Restoration, and the West Window (15C), the glass of which was reassembled in c 1845 after having been found in a shattered heap in a cottage. Also noteworthy are the hammer-beam roofs, and an ancient oak chest of two compartments (one for papers, the other for plate) and an attached alms box; keys to the three locks are held each by the vicar and two churchwardens.

4m. **Ruthin** (4000 inhab. *Inf.*), on a hill overlooking the Clwyd, was originally Rhudd-din, meaning Red Fortress, and the town's early history is that of its castle, now a hotel. For today's visitor, though, the main appeal is likely to be the town's several attractive old buildings, notably around St. Peter's Square. Here, on the S, the *Court House*, now a bank and largely facsimile, dates in origin from 1404 when it conveniently served both as law court and prison, even having the gallows attached to the building; a short length of the gibbet still projects from below the eaves. On the W side of the square stands *Exmewe Hall*, also now a bank, with, in front, Maen Huail, a stone on which King Arthur (not always, it seems, a paragon of chivalry) is said to have executed Huail, a rival in a love affair. The hall was built in c 1500 by Thomas Exmewe, later Lord Mayor of London, and was at one time the home of Gabriel Goodman (see below). At the square's NE corner the largely 14C *Church of St. Peter* was made collegiate in 1310 by Lord Grey of Ruthin and still styles its incumbent as Warden. The choir was destroyed in 1663 and the spire is an addition of 1859. The church's two principal features are the churchyard gates by the Davies brothers and, inside, the splendid oak *Roof of the N aisle (the original nave), with 500 carved panels, each one different, presented by Henry VII to men of Wales who had helped him ascend the English throne. In the church, too, on the N wall of the choir, is a bust of Gabriel Goodman (died 1601), a benefactor of the town, Dean of Westminster and one of the translators of the New Testament. The Cloisters, N of the Church, dating in origin from the 13–14C and once part of the original college, are now the residence of the Warden. The *Old Grammar School* (now a community centre),

N of the cloisters, and *Christ's Hospital Almshouses* to the E, were both founded by Dean Goodman. In Castle Street, *Natclwyd House*, in part 14C, presents a fine half-timbered frontage. *Ruthin Craft Centre* (Park Road), with many individual studios, offers work by leading craftsmen.

A hotel has been grafted on to the *Castle* (no adm. except for guests), and medieval banquets are now held in the reconstructed hall.

History. The first castle was probably early Norman, built perhaps by Hugh Lupus soon after the Conquest. In 1277, under the Treaty of Conwy, Edward I granted the site to Dafydd, brother of Llewelyn the Last. Dafydd undoubtedly carried out some building, but when in 1282 he supported his brother's uprising Ruthin was taken for Edward I by Reginald de Grey who between 1282 and c 1296 built the rectangular fortress which survives as today's ruin. In 1400 the then Lord Grey seized some Glendower land, an act which sparked Owen Glendower's revolt, one of the first incidents of which was Glendower's unsuccessful attack on Ruthin. During the Civil War Ruthin was garrisoned for Charles I but taken by General Mytton and dismantled in 1647.

Llanrhydd, 1m SE of Ruthin, was the home of Stanley Weyman (1855–1928), the novelist, who died here.

RUTHIN TO CERRIGYDRUDION (B5105, SW 13m). This road runs across the southern part of *Clocaenog Forest* (FC) reaching NW towards Llyn Brenig. From near *Pont Petryal* (7m from Ruthin) there are forest walks starting from a FC Visitor Centre in an old keeper's cottage (Tel: 08245–208). For *Cerrigydrudion*, see Rte 13.

Leaving Ruthin A494 leads S, in 2m passing between (E) *Llanfair-Dyffryn-Clwyd*, with a 15C church housing a 17C Communion table and a mosaic window of 15C glass, and (W) *Efenechdyd* where the small church has an unusual tub-font dating from early Norman or possibly even Saxon times.—*7m*. Derwen is 1m N of the main road. Here, in the churchyard, there is a particularly fine Celtic cross, while the pride of the church is its 15C rood screen and loft.—The road now leaves the Clwyd, just before Corwen joining A5, to the W of A494 just before the road junction being the estate of *Rug*, once a home of Owen Glendower and later the seat of the Vaughans. The ancient though much restored chapel seen from the road was built by William Salesbury in 1634.—*5m*. **Corwen**, see Rte 13.

6   Conwy to Betws-y-Coed and Ffestiniog

As far as Betws-y-Coed this Route travels the VALE OF CONWY, a fertile valley, below rising woodland and moor on both sides, which generally defines the eastern boundary of Snowdonia National Park. There is a choice of two scenically similar roads—Rte 6A following the river's E bank, Rte 6B the west—both with places of interest and conveniently linked by bridges at Tal-y-Cafn and Llanrwst. Boat excursions in summer from Conwy.

Rte 6C describes the road onward from Betws-y-Coed to Ffestiniog, some 30m distant from Conwy.

A.   East Bank of the Conwy

A55 to Llandudno Junction. A470 to Betws-y-Coed. Total distance
18m.—*1m.* **Llandudno Junction**.—*4m.* **Bodnant Garden**—*7m.*
Llanrwst.—*6m.* **Betws-y-Coed**.

From **Conwy**, the Conwy Estuary is crossed to **Llandudno Junction**
(for all three, see Rte 1B. For Llandudno, see Rte 2), just beyond
which A470 bears south.—*2m. Glan Conwy* where Felin Isaf Mill
(Tel: 0492–580646) is a picturesque restoration to its 19C condition
(machinery of 1730) of a 17C flour mill.—*3m.* ***Bodnant Garden** (NT.
Tel: 0492–650460), the garden of Bodnant Hall (c 1790, but later
enlarged), was laid out in 1875 by Henry Pochin, a Lancashire
industrialist with a passion for trees, and later extended by his
daughter (who married the 1st Lord Aberconwy) and grandson, the
2nd Lord Aberconwy, who gave the greater part to the National Trust
in 1949. Later, the Trust acquired further land by purchase and by
gift from the 3rd Lord Aberconwy. Covering some 80 acres and
sloping to the SW with splendid views towards Snowdonia, the
garden, with both formal and informal areas—an upper garden of
terraces and sweeping lawns; a lower part, the Dell, formed by a
small valley and with a pinetum and wild garden—ranks with the
finest in Britain.

In under 1m *Tal-y-Cafn Bridge* crosses the river for *Caerhun* (see
Rte 6B).—*4m. Cadair Ifan Goch* (672ft)—the Seat of Red Ifan, a giant
who stood with one foot here and the other on Pen-y-Gaer across the
river—approached by a road running E from Maenan Abbey Hotel
and then a path, is a NT property commanding fine views. The hotel
name, Maenan Abbey, recalls the site to which the Cistercian monks
of Conwy were moved by Edward I in 1283 and where they remained
until the Dissolution.

3m. **Llanrwst** (3000 inhab.), a place with a long and as often as not
violent history, is today a market and general centre serving a wide
district. For Gwydir Castle and Gwydir Uchaf Chapel, both just
across the river, see Rte 6B.

History. The town's name derives from St. Grwst (Restitutus), a 6C missionary
active in these parts and to whom the church has long been dedicated. The
early settlement was destroyed in a battle of 954 when the sons of Hywel Dda
invaded Gwynedd but were here defeated by the northern princes; a second
time during Owen Glendower's revolt, after which the place was as good as
abandoned for several decades; and yet again during the Wars of the Roses
(1455–85) when there was continual fighting between the Lancastrians of the
Conwy valley and the Yorkists of Clwyd. With more settled times Llanrwst
became modestly prosperous, its story during the 16 and 17C being associated
with the Wynne family of Gwydir Castle across the river. By the mid 19C the
town had almost twice today's population, its main activities being wool,
malting, tanning and the manufacture of harps. William Salesbury, who in 1567
first translated the new testament into Welsh, lived here.

From the town square a short narrow road leads past *Jesus Hospital
Almshouses*, founded in 1610 by Sir John Wynne 'for 11 old men and
an old woman for their bedmaker', to the *Church of St. Grwst*, dating
from 1470 (tower and N aisle 19C) and successor to a thatched
building of 1170 destroyed in the fighting of 1468. The fine rood
screen and loft came from Maenan Abbey. **Gwydir Chapel*,
adjoining the church, and not to be confused with Gwydir Uchaf
Chapel across the river, was built in 1633, it is said to a design by
Inigo Jones, by Sir Richard Wynne, who was treasurer to Henrietta

Maria, wife of Charles I. The elaborate roof, the panelling and screens, and the various Wynne monuments are noteworthy, these last including several 17C brasses. The huge stone coffin is said to be that of Llewelyn the Great (died 1420), whose remains the monks brought with them from Conwy to Maenan, the coffin being moved here at the Dissolution. Beside this lies the effigy of Howel Coetmor, an early owner of Gwydir Castle, who fought at Poitiers in 1356 and was killed in Flanders in 1388. In the churchyard, note a stone in the wall (right, on entering), bearing a Lamb and Flag said to have come from Yspytty Ifan, once a centre of the Knights Hospitaller of St. John.

Across the graceful, if for traffic inconvenient, Old Bridge, said to have been built in 1636 by Inigo Jones and modified in 1703 when a section was carried away, stands *Tu Hwnt i'r Bont* (The House over the Bridge), a 15C stone building once used as a courthouse but later divided into two cottages. Owned by the National Trust, the house is now let as a tea-room and shop. The nearby Gorsedd stones commemorate the National Eisteddfod held in Llanrwst in 1951.

Just S of Llanrwst, B5427 (becoming B5113) angles SE to (8m) *Pentrefoelas* on Rte 13, on the way commanding extensive views.

Betws-y-Coed, see Rte 6C, may be reached either by A470 in *6m*, passing, in 1¹⁄₂m, a small road climbing S to *Capel Garmon Burial Chamber* (see Rte 13); or in 4m by crossing the river to join Rte 6B.

B.   West Bank of the Conwy

B5106. Total distance 14m.—*4m*. **Tyn-y-Groes.**—*1m*. **Caerhun Church.**—*4m*. **Trefriw.**—*2m*. **Gwydir Castle.**—*3m*. **Betws-y-Coed**.

Conwy (see Rte 1B) is left through *Gyffin* (see under Conwy).—*4m*. **Tyn-y-Groes**, with, just to the E, Tal-y-Cafn bridge for *Bodnant Garden*, see Rte 1A.—*1m*. **Caerhun Church**, reached by a lane towards the river, dates from the 13–14C, the nave and S walls being the oldest parts. The churchyard occupies the site of the Roman Kanovium, a riverside fort along the road between Deva (Chester) and Segontium (Caernarfon) which was abandoned around the middle of the 2C but reoccupied in the 4C. Later, the Welsh named this place after Rhun, a warrior son of Maelgwn Gwynedd, but of this Roman and very early Welsh past vitually nothing visible survives though a clump of trees some 50 yards NE below the churchyard wall marks the site of the baths.—*1m*. *Tal-y-Bont*, 1m W of which *Pen-y-Gaer* (1225ft) is a hillfort associated in legend with Cadair Ifan Goch on the E bank (see Rte 6A). The hillfort sprawls over an internal area of nearly five acres, with hut circles, and on the vulnerable S and W slopes there was a massive rubble rampart, below this being four ditches and earthworks. From Tal-y-Bont, a lane and a path lead 4m SW to the reservoir of *Llyn Eigiau* at 1219ft.

2m. **Trefriw Wells** (Tel: 0492–640057) is a spot with a story reaching back to Roman times when, sometime between 100 and 250, the 20th Legion, perhaps prospecting for minerals, opened up a cave in which there was a chalybeate spring (rich in iron). Later covered by a landslip, the cave was reopened during the 18C by Lord Willoughby de Eresby who in 1743 built and exploited a stonework (cyclopean) bathhouse which became so popular that by 1874 there was a Victorian pumproom and bath and the bottled waters were sold worldwide. By the mid 20C, though, faced with the competition from modern drugs, Trefriw Wells had lapsed into disrepair, until rescued in 1972 and today not only on the tourist map but also, thanks to a reviving interest in natural sources, once again marketing its water. Visitors can see the original Roman cave (and sample the water direct from the rock basins) and also admire the 18C cyclopean bathhouse with its original slate bath.—*1m*. **Trefriw** is a small town associated with Llewelyn the Great who had a home here and who is also said to have built a church here to please his wife who flatly refused to climb to the church at Llanrhychwyn (see below). Today the chief attraction is *Trefriw Woollen Mill* (Tel: 0492–640462), opened in c 1830 and until 1900, when hydro-electric turbines were first installed, using wheels directly driven by the river Crafnant. Visitors view all the processes in the manufacture of tapestries and tweeds from raw wool, the whole well explained by an illustrated self-guide leaflet.

SOME RESERVOIRS. In addition to Llyn Eigiau, mentioned above, there are several reservoirs in the wild country to the W of Trefriw. *Llyn Cowlyd*, the largest, is reached by a path (3m) which crosses the bleak ridge of Cefn Cyfarwydd (1407ft).—*Llyn Crafnant* (603ft) is the reservoir for Trefriw whence it may be reached in 2m by a narrow lane.—*Llyn Geirionnydd*, at 616ft, is the closest and most accessible, reachable by roads or lanes from Trefriw, Llanrwst or the Betws-y-Coed to Capel Curig road a short way W of Swallow Falls. All these approaches are narrow and steep, especially that from Trefriw which is a lane not suitable for larger cars. This lane passes the remote little hill church of *Llanrhychwyn*, said to have been the place of worship of Llewelyn the Great, at least until, on his wife's insistence, he built a more accessible church at Trefriw. Today's quaint and simple church has a double nave (13–16C), a 12C font and fragments of medieval glass. The reservoir, at the NW corner of Gwydir Forest, has a picnic site from which starts a trail (3/4m) passing lead workings (1840–1914), the levels of which are dangerous and should not be entered, the ruin of the mine's explosive store, and the old tramway. At the N end of the lake there is a monument to Taliesin, the 6C bard, who however seems to have had no known association with this district.

2m. **Gwydir Castle** (Tel: 0492–640261) is a generally 16 and 19C mansion built around a 14C hall. But the castle's roots go much deeper; to a fortification of the 7C and to an early 14C tower built by that Howel Coetmor whose effigy lies just across the river in Llanrwst's Gwydir Chapel. Later the estate was acquired by Maredudd ap Ievan of Dolwyddelan (died 1525) and it was he who built the hall. John Wynne (died 1559), one of Maredudd's 26 children, enlarged the house which remained in the family until 1674. The family had a close association with Charles I and his queen, Henrietta Maria, to whom Sir Richard Wynne was treasurer. After various owners and several fires, the house was bought in 1944 by the late Arthur Clegg, who, with his son, restored and furnished Gwydir. Some of the roof timbers have a long story, having originally been in the monastery at Conwy, later used in the construction of Maenan, and finally incorporated here after the Dissolution. The gardens, known for their peacocks, include splendid cedars planted to celebrate the wedding of Charles I.

Gwydir Uchaf Chapel (WHM. Key from adjacent Forestry Commission office during normal working hours), to the W of the road a short distance S of Gwydir Castle and not to be confused with Gwydir Chapel in Llanrwst, was built by Sir Richard Wynne in 1673. The chapel still retains many of its original features, outstanding being the *Painted Ceiling, one of the most remarkable examples in Britain of this genre of 17C art and portraying such themes as the Creation, the Trinity and the Day of Judgement.

3m. **Betws-y-Coed**, see Rte 6C.

C.   Betws-y-Coed to Ffestiniog

A470. Total distance 13m.—*6m.* **Dolwyddelan Castle**.—*4m.* **Blaenau Ffestiniog**.—*3m.* **Ffestiniog**.

Betws-y-Coed (700 inhab. but many more in summer. *Inf.*) is a sprawling and straggling overgrown village on the Llugwy just above its confluence with the Conwy and 1½m below the meeting of the Conwy and Lledr. With these three valleys of glen and river scenery, all parts of Snowdonia National Park and of beautiful Gwydir Forest (famed for its walks), and lying on the main A5 approach to Snowdonia proper, it is hardly surprising that Betws-y-Coed is a bustling holiday centre, liable in summer to be swamped by people, cars and coaches. The place's origins, though, are very different, the name meaning Prayer House in the Forest, this origin recalled by the *Old Church* (just E of the station), the Bede, or Prayer House, in use from the 14C or earlier until the construction of the town's new church during the 19C. This old church, with a 14C nave and choir and a 19C single transept, houses a 12C font, remains of 15 or 16C glass, a pulpit made up of 15–17C fragments, and the effigy, in unusual studded armour, of Dafydd Goch (c 1380), grandson of the Prince Dafydd who was executed by Edward I in 1283; Dafydd Goch's home was Fedw Deg, on the hill within the confluence of the Conwy and Lledr rivers.

The tourist heart of Betws-y-Coed is the complex beside the station, here being large car parks, craft shops, a railway museum, a motor museum, and, in the Old Stables, a *Visitor Centre* (Tel: 06902–426) which includes Tourist Information, an aquarium, and exhibitions on Snowdonia National Park and by the Forestry Commission and the Royal Society for the Protection of Birds. The *Conwy Valley Railway Museum* (Tel: 06902–568), at the Old Goods Yard, shows much material from the period of the old London and North Western Railway. There are also dioramas, working model railway layouts, steam and diesel locomotives and the opportunity of a short, scenic ride. The *Motor Museum* (Tel: 06902–632), housed in old farm buildings, shows a private collection of vintage and later thoroughbred cars.

Betws-y-Coed is known for its generous choice of river valley and forest walks, some of which, it should be noted, pass close to dangerous disused mine shafts. Among the many spots visited by walks are *Pont-y-Pair* (Bridge of the Cauldron), the bridge, perhaps 1470, crossing the Llugwy in the N part of the town; *Miners' Bridge* (³⁄₄m W), a picturesque footbridge used by generations of miners, 50 yards above a ford where the Roman Sarn Helen crossed the river; *Artists' Wood* (walk starts and finishes at Miners' Bridge), so called because of its popularity with 19C artists such as David Cox and

Turner; *Swallow Falls*, a FC *Arboretum* and *Ty Hyll*, for all of which see Rte 7; and the forest upland across to Gwydir Castle on Rte 6B, passing relics of the era of lead mining.

For Betws-y-Coed to *Bangor*, see Rtes 7 and 9; to *Llanberis*, see Rtes 7 and 8; to *Beddgelert* and *Penrhyndeudraeth*, see Rte 7; to *Corwen*, see Rte 13; to *Denbigh*, see Rtes 4 and 13.

A5 leads SE out of Betws-y-Coed, at the town's edge crossing the Conwy by Telford's graceful iron Waterloo Bridge of 1815, the year of the battle. Immediately beyond, A470 breaks away and soon recrosses the Conwy, just before this bridge being a sign to *Fairy Glen* in which the Conwy drops through a narrow wooded gorge. A470 now ascends the lovely valley of the Lledr river, at first green and pastoral but soon becoming rocky and wilder while to the S opens the valley of the Gwibernant up which a road leads in 1 1/2m to Ty Mawr (NT. Tel: 06903–213), farmhouse birthplace of Bishop William Morgan (c 1545–1604), first translator of the Bible into Welsh. There is also a (1m) nature trail. For the alternative approach from Penmachno, see Rte 13.—*4m* (from Betws-y-Coed *Pont-y-Pant*, crossing place of the Roman Sarn Helen from Tomen-y-Mur (Rte 16) to Kanovium (Rte 6B).

2m. **Dolwyddelan Castle** (WHM. Tel: 0222-465511) stands as a stark, square isolated keep on a ridge above the road.

History. The castle was built in c 1170, possibly by Iorwerth, father of Llewelyn the Great who may have been born here in 1173 and who later certainly used Dolwyddelan as a home. In 1281 Llewelyn the Last was here, but two years later the castle was taken by Edward I and strengthened. In 1488 the place was acquired by Maredudd ap Ievan (see Gwydir Castle), who built the village church in which his kneeling effigy in brass can be seen. After Maredudd's death the castle decayed into ruin though a modern roof and battlements were added during the 19C.—An exhibition tells the story of the castles of the Welsh princes.

The ruins comprise a small ward, with a W tower and keep, this last (12C) being the oldest part with, as its most interesting feature, its curious defensive entrance. This entrance was at the first floor and was covered by a small barbican, now very ruined, reached from outside by steps along the face of the keep; inside the barbican there was a pit, covered by a drawbridge. Inside the keep the main room was originally covered by a gabled roof which was nevertheless still enclosed by the keep walls which rose above it. Traces of this can still be seen, although it was later replaced, probably by Maredudd, by a flat roof and upper room. The castle's curtain wall is early 13C, but the inner walls of the W tower date from the end of that century.

To the N of Dolwyddelan rises *Moel Siabod* (2860ft), as A470 crosses the river at Roman Bridge, which has in fact no clear Roman association, before passing over bleak hills by the *Crimea Pass* (1263ft), a name recalling a now vanished inn. On the descent which follows, two unusually interesting slate mines can be visited, the first being ***Gloddfa Ganol** (Tel: 0766–830664), starkly impressive massive site of what was once the world's largest slate mine. The complex includes machinery; panorama walks above the quarry workings 350ft below; three cottages of c 1840, furnished in the styles of the late 19C, 1914–18, and as used until the late 1960s; and a museum telling the story of the slate mining industry and in which a former miner demonstrates slate-splitting and other skills. Additionally there are the huge blasted caverns, demonstrations of opencast blasting, a craft shop and a natural history collection.—

Llechwedd Slate Caverns (Tel: 0766–830306), a short way farther down the hill, offer two underground experiences. The Underground Tramway visits parts of the mine where 19C mining conditions have been recreated, while the Deep Mine Tour, using the inclined railway, descends to the lower levels with their caverns and lake. On the surface, in the slate mill, there are various exhibitions as also demonstrations of slate-splitting.

4m (from Dolwyddelan) **Blaenau Ffestiniog** (5500 inhab. *Inf.* High Street. Tel: 0766–830360) lies darkly below hills scarred by quarrying. The principal local attraction, 2m SW at Tan-y-Grisiau off A496, is the Central Electricity Generating Board's *Ffestiniog Pumped Storage Scheme*, opened by the Queen in 1963 and the first of this type built for the Board (Tel: 0766–830465). At this level visitors can enjoy the Exhibition, with an audio-visual programme and working models, or tour the power station, while for the more ambitious there is the drive (charge) 1000ft up the mountain to the upper reservoir's *Stwlan Dam* with its sweeping views of Snowdonia. The lower reservoir (Tan-y-Grisiau) was formed by damming the river Ystradau.

For the Ffestiniog Railway, running between Porthmadog and Blaenau Ffestiniog, with a request halt at Tan-y-Grisiau (for the power station), see Rte 15.

Manod, the straggling southward extension of Blaenau Ffestiniog, has huge underground quarries which, air conditioned and fitted with brick chambers, in 1940–45 housed most of the National Gallery's paintings.—*3m.* **Ffestiniog**, see Rte 15.

7   Betws-y-Coed to Beddgelert and Penrhyndeudraeth

A5 to Capel Curig. A4086 to Pen-y-Gwryd. A498 to Beddgelert. A4085 to Penrhyndeudraeth. Total distance 23m.—*5m.* **Capel Curig.**—*4m.* **Pen-y-Gwryd.**—*7m.* **Beddgelert.**—*7m.* **Penrhyndeudraeth**.

To Capel Curig up the wooded valley of the Llugwy. From Capel Curig to Pen-y-Gwryd across high moor, then descending beautiful Nant Gwynant, a valley of lush meadows and woods with mountains lifting high on both sides.

Betws-y-Coed, see Rte 6C.—*2m. Swallow Falls* (fee), a cataract breaking its way through surroundings of rock and woodland. A short way beyond there is a Forestry Commission picnic site and car park for the *Gwydir Forest Arboretum* (Tel: 0492–640578) which, opened in 1950, now shows more than 40 tree species. Beyond, where the road crosses the river, the stone building known as *Ty Hyll* (Ugly House)—owing its name to its rough appearance, the result, it is said, of hurried construction in order to grab a freehold on what was common land—was once an overnight stop for Irish drovers bringing cattle from Holyhead to markets in England. These drovers followed what is now the old road along the river's S bank, rather less than 1m along which, between the road and the river, are the tree-covered earthworks of *Caer Llugwy*, or, on some maps, *Caer Bryn y Gefeilliau*, a Roman station occupied apparently for only some 50 years between 90 and 140. From Ty Hyll a small road climbs N to (see Rte 6B) Llyn Geirionnydd, descending beyond into the Vale of

Conwy. A5 continues with the N bank of the Llugwy, soon passing on the left *Pont Cyfnyg* (Narrow Bridge) where the S bank old road rejoins. Soon there appears to the left one of the finest and most famous views of Snowdon.

3m. **Capel Curig**, encircled by mountains and at the junction of the important mountain roads to Beddgelert (this Rte) and Llyn Ogwen and Bangor (Rte 9), is a centre for walks, these including heights such as Moel Siabod (2860ft; 2½m SW); Pen Llithrig-y-Wrach (2621ft; 3m N); and the Glyders immediately to the west. Here at Capel Curig the *National Mountaineering Centre* (Tel: 06904–214) occupies Plas-y-Brenin, a building dating from 1800, the Capel Curig Inn until 1871 and then the Royal Hotel. The centre offers training in all aspects of mountaineering as well as in other outdoor activities, including day courses in skiing and canoeing.

From Capel Curig A4086 is followed along the N shore of Llynau Mymbyr and up the moorland valley of Nant-y-Gwryd. To the S Moel Siabod presents its least attractive slope while on the N the Glyders are not here impressive, but, in contrast, ahead rises the fourfold peak complex of Snowdon.—*4m.* **Pen-y-Gwryd Hotel**, at 850ft, is a lonely spot at the fork with A4086 which, after a brief climb, drops down the Pass of Llanberis (see Rte 8). Popularly known as PYG, Pen-y-Gwryd has long been known to climbers and shows mementoes of the Everest team of 1953 who trained in this area. The Romans, too, knew this place and traces of a square earthwork spanning both roads just below the fork recall that this often bleak junction was once a temporary fort or marching camp.

This Route now follows A498 descending **Nant Gwynant*, a lovely valley, part wooded, with two lakes and with mountains lifting on either side. Just below Pen-y-Gwryd there is a car park and view point high above *Cwm Dyli*, at this valley's foot being a power station while the great face of Snowdon towers above.—*3m.* *Llyn Gwynant* (217ft) is nearly 1m in length. Here the road skirts the SE shore between the lake and Hafod Lwyfog, an estate given to the National Trust in 1938 by the architect Sir Clough Williams-Ellis; it includes the house (reconstruction of 1638. No adm.) which was the birthplace of Sir John Williams, goldsmith to James I. Beyond the S end of the lake is the hamlet of *Glenaber* (or *Plas Gwynant*), below which to the N opens the great hollow of *Cwm-y-Llan* with the peaks of Snowdon at the cwm's head, the slopes of Lliwedd to the right, and, to the left and closer, those of Yr Aran. The Watkin Path (see Rte 8B) up Snowdon starts at the bridge over the Glaslyn (Pont Bethania), this path in 1m entering the Cwm-y-Llan National Nature Reserve, an ice-fashioned landscape of some 12,000 years ago.—For the small Nantmor valley road, heading E from Bethania and then S and enabling Beddgelert to be bypassed, see immediately after Pont Aberglaslyn below.

The road now fringes the N shore of Llyn Dinas (176ft) to pass, N of the road and just below the lake, *Dinas Emrys*, a hill on top of which are vestiges of 12C ramparts. More interesting, though, is the legend which haunts this place, for it was here that the luckless Vortigern tried to build his tower while Merlin told of the red and white dragons (see Legend). Romantics may accept the discovery here of Iron Age relics as backing for the legend. Opposite, the southern slopes of Nant Gwynant—hills which in 1958 were used for the filming of 'The Inn of the Sixth Happiness', starring Ingrid Bergman—were in the 18 and 19C busy with copper mining, a prosperous past recalled today by *Sygun Copper Mine* (Tel: 076686–

595), off A498 approaching Beddgelert. Here guided tours, which include the large chambers hewn into the hillface, backed by a Visitor Centre with video presentation, photographs and models, combine to explain the successive steps in the mining process and also to give some idea of the working environment.

4m. (from Llyn Gwynant) **Beddgelert** is a scattered and straggling village in a wooded and pastoral setting below rocky heights at the confluence of two mountain streams, the Glaslyn and the Celwyn. It is also at the junction of three valleys (Nant Gwynant, described above; Nant Celwyn, the road to Caernarfon, Rte 10; and Aberglaslyn, see below), all carrying main roads, the result being that in summer Beddgelert can be swamped by visitors and its narrow bridge clogged by traffic.

History and Legend. A Celtic monastery was founded here in the 6C, this becoming one of the foremost houses in Wales. In the 12 or 13C the monastery was succeeded by a small Augustinian priory founded by Llewelyn the Great, but this disappeared with the Dissolution. Beddgelert was, however, more than a religious centre, in medieval times ranking also as something of a port, a role made possible by the fact that the Glaslyn was navigable at least as far as Pont Aberglaslyn and remained so until the construction of the Porthmadog embankment in the early 19C.—The village owes its name (Grave of Gelert) to a legend first made familiar by the verses of William Spencer in 1800. Gelert was the trusted hound of Prince Llewelyn, who, departing for the hunt, left Gelert in charge of his infant son. Returning, and finding the child missing, the cradle in disorder and Gelert with blood-stained muzzle, Llewelyn slew the hound—only, soon after, to find the child safely sleeping, beside him being a dead wolf killed by the faithful Gelert.

Of the Augustinian priory all that remains is the village *Church*, once the priory chapel and still showing some 13C work in the triple lancet windows at the E end and in the arcade between the nave and its N chapel. The reputed grave of Gelert—the stones apparently erected by a visitor-conscious landlord of The Goat during the 18C—is in a meadow 1/4 S of the village, reached by a path from the bridge. But it is to walkers that Beddgelert has perhaps the most to offer, the choices ranging from modest local walks along the rivers and through the woods to ascents of heights such as Moel-y-Dyniewyd (1254ft) or Moel Hebog (2566ft), or, more ambitiously, Yr Aran (2451ft) or Snowdon by either the Watkin Path or the Pitt's Head approach, for both of which see Rte 8B.

Below Beddgelert the road soon enters the **Pass of Aberglaslyn** (NT), a narrow defile in which the torrent of the Glaslyn and the road run side-by-side between steep slopes of fir. This is where the Glaslyn leaves the mountains and, as noted above, until the early 19C the river was navigable as far as *Pont Aberglaslyn.* At this bridge A498 (Rte 10) continues S to Porthmadog while this Route, now A4085, crosses the bridge.

Just beyond the bridge a small road (the old Ffestiniog road) branches E for *Nantmor* at the foot of Cwm Bychan, the head of which was during the 18 and 19C the site of an important copper mine. Beyond comes *Bwlch Gwernog,* whence another small road heads N along the wooded Nantmor valley (with forest walks) to reach Nant Gwynant between Llyn Gwynant and Llyn Dinas, for both of which see above. Climbs from Bwlch Gwernog include Cnicht (2265ft) and Maelwyn Mawr (2527ft), the two separated by the deep Cwm Croesor.

From Pont Aberglaslyn A4085 skirts the reclaimed Traeth Mawr (see Rte 10).—*7m.* (from Beddgelert) **Penrhyndeudraeth** is a small town with a station of the Ffestiniog Railway.

For Penrhyndeudraeth to *Ffestiniog* and *Bala*, as also for *Portmeirion* and *Porthmadog*, see Rte 15.

8   Pass of Llanberis. Snowdon

This Route describes first (Rte 8A) the Pass of Llanberis, the steep narrow cleft which defines Snowdon's NE flank and carries the road which passes the starting points of three of the six principal ascent paths as also, at Llanberis, the valley station of the Snowdon Mountain Railway. Rte 8B describes Snowdon itself.

Snowdon Sherpa Bus. Much of northern Snowdonia is served by the Snowdon Sherpa bus service, the network's E and SE boundary being Llandudno to Porthmadog via Llanrwst, Betws-y-Coed, Capel Curig and Beddgelert, with links to Caernarfon, Llanberis and Bangor. Parking can be difficult around Snowdon, with Pen-y-Pass car park often full and on-road parking prohibited between Pen-y-Gwryd and Nant Peris. There is parking at Llanberis Lake Railway Station and at Nant Peris for visitors who use the Sherpa service, which not only allows the best of the scenery to be seen but also offers flexibility for walkers. Information from local Tourist Information offices.

A.   Pass of Llanberis
(Pen-y-Gwryd to Caernarfon)

A4086. Total distance 13m.—*1m. Pen-y-Pass.—3m. Nant Peris.—2m.* **Llanberis.**—*7m.* **Caernarfon**.

From Pen-y-Gwryd (see Rte 7) the Llanberis road, cut into this hillside in c 1850 and affording a splendid view down Nant Gwynant, loops first SW and then NW round Moel Berfedd.—*1m. Pen-y-Pass* (1169ft), at the crest of the pass, is a youth hostel, a mountain rescue centre, and the starting place for the Pyg and Miners' tracks to the peaks of Snowdon. From here the road starts its descent through the ***Pass of Llanberis**, one of the wildest and most desolate valleys in Wales, a narrow defile below towering black walls of rock and in places almost blocked by boulders and debris. At *Pont-y-Gromlech*, just over a mile below the summit, the road crosses the tumbling Peris, by the bridge being a parking area below precipitous crags much used by rock climbers. Soon, to the W, the arms of Crib Goch open to give a fine view of **Cwm Glas* (approached by a footbridge ¹/₂m below Pont-y-Gromlech), with its two tarns (2200ft and 2700ft) overhung by majestic precipices an awesome place and one of particular interest to geographers and geologists for its clear evidence of glacial action.

3m (from Pen-y-Pass) *Nant Peris*, or Old Llanberis, where there is a simple cruciform church (part 12C), with a 15C timber roof, a screen with an old alms box, and a curious window in the W wall. The Well of Peris, in a field across the road, was until comparatively recent times much visited for both healing and wishing, a successful request being signalled by the appearance of a sacred fish; or so Pennant reported in 1781. Skirting Llyn Peris, the road soon kinks round *Dolbadarn Castle* (WHM. Tel: 0222-465511), the main feature here being the circular keep thought to have been built by Llewelyn the Great in the early 13C. Later, from 1255 for over 20 years, this was the prison of Owain Goch, older brother and defeated rival of Llewelyn the Last.

2m. **Llanberis** (1500 inhab. 350ft. *Inf.* Oriel Eryri. Tel: 0286–870765) is a straggling and scattered community (the centre of which is off the W of the main road) at the S end of Llyn Padarn, here separated by a narrow isthmus from the smaller Llyn Peris. The natural beauty of the surroundings has long been marred by the nevertheless impressive great scars of huge slate quarries which, tier above precipitous tier, climb to a height approaching 1500ft. Quarrying finished in 1969, but in 1974 slate began again to litter the slopes as work began on excavating the deep caverns which now hide the Central Electricity Generating Board's *Dinorwig Pumped Storage Scheme*, the largest of its kind in Europe, with its upper reservoir of Marchlyn Mawr (2m NE) 1600ft above Llyn Peris, the lower one (Visitor Centre beside Llyn Peris: Tel: 0286-870935).

Although best known as the valley station of the Snowdon Mountain Railway (see Rte 8B), Llanberis offers various other attractions, first, on the main road, being *Oriel Eryri* or the *Museum of the North*, the National Museum of Wales's environmental gallery (Tel: 0286–870636). Three other attractions will be found close to one another on the far side of the isthmus separating the two lakes. The *Welsh Slate Museum* (Tel: 0286–870630), a branch of the National Museum of Wales, is housed in workshops of the former Dinorwig quarry which functioned from 1809 to 1969, at its peak in 1900 employing some 3000 people. Much of the machinery has been preserved (the wheel, over 50ft in diameter, is one of the largest in Britain) and visitors can see the foundry; smithy; the pattern, woodworking and fitting shops; the sick bay and suchlike, while in summer there are demonstrations and films. *Padarn Country Park* (Tel. in summer: 0286–870892), opened in 1970 and one of the first of its kind in Wales, extends along the shore of Llyn Padarn and includes a network of nature and industrial trails using the paths worn by generations of quarrymen, while the former quarry hospital shows surgical equipment and also houses a woodland display. Lastly there is *Llanberis Lake Railway* (Tel: 0286–870549). Originally the quarry railway to Port Dinorwic on the Menai Strait, and at first (1840) worked by a combination of animal and gravity power, the line later became 4ft gauge and steam-operated. Saved by enthusiasts, and now narrow gauge but still steam, today's line offers a 40 minute return journey the length of the N shore of Llyn Padarn. Passengers may leave the train at the halfway station (Cei Llydan), with a picnic site, and catch a later train.

Walks from Llanberis include the waterfall of *Ceunant Mawr* (³/₄m) and the smaller Ceunant Bach, a little farther upstream. The main longer distance walk is that up Snowdon (see Rte 8B) and there are also tracks to Llyn Cwellyn (4m, Rte 10) and Beddgelert (9m, Rte 7).

Beyond Llanberis the road skirts the S shore of Llyn Padarn, soon emerging from the mountains and in rather over *2m* passing close to *Bryn Bras Castle* (Tel: 0286–870210), a rambling castellated complex built in the 1830s around an early 18C predecessor and known for its extensive gardens and panoramic walks. Just N of *Waun* (1m N across the river Seiont), Ffynnon Cegin Arthur is a chalybeate well with medicinal properties ascribed to King Arthur.—*5m.* **Caernarfon**, see Rte 10.

The summit of Glyder Fawr in winter with Snowdon in the background

B. Snowdon

SNOWDON, the highest mountain in England and Wales, is despite its name generally free from snow between April and October, though drifts may linger in the gullies until early summer. The massif forms a cluster of five peaks, linked by sharp ridges, and presents fine escarpments in all directions, especially towards the E where the beautiful lakes of Glaslyn and Llyn Llydaw are overhung by sheer walls of rock. The principal heights, in their starfish formation, are *Yr Wyddfa Fawr* (3560ft), the central peak, now crowned by a cairn; *Crib-y-Ddysgl* (3493ft), ½m N, skirted by the Llanberis Track; *Crib Goch* (3023ft; Red Ridge), 1½m NE, a splendid pile of rock, rich in pinnacles and buttresses; *Lliwedd* (2497ft), the long craggy ridge running SE, with a well-known rock wall; and *Yr Aran* (2451ft), the outlying S peak, forming a spur towards Beddgelert. Between these mountains are six cwms or hollows, of which *Cwm Dyli* and *Cwm Glas*, separated by Crib Goch, are the most impressive. Tracks cross all the ridges; exposed and liable to high winds, these are suitable only for the experienced.

Legend and History. To the ancient Welsh the mountain was Eryri, the High Land. Its English name of Snowdon it owes to the Saxons, who spoke of the distant Snow Dun, the Snow Hill or fortress. Its present Welsh name Yr Wyddfa Fawr (Great Tomb) it owes to the legend that the summit was the tomb of the giant Rhita Fawr, slain by King Arthur. Arthur is supposed to have been mortally wounded on Bwlch-y-Saethau, and from this it is natural to accept Llyn Llydaw below as the lake into which Excalibur was thrown. Another legend is that of Vortigern and Merlin at Dinas Emrys in Nant Gwynant (see Rte 7). That prehistoric man lived on the lower slopes is known from material found near Llyn Llydaw. In medieval times Dolbadarn became a castle of the Welsh princes, and the mountain is mentioned by Giraldus. Llewelyn the Last retreated into Snowdon before his final defeat and death; Edward I created a Royal Forest of Snowdon; and Owen Glendower is thought to have found refuge here. Thomas Johnson, a naturalist, is recorded as having ascended Snowdon in 1639, and Halley is said to have made astronomical experiments on the summit in 1697. It was in the 17C, too, that the first mining began. An ascent from Llanberis is fully described by Pennant (1726–98), and Wordsworth writes of leaving 'Beddgelert's huts at couching time' to witness sunrise from the peak ('Prelude'). Victorian times were prosperous for guides and their ponies (George Borrow took his step-daughter up the mountain in 1859, this being a highlight of the tour which led eight years later to the publication of his classic 'Wild Wales'), but this era ended with the building of the railway in 1896.

Ascent of Snowdon

Snowdon is ascended by the Snowdon Mountain Railway from Llanberis, or by any of the six signed traditional walkers' tracks, beginning at various points around the base of the mountain. Of these the finest and steepest are the *Watkin Path* from Nant Gwynant and the *Pyg Track* from Pen-y-Pass, to which the *Miners' Track*, also from Pen-y-Pass, is an interesting alternative skirting Llyn Llydaw and passing mine workings. The *Pitt's Head Track* and the *Snowdon Ranger Track*, both from the Beddgelert to Llyn Cwellyn main road, afford views of the lesser known W escarpments. The *Llanberis Track* is the easiest but least interesting ascent.—The above ascents, all outlined below, are safe in clear weather, but it should be remembered that Snowdon is notorious for its sudden mists, and that parts of the group are dangerously precipitous and craggy. The inexperienced should not stray from the paths.

The **Snowdon Mountain Railway** (Tel: 0286–870223) operates between Easter and the end of October, every Mon.–Fri. and most Sat. and Sun., the first train leaving Llanberis at 09.00 and the service then being roughly half-hourly until mid to late afternoon. Return journey about 2½ hours, including half-an-hour on the summit. The service is subject to weather and the number of passengers (normal minimum 25); long waits must be expected at peak seasons.—This narrow-gauge rack-and-pinion line, the only such in Britain, and with a maximum gradient of 1 in 5½, was opened in 1896 and is today operated by seven steam locomotives (some 1895–96, some 1922–23) and two Diesels of 1986.

A sharp ascent begins soon after the station. A viaduct is crossed, with a good view of the·Ceunant Mawr Falls and, beyond, the Ceunant Bach Fall is also seen. After passing *Hebron* (1¼m; 930ft) the line ascends the long N spur of the mountain and crosses the Llanberis Track, Moel Eilio and Y Foel Goch being seen to the right. Beneath *Halfway* (2½m; 1600ft), to the right is the deep valley of Cwm Brwynog (Cwm of Rushes), with its amphitheatre of cliff. The foot track is again crossed just beyond *Clogwyn* (3¾m; 2550ft) and there is a glimpse left into the precipitous gorge of Cwm Glas Bach with the Pass of Llanberis beyond. Curving to the right to ascend a slope above the cliffs of Clogwyn-du'r-Arddu (Black Precipice), with a tarn at their foot, the line affords a fine view extending as far as Anglesey. It then crosses the Snowdon Ranger Track (3200ft) and reaches the saddle. *Snowdon Summit* station is just below the cairn of Yr Wyddfa.

Llanberis Track. From Llanberis (Victoria Hotel). 5m in 3 hours. The track, originally a Victorian pony trail, never diverges far from the railway and generally affords the same views. A detour on the left beyond the second railway crossing leads to the cliff edge, with a splendid view of *Cwm Glas*. Near the summit *Bwlch Glas*, where the Pyg and Snowdon Ranger tracks join, is another viewpoint.

Pyg Track. From Pen-y-Pass. 2½ hours. This popular route was so named at the turn of the century by climbers from Pen-y-Gwyrd Hotel (PYG), who wished to distinguish it from the Miners' Track. It is also often spelt Pig Track, some justification being that one translation of *Bwlch Moch*, reached at 1850ft, could be Pigs' Pass. Llyn Llydaw and the sheer cliffs of Yr Wyddfa and Lliwedd here come into view, and the track skirts the hillside under the crags of Crib Goch. Later a shoulder is crossed, looking down 400ft into the cwm which contains Glaslyn, the Miners' Track being met above the W end of the lake. The joint path bears right up zigzags to meet the Llanberis track at *Bwlch Glas*.

Miners' Track. From Pen-y-Pass. 3 hours. The mine is Glaslyn, where copper was mined from the second half of the 18C until 1916. Its situation was so remote that the miners lived at the mine, returning on foot at weekends across the Glyders to their homes in Bethesda.—From Pen-y-Pass the track passes the small *Llyn Teyrn* (1238ft) then crosses the NE end of *Llyn Llydaw* (1416ft) by a causeway. The lake, more than 1m long, is dominated at its head by Lliwedd. The track skirts the N shore for ½m, then turns NW, passing the abandoned copper workings near the smaller *Glaslyn* (1971ft). From Glaslyn the path zigzags up to the Pyg Track, a route up which the miners carried their sacks to Bwlch Glas, whence the ore was dragged on sledges down to Llyn Cwellyn.

Watkin Path. From Nant Gwynant. 3 hours. Sir Edward Watkin was a Victorian railway entrepreneur whose dream was a train from Manchester to Paris, and who constructed nearly 2m of Channel Tunnel before the government stopped the project. He retired to Nant Gwynant and soon built a path upwards from the South Snowdon Slate Quarries; it was opened by Gladstone in 1892. The path is perhaps the finest ascent, but it is steep and not for the inexperienced.—From the road, near the Glaslyn bridge, a cart-track is followed to a fork (5 min.). Here the branch to the left is taken, climbing above waterfalls to the right. At 850ft the stream is crossed to a ruined house, a short way beyond which is *Gladstone Rock* (inscription), from which Gladstone, aged 83, opened the path, the theme of his speech being Justice to Wales. The cart-track ends at the old quarry, the point where the Watkin Path proper bears right and begins to ascend the long SW slope of Lliwedd. Approaching the ridge a short detour to the right affords a sudden and magnificent view from the edge of the precipice looking into Cwm Dyli. The narrow saddle which the track follows between Lliwedd and Yr Wyddfa is *Bwlch-y-Saethau* (2690ft), the Pass of the Arrows, traditionally a burial place of King Arthur. The ridge broadens, and another short detour gives a fine view of Glaslyn below.

Pitt's Head Track. From *Pitt's Head Rock* (2½m N of Beddgelert on A4085) or from *Rhyd-Ddu*, 1m farther north. 3 hours. From the point where the two tracks meet (c 1m) there is a gradual climb NE over open moor to the W extremity of the *Llechog* ridge (2400ft). Where the track is faint, there are small cairns. The precipitous N face of Llechog is followed, with views down to the tarns in Cwm Clogwyn, the ridge narrowing into the rocky razor-edge of *Bwlch-y-Maen* (3056ft), the Stone Pass. The Watkin Path is joined just below the summit.

Snowdon Ranger Track. From Snowdon Ranger hostel on Llyn Cwellyn. 2^1/$_2$ hours. After about ^{3}/$_4$m the path to Llanberis is crossed. The slope of Moel Cynghorion is to the left, while to the right is the marshy ground of Cwm Clogwyn with its five tarns. From *Bwlch Cwm-Brwynog* (1600ft), the steep ridge of *Clogwyn-du'r-Arddu* is ascended, and the Llanberis track is met near Bwlch Glas.

An exhilarating high-level route is the ***Snowdon Horseshoe**, the traverse of the long precipitous ridges connecting Crib Goch and Lliwedd with Yr Wyddfa. This route, which involves some scrambling, should only be attempted in fine weather and by experienced walkers briefed with local information.

9 Capel Curig to Bangor

A5. Total distance 14m.—*5m*. **Ogwen Cottage.**—*4m*. **Bethesda.**—*3m*. **Llandegai.**—*2m*. **Bangor.**

As far as Ogwen Cottage, and down Nant Ffrancon, the road is through grand mountain scenery.

For **Capel Curig**, see Rte 7.—The road ascends the N bank of the Llugwy into country of increasing grandeur, the old road, now a grass-grown track, providing a pleasant alternative for walkers along the other bank. To the N are the slopes of Pen Llithrig-y-Wrach and Pen Helig, with the two Carneddau beyond in the distance, while to the S Snowdon is soon hidden behind the long eastward extremity of the Glyders, the projection nearest to the road being Gallt-yr-Ogof, the Cliff of the Caves. Soon the great rock-pyramid of Tryfan comes suddenly into view, with the mountains beyond Llyn Ogwen (Y Foel Goch, and, later, Y Garn) in the background. The road crosses the Llugwy, descending from its source of Fynnon Llugwy a mile away to the N, while to the S opens the great Cwm Tryfan. *Llyn Ogwen*, a lake 1m long and nowhere more than 10ft deep, is grandly set in a deep hollow between the black, rock-strewn slopes of Tryfan and the Glyders to the S and, to the N, Pen-yr-Oleu-Wen, the precipitous S spur of Carnedd Dafydd.

5m. **Ogwen Cottage**, at Pont Pen-y-Benglog (993ft), is a mountain school, while adjacent Idwal Cottage is a youth hostel. This area is the southern end of the National Trust's huge Carneddau Estate of over 15,000 acres, the estate including Llyn Idwal, the head of Nant Ffrancon and several mountains, amongst these being the N slopes of the two Glyders, Tryfan, Carnedd Dafydd and the NW slopes of Carnedd Llewelyn.

*Cwm Idwal Nature Reserve, ^{1}/$_2$m S, is reached by a path behind Ogwen Cottage. Established in 1954 as the first reserve to be declared in Wales, and now leased by the National Trust to the Countryside Council for Wales, this natural amphitheatre (1223ft) below volcanic rock walls piling up another 2000ft or more, is scenically awesome, botanically of a particular interest (Alpines), and, as might be expected of such a place, a source of legend. Hollowed out by the same inexorable glacier which on its further descent carved Nant Ffrancon, Cwm Idwal is largely filled by *Llyn Idwal*, a sombre lake below the main precipice of Glyder Fawr, to the right of which opens a great fissure with overhanging sides, known as Twll Du, or the Devil's Kitchen. In legend Prince Idwal, son of Owain Gwynedd, was drowned here by his foster-father; his spirit still haunts the lake, and that of his murderer the Devil's Kitchen. A nature trail, 2m in length, makes the circuit of the lake, feral goats being among the wildlife here.

Ogwen Cottage is a focus for many demanding walks and climbs. But this is also the heart of one of the wildest districts in Wales, notorious for precipices, boulders, treacherous scree and uncertain weather, and advice should be sought before setting out for any distance or height. Walks and climbs include *The Glyders* (3279 and 3262ft); *Y Garn* (3104ft); *Elidir Fawr* (3029ft) above Marchlyn Mawr, the upper reservoir of the Dinorwig Power Station at Llanberis; the *Miners' Track*, the route from Bethesda used by the copper miners employed at Glaslyn (see Rte 8B); *Tryfan* (3010ft), with its three precipitous faces; and, to the NE, *Carnedd Dafydd* (3426ft) and *Carnedd Llewelyn* (3484ft), named after the two brother princes who confronted Edward I, and, after Snowdon, the two highest mountains in Wales.

Immediately beyond Ogwen Cottage the road crosses the Ogwen which here spills out of its lake and, joined by the stream from Llyn Idwal, plunges down into the head of Nant Ffrancon in a series of cataracts known as the Benglog Falls (Falls of the Skull). The road, engineered by Telford in 1815–30, now enters ***Nant Ffrancon**, possibly named after Adam de Francton, traditionally the name of the man who killed Llewelyn the Last, but more probably deriving from Nant yr Afanc, meaning the Valley of the Beavers. Glacially immediate successor to Cwm Idwal, the valley is bounded by rocky mountains, those on the W side cut by tributary glacial cwms.

Just beyond (*2m*) the hamlet of *Tyn-y-Maes* a bridge crosses the Ogwen, the small road on this side of the river being one built in the latter part of the 18C for the benefit of Irish Members of Parliament making for London. The scenery now quickly changes, the rocks giving way to the woods of Ogwen Bank (E) while to the W are the Penrhyn Slate Quarries.

2m. **Bethesda** (4500 inhab.) owes its growth to the 19C development of slate quarrying, and its present name (previously it was Glanogwen), deriving from a Nonconformist chapel in the main street, to the religious fervour of the same period. The *Penrhyn Slate Quarries* (Groups only; by appointment) were developed in c 1770 by Richard Pennant, the 1st Baron Penrhyn. The biggest opencast system in the world, the quarries form a vast amphitheatre, a mile long and some 1200ft deep, hewn in terraces out of the N end of Bron Llwyd. The mules and carts of the early days were superseded in 1801 by a special railway to Port Penrhyn, immediately E of Bangor.—For (*3m*) **Llandegai** and **Penrhyn Castle**, see Rte 1C.—*2m.* **Bangor**, see Rte 3.

10 Bangor to Caernarfon and Porthmadog

A487 to Caernarfon. A4085 to Beddgelert. A498 to Porthmadog.
Total distance 29m.—*5m.* **Port Dinorwic.**—*4m.* **Caernarfon.**—*5m.*
Betws Garmon.—*7m.* **Beddgelert.**—*2m. Pont Aberglaslyn.*—*5m.*
Tremadog.—*1m. Porthmadog.*

Mountain and woodland on both sides between Betws Garmon
through Beddgelert to Pont Aberglaslyn; then mountains to the W
and reclaimed estuary to the east.

For **Bangor**, see Rte 3.—*5m.* **Port Dinorwic**, today a yachting centre
and marina, is a place which has had its touches of history, starting in
the 1C when, it seems reasonably certain, both Suetonius and
Agricola chose this as their crossing point for their assaults on
Anglesey. Some eight centuries later the raiding Norsemen habitu-
ally sheltered here from both weather and tides, their example
followed by generations of fishermen until in the 19C Dinorwic
became the port at the end of the slate railway from the great
quarries above Llanberis (the Llanberis Lake Railway, see Rte 8A, is
all that survives).

4m. **CAERNARFON** (9000 inhab. *Inf.* Oriel Pendeitsch, opposite
castle entrance. Tel: 0286–672232), on the right bank of the mouth of
the Seiont near the SW end of Menai Strait, is a historic place visited
for its great castle, for its rectangle of town walls protecting the 13C
Edwardian Borough, still the main shopping area, and for the Roman
site of Segontium. The Romans were at Segontium from c 77 to c 380,
and on Twt Hill, in the E of the town, evidence has been found of a
Celtic settlement. Otherwise the story of Caernarfon is essentially
that of its castle.

Bangor Street enters the town from the NE, soon reaching Turf
Square, once the site of the pillory and stocks. From here High Street
leads W through the medieval walls while Bridge Street continues S
into the large CASTLE SQUARE, also known as Y Maes, with statues of
David Lloyd George (by W. Goscombe John), local MP from 1890 to
1945, and of Sir Hugh Owen (1804–81), a pioneer of Welsh university
education. The Castle, the quays along the mouth of the Seiont, and
the walled town are all immediately W and NW of Castle Square; it is
well worth while to go down to the quay, often busy with fishing
boats and yachts (embarkation also for Menai cruises), from where a
far better impression of the great walls and their defensive strength is
gained than is apparent from the somewhat cramped town side.

*Caernarfon Castle (WHM. Tel: 0222-465511), occupying an area
of three acres within the angle of the Seiont and the Menai Strait, is,
despite its low-lying site, a massive and commanding example of
medieval fortification.

History. The first castle was a Norman motte-and-bailey of c 1100, taken by the
Welsh princes not long after its construction and remaining in Welsh hands until
1283, when Edward I set James of St. George to building the castle that stands
here today. The castle was completed in three main stages, the first being up till
1292, the second 1295 to 1308 when the master mason was Walter of Hereford,
and the last 1309 to 1323. The associated English Borough was granted its
charter in 1284. The use of polygonal towers has few English precedents, and
that of banded masonry none. Both these are features of the walls of Con-
stantinople, and, together with the use of the decorative eagle, suggest an
intention to recall Segontium's tradition as the birthplace of Constantine the
Great (what was believed to be the body of Constantine's father, Constantius I,
killed at York in 305 while on an expedition against the Picts and Scots, was
found in 1283 and reburied at Edward's behest). Edward II was born here in

1284, but not in the Eagle Tower as popularly supposed. The story of his presentation to the conquered Welsh as a Prince of Wales who could speak no English' is almost certainly apocryphal, and cannot in fact be traced earlier than 1584. In 1294 during Madog's rebellion the town was sacked by the Welsh, who breached the wall below Eagle Tower. In 1399 Richard II was here after his landing from Ireland, and in 1403 Caernarfon was unsuccessfully attacked by Owen Glendower. The Parliamentarian William Prynne was imprisoned here in 1637, and during the Civil War the castle changed hands three times, finally falling to Parliament. After 1660 it was dismantled. In 1911 the future Edward VIII was invested here as Prince of Wales, as was also Prince Charles in 1969.

Despite its externally complete appearance, the castle today is little more than a shell. It comprises two irregular wards, the upper or outer (E) of which encloses the site of the Norman motte. There are two gates, the King's Gate (N) at the join of the wards, and the Queen's Gate at the E extremity. The many angles of the walls are marked by polygonal towers, crowned by picturesque turrets, Eagle Tower at the castle's W end having three of these. The walls and towers along the S side, between and including Eagle Tower and North East Tower, represent the earlier building phase (up to 1292), although the upper parts of Eagle Tower were completed later. An interesting defensive feature is the almost continuous system of mural passages, carried round the inner faces of the towers and pierced with loopholes. On the S face of the castle these passages are doubled, this affording, in conjunction with the looped merlons of the rampart walk, positions for three tiers of archers.

The description below follows an anticlockwise circuit, starting with the lower ward. Visitors have a choice between using the mural passages or returning to the courtyard after each tower.

The ENTRANCE, on the N side, is through the *King's Gate*, above which is a mutilated statue of Edward II. The gate was formerly approached by a drawbridge, traces of which and of its associated defences (portcullis, arrow slits) can still be seen. The entrance passage is flanked by strong octagonal towers, and the gatehouse would have incorporated quarters for the constable, with a hall, chapel, and living rooms. Beyond the entrance a range of buildings (now destroyed, except for *Prison Tower*, an inwards extension of the W gatehouse tower) would have separated the two wards.—LOWER WARD. Along the wall between the W gatehouse and the next tower (*Well Tower*) was the site of the kitchens. From the basement of Well Tower hooded fireplaces can be seen above. A postern here was perhaps for direct delivery of kitchen supplies. The westernmost tower is *Eagle Tower* (exhibitions), the largest of the castle, with walls 15ft thick and an internal diameter at ground level of 34ft. On the first floor there is a small room in which Edward II was once thought to have been born; in fact the tower would not by 1284 have reached this height. Stairs ascend to the roof with its three turrets. Stone eagles are among the weathered figures on the turret battlements, but only one (W) is recognisable. In the basement of the tower is the castle watergate. Next comes *Queen's Tower*, housing the *Museum of the Royal Welch Fusiliers*, telling the story of the regiment since its founding in 1689. Below the Queen's Tower the Hall (100ft by 34ft) filled the SE of the ward.—UPPER WARD. *Chamberlain Tower*, with an exhibition on the Castles of Edward I, also contains a chapel (first floor, NE); *Black Tower* has small ten-sided rooms; and at *Cistern Tower* there is a stone tank. *Queen's Gate*, at the E end of the castle, was originally approached by a drawbridge, evidence of which can be seen from a railed platform high above the quay. The next tower, the small *Watch Tower*, is entered through *North East Tower* beyond, which houses a Prince of Wales Exhibition. The last tower is *Granary Tower*, between which and King's Gate the wall has arrow slits, so designed that two or three archers could shoot out of a single opening.

The **Town Walls**, nearly 1/2m in circumference and strengthened by towers, enclose a roughly rectangular area to the N of the castle, to which, forming a single scheme of defence, they were joined at North East and Eagle towers. The town within, with several 16–19C houses, still retains the regular pattern standard to Edward I's English Boroughs. The walls are almost complete, and had E and W gates at either end of what is today's High Street. The tower at the W gate (also known as *Porth-y-Aur* or Golden Gate) is now the head-quarters of the Royal Welsh Yacht Club (founded 1847). At the E end the gate is also known as *Porth Mawr* or Great Gate. Below, in Greengate Street, the little window in the SE corner of the arch is that of the cell which until 1835 served as town lock-up. The most interesting building around the walls is the *Chantry of St. Mary* (or Old Church), structurally incorporated within the walls at their NW

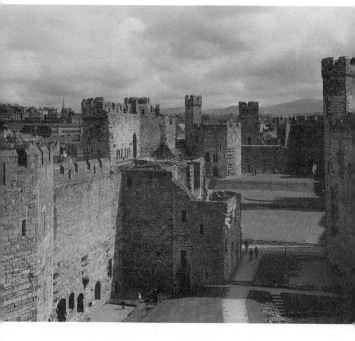

Caernarfon Castle, begun by Edward I in 1283

angle where the adjoining tower serves as vestry and bell-tower. The church (restored) was built in the 14C by Henry de Elierton, later master mason of the castle.

Victoria Dock is just beyond the NW angle of the walls, here being Caernarfon's *Seiont II Maritime Museum* (Tel: 0286–830932), with a general museum section and two ships, the 'Seiont II', a steam dredger of 1937, and the 'Nantlys', built in 1920 and the last of the Menai Strait ferries.

The Roman fort of **Segontium** (NT and WHM. Tel: 0222-465511 or 0286-5625) is ½m SE of Castle Square beside A4085 to Beddgelert. Probably founded in 78 by Agricola as a fort for auxiliary troops, Segontium remained occupied until c 380, one reason for its eventual abandonment possibly being the withdrawal of troops from Britain by Magnus Maximus, who came to Britain as an official of Theodosius and was then declared emperor by the disaffected legions (he would later become Macsen Wledig of the 'Mabinogion'). There is a tradition that Constantine the Great was born here, although in fact he was probably born in c 288 at Nis, in what is today Yugoslavia. Bar the ground plan outlined by foundations, little remains to be seen of the fort. Of considerably more interest are the *Museum* (Tel: as above), covering not only this site but the Romans generally, and, just E, *Llanbelig Church*, dedicated to Peblig (Publicus), son of Magnus Maximus, and interesting for the continuity it provides from the days of early pagan worship; it stands close to the Roman Mithraeum (located in 1959, but now covered; plaque on house), while the modern cemetery across the road spreads over its Roman predecessor. The oldest part of the church is the S wall, which is probably 13C; the transepts and choir are mainly 14C; and the lower part of the tower (which was once whitewashed as a navigation mark for ships) is 15C.

A4085, leaving Caernarfon, passes Segontium and Llanbelig, crosses the Seiont, and ascends generally following the line of a Roman road. Ahead to the SE rises Moel Eilio (2300ft) and to the S Mynydd Mawr (2290ft).—*5m. Betws Garmon*, at the boundary of Snowdonia National Park, possibly derives it name from St. Germanus. Beyond, the road, beside the Gwyrfai and approaching wilder scenery, reaches *Llyn Cwellyn* (464ft), on the farther side of which the bold crag of *Castell Cidwym* (Wolf's Castle) rises sheer from the water. About halfway along the lake is the *Snowdon Ranger Hostel*, starting point of one of the recognised routes up the mountain. The house was opened as an inn early in the 19C by a mountain guide, doubtless the pioneer of the track; later the place became a monastery, and it is now a youth hostel.—*4m. Rhyd-Ddu* (600ft) is a pleasantly situated hamlet from which a path joins the Snowdon Pitt's Head Track.

From Rhyd-Ddu B4418 passes in ½m (left) a path leading to Beddgelert Forest, with many walks. In another ½m this road reaches *Llyn-y-Dywarch*, mentioned by Giraldus as possessing a floating island; it still occasionally happens that a piece of the peat shore breaks away and drifts about.

Pitt's Head Rock, 1m S of Rhyd-Ddu, starting place of the similarly named Snowdon ascent, is so called because of its supposed resemblance to the statesman's profile. The watershed here is at 650ft, and the road now descends Nant Colwyn, with *Beddgelert Forest* (FC walks) on the W, dropping over 500ft in 2¾m to (*3m* from Rhyd-Ddu) *Beddgelert* and, *2m* farther, *Pont Aberglaslyn*, for both of which see Rte 7.

At Pont Aberglaslyn Rte 7 crosses the bridge to Penrhyndeudraeth, while this Route continues south. On the E are the wide, marshy flats of *Traeth Mawr* (7000 acres). Until the early 19C a broad estuary navigable up to Pont Aberglaslyn, this became reclaimed land between 1807–11 when W.A. Madocks MP (1774–1828) built his great embankment (The Cob) across the mouth of the Glaslyn. Beyond the flats rise Cnicht and the Moelwyns, while to the W of the road is Moel Ddu (1811ft).—*3m* (from Pont Aberglaslyn) *Glaslyn Hotel*, beyond which the road skirts a range of steep, wooded cliffs. This is the *Coed Tremadog Nature Reserve*, a large area of oak, also botanically interesting because of the plants which have survived thanks to the absence of sheep. *Tan-yr-Allt*, beside the road just before Tremadog, was the residence of W.A. Madocks.

Tan-yr-Allt was the scene of the 'Tremadog Incident', long a perplexity to Shelley's biographers. In September 1812 the poet, attracted by Madocks's 'generous project', symbolising a pre-eminence of mind over matter, came here with Harriet to offer his assistance. They occupied a house (now pulled down) at the W end of the grounds, and here much of 'Queen Mab' was written. One night the following February, according to Shelley and Harriet, the house was forcibly entered, shots were fired, and Shelley's life was attempted. Thereupon the pair departed. The incident is now explained as a successful ruse to scare Shelley away, adopted by certain shepherds who objected to the poet's habit of putting sick or injured sheep out of pain when he came across them on his walks.

2m. **Tremadog** was built by W.A. Madocks between 1805–07, and, largely unaltered, remains a good example of early 19C town planning. T.E. Lawrence (Lawrence of Arabia, 1888–1935) was born here (plaque).—*1m*. **Porthmadog**, see Rte 15.

11 Anglesey

The name Anglesey is generally accepted as meaning Island of the Angles, although some authorities derive it from the Norse 'öngull' for fiord. In Welsh it is Ynys Môn (the Mona of Tacitus, Ynys meaning 'island' and Môn perhaps stemming from a Celtic word for 'end'), to which is often added 'Mam Cymru' (Mother of Wales), a title arising from the island's extensive cornfields. Anglesey was occupied by man in very early times–Middle Stone Age remains of perhaps 7000 BC have been found, while later prehistoric sites abound—and, at the close of the prehistoric period, was the chief centre of the Druids, attacked by the Roman Suetonius Paulinus in 61 and virtually exterminated by his successor Agricola in 78. Later (7–13C), Anglesey was a stronghold of the princes of Gwynedd with their capital at Aberffraw, despite which, though, the island's coasts endured some 200 years (850–1050) of Norse raids.

Scenically, Anglesey is for the most part undulating and somewhat monotonous, though there are some pleasant stretches of coast, especially along the north east. Through the island run the main road and railway to Holyhead, an industrial town and port with the passenger and car ferry service to Dun Laoghaire in Ireland. Otherwise, Anglesey is visited largely for its many prehistoric sites, for the mansion of Plas Newydd, for the impressive Edwardian castle at Beaumaris and for some unpretentious resorts.

The direct road from the Menai bridges to Holyhead (Rte 11A) is of limited interest. Visitors in search of the best of the island should explore around the circuit described as Rte 11B.

Tourist Information. Station Site, Llanfair PG, LL61 5UJ. Tel: 0248–713177.

A. Bangor to Holyhead

A5. Total distance 23m.—*3m*. **Llanfair PG.**—*6m*. **Llangefni.**—*11m*. **Valley.**—*3m*. **Holyhead**.

The MENAI STRAIT, with for the most part green and pleasant banks, is a channel some 13m long and varying in width between a mile and 200 yards. The principal towns on the mainland are Bangor (N) and Caernarfon (S); and, on the island, Beaumaris at its SE corner. Near Bangor the strait is crossed by two distinguished bridges—one road, the other (1m SW) combined rail and road—the main A5 using the latter. The *Menai Suspension Bridge* (road only) was built by Thomas Telford in 1819–26. Before this, crossing had been by ferry but the herds of cattle for sale on the mainland had had to swim. Not surprisingly perhaps, there was fierce opposition from the many interests whose livelihood depended on the ferries, as also from ship-owners determined that the passage of their tall ships should not be impeded, this insistence resulting in the road being at a height of

100ft. The bridge was considerably rebuilt in 1938–41 when the structure was strengthened, the roadway widened, and the number of supporting chains reduced from 16 to four. The bridge measures 579ft between the piers and 1000ft overall. *Britannia Bridge*, 1m SW, originally a tubular railway bridge built by Robert Stephenson between 1846–50 and similar to his bridge at Conwy, was burnt out in 1970 and the rail link was only restored with the completion (on the stonework of the original) of a new conventional bridge in 1972, this now with an extra deck which carries the A5 road. The statue to Lord Nelson, on the N shore just W of the bridge, was erected in 1873 by Admiral Lord Clarence Paget as an aid to navigation.

Motorists may choose either bridge, Telford's crossing direct to the small town of Menai Bridge while Stephenson's heads for Llanfair PG.

At **Menai Bridge** (3000 inhab.), *Pili-Palas* (Tel: 0248–712474), just NW on B5420, is the home of both local and exotic butterflies and insects, while on Church Island, immediately W of the town and reached by a causeway, there is a small 14C church, a foundation of 630 by St. Tysilio, perhaps later visited by Archbishop Baldwin and Giraldus, thought to have landed here in 1188.

A5, leaving Britannia Bridge, loops northward, soon passing (right) the *Anglesey Column*, 90ft high and commemorating the 1st Marquess (1768–1854) who commanded the cavalry at Waterloo where he lost a leg; the column was erected in 1817, the statue by M. Noble being added in 1860. For more about this remarkable marquess, see Plas Newydd on Rte 11B.

3m (from Bangor) **Llanfair PG** is an accepted abbreviation for *Llanfairpwllgwyngyllgogerychwyrndrobwllllantysiliogogogoch* (St. Mary's Church in a hollow by the white hazel close to the rapid whirlpool by the red cave of St. Tysilio), a name probably invented as a tourist lure, which to some extent it still is, though, with the station now closed, the longest platform ticket in the world, once the principal souvenir, now has to be bought at local shops, thus losing both authenticity and usefulness. The first Women's Institute in Britain was founded here in 1915. Today the main attraction is the *James Pringle Woollen Mill* (Tel: 0248–717171), a huge retail complex which includes Tourist Information (Tel: 0248–713177), a restaurant, a gift shop and other facilities.

For *Plas Newydd*, ½m SW, see Rte 11B which starts from Llanfair PG.—At *Penmynydd*, 2m NW, the mansion (present building 1576; no adm.) was for centuries the home of the Tudors. Here was born Owen Tudor, believed to have married Catherine of Valois, widow of Henry V, their grandson being Henry VII. In the 14C church is the alabaster tomb (c 1385) of Gronw Tudor, uncle of Owen, and of his wife, the alabaster of which is chipped, due to a tradition that it could alleviate eye disease.

4m. *Pentre Berw*, beyond which the road crosses the Malltraeth Marsh and the river Cefni.—*2m*. **Llangefni** (3500 inhab.), 1m N of A5, is the main market and administrative town of Anglesey. Here a gallery (Tel: 0248–724444) shows works by Welsh artists, in particular the Anglesey wildlife artist Charles Tunnicliffe. Tregarnedd (no adm.), a farm to the SE of the town, marks the site of the home of Ednyfed Fechan, minister of Llewelyn the Great (his graveslab can be seen at Llanelian-yn-Rhos on Rte 1B), while to the NW, by B5111, Cefni Reservoir, known for migrant wildfowl, offers a picnic area and a hide.—*4m. Gwalchmai*, briefly famous as being the first village in Anglesey to have electricity (supplied by a local watermill), is today

known as the home of the annual Anglesey Agricultural Show.—7m.
Valley, thought to have been given its name by Telford when cutting
his road through a small hill here, was, centuries earlier, a home of
Iron Age man whose weapons and horse trappings found here are
now in the National Museum of Wales. Today Valley is perhaps best
known for its military airfield, built in 1941 and in turn fighter base,
trans-Atlantic terminal, flying school and missile practice camp.—
Beyond Valley A5 and the railway together cross a causeway 1200
yards long to Holy Island (see also below) on which are the port of
Holyhead, the conspicuous mountain of the same name with dramatic cliff scenery, and several archaeological sites. *Penrhos Nature
Reserve*, at the W end of the causeway and with a 2m nature trail, is
of interest for its variety of birds.

   3m. **Holyhead** or Caer Gybi (10,500 inhab. *Inf.* Marine Square. Tel:
0407–762622), in origin a Roman fort and Celtic Christian settlement,
is today mainly a commercial and industrial town, but also something

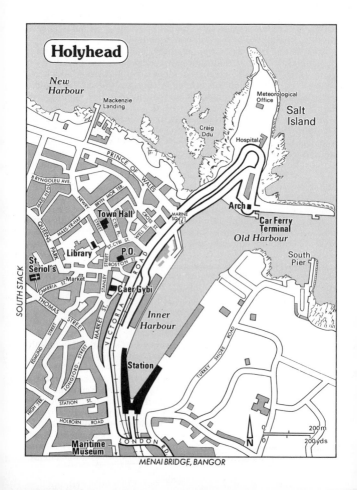

of a resort, owing its growth and importance to its harbour. A5 enters the town as London Road, curving across the railway by the station, just SW of here, in Rhos-y-Gaer Avenue, being the *Maritime Museum* (Tel: 0407–762622), devoted largely to the port, with some emphasis on the Irish mail, but also with much else of general maritime interest. On the W side of the station there is a road fork, with Victoria Road (see below) to the right and the shopping zone of Market Street and Stanley Street to the left.

The visible evidence of Holyhead's birth, and the source of its Welsh name—the small Roman fort of *Caer Gybi*—survives in the area between Stanley Street and Victoria Road; a survival of particular interest because the Roman walls were used by St. Cybi as early as the 6C to protect the church he founded here. The fort, dating from the 3–4C and possibly built as a protection against raiding pirates, forms a rectangle with rounded towers at the corners; except on the E the walls are largely intact but the NE and SE towers were much rebuilt in the 18 and 19C respectively. The church here today is mainly 15–17C, though the restored choir is 13C; the Stanley Chapel is worth a visit for the figure of W.O. Stanley by Hamo Thornycroft (1897) and the window by Burne-Jones and William Morris. The smaller church to the S, known as Egylwys Bedd (Church of the Tomb), is said to shelter the grave of a 5C pirate captain.

Victoria Road reaches Marine Square, beyond being the port, while the road to the W, crossing open green slopes, skirts the New Harbour (Coast Guard. Sailing clubs), opened in 1873 and protected by a breakwater 1860ft long.

Port of Holyhead. Packet boats between Holyhead and Ireland are mentioned as early as 1573. Important later dates were 1801, when Holyhead was officially selected as the Irish packet station, at first to Howth but after 1834 to Dún Laoghaire; 1808, completion of the South Stack lighthouse; 1820, when steam began to replace sail; 1826, the opening of the Menai road bridge; 1850, the opening of the Menai railway bridge; 1873, completion of the New Harbour; 1880, when the Inner Harbour was opened; 1965, when the car ferry service was introduced; and 1970–71 when there was no rail traffic because of the destruction by fire of the Menai railway bridge. Recent developments have been the construction of a new terminal at Salt Island and the growth of container traffic.—An arch (1821) at the entrance to Admiralty Pier, protecting the Inner Harbour, marks the end of A5 and commemorates the landing here by George IV.

The remainder of **Holy Island** is worth touring, both for its cliff scenery and its prehistoric remains, and the following round is suggested. From Holyhead, Cambria Street, passing the prominent, modern St. Seriol's Church, leads towards South Stack, rounding *Holyhead Mountain*, or *Mynydd Twr* (710ft), with many paths, a hill-fort, and views which can include Snowdonia, and sometimes the Isle of Man and the Mountains of Mourne in Ireland. Approaching the coast the road turns right and climbs towards South Stack, about halfway up being a car park (left). Across the road from here are the *Holyhead Mountain Hut Circles*, named and sometimes signposted as 'Irishmen's Huts' (Cytiau Gwyddelod) in obedience to a tradition, without any archaeological backing, that the huts were those of the Goidelic (Irish) Celts driven out by the Brythonic Celts in the 5C. The huts represent an extensive settlement of the 2–4C. Originally the settlement may have occupied something like 20 acres, but today only 20 huts remain, of which 14 are in the main group. The huts are circular or rectangular, some of the former having traces of central hearths and slabs indicating the positions of beds and seats.

The road (narrow, steep, and often very crowded) ends at a small parking area above *South Stack Lighthouse*. Steps lead down to a small suspension bridge which crosses to the stack. The automated lighthouse (91ft high and 197ft above high water) was built in 1808 by David Alexander, who also built Dartmoor prison. The steps, with an associated nature trail, enable the seabird colonies to be well seen.

The road back passes the hut circles, just below which there is a T junction, the right arm of which is signed Trearddur. In 1/2m, a short way up a road to the left, are the *Penrhos Feilw Standing Stones*, two stones 10ft high, traditionally at the centre of a circle though nothing of this is now visible. In another 3/4m the coastal road reaches the head of the small bay of *Porth Dafarch* with a road junction at which there are traces of hut circles. Rather less than 2m farther E, at Trearddur Bay, the road meets B4545. Here, if B4545 is crossed, the road soon bears N and in about 1m reaches *Trefignath Burial Chamber*, consisting of a long passage, once divided into several chambers. Today the E chamber is the best preserved and is flanked by two upright stones. *Ty Mawr Standing Stone* is 1/2m farther up this road. If B4545 is taken SE for 1m, a side road bears S for *Rhoscolyn*. Here St. Gwenfaen founded a church in the 6C, and her well on the W slope of Rhoscolyn Head was long supposed to cure mental disorders.

B.   Circuit of the Island

The circuit described below is a clockwise one, starting from **Llanfair PG** (for which, as also for the approaches from Bangor, see Rte 11A) and ending at Menai Bridge.

A4080 and A5 to Valley. A5025 to Pentraeth. B5109 to Beaumaris, with minor roads to Penmon and back. A545 to Menai Bridge. Total distance 76m.—*9m.* **Newborough.**—*4m.* **Llangadwaladr.**—*2m.* *Aberffraw.*—*4m.* **Rhosneigr.**—*9m.* **Valley.**—*10m.* **Tregele.**—*6m.* **Amlwch.**—*9m.* **Benllech.**—*8m.* **Beaumaris.**—*8m.* **Penmon** and back.—*7m.* **Menai Bridge.**

A4080 bears S out of Llanfair PG, in a little over 1m reaching ***Plas Newydd** (NT. Tel: 0248–714795), a magnificent mainly 18C mansion beside Menai Strait, seat of the marquesses of Anglesey and since 1976 belonging to the National Trust. In addition to splendid rooms, furniture, and portraits, the house contains important works by Rex Whistler, including his largest wallpainting, and a museum devoted to the militarily renowed 1st Marquess who, as Lord Uxbridge, led the British cavalry at Waterloo.

History. The original house here was built in the early 16C by the Griffith family of Penrhyn, the estate later descending by marriage to the Bagenal, Bayly, and (1737) Paget families. An early Paget, a chief adviser of Henry VIII, had acquired the large estate of Beaudesert (demolished 1935) in Staffordshire and been created Baron Paget, the creation containing the unusual provision that the title should, if necessary, continue through the female line. This happened as the result of the marriage in 1737 between Caroline Paget and Sir Nicholas Bayly, their son becoming 9th Baron Paget in 1769 when the 8th Baron died childless. In 1784 he was created 1st Earl of Uxbridge, a title which in the first creation had already been held by the 7th and 8th barons Paget. From various sources this new 1st Earl of Uxbridge acquired immense wealth, and it was he who between 1783 and 1809 refashioned Plas Newydd from a medieval manor into an 18C mansion. The first phase was 1783–86 when, to match that at the S end, another octagonal tower was built at the N end of the E front. In the second phase (1793–99) James Wyatt and Joseph Potter of Lichfield achieved a new entrance front on the W, created the Classical and Gothick interiors of the present main block, and built the stables. Potter added the N wing between 1805–09. The grounds owe much to Humphry Repton, commissioned in 1798 to advise on the layout. In 1812 the estate passed to its most illustrious owner, the 2nd Lord Uxbridge, commander of the cavalry during the retreat to Corunna and at Waterloo and after the latter battle created 1st Marquess of Anglesey. Towards the end of the battle his leg was smashed, upon which he exclaimed to Wellington, riding beside him, 'By God, sir, I've lost my leg!', Wellington replying, momentarily glancing away from the retreating French, 'By God, sir, so you have!' What must surely be a unique monument is the one in the town of Waterloo commemorating this leg. The Marquess eloped with Wellington's sister-in-law, fathered 18 children, and died aged 84 (see also Cavalry Museum below). In the 1930s the 6th Marquess removed the battlements from the parapets, shortened the pinnacles on the E front, giving them Tudor caps to match those on the entrance side, remodelled the N wing, and created a long dining room, decorated by Rex Whistler, a close friend of the Pagets, between 1936–40. In 1976 the 7th Marquess gave the house and surrounding land to the National Trust.

The car park is beside the early 19C dairy, with a National Trust shop and information centre. There is a longish walk down to the house, during which, beyond the sweep of grass on the left, can be seen the turreted and castellated stables (Joseph Potter, 1797), with, in front, the large stones of a prehistoric burial chamber.

The *Gothick Hall* (1796–98) is a lofty rectangular room rising through two storeys and having a gallery. Pictures here include a contemporary portrait of the 1st Baron Paget; a portrait by Van Dyck; and two large works by Snyders. Another portrait is of Caroline Paget. The banners, both of the Royal Horse Guards, are of the Peninsular and Waterloo campaigns. The *Music Room*, also 1796–98 and the finest room in the house, occupies the site of the hall of the original building. The carved woodwork here, as elsewhere in the house, is that of Potter's craftsmen. Among the portraits are four by Hoppner (of the 1st Marquess, his sister and his second wife, and his younger brother Sir Arthur Paget), one by Lawrence of the 1st Marquess, and one by Romney of the Earl of Uxbridge. The *Hall and Staircase*, and the remaining rooms, are generally in the Neo-Classical style (note for instance the Doric columns) associated with Wyatt. In the hall there are two portraits of early Pagets, one attributed to Leandro Bassano and the other (1578), of the wife of the 2nd Lord Paget, by Marc Gheeraedts. The eight canvases of scenes of the Duke of Marlborough's campaigns are by Laguerre, and the full-length portrait of Wellington is by John Lucas. On the top landing there are Elizabethan portraits of the 1st Lord Paget (1549), of a young man (1585), and of Henry VIII and Queen Elizabeth. The *Landing and Gallery* and passages have more pictures, notably a portrait of Lady Caroline Paget by Rex Whistler; a group of the 1st Marquess's children, painted by Wilkin; early 19C watercolours of Beaudesert and Anglesey, the latter part of a set by John 'Warwick' Smith; and one, in the passage leading to Lady Anglesey's bedroom, of Florence Paget (the 'Pocket Venus') as a child (Henry Graves, 1850). She was the central figure of a Victorian scandal; courted by the Marquess of Hastings and by Henry Chaplin, both wealthy gamblers and rivals also of the turf, Florence accepted Chaplin but promptly eloped with and married Hastings, who however soon died of dissipation leaving Florence a widow at twenty-six. *Lady Anglesey's Bedroom*, occupying the octagonal SE tower, affords views along Menai Strait, including the family's private harbour (the 1st Marquess and his father always kept three yachts at Plas Newydd). The plaster frieze and chimneypiece date from the redecoration of 1793–99, but the present colour scheme was introduced in the 1930s by Lady Marjorie Manners, wife of the 6th Marquess, with the advice of Sibyl Colefax, a leading decorator of that period. *Lord Anglesey's Bedroom* also has a frieze and chimneypiece of the 1790s. The late 17 or early 18C state bed came from Beaudesert and the marine pictures are 19C English and Dutch.

The tour of the house returns down a spiral staircase of 1795 to the Gothick Hall, beyond which is the *Ante Room*, of Neo-Classical design by Wyatt. The portrait of the 1st Earl of Uxbridge as a young man is by an unidentified artist, but the one opposite, of one of his sons, is by Lawrence. Among the furnishings are Louis XV chairs; a pair of Napoleonic Sèvres vases, with campaign scenes; gilt console tables in the style of Robert Gumley and James Moore, two leading craftsmen of the early 18C; and two gilt gesso pier glasses, bearing the Paget crest in medallions. The *Octagon Room* has an identical frieze to that in the Ante Room. Furnishings include early 19C Rococo games tables, one with a chessboard bearing the lions and eagles of the Paget arms; Louis XV chairs upholstered in a pattern of naval scenes; an 18C pier glass in the style of William Kent. The picture of the Menai Bridge was painted two years after its opening. The *Saloon* represents various periods. The bay window forms the base of a round tower added in 1751; the general form of the room may date to the alterations of 1783–86; the frieze, window mouldings, and double doors are Wyatt's of 1795. The marble chimneypiece was probably bought in 1796 from the elder Richard Westmacott. The room contains some interesting pictures, among these being four large pastoral scenes by B.P. Ommeganck; Queen Victoria and her suite riding at Windsor by R.B. Davis (1837); and the 1st Marquess, by an unknown artist. The two busts, both by Reid Dick (1921 and 1925), are of Lady Caroline Paget and her mother, the 6th Marchioness. Outstanding among the furniture are the gilt pier tables and glasses (early 18C). In the *Breakfast Room* the frieze and pairs of double doors are all of c 1795–98, and the chimneypiece is almost certainly by Westmacott. Most of the pictures are seascapes.

The *Rex Whistler Exhibition*, in the octagonal tower added in 1783–86, comprises a number of portraits of the family and also examples of Whistler's skills as book illustrator, stage designer, and decorative artist. Beyond, the long dining room created by the 6th Marquess is now the *Rex Whistler Room, containing the artist's last and largest mural, in trompe l'oeil. The basic theme is an estuary with Renaissance cities, their buildings of every style and period, some genuine, others inventions. Throughout there are frequent references to the family, and Whistler includes himself as a young man sweeping leaves. In the small room beyond can be seen architectural drawings for the house, including Wyatt's and Potter's designs. The *Cavalry Museum* is in two parts. One room is devoted to the 1st Marquess and includes a portrait by Winterhalter, while in the second room there is a vast picture of Waterloo (Denis Dighton), of particular interest for the accuracy of the uniforms. Here too is an Anglesey Leg, an artificial limb invented and patented by James Potts of Chelsea and used by the Marquess. Beyond the Cavalry

Museum is the *Ryan Collection of Militaria*, the emphasis here being on uniforms and helmets.

2m (from Llanfair P.G.) *Cefn Bach* is a hamlet at a crossroads. The road N soon reaches the path to ***Bryn Celli Ddu**, a well-preserved burial chamber of 2000–1500 BC. The mound is modern protection and covers only a small part of the area of the prehistoric mound, which was 160ft in diameter. The polygonal chamber, roofed by two stones and approached through an open outer passage (6ft long) and an inner passage (20ft long), was within but not in the centre of a circular area. It was surrounded by four concentric stone circles, three of which were within the cairn while the fourth marked the base. An incised stone found here, now in the National Museum of Wales, has been replaced by a replica. The road S from the crossroads in 1m reaches Menai Strait at *Moel-y-Don*, one of two claimants (the other is Abermenai Point) to be the place at which Suetonius and, later, Agricola crossed to meet and defeat the Druid-led Celts massed on Anglesey's shore.—About 1½m farther along A4080, another small crossroads is reached from which a lane, marked by a lodge (key for church) and stone gate-posts, leads down to a somewhat vague T junction at which stands the primitive little disused church of *Llanidan*, known for its stoup which never dries up and reputedly had miraculous healing powers. It is believed that there has been a church on this site since 616, when the first may have been founded by St. Nidan, possibly a missionary from Scotland. The present building (?13–15C) was originally double-aisled but in 1844 the bulk of the E part was demolished, leaving only the arcade still standing in the churchyard.

2m. **Brynsiencyn**, once a Druid centre, is today the home (down on the Menai Strait shore opposite Caernarfon) of the unusual and imaginative *Anglesey Sea Zoo* (Tel: 0248–430411), a complex offering close and informative viewing (open and from above; not as in an aquarium) of marine life, among the highlights being conger eels, sea bass, crowds of lobsters, shoals of herring, a tank of flat fish and, of unusual interest, lobster breeding. Children are particularly welcome, and there is also a seafood retail shop.—Just beyond Brynsiencyn a road bears NW almost at once reaching *Caer Leb*, an Iron Age pentagonal enclosure defended by a double rampart, at which excavation during the 19C found remains of a rectangular building and a circular hut. Beyond Caer Leb this minor road crosses another similar road to reach (¾m from Caer Leb) *Bodowyr Burial Chamber*, with a capstone balanced on three uprights. Along A4080, in another mile, a track leads N for about 300 yards to reach *Castell Bryn-Gwyn*, a site—essentially a rampart and ditch enclosing a circular area of some 180ft diameter—archaeologically traced to activity spanning from New Stone Age times until the Roman invasion.—*2m* (from Brynsiencyn) *Dwyran*, just S of which is *Bryntirion Open Farm* offering guided tours.

3m. **Newborough**, formerly Rhosyr, is a small town which received its charter and English name from Edward I in 1303 when he transferred there people displaced by the construction of Beaumaris. From the 17C until the 1920s the weaving of marram grass ropes, baskets and mats was a thriving local cottage industry. Around the town, except to the NE, spreads the **Newborough Warren-Ynys Llanddwyn Nature Reserve**, where the main interests are forest, marsh and dunes. The reserve comprises five sections (see below) and can be seen by using a choice of approved paths. The only motor road through the main reserve runs from Newborough for 2m through the forest to a car park and picnic area (in summer, information and leaflets) near the shore.

Malltraeth Pool, at the N tip of the reserve, is beside A4080, rather under 2m NW of Newborough; protected by an embarkment built by Telford as a sea defence, the pool is mainly a bird sanctuary.—South from here is *Cefni Saltmarsh*, sandwiched between Malltraeth Sands and Newborough Forest and known for its sea plants and grasses.— To the E and S of the marsh stretches *Newborough Forest*, planted in 1948 at which time sand frequently blocked roads and covered crops; now, thanks to the trees (mostly Corsican pine) and other anti-erosion measures, this drifting is a thing of the past.—*Ynys Llanddwyn*, a promontory nearly 1m long at the S of the reserve, is geologically known for its pre-Cambrian rocks, among the oldest in Britain (more than 600 million years). In the 5C this promontory was the retreat of St. Dwynwen, patron of lovers, but the ruined church seen today dates only to the 16C. The lighthouse was built in 1873, before which the nearby tower (1800) was all that marked this hazard.—*Newborough Warren*, the large SE section of the reserve, was, until the ravages of myxomatosis, the home of so many rabbits that as many as 80,000 were trapped annually. In the 13C this was agricultural land, and Abermenai, at the SE tip and at the W end of the Menai Strait, was an important anchorage. Abermenai—a rival claimant to Moel-y-Don as the crossing point of the Romans—also has a place in legend, as the port from which Bronwen, daughter of Llyr and 'fairest maiden in the world', and her new lord, Matholwch, King of Ireland, set sail with 13 ships after their nuptial feast and bedding at Aberffraw. Storms during the 14C caused sand to cover the fields and block the anchorage, the warren ever since remaining a wilderness of dunes. The decrease in rabbits has brought an increasing spread of vegetation, marram grass being the principal plant.

Within the 2m beyond Newborough, A4080 crosses a finger of the forest, skirts Malltraeth Pool, and crosses the Cefni at the head of its estuary.—*4m*. **Llangadwaladr** has a 13–14C church, interesting for a stone (nave wall, N) commemorating Cadfan (Catamanus), a king or prince of Gwynedd who died c 625. Translated, the Latin inscription reads 'Cadfan the King, wisest and most renowned of all kings'. The village's name is that of Cadfan's grandson Cadwaladr, defeated by the Northumbrians near the Tyne in 634. About 2m NNE of here, reached by side roads, is the burial chamber of *Din Dryfol*. In poor condition today, the chamber seems originally to have been some 50ft in length.—*2m*. *Aberffraw* was the capital of Gwynedd from about the 7–13C, but of this past there is now no trace other than perhaps a Norman arch reset in the church and traditionally a part of the palace of the princes. On a small rocky island, 1¹⁄2m SW, reached by causeway at low tide, the little church of St. Cwyfan (restored 1893) stands on 7C foundations.—*2m*. *Barclodiad-y-Gawres Burial Chamber*, on the N side of the small Trecastell Bay, is interesting for sharing with Bryn Celli Ddu the distinction of being a burial chamber with mural art, five of the stones here being incised with designs. The chamber, re-arranged to protect the stones, comprises a 20ft long passage, a central chamber, and side chambers. The original mound, remains of which can be seen, would have been some 90ft in diameter.—*2m* **Rhosneigr** is a small seaside resort, in the 18C notorious for the ship wreckers who hid in the Crigyll estuary to the north. Hanged in 1741 they are the subject of a ballad by Lewis Morris.—The loop of A4080 serving Rhosneigr is completed N of the railway at *Llanfaelog*, ³/₄m NE of the church of which is *Ty Newydd Burial Chamber*, with a capstone resting on three uprights. A4080 continues N to join A5; about half-way between Llanfaelog and A5 (right, beside the road, opposite a house called Maen Hir) there stands an inscribed stone.

4m (from Rhosneigr). Junction with A5, Rte 11A now being followed W for *5m* to **Valley** (Dyffryn), from where A5025 is taken northwards.

2m. *Llanynghenedl*, 2m E of which, near the S end of Llyn Llywenan (well signed; reached by B5109 and a small road N beyond Bodedern) are *Presaddfed Burial Chambers*, one collapsed, the other with capstone and uprights.—*4m. Llanfaethlu*.

DIVERSION TO LLYN ALAW (5m. E). At *Llanddeusant*, reached in 2m, *Llynnon Mill* (Tel: 0407–730687) is a stone tower working windmill of 1775, the only example on Anglesey, while, about 1m E, *Howel Mill* (Tel: 0407–730595) is an ancient working watermill—also an only example—in a picturesque and remote setting and with recorded origins of 1335.—A minor road NE out of Llanddeusant in 2m reaches the hamlet of *Llanbabo* where the 12C church preserves a figure of St. Pabo, thought to have been a 6C Celtic mainland chief forced to seek safety in Anglesey. *Llyn Alaw*, a reservoir of 1966, some 3m long by ¹/₂m broad, lies immediately E of Llanbabo, at the lake's SW corner (minor road from Llanbabo) being a small information centre, a pleasant picnic site and a bird-watching hide.

4m. **Tregele** is a hamlet at a crossroads for various places of interest but principally, just to the N, *Wylfa Power Station*, with an information centre, guided tours, an observation tower and exhibition on Wylfa Head, and a cliff walk (Tel: 0407–710471). *Cemlyn Bay*, a shingle beach rather over 1m W of Tregele, is part of a National Trust coastal property which includes a bird sanctuary, chiefly for winter migrant wildfowl, and *Carmel Head*, 2¹/₂m farther W (no road), marks the NW extremity of Anglesey. The *Skerries*, a group of islets 2m NW, have carried a lighthouse since the 18C (it was then a coal fire in a grate) and until the 19C all passing ships had to pay a toll. A mile to the S of Tregele, in a district of burial chambers and standing stones, *Llanfechell* was the home of the 18C diarist William Bulkeley.

1m. **Cemmaes**, on the bay of the same name, is a modest resort. The church at *Llanbadrig* (1m N), said to have been founded by St. Patrick on a journey to Ireland, possibly as thanks for being saved in a shipwreck on Middle Mouse Rock, was restored in 1884 by Lord Stanley, the local landowner; a Muslim, he insisted on Islamic style in, for example, the tiles. Beyond, *Llanlleiana*, the northernmost point in Wales, is thought to be named after a female recluse who founded a chapel here in the 5 or 6C. The headland, which is National Trust property, includes the hillfort of Dinas Gynfor.

5m. **Amlwch** (3000 inhab.) is a port and resort whose fortunes have fluctuated with those of the copper mines of *Parys Mountain* to the south. Intermittently worked since Roman times, the mines were at their most prosperous in the late 18 and early 19C, at which time Amlwch was the most populated part of Anglesey. Abandoned in the later 19C, due to exhaustion, unstable prices, and foreign competition, there are now plans to re-open. Meanwhile the mountain is a bleak, deserted place with many dangerous shafts. The small port, built for the mines in 1793, has however now regained importance with the construction of the *Shell Marine Terminal* which began in 1973.

The Parys Mountain mining company is also known for its penny and halfpenny tokens (1787–93). Minted when provincial tokens were introduced because of the shortage and poor quality of official copper currency, the Parys tokens became known both for their quality and for their design.

The church of St. Eilian (³/₄m E) is 15C, with a 12C tower. It contains a 15C rood screen and loft; 15C seats and book desks; wooden dog tongs; and an ancient painting of St. Eilian (?), whose chapel adjoins the choir. In this chapel there is a curious semicircular piece of furniture, once believed to bring good luck to those who could turn round within it without touching the sides. St. Eilian's Well, near the sea, was thought to have healing powers.

2m. Penysarn, 2m SE of which is Traeth Dulas, the now almost land-locked estuary of the small river Dulas. The village of Dulas was the home of the Morris brothers (monument), men of letters and patrons of the arts, and on Ynys Dulas, beyond the estuary, there is a 19C tower which once served as a marker for ships.—Continuing S from Penysarn, A5025 in *2m* crosses the river at *City Dulas*, 2m SW of here being *Llandyfrydog*, the church of which is mentioned by Giraldus as the scene of a sacrilege in 1098 when Hugh Lupus locked his dogs in the church; however, he paid a high price, for the dogs went mad and their owner was killed within the month.—*1m. Rhos Lligwy* where this Route briefly leaves A5025 to continue E towards the small resort of *Moelfre*, off which in 1859 the 'Royal Charter', returning to Liverpool from Australia, was wrecked with the loss of 452 lives. Charles Dickens came here soon afterwards and used the tragedy as the basis of a story in 'The Uncommercial Traveller'.

About half-way between Rhos Lligwy and Moelfre there is a crossroads the S arm of which quickly reaches a group of three ancient sites—a fortified settlement, a ruined chapel and a burial chamber—which between them span perhaps 3000 years of human occupation. The fortified settlement, ***Din Lligwy** (¹/₂m walk), Iron Age and at about the centre of the time-span, is by far the most interesting of the three and, indeed, the most exciting ancient site on Anglesey, if only because this survives as a place in which ordinary people lived, as distinct from the many burial chambers marking their deaths. Probably built (or rebuilt) by local people during the closing years of the Roman occupation, the site covers about half an acre and much can still be seen of the stonework of circular and rectangular buildings inside an irregular defensive wall. Some of these buildings, or rooms, still have substantial walls, some show massive doorway posts, others traces of drainage systems across the floors and through the walls. *Capel Lligwy*, the chapel to the NE, built by whatever people lived here some 800 years after Din Lligwy flourished, is now a sad, roofless place (12C; upper walls rebuilt 14C) with a simple Norman-arched doorway, a crude hollow stone which was presumably a font, and a chapel with a crypt added during the 16C. Just S of these two sites, on the right beside the road, is *Lligwy Burial Chamber*, a monument preceding Din Lligwy by perhaps 2000 years and one, also, with a long continuity of use, excavation in 1908 revealing the remains of some 30 people thought to have been buried in both Stone and Bronze Age times. The huge capstone (18ft by 15ft by 3ft 6ins and weighing 28 tons) is, not surprisingly perhaps, supported by low uprights over a natural fissure, the greater part of the chamber thus being below ground.

Beyond the burial chamber, the road soon rejoins A5025 just SW along which, at *Llanallgo*, the church contains a memorial to the victims of the 'Royal Charter' (see above), buried in nine different churchyards. *Traeth Bychan*, the bay to the SE, was in 1939 the scene of another sea disaster when the submarine 'Thetis', on trials, failed to surface and 99 men lost their lives.

4m (from Rhos Lligwy) **Benllech**, a family resort with some 2m of sand. The poet Goronwy Owen was born in the parish. *Red Wharf Bay* (Traeth Coch) to the S has 3m of sand at low tide and Castell Mawr, on the N headland, is a hillfort which, on the evidence of coins found here, may have been occupied by the Romans.—*2m. Pentraeth* was on the coast until stranded inland by land reclamation. Here B5109 is taken eastward, in about 2½m passing *Llansadwrn*, where, set in the chancel wall, the church contains a memorial of 520, unusual for being both to a holy man (Beatus Saturninus, Blessed Sadwen) and also to his saintly wife.

6m. **Beaumaris** (2000 inhab.) is a small resort and important yachting centre, pleasantly situated on Menai Strait with a view across Lavan Sands (see Rte 1C) to the mainland mountains. The town's earlier history is that of its great castle, today a major tourist attraction. The growth of tourism during the 19C brought the construction of a pier, the founding of the yacht club (Beaumaris is the home of the Royal Anglesey), and the building of Victoria Terraces, designed by Joseph Hansom of Hansom cab fame. Bathing is poor (shingle). In summer there is a passenger ferry to Bangor and Menai Bridge.

The **Castle* (WHM. Tel: 0222-465511), now an extensive ruin, occupies an open site on level ground close to the shore. It is a concentric castle of almost perfect symmetry, encircled by a once tidal moat, and is particularly interesting for its sophisticated defences, which were, however, virtually never used. The outer curtain is superficially square, but since each of the four sides has a slight salient the form in practice is a flattened octagon, this allowing attack from any direction to be met. This outer wall is strengthened by towers. The more massive square inner defence is higher, permitting simultaneous firing from both outer and inner walls. The inner wall, also with towers, is noteworthy for its almost continuous internal passage. Another defensive trick is that the outer gateways are out of alignment with their gatehouses, this forcing an attacker to make an oblique approach.

History. Prince Madog had sacked Caernarfon in 1294, and it may have been this that prompted Edward I to start building Beaumaris, the last of his Welsh castles, the following year. At the same time the associated English Borough was granted its charter, taking the name Beau Marais (Beautiful Marsh) from an area soon to be drained by the castle moat system. The architect was James of St. George and, although the castle was never completed, it was declared to be in a state of defence by 1298. Architecturally, the inner part of the S gatehouse remained unfinished, the hall in the inner ward was scarcely started, and the towers were never properly roofed. In 1403 the castle was taken by Owen Glendower, but it was retaken in 1405. During the Civil War it was held (by a Bulkeley, the leading local family) for Charles I, but capitulated to General Mytton in 1646. At the Restoration Lord Bulkeley was reinstated as Constable, but the castle was abandoned in 1705. It nevertheless remained a Bulkeley possession until 1925 when it was made over to public ownership.

The moat, much wider than it is now, communicated with the sea by a short Dock; an iron ring to which boats were tied can still be seen. This dock was defended on its E side by a projecting wing known as Gunner's Walk, in a bastion of which was the castle mill, the sluice and spillway of which remain. A wooden bridge, replacing the former drawbridge, crosses the moat to the Outer Ward, which also had another gate at its NE, a triple doorway which was never completed and is little more than a postern. Note the out-of-alignment arrangement, referred to above, of the gates and their gatehouses. The outer rampart walk, including twelve towers, affords fine views. The Inner Ward is entered by the S gatehouse, guarded by a small rectangular barbican. The large gatehouses seem to have provided most of the living accommodation, that on the N containing on its first floor what was intended to be the hall. The basement of the NE tower may have served as a prison. The tower on the E face of the inner ward contains the beautiful Chapel, apsidal and vaulted and with a trefoiled arcade and doorway.

The *Bull's Head Hotel*, close to the castle, dates in part from 1472. During the Civil War it was commandeered by General Mytton, and later both Dr Johnson and Charles Dickens are said to have stayed here. The *Courthouse* (visited in association with Beaumaris Gaol), on the corner of Castle Street opposite the castle, was built in 1614. Also opposite the castle is the *Museum of Childhood* (Tel: 0248–712498), a treasure of toys and childhood nostalgia spread around nine rooms and spanning roughly the last 150 years.—Farther along Castle Street, Steeple Lane leads to *Beaumaris Gaol* (Tel: 0248–810921), built in 1829 to designs by Hansom and now a museum. Here can be seen the cells, including the punishment and condemned cells, a treadmill, and an exhibition of documents illustrating prison life in the 19C. The *Church of St. Mary* (restored) dates from the early 14C, the nave having curious window-tracery and circular clerestory windows enclosing quatrefoils. The choir was rebuilt in 1500, but some original glass fragments have been set in the S window. Among the monuments are the 16C altar-tomb of Sir Richard Bulkeley and his wife; a monumental stone to the father of Sir Philip Sidney; and, brought here from Llanfaes (see below), the carved stone coffin of Joan, wife of Llewelyn the Great and daughter of King John.

On rising ground NW of Beaumaris the *Bulkeley Monument* (1875) commemorates the family who were for generations Anglesey's leading landowners; their seat was *Baron's Hill*, between the monument and the town.

From Beaumaris this Route runs N to Penmon Priory (c *4m* by B5109 and then minor roads) before returning through Beaumaris to Menai Bridge.

Llanfaes, now a village, was until the 13C a commercial centre and port of some importance. In 1237 Llewelyn the Great founded a priory here over the tomb of his wife Joan; in 1295 Edward I removed all the inhabitants of Llanfaes to what is now Newborough and used the town's stonework as material for Beaumaris castle; and at the Dissolution the contents of the priory, including Joan's coffin, were removed to St. Mary's in Beaumaris.—*Castell Llieniog* (E of B5109, about 1m from Llanfaes) is a motte, perhaps erected by Hugh Lupus when he overran Anglesey in 1098, with fragments of a small square tower which withstood a Royalist siege in the Civil War. To the S is the site of a battle of 819 in which the invading Saxons under Egbert gained a short-lived victory over the Welsh.

Penmon Priory was founded by St. Seiriol in the 6C. The church was rebuilt between 1120–70, and in 1237 Llewelyn the Great granted the monastery and its property to the prior and canons of Priestholm (Puffin Island), who then apparently moved to Penmon, reorganising the community as Austin Canons. The church and domestic buildings are now separate, the former serving as parish church and the latter in the care of Welsh Historic Monuments.

The *Church of St. Seiriol*, successor to an earlier wooden church burnt by the Danes in 971, dates, as noted above, mainly from 1120–70, the nave being the oldest part (c 1140), while the choir, longer than the nave, is a rebuilding of c 1220–40. There is a fine Norman (c 1150) pillar piscina in the nave, used as a font until the present one (also in the nave), originally the base of a pre-Norman cross (S transept), was adapted during the 19C. Another cross, of c 1000 and with intricate though mutilated carving including a Temptation of St. Anthony, previously stood above the church on a hill to the north-west. The remains of St. Seiriol, originally on Puffin Island, were probably placed under the altar in this church.—The outside area immediately S of the choir represents the site of a small cloister, the W side of which was the prior's house, now much altered and privately occupied. The *Domestic Buildings*, on the S of this cloister and with a mounting block beside the road, are a once three-storey 13C wing containing the refectory on the ground floor, a cellar below and a dormitory above. In the refectory, near the SE corner, can be seen traces of the seat used by the monk who read aloud during meals.

The square *Dovecot* of c 1600, with a domed roof and open cupola and containing around 1000 nests, was probably built by Sir Richard Bulkeley of Baron's Hill. From across the road from the dovecot, a path leads to *St. Seiriol's Well*, probably at the site of the 6C priory. The upper part of the small building covering the well seems to be 18C, but the much older lower part may well incorporate something of the original chapel, while the adjacent foundations of an oval hut could well be those of the saint's cell.

A small road (fee for cars) continues for rather less than a mile to the headland of *Trwyn Du*, this road providing interesting continuity with the past for it is still used by the same quarries from which James of St. George extracted the stone for Beaumaris and which, centuries later, provided footings and piers for Telford's and Stephenson's Menai bridges. Trwyn Du is a modest enough headland—with some cottages, a disused lifeboat station, an automatic light-house of 1837 and a mournful bell—but it provides a good view across to *Puffin Island*, once known as Priestholm and today also called Ynys Seiriol after the saint who established his settlement here in the 6C. The once large puffin population declined seriously when in the early 19C the pickled young birds were a popular delicacy. On the island there are fragments of monastic settlement.

Small roads W from Penmon lead in 3m to *Bedd Arthur* (500ft), a bluff with a rampart enclosing traces of hut circles.

This Route returns from Penmon to (*4m*) Beaumaris, from where A545 skirts the wooded shore for 7m for Menai Bridge, see Rte 11A.

12 The Lleyn

The **LLEYN** (the Peninsula), some 25m long and from 5 to 10m broad and dropping SW towards the Irish Sea, provides the southern arm for Caernarfon Bay and the northern for Cardigan Bay. Scenically this is mainly mixed agricultural and wooded country, broken by groups of hills or mountains, those in the SW affording some sweeping coastal views. The highest ground is towards the NE where Yr Eifl lifts dramatically to 1850ft. Along the Cardigan Bay coast there are popular resorts such as Abersoch, Pwllheli and Criccieth, but elsewhere, and particularly inland, the Lleyn is generally quiet, with something of a character of its own and a stronghold of the Welsh language. Among places of specific interest are, along the N coast, the church at Clynnog Fawr and, for those willing to climb, the Iron Age hillfort-village of Tr'er Ceiri; Bardsey Island off the peninsula's tip; and, along the Cardigan Bay coast, the medieval hall house of Penarth Fawr, Llanystumdwy and its associations with Lloyd George, and the native Welsh castle at Criccieth.— During the Dark Ages and throughout the medieval centuries, all roads through the Lleyn were trodden by the pilgrims making their way to Bardsey, some 20,000, if tradition is to be believed, dying on the island.

The Lleyn is described below as an anticlockwise circuit from Caernarfon.

> A487 to Glanrhyd (Llanwnda). A499 to Llanaelhaearn. B4417 and B4413 to Aberdaron. Unclassified to Abersoch. A499 to Pwllheli. A497 to Criccieth. B4411 and A487 to Caernarfon. Total distance 74m.—3m. Glanrhyd (Llanwnda).—7m. **Clynnog Fawr.**—4m. **Llanaelhaearn** (Tre'r Ceiri).—6m. **Nefyn.**—13m. **Aberdaron.**—9m. **Abersoch.**—7m. **Pwllheli.**—7m. **Llanystumdwy.**—2m. **Criccieth.**— 13m. Glanrhyd (Llanwnda).—3m. **Caernarfon.**

For **Caernarfon**, see Rte 10.—3m. Glanrhyd is a road fork at which this Route bears right on A499. The other road (A487) is described as the return leg of this Route.—2m. Llandwrog is just W of A499.

From here a diversion can be made N to Belan, the road W out of Llandwrog soon reaching the shore at Dinas Dinlle, an isolated grass hill the top of which is formed into a roughly oval fort by two ramparts and a ditch. Probably used by both British and Romans, the fort is also interesting for featuring, together with the islets of Arianrhod and Maen Dylan to the S, in legend, this being the place where the heroic youth Lleu Llaw Gyffer, destined to become Lord of Gwynedd, 'was reared till he could ride every horse, and till he was perfected in feature, growth and stature'. Beyond, the road follows the shore through an area of shoddy building and across alluvial flats, passing Caernarfon Airport (picnic area; Snowdonia flights; museum. Tel: 0286–830800), to reach Fort Belan (no adm.) on the promontory which, with Abermenai to the N, forms the narrow entrance to Menai Strait. The fort was built by Thomas Wynne (of Glynllifon, SE of Llandwrog), 1st Baron Newborough, in 1775 as a garrison for his Royal Caernarvonshire Grenadiers, a force of 400 men raised and equipped at his own expense; a patriotic gesture which, by the time of his death in 1807, had cost him a quarter of his fortune.

5m. **Clynnog Fawr**, a typical Lleyn village, in which the Church of St. Beuno is of outstanding interest. Founded by Beuno in c 616, and soon one of the first and most important stages along the pilgrimage path to Bardsey, the church seems at first to have been monastic, but by 1291 it had become collegiate, remaining such until the Dissolution. The present building dates from the early 16C, interesting external features being the N porch with its outside stair and, at the SW angle of the chapel, a stone sundial of Anglo-Saxon type. Noteworthy inside are, in the choir, the contemporary stalls and the book-desks with linen-pattern panelling; a rather plain rood screen of 1531, with the base of its former loft curiously prolonged into the S transept, where it is entered by a door communicating with a turret stair; dog tongs of 1815 and a dugout chest known as St. Beuno's Chest. From the tower, a 17C passage (long used as the village lock-up) leads to St. Beuno's Chapel, which sheltered the tomb or shrine of the saint, destroyed by fire in 1856 but until then worshipped as miraculous. Restored in 1913, this chapel is of later date than the church, but the line of the foundations of an earlier building discovered during the restoration is marked by grey floor-slabs. The stone with a cross is traditionally the original stone set up on the ground given to Beuno by Gwyddaint, Prince of Gwynedd, but seems more likely to have been a medieval boundary marker or perhaps a pilgrim prayer-stone. *St. Beuno's Well*, beside the road on the left just S of the village, was a healing spring (Pennant described seeing a paralytic treated here). There are stone benches, steps down to the water, and niches probably intended for clothes.

Soon the road begins to leave the coast, ascending gradually, with the steep slopes of Gurn Goch (1607ft) and Gurn Ddu (1712ft) to the E and a view seaward across to Holyhead.—*4m*. **Llanaelhaearn**, a village at the foot of Yr Eifl, has a church entirely furnished with box-pews, and an ancient stone in the N transept inscribed 'Aliortus Elmatiacos hic jacet'. From the village, A499 cuts across S to Pwllheli while this Route follows B4417 along the S slopes of *Yr Eifl* (The Forks; 1849ft), so called because of the triple peaks. The central peak, Yr Eifl proper, is flanked on the NW by a precipitous and much quarried summit (1458ft) falling to the sea. To the SW below this, *Nant Gwrtheyrn* is also known as Vortigern's Valley, one of a number claiming to be the final refuge sought by that ill-starred royal bungler. Not that he had much luck here, for, legend relates, his palace was destroyed by fire cast from the sky while its owner drowned when, as a result, forced to leap into a wild sea.

Just S of Llanaelhaearn (³/₄m) a path off B4417 climbs what seems a long mile to the hillfort-village of *Tre'r Ceiri* (1591ft). Dating from the 2C, but perhaps earlier, this well-preserved site covers some five acres, enclosed by a rampart with an internal parapet. Inside there are the remains of some 50 huts of varying shape, size and, probably, period, while the enclosures to be seen outside the rampart were probably for cattle. The cairn, on the summit to the NW, is Bronze Age in origin.

2m. *Llithfaen*, whence a small road heads N for Nant Gwrtheyrn, see above. The quarrying village in the valley, deserted in 1954, has been acquired by a trust for use as a centre for Welsh language studies.—*4m*. **Nefyn** (2000 inhab.), on the cliff, and *Morfa Nefyn* 1m W, with the adjacent sandy bays of *Porth Nefyn* and *Port Dinllaen*, together form a quiet summer resort area. Porth Dinllaen, a fine natural harbour, might have become the port for the packets to Ireland, but in 1839, as the result of a single vote in the House of Commons, the choice fell on Holyhead. In Nefyn there is a *Maritime Museum* (Tel: 0758–720308) in Old St. Mary's Church, Church Street, at the centre of the village, recalling the busy seafaring days of the 19C.—*5m*. *Tudweiliog*, rather over 1m beyond which a road (signed Sarn) bears SE and passes, on the right in about 500 yards, a sizeable burial chamber.

8m. **Aberdaron** (1000 inhab.), 2m short of the tip of the Lleyn and today a quaint holiday and fishing village, was long a gathering place for pilgrims on their way to Bardsey, an era recalled by a 14C building which, as a café and souvenir shop, today still caters for travellers, if perhaps of a less single-mindedly pious breed. The church, the yard wall of which is washed by the sea at high tide, consists of a 12C nave and choir, and a wide S aisle added in the early 16C. Gruffydd ap Rhys is said to have sought sanctuary here when the Normans swept into southern Wales.

Aberdaron's perhaps best-known native is Richard Roberts Jones (1780–1843), a son of a local carpenter. Known as Dic Aberdaron, he was a strange vagabond and natural self-educated linguist, said to have spoken 35 languages and renowned for having compiled a dictionary in Welsh, Greek and Hebrew; it can be seen at St. Asaph cathedral where its author is buried.

Roads run SW to within a short distance of *Braich-y-Pwll* and *Pen-y-Cil*, the two extremities of the Lleyn and both belonging to the National Trust. The former was the spot from which pilgrims once embarked for Bardsey, a holy well (the pwll) and the ruins of a chapel today recalling how piously active this place must once have been.

Bardsey Island (no regular access), 450 acres rising to 500ft, is 2m off the tip of the Lleyn. The name is of Norse origin, and the Welsh name Ynys Enlii, meaning Island of the Currents, reminds that the narrow strait is treacherous. Known also as the Island of 20,000 Saints, Bardsey was an important pilgrimage objective from the 5 or 6C onwards, three pilgrimages here being reckoned as the equivalent of one to Rome. St. Cadfan, from Britanny, is said to have founded the first monastery here in 429; in c 545 St. Dyfrig is thought to have died and been buried here, though Llandaff cathedral also claims his relics; and after the destruction in 607 by Ethelfrid of Northumbria of the great monastery of Bangor-is-y-Coed, the surviving monks may have found refuge here. In the N part of the island are the 13C remains of the Augustinian St. Mary's Abbey, in the churchyard of which lie some of the 20,000 'saints' reputedly buried on the island. Owned since 1979 by Bardsey Island Trust, the emphasis today is on nature, the island being an official Site of Special Scientific Interest and the home of a Bird and Field Observatory. Limited self-catering accommodation (Trust Officer, Stabal Hen, Tyddyn Du, Criccieth, LL52 0LY. Tel: 0766–522239).

From Aberdaron an unclassified road is taken E, this in *3m* reaching *Y Rhiw*, a hamlet on a miniature pass commanding a wide view, including the great four-mile-long sweep of Porth Neigwl, or Hell's Mouth, both arms of which are in large part protected as National Trust properties. From here the road drops steeply, at the foot of the hill being *Plas-yn-Rhiw* (NT. Tel: 075888–219), a small, part medieval, part Tudor and part Georgian manor house with beautiful gardens and woodland.—*5m. Llangian*, where in the churchyard (roughly in line with the S centre window of the church) there is a particularly interesting 5C stone, inscribed Meli Medici/Fili Martini/ Jacit/ (Here lies Melus the doctor, son of Martinus), the earliest mention of a doctor in Wales.

1m. **Abersoch** is a still small but growing resort at the end of the coastal road from the north east. Attractively situated with its harbour at the mouth of the river Soch, with two large and sandy beaches, and important also as a yachting centre, the town can become overcrowded in summer. Boat excursions to the *St. Tudwal's Islands* (2m SE), on the northern of which are the chapel remains of a small medieval priory. At *Llanengan*, 1½m SW of Abersoch, there is a 15C church (but tracing its origin to a foundation of the 6C), with two naves, each crossed by a rood screen, one of which has an elaborately carved loft. Noteworthy also are the builder's 'credit' on the crossbeam of the vaulting of the S nave; the tower, with bells from Bardsey; the old return-stalls, the 17C altar rails, and a dugout chest. South of Llanengan, a road continues for 2m into the headland of *Mynydd Cilan* with good coastal scenery.

3m. Llanbedrog is a modest resort sheltering below the bold promontory of Mynydd Tir-y-Cwmwd (434ft), paths across which offer views of St. Tudwal's Islands.

Just before Pwllheli, A497 bears NW, in 2m passing *Bodvel Hall*, the birthplace of Dr Johnson's friend Mrs Thrale. At *Bodfuan*, 1m beyond, the church of 1894 claims descent from a shrine founded in 595 by St. Buan, to whom a cross has been erected.

4m. **Pwllheli**, pronounced Pool-thelli and meaning Salt Water Pool (400 inhab. *Inf.* Tel: 075881–3000), today, as a popular and crowded resort, gives no hint that it received its first charter as long ago as 1355. The main town lies along A497, about ½m back from the long sand and shingle beach area with a promenade opened in 1890. At its E end this seafront ends at a narrow hook of land forming one of the protecting arms of the almost landlocked harbour.

In 3m a minor road branches N for **Penarth Fawr** (WHM. Tel: 0222–465511), a 15C hall-house; the single room which served as the home of a family of some substance, probably numerous and with their several servants also all under the same roof. But properly to picture those late medieval days the imagination must place a tall screen along the open passage below the platform, with the lord and his family living on one side, the servants on the other; and those elegant windows and fireplaces installed in the 17C must in imagination be replaced by slits and an open hearth.—From Penarth Fawr, anyone with a feel for holy wells will continue N for 2m to *Llangybi*, a name recalling that Anglesey saint who founded his Christian church within the walls of the Roman fort at Holyhead. Here at Llangybi, Fynnon Gybi (300 yards from the church; path) is a holy well sheltered within a building generally accepted as being at least in part early Christian in origin; the beehive vaulting here is thought to be unique in Wales, though found in Ireland. The well is adjacent to another roofless building, which, although it does not look all that different, is in fact an 18C cottage.

Continuing E, A497 in *4m* reaches **Llanystumdwy**, noted as the home of Earl Lloyd George of Dwyfor (1863–1945). A Heritage Trail includes Highgate, his uncle's cottage in which he spent his early years (furnished now in 1860s' style); his riverside grave; and a museum (Tel: 0766–522071), originally a building designed by Clough Williams-Ellis to house gifts from foreign leaders but in 1990, centenary of the statesman's first election to parliament, greatly enlarged and now showing documents, photographs, a Victorian schoolroom and a range of historic and domestic memorabilia. *Gwynfryn*, ¾m NW, is the house to which Shelley moved in 1813 after the curious incident at Tremadog.

2m. **Criccieth** (1500 inhab. *Inf.*), a family resort near the corner of Cardigan Bay, here Tremadog Bay, enjoys a particularly fine outlook down the Lleyn, NE towards Snowdonia, and across the water to Harlech and the mountains behind. The *Castle* (WHM. Tel: 0222–465511), perched on a rocky green hill above the town, is interesting for being a native Welsh stronghold built in c 1230, strengthened by Edward I in 1284, and Welsh again in 1404 when taken by Owen Glendower. The ruins consist mainly of a curtain enclosing the small rectangular inner ward (the oldest part of the castle) and the bold N gatehouse flanked by towers. The large outer ward, of which less remains, dates from c 1260. The Leyburn Tower (W) was probably the home of the constable, while the Engine Tower (N) was the launching site (from an upper floor, now disappeared) of missiles.

B4411 N out of Criccieth in *4m* joins A487, a short way SE down which is *Dolbenmaen* with, opposite the church, a large motte, probably the 11C or earlier seat of the local rulers before they built their castle at Criccieth. A487 followed N in *6m* reaches *Pen-y-Groes*, until the beginning of the present century the centre for the slate and copper mines the forlorn traces of which litter the hills to the east. However, slate working survives at the *Inigo Jones Slate Works* (Tel: 0286–830242) where the old skills can still be watched.—*3m. Glanrhyd*, where this circuit of the Lleyn is completed.—*3m.* **Caernarfon**.

13 Chirk to Llangollen, Corwen and Betws-y-Coed

A5. Total distance 37m.—6m. **Llangollen.**—10m. **Corwen.**—9m.
Cerrigydrudion.—5m. **Pentrefoelas.**—7m. **Betws-y-Coed.**

Mainly undulating agricultural country and moor, with occasional
distant views of mountains.

Chirk, a pleasant small place on the English border, traces its origins
to a castle built here in the 11C, of which all that remains is a small
motte near the mainly 15C church. Beyond the S edge of the town
and well seen from the A5, two adjacent viaducts impressively span
the Ceiriog valley some 30ft below, one (1848) carrying the railway,
while the other, Telford's aqueduct of 1801, carries the Shropshire
Union Canal. (For a view from level or above, see Vale of Ceiriog
below).

The ironwork gates, made in 1719, of Chirk Castle

*Chirk Castle (NT. Tel: 0691–777701), 2m W of the town, stands
massively and splendidly within a large park entered (from the E)
through ironwork gates of 1719 which are an outstanding example of
the work of the Davies brothers. Originally these gates stood in front
of the castle, a complete and still inhabited pile, possibly designed by
James of St. George in c 1290–95 and completed in c 1310 by Roger
de Mortimer, on whom the land had been conferred by Edward I.
The estate was bought in 1595 by Sir Thomas Myddelton, Lord
Mayor of London and brother of the engineer, Sir Hugh. Originally

square, the castle early lost its southern wall and is now rectangular in plan with a round bastion at each corner and a half-bastion at the centre of each face. The interiors have been frequently rebuilt and today's visitor sees decorative styles ranging from the 16 to the mid 19C. The park has a lake, N of the castle, near which a stretch of *Offa's Dyke* is clearly seen.

VALE OF CEIRIOG (B4500. 6m from Chirk to Glyn Ceiriog). Leaving Chirk the road offers a good view from above of the viaducts mentioned above, then ascends the Vale of Ceiriog cutting W into the *Berwyns*, a beautiful district of wooded hills reaching westward towards Bala and offering, to anyone not averse to steep and narrow lanes, unexpected tree-clad and pastoral glimpses and vistas. At **Glyn Ceiriog**, where B4500 turns S, the *Chwarel Wynne Slate Mine and Museum* (Tel: 069172–343) tells the story of the slate industry by means of a video film and also a tour of the underground workings, and also offers a nature trail. The local (Dyffryn Ceiriog) Male Voice Choir welcomes visitors to rehearsals (Tel: 0691–772627).—From Glyn Ceiriog small roads wander southward through the eastern Berwyns to join Rte 19C in some 10m at Llanrhaeadr-ym-Mochnant, while steep and narrow lanes provide a scenic approach to Llangollen.

A5 runs N out of Chirk in 1½m crossing the Shropshire Union Canal. Visitors to Chirk Castle aiming for Llangollen may leave the park by the N exit and then follow a minor road to join A5 by the canal crossing.

Just beyond the canal crossing, A483 leads off N for **Ruabon** (5000 inhab.), a largely industrial place but with a church (said to have been founded by St. Mabon in the 6C) in which are some restored 14C murals and also monuments by Nollekens and Rysbrack to members of the Williams-Wynne family, whose seat was at *Wynnstay* (rebuilt after a fire in 1858; no adm.) immediately south-east. This name is a substitution for the earlier Wattstay deriving from Wat's Dyke which runs through the park. From Ruabon, Llangollen can be reached by A539 along the N side of the Dee (Vale of Llangollen).

3m (from Chirk, along A5) *Froncysyllte* where a side road N drops down to the Dee far below Telford's *Pontcysyllte Aqueduct* (1795–1805), which, 1007ft long and supported by 18 piers, carries the Shropshire Union Canal across the valley at a height of 121ft. There are boat excursions from Llangollen (Groups. Tel: 0978–823215) and the footpath is a section of the Offa's Dyke Path.

3m. **Llangollen** (2500 inhab. *Inf.* Town Hall. Tel: 0978–860828), in summer crowded and often a traffic bottleneck, lies mainly on the S bank of the Dee, here flowing below wooded hills on one of which, to the N, is perched the conspicuous Castell Dinas Bran.

Llangollen is the home of the annual (July) *International Music Eisteddfod*, first held in 1947 and now each year attracting around 150,000 visitors from all over the world. The competitions include events for choirs, soloists, folk singing, dancing and suchlike. For further information: Secretary, International Eisteddfod Office, Llangollen, LL20 8NG. Tel: 0978–860236.

Although a modest enough town, Llangollen, with its environs, is surprisingly rich in the number and variety of its places of interest. SOUTH OF THE RIVER. A5 crosses the town as, successively, Queen Street, Regent Street, and Berwyn Street. Butler Hill, S off Queen Street, leads to *Plas Newydd* (Tel: 0978–860234), a picturesque half-

timbered house which was the home from 1780 of Lady Eleanor
Butler (died (1829) and the Hon. Sarah Ponsonby (died 1831), better
known as the 'Ladies of Langollen'.

The two 'Ladies of Langollen' were eccentric Irishwomen, who left their homes
secretly in order to devote their lives to 'friendship, celibacy, and the knitting of
blue stockings'. They became famous for their peculiarities of dress, their
beneficence, and their collection of old oak and curios, to which it became
recognised practice that their many visitors should contribute. Wellington, De
Quincey (as a boy), Walter Scott (who made the house a scene in 'The
Betrothed'), and Wordsworth were among such visitors; Wordsworth's somewhat tactless sonnet, with its description of the house as a 'low browed cot' and
its oblique reference to the ladies' age, is said to have given offence. A third
member of this distinctly odd household was Mary Carryl, the ladies' maidser-
vant, who somehow managed to buy the freehold of Plas Newydd with her
savings, leaving it to her employers on her death in 1809.

Sadly, the greater part of the collection was dispersed in 1832, but
some memorabilia survive and the house in any case merits a visit for
its carved panelling, stained glass and Spanish leatherwork gifted by
the Duke of Wellington.

Church Street, opposite Butler Hill, leads to the Church of St.
Collen, dedicated to a 6C saint whose cell survived here until 1747
when it was demolished, its stones being incorporated in the construction of the tower. Important in its own right during the 12C, the
church was made subordinate to Valle Crucis (see below) early the
following century. Inside the church the main features of interest are
a 14C tomb-niche and the 15C hammer-beam roofs, while in the
churchyard there is a monument erected by the Ladies of Llangollen
to their faithful servant Mary Carryl, this also later serving to mark
their own burial place.

Castle Street descends N from the point where Regent Street
becomes Berwyn Street, passing on the left the European Centre for
Traditional and Regional Cultures (Tel: 0978–861514), a research
centre ofering a programme of exhibitions, a wide choice of courses
and a library noted especially for its important collection of works on
the Arthurian legends. Beyond, Castle Street continues past the
Town Hall (Tourist Information) to reach Llangollen Bridge, dating in
part (E side) to the bridge built in 1347 by John Trevor, who later
came Bishop of St. Asaph. Rebuilt in Tudor times, the bridge has in
turn been widened for 18C coaches and strengthened for modern
traffic.

NORTH OF THE RIVER. There are two places of interest (Llangollen
Railway and the Canal Museum and Centre) immediately N of the
bridge; other places (including Castell Dinas Bran and Valle Crucis
Abbey) are up to 2m farther.

Llangollen Station is now the home of the Llangollen Railway
Society which since 1975 has enthusiastically brought back to life the
station and some of the track of the Ruabon to Barmouth line which
operated from 1865 to 1968. The station, with a collection of steam
engines, coaches and much else, is a museum in itself, and steam and
diesel trains now run along the Dee valley as far as (2m) Berwyn,
with a planned extension to Glyndyfrdwy and Carrog (Tel: 0978–
860951 with an answering service). The Canal Museum (Tel: 0978–
860702), just above the station in an early 19C warehouse on the
Shropshire Union Canal, tells the technical, commercial and social
story of the great days of Britain's canals. And a taste of this past can
be experienced by taking a horse-drawn boat trip of some 45

minutes westward to the Pentrefelin Basin and back (Tel: 0978–860702).

The ruin of *Castell Dinas Bran* (1000ft), conspicuous to the N above Llangollen, can be reached by a waymarked route from near the Canal Museum. An Iron Age hillfort, and, later, a Welsh and for a brief period Norman wooden castle probably preceded the stone castle which seems to have been built in about 1236 and which, apparently little used, is known to have already been a ruin by 1578. In legend, though, this was the home of the lovely Myfanwy Fechan who spurned the love of the poet Hywel ap Einion and drove him to write a love poem, set to music in the 19C by Joseph Parry and now in the repertoire of many male voice choirs. The climb is rewarded more by the views than by the ruin, which consists chiefly of the wall surrounding the hilltop, together with the entrance passage, flanked by towers, at the NE angle. Much of the stone came from the ditch hacked out of the rock on the E and south.

A542, followed W and N, passes the International Eisteddfod Ground on the right and reaches Pentrefelin, with the *Llangollen Motor Museum* (Tel: 0978–860324) showing mainly pre-war vehicles and motor trade memorabilia. From here B5103 continues beside the river for ¹/₂m to Telford's *Horseshoe Weir* and to *Llantysilio Church* (for both of which see below), while A542 leaves the river and heads N, quickly reaching the ruins of Valle Crucis Abbey.

*_Valle Crucis Abbey_ (WHM. Tel: 0222-465511) was a Cistercian house founded in 1201 by Madog ap Gruffydd, an ambivalent prince of Powys who tended to side alternately with his own people and the English. A serious fire later in the same century led to major alterations, and the tower collapsed in 1400. The abbey was dissolved in 1535, but, despite centuries of neglect, the surviving ruins are quite extensive and include both the church and some of the domestic buildings.

The Church adheres to the common early Cistercian plan of aisled nave, transepts with E chapels, and short aisleless choir; the N transept has been walled off from the crossing. In the walls of the N aisle can be seen the original masonry, heightened by small flat stones added after the fire. The W front is a beautiful composition (c 1250–75), with three fine plate-tracery windows enclosed in a common frame, and with a delicate rose-window in the gable. The E end (c 1240) is notable for the manner in which its external pilaster buttresses split above the bottom row of lancets so as to embrace an upper pair. To be noted in the church are the remains of the pulpit (including the stairway) under the vanished W arch of the crossing; the base of the altar; the curious recess, with remains of a shafted screen, on the N side of the choir; the bases of altars in the two chapels on the E side of the S transept; and the arch (at the end of the S transept) by which the dormitory was entered from the now vanished night-stairs. The piers of the crossing were heavily buttressed after the tower fell in 1400. In front of the choir there are six mutilated tombs, said to include those of Myfanwy Fechan, the legendary beauty of Castell Dinas Bran, and Iolo Goch, the bard of Owen Glendower.

Domestic Buildings. The S transept is adjoined by the Sacristy, to the S of which is the vaulted *Chapter House (rebuilt c 1315–50), in three parallel aisles. In the central one of these is the door from the Cloister, S of which is the day-stair (blocked) to the dormitory, while to the N the curious little vaulted space may have been for books. The passage immediately S of the chapter house led perhaps to the

The ruins of thirteenth-century Valle Crucis Abbey

infirmary. To the S of the Dormitory, which occupies the whole length of the upper floor, is the Reredorter, while the NE corner of the dormitory was apparently the Abbot's Lodging. The S and W cloister ranges are no more than foundations.

Eliseg's Pillar, ¼m N of the abbey, a tall broken shaft 8ft high, stands atop what may well be a burial mound. The pillar's interest lies in its Latin inscription, originally of 31 lines but now so badly weathered that parts only of 15 remain. Luckily a scholar of 1696 made a record, so it is known that the cross was erected early in the 9C by Cyngen (Concenn), who died in c 854 on a pilgrimage to Rome, in memory of his great-grandfather, Eliseg, who annexed Powys from the English. It may be that the mound marks Eliseg's grave, and it may also be that it is from this cross that this valley and the abbey take their names.

To the E of the valley rises the range of *Eglwyseg Mountain*, at the S end being the ridge of the Eglwyseg Rocks, a series of terraced limestone cliffs of rounded promontories with gullies between. Offa's Dyke Path runs much of the length of the mountain, as does also a small road from Pentrefelin to World's End. The ridge is well seen from *Horseshoe Pass* on A542 beyond Valle Crucis, this road continuing N to join Rte 14.

This Route now continues westward from Llangollen along A5. Visitors to Valle Crucis may return to Pentrefelin, there taking B5103 to join A5.

2m (from Llangollen) *King's Bridge (Berwyn)* crosses a delightful stretch of the Dee, above Chain Bridge, the earlier crossing here, restored 1929. Just across King's Bridge are Telford's *Horseshoe Weir*, built in 1806 to supply water to the Llangollen branch of the Shropshire Union Canal, and Norman *Llantysilio Church*. Robert Browning worshipped here in 1886, a fact recorded by a brass on the S wall placed here by Lady Martin (Helena Faucit, the actress; died 1898), herself commemorated in a more modern chapel N of the choir. Sir Theodore (died 1909) and Lady Martin lived at the adjacent house.—The road runs between two high areas of moorland, the Berwyns being to the S and Llantysilio Mountains to the N, in *4m* reaching *Glyndyfrdwy*, once an estate owned by Owen Glendower and the place from which he derived his name. A mound, 1½ W between the road and the river, was almost certainly the site of his fortified manor. *Carrog*, just beyond across the river, is reached by a fine stone bridge of 1660.

4m. **Corwen** (2200 inhab.), a small market town below a steep wooded hill, has its place in history as Owen Glendower's headquarters, where he gathered his forces before the battle of Shrewsbury. The Church (part 13C, restored) contains in the choir a curious raised monumental slab (14C) to a former vicar, and a Norman font. On the outer lintel of the priest's door (S choir) is an incised dagger, known as Glendower's Sword and supposed to mark the point of impact of a weapon thrown by Glendower from the hill above in a moment of anger with the townsfolk. In fact it dates from the 7–9C. There is another dagger-mark on a 12C cross outside the SW corner of the church. Across the river, the hill of *Caer Drewyn* (½m walk from swimming pool), with a stone rampart ½m in circumference, probably dates to the immediate post-Roman period.

For Corwen to *Rhyl*, see Rte 5; to (N) *Wrexham* and *Chester*, and (S) *Bala*, *Dolgellau* and *Barmouth*, see Rte 14.

Beyond Corwen, A5 crosses the Dee, and within the next 2m the junctions with the above Routes 5 and 14 are passed. The valley of the Alwen is followed to (*4m*) *Maerdy*, where A5 enters that of the Ceirw. About 1m beyond Maerdy, on the S (sign to Cwmain), a small road crosses a picturesquely set single-arch bridge 50ft above the broken course of the river.—*5m* **Cerrigydrudion** is a village on a loop off the main road. The name, often wrongly written as 'druidion', means Place of the Brave and has no connection with Druids. Here B4501 leads N for (4m) Llyn Brenig (see Rte 4). *Caer Caradog*, 1m E of Cerrigydrudion, is a hillfort where the British chief Caractacus (Caradog) is said to have been betrayed to the Romans by Cartismandua, Queen of the Brigantes, after his final defeat by Scapula in 51. For the next 5m the road crosses rather dull moorland, relieved however by distant views of Snowdonia. A mile farther on Snowdon itself comes into view. *Glasfryn* is just before the summit level (908ft).—*5m*. **Pentrefoelas**. The Levelinus Stone, now in the National Museum of Wales and replaced by a replica, stood just N near the farm of Hen Voelas. It may have marked the grave of Llewelyn ap Sysyllt, slain in 1021. Several roads converge near the village.

Rte 4 (A543) from *Denbigh* joins here.

The road leading NW (B5113) reaches *Llanrwst* in 8m, crossing a high point of 1056ft and commanding exceptional views.

One mile W of Pentrefoelas, B4407 bears S, ascending the narrow valley of the Upper Conwy and in 2m reaching the secluded village of *Yspytty Ifan*, which once belonged (yspytty = hospitium) to the Knights Hospitaller of St John. In the church (rebuilt 1858) there are recumbent effigies (15–16C) of the Rhys family, one of these being of Rhys ap Meredydd who carried Henry Tudor's Red Dragon standard at Bosworth. The road continues SW, following the Conwy almost to its source in *Llyn Conwy*, about 4m beyond Yspytty Ifan and ½m N of the road. Until the Dissolution this upper valley was officially sanctuary and, despite the presence of the Hospitallers, notorious for its lawlessness. Beyond, traversing open moor, the road joins Rte 15 at *Pont-ar-Afon Gam*.

A5 soon crosses the river, following it down a deepening wooded glen and soon passing a small road which ascends NW to reach (1½m) *Capel Garmon Burial Chamber* (c 1500 BC), the remains of a long barrow with three chambers, one with its capstone still in position. The stone base which surrounded the mound can be seen, with the long entrance passage.—In rather over another mile A5 reaches a road junction (B4406) above Conwy and Machno Falls (paths) by the confluence of these rivers in the steep, wooded valley below.

B4406, running SW above the tight wooded valley of the Machno, soon reaches *Penmachno Woollen Mill* (Tel: 06902–545). Here, in a lovely setting, a small road bridge crosses the river just above a packhorse bridge, the road beyond descending through woods above the left banks of the Machno and Conwy (not visible from the road) to join the Betws-y-Coed to Ffestiniog road (Rte 6C). B4406 soon reaches *Penmachno*, where the church houses a *Collection of Early Christian Stones, one of the most important in Wales. One stone is inscribed with the sacred Chi-Rho (Christos) monogram; a second commemorates 'a citizen of Venedos' (an ancient name for Gwynedd), cousin of Maglos the Magistrate; and a third states that it was erected during the time of the Roman consul Justinius. Inscribed in Latin and dating from the 5–6C, the stones suggest that some form of Roman administration was surviving here even at this late date. For *Ty Mawr*, which can be approached from Penmachno, see Rte 6C. Beyond Penmachno B4406 rounds the W side of Llyn Conwy to meet Rte 15 at *Pont-yr-Afon-Gam* (8m from A5).

7m (from Pentrefoelas) **Betws-y-Coed**, see Rte 6C.

14 Chester to Bala, Dolgellau and Barmouth

A483 to Wrexham. A525 and A5104 to Corwen. B4401 to Bala. A494 to Dolgellau. A496 to Barmouth. Total distance 68m.—*9m*. **Gresford**.—*3m*. **Wrexham**.—*5m*. **Bwlchgwyn**.—*5m*. **Llandegla**.—*9m*. **Corwen**. *12m*. **Bala**.—*5m*. **Llanuwchllyn**.—*12m*. **Dolgellau**.—*4m*. **Bont-ddu**.—*4m*. **Barmouth**.

Pleasant if unexciting scenery as far as Bala, after which there is higher moor and mountain on both sides. From Dolgellau to Barmouth the road fringes the wooded Mawddach estuary. Views of Cader Idris (2927ft).

Chester (see 'Blue Guide England') is left by Grosvenor Bridge.—*6m*. **Pulford**, just beyond which the border is crossed into Wales.—*3m*.

Gresford has a modest place in literature through figuring in 'The Angler' in Washington Irving's 'Sketch-Book'. Gresford colliery, closed in 1973, was the scene of a disaster in 1934 when 266 miners were killed in an explosion; the winding-wheel forms part of a memorial.—*3m.* **Wrexham** (see Rte 4), which may be bypassed.

5m. **Bwlchgwyn** is the home of the *Geological and Folk Museum of North Wales* (Tel: 0978–757573), providing a good geological background to the varied countryside of northern Wales, this complemented by folk material illustrating man's developing role in the area. There are indoor and outdoor sections, the former including a reconstruction of a Welsh kitchen of about 1900, while outdoors massive geological specimens contrast with industrial relics such as pit-head winding gear, a stone crusher, kilns and suchlike. A disused silica quarry now provides a mixed geology and flora trail.—From (*5m*) the village of *Llandegla*, where there is a holy well once famed for curing epilepsy, this Route chooses A5104 which traverses a district once known as the Hundred of Ial (Yale), in 2¹/₂m reaching *Plas-yn-Yale*, former home of the Yale family and birthplace of Elihu's father, and, a short way beyond, *Bryngeglwys* where the church has relics of the family—*9m* (from Llandegla) Junction with Rte 5 (A494) from Ruthin and, just beyond, with Rte 13 (A5) from *Corwen*, which is ¹/₂m east.

Here there is a choice of roads onward to Bala, A494 being the main approach (10m), though this Route takes B4401 out of Corwen, an approach some 2m longer and slower but more attractive along the fertile Vale of Edeyrnion below the NW slopes of the Berwyns.— *4m. Llandrillo* is a starting point for walks into the hills, Craig Berwyn (over 2100ft) being 4m south-east.—The fine mass of Arenig Fawr comes into view ahead before the river Dee is crossed to (*4m*) *Llandderfel* where the 15C church has a contemporary rood screen and one parapet of its loft, and also two curious wooden relics, a headless animal and a piece of a pole. Known as St. Derfel's Horse and St. Derfel's Staff, these are said to be all that is left of an equestrian figure of the saint the rest of which was taken to London to form part of the fire in which Friar Forest, Catherine of Aragon's confessor, was martyred in 1538.

4m. **Bala** (2000 inhab. *Inf.* High Street. Tel: 0678–520367), set back from the N end of Bala Lake, is a pleasant local and holiday centre fortunate in having an attractive tree-lined main street (High Street, A494) broad and straight enough to ease the flow of through traffic.

History. The town's name derives from the Welsh 'bala', meaning 'outlet', because the Dee here flows out of Bala Lake. The motte in the town, as also the smaller one at the NE corner of the lake, is probably Norman, though some opinion suggests that it is Iron Age and that the Romans, who were certainly in this district (e.g. at Caergai, see below), made use of it. The town was the centre of the more or less independent district of Penllyn within the Kingdom of Powys, and when the castle was taken in 1202 by Llewelyn the Great he annexed Penllyn to Gwynedd. Little else is known of Bala's history until the 18C when it became prosperous as a centre of the woollen industry, Pennant writing of a 'vast trade in woollen stockings' and of women and children 'in full employ, knitting along the roads'. This prosperity died in the early 19C with the Industrial Revolution. Bala's repute as a religious centre was more enduring, the town's best known figure being the Rev. Thomas Charles (Charles of Bala, 1755–1814), pioneer of the Methodist movement in north Wales, founder of the British and Foreign Bible Society, and a leader of the Sunday School movement. Other local religious figures were Hywel Harris (1714–73), a Dissenter whose persecution here was marked by riots in 1741 (see also Trefecca); Dr Lewis Edwards, who in 1837 started an academy for young preachers, later the

Theological College for Calvinist Methodists and today a Christian Movement Centre; and the Rev. Michael Jones, who in 1865 fitted out a ship which took 153 people, most of them from Bala, to Patagonia where they could be free to practise their nonconformism. They founded the town of Trelew, with which Bala still keeps close touch. In 1967 the National Eisteddfod was held in Bala.

East of A494 on the N edge of the town the large car park was once part of the Green, the town's market and the scene of large Methodist gatherings. Gorsedd stones nearby recall the National Eisteddfod in 1967. To the W, a short way up A4212, stands the former *Bala Theological College*, while the ancient, perhaps Iron Age motte, *Tomen-y-Bala*, is just E of the N end of High Street. Farther on (right) stands a bronze statue (Goscombe John) of Thomas Ellis (1859–99), long Member of Parliament for Merionethshire. Roughly opposite the White Lion Hotel is the house (tablet) where Thomas Charles lived. From here Tegid Street leads to the N extremity of Bala Lake, on the way passing, in front of the Welsh Presbyterian Church, a statue of Thomas Charles.

For *Bala Lake*, see below. For Bala to *Ffestiniog* and *Porthmadog*, see Rte 15; to *Lake Vyrnwy*, see Rte 19B; to *Bwlch-y-Groes* and *Dinas Mawddwy*, see Rte 20B.

Bala Lake (530ft) is known in Welsh as Llyn Tegid, a name deriving from Tegid Foel (Tegid the Bald), a shadowy figure who in the 5C was Lord of Penllyn, the ancient local district, and perhaps husband of Ceridwen, mother of the bard and seer Taliesin. The lake, lying pleasantly though undramatically below green hills backed by mountains, is several times mentioned in literature. Tegid Foel is a character in the 'Mabinogion'; Giraldus, who calls the lake Penmelesmere, possibly from the old English 'pemmel' meaning 'pebble', records that it 'rises by the violence of the winds'; it appears in Spenser's 'Faerie Queen'; and Tennyson in 'Geraint and Enid' refers to the sudden floods in the Dee valley caused by the SW wind 'that blowing Bala Lake fills all the sacred Dee'. This flooding has now been checked by the building of sluices below the river outlet, but in strong winds Bala can still be very rough. The lake (3¾m long by ½m broad) is the largest natural sheet of water in Wales, though it is smaller than the artificial Lake Vyrnwy. It is fed by several streams, one being the Dyfrdwy (Little Dee) at the S end, and empties into the Dee which flows through Llangollen to its estuary NW of Chester. Bala is thought to be the only lake in which are found gwyniad, white fish of salmon species. The main road, skirting the W bank, is described below. Along the E bank run a narrow, rather enclosed road, and also the *Bala Lake Railway* (Tel: 06784–666), which operates along a section of the former Great Western Railway's Ruabon to Barmouth line. In 1972 a local company laid 1ft 11½ inch track, and today both steam and diesel trains run the length of the lake between Llanuwchllyn (the main station) and Bala (station at NE tip of the lake).

1m. **Llanycil**, where the churchyard contains the graves of Thomas Charles, Lewis Edwards, and the Rev. John Parry (1812–74), compiler of a Welsh encyclopaedia. In another 2m the road crosses the Llafar, by the lake being *Glanllyn*, a main centre of the Welsh League of Youth (see below), then leaves the lake and passes below *Caergai* (no adm.), a 17C manor standing within the earthworks of a Roman camp occupied c 98–117 and also traditionally site of the home of Sir Kay of Arthurian romance; Sir Rowland Vaughan (1590–1667), Royalist, hymnologist, and translator, lived here. Beyond, the Lliw, Bala Lake's longest feeder, is crossed. For the lonely and beautiful road ascending this river and crossing high moor and afforestation to Bronaber, see Rte 16. *Castel Carndochan*, S of the river 1½m up the valley, is a Norman motte, still with something of its foundations, and a 14C effigy in the church at (*4m*) **Llanuwchllyn** is probably that of one of the castle's owners. This church (rebuilt 1872) also contains a portable, wooden immersion baptistery of the 1850s; a brass communion plate, bearing a relief of the Temptation, said to have belonged to Cymmer Abbey; and a tablet to Rowland Vaughan of Caergai. The *Bala Lake Railway Station* (workshops etc.) is at the far end of the village, while at the main road entrance to Llanuwchllyn stand statues of Sir Owen M. Edwards (1858–1920) and of his son, Sir Ifan, both active in helping youth, the father as an educationalist and writer of children's books and the son as founder of Urdd Gobaith Cymru, the Welsh League of Youth, broadly an amalgam of youth movements and organisations, and practically concerned with activities which range from an annual eisteddfod to all manner of outdoor endeavours (see also Glanllyn above). For the high scenic road through Llanuwchllyn to *Bwlch-y-Groes* and *Dinas Mawddwy*, see Rte 20B.

Generally following the course of its Roman predecessor, A494 now ascends the river Dyfrdwy through rather desolate country overshadowed on the S by Aran Benllyn (2901ft) and Aran Mawddwy (2970ft), volcanic peaks the names of which recall the semi-independent districts of Mawddwy (see Rte 20B) and Penllyn (see Bala, History, above). Reaching the watershed at 770ft, the road descends the wooded Wnion valley, with Cader Idris prominent ahead.—*9m* (from Llanuwchllyn) *Bont Newydd*, where a road S through Brithdir, avoiding often-crowded Dolgellau, connects to the main roads to Dinas Mawddwy and Machynlleth.—*3m*. **Dolgellau**, see Rte 16.

For the first 3m beyond Dolgellau there is a choice of roads, N or S of the Mawddach Estuary, the S road being slightly shorter but crossing a tollbridge.

The northern road in 1½m reaches the bridge over the Mawddach, just before which are the modest but evocative remains of *Cymmer Abbey*, a Cistercian house founded in 1199 by monks from Cwmhir (the name, pronounced Kummer, was in full once Kymer deu dyfyr, meaning Meeting of the Waters). The ruins are principally those of the abbey's never completed 13C church, survivals being the N nave arcade, three lancets at the E end, battered sedilia, and a piscina in the S wall. Of the cloister and domestic buildings little remains, but something of the chapter house is in the local farm's yard, and the farm itself is probably on the site of the guest house, important at an abbey where travellers must frequently have been delayed by river floods. For Precipice Walk, which can be reached from here, see Rte 16, Dolgellau. For the Mawddach valley northwards, also see Rte 16.—In the churchyard at *Llanelltyd*, across the bridge, is buried Frances Power Cobbe (1822–1904), social writer and suffragist. Beyond, and running below the ridge which carries New Precipice Walk, A496 in 1½m reaches the N end of the Mawddach tollbridge referred to above. At *Penmaenpool*, at the S end of the bridge, the signal box of the old railway (1865–1965, originally the Aberystwyth and Welsh Coast Railway) has been converted by the Royal Society for the Protection of Birds and the North Wales Naturalists' Trust as a Nature Information Centre. Rte 21, from Machynlleth and Tywyn, joins here from the south.

4m (from Dolgellau) *Bont-Ddu* lies below hills through which runs a gold seam. Intermittently worked since Roman times, the mines have long been commercially abandoned though gold from here has been used in recent royal wedding rings, including that of the Queen. The road briefly leaves the shore, regaining it in 3m for a fine view of the Cader Idris massif across the estuary.—*4m.* **Barmouth**, see Rte 17.

15 Bala to Ffestiniog and Porthmadog

A4212 and B4391 to Ffestiniog (Pont Tal-y-Bont). A487 to Porthmadog. Total distance 23m.—*3m. Frongoch.—7m. Pont-yr-Afon-Gam.—3m.* **Ffestiniog**.—*3m.* **Maentwrog.—***4m.* **Penrhyndeudraeth.**—*3m.* **Porthmadog**.

Moor and mountain. After Pont-yr-Afon-Gam fine views down to the Vale of Ffestiniog and the coast.

Leaving **Bala** (see Rte 14) A4212 ascends the pleasant open valley of the Tryweryn, in *3m* reaching a road fork at *Frongoch* from where an upland road bears N for Cerrigydrudion on Rte 13; a memorial along this road commemorates Bob Tai'rfelin, singer of folk songs.—*2m.* **Llyn Celyn**, in a beautiful setting of moor and mountain, is a reservoir completed by Liverpool Corporation in 1965 to regulate the flow of the Dee and supply water largely to Liverpool and the Wirral. The dam (2200ft long) is at the E end, and fish, which formerly swam up the river, are now collected in a trap and spawned for stocking. The main road runs with the N shore, by the NW arm passing a chapel and memorial garden commemorating the chapel and burial ground drowned by the lake; some of the stone from the submerged chapel is incorporated into this new one.

About 1½m beyond the W end of Llyn Celyn a road fork is reached, the road to the left (A4212) following the track of the old railway past little Llyn Tryweryn to *Trawsfynydd* on Rte 16. The old bridge near this road fork is said to be Roman in origin.

Almost due S rises *Arenig Fawr* (2800ft) which, isolated and barren, prompted George Borrow to write that of all the hills he saw in Wales none made a greater impression. On the summit a tablet on a cairn commemorates the crew of a United States Air Force Flying Fortress which crashed here in 1943. The mountain can be climbed by following A4212 for 1m, then a track.

Now following B4391 across rather desolate moor, this Route reaches a watershed at 1507ft (*2m* from the fork) and, in another *3m*, *Pont-ar-Afon-Gam*, where the moorland road (see Rte 13) from Penmachno and Yspytty Ifan comes in from the north. A short distance beyond this junction there is a car park beside a *Viewpoint high above the deep slate cleft of *Rhaeadr Cwm* with its several cataracts.

Llyn Morwynion (Lake of the Maidens. 1292ft) is ¼m N over the hill. The story goes that the men of Ardudwy, who had made a foray into Clwyd, were returning with their captive women when they were overtaken here by the pursuing men of Clwyd and slain. But so enamoured had the women become of their captors that, rather than return with their own men, they drowned themselves in the lake. Another story is that this is where the maidens of Blodeuwedd were drowned, after their mistress, who had murdered her husband in order to be with her lover, had been turned into an owl.

The descent into the Vale of Ffestiniog affords a superb view across Traeth Bach to Tremadog Bay and the long line of the Lleyn.—*3m.* **Ffestiniog**, at 600ft, is boldly situated on a bluff between the Vale of Ffestiniog and the valley of the Cynfal. The knoll behind the church, reached by a path beside the S wall of the churchyard, affords a view which, though now marred by the Trawsfynydd nuclear power station, still includes the full perspective of the valley and the sea and coast beyond. A hill SW of the village, on which is the tomb of the 4th Baron Newborough, is another viewpoint, while a local walk (sign by the church) is to the *Cynfal Falls*, just S below the town; above the falls a rock is known locally as Pulpud (pulpit) Huw Llwyd, recalling a local mystic who preached from here. The walk can be continued up the valley via Bont Newydd to Rhaeadr Cwm.

For Ffestiniog to *Blaenau Ffestiniog* and *Betws-y-Coed*, see Rte 6C; to *Dolgellau*, see Rte 16; to *Harlech* and *Barmouth*, see Rte 17; for the *Ffestiniog Railway*, see Porthmadog, below.

The Porthmadog road descends to the valley, at *Tal-y-Bont* merging with A496 from Blaenau Ffestiniog and in *3m* reaching **Maentwrog** (see Rte 17 which here comes in from Barmouth and Harlech). A487 crosses the river Dwyryd, on the farther side, at the foot of the old road from Beddgelert, being *Tan-y-Bwlch*. The estate (Plas Tan-y-Bwlch) formerly belonged to the Oakley family, owners of the Blaenau Ffestiniog quarries, but is now the Snowdonia National Park Residential Study Centre, with, in summer, an information facility. Here, too, are nature trails, one of which (Llyn Mair) runs through a part of the nature reserve which protects something of the original oak woods that once covered much of Wales.

4m. **Penrhyndeudraeth**, see Rte 7.—*1m. Minffordd*, for (1m S) ***Portmeirion** (Tel: 0766–770228), an astonishing and, in other than sunny weather, somewhat incongruous private village and tiny harbour in Italianate style, the achievement of the Welsh architect Sir Clough Williams-Ellis (1883–1978) who, acquiring this then run-down estate in 1925, determined 'to show that one could develop even a very beautiful site without defiling it and indeed ... even enhance what nature has provided for your background'. Sir Clough's work here has generally been of two periods, one before the 1939–45 war and the other from 1954 onwards, the more conspicuous buildings being the Campanile, half-Romanesque and half-Baroque, and the Bath House Colonnade (18C), brought from Bristol in 1957 when the house itself was in danger of demolition. The village is surrounded by grounds (mainly rhododendrons); there is a long, sandy beach (dangerous bathing); and, in addition to the hotel, restored and reopened in 1988 after a fire in 1981, there are cottages of unique character for renting. Portmeirion pottery is famous.

2m. **Porthmadog** (3000 inhab. *Inf.* High Street. Tel: 0766–512981) is reached by crossing *The Cob* (toll), the 1m-long embankment carrying the road and the Ffestiniog Railway across the mouth of the Glaslyn which was built by W.A. Madocks MP (1774–1828) as part of the reclamation of the 7000 acres of Traeth Mawr (see towards the end of Rte 10). Today primarily a holiday and sailing centre, Porthmadog was once important as a port (largely for the Blaenau

Picturesque Portmeirion designed by Sir Clough Williams-Ellis

Ffestiniog quarries) and this past is recalled at the *Gwynedd Maritime Museum* (Tel: 0766–512981) in a surviving slate shed on one of the harbour wharves. *Porthmadog Pottery* (Tel: 0766–512137) offers exhibitions and demonstrations and also encourages visitors to try their hand at the wheel or with the paint brush, while for train enthusiasts Porthmadog is the home of two railways.

The **Ffestiniog Railway* (Museum at Porthmadog station. Tel: 0766–512340), climbing and running high above the estuary and the Vale of Ffestinog and affording exciting coastal and mountain views, reaches Blaenau Ffestiniog (see Rte 6C) in 13½m and one hour. Opened in 1836 as a horse-drawn tramway for the Blaenau Ffestiniog slate quarries, and adapted for passengers in 1865, the line had a gauge of 1ft 11½ ins and, with a total rise of 700ft, was skilfully engineered so that the gradient (maximum 1:70) enabled laden trains to descend by gravity. Closed in 1946, the line has been re-opened in stages since 1954, one major achievement being the construction of nearly 3m of new alignment, made necessary by the drowning by the Tan-y-Grisiau Reservoir of a section of the original course. Trains may be steam or diesel and there are a number of stations along the route.—The *Welsh Highland Railway* (Tel: 0766–513402), with its terminus within the NE angle of the British Rail line and A487, represents the restored survival of a short section of the scenic narrow-gauge line which from 1923 to 1937 linked Porthmadog (via Aberglaslyn, Beddgelert and Rhyd-Ddu) with Dinas near Caernarfon. At present about a mile of track from Porthmadog is open, served by steam or diesel locomotives, but extension is planned. The sheds and workshops are open to visitors.

For Porthmadog to *Caernarfon* and *Bangor*, see Rte 10. For the *Lleyn*, to the SW, see Rte 12.

16 Dolgellau to Ffestiniog

A470. Total distance 17m.—*2m. Llanelltyd.—3m. Ganllwyd.—5m. Bronaber.—2m. Trawsfynydd.—3m. Junction A470/A487 (for* **Maentwrog**).—*2m.* **Ffestiniog**.

The first half of the road is up the beautiful Ganllwyd valley, beside the rivers Mawddach and Eden and through the forest of Coed-y-Brenin. Afterwards the country opens up giving some views of mountains. For much of the way the road runs just W of the Roman Sarn Helen.

Dolgellau (2000 inhab. *Inf.* The Bridge. Tel: 0341–422888), its name pronounced Dol-gethly and meaning perhaps Meadow of the Hazels, is the chief centre and market town for a wide surrounding mountain district and thus very Welsh in both custom and language. Pleasantly situated on the S bank of the Wnion, at the foot of the mass of Cader Idris, within easy reach of varied but always beautiful scenery, and at the junction of several main roads, the town can be a magnet for tourists and its narrow streets and bridge a traffic bottleneck in summer.

History. Owen Glendower held a Welsh parliament here in 1404, and later in the same year here signed an alliance with Charles VI of France, but otherwise Dolgellau figures little in history. The Vaughan (Fychan) family were long the most important landowners, their seats being at Nannau (2m N) and Hengwrt (1m NW). One distinguished member of the family was Robert Vaughan (1592–1667), the antiquary, who lived at Hengwrt and was known for his priceless collection of manuscripts, now in the National Library of Wales; the remains of his house can be seen.

Dolgellau bridge, with its seven arches, dates largely from 1638. On the S side, the small town of grey-walled, slate-roofed houses clusters mainly around Eldon Square and the smaller Queen's Square, perhaps the main building of note being the *Church of St. Mary*, rebuilt except for its tower in 1776 and containing a recumbent effigy of Meurig ap Ynyr Fychan, a Vaughan ancestor. There are a number of local walks (detail and leaflets from Tourist Information), two favourites being Precipice Walk and Torrent Walk. *Precipice Walk*, c 3m N, is a path some 3m in total length encircling the steep high ridge of Foel Cynwch, 1000ft above the river Mawddach and with on its E side the wooded small Llyn Cynwch. The walk affords superb views of Cader Idris and the length of the Mawddach estuary towards Barmouth. One approach is from Cymmer Abbey (see Rte 14), but the shorter one is from a parking area on the Dolgellau to Llanfachreth road near the entrance to Nannau Park, ancient seat of the Vaughans.

An older house on this site belonged to Howel Sele, whose Lancastrian sympathies brought him into conflict with his cousin Owen Glendower. It is said that Sele, while out hunting, shot at Glendower but missed. Glendower then killed Sele, hiding the body in a hollow oak, later to become 'the spirit's blasted tree' of Walter Scott's 'Marmion', and the 'hollow oak of demonrie' of Lord

Lytton's 'Arthur'. What may have been the original oak was destroyed by lightning in 1813.

Torrent Walk, 1½m E of the town, is a 1m walk up the mossy, fern-clad glen of the Clywedog, starting from the point where this stream runs into the Wnion and ending at the bridge at the junction of A470 with the road to Brithdir.

For Dolgellau to *Barmouth* (W) and to *Bala* (NE), see Rte 14; to *Machynlleth*, see Rte 20A; to *Machynlleth* via the coast (*Tywyn*), see Rte 21; to *Dinas Mawddwy*, see Rte 20B.

CADER IDRIS, lifting high (2927ft) to the SW of Dolgellau, means Chair of Idris, who was according to tradition and the bards a giant variously celebrated as warrior, poet and astronomer. Tradition further insists that anyone sleeping the night in the chair, the precise position of which is obscure, may expect to wake up as either a poet or a lunatic. More historically, if still shadowy, it seems that Idris was a descendant of Cunedda, through Meirion (who gave his name to Merioneth), and that he was killed in about 630 fighting the Saxons.—A hoard of Iron Age ornaments in the La Tène style, found under a boulder on the mountain in 1963, is now in the National Museum of Wales.

Though exceeded in height by many Welsh peaks, Cader Idris, thanks largely to its accessibility, almost levels with Snowdon in visitor popularity. The main core of the mass is a ridge, some 8m long, the summit being *Pen-y-Gadair*, while the ridge itself, steep on all sides, presents almost perpendicular walls of rock towards the N with an average drop of 900ft. To the S the ridge descends, for the most part in abrupt grassy slopes, down to the Dysynni valley, part of the fault (geologically known as the Bala Fault) which includes Bala Lake and Tal-y-Llyn. On this S side there is also an impressive cwm, enclosed by Craig-y-Cau and Pen-y-Gadair and containing the dark lake of *Llyn-y-Cau*.—Of the massif's lesser heights, *Mynydd Moel* (2804ft) is 1m NE of the summit, while *Tyrau Mawr* (2167ft), 2¼m W, commands a view at least equal to that from Pen-y-Gadair. To the NW of Pen-y-Gadair there is another deep cwm in which lies *Llyn-y-Gadair*, the narrow wall of rock, 1000 to 1300ft high and separating the basin of this lake from that of Llyn-y-Cau, being the most striking feature of the mountain.—Cader Idris has been a national nature reserve since 1955, of particular interest to geologists for its Ordovician lavas and to botanists as one of the most southern areas in Britain for arctic-alpine plants.

There are five recognised ascents, three of these being from the N from near Dolgellau, and two from the S from the area of Tal-y-Llyn lake. Local advice should be sought regarding current conditions and as to which path best suits individual requirements (Visitor Centre, The Bridge, Dolgellau. Tel: 0341-422888).

For Dolgellau to (2m) *Llanelltyd*, see Rte 14.—A470 (but see alternative road below) ascends the lovely *Ganllwyd Valley*, following the W bank first of the Mawddach and then of the Eden, the ridge above the opposite bank of the former being Foel Cynwch, with Precipice Walk high up on its slope. In 2m, where the Wen and Las streams flow into the other side of the Mawddach, the road enters the wooded Ganllwyd Valley proper, in ¾m, just beyond the Tyn-y-Groes Hotel, passing above the bridge by which the alternative road (see immediately below) joins this main road.

A quiet and pleasant alternative is provided by the small road which ascends the E bank of the Mawddach, passing, first, close to Cymmer Abbey (see Rte 14). In 2¹/₂m, with the Mawddach bearing away NE, the Las stream is crossed, just the other side being a road which leads E to reach in ¹/₂m the Forestry Commission's *Glasdir Arboretum*. Returning W, the Mawddach is crossed, the Eden then being followed N to the next bridge across to A470.

3m (from Llanelltyd) *Ganllwyd*, the hamlet which gives this valley its name and immediately W of which is the National Trust's Dalmelynllyn estate, best known for the waterfall of *Rhaeadr Ddu*, easily reached (¹/₂m) by a path. Continuing beside the W bank of the Eden, A470 soon reaches *Pont Dolgefeiliau* (picnic site), the name meaning Meadow of the Smiths and recalling that in the early 19C this was where the drovers had their cattle shod before starting the long drive towards London.

From Pont Dolgefeiliau a branch roads leads in ¹/₂m to the Forestry Commission's **Maesgwn Visitor Centre** (Tel: 0341–422289) in the heart of the *Coed-y-Brenin*, a forest most of which was part of the ancient Nannau Estate. The first owner (c 1100) was Cadwgan, Prince of Powys, the property later passing to the Vaughans. After land had been bought from the Vaughans, the Forestry Commission started planting in 1922, and in 1935, to celebrate the Silver Jubilee of George V, the name was changed from Vaughan Forest to Coed-y-Brenin, the Forest of the King. The total area of forest, on both sides of A470 and with a number of outlying sections, is some 21,700 acres, of which about 15,500 are planted, most of the remainder being agricultural land. The Maesgwn Centre provides an admirable survey of all the main aspects of the forest—past, present and planned—and includes also much about local gold mining.

The varied scenery—the most accessible area being that to the E of A470—includes forest proper, pasture, moorland and the wooded glens through which tumble the Eden, Gain, Mawddach and Wen. A map obtainable at the Visitor Centre describes a network of many miles of paths and some motorable roads, particularly popular objectives being the cascades of *Rhaeadr Mawddach* and *Pistyll Cain*, both near former gold workings. For an alternative approach from the N (from Bronaber), see below.

A470 crosses the Eden at Pont Dolgefeiliau, gradually leaving the river's E bank and in 1¹/₂m, at *Bryn Eden*, exchanging the forest for open moor, with views of the Rhinogs to the west.—*5m.* (from Ganllwyd) *Bronaber* is a scattered hamlet from which a choice of small roads traverse the lonely moorland from the east.

A road ascends E through a holiday village, on the hilltop above which a fork offers a choice. The righthand road, soon passing a chapel, leads across moor and through forests to (3m) a farm where the road ends. From here a path descends (25 minutes) to the cascades of *Rhaeadr Mawddach* and *Pistyll Cain* (see above). The lefthand road soon arrives at another fork. Here the righthand road (Abergierw) drops to the river Gain with, before the bridge, two antiquities. *Llech Idris*, to the right, is a tall standing stone, probably set up in prehistoric times though later given the name of the 7C warrior of Cader Idris. To the left is *Bedd Porius*, the grave of Porius, now no more than broken fragments marking the site of a 5–6C inscribed stone (in Latin, 'Porius, a simple man, lies here') now housed in the National Museum of Wales. The lefthand road at the fork wanders across remote high moor and afforestation to (12m from Bronaber) Llanuwchllyn (see Rte 14) at the S end of Bala Lake.

2m. Trawsfynydd is a village beside the lake of the same name created in 1930 as part of the Maentwrog hydro-electric scheme and now dominated at the N end by a nuclear power station (Sir Basil Spence, 1959–64; tours Tel: 076–687331). A nature trail (leaflet from the power station) makes the 3m circuit of the lake. In the village there is a statue to Hedd Wyn, a shepherd poet whose winning of the bardic chair at the 1917 Eisteddfod was declared after he had been killed in Flanders; and from here A4212 bears NE to meet Rte 15 in 8m just W of Llyn Celyn.

Just over ¹/₂m beyond the power station, and just before the A470/A487 junction, a small road leads E to reach in 1m a spot which, however bypassed and insignificant today, nevertheless has its roots in the Roman and Norman past as also in early Welsh legend. Here is a tiny *Roman Amphitheatre*, interesting for being the only example in Britain serving an auxiliary fort, while, a short way SW, the mound of *Tomen-y-Mur* (Mound of the Wall) was probably an early Norman motte raised inside the walls of this 1C Roman auxiliary fort on Sarn Helen. And in legend, in those shadowy years between the departure of the Romans and the arrival of the Normans, this was a seat of the princes of Ardudwy; the place, too, from which the men of Ardudwy set out on that raid into Clwyd which ended in the drowning of the maidens in Llyn Morwynion (see Rte 15).

3m. (from Trawsfynydd village) Junction of A470 and A487. For **Maentwrog**, 2m along the latter, see Rte 17. A470, crossing the Cynfal at Bont Newydd, in *2m* reaches **Ffestiniog**, see Rte 15.

17 Barmouth to Maentwrog

A496. Total distance 21m.—*8m.* **Llanbedr.**—*2m.* **Llanfair.**—*2m.* **Harlech Castle**—*3m.* *Llanfihangel-y-Traethau.*—*6m.* **Maentwrog**.

At first the road runs through the district of Ardudwy, the narrow land between the mountains and the sea which was the home of a people who, after the departure of the Romans, seems to have moved to Tomen-y-Mur (Rte 16). Beyond the flat coast with its many caravan sites, there is a seaward view across to the Lleyn, while ahead, beyond Llanfair, appear the mountains of Snowdonia. Inland there is moorland, dull as seen from the road but, deeper in, with some wild scenery; the best parts of this inland country, with many prehistoric remains, are indicated below as diversions eastward off A496.

Barmouth (2000 inhab. *Inf.* Station Road. Tel: 0341–280787), in Welsh Abermaw or Y Bermo, is a popular and at times uncomfortably overcrowded resort which manages to preserve something of its 19C origins amid an extrovert funfair ambience. Situated at the N extremity of the estuary of the Mawddach, on a narrow strip between the sea and the hills, the town's most obvious attraction is its waterfront and beach with 2m of sands. This area is rather awkwardly separated from the rest of the town by the railway.

A496—here from S to N the sequence Church Street, High Street and King Edward Street—represents, together with Jubilee Road (parallel to and just seaward of Church and High streets) the main street on the railway's landward side. On the steep slopes above, and especially above Church Street, cluster the houses of the old town. Above, again, is *Dinas Oleu*, 4¹/₂ acres of cliffland of particular interest as the first property acquired by the National Trust, the gift, in 1895, of Mrs. F. Talbot.

The fine beach is backed by the Promenade, a wide motor road and walk extending some 2m between Llanaber and the harbour, near the latter being *Ty Gwyn* (rebuilt but still showing an old door), a house perhaps built for Henry Tudor and said also to have been used by a Vaughan when plotting with Jasper Tudor to put Henry on the English throne. Here, too, is the *RNLI Museum* (Tel: 0341–280787).

Three walks are popular, one being the *Railway Bridge* footpath across the estuary. The bridge is 800 yards long, with an iron swingbridge at its N end where the navigable channel hugs the shore, and the view, which embraces the massif of Cader Idris, is striking enough to have prompted Wordsworth, who was here in 1824, to write of this 'sublime estuary'. The estuary can also be crossed by ferry (not cars) to Penrhyn Point, terminal of the Fairbourne small-gauge railway (see Rte 21). *Panorama Walk*, reached by a lane off the main road 150 yards short of the railway bridge, undulates for some 3m along a steep slope 300–500ft above the estuary, while a third walking area is provided by the high ground above the town, which, municipally owned, has been laid out with paths.

Leaving Barmouth, A496 in *2m* reaches *Llanaber* where the church, between the road and the sea and dating from the early 13C, is well worth a visit, if only for the interior work which is surprisingly elaborate for what was, at the time of the church's building, a remote corner of Wales. Note, for example, the choir and the S doorway with its clustered shafts. There are some unusual features here, too, such as the single E lancet, the contemporary outer door to the porch and the construction, due to the sloping site, on three levels, with five steps from the nave to the choir and two more to the sanctuary. Noteworthy also are an old alms chest; the 16C roof timbers; a cross on the W wall which is part of an ancient graveslab; and two venerable stones (before 10C), one of which, inscribed 'Caelexti Monedo Regi', though mentioned by early writers on Wales, is of undetermined provenance.—*3m*. *Llanddwywe* is associated with a branch of the Vaughan family, one of whom, Gruffyd, in 1615 founded a chapel in the church (W side of the road), both the chapel and its monument to Gruffyd being ascribed to Inigo Jones. Opposite the church a driveway leads in nearly 1m to the one-time Vaughan mansion of *Cors-y-Gedol* (1593), largely remodelled but with a gatehouse of 1630 said to be a design by Inigo Jones. The small gated-road round the S of the house soon reaches, on the right beside the road, *Cors-y-Gedol Burial Chamber* (or, on some maps, Arthur's Quoit), now little more than a large perched capstone.

The road westward beside the church is the motor approach to the area of *Morfa Dyffryn National Nature Reserve* (permit required; known for its dunes flora) within an inverted triangle (apex at the car park) which fringes the shore for almost 2m northwards.

The straggling built-up area of **Dyffryn Ardudwy** begins immediately beyond Llanddwywe, at the S end, on the E side of the road, being *Dyffryn Cairn*, one of the more important burial chambers in this part of Wales and one from which excavation in 1962–63 produced pottery and other finds, now in the National Museum of Wales. Calculated to have been 100ft long, narrowing in width from 54ft at its W end to 35ft at its eastern, the surviving visible remains are simply some of the base stones of the cairn and the two burial chambers. The W chamber, with its own cairn, traces of which can be seen, is thought to have been the first built and to have later been covered by the cairn of the larger E chamber.—In the church at *Llanenddwyn*, the western part of Dyffryn Ardudwy, is buried

Colonel Jones of Maes-y-Garnedd (see below); brother-in-law of
Oliver Cromwell, he signed the death warrant of Charles I and was
himself executed as a regicide at the Restoration.

3m. **Llanbedr**, beside the river Artro, is the home of *Maes Artro*
(Tel: 034123–467), a craft village and visitor centre set up in a RAF
wartime camp built in 1941, an era recalled by an exhibition. There is
a variety of craft shops, while other attractions include an adventure
playground and woodland with nature trails. But connoisseurs of
ancient stones will also visit Llanbedr church in which a stone,
bearing a spiral design probably of the Bronze Age, interestingly
indicates religious use spanning pagan to early Christian times.

From Llanbedr diversions can be made both W and E, the latter
being into some wild country.

The WESTWARD DIVERSION (4m return), passing some Standing
Stones, is to *Shell Island* (fee), in fact more peninsula than island and
a spot noted for its variety of shells (some 200 have been identified)—
a feature which gives the island its Welsh name of Mochras—its
variety of birds, both local and migrant, and its wealth of wild flowers
numbering some 170 different species. Additionally, visitors can
enjoy sandy bathing beaches, dunes, camping, fishing and boating,
while other needs are met by shops, tavern, snack bar and
restaurant.—From here, exposed at low tide, extends *Sarn Badrig*, or
St Patrick's Causeway, a broken line of rocks running away SW and
fabled as having once been a road to the Lowland Hundred (see Rte
21).

The EASTWARD DIVERSION (11m return; narrow road) gradually
ascends the valley of the Artro, which, with its tributary Cwmnantcol,
embraces *Rhinog National Nature Reserve*, in large part a wild area
of ledges, scree and boulders building up to Rhinog Fawr (2362ft).
There are several tracks and a walk circuit may be made by way of
Bwlch Tyddiad (Roman Steps, see below) and Bwlch Drws Ardudwy
(detail from the Reserve Warden, 43 Bro Enddwyn, Dyffryn
Ardudwy. Tel: 03417–555).

The lane up Cwm Nantcol, with a nature trail, finishes at *Maes-
y-Garnedd* (4m from Llandbedr), birthplace of the regicide Colonel
Jones (see above), a track continuing NE and in 1m reaching Bwlch
Drws Ardudwy, the pass below Rhinog Fawr (N) and Rhinog Fach (S).

The narrow road up to the Artro in 4m (from Llanbedr) skirts the
beautiful tarn of *Llyn Cwm Bychan* before ending at a farm (parking),
whence a path (once a packhorse trail) in what can seem a long mile
reaches the start of the so-called *Roman Steps* (Bwlch Tyddiad), a
strange broken ascent of flat unhewn slabs, in places edged by
smaller uprights. Of obscure origin, the steps are variously attributed
to British, Roman and medieval builders.

2m. **Llanfair** was between 1853 and 1906 prosperous with deep slate
quarries, recalled today by *Old Llanfair Cavern* (Tel: 0766–780247)
offering a guided tour through two levels. Ahead now is a view of the
Snowdon mountain group.

2m. ***Harlech Castle** (WHM. Tel: 0222-465511), backed by its
small town, rises four-square on its rock platform some 200ft above
the marshes of Morfa Harlech, from which the sea has retreated, here
for over ½m. The castle is a notably complete and well-preserved
example of Edward I's system of concentric fortification.—Access is
from either above or below. The approach from below (car park) is
through the old watergate and involves a long steep climb. B4573,

from N or S, is the easiest road to the town and the castle's upper entrance, the road from the station, immediately below the castle, being very steep and twisty. Parking close to the castle's upper entrance is limited.

History. The name means Bold Rock, a name and a place known in legend which tells that Bendigeidfran, the King, sat with his siblings upon the rock of Harddlech and watched 13 ships coming from Ireland, 'beautiful, seemly and [with] brave ensigns of brocaded silk'. In those Dark Ages days the estuary waters, now some 3m to the N, would have lapped this towering rock, as indeed was still the case when this site was chosen by Edward I in 1283.

Edward's castle was started by James of St. George in 1283 and completed by 1289, its builder staying on as constable until 1293. The town received its charter as an English Borough in 1285. With a garrison of only 37 men the castle withstood a siege by Madog in 1294–95, but was not again besieged until 1404 when it was taken, but only after some treachery and bribery, by Owen Glendower. For four years, until retaken for the English in 1408, Harlech served as Glendower's capital. In 1460 Margaret of Anjou took refuge here after the battle of Northampton, and, although she soon moved on to Scotland, the castle remained in Lancastrian hands until taken by the Yorkists in 1468. It was the last stronghold in England and Wales to fall, and then only after enduring a siege of seven years. Among the survivors was a boy of 12, later to become Henry VII. The castle's stubborn resistance is said to have inspired the song 'The March of the Men of Harlech'. By the 16C Harlech had become a ruin, but during the Civil War, defended by Colonel William Owen, it held out for Charles I until, the last Welsh fortress to fall, it was taken by General Mytton in 1647. The castle was then allowed to lapse into ruin.

The ENTRANCE is across the wide moat from the site of the barbican to a doorway flanked by two towers in the outer curtain. The outer defence here consists of a revetted terrace with a breastwork, rather that the full wall found at some other castles. Another surprising feature is that the gateways of the outer and inner defences are in line, there being no attempt, as for example at Denbigh and Beaumaris, to construct an oblique approach. The GATEHOUSE, three storeys high, is the principal feature of the castle. The residence of the constable, it had living rooms on the upper floors. It has two huge half-round towers facing outwards, and two large drum-towers, rising a further storey, at the inner corners. The rooms include an oratory, which was also a portcullis chamber, and a second oratory above that. This gatehouse, and the NE tower, were the only parts of the castle still roofed in the later 16C, the former then being used as judges' lodging and the tower as a prison.

A central passage admits to the INNER WARD, which is roughly oblong, enclosed by walls 40ft high with a round tower at each corner. The rampart walk is corbelled across the flattened inner faces of these towers, the outer two of which carry circular watch-towers. The SE and NE towers are similar, each having a dungeon entered originally by trapdoor from the room above. The rooms, not uniform in shape, are approached by wall stairs, at the top being privies. The outer towers represent the last part of the castle to be built and contain pentagonal rooms of one size. Various rooms can be traced around the interior of the ward. On the W side are the Kitchen (S) and Great Hall (N). On the S side are the Granary (E) and, adjoining the kitchen, the site of a room known as the Ystumgwern Hall, so called because it was brought here complete from the residence of that name (4m away) of Llewelyn the Last. Opposite, against the N wall, are the Chapel (W) and Bakehouse (E).

Between the chapel and bakehouse a passage with a postern leads to the OUTER WARD with, straight ahead, another postern, flanked by towers, that gave access to the precipitous CASTLE ROCK. On the N and W sides of the castle, following more or less the lower edge of the rock and connected by steep walls to the NE and SW corners of the outer ward, was a third line of defence, a wall added c 1295 after Madog's unsuccessful siege. The W part of the rock is now reached by a gate behind the NW tower. Beyond can be seen the remains of a wall which ran from the tower to the precipice; also, to the S of this wall and a little below the castle, platforms on which stood defensive engines. A path descends to the Upper Gate, once with a drawbridge, and hence, with a protecting wall, down to the Watergate.

3m. Llanfihangel-y-Traethau is reached either by A496 across the flat Morfa Harlech, or, more pleasantly, by the higher B4573 which, just outside Harlech, skirts *Coed Llechwedd*, a woodland property given to the National Trust in 1937 in memory of the Irish writer A.P. Graves (1846–1931). At Llanfihangel-y-Traethau a narrow lane climbs to the small church above the village. When first built the church stood on a tidal island, and, although the sea receded in the later Middle Ages, there was still flooding until the building of a seawall in 1805. In the churchyard, close to the porch, stands a 12C stone, its Latin inscription recording that it marks the grave of the mother of the builder of the church during the time of King Owain Gwynedd (1137–70). Portmeirion can be seen across the water.— A496 crosses the railway, passes the hamlet of *Talsarnau*, and reaches the head of the Traeth Bach estuary, where a road branches N and W to cross the Dwyryd by tollbridge and in 1m reach *Penrhyndeudraeth*. Here, and beyond, the train of the Ffestiniog Railway may be seen high on the hill across the valley.—*5m.* (from Llanfihangel-y-Traethau) *Maentwrog Power Station* is a small power station in woods, linked by pipe with Llyn Trawsfynydd.

A path here follows a glen to (1¹/₂m) *Rhaeadr Ddu*, the Black Cascade, a twisted water slide set among rocks and trees.

1m. **Maentwrog**, a pleasant village below wooded hills, gets its name from its ancient stone, the 'maen' of Twrog, which stands in the churchyard and traditionally commemorates (there is no inscription) a 7C holy man known to have been a companion of St. Beuno. The stone, though only 4ft high, may be a prehistoric standing stone. Also in the churchyard is the grave of Archdeacon Prys (died 1624), once minister here and author of the Welsh translation of the Psalter still in use.

For Maentwrog to (W) *Porthmadog* and (E) *Ffestiniog* and *Bala*, see Rte 15; to *Trawsfynydd* and *Dolgellau*, see Rte 16.

18   Shrewsbury to Machynlleth and Aberystwyth

This Route cuts across central Wales at the principality's narrowest part, within which, however, there are three roads. There is little to choose between the three, but Rte 18A is marginally shorter than the other two, while Rte 18C is the most scenic. A fourth route (but cutting out Machynlleth) would be the straight line provided by A470 and A44 from Llanidloes on Rte 18C. For this choice, see Rte 23A.

A.   Via Welshpool and Mallwyd

A458 to Mallwyd. A470 to Cemmaes Road. A489 to Machynlleth. A487 to Aberystwyth. Total distance 70m.—*18m*. **Welshpool**.—*9m*. *Llanfair Caereinion*.—*16m*. **Mallwyd**.—*11m*. **Machynlleth**.—*6m*. *Furnace (Eglwysfach)*.—*2m*. *Tre'r Ddol*.—*2m*. *Tal-y-Bont*.—*6m*. **Aberystwyth**.

In large part agricultural scenery, but some moor between Llanfair Caereinion and Mallwyd. Green valley of the Dyfi to Machynlleth. After Machynlleth, wood and moor inland and estuary flats to seaward.

Shrewsbury, see 'Blue Guide England'.—*12m*. *Middletown*, a village just in Wales, lies below the Breidden Hills (1234ft) which derive the second syllable of their name from the forts (duns) found on two of the hills, Middletown immediately N of the village, and Breidden beyond. The latter, thought to have been the site of a battle between the Welsh and the English in 1292, bears an obelisk commemorating Admiral Rodney's victory over the French off Domenica in 1782. At (*4m*), *Buttington*, traditionally the site of a battle in 894 between the Saxons and the Danes, the church has a font made from a capital from the abbey of Strata Marcella, now disappeared (see Powysland Museum, Welshpool, below). The Severn is crossed just beyond the village.

2m. **Welshpool** (5000 inhab. *Inf.* Vicarage Gardens Car Park. Tel: 0938–552043), on the Shropshire Union Canal, enjoys the Welsh name of Y Trallwng, as such being granted a charter by the Prince of Powys in 1263. This, however, was largely a confirmation of earlier privileges, notably the already long-established Monday market for which the town is still known today. The town is entered by Salop Road. Just before the church is a cottage said to be the birthplace of Grace Evans, who helped Lady Nithsdale, daughter of the Marquess of Powis, in the romantic rescue of her husband from the Tower of London in 1716 (see Powis Castle below). The *Church*, restored by Street in 1871, shows work dating from the 13–19C, the earliest parts being the W tower and the choir, the roof of which is decorated with armorial designs. The main theme of the nearby *Powysland Museum* (Tel: 0938–554759), founded in 1874, is the social history of Powys. But there is also archaeological material, which includes local Roman finds and fragments from the local abbey of Strata Marcella, founded in c 1170 for Cistercians by Owain Cyfeiliog, Prince of Powys (who died as a monk here), ransacked at the Reformation, and of which nothing now remains. Near the station (to the SE beyond the canal) can be seen remains of the early Norman motte-and-bailey castle, the bailey now being the bowling green.

Welshpool is about half-way along the 35m—long *Montgomery Canal*, which comes in from the NE and continues SW to end at Newtown. Dug in three stages—1796, 1797 and 1821 when the extension to Newtown was completed—the canal was intended to support agriculture as also to move limestone, coal and other goods. Abandoned by 1944, largely as the result of rail competition, considerable lengths have now been restored and the waterway now offers towpath walks, boating (including in summer a narrowboat cruise from Welshpool's Severn Street wharf. Tel: 0938–553271), wildlife, and the industrial archaeology of locks, wharves, warehouses and limekilns.

For the *Welshpool and Llanfair Railway*,, see below.

Guilsfield, 3m N, is worth a visit for its large 15C church, of particular interest here being the unusual upper chamber over the S porch; the clustered pier shafts; the carved heads on the beams in the S aisle, these coming from a predecessor church; the 19C vaulting, with each panel different; and a Jacobean or earlier churchwarden's chest.

Long Mountain stretches for some 4m along the Welsh side of the border to the E of Welshpool. It is crossed by Offa's Dyke; the highest point, *Beacon Ring* (1338ft), on the E side and commanding a length of Roman road, is a hillfort; and at *Trelystan*, to the S, there is the oddity of a 15C wooden church which, in 1856, was cased in brick.

*Powis Castle (NT. Tel: 0938–554336), 1m SW of Welshpool, has been inhabited for some 500 years, and, although in part rebuilt during the 16 and 17C, still keeps the general aspect of its 13–14C origin. Standing in fine grounds which include famous terraced gardens, Powis shows late 16C plasterwork and panelling, a 17C staircase, early Georgian furniture, some notable portraits, and its important Clive (of India) Museum.

History. It seems probable that the remains of a Norman motte-and-bailey in the park are those of the original castle here (c 1100), destroyed by Llewelyn the Great in 1233 during his struggle with his rival, the local Gruffydd ap Gwenwynwyn, and again and finally in 1275. Under the Treaty of Conwy (1277), Edward I granted the Gwenwynwyn family the barony of De la Pole, but required that they renounce Welsh princely titles. Agreeing, the family then built the castle which is the nucleus of today's. The barony died out in 1551, and in 1586 the castle was bought by Sir Edward Herbert, a younger son of the Earl of Pembroke, and it was he who put in hand the conversion to Elizabethan taste and standards. Sir Edward's son, William, created Baron Powis in 1629, defended the castle for Charles I during the Civil War, but it fell to Parliament in 1644. The 3rd Baron (1667) undertook further rebuilding, but, as a supporter of James II, had to flee the country in 1688, and it was his wife who, as a Lady of the Bedchamber, smuggled out the future Old Pretender shortly before his father's hurried departure.

In 1784, through marriage, the estate passed to Edward Clive (later, in 1804, Earl of Powis), son of Lord Clive or India, and in 1807 the family took the name of Herbert. It was the 4th Earl who was responsible for much remodelling of the interior (by G.F. Bodley in 1891–1904), and it was in 1952 that Powis came to the National Trust.

Ballroom. 18C decoration. Italian tapestry (1545), depicting the embassy of the Venetians to Cairo in 1502. French strongbox (17C). The **Clive Museum*, beyond the ballroom, shows some 300 relics (art treasures, jewels, weapons, letters, diaries) from the Indian careers of Robert Clive (Clive of India, 1725–74) and of his son Edward Clive (1754–1839) who, as Governor of Madras, acquired much memorabilia of Tipoo Sahib, Sultan of Mysore, defeated and killed by the British in the storming of Seringapatam in 1799.

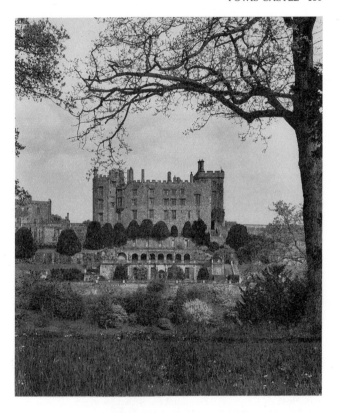

Powis Castle, with its attractive terraced gardens

Billiard Room. Pewter belonging to the 1st Baron Powis, which replaced silver sold during the Civil War. Portraits. *Staircase Hall.* Bust of Spencer Perceval, Prime Minister, by Nollekens (1814). *Dining Room.* This was formerly three rooms, and original plaster-work survives in the window recess and the doorway to the servants' staircase. Other decoration is Bodley's. Early 19C mahogany wine table. Among the portraits are two by George Romney and one by Joshua Reynolds; also others by N. Dance, J.M. Wright, M. Dahl, and R. Marientreu. *Library.* Ceiling painting by Lanscroon. Among the five daughters of the 3rd Baron (1st Marquess) depicted, the young-est, as Lady Nithsdale, rescued her husband in 1716 from the Tower of London; accompanied by her servant, she visited her husband, who, donning female's clothes brought by his wife, walked out with the servant. Portrait (unknown 17C artist) of 'Old Parr', who died in 1635 reputedly aged 152. Also a portrait of Lord Herbert of Cherbury, who surrendered Montgomery Castle to Parliament. *Oak Drawing Room.* Some original 16C plasterwork in W window aperture. Other decoration and the inserted oriel window are by Bodley. William and Mary and early 18C furniture. Sèvres china, once belonging to Tipoo

Sahib. Portraits include Charles II by Godfrey Kneller; 1st Earl of Powis as a boy, by Thomas Gainsborough; 1st Lord Clive, by N. Dance. *Gateway Room.* Mortlake tapestries of the life of Nebuchadnezzar (remainder of set is in Long Gallery). English 15C Book of Hours. Insignia of Lord Clive's Order of the Bath. Family and other portraits. *State Bedroom.* Decoration includes crowns and CR, presumably in honour of Charles I or II. Main decoration is mid 17C. Brussels tapestries (late 17C), illustrating the life of Süleyman the Magnificent. Mahogany bed (18C). Queen Anne chairs. Two toilet sets of c 1700 in cloisonné enamel on brass.

Long Gallery, with 16C plasterwork. The painted wainscot is mid 17C. Furniture includes late 17C chairs; French walnut chest with carved portraits (1538); a 16C table, the top of which is inlaid with marble and semi-precious stones. Marble figures of the Elements (c 1700). Greek vases of the 4C BC. Mortlake tapestries, belonging to the set in the Gateway Room. Portraits (mainly family). The *Staircase* and landings were probably designed by William Winde (late 17C). The staircase murals are signed and dated by Lanscroon, 1705; on the right Vulcan forging the arms of love for Venus, and, on the left, Venus in Neptune's chariot, with Bacchus. On the landing the sword of the Lords of the Marches, said to date from c 1500. *Blue Drawing Room.* Ceiling, by Lanscroon, with the daughters of the 2nd Marquess attended by allegories of Africa, Asia and America. Early 18C panelling. Brussels tapestries, depicting Clasical scenes (one signed Marcus de Vos, late 17C). Black lacquer commodes, attributed to Pierre Langlois, c 1760. Enamel bowl and a large dish, both bearing the initials P.R. (Pierre Raymond of c 1513–1584, first of a distinguished line of Limoges enamelists). Among the pictures are family portraits by M. Dahl, P. Batoni and J.M. Quinkhard, and there is also a Madonna and Child attributed to Andrea del Brescianino.

The *Gardens*, of the later 17C, surviving in largely original form, are famous for their four terraces, nearly 200 yards long, possibly designed by William Winde. The Orangery, at the centre of the terraces, carries a balustrade with urns and early 18C lead statues (? Van Nost, or Cheere) of shepherds and shepherdesses. Within the grounds, but outside the gardens, a Douglas fir (185ft) is the tallest tree recorded in Britain.

Welshpool is left by A458, descending into the valley of the Einion (also called the Banwy) and running close to the line and stations of the *Welshpool and Llanfair Railway* (Tel: 0938–810441), the headquarters of which are at the station at *9m* **Llanfair Caereinion**. This railway (2ft 6in gauge) linked Welshpool and Llanfair Caereinion from 1903 to 1931 (passengers) and 1956 (goods). Re-opened by enthusiasts in 1963 to Castell Caereinion, and in 1972 to Sylfaen, the extension to Welshpool was achieved in 1981. Among the steam engines are two built for this line in 1903, one belonging to the German army and one from a West Indian sugar plantation. The *Church* of this small market town was rebuilt in 1868 as successor to a derelict 13C predecessor, of which, however, the doorway survives. Other survivals include the font, the oak vaulting of the choir, and the recumbent effigy (?14C) of a knight, unusual for being hollow as also for having the inscription on the low-slung sword-belt rather than on the shield. Outside the porch, the sundial of 1765 is the work of Samuel Roberts, a local clockmaker. while below the church, on the river bank, *St. Mary's Well* was once known for its healing properties.

Meifod, 4m NE of Llanfair Caereinion, a village in a tranquil pastoral and wooded valley, is celebrated in Welsh poetry, because here, or nearby, there was once a summer residence (maifod) of the princes of Powys. The *Church* here, consecrated in 1155, is of several periods ranging from the 11 to the 19C, the oldest part being the 11C piers ahead and left of the entrance. But older still (9–10C) is a graveslab in the S aisle, bearing the early Christian XP symbol and also some Norse features. The churchyard is exceptionally large and is thought once to have included at least one if not two other churches.

5m. Llanerfyl with, in the village churchyard beneath a yew, a 5C or 6C gravestone. From here the road ascends the N bank of the river (now unequivocally the Banwy and no longer associated with the Einion), in *3m* crossing the tributary Twrch and in another *4m* the watershed (957ft) between the Severn and the Dyfi. From here the pleasant valley of the Dugoed is descended, the road soon making a sharp curve where it crosses a glen. The name *Llidiart-y-Barwn* (Baron's Gate) here recalls that it was in these woods that Baron Owen was murdered in 1555 (see Rte 20B, Mallwyd).

4m. **Mallwyd**, see Rte 20B, which describes the road N to *Bala* and also S (*11m*) to **Machynlleth**, for which town see Rte 20A.

Beyond Machynlleth this Route, now A487, drops gently with the wooded valley of the Dyfi to reach (*6m*) *Furnace (Eglwysfach)* where, beside the road, the Dyfi Furnace (WHM. Tel: 0222-465511) is now preserved as industrial archaeology. Using the power of the Einion cascade, this site was first used during the 17C for refining silver, this being followed in the mid 18C by the construction of the present building as an ironworks blast furnace, the water driving the bellows. From here a small road ascends (N) the pretty *Cwm Einion*, or Artists' Valley, with, in 1m, a waymarked forest walk, while bird enthusiasts will make for the *Ynys Hir* reserve (RSPB. Sign in Eglwysfach.) —*2m. Tre'r Ddol.* Here, in a disused 19C Wesleyan chapel (Yr Hen Gapel. Tel: 0970–86407), there is a museum devoted to 19C religious life and its far-reaching social effects; founded by the late R.J. Thomas, the museum is now a part of the National Museum of Wales.

From Tre'r Ddol there is a choice of roads to Aberystwyth; either direct along A487, or, using B4353, by a westward loop around Dyfi Nature Reserve.

To ABERYSTWYTH DIRECT (A487. 8m). *2m. Talybont*, at the foot of the scenic drive via Nant-y-Moch reservoir to Ponterwyd (see Rte 23A). Also from Talybont a lane climbs NE on to moorland, in rather over 1m reaching, on the right, *Bedd Taliesin*, the stones seemingly of a burial chamber and traditionally the grave of Taliesin, a (possibly mythical) bard and seer of the 6C.—*6m.* **Aberystwyth**, see Rte 22.

To ABERYSTWYTH BY WESTWARD LOOP (B4353 and A487. 11m). From Tre'r Ddol B4353 heads W across *Dyfi National Nature Reserve* (restricted access: dangerous tidal paths), established in 1969 and 1972 and comprising the Estuary, with wildfowl and migrant waders; Cors Fochno, or Borth Bog, either side of the road, an area of raised bog much used for botanical research; and, where the road curves at the NW, Ynyslas Dunes, with parking, information and a nature trail.

Southward, between Ynyslas and the straggling resort village of *Borth*, the road runs beside a storm beach which, millennia ago, was forest. Beyond Borth there is a road choice between B4572 or B4353. The former crosses hills above cliffs, below which, at Wallog, *Sarn Cynfelyn* is a rock causeway said to be the remains of a road leading to the drowned Lowland Hundred (see Rte 21). The latter runs through the village of *Llandre*, in the woods above which is Castell Gwallter, the motte of an early Norman castle (destroyed by the

Welsh in 1137) the name of which recalls its builder, Walter de Bec.
Beyond, B4353 joins A487 for the 4m run into **Aberystwyth**, see Rte
22.

B. Via Welshpool, Newtown
and Cemmaes Road

A458 to Welshpool. A483 to Newtown. A489 to Caersws. A470 to
Cemmaes Road. A489 to Machynlleth. A487 to Aberystwyth. Total
distance 73m.—*18m.* **Welshpool.**—*13m.* **Newtown.**—*5m.*
Caersws.—*16m.* **Cemmaes Road.**—*5m.* **Machynlleth.**—*16m.*
Aberystwyth.

After Welshpool the general course of the valley of the Severn is
followed as far as Caersws. Byond, there is increasing moorland,
this, beyond Machynlleth, giving way to mixed wood and moor
inland with estuary flats to seaward.

For **Shrewsbury** to (*18m*) **Welshpool**, see Rte 19A.—*5m. Berriew*, a
pleasant half-timbered village on the Rhiew, is traditionally
associated with St. Beuno after whom a large glacial boulder is
named. It is said that, when communing by the Severn, he heard
English voices across the water and successfully warned the villagers
of this pagan threat. Near *Garthmyl, 1m* farther, the Severn can be
crossed; beyond the bridge, a road running N parallel to the railway
in 1m reaches the remains of a small Roman fort, probably a stage
between Viroconium and Caersws and apparently in use until the
4C.

Montgomery (1000 inhab.), in Welsh Trefaldwyn, 2½m SE of
Garthmyl, is a very small market town, attractively Georgian in
character and straddling a hill below the ruins of its castle; this castle,
a preserved length of Offa's Dyke, and the basically 13C church are
the three sites of specific interest.

History. Offa's Dyke cut through here in about 784 (a section is preserved in
Lymore Park, E of the town). Some 300 years later, in c 1072, another
fortification was started, Roger de Montgomery's Norman castle, the site of
which is almost certainly the motte-and-bailey 1m NW and known as Hen
Domen (see below). The present castle was built by Henry III in 1223 and the
town received its charter four years later. Both town and castle are closely
associated with the Herbert family. The 1st Lord Herbert of Cherbury (1583–
1648), philosopher and diplomat, spent his youth here and it was he who in 1644
surrendered the castle to Parliament. But it was demolished in 1649 because the
2nd Lord Herbert was a Royalist. Another Herbert, the 1st Lord's brother
George Herbert (1593–1633), the poet, was born either in the castle or in the
town. What was left of the castle pretty well collapsed during the 19C.

Of Henry III's *Castle* not much survives—something of a twin-
towered gatehouse, the lower courses of wards, a ditch, a deep
well—but the site is as it should be: a long, narrow and rocky ridge
projecting boldly towards the N and, accessible virtually only from
the S, of unusual strength. Inside the mainly 13C *Church* (tower
rebuilt in 1816) the most noteworthy feature is a double *Screen and
Loft, the original 15C part being the W side of panels with traceried
tops, five each side of the door. The loft is thought to be made up of
sections from the mother priory at Chirbury (2½m NE in England)
where the church preserves the 13C nave arcades of a small priory of
Austin Canons founded in c 1180, probable provenance also of
Montgomery's church's 15C stalls and misericords. Also in the
church are the fine Renaissance tomb (1600) of Sir Richard Herbert

and two recumbent effigies, the smaller figure probably being Sir Edmund Mortimer (died 1409), grandson of Owen Glendower, and the other Sir Richard Herbert (died 1534), grandfather of the occupant of the Renaissance tomb. Less distinguished, but of more interest perhaps, is the occupant of the Robber's Grave on the N side of the churchyard; for here the grass is said never to grow above the grave of John Newton Davies, an innocent man hanged in 1921.

On the adjacent hill to the W is the hillfort of *Fridd Faldwyn* (750ft), while *Town Hill* (1050ft), ³⁄₄m SW of Fridd Faldwyn and crowned by the county war memorial, commands a view which includes Cader Idris.

A483 may be regained by B4385 and B4386. Just N of the former (1m from Montgomery, in trees on the left side of a road leading N from a small crossroads) the motte of *Hen Domen* probably represents Roger de Montgomery's castle of 1072.

B4386 meets A483 near where the latter crosses the Severn (*4m* from Garthmyl), near here, on the steep narrow ridge to the NW, being the slight remains of *Dolforwyn Castle*, started by Llewelyn the Last in 1273. **Kerry**, 2¹⁄₂m S and reached by B4368, is a small place in the heart of a sheep-rearing countryside and the origin of the name of a well-known breed distinctive for the black spots on their faces and legs. The *Church* here was dedicated in 1176 amid, it is said, disorderly scenes as the retainers of Giraldus and those of the Bishop of St. Asaph disputed over local episcopal jurisdiction. Of this early Norman church, however, there survive only the N arcade and, possibly, part of the tower (most of which was rebuilt in the 14C), with its buttresses of varying pattern and picturesque boarded top. Inside are a chained Welsh Bible (1690); a 15C font, with the Instruments of the Passion; a 14C piscina (S choir); and a pulpit which, though modern, bears some 15C tracery.

3m (from A483 Severn bridge), or 2¹⁄₂m by A489 from Kerry, **Newtown** (Drenewydd. 10,000 inhab. *Inf.* Central Car Park. Tel: 0686–625580) is a busy but pleasant enough market town on the Severn and with several places of varied interest to visitors.

History. Despite its name, Newtown traces its origins to about 973 and to a motte-and-bailey castle. Edward I granted the associated borough a charter in 1280, this marking the start of a commercial progress which peaked in the 19C by which time the town was a weaving and textiles centre and the home of the Welsh flannel industry. Notable dates include 1648 when Charles I sheltered here after defeat at Naseby; 1771, birth of Robert Owen (see below); 1821 when the Montgomery Canal reached Newtown; and 1859–63 which saw Newtown served by railways to Llanidloes, Oswestry and Aberystwyth.

Just beside Tourist Information (Central Car Park) stands the 1960s *Davies Memorial Gallery*, commemorating the Davies sisters of Gregynog (see below) and used for a variety of touring and temporary exhibitions, to the S of this, and near the Council Offices, being the motte of the motte-and-bailey to which Newtown traces its origins.

From the Central Car Park, Wesley Place leads NE into Broad Street, about 150 yards NW up which Long Bridge crosses the Severn. Just across the bridge, at 5–7 Commercial Street, in a building which in the days of handloom weavers served as both dwelling and workshop, is the *Textile Museum* (Tel: 0686–625580), telling, progressively, the story of Newtown's one-time key industry. The theme of the ground floor is 'Fleece to Flannel' while the upper level provides a record of the prosperous period which spanned from the 1790s to the mid 1930s.

From opposite where Wesley Place meets Broad Street, Old Church Street leads to ruined *St. Mary's Church*, built in the 13C but abandoned in 1856 because it was too small and also liable to flooding. The tower and other remnants were restored in 1939, and in the yard, beside the church wall, is the tomb of Robert Owen (1771–1858), factory reformer, founder of the cooperative movement, and Newtown's most cherished native. Owen was born at what is now the *Robert Owen Memorial Museum* (Tel: 0686–626345), farther E along Broad Street on the corner with Severn Street. Here there is a reconstruction of the room in which Owen was born, while displays record his life, starting with his birth here, tracing his many wanderings and experiments (notably in Scotland at New Lanark), and concluding with his return to and death in Newtown in 1858. Just round the corner in High Street there is a museum of a very different kind, namely the *W.H. Smith Shop and Museum* (Tel: 0686–626280), the former in part restored, as a contribution to European Architectural Heritage Year (1975), to its elegant style of 1927, while the museum tells the story of the firm from its beginnings in 1792 in London's Little Grosvenor Street.

Broad Street, continuing SE, becomes Short Bridge Street. Here, on the left, is a small triangular *Robert Owen Memorial Park* with a charming figure of the reformer.

ENVIRONS OF NEWTOWN. The village of *Tregynon*, 4m N, has a place in the history of the early use of concrete, two cottages and the school here being considered to be among the world's first concrete buildings (1870).—*Gregynog Hall* (Tel: 0686–626521) has since 1960 been an educational residential centre of the University of Wales. Following predecessors dating back to the 12C, the hall was largely rebuilt in the 19C and in 1920 the estate was bought by the sisters Gwendoline and Margaret Davies (the latter gave it to the university) and developed as a music and discussion centre, with, also, a press which produced fine limited editions and soon became a leader among private presses. The sisters were also art collectors, the bulk of their collection now being in the National Museum of Wales, though some works, notably two Rodin busts, are still here at Gregynog.

Fronlas Farm Park, 1m W of Newtown off Llanidloes Road, a part of the Agriculture Department of Montgomery College, offers a farm tour, nature trails, a pets' corner, and pony and tractor rides (Tel: 0686–624187).

This Route leaves Newtown by A489, in *5m* reaching **Caersws**, on the site of a 1C Roman station, well defended by the Severn and the Garno and at the hub of road links with Castell Collen, Y Gaer, Pennal and, away to the N, Deva (Chester). The fort, the earthworks of which survive on the NW side of the town beside A470, is known to have been garrisoned by troops from Spain. A more modern claim to interest is that Caersws was for 20 years the home of the poet John Ceiriog Hughes, then manager of the local Van Railway (plaque on house just S of the station).

For the more scenic 'Mountain Road' to Machynlleth via Llyn Clywedog, see Rte 18C.

Caersws is left by A470, this soon passing just W of the village of *Llanwnog*, with, in the churchyard, the grave of John Ceiriog Hughes. The church itself has a 15C rood loft, still with its stairs, and also some fragments of 15C glass in a window on the N side.—The scenery now starts to become moorland in character as the road follows the glen of the Garno to (*5m*) *Carno*, which has its place in history, for it was here in 1081 that Gruffydd ap Cynan and Rhys at Tewdwr, both returning from exile, joined forces, defeating their rivals and winning respectively the crowns of northern and southern Wales.—*3m. Talerddig*, just before which the watershed (731ft)

between the Severn and the Dyfi is crossed.—*3m Llanbrynmair*, 1m S
of which is *Llan*, birthplace of Abraham Rees (1743–1825), the
encyclopaedist, and long the home (1806–57) of the Rev. Samuel
Roberts, social reformer and tireless advocate of postal innovations.
The early 15C church here is a curiosity, with its wooden tower
enclosed inside the nave.—*5m* **Cemmaes Road**, from where to (*5m*)
Machynlleth see Rtes 20B and 20A. For Machynlleth to (*16m*)
Aberystwyth, see Rte 18A.

C.   Via Welshpool, Llanidloes and Llyn Clywedog

A458 to Welshpool. A483 to Newtown. A489 to Caersws. A470 or
B4569 to Llanidloes. B4518 and unclassified to Machynlleth. A487
to Aberystwyth. Total distance 76m.—*18m*. **Welshpool.**—*13m*.
Newtown.—*5m*. **Caersws.**—*7m*. **Llanidloes.**—*17m*. **Machynlleth.**—
16m. **Aberystwyth.**

After Welshpool the general course of the valley of the Severn is
followed as far as Caersws. The 'Mountain Road' between
Llanidloes and Machynlleth, across high, remote moorland. After
Machynlleth wood and moor inland, estuary flats to seaward.

For **Shrewsbury** to (*18m*.) **Welshpool**, see Rte 18A. Beyond, to (*18m*.)
Caersws, see Rte 18B.

There is a choice of roads between Caersws and Llanidloes. Along
A470, the more southerly choice, *Llandinam*, reached in 2m, was the
home of David Davies (1818–90), a local lad who became a leading
industrialist, developing the coal industry and founding the docks at
Barry; he is remembered by a bronze statue (by Sir Alfred Gilbert,
best known for London's Piccadilly Eros) at the E end of the bridge
over the Severn, now little more than a stream and here usually given
its Welsh name Hafren.—Along B4569, the northerly choice,
Trefeglwys, reached in 5m, was the birthplace of Benjamin Piercy
(1827–88), an engineer who built many of the railways in Wales and
also those in Sardinia.

7m. **Llanidloes** (2300 inhab. *Inf.* Longbridge Street. Tel: 05512–
2605), at the confluence of the Severn (or Hafren) and its larger
tributary the Clywedog, has roots deep in the religious and social
upheavals of the 18 and 19C. John Wesley preached here in 1748,
1749 and 1764, and in the following century, in 1839, the town was a
centre of the Chartist riots. Today the striking half-timbered *Old
Market Hall*, built in c 1600 and a rare example of a Welsh free-
standing market hall, is a focus for the past. The upper floor,
originally used as a court house, was in the 18 and 19C the meeting
place of Quakers, Methodists and Baptists before they built their own
chapels, and the building now houses the *Museum of Local History
and Industry* (Tel: 05512–2605), with an emphasis on textiles, lead
mining and the Chartist riots. Against the building's exterior stands
the John Wesley Stone from which Wesley preached during his three
visits. The *Church*, dedicated to the 7C St. Idloes, was restored and
enlarged in 1881 but nevertheless retains much of its early structure,
though the early 13C N arcade, with heavily moulded arches and
clustered piers, and the 15C hammer-beam roof may both have been
brought here from Cwmhir Abbey. The 14C tower also merits

attention, for its pronounced external batter and, inside, the vaulted base with curious slate masonry.

From Llanidloes A470 and A44 lead direct to Aberystwyth (see Rte 23A).

Hafren Forest, on the E slopes of the massif of Plynlimon and covering over 17 square miles, is some 6m W of Llanidloes and offers several waymarked walks ranging from 1m to 8m through the forest, along the upper Severn and up on to Plynlimon.

B4518, the start of what is sometimes called the 'Mountain Road', heads NW out of Llanidloes, in 2m reaching a fork offering a choice between skirting the E or W shore of **Llyn Clywedog**, a beautiful reservoir created between 1964–68 to regulate the flow of the Clywedog and Severn, thus both meeting water demand and, by catching and storing winter rain, preventing flooding along the Severn's lower reaches. For the W bank road, see below. On the E side, B4518 runs some distance from the reservoir's shore, on the road's right rising *Fan Hill* (1580ft) on the slopes of which can be seen (a road rounds the hill) the chimneys of the now disused Van Lead Mine, once one of the most prosperous in this part of Wales and still with the forlorn remnants of terraced houses and even chapels. It was near here, at a farm called Crowlym, that the first Sunday School in England and Wales was started in 1770 by Jenkin Morgan. To the road's left, crowning a promontory which now juts into the reservoir, is the hillfort of Dinas (1461ft), and some 2m beyond this, at the N end of the narrowing finger where the river Clywedog becomes a reservoir, the hamlet of *Staylittle* (7m from Llanidloes) owes its odd name to three blacksmiths who shod horses so quickly that their smithy came to be called Stay-a-Little.

The road along the W shore of Llyn Clywedog, only some 2m longer, is scenically rather more rewarding and also offers picnic sites, view points, the dam (237ft high), and walks, one of these, just below the dam, being the Clywedog Gorge Trail which includes the remains of Bryntail lead mine, an early mine, which was reopened in the mid 19C (the period of today's remains) but finally closed in 1884. Immediately beyond the dam the road rounds the hillfort of Pen-y-Gair (1250ft), then, continuing round the lake, enters *Hafren Forest* (see above), at a T junction here bearing right and in another 2m rejoining B4518 just N of Staylittle.

Just N of Staylittle a road junction is reached from which B4518 continues due N to meet Rte 18B in 7m at Llanbrynmair. This Route, though, bears W along an unclassified road to reach in ½m a view point above *Ffrwd Fawr*, with an awesome barren abyss. Beyond, the road makes its lonely way across high open moor (road highest point 1671ft) before descending along the N flank of the Plynlimon plateau to reach (*10m* from Staylittle) **Machynlleth**, for which see Rte 20A. For A487 to (16m) **Aberystwyth**, see Rte 18A.

19 Lake Vyrnwy and its Approaches

A. Lake Vyrnwy

Lake Vyrnwy (pronounced Verny), or Llyn Efyrnwy, at a height of 825ft and scenically situated below wooded hills, is a narrow strip 4m in length and less than ½m wide. The lake (dam at S end), a reservoir for the water needs of Liverpool, was formed in 1886–90; tablets in the roadside rock-face at the N end of the dam record the various stages of the work and of the associated pipeline projects. Prior to the construction of the reservoir, the river Vyrnwy, a chief Welsh tributary of the Severn, was here a small stream meandering across a marshy flat formed by the sands and gravels which had silted a lake basin scooped out in glacial times. The present dam, 390 yards long and 144 feet high, rests on the bar of glaciated rock that retained the early lake, and the reservoir can thus be regarded as the restoration of an ancient natural feature. The lake's surface area is 1121 acres, its storage capacity is 12,131 million gallons, and the catchment area covers some 36 square miles.

A wooded road circuits the lake, crossing the dam on a series of arches through which surplus water escapes in cascades. The original hamlet of *Llanwddyn* was drowned, but a new village has grown below the dam. On the NE shore, about 1m from the dam, a picturesque tower marks the entrance to the *Hirnant Tunnel* (2¼m long) which forms the first section of the aqueduct, 75m long, that carries the water to Liverpool. Farther on, at the mouth of the Cedig, is the site of the drowned village. The road from Bala by way of Cwm Hirnant reaches the lake at its N tip; and that from Bwlch-y-Groes at Pont Eunant, 1m farther on the W shore, the site of submerged Eunant Hall.

Approaches to Vyrnwy from Bala and Oswestry (see 'Blue Guide England') are described below, those from Bala being very scenic.

B. Approaches from Bala

VIA LLANGYNOG. B43491 and B4396. 19 miles.—The road skirts the N tip of Bala Lake, almost immediately afterwards passing the road to Cwm Hirnant (see below). Beyond, in another 3m at the junction with B4402/01, it climbs through woods, reaching open moor and (*8m* from Bala) *Milltir Gerig Pass* (1595ft), a saddle in the long Berwyn range. The descent is above the precipitous valley of the Eirth.—*3m* **Llangynog**, a name recalling Cynog, son of the 5C prince, Brychan, is a long village beautifully set below mountains at the meeting of the Eirth and Tanat glens. The lead mines and slate quarries are now closed, the former due to flooding.

The valley of the upper Tanat, cutting NW as a wooded and pastoral finger into the mountains, in 2½m reaches the little Norman church of *Pennant Melangell*. Inside are two 14C recumbent effigies, one said to be of a Welsh prince and the other of St. Melangell; an 18C wooden candelabrum; and a rood screen of c 1500. The loft of the screen has on its bottom beam mutilated carvings illustrating the 7C legend of St. Melangell (or Monacella), according to which a hare, hunted by Brochwel Ysgythrog, Prince of Powys, took refuge under her robe. As a result Melangell became the patron saint of hares, thenceforward known as 'St. Monacella's lambs' and treated as sacred in the district. Recent excavations have revealed, below the rebuilt apse and in line with the original, a grave which may well be that of the saint, while fragments identified as parts of her shrine are to be incorporated in a reconstruction. The valley ends in a rounded cwm, with the white thread of *Blaen-y-Cwm* waterfall.

The valley below Llangynog is that of the middle Tanat.—*2m. Penybontfawr*, where the Tanat Valley and Llansilin approaches from Oswestry are met. For *Llanrhaeadr-ym-Mochnant* and *Pistyll Rhaeadr*, see Rte 19C. From Penybontfawr B4396 ascends Cwm Hirnant (not to be confused with the other Cwm Hirnant described immediately below), in *6m* reaching **Lake Vyrnwy**.

VIA CWM HIRNANT, Unclassified road. 9 miles. A beautiful drive through remote wood and moorland scenery.—B4391 is taken E out of Bala, then, soon after leaving the lake, an unclassified road which climbs S up the thickly wooded *Cwm Hirnant* (FC picnic site). Emerging from the woods, the road continues to climb across high moor (1641ft) before, again in woods, descending beside the tumbling Nadroedd stream to reach the N extremity of **Lake Vyrnwy**.

VIA BWLCH-Y-GROES. A494 or B4403, then unclassified roads. 14 miles.—*5m.* **Llanuwchllyn** may be reached either by A494 along the W shore of Bala Lake (see Rte 14 for this road as also for the village) or by B4403 along the E shore. From Llanuwchllyn an unclassified road ascends high up on the side of Cwm Cynllwyd for (*5m.*) *Bwlch-y-Groes* (1790ft. Rte 20B), the highest road pass in Wales. Just beyond the summit a road branches E away from the Dinas Mawddwy road to descend beside the Eunant stream, first across moor and then through woods, to (*4m.*) **Lake Vyrnwy**.

C. Approaches from Oswestry

VIA LLANSILIN. B4580 and B4396. 18 miles.—*3m. Rhyd-y-Croesau*, where the Welsh border is crossed.—*2m. Llansilin*, where Hugh Morris (1622–1709), the Royalist satirical poet, is buried.—*5m.* **Llanrhaeadr-ym-Mochnant**, of which Bishop Morgan (1545–1604), who in 1588 here made his translation of the Bible into Welsh, was vicar. In the church there is a Celtic cross-slab (9–10C).

From the village a narrow, and in summer crowded, road leads in under 4m to **Pistyll Rhaeadr** (parking), said to be the highest falls in Wales and of which Borrow wrote 'I never saw water falling so gracefully, so much like thin beautiful threads as here'. The falls descend some 240ft by a series of leaps, of which the first is an unbroken drop of more than 100ft, falling into a cauldron from which the second cascade issues through a gap in the rock.—A track leads N for 1½m to *Llyn Llyncaws* (2000ft), a small tarn in a rock amphitheatre, and thence (½m) to *Moel Sych* (2713ft), the highest point in the Berwyns.

2m. Penybontfawr to (*6m.*) **Lake Vyrnwy**, see Rte 19B.

VIA TANAT VALLEY. A483, A495, and B4396. 22 miles.—A483, S out of Oswestry, in *4m* reaches *Llynclys*, from where A495 and B4396 are followed to (*2m*) *Llanyblodwel*. Soon the road reaches the N side of the Tanat and crosses into Wales. At *Sycharth*, 1m N and reached by the first road beyond the border, a motte is all that marks the site of a principal residence of Owen Glendower, described in a poem by the bard Iolo Goch as having nine halls, many guest rooms, and a church. It was destroyed in 1403 by the future Henry V.—*4m. Llangedwyn,* where the church contains the recumbent effigy of a vested priest and a font, both from the previous church. At the E exterior of the church there is a medieval stone cross. Llangedwyn Hall, N of the road, was the residence of Sir W. Williams Wynn, the generous friend of the poet Southey, who, with Bishop Heber, visited him here. He gave the poet an allowance from 1797 until 1806, and in 1807 arranged a government pension.—*3m.* Junction with B4580, up which (1m) is *Llanrhaeadr-ym-Mochnant* (see above).—*3m. Penybontfawr* to (6m. **Lake Vyrnwy,** see Rte 19B.

VIA LLANFYLLIN. A483 to Llynclys: A495 to Llansantffraid-ym-Mechain: B4393 and A490 to Llanfyllin: B4393 to Lake Vyrnwy. 24 miles.—To just short of (6m.) *Llanyblodwel,* see immediately above.—*3m.* (by A495) *Llansantffraid-ym-Mechain,* a short way into Wales and on the Vyrnwy, has a church with a Jacobean window (1619). Beyond the hamlet B4393 is taken for (2m.) *Llanfechain,* where the church, dedicated to St. Garmon (Germanus), contains an inscribed pulpit of 1636 and an iron chandelier of 1727.

4m. **Llanfyllin** (1250 inhab.), a town which received its first charter in 1293, straggles along the upper Cain valley below steep wooded hills. About ¹/₂m W of Llanfyllin the road forks, the right branch in 4m reaching Penybontfawr. The left branch (B4393) leads SW, ascending Nant Alan.—*5m. Llanfihangel-yng-Ngwynfa,* just S of the road, has a church containing old armorial pew backs (on the walls) and, in the vestry, grave-slabs of c 1400. In the churchyard there is a memorial to Ann Griffiths (1780–1805), well known as a writer of hymns in the Welsh language. Her home at *Dolwar Fach* (2m S) can be seen—After an ascent to 1104ft the road drops to (4m.) **Lake Vyrnwy**.

20 Machynlleth to Bala

A. Via Dolgellau

A487 and A470 to Dolgellau. A494 to Bala. Total distance 32m— *5m. Corris.*—*3m. Minffordd.*—*4m. Cross Foxes.*—*3m.* **Dolgellau.**— *17m.* **Bala.**

The narrow wooded valley of the Dulas is followed by moor, a fine view of Cader Idris, and a craggy stretch along the mountain's E foot.

Machynlleth (2000 inhab. *Inf.* Canolfan Owain Glyndwr. Tel: 0654– 702401), pronounced Mahun'hleth, in the green valley of the Dyfi, is a market and shopping centre serving a wide district, and also, being at the heart of much lovely scenery, a popular but generally not overcrowded holiday base. The town centre is the *Clock Tower* of 1872, from which Maengwyn Street, the broad main street, runs E to reach on the left side the *Owen Glendower Institute (Canolfan Owain Glyndwr)*, a 16C building said to be on the site of a predecessor in which Glendower held his first parliament in 1404. Today the building houses Tourist Information and exhibitions. Opposite is the entrance to *Plas Machynlleth* (1653), which, with its fine grounds, was presented to the town by Lord Londonderry. The hall now houses local government offices while the grounds are a public park and recreation area. Farther E, on the S side of Maengwyn Street, the so-called *Mayor's House* is a half-timbered building of 1628.

For Machynlleth to (S) *Aberystwyth* and (E) *Llanidloes, Newtown, Welshpool* and *Shrewsbury,* see Rte 18; to *Dinas Mawddwy* and *Bala,* see Rte 20B below; to *Tywyn* and *Dolgellau,* see Rte 21.

A487 (Doll Street) passes the station and crosses the Dyfi by a bridge first built in 1533 but rebuilt in c 1800. Beyond, A493 bears W as Rte 21, while this Route heads N, climbing the wooded, narrow and winding valley of the river Dulas to reach in *3m* the **Centre for Alternative Technology** (Tel: 0654–702400). Of particular interest in a world increasingly concerned with its environment, this Centre is an independent educational charity; not a museum, but a community actually living and working with alternative technology. Among the functioning themes are solar power, including a solar-heated cottage; windmills and water-wheels; a conservation house, with super-insulation, heat pumps and quadruple glazing; organic horticulture; fish culture and bee keeping. A short way farther up the road, *Tan-y-Coed*, a Forestry Commission picnic site, is the starting place for waymarked forest walks (Cwm Cadian) which may be extended to the moorland ridge (2187ft) beyond and down to the valley of the Dysynni.

2m. Corris, a village sharply below the road at the junction of the Dulas and a small tributary, was in the 19C a part of a district busy with slate quarrying, associated with this being a rail line between Aberllefenni (E of Corris) and Machynlleth. Now long disused, the line (which provided two engines of 1878 and 1921 for the Talyllyn railway) is recalled by a small museum in Corris, while some of the quarry buildings can be seen along a trail (2m) which starts from a Forestry Commission picnic site (Foel Friog) between Corris and Aberllefenni.—After Corris, A487 bears NW, turning away from the Dulas and climbing past slate workings to reach a height of 666ft, with a splendid view of Cader Idris.

3m, Minffordd, at the junction with B4405 which has ascended the Dysynni from near Tywyn. For this beautiful road (with the Talyllyn Railway, Castell-y-Bere, Llanfihangel-y-Pennant and Tal-y-Llyn lake) see Rte 21. Minffordd is immediately below Cader Idris, the road now climbing NE, with craggy heights on either side, to reach a pass at 938ft.—*4m. Cross Foxes*, where A470 comes in from the E from Dinas Mawddwy. In another 1½m, at the head of Torrent Walk (see Rte 16), B4416, diverging NE through Brithdir, offers a shortcut avoiding Dolgellau, which can be a bottleneck in summer.—*3m.* **Dolgellau**, for which, with Cader Idris, see Rte 16. For Dolgellau to (*17m*) **Bala**, see Rte 14.

B.   Via Dinas Mawddwy and Bwlch-y-Groes

A489 to Cemmaes Road. A470 to Dinas Mawddwy. Unclassified over Bwlch-y-Groes to Llanuwchllyn. A494 or B4403 to Bala. Total distance 30m.—*5m.* **Cemmaes Road.**—*8m.* **Dinas Mawddwy.**—*7m.* **Bwlch-y-Groes.**—*5m.* **Llanuwchllym.**—*5m.* **Bala.**

As far as Dinas Mawddwy the road follows the pastoral valley of the Dyfi, with high ground on either side. Beyond Dinas Mawddwy the narrow and steep unclassified road climbs through wild scenery across Bwlch-y-Groes (1790ft), the highest road pass in Wales. Motorists preferring the main road can continue on A470 to Dolgellau, and thence to Bala.

Machynlleth, see Rte 20A above.—*2m. Penegoes* was the birthplace of the painter Richard Wilson (1714–82), and is today the home of Felin Crewi, a restored 17C water-mill (Tel: 0654–703113).—*3m.* **Cemmaes Road**, where A470 (Rte 18B) comes in from the east. At *Cemmaes*, 1½m farther, there is a memorial in the church to Dr Daniel Evans (died 1903), the first Professor of Welsh at University College, Aberystwyth.—*6m*, **Mallwyd**, where A458 (Rte 18A) joins from the east and where the name of a hotel, the 'Brigands Inn', recalls that in the middle of the 16C this neighbourhood was terrorised by a large gang, known from the colour of their hair as the 'Red Robbers of Mawddwy'. Eighty of these brigands were seized and executed in 1554, mainly through the efforts of Baron Lewis Owen, who, the following year, was murdered by the gang's survivors at Llidiart-y-Barwn (the Baron's Gate), about 2½m up A458. After this, the gang was exterminated. The church here, dating from 1641, but certainly on much older foundations, is also of modest interest. The rib of some unidentified prehistoric beast, dug up locally during the 19C, hangs over the wooden E porch, while John Davies (1570–1644), the lexicographer and assistant to Bishop Parry in producing the Welsh Authorised Version of the Bible, is buried in the churchyard. Minister here from 1604–44, John Davies was also something of a practical engineer, building Pont Minllyn, a picturesque twin-arched foot and packhorse bridge about half-way between Mallwyd and Dinas Mawddwy close to *Meirion Mill* (Tel: 0650–521311), a working wool mill which, in part occupying the buildings of what was once Dinas Mawddwy station, is just the other side of the main road river bridge. The mill includes a shop, a restaurant and a gallery of local arts and crafts, while the railway (the Cemmaes-Mawddwy Line, opened in 1868) is recalled by the station buildings, the reconstructed fine wrought-iron gates and a section of track maintained as a walk.

Dinas Mawddwy village, rather under *2m* from Mallwyd, was long ago the centre of one of two more or less independent districts within the princedom of Powys, the other being Penllyn to the north (see Rte 14, Bala Lake). Mawddwy remained with Powys until the Edwardian conquest, when it became a part of the shire of Merioneth, although retaining the dignity of its own mayor and council until 1668. Today a walking and fishing centre, the village nestles in a lovely amphitheatre below wooded hills and mountains at the junction of the Dyfi and the Cerist. Much of the hillsides is covered by rhododendrons, and in season the colour across the valley to the E can be breathtaking.

Motorists not wishing to take the direct Bala road across Bwlch-y-Groes can use the longer main road route via Dolgellau (10m). This road, for its first part very scenic, with steep cwms and waterfalls, ascends the valley of the Cerist, above the N bank in 1m being National Trust property, given in 1947 by Squadron Leader J.D.K. Lloyd and his brother Dr W.E.B. Lloyd as a memorial to the men of Bomber Command who lost their lives during the war. Beyond, the road climbs steeply to the top of *Bwlch Oerddrws* (Cold Door Pass; 1178ft), beyond which the country, though becoming open and bleak, is backed by a magnificent view of Cader Idris. At *Cross Foxes Hotel*, Rte 20A is joined.

1m. Aber-Cywarch, from where a small road ascends the narrow valley of the Cywarch for 2m. From the end of this road a path climbs NE up the steep slope of Hengwm valley for Dyrysgol and the range of the Arans.—Near (*3m.*) *Llanymawddwy* there are some fine waterfalls, notably Pistyll Gwyn, 1¼m W on the Pumryd. The scenery grows wilder, the Dyfi is crossed, and the valley ends in a cwm of precipitous mountain slopes, 800–1000ft high, deeply scarred by watercourses. The Dyfi, from its source in the tarn of Craiglyn Dyfi (2½m NW), comes in through *Llaethnant* (Milk Valley) in a succession of cataracts, and the black, rocky peak of Aran Mawddwy stands out beyond the head of the glen. The road now climbs the steep side of the deep *Glen of the Rhiwlech* (over 1000ft in under 2m), passing the eastward road to Lake Vyrnwy (see Rte 19B) and reaching the summit of (*3m*) **Bwlch-y-Groes** (1790ft; parking), the highest point on any road in Wales. To the W the dominant feature is the range of the Arans, a volcanic ridge running between Bala Lake and Dinas Mawddwy, the names of the peaks of which—Aran Benllyn (2901ft) and Aran Mawddwy (2970ft)—recall the two semi-independent districts referred to under Dinas Mawddwy above.

The descent is down the precipitous wall of Cwm Cynllwyd to (*5m*) the lake level at **Llanuwchllyn**, from where **Bala** can be reached in *5m* either by A494 along the N shore of Bala Lake, or by B4403 skirting the S shore and accompanied by the little Bala Lake Railway (for Llanuwchllyn, the above roads, and Bala, See Rte 14).

21 Machynlleth to Tywyn and Dolgellau

A493. Total distance 34m.—*11m.* **Aberdyfi**.—*4m.* **Tywyn.**—*2m.* Bryncrug (for the Fathew and Dysynni valleys).—*9m.* **Fairbourne.**— *8m.* **Dolgellau.**

A pleasant coastal road with some good views. Interesting and scenic diversions from Bryncrug up the valleys of the Fathew and Dysynni rivers towards the S foot of Cader Idris. Beyond Fairbourne the main road runs between the Mawddach Estuary and the NW side of Cader Idris.

Machynlleth (see Rte 20A) is left by the bridge across the Dyfi (first built 1533, rebuilt c 1800), on the far side of which A487 (Rte 20A) continues N, while this Route bears W along A493 to (*4m.*) **Pennal**, a village near the site of a Roman fort, traces of which, with a later motte, can be seen S of the road.—*3m.* Gogarth, where the estuary of the Dyfi is reached. For the Dyfi National Nature Reserve, see Rte 18A.—*4m.* **Aberdyfi** (1000 inhab. *Inf.* The Wharf. Tel: 0654–767321), the name frequently anglicised to Aberdovey, is a modest small resort with good sands and well-known for golf and, more particularly, sailing, the latter the theme of the *Outward Bound Sailing Museum* (Tel: 0654–767464) on the waterfront.

The song, 'The Bells of Aberdovey', became popular through Charles Dibdin's opera 'Liberty Hall' (1785). The legend is that of the Lowland Hundred, or Cantref-y-Gwaelod, a low-lying land protected by dykes. On one stormy night its prince, Seithenyn, was so drunk that he forgot to close the sluices, and the cantref, or hundred, was drowned. But its bells still peal below the water, and Sarn Badrig (Rte 17) and Sarn Cynfelin (Rte 18A), geologically glacial deposits, are said to be ancient roads which once led to this lost land. The earliest mention of this catastrophe is in a 13C manuscript, but the story held a strong attraction for writers of the 17–19C who added their own romantic embellishments. See also James Elroy Flecker's poem 'The Welsh Sea'.

4m. **Tywyn** (*Inf*. High Street. Tel: 0654–710070), or Towyn (the yw or ow pronounced as in 'now' and the name meaning Sand Dune), is essentially an inland small town which has grown into a seaside resort, with a sand and shingle beach reaching S as far as Aberdyfi's golf links, and caravan parks and holiday camps to both the N and the south. Tywyn's ancient roots live on in the *Church of St. Cadfan* at the N end of the town. Named after the founder (in 429) of the monastery on the island of Bardsey off the tip of the Lleyn, the church has an early Norman nave (probably 11C), with massive short piers, curiously primitive whitewashed arcades, and tiny splayed windows in the clerestory. There is also some early work in the N aisle, though the rest of the church is rebuilding of 1844. But the church's most interesting feature is the so-called St. Cadfan Stone, probably of the 7C and bearing an inscription thought to be the oldest example of written Welsh and certainly older than any extant manuscript. Also interesting, inside the church, are, N of the choir, two recumbent effigies of the 14C, one of a knight seemingly in the act of drawing his sword, the other of a vested and hooded priest, while on the church's exterior there are two old horizontal slabs curiously incorporated into the 19C tower, the one on the S side showing an inscribed cross.

Tywyn is probably best known for the *Talyllyn Railway* (Tel: 0654–710472), the principal station of which, Tywyn Wharf, is at the SW end of the town on the Aberdyfi road. The line, opened for freight in 1866 and for passengers the following year (over 23,000 were carried in 1877), was built to carry slate from the quarry above Abergynolwyn (7m NE) down to Tywyn, where it was transferred to main line trains. The quarry closed in 1947, after which (in 1950) the Talyllyn Railway Preservation Society was formed, the result being a railway service which was the first in the world to be operated by volunteers. With a gauge of 2ft 3ins, with venerable and historic steam engines (1865 and later), and with carriages of many shapes, sizes and origins, the track ascends the pleasant valley of the Fathew (for the road, see below) as far as Nant Gwernol (no road access; waymarked forest walks), the full return journey requiring some two hours. With several stations and halts (parking and other facilities at Abergynolwyn and Dolgoch), however, the timetables permit a good deal of individual choice and flexibility. Other attractions of the railway include a letter service with special stamps and postmarks; and, at Tywyn, a shop and the Narrow Gauge Railway Museum with a notable collection of material, including engines and rolling stock, relating to narrow gauge railways generally.

Beyond Tywyn, while the mainline railway and a minor road skirt the shore crossing the mouth of *Broad Water*, a lagoon into which the Dysynni flows, the main road runs inland to (*2m*.) *Bryncrug*, burial place of Mary Jones (see Dysynni Valley just below) and starting point for diversions up the interesting and scenically pleasant Fathew and Dysynni valleys. A circuit may be made.

FATHEW VALLEY. The road is B4405 which in 3m at *Dolgoch*, with a waterfall, meets the Talyllyn Railway which it accompanies to *Abergynolwyn*, reached in another 2m. Above was the Bryneglwys Slate Quarry (closed 1947), for which the line was built. Here the upper course of the Dysynni is met and a road follows the river NW through a cut in the hills to its main valley just S of Castell-y-Bere (see below). B4405 continues NE, ascending the upper Dysynni for 2 ½m to the river's source in *Tal-y-Llyn Lake*, 1m long and ¼m wide, below the S slopes of Cader Idris. The village of the same name, at the S end of the lake, has a little church with a timbered roof, perhaps of the 15C, curiously boarded and painted in the choir. A short way N of the lake the road meets Rte 20A.

DYSYNNI VALLEY. The unclassified road up the S side of the valley in 3m reaches the bold buttress of *Craig Aderyn* (Bird Rock) which, though now well inland, is a breeding place for cormorants, an interesting natural continuation from the times when this valley was an arm of the sea. In rather over 1m farther, the Dysynni valley, with its road to Abergynolwyn, turns SE, the ancient Welsh fortress of *Castell-y-Bere* being a short way N of the turning. Started by Llewelyn the Great in about 1221, and taken by the Earl of Pembroke in 1283, the castle was rebuilt by Edward I who, however, held it only until 1285 when it was retaken by the Welsh by whom it was apparently razed. The now only fragmentary remains on a defensive ridge form a long narrow enclosure, at the end of which a postern protected by a tower can be traced. The borough established here in 1285 by Edward I seems not to have survived the retaking of the castle by the Welsh. The scattered hamlet of *Llanfihangel-y-Pennant* is a short way beyond Castell-y-Bere. Here, in a beautiful setting below mountains, the road crosses the Cader river by a modern bridge beside an old one, on the far side being the ruin of *Mary Jones's Cottage*, with a memorial. Daughter of a weaver, Mary Jones was born in 1784. When 10 years old, she started to save for a Welsh bible, a task which took her six years. She then walked barefoot across the mountains to Bala where, so she had been told, she would be able to buy a bible from Thomas Charles, only to find that none was available. Thomas Charles, however, gave Mary his own bible and, as a result of this incident, founded the British and Foreign Bible Society. Mary Jones lived to the age of 88 and is buried at Bryncrug, while her bible is preserved in the Society's headquarters in London. The cottage marks the end of the road.

After Bryncrug A493 crosses the Dysynni, just beyond the bridge (S) being a motte, all that survives of an early seat of the princes of Gwynedd, in use before the construction of Castell-y-Bere.—2m. *Llanegryn*, where the little church, on a hill to the NW, has a Norman font and also a magnificent *Rood Screen and loft, according to one tradition, brought here by the monks of Cymmer Abbey at the Reformation but more probably an example of superb local craftsmanship of somewhere between the early 14 to 16C. Note also, on the S exterior wall of the choir, to the left of the window, an incised cross, possibly a consecration cross from an earlier church.—The road reaches the coast shortly before (2m.) *Llangelynin Church*, a very primitive mainly 12C structure above the sea, dedicated to St. Celynnin, a local saint of the 7C, and containing several curiosities: a unique double horse-bier; murals of ancient but unknown date, discovered during restoration in 1917; old pews with painted names; and a stoup, once reputed to be miraculously kept filled with water.

5m. **Fairbourne** is a growing holiday resort with sands stretching away N for 2m to Penrhyn Point, marking the S side of the narrow entrance of the Mawddach Estuary. Barmouth, on the other side, can be reached either by ferry (not cars) or by footpath across the mainline railway bridge (see Rte 17), access to this being by a road

1m east. The *Fairbourne Railway* (Tel: 0341–250362), with a gauge of
only 15 inches the smallest of Wales's little trains, started in the 19C
as a horse-drawn tramway (2ft gauge) used for carrying materials for
the construction of the village. The gauge was changed to 15ins in
1916, and, rescued by enthusiasts after disuse during the last war, the
train today boasts 1st, 2nd and 3rd Class coaches which carry their
passengers between Fairbourne and the ferry. An added attraction is
provided by the 'Butterfly Safari' on Fairbourne platform, with also a
free-flight aviary and enclosures for lemurs, racoons and similar
small animals.

2m. Arthog, to the E above which, surrounding twin lakes, is the
National Trust property of Cregennan (705 acres), given in 1959 by
Major C.L. Wynne-Jones in memory of his two sons killed in the
war.—*4m. Penmaenpool* with its footbridge and nature information
centre (see Rte 14).—*2m.* **Dolgellau**, see Rte 16.

22 Aberystwyth

ABERYSTWYTH (9000 inhab.) combines several features, being the
main town on Cardigan Bay and thus a general centre serving a wide
area; a lively seaside resort; the base of the Vale of Rheidol Railway;
with its castle, a place of some historical interest; and the home of the
National Library of Wales and of the University College of Wales.

Tourist Information. Terrace Road (below museum). Tel: 0970–612125.

History (Town and Castle). The present suburb of Llanbadarn Fawr is on the
site of a 6–8C bishopric and settlement, which can be regarded as the parent
village of Aberystwyth, in fact known as Llanbadarn until the 15C. In 1110
Gilbert FitzRichard of Clare built a primitive castle, the earthworks of which can
still be seen about 1½m S of the present castle on a site which at that date was
near the mouth of the Ystwyth. For over a century this early castle endured a
violent history, being burnt down no fewer than five times, usually in disputes
between Welsh princes, the last recorded incident being the taking of the castle
by Llewelyn the Great in 1221. The present castle, dating with its associated
borough from 1277, was started by Edmund of Lancaster, brother of Edward I.
Progress, slow in any case, was halted in 1282 when the Welsh took and briefly
held the castle, but by 1284 the place was fit enough to receive a visit by
Edward I, and, ten years later, in 1294, strong enough to withstand a Welsh
siege. During Owen Glendower's revolt the Welsh destroyed the town in 1401
but failed to carry the castle until 1404, after which it remained a Glendower
headquarters for four years. Coins of Welsh silver were minted here between
1637–42 (remains of the mine survive at Cwmsymlog, 3½m E, Ordnance
Survey 135–704838), and during the Civil War Aberystwyth was held for
Charles I until the castle was surrendered in 1646 and blown up in 1649. At the
close of the 18C the discovery of a chalybeate spring sparked a short-lived
attempt to turn Aberystwyth into a fashionable spa.

Choirs. Two choirs welcome visitors to their rehearsals. *Aberystwyth and
District Choral Society* and *Cor Meibion*. Days and times from Tourist Information.

The general pattern of the town is a seafront, running generally N to
S and broken by the castle headland, backed by a zone of pleasant
and mostly small streets (the main axis of which is Great Darkgate
Street linking Terrace Road at the NE with Pier Street and Bridge
Street at the south-west), with to the E the station and to the SW the
harbour. The district of Penglais (National Library, and new University College) is on rising ground to the north-east.

From the seafront there can be a view embracing virtually the whole of Cardigan Bay, from Snowdon and the Lleyn in the N to Strumble Head and the Presely Hills in the south. Beyond the N end of the town rises *Constitution Hill* (400ft), climbed by a path or by the Aberystwyth Electric Cliff Railway, 'a conveyance for gentlefolk since 1896' (Tel: 0970–617642), from the top being an even wider view, this, since 1985, enhanced by a camera obscura (times as for railway).

Along the curve of Marine Terrace are the bandstand and, farther SW, the Pavilion and Pier, while, just W again and beside New

Promenade—and the most conspicuous feature along the seafront—is the old building of the *University College of Wales* (see below). Originally intended to be a hotel, the building was restored after a fire of 1885 and now houses various departments of the university. In front, both in their robes of office, stand Thomas Charles Edwards (1837–1900), the first Principal, and the Duke of Windsor who was Chancellor when Prince of Wales.

The **Castle** ruins occupy the low hill of a promontory immediately S of the college. For the castle's history see above. The open site is an unusual diamond shape, with a large inner ward above and surrounded by a narrow outer ward. Of the outer ward there survive most of the length of the curtain (but much restored) and remains of the E and NW gates and of the angle towers. The inner ward, its line marked by an embankment, has virtually disappeared except for its E and NW gates and fragments of angle towers. To the E of the E angle of the outer ward there was a barbican, now marked by a mound, and it is thought that the War Memorial at the tip of the promontory may stand on the site of outlying defences. The *Harbour*, SE of the castle and fed by both the Rheidol and the Ystwyth, is used by both fishing and private craft.

In the town proper the **Ceredigion Museum** (Tel: 0970–617911) is interestingly housed in the Coliseum, a restored Edwardian theatre in Terrace Road. The basic theme here is the story of Ceredigion (Cardigan), this being told through a good folk collection which includes material illustrating local crafts, mining, seafaring, agriculture, housing (a cottage interior of 1850), and much else. For the *Vale of Rheidol Railway* (from the British Rail Station), see the end of this Rte.

The **University College of Wales** was founded in 1872, mainly through the efforts of Sir Hugh Owen (1804–81). For the original buildings on the seafront, see above. Other buildings lie to the E of the station, but the main recent development (buildings generally dating from 1959 onwards) has been on Penglais Hill in the NE outskirts of the town. Here the *Aberystwyth Arts Centre* (Tel: 0970–622887), which includes a concert hall and the university theatre, throughout the year mounts a programme of wide-ranging exhibitions, while the *Catherine Lewis Gallery and Print Room* (University College's Hugh Owen Library) not only shows a permanent collection of 15–20C graphic art but also organises a series of changing exhibitions (Tel: 0970–623591).

The ***National Library of Wales** (Tel: 0970–623816) occupies a commanding site on Penglais Hill, the land of which was presented by Lord Rendel. Begun in 1911, the buildings span from that date to modern times. There is a regular programme of exhibitions.

The movement for a national library was contemporary with the founding of the University College in 1872, and a Royal Charter was granted in 1907. Under this, the task of the library is to collect, preserve and make available all books, manuscripts etc. in Welsh and other Celtic languages, or which deal with the Welsh and other Celtic people; also to hold works on all subjects and in all languages which help to achieve the purpose for which the University of Wales and other Welsh educational institutions were founded. In 1912, under the Copyright Act, the library became one of the six libraries entitled to claim a copy of all books, pamphlets, maps etc. published within the British Isles.

Among the library's chief treasures are the 'Black Book of Carmarthen' (12C), the oldest manuscript in Welsh; the 'Book of Taliesin' (13C); the 'White Book of Rhydderch' (13–14C), containing the oldest

known versions of the Mabinogion tales; Latin and Welsh manuscripts of the Laws of Hywel Dda; early manuscripts of Geoffrey of
Monmouth's 'Chronicle'; the Henwrt manuscripts of Bede's 'Ecclesiastical History of Britain' (12C) and Chaucer's 'Canterbury Tales'
(c 1400); the so-called 'Bangor Missal', really a Sarum missal of the
late 14C or early 15C and finely decorated; one of the only two
vellum copies of 'The Great Bible' of 1539; a 15C 'Passionale'
probably made for Henry VII.

As noted above (History), the suburb of **Llanbadarn Fawr**, 1m SE
off A44, was the ancient parent village of Aberystwyth and in the 6–
8C the *Church* was the seat of a bishopric founded by St. Paternus
(Badarn or Padarn) but in the 8C merged into that of St. David's.
Today's aisleless cruciform church (with the tomb of St. Padarn and
an exhibition)—140ft long, 90ft across the transepts and with a
central tower 40ft square—is one of the largest in Wales. Except for
the sanctuary, which may be a 15C extension, the church is a plain
building of the early 13C, its austerity relieved, however, by a
beautiful S doorway, and unusual features being the arrangement of
the three lancets at the W end, and the three on the S of the S
transept. The church shows two venerable Celtic crosses, the smaller
of which, and much mutilated, is by far the older, tradition insisting
that, before its Christian shaping, it was a prehistoric standing stone.
The larger may date to the 7 or 8C. Legend associates both stones
with St. Samson, agriculturist brother of St. Paternus. Samson, it is
said, was threshing corn on a farm two miles or so away, using the
stones as a flail, when the head flew off and landed at Llanbadarn,
whereupon, losing his saintly patience, Samson hurled the shaft after
it. Also associated with this church, though many centuries later, is
the 14C poet Dafydd ap Gwilym, said to have been born in this
parish.

The **Vale of Rheidol Railway** (from British Rail station. Tel: 0970–
625819), gauge 1ft 1½ins and steam hauled, was opened in 1902 by a
private company partly to carry lead from the Rheidol valley mines
and partly in response to tourist demand. Later operated by British
Rail, the railway was in 1988 acquired by the Brecon Railway (see
also Rte 31).

The line ascends the lovely Vale of Rheidol for 12m (single journey
one hour; three hours return) from Aberystwyth to Devil's Bridge and
is the best way to enjoy the Vale as the main roads (Rtes 23A and
23B) run well above and clear of the valley. For the minor road along
part of the N side to Rheidol Power Station, see Rte 23A. After
Llanbadarn, the line keeps to the S bank of the river, beyond Capel
Bangor, as the valley narrows and winds, affording constantly
changing views, including, after Aberffrwd, the Rheidol Falls. The
average gradient is 100ft per mile, this becoming 1:50 after Aberffrwd. For *Devil's Bridge*, see Rte 23B.

For Aberystwyth to *Machynlleth* and beyond, see Rte 18; to *Rhayader* and
Builth Wells, see Rte 23; to *Carmarthen*, see Rte 41.

23 Aberystwyth to Rhayader and Builth Wells

Between Aberystwyth and Rhayader there is a choice of roads, both scenic with moor, forest and the beautiful valley of the Wye. These alternatives are either via Ponterwyd (near a silver-lead mine museum) and Llangurig, with, if wished, a diversion to Llanidloes (31m to Rhayader); or a more southerly choice via Devil's Bridge, followed by a wild and remote mountain road (29m to Rhayader). The two Routes, here only 3m apart, are linked by a road between Ponterwyd and Devil's Bridge.

A. Via Ponterwyd and Llangurig

A44 to Llangurig. A470 to Builth Wells. Total distance 44m.—*10m.* **Ponterwyd**.—*5m. Eisteddfa Gurig.—4m. Pant Mawr.—3m.* **Llangurig**.—*9m.* **Rhayader**.—*7m. Newbridge-on-Wye.—6m.* **Builth Wells**.

For **Aberystwyth** and (*1m*) *Llanbadarn Fawr*, see Rte 22.—*3m. Capel Bangor*, from where a minor road ascends the Vale of Rheidol beside the N bank of the river, in 4m reaching *Rheidol Power Station* (Tel: 097084–667), the focus of a number of attractions this side of the valley, these including power station tours, an information centre, a fish farm and various walks. For the Vale of Rheidol Railway, across the river, see Rte 22.—*4m. Bwlch Nant-yr-Arian*, with a Forestry Commission Visitor Centre, starting-point for walks in Rheidol Forest.—*1m.* *Llywernog Silver-Lead Mine* (Tel: 097085–620), describing itself as a 'boom-days museum', is based on the mine which opened here in the 1740s and reached its greatest prosperity during the 19C, albeit only to be abandoned in the 1880s. Restoration started in 1973 and the museum now offers a Miners' Trail embracing working water wheels, 18 and 19C mining and agricultural machinery, exhibitions, underground workings and much else.—*1m.* **Ponterwyd** is a hamlet where the upper Rheidol is crossed and from where roads N and S enable two diversions, both scenic and interesting, to be made. The name of an inn here, the Borrow Arms, recalls that it was here that George Borrow dried out after floundering through peat bog, much of which is now covered by the reservoirs of Dinas and Nant-y-Moch (see immediately below).

NORTHWARD DIVERSION. 13m to Talybont on Rte 18A. This 'Scenic Route' through a bare mountain landscape below the W flank of Plynlimon passes above the small *Dinas Reservoir* and in 4m reaches *Nant-y-Moch Reservoir*, an irregular, narrow crescent of water some 3m long representing the upper part of the Rheidol hydro-electric scheme. The reservoir (named after a chapel drowned here), with its dam (170ft high and 1150ft long), was inaugurated in 1965. The dam is crossed and the road skirts the S and W shores, the scenery here being broken and softened by plantations. Leaving the reservoir, the road bears W, crossing a watershed at 1300ft and then dropping down the scenic Cwm Ceulan to reach Talybont, 9m beyond the dam.

SOUTHWARD DIVERSION. A4120. 3m to Devil's Bridge on Rte 23B. The place of interest along this road is the church of *Ysbytty Cynfyn*, set within the remains of a stone circle (only five stones survive) and thus providing on the same site a fascinating continuity of ritual building, pagan and Christian, spanning from prehistoric to present day times. Cynfyn was a hospice (Ysbytty) of the abbey of Strata Florida. A path from the church leads in ten minutes to the *Parson's Bridge*, below which the Rheidol forces through a narrow passage.

Beyond Ponterwyd, A44 rises steadily along the S slopes of **Plynlimon** (2468ft), a large moorland dome on which are the sources of five rivers: Severn, Wye, Dulas, Llyfnant and Rheidol. Featureless, notorious for its bogs and mists, and with several abandoned mines, Plynlimon is not for the inexperienced or ill-equipped walker.—*5m. Eisteddfa Gurig* (1359ft) is the road pass and watershed. Beyond, the road descends beside the Tarenig, with afforestation to the S, just in these woods, 2m below the pass, being traces of a small Roman outpost fort. In another mile the Wye, dropping down from the N, is crossed and then followed past *Pant Mawr* to (*7m*), in gentler scenery, the village of **Llangurig**, the name recalling St. Curig, a holy man who died in 550. The church (dedicated to the saint), although a rebuilding of 1879 by George Gilbert Scott, nevertheless preserves some older parts, notably the 14C tower and, from the 15C, the arcade between the nave and the N aisle, the choir arch, and the tracery of the E window. For *Llanidloes*, 4m NE, see Rte 18C.

Keeping to the E bank A470 continues to descend the now narrowing and increasingly beautiful Wye valley.—*9m.* **Rhayader** (1500 inhab. *Inf.* West Street. Tel: 0597–810591) is in Welsh Rhaeadr

Claerwen dam, 1166ft long

Gwy, the 'Waterfall of the Wye', a name which recalls falls here that virtually disappeared when the river bridge was built in 1780. The castle built here by Rhys ap Gruffydd in the 12C has also long disappeared, and Rhayader today is a country centre much used by holiday visitors attracted by pony trekking, fishing, walking, an open working hill farm (*Gigrin*) and the beautifully situated reservoirs a short distance to the west.

The diarist Francis Kilvert was in 1876–77 vicar of *St. Harmon*, 3m N, where his church preserves a Norman font.

The ***Elan Valley and Claerwen Reservoirs**, completed respectively 1892–96 and 1952 and supplying water to the Birmingham district, are reached in 3m by B4518 SW out of Rhayader. An alternative approach, from the N, is from Pont-ar-Elan on B4574 towards the end of Rte 23B, this and the approach from Rhayader allowing a scenic circuit to be made. In a setting of mixed woodland and rocky, bare hills, the Elan reservoirs comprise a chain of five narrow lakes, each with its dam, extending some 9m from N to south. The flooding of the valley provided the theme for Francis Brett Young's novel, 'The House under the Water'. Claerwen reservoir, aligned roughly E–W and nearly 4m long, fills its own river's valley to the west.

Roads skirt the entire length of the reservoirs, and there are a number of parking areas. The road from Rhayader in 3m reaches *Elan Village* on the S bank of the Elan, here being a Visitor Centre (Tel: 0597–810898). Just beyond is the dam on the E side of the reservoir of *Caben Coch*, and in another mile comes the *Garreg Ddu Viaduct* (built above a part-submerged dam wall) where there is a choice of roads, either S and then W to Claerwen reservoir or northward beside the Elan chain.

The Claerwen road skirts the W shore of Caben Coch, towards the S of which, if the water is low, can be seen the garden walls of Nant Gwyllt, the house in which Shelley and Harriet lived in April–June 1812 and which also inspired Francis Brett Young's novel. At the lake's end the road curves W, to follow the river Claerwen and in 2m reach *Claerwen Reservoir* with its dam 1166ft long.—The other road from Garreg Ddu viaduct heads N beside this narrowing reservoir, below which lies Cwm Elan, the house where, after his expulsion from Oxford in 1811 because of his pamphlet 'The Necessity of Atheism', Shelley visited his cousin Thomas Grove and wrote that 'all was gloomy and desolate'. Next, the *Pen-y-Garreg* reservoir dam (528ft long, 123ft high) is reached, with a car park from which an attractive short walk leads to the foot of the dam. The roads along either side of this reservoir meet at the dam (513ft long, 120ft high) at the foot of *Craig Goch* reservoir, clear of woodland and in open moor. From here the road N runs above and a short way back from the reservoir, at its head (*Pont-ar-Elan* on B4574) meeting Rte 23B.

Southward from Rhayader, A470 descends the glen of the Wye which in 2m is joined from the W by the Elan.—*3m. Llanwrthwl*, where the church is successor to one built by St. Gwrthwl, an early Christian holy man who surely knew the ancient stone which still stands in the churchyard near the porch as a reminder of ritual of millennia ago. Doldowlod House, between the road and the river 1¹/₂m farther S, was once the home of the engineer James Watt. The valley opens out before (*4m*) the straggling village of *Newbridge-on-Wye*, just S of which the river cascades into one of its most broken and beautiful reaches.—*5m. Llanelwedd*, site of the Royal Welsh Agricultural Society showground (July). Rte 24 comes in from the E, and the road crosses the Wye by a bridge of six arches, built in 1779 but since widened.

1m. **Builth Wells** (1500 inhab. *Inf.* Groe Car Park. Tel: 0982–553307), in Welsh Llanfair-ym-Muallt, lies on the S bank of a pastoral stretch of the Wye.

History. The town probably originated as a settlement below the early Norman motte-and-bailey castle, thought to have been built by Bernard of Newmarch in 1091. The castle was partly destroyed by Llewellyn the Last in 1260, and in 1282 the refusal of the garrison (in Welsh history the 'traitors of Bu-allt') to allow Llewelyn sanctuary led to his death at nearby Cilmeri. At about this time Edward I built a stone castle here; known to have still been in good repair in the time of Henry VIII, it was probably destroyed under Elizabeth I. Later, Builth became an important stage along the cattle route to England (it still has a weekly cattle market), and for a period the town was known for mineral springs.

Of Edward's stone castle virtually nothing has survived and *Castle Mound*, just beyond the S end of the bridge, really represents Bernard of Newmarch's large motte-and-bailey of 1091. The earthworks are notable for the unusual width of their ditches, and for the way in which the bailey is divided by another ditch. The *Church*, W of the riverside car park, was rebuilt after 1875 except for the restored 12C tower. In the porch there is an effigy of John Lloid (died 1585), one of Elizabeth I's squires.

For Builth Wells NE to *Llandrindod Wells* and *Knighton* and SW to *Llandovery* and *Swansea*, see Rte 24; to *Abergavenny*, see Rte 25.

B.   Via Devil's Bridge

A4120 to Devil's Bridge. B4574 to Rhayader. A470 to Builth Wells.
Total distance 42m.—*11m.* **Devil's Bridge.**—*2m.* **The Arch.**—*11m.* *Pont-ar-Elan.*—*5m.* **Rhayader.**—*13m.* **Builth Wells.**
   For the Vale of Rheidol Railway, see Rte 22.

Aberystwyth, see Rte 22, is left by A487/A4120 which, after crossing the Rheidol, skirts the E side of a hill (415ft) crowned by a hillfort and an unsightly monument to the Duke of Wellington.—*1m.* **Penparcau**, a suburban village and crossroads from which A487 (Rte 41) leads S while this Route continues E, gradually ascending along the S side of the Rheidol valley, with occasional views down to the river and across to the steep N side. The highest point reached is 989ft; beyond, during the descent, hills mask the valley.

10m. **Devil's Bridge**, a popular beauty spot with a hotel, a huge car park, and the terminus of the Vale of Rheidol Railway, is in a romantic landscape of wooded glen, rocks and torrent. Here the Rheidol abruptly changes direction from S to W, at the bend being joined from the E by the Mynach, which drops 300ft through a rocky chasm in a series of cataracts which in spate become an almost continuous fall. An iron bridge (1901) spans the stream at the lip of the falls. Just below this is the stone bridge of 1753, and, lower still, the original and ancient *Pont-y-gwr-Drwg* (Bridge of the Evil One), traditionally ascribed to the Devil. It may in fact have been built by the monks at Strata Florida (the abbey is 8m S, and its hospice of Ysbytty Cynfyn under 2m N), and Giraldus writes of crossing a bridge here in 1188, a few years after the founding of the abbey. The *Mynach Falls* (fee for non-residents) are in the grounds of the Hafod Arms Hotel. Paths offer views of the basin above the falls, of the three bridges, and of the distant Gyfarllwyd Falls up the Rheidol. Farther down, the whole series of the Mynach Falls is seen from a platform, from where steps descend steeply to a foot-bridge across the river at the foot of the falls.

For Devil's Bridge to *Ysbytty Cynfyn* and *Ponterwyd*, see Rte 23A.

  B4343, leading S from Devil's Bridge and crossing the valley of the Ystwyth, in 8m reaches the abbey of *Strata Florida*, see Rte 41B.

Devil's Bridge is left by B4574 which climbs into woodland to (*2m*) **The Arch**, with a Forestry Commission picnic site, trails and a view point. The stone arch was put up in 1810, to honour the Golden Jubilee of George III, by Thomas Johnes (1748–1816) of Hafod Uchtryd (demolished 1958), 2m south. When in 1783 Johnes inherited the estate, in, apparently, neglected condition, he resolved to transform the place through sound farming and afforestation, in the latter context becoming a pioneer and between 1786 and 1813 planting over four million trees, mostly larch. He can thus be said to have anticipated the present Forestry Commission estate. Johnes was also a scholar and published his own translations of Froissart's and Monstrelet's 'Chronicles' from his private press.

  After The Arch the road leaves the forest for lonely, open moor, ascending the Ystwyth and passing large abandoned lead mines, notably at (*4m*) *Cwmystwyth* where lead was mined first in Roman times, later by the monks of Strata Florida, and finally during the 17–19C when this was one of the most advanced lead and silver mines in Europe. The desolate site—with remains which include workshops, a mill of 1898, a turbine house and tramways—is dangerous because of concealed adits and shafts, but much can be seen from the road. Still in remote and desolate country, B4574 crosses the watershed at 1320ft to descend the Elan to (*7m*) *Pont-ar-Elan*, a road junction above the head of Craig Goch reservoir into which the Elan flows. The small road leading S offers an alternative approach to Rhayader via the beautiful Elan Valley reservoirs (see Rte 23A).—*5m.* **Rhayader**, for which, as also for Rhayader to (*13m*) **Builth Wells**, see Rte 23A.

24 Knighton to Llandrindod Wells, Llandovery and Swansea

A488 to Penybont. A44 to Cross Gates. A483 to Llandovery. A40 to Llandeilo. A476/A48, or A483/A48 to Swansea. Total distance excluding diversions 82m.—*5m.* **Monaughty.**—*9m.* **Penybont.**—*2m.* **Cross Gates.**—*3m.* **Llandrindod Wells.**—*7m.* **Builth Wells.**—*12m.* **Llanwrtyd Wells.**—*10m.* **Llandovery.**—*12m.* **Llandeilo.**—*14m.* **Pontardulais.**—*8m.* **Swansea**.

Gradually increasing moorland and afforestation, the road running below the Cambrian Mountains to the N and Mynydd Epynt and the Black Mountain to the south.—Several worthwhile diversions.

Knighton (2200 inhab. *Inf.* Offa's Dyke Heritage Centre, The Old School. Tel: 0547–528753), today a quiet border market town on the steep Welsh bank of the small river Teme, recalls a more turbulent border past through two mottes—one, first mentioned in 1181, at the top of the town; the other, Bryn-y-Castell and possibly an outlying defence of the first, in the valley just E of the station—and through *Offa's Dyke* which crosses the SW of the town and gives it its Welsh

name of Tref-y-Clawd, the Cantref on the Dyke. A good section of
the dyke can be reached by a short path beside the Heritage Centre.

KNIGHTON TO NEWTOWN (on Rte 18B). B4355. NW, 20m. This hill
road ascends the Welsh bank of the Teme, in 3m reaching *Knucklas*
with a hillfort. At *Beguildy*, reached in another 5m, the church
preserves a rood screen with the base of its loft. From here Newtown
can be reached either direct by B4355, or, alternatively, by small
roads, briefly in England, leading generally N and in 1m reaching the
remote church of *Betws-y-Crwyn* (at 1300ft) with a fine rood loft and
panelled roof. Hence, minor roads continue to (in another 3m)
Anchor Inn on the border. From here B4368 is taken for Kerry (Rte
18B), across the valley on the ascent from Anchor Inn being a
distinctive earthwork called *Castell Bryn Amlwg*, overlooking the
junction of two streams which once marked the meeting place of the
former counties of Montgomery, Radnor and Shropshire.

5m. Monaughty, to the W of the road, is a stone Tudor farm which
was once a monastery grange. It is said that a tunnel once ran
between the grange and Pilleth (see immediately below), this being
used as an escape route by the monks when attacked, a not
uncommon occurence in this border district.

MONAUGHTY TO PRESTEIGNE. B4356. SE, 7m. *Pilleth*, reached in 1m,
was in 1402 the scene of an important battle in which Owen
Glendower defeated and captured Sir Edmund Mortimer, fighting for
Henry IV, thus establishing his claim to be the Welsh national leader.
Mortimer, advancing from the E along the flank of the hill, seems to
have been ambushed by Glendower, who was hiding on the reverse
slope above, the English (according to Shakespeare's 'Henry IV, Part
One') losing a thousand men whose bodies were so mutilated by the
Welsh women 'as may not be without much shame retold or spoken
of'. Probably wisely, Mortimer then sided with Glendower. *Castell
Foel-Allt*, beside the river below Pilleth church, is a motte-and-bailey
remain dating from the 11C.
    From *Whitton*, 1m farther, B4356 continues SE for Presteigne, but a
diversion may be made S and then, at the first crossroads, NW to (4m
from Whitton) the hamlet of *Cascob* where the church has a mound at
its W end which is generally thought to represent the remains of a
tower burnt by Glendower. The present tower is of unusual ground
plan, being twice as long from N to S as from E to west. Inside the
church are a triangular aumbrey and a square piscina (both 13C), a
14C font, and a restored rather plain 16C rood screen.
    Presteigne (1300 inhab) is an attractive and locally typical old
border town—the Lugg which skirts the N edge of the town is the
actual border—with half-timbered houses, notable among these
being the *Radnorshire Arms* of 1616, once the home, it is said, of John
Bradshaw (1602–59) whose signature headed those on the death
warrant of Charles I. The Lugg bridge dates from the 17C. The
Church is 14–16C, but has interesting earlier fragments; a jamb and
segment of choir arch (E end of N aisle) are pre-Norman, and there
are two early Norman window fragments in the N wall. Also
noteworthy are a mosaic of late old glass (S chapel); a late 13C sepulchral
slab (N aisle); and an early 16C Flemish tapestry representing the
Entry into Jerusalem. The low hill W of the town known as *The
Warden*, now a public park, is the site of the Norman castle destroyed
by Llewelyn the Last in 1261.—At *Norton*, 2m N, the church has a

bell-turret supported on timber framing, and a tree stump by the churchyard entrance still bears manacles suggesting its use as a pillory or whipping post.

2m. (from Monaughty) *Bleddfa* where, as at Cascob (see above), the church shows a mound at its W end. Excavation in 1962 revealed a small doorway and the base of a tower, probably that of the earlier church destroyed by Owen Glendower at about the same time as the battle at Pilleth. From here the road now climbs along the N flank of *Radnor Forest*, a plateau (2160ft) some 5m square and well afforested on this side, to reach a height of 1201ft before descending to (*4m*) *Llanfihangel Rhydithon*, 2m beyond which a road (sign) leads S for 1m to *The Pales*, a Quaker house of 1771.—*3m. Penybont.*

PENYBONT TO OLD RADNOR. A44. E, 11m. At *Llandegley*, reached in 2m, the church has a 15C screen and a blocked priest's doorway with a curious seven-foiled head. The Pales (see above) is ½m north. For the next 8m the road loops around the S of the moor and forest upland of Radnor Forest, in 4m reaching the junction with A481 to Builth Wells with, just to the N, a conspicuous tumulus.

TO BUILTH WELLS. A481. SW, 11m. This road almost immediately reaches its highest point (1243ft) above the little tarn of *Llyn Heilyn*, after this dropping through open scenery into the upper valley of the Edw. This stream is crossed at *Hundred House Inn*, ½m beyond being *Maud's Castle*, a motte-and-bailey, now a farm, mentioned in the first half of the 12C. The undulating road passes below (N) *Caer Einon*, a hillfort on an 1100ft spur, and reaches the valley of the Wye. For *Aberedw*, 3m S on the E bank of the Wye, see Rte 25A. At *Llanelwedd* Rte 23 is joined.

Llanfihangel-nant-Melan, about 1m beyond which (steep rise by a road bend) a motorable lane (NW), keeping right at a fork, leads in 1m into woods in which a cascade, attractively named *Water-break-its-Neck*, tumbles through a narrow ravine. A pleasant walk can be made around the top of the ravine, and a track and path cross Radnor Forest to respectively Llanfihangel Rhydithon and Bleddfa (8m) on A488 (see above).

New Radnor, once the county town of Radnorshire, is now a large village the most interesting feature of which, both visually and historically, is the large *motte-and-bailey* beside the church. Visually this represents a castle built in the 11C, destroyed by King John, rebuilt by Henry III, and finally ruined by Owen Glendower in 1401; historically, the castle was the starting-point in 1188 of Archbishop Baldwin's tour through Wales with Giraldus to preach the Third Crusade. In the 13C the town was laid out to the Edwardian plan of square blocks, but of this street plan virtually nothing now survives, although just outside the SW of the town something can be seen of the protective boundary earthwork.

Old Radnor, 2½m beyond New Radnor and on a hill to the S of the road, was once a base of Harold Godwinson, or King Harold, defeated and killed by William of Normandy (William the Conqueror) at Hastings in 1066. The small motte in a field some 300 yards SE of the church represents the site of his castle, and must also have been the 'Cruker Castle' mentioned by Giraldus. The *Church, though essentially English in style (the border is little more than a mile away), is nevertheless one of the finest parish churches in Wales, with its imposing W tower a good example of late 14C work though showing in the N aisle and S chapel traces of an earlier style. Inside there is much of interest, such as the parclose screens N and S of the choir; the rood screen, still with the base of its loft; the ancient stalls and desks, one of the latter still with chain and clasp; the organ case of c 1500, with linenfold and Tudor roses; and the huge, rudely circular *Font, one of the largest in Britain, made from a glacial boulder which may once have served as a prehistoric pagan ritual stone. The floor slab with a floreated cross at the entrance to the choir is 13C; and in the N chapel are, at the E end, a late 15C St. Catherine window, an Easter sepulchre built into the N wall, and a massive medieval vestments chest.

2m. (from Penybont) **Cross Gates** (or Crossgates) is a road junction (A44 and A483) at which anyone with a feel for ruined and historic abbeys as also for small churches will consider a northward diversion which may be made as a circuit of some 17 miles, described immediately below.

NORTHWARD CIRCUIT FROM CROSS GATES. A483 is briefly followed N before a minor road branches left to reach (in 5m from Cross Gates) the fragmentary remains of **Cwmhir Abbey**, sleeping in a beautiful pastoral setting in the winding valley of the Clywedog (Cwmhir means 'long valley'). The abbey was founded in 1143 for Cistercian monks from Whitland, and a second foundation followed in 1176. It was also twice destroyed, first by Henry III in 1231, and again in 1401 by Owen Glendower who is said to have suspected that the monks were Englishmen in disguise. Although after Henry III's attack an ambitious rebuilding was planned, in fact the choir was never built, the transepts were left unfinished, and the great nave (242ft long) was wrecked by Glendower. The 15C was one of steady decline and by the time of the Dissolution there were only three monks in residence. Today's remains comprise little more than the foundations of the nave and some battered lower courses of its wall, but visitors ready to accept tradition will accept also that the body of Llewelyn the Last was brought here from Cilmeri in 1282 for burial below the altar, a position today marked by a blackthorn.

From Cwmhir minor roads amble generally NE for 4m to meet A483 just N of *Llananno* where the church contains an early 16C *Rood Screen and loft, though with some later work (1933), distinguishable by its darker tone. Twenty-three recessed figures, supported above and below by delicate wood tracery, face into the nave. There is also a churchwarden's pew of 1681. If the church is closed, something of the screen can be viewed through the N windows.—At *Llanbister*, 1m S by A483, the 12 or 13C church, known to be a foundation of the 6C, adapts to its sloping site by interior flights of steps, and is curious also for having its tower at its E end, the entry being by a door N of the altar. Also to be noted are a stoup and piscina, both 13C; what is left of the carved 16C rood screen; the 17 or 18C W gallery; and the modern baptistery for immersion.—Farther S, roughly half-way back to Cross Gates, the church at *Llanddewi Ystradenny* (St. David beside the Road), although a rebuilding, retains a 12C doorway.

From Cross Gates this Route follows A483 southward, almost at once passing the church at *Llanbadarnfawr*, with a 12C S doorway and fine carved *Tympanum of c 1140. The left supporting capital bears two naked figures, presumably Adam and Eve, with the Devil below, while another interesting feature is a Roman stone, inscribed with the name of Valerius Flavinius, inserted in the left wall of the porch.

Almost certainly coming from Castell Collen, the stone was found embedded in the wall of the earlier church during rebuilding in 1878 and suggests that the original church in all probability used Castell Collen as a quarry.

3m. **Llandrindod Wells** (4000 inhab. *Inf.* Town Hall. Tel: 0597–822600), though no longer a spa, is still a not-unfashionable holiday centre which, with its wide streets and large hotels, retains much of its spacious Edwardian character. The town is divided into two by the railway, Rock Park being to the W and the main street (Temple Street), with the town's two museums, to the east.

History. Although today's Llandrindod Wells dates only from the late 19C, the town in fact has ancient roots. The Romans were nearby at Castell Collen and probably knew the springs (saline, sulphur, magnesian and chalybeate), and the parish church of the Trinity, which gives the town its name, traces its origins to the 12C. The saline spring is recorded in 1696, the sulphur spring in 1736, and in 1748 the springs were the subject of verses in the 'Gentleman's Magazine'. At this time, the place was no more than a scattered hamlet, but a hotel was built in 1749 and, until closed in 1787, gave Llandrindod a few years' notoriety as a haunt of gamblers and rakes. It was the arrival of the railway in 1867 that changed everything, and by the end of the century the spa had developed, welcoming as many as 80,000 visitors a year, a prosperity which was to last, if later in decline, until the Second World War.

The *Llandrindod Museum* (Tel: 0597–824513), in Temple Street, is largely though not exclusively devoted to finds from the Roman fort of Castell Collen, other exhibits including the Paterson Doll Collection, with dolls from many parts of the world. At the *Automobile Palace*, also in Temple Street, can be seen the Tom Norton Collection of Bicycles and Tricycles (Tel: 0597–822214), covering the period from 1867 to 1938, while, beyond the railway, something of Llandrindod's elegant past can be recaptured at *Rock Park Spa* (Tel: 0597–824307), with 18 acres of park and the 19C Pump Room where the visitor can sample the waters or enjoy a Welsh tea. Here too there are frequent craft markets while the former Bath House now offers an exhibition on this and other Welsh spas.

The Roman fort of **Castell Collen**, 1¼m NW of the town, is reached from A4081 (lane N, immediately W of the Ithon bridge). The fort seems to have known four phases, namely an original turf and timber site of 75–78, the work of Julius Frontinus during his campaign against the Silures; stone construction of the mid 2C; a contraction in size in the early 3C; and a strengthening in the late 3 or early 4C. Today the rectangular earthworks of a fort of between three and four acres are clearly detectable, while to the W can be traced something of the area abandoned in the 3C.—*Cefnllys*, 1m E of Llandrindod Wells, has a 13C church, the roof of which was removed by the rector in 1893 because he wanted his parishioners to attend his church at Llandrindod, now at its height as a spa; but so indignant were the parishioners that they reroofed their church two years later. On the motte above the church once stood a castle built in 1242.

Llandrindod Wells is left by A483 southward. Between Llandrindod and (*2m*) *Howey*, to the W of the road and beyond the railway, aerial photographs have revealed evidence of a Roman road and temporary camp, while at *Disserth*, just W off the main road, the church has a curious three-level pulpit and a box-pew, both of the 17C. The *Carneddau Hills* (1430ft), to the E of the road, provide good walking and are of geological interest for the way in which the Llandovery and Lower Silurian flags here have been disrupted by volcanic intrustions, while ice markings, perched blocks and moraines indicate later glacial action.—For *4m Llanelwedd* and *1m* **Builth Wells**, in the Wye valley, see Rte 23A.

Beyond Builth Wells A483 runs between the long ridge of Mynydd Epynt (1650ft; Ministry of Defence ranges) to the SE and the southern end of the Cambrian Mountains to the north-west. Both areas include high moor and forest and are crossed by a number of motorable minor roads, those through the Cambrian Mountains serving some of the remotest country in Wales.—*2m. Cilmeri* is where Llewelyn the Last, denied help by the garrison at Builth, was killed in 1282 during a skirmish with the English. A roadside monument (1956, replacing one of the 19C) stands on the spot where he is supposed to have fallen, one tradition holding that he is buried here, another that his remains were taken to Cwmhir Abbey. Glan Irfon, ¼ m S of the road, was a home of the eccentric Lady Hester Stanhope (1776–1839).—*4m. Garth*, from where there is a choice of roads for the next five or six miles. The main road loops N through *Beulah*, a village which has given its name to a breed of sheep; from here an unclassified road NW in 5m joins the drover road (see below) at Abergwesyn. The valley road, 1m shorter, passes through **Llangammarch Wells**, in parkland scenery at the confluence of the Irfon and Cammarch. The village gained its onetime reputation as a spa because its water was found to contain barium chloride, not found elsewhere in Britain and recommended for cardiac and rheumatic complaints; the now disused pump house and the well are in the grounds of the Lake Hotel. Somewhat surprisingly for so modest a place, Llangammarch claims association with a number of people who, if on the whole obscure, nevertheless have their niches in specialist segments of history. One such was John Penry, Puritan writer and publisher, born here in 1559 (traditionally at the farm of Cefn Brith, 2m S of the village) and hanged in London in 1593 after conviction for sedition. Another native was the Royalist Bishop Howell (1588–1646), while Theophilus Evans (1694–1767), author of a popular book on Welsh antiquities said to have achieved 30 editions, was vicar. The book, translated into English under the title 'View of the Primitive Ages', was highly imaginative and pleased the Welsh by its assertion that Arthur was as historic a figure as Alexander the Great.

6m. **Llanwrtyd Wells**, once a spa known for its sulphur and chalybeate springs, is now a modest country holiday and pony trekking centre. The small modern town is on the main road and the old village about a mile NW up the valley of the Irfon. The *Cambrian Factory* (Tel: 05913–211), a Welsh Tweed centre beside A483, was founded in the 1820s, then producing flannels which were marketed locally. But in its modern form the factory dates from 1918 when it was opened by the Royal British Legion for the benefit of war-disabled. Considerably extended in 1944, and again in 1970, the factory now offers visitors an informal view of all the production processes as also a high-class shop.

From Llanwrtyd Wells a former drover hill road, today with Forestry Commission picnic sites and walks, can be followed N and W through forest and across remote moorland to (18m) Tregaron on Rte 41B. The narrow rocky glen of the Irfon is ascended through *Abergwesyn*, some 2m beyond which the road bears W across a corner of Towy Forest before breaking out on to moor, crossing the Towy, passing a road S to the N tip of *Llyn Brianne* (see below), and reaching a watershed at over 1500ft. From here the road drops with the Berwyn down to Tregaron in the valley of the Teifi.

Beyond Llanwrtyd Wells, A483 ascends through remote country to cross the *Sugar Loaf Pass* (949ft).—At (6m) *Llanfair-ar-y-Bryn* the 13–15C church is built within the walls of a Roman station, possibly the Luentium of Ptolemy. The Rev. William Williams (see below) is buried in the churchyard.

4m. **Llandovery** (2000 inhab. *Inf*. Central Car Park, Broad Street. Tel: 0550–20693), a leading market town, owes its Welsh name of Llanymddyfri (Church amid the Waters) to its situation at the confluence of the Gwydderig and the Bran and about 1½m above that of the Bran and the Towy, this last, with a course of 68m, being the longest river entirely in Wales. Of the Norman *Castle* around which a settlement developed into a small town a few remains (an oval motte, a roughly square bailey, and some later masonry) stand beside the large parking area in the S of the town; partly burnt by Gruffyd ap Rhys in 1116, the castle does not seem to have been long held by the English. Two churchmen are associated with the town, one being Rhys Pritchard (1579–1644), celebrated for his preaching (he was known as the Vicar of Llandovery) and as the author of 'The Welshman's Candle', a paraphrase of the Gospels in Welsh quatrains; born in Llandovery, in 1602 he became vicar of the local parish of Llandingat. The other churchman was William Williams ('Williams Pantycelyn', 1717–91), a revivalist and hymn writer who was born at Cefncoed, 4m north-east.

LLANDOVERY TO LLYN BRIANNE. N, 11m. Ascending the upper Vale of Towy, roads follow either side of the river to meet in 8m at *Craig Bron-y-Cwrt* where a minor road breaks away first NW and then SW to follow the Cothi down to Dolaucothi and Pumpsaint on Rte 27. From Craig Bron-y-Cwrt the road up the Towy left bank is taken, this in 2m reaching the farm of Ystradffin, just W of which is *Twm Shon Catti's Cave*, the retreat of 'Tom John, son of Catherine' (1530–1620), a poet whose youthful freebooting escapades gained him the title of the Robin Hood of Wales. Later, he settled down, married the heiress of Ystradffin and even became a magistrate. *Llyn Brianne*, with a dam at its S end and over 3m long from the dam to the N tip of its long narrow E finger, boosts the water supply of Swansea.

For Llandovery to (E) *Brecon* and (W) *Lampeter* and *Aberaeron*, see Rte 27.

Beyond Llandovery, there is a choice of roads SW either side of the Towy to (6m) **Llangadog**. A40, a straight Roman stretch N of the river, should be followed for Rte 27 (A482) to Dolaucothi, Lampeter and Aberaeron which bears away W at *Llanwrda*, 4m from Llandovery. From Llanwrda there is also a road NW across to (5m) Talley Abbey (see Diversions from Llandeilo, below). Llangadog is a modest market town sandwiched between the rivers Sawdde and Bran just above where they join the Towy. *Mandinam*, 2m E, was the home of Joanna Bridges, Jeremy Taylor's second wife (1656), rumoured to have been a natural daughter of Charles I. *Carn Goch*, 3m S of Llangadog, is an exceptionally large hillfort, with a stone rampart and earthworks covering some 15 acres.

After Llangadog there is again a choice of roads, the more direct choice for Swansea being A4069 which ascends the Sawdde and crosses the long open moorland of Black Mountain before dropping to the industrial centre of Brynamman. But this Route takes the more interesting road through (6m) **Llandeilo** (1600 inhab.) at the hub of a number of worthwhile diversions. Sprawled on the slope of a hill above the Towy, the town takes its name from St. Teilo who is said to have died in a monastery here in 560. Of this era there is no trace, but Llandeilo's *Church*, in origin 13C but largely a rebuilding of 1840, preserves the heads of two stone crosses of the 9 and 10C, while the little church of *Llandyfeisant* (Coed-y-Castell; visitor centre of the West Wales Trust for Nature Conservation), reached in ½m by a path leading W from the bridge (1848) along the N bank of the Towy, is said to stand on the site of a Roman temple.

DIVERSIONS FROM LLANDEILO. As noted above, Llandeilo can be a hub for various diversions from this main Route, including the estate of Dynevor, immediately W of the town; a westward circuit of 12m passing much of varied interest; Talley Abbey, 7m north; and Carreg Cennen castle, 4m south-east.

The estate of **Dynevor** (Dinefwr), just W of Llandeilo and today comprising the Park, the Old Castle and Newton House (sometimes called the New Castle), has roots deep in Welsh tradition and history.

Archaeology has revealed that the site of the Old Castle was once an Iron Age hillfort; legend, as told by Spenser, places Merlin's grave 'amongst the woody hill of Dynevowre'; tradition tells that in 876 Rhodri Mawr built a castle here as a base in his stand against the Norsemen; and it is fact the Hywel Dda (died 950), grandson of Rhodri Mawr and great codifier of the law, was lord of Dynevor. It is fact, too, that the books of the law refer to the white cattle, associated with Dynevor since shadowy times (the breed may have been brought over by the Romans for sacrificial purposes) until as recently as 1970 and, under National Trust auspices, hopefully to be returned to the park.

Rhys ap Tewdr (died 1093), a descendant of Hywel Dda, ruled his princedom of Deheubarth from here, while the great Rhys ap Gruffydd (died 1197) is credited with building the first stone castle. As capital of Deheubarth, Dynevor was a constant target for both the Normans and the English and an English siege of 1257 was raised by Llewelyn the Last. But not even Dynevor could withstand Edward I and traces of his borough still survive near the Old Castle.

Later, in the 15C, a manor house (on the site of the present Newton House) superseded the Old Castle and by the 17C the family name of Rhys had become anglicised to Rice.

The *Park* (NT. Tel: 0558–822800) was in part landscaped by 'Capability' Brown in 1775, his main contributions being the strategically planted clumps of trees and the opening of elegant vistas. Acquired by the National Trust in 1987, the park is being rescued and restored (including, hopefully, the return of the white cattle), a second step being the provision of visitor facilities.—The *Old Castle* (WHM), long the heart of Dynevor, is also the object of major conservation work. Meanwhile the ruins—essentially a circular keep, a drum-tower and some fragments of wall—can be well seen from B4300 to the S (see Westward Circuit below).—*Newton House* (private), or the New Castle, successor to the 15C manor, dates from about 1660 but with substantial later alterations.

A **Westward Circuit.** A pleasant and varied round of 12m can be made either side of the Towy to the W of Llandeilo, starting along B4300, to the N of which the ruin of *Dynevor Old Castle* can be seen on the hill above the valley. Soon afterwards, the mansion of *Golden Grove* (Gelli Aur) stands above the road on the S side. Now part of an agricultural college, the present building (by Joseph Wyatville, c 1824) is successor, though on a different site, to a mansion burnt down in 1769 in which Jeremy Taylor found a refuge with Richard Vaughan, 2nd Earl of Carbery, the mansion's owner, during the ten disturbed years of 1645–55. It was while he was here that Taylor wrote many of his best works, including 'Holy Living', 'Holy Dying' and 'Golden Grove', at the same time successfully running a school. The Park is now an official Country Park (Tel: 05584–885) with an arboretum, nature trails, deer park, play area and exhibitions and displays.

B4300 continues W—with a view ahead of *Paxton's Tower*, a folly built in 1811 by Sir William Paxton in honour of Lord Nelson and now owned by the National Trust—this circuit, however, bearing N along B4297 to cross the Towy for, just the other side of the river, the ruin of the early Welsh *Dryslwyn Castle*. With traces of a chapel, a hall and a round keep (and with more excavation planned), the ruins are of particular interest for being to some extent the result of deliberate undermining by besiegers in the late 13C, an operation which, it is recorded, cost the lives of many of the sappers. The return to Llandeilo may be made along A40, with, on the S side before the turn to Llangathen, the hill of *Grongar* with a hillfort. The charms of this modest hill, as also of Dryslwyn, were sung by the poet John Dyer (1700–58) who was born at nearby Aberglasney. In the church of *Llangathen* there is a monument to Bishop Rudd of St. David's (died 1615), who also lived at Aberglasney.

The remains of **Talley Abbey** (WHM. Tel: 0222-465511), 7m N of Llandeilo, are reached by B4302 up the pleasant valley of the river Dulais. Talley—the name deriving from Tal-y-Llychau, or Head of the Lakes, because of the abbey's situation on the more southerly of two small lakes—was founded in the late 12C by Rhys ap Gruffyd for Premonstratensian canons and was the only house in Wales of this Order. Although ejected as early as c 1200 by the powerful Cistercians of Whitland, the canons successfully appealed to the Archbishop of Canterbury and had returned by 1208. The skeleton of the abbey's church tower is the most significant remain, together with something of the nave, choir and transepts with their chapels, as also, to the S of the nave, the lower courses of cloisters. Talley claims, as does also Strata Florida, to be the burial place of Dafydd ap Gwilym (c 1320–80), described by Borrow as 'the greatest of his country's songsters'.

*Carreg Cennen Castle (WHM. Tel: 0222-465511), 4m SE of Llandeilo, is dramatically sprawled along a precipitous limestone rock rising 300ft above the ravine of the river Cennen, a situation which means that there is a long, steep climb from the car park, rewarded, however, by a view over much of Brecon Beacons National Park and Black Mountain.

History. There must have been a fortress on a site such as this from very early times, and indeed tradition ascribes one castle here to Urien, a knight of Arthur's Round Table. The present castle, the name of its builder unknown, dates from the late 13C or early 14C. It was taken by the Lancastrians during the Wars of the Roses, but in 1462 was destroyed by William Herbert of Raglan because it had become a nest of brigands.

The castle, without a keep, was four-sided with inner and outer wards. The ruins are entered on the N by a gatehouse with a portcullis at each end. The solid tower at the SW angle of the quadrangle is scarcely more than a buttress, and the SE corner, above the cliff, is unprotected. Strangely, the hall is placed on the N and weakest sector of the curtain. Perhaps the most remarkable feature of the ruins is the long passage, cut through the rock and lit by loopholes, that leads to the so-called well, a kind of cave deep beneath the ruins which, though it may have served as a cistern, apparently contains no spring.

A farm below the castle is a rare breed centre.—At *Llwyndewi Farm*, 1m S of Trap which is 1m W of Carreg Cennen's car park, barns and cowsheds have been converted as an arts and crafts centre (Tel: 0269–850362).—About 1m S of the castle, the river Loughor issues from a limestone cave, sometimes known as the *Llygad Llwchwr*, or the Eye of Loughor.

From Llandeilo Swansea can be reached in 22m by a choice of roads which meet at Pontardulais.

VIA CROSS HANDS. A476 and A48. There is an ascent over bleak moorland to *(8m)* Cross Hands where, in the early 1970s, two huge coal slagheaps were levelled to provide a largely recreational area. From here A476 continues S to Llanelli on Rte 35, but this Route bears SE on A48, touching the M4 motorway.—*6m.* **Pontardulais**, where the Loughor is crossed just above the flats of its winding estuary, is an industrial town which in the 1840s was a centre of the Rebecca riots. For rehearsals of the well-known male voice choir, Tel: daytime 0972–898331 or, evening, 0972–586330. From Pontardulais a road S (B4296) through Gorseinon and Gowerton offers an approach to the Gower (Rte 39) avoiding Swansea.

VIA AMMANFORD. A483 and A48. First the valley of the Cennen is followed, then, before *(5m.)* *Llandybie*, that of the Loughor.—*2m.* **Ammanford** (6500 inhab.), in Welsh Rhydaman, is a busy industrial valley town. From here A483 and A48 lead SW and then S to *(7m.)* **Pontardulais**, see above.

8m. **Swansea**, see Rte 38.

25   Builth Wells to Abergavenny

The alternative Routes described below run roughly parallel and up to 8m apart, meeting at Tretower, with its medieval manor and ruined Norman castle, 7m N of Abergavenny. Rte 25A, descending a particularly lovely reach of the Wye, is for its first dozen or so miles scenically the more attractive. Rte 25B, on the other hand, includes the interesting cathedral town of Brecon, with access to some beautiful country to its south. The best of both Routes will be achieved by choosing Rte 25A as far as Bronllys, then using a section of Rte 33 to cut across to Brecon, thence continuing to Tretower and Abergavenny by Rte 25B.

A.   Via Talgarth and Tretower. Wye Valley

A470 to Llyswen. A479 to just beyond Tretower. A40 to Abergavenny. Total distance 33m.—*7m. Erwood Bridge.—1m.* **Erwood**.—*4m. Llyswen.—3m.* **Bronllys**.—*1m.* Talgarth.—*10m.* **Tretower**.—*2m.* **Crickhowell**.—*5m.* **Abergavenny**.

Between Builth Wells and Llyswen the road descends the wooded and pastoral valley of the Wye, this being followed, between Talgarth and Tretower, by the upland W slopes of the Black Mountains. Beyond Tretower, the pleasant valley of the Usk.

Builth Wells, see Rte 23A. The main road (A470) follows the W bank
of the Wye. An alternative—quieter, scenically equally attractive,
and passing Aberedw (see below)—is provided by B4567 down the E
bank from Llanelwedd, just NE of Builth Wells. The first bridge
(Erwood) is 7m S by A470, and 3m S of Aberedw.

By A470, soon after (*4m*) *Alltmawr*, the *Aberedw Rocks*, an outcrop
of the Silurian formation rising in terraces of slabs to a height of
nearly 600ft, can be well seen across the river.—*3m. Erwood Bridge*.

From across the bridge, B4567 leads N below Aberedw Rocks, in 3m reaching
the village of **Aberedw** at the wooded foot of the glen of the Edw. There are
fragments of a small castle, but the church, probably late 13C but restored in
Tudor times and typical of the primitive Welsh mountain type, is more
interesting. The large N porch once served as parish hall, being closed by doors
the hinges of which can still be seen, while notable inside are the hammer-
beam roof and a late 14C rood screen surmounted by some curious 17C
balustrading. *Llewelyn's Cave*, in woods across the Edw and a traditional hiding
place of Llewelyn the Last, was perhaps earlier a retreat of St. Cewydd, a local
saint. At *Llanbadarn Garreg*, 2¹/₂m up the Edw valley, the church is 15C and
virtually untouched.

1m. **Erwood**, the name, pronounced Errod and a corruption of the
Welsh Y Rhyd (the Ford), recalling a past when the shallow crossing
here was much used by drovers and their herds. Here, too, in 1841,
the magazine 'Punch' was born, the brainchild of Henry Mayhew
(the first joint-editor) and others who were visiting here.—*4m.*
Llyswen and (by A479) *3m.* **Bronllys** where Rte 33 is crossed and
where the church, a 19C rebuilding, has a detached 14C tower.
Bronllys Castle, just SE and balancing on an earlier motte, is a lone
cylindrical tower of c 1200, with later alterations but a possibly earlier
vaulted basement.

1m. **Talgarth** (2000 inhab.), a small market town of some character,
stood athwart the Norman thrust into Wales (under Bernard of
Newmarch) and still shows defensive features, notably in the tower
(14C in its present form) of the church and in another tower, this one
of the 11–13C and later serving as the jail, beside the bridge and now
incorporated into a house. Talgarth is associated with Hywel Harris
(1714–73, and buried here), a Methodist revivalist who in 1752
established at Trefecca House, 1¹/₄m SW by B4560, 'The Connexion',
a community organised on communal religious-industrial lines.
Today the house is a college (Tel: 0874–711423) with a museum
which includes rare books published by the Connexion press, field
pulpits and much else relating to the community.

Llangorse Lake, rather over 4m S of Talgarth by B4560, is some 4m in
circumference and, after Bala, the largest natural lake in Wales. Shallow and
reedy, and today popular for water sports, the lake is the result of glacial action.
It also has the distinction of being the only place in Wales where definite traces
have been found (on a crannog-island off the N shore) of prehistoric lake-
dwellings, an ancient settlement which may well have been the source of the
local legend of a drowned township. The best general view of the lake is from
B4560 above the lake's SE end, the road from here continuing to Bwlch on Rte
25B.—To the N of the lake there are three churches of modest interest, starting
with the one in the village of *Llangorse* which is of the 14 and 15C. A short way
NW, the churches of *Llanfihangel Tal-y-Llyn* and *Llan-y-Wern* both contain 17C
survivals of the floreated cross motif (see Rte 26A, Brecon Cathedral), while the
oval shape of the churchyard of the latter suggests that this was a very early
Celtic foundation.
  In the hamlet of *Llanelieu*, at 800ft 2m E of Talgarth, the church retains its
medieval S door and ironwork. Inside, there is a double rood screen, with
something of the floor of its loft, while at the back is the original boarded and
painted tympanum, rising above the tie-beam of the roof. Cut on the front of the
tie-beam is the socket for the rood. The tympanum is pierced by a number of

small openings, presumably serving as squints for the occupants of the gallery. The church owes its name to St. Ellwy, a granddaughter of King Brychan of Brecknock, said to have had a castle near here.

A479, leading S out of Talgarth, now crosses the W slopes of the Black Mountains, representing the eastern extremity of Brecon Beacons National Park.—*3m. Pen-y-Genffordd*, above which *Castell Dinas*, originally a hillfort, was later a motte-and-bailey castle complementing Tretower Castle at the foot of the glen. From here a track ascending the S bank of the Rhiangoll stream heads towards (3m) Waun Fach (2660ft), the highest point of the Black Mountains. *Ty Isaf Burial Chamber*, ¼m E of the road, ¾m S of Pen-y-Genffordd, is on private land, but the mound and stones can be seen from the lane.— The road descends beside the Rhiangoll to (*5m*) *Cwm-Du*, where the church has a late 14C tower, a sanctuary arch (though none to the choir), a curious small porch towards the S, and (S exterior) an early inscribed stone.

2m. **Tretower** is an Usk valley village known for its medieval manor and, adjacent, ruined Norman castle (both WHM. Tel: 0222-465511).

*Tretower Court, entered through a gatehouse of about 1480 and an exceptionally complete and picturesque example of a late medieval manor house, was the seat of the Vaughans. The oldest part, the stonework on the N, is 14C, and the woodwork is possibly 15C, a time when Sir Roger Vaughan made extensive alterations, but preserving the house's earlier character. The wall-walk, originally a defensive structure, was given its roof and windows during the 17C. For today's visitor the outstanding features are the rich oak woodwork, well seen in the spacious empty rooms, and the unusually generous provision of garderobes. *Tretower Castle*, Norman-built early in the 12C, was, with Castell Dinas at the head of the Rhiangoll glen, intended to guard this pass against the incursions of the unconquered Welsh. Nevertheless it was successfully besieged by Llewelyn the Last and was partly destroyed by Owen Glendower in 1403, after which it seems to have been abandoned. The layout—a massive cylindrical tower of about 1235 planted within the enclosure of an earlier (mid 12C) square keep, which had been partially demolished—is unusual if not unique. The large ward, on the E, now encloses a farmyard.

1m. Junction with Rte 25B, the onward road is now the A40 along which, in about another mile, can be seen cist stones, once covered by a long barrow.—*1m.* **Crickhowell** (1400 inhab,) takes its name from the hillfort (crug) of Hywel on the hill known as Table Mountain 1m to the north. Worth noting on the way through the small town are, on the W of the road at the N entrance to the town, the picturesque 15C gateway of a now vanished mansion of the Herberts; the *Church* of the 14C, with a shingle spire unusual in Wales; and the motte and two shattered towers of the Norman *Castle*. The river Usk, to the W, is spanned by a medieval bridge of 13 arches.

Beyond Llangattock, the Beaufort road in 1½m (first cattle grid) reaches *Craig-y-Cilau Nature Reserve*. Access is by a track from the grid, a path then running the length of the reserve (1¼m) below the 400ft escarpment. The reserve (157 acres) is one of the best botanical sites in the Brecon Beacons National Park, with over 250 recorded species, and is also known to be the breeding place of some 49 kinds of bird. The reserve also includes entrances to a cave system of about 12m, but access is only for members of approved clubs.

On the E side of A40, 1m S of Crickhowell, there is a fine standing stone. Approaching Abergavenny, a steep and narrow road (National Trust sign) climbs up on to the *Sugar Loaf* (1955ft), a National Trust property of 2130 acres given in 1936 by Viscountess Rhondda. From a car park there is an easy upland walk of about 1½m to the highest point.—*5m.* **Abergavenny**, see Rte 28.

B.   Via Brecon and Tretower

B4520 to Brecon. A40 to Abergavenny. Total distance 33m.—*5m. Mynydd Epynt watershed.*—*10m.* **Brecon**. *8m.* **Bwlch**.—*3m.* **Tretower**.—*7m.* **Abergavenny**.

From **Builth Wells** (see Rte 23A) B4520 climbs across the open upland of *Mynydd Epynt*, with Ministry of Defence ranges to the west.—*5m.* From the watershed (1560ft), with a road across to Garth on Rte 24, the E edge of the ranges is skirted before the descent into the valley of the Honddu.—*8m. Llandefaelog Fach*, where the church preserves a 10C Celtic cross-slab bearing the name and figure of one Briamail.—*2m.* **Brecon**, see Rte 26A.

A40 is now followed SE to reach, in *3m, Llanhamlach* where the church, although rebuilt, still houses an unusually well-preserved effigy of a lady, a 10–11C slab representing the Crucifixion, and, in the N porch, several grave-slabs showing the floreated cross motif (see Rte 26A, Brecon Cathedral). Just beyond, *Ty Illtud* (¼m E of the junction with minor road to Pennorth) is a prehistoric long cairn with a well-preserved mound containing a small chamber and capstone. The carved crosses on the capstone supports are medieval.—*3m. Llansantffraid*, with, in the churchyard near the E wall, the tomb of Henry Vaughan (1622–95), self-styled the 'Silurist' (the Silures were the early tribe of this district), born at Seethog, 1½m farther on. The tomb bears the Vaughan crest of three heads, said to recall the birth in c 1100 of Vaughan triplets who survived despite some umbilical strangulation. Henry Vaughan was himself a twin. For *Talybont Reservoir*, 2m SW, and beyond, see end of Rte 26B.—*2m.* **Bwlch**, ½m NW of which (off B4560) is *Castell Blaenllynfi*, the fragmentary remains of a Norman castle of the De Braose family. For *Llangorse Lake*, 2m farther N, see Rte 25A. *Llangynidr Bridge*, 1m S below Bwlch, is a particularly attractive four-arch bridge across a lovely stretch of the Usk.

The road now drops, rounding the wooded hill of Myarth, passing (*3m*) **Tretower** (see Rte 25A), plainly seen immediately E, and , just beyond, reaching the junction with A479. For Tretower to (*7m*) **Abergavenny** see Rte 25A.

26 Brecon and the Brecon Beacons

This Route, in two parts, first describes the city of Brecon, together with the Roman fort of Y Gaer, 3m to the west. The second part covers the Brecon Beacons, with Talybont and Taf Fechan forests, and suggests a motor circuit around the foot of the area.

A.   Brecon

BRECON (7000 inhab. *Inf.* Market Car Park. Tel: 0874–2485 or 5692), in Welsh Aberhonddu, sprawls over raised ground N of the river Usk at its junction with the Honddu and the Tarell. Of ancient origin, the town is visited largely for its interesting 13–14C cathedral, and also as a base for touring the Brecon Beacons and the national park of the same name.

History. The Romans were here (at Y Gaer, 3m W) in about 75, and in the 5C, after the Roman departure, the Brecon area was controlled by the chieftain Brychan, from whom it derives its name. During the reign of William II, at the close of the 11C, the Norman Bernard of Newmarch built his castle here, and it was around this that the town began to grow, gaining its first charter, from Humphrey de Bohun, Earl of Hereford, in 1276. Brecon was besieged by Llewelyn the Last in 1282, and later the neighbourhood suffered raids by Owen Glendower, but by the 15C the town had developed a considerable cloth trade. During the Civil War Brecon's attitude was unequivocally neutral, the citizens even demonstrating this by demolishing the town walls and much of the castle.—Among natives of Brecon were Sir David Gam (fell at Agincourt, 1415), supposed to have been the original of Shakespeare's Fluellen; Dr Hugh Price (1495–1574), founder of Jesus College, Oxford; Dr Thomas Coke (1747–1814), founder of the American Methodist Episcopalian Church; Mrs Sarah Siddons (1755–1831), the actress, and her brother, the actor Charles Kemble (1775–1854). Henry Vaughan (1622–95), the 'Silurist', worked here as a physician for some years.

St. Mary's Church, at the town centre, shows a bold 16C tower and a nave arcade which retains a single fluted Norman capital on the N side. Adjacent, the *Sarah Siddons Inn* was the birthplace of the actress in 1755 (it was at that time the 'Shoulder of Mutton'), and the actor Owen Nares died here in 1943, while, as a third theatrical link, it was in the *Roman Catholic Church* in Glamorgan Street, S of St. Mary's, that the opera singer Adelina Patti married Baron Cedarström, her third husband, in 1898.

Within the angle of Glamorgan Street and Captain's Walk, the Classical Shire Hall (1842) contains the **Brecknock Museum** (Tel: 0874–4121), concerned principally with the former county of Breconshire, until the late 1930s generally known by its earlier name of Brecknockshire. Among the varied exhibits are agricultural and domestic machinery and implements; archaeological material telling the story of man in Brecknock; a copy of a town charter granted by Queen Mary and, interestingly, her husband Philip II of Spain; Roman and Early Christian stones; a reconstructed Assize Court; the town stocks, last used in 1826; a *Collection of love-spoons, the traditional Welsh courting gift up to about the 17C; costumes, with contemporary photographs; and a natural history section.

Captain's Walk, descending towards the Usk and passing some remains of the old town wall, is said to have been a favourite promenade for French officers interned at Brecon during the Napoleonic wars. The *South Wales Borderers Regimental Museum* (Tel: 0874–3111. Ext. 310), at the Barracks on A40 rather over ¼m SE, covers some 280 years of history which saw the award of no fewer than 16 Victoria Crosses.

The *Cathedral*, or the Priory Church of St. John the Evangelist, stands on high ground above the Honddu in the northern part of the town.

History. The priory was founded, very probably on the site of an earlier church, by Bernard of Newmarch at the close of the 11C as a cell of the Benedictine monastery of Battle in Sussex, an association recalled by a village called Battle 3m north-west. Giraldus was Archdeacon of Brecon in c 1172, but of the early church of this Norman period little remains other than parts of the nave walls immediately W of the crossing. The choir and transepts were entirely rebuilt in the first half of the 13C, the tower being added at the same time; and during the 14C the nave, together with the N and S aisles, was newly built and the E chapels of the transepts were reconstructed to a larger scale. The church was restored in 1862–65 by Sir Gilbert Scott.

In 1923 the church was promoted to be cathedral of the dioceses of Swansea and Brecon, and in 1927 such parts of the priory domestic buildings as had survived the Reformation were restored by W.D. Caröe and rededicated for cathedral chapter use.

The NAVE is normally entered by the NW porch, above which is an upper chamber. The present beautiful vista up the whole length of the church was before the Reformation broken by a rood screen, reached by the still remaining staircases W of the crossing. The screen divided the church into two, the E part being for the monks and the W serving as parish church; above the screen was suspended a great rood, the Crog (Cross) Aberhonddu, of miraculous virtue, which gave the church its third title, Church of the Holy Rood, and which is celebrated by the Welsh bards of the 15C. At the W end of the nave are a Norman font; a remarkable stone cresset with 30 cups, unique in Wales and the largest found in Britain; a stone thought to have been used by archers for sharpening their arrows; and several sepulchral slabs, notable for their retention as late as the 17C of the medieval floreated cross, a practice common in this neighbourhood though rare elsewhere. Similar slabs will be found in other parts of the cathedral. The *North Aisle*, the former Chapel of the Corvisors (shoemakers) and Tailors, has a beautiful 14C tomb-niche and recumbent effigy; an old parclose screen; a dormer window portraying three early Welsh saints, Cynog, Brychan, and Alud; and a case of old religious books, including a rare breeches-bible (this word used instead of fig leaf, for the covering of Adam and Eve). In the *South Aisle*, the former Chapel of the Weavers and Tuckers, are the tombs of Sir David Williams (died 1613) and his wife Elizabeth Vaughan; the wooden effigy of a lady (c 1555), the only surviving figure from a tomb made up of three tiers of oak beds; and, at the W end, a medieval cope chest. The *North Transept* was known formerly as the Chapel of the Men of Battle, and the *South Transept* as that of the Red Haired Men (the Normans).

The *CHOIR, the vaulting of which was first completed by Gilbert Scott, contains the most beautiful work in the cathedral. The E window, of five large lancets, completely fills the wall space, while at the sides are graduated triplets of unusual character. The full effect of those on the N, however, is impaired by the later (14C) blocking of their lower parts. Also worth noting are the exquisite 13C sedilia; the rare triple piscina; the trefoiled niches (concealed by the reredos), N and S of the altar, that seem once to have opened on the outer air but perhaps afterwards served as aumbries; and the supulchral slab on the N wall of the sanctuary, with a curious carving of the Crucifixion. The reredos (W.D. Caröe, 1937) has figures of saints and others in relief. Rich archways at the W end of the choir open into the transept chapels on either side. In the *Havard Chapel* (N), with a 14C doorway to the sanctuary combined with a squint, is the tomb of Walter Awbrey (?1312), with an inscription in old Saxon and Norman French characters. Here also are four old benches (two now cut down for footstools) that formerly took the place of fixed altar rails at the celebration of Holy Communion. This is now the regimental chapel

(1961) of the South Wales Borderers. The *Chapel of St. Lawrence* (S), after lying in ruins for 300 years, was rebuilt by Caröe in 1930; it contains a small 13C piscina.

The domestic buildings of the priory (entered from the SW door), after serving as stables etc. for three centuries, have been skilfully fitted up by Caröe as the canonry, deanery, and chapter house.—On the steep bank of the Honddu above the church are the pleasant *Groves*, a public park, once a retreat of Henry Vaughan.

The **Castle** (no adm.), between the cathedral and the Usk bridge, is in two parts. The main ruin, in the grounds of the Castle Hotel, dates from a reconstruction during the reign of Edward I and consists of one side of the Great Hall and of the *Ely Tower*. It was in this tower that in 1483 the Duke of Buckingham, a lord of Brecknock, held prisoner Morton, Bishop of Ely, who had been arrested on the accession of Richard III. Morton succeeded in persuading his gaoler to rebel, but the venture failed and Buckingham was executed though Morton escaped, to become, under Henry VII, Archbishop of Canterbury, Lord Chancellor and Cardinal. On the rise opposite the hotel are the motte and part of the bailey of Bernard of Newmarch's original 11C castle, still with fragments of keep and gatehouse (see also Y Gaer below).

The suburb of **Llanfaes** is SW of Brecon beyond the attractive old seven-arch Usk bridge. Here *Christ College*, originally a Dominican friary, was refounded by Henry VIII in 1541 as a collegiate church and school. The buildings are largely modern, but incorporate the 13C monastic church, the nave of which is in ruins while the choir is now the school chapel. The former refectory is the school dining hall, and another old room serves as library.—Visitors are welcome at rehearsals of Aberhonddu Male Voice Choir (Tel: 0874–3908).

The remains of the Roman fort of **Y Gaer**, 3m W of Brecon, can be reached on foot by the track of the Roman road S of the now disused railway. By car, the Cradoc road is taken W out of the town, this road running below the hill of *Pen-y-Crug* (1088ft) with a hillfort. At Cradoc the left fork (signed Aberyscir) passes, on the left by the railway bridge, a 13ft-high standing stone and soon reaches a small crossroads, the left turn from which leads to a farm where permission to park and visit Y Gaer should be asked. Probably known to the Romans as Cicutium, the fort occupies a site bounded on the S by the Usk, on the W by the Yscir stream, and on the other sides by a ditch. It was first built in c 75 at the time of the final Roman conquest of Wales, rebuilt in c 105 and again in c 140, and finally abandoned in c 290, among the garrisons having been the Vettonian Spanish cavalry and the 2nd Legion. Some eight centuries later, much of what remained of the masonry was used by Bernard of Newmarch in the construction of his castle at Brecon. Excavated by Sir Mortimer Wheeler in 1924–25, most of what was exposed was later covered, but the outer face of the N wall, in good condition and up to 10ft high, can be seen; and the other walls, with the usual rounded angles, and something of the N, E and especially W gates can be traced.—The village of *Battle*, 1m N of the fort, recalls that Brecon priory, later to become the cathedral, was originally a cell of Battle Abbey in Sussex. Dr Thomas Coke (see History, above) is buried here.

For Brecon to (N) *Builth Wells* and (S) *Abergavenny*, see Rte 25B; to *Aberaeron*, see Rte 27; to (E) *Hay-on-Wye* and (W) *Swansea*, see Rte 33; to *Merthyr Tydfil*, see Rte 26B below.

B. Brecon Beacons Talybont and Taf Fechan Forests

Together the Brecon Beacons with Talybont and Taf Fechan Forests make up a splendid area of mountain, forest, moor and water, bounded on the W by A470 (Brecon to Merthyr Tydfil, see below), on the S by A465 (Merthyr Tydfil to Abergavenny, see Rte 31), and on the E by A40 (Brecon to Abergavenny, see Rte 25B). There is a network of walks, and a Motor Circuit, suggested below, can be made which takes in much of the best of the scenery.

The BRECON BEACONS, which are only one relatively small part of Brecon Beacons National Park, fill the NW section of this area. The Beacons themselves—given, with over 6000 surrounding acres, to the National Trust in 1965 by Sir Brian Mountain—have two principal summits, barely ½m apart, these being *Pen y Fan* (N, 2907ft) and *Corn Ddu* (S, 2863ft), a distinctive pair of sandstone peaks facing sharply N and on this side broken by cwms. Southward the slopes are for the most part gentle, while a range extending E in nearly 1m reaches the lesser peak of *Cribyn* (2608ft). Continuing E from Cribyn the ridge is broken by *The Gap*, a col between the N–S ridges of Bryn Teg and Cefn Cyff across which runs the track which may once have been a Roman road and which later, until the 19C, became the main link between Brecon and Merthyr Tydfil.

The Beacons are very popular with walkers, being crossed by several recognised routes which, because of the relative compactness of the area, can be combined as wished (Information from Watton Mount, Brecon, LD3 7DF. Tel: 0874-4437, or Mountain Centre, near Libanus. Tel: 0874-3366. Also, by post with large stamped addressed envelope, National Park Office, 7 Glamorgan Street, Brecon, LD3 7DP).

Talybont and **Taf Fechan forests**, with their long narrow reservoirs of the same names and, on the lower SE slopes of the Beacons, the two beautifully situated *Neuadd Reservoirs*, angle as valleys across the middle of the area. The valleys, which are water catchment zones, were first planted by the Forestry Commission in 1937; large scale planting of conifers started in 1945, but the earlier oak, ash and other trees have been preserved. A number of car parks and picnic sites have been provided.

MOTOR CIRCUIT FROM BRECON. 37m.—*6m.* Brecon Beacons National Park **Mountain Centre** is at 1000ft on the upland **Mynydd Illtyd Common** in the SW angle between A40 and A470. The main access, suitable for larger vehicles, is by a minor road from Libanus on A470. A more leisurely approach is by way of a minor road (sign) off A40 just beyond the roundabout on the W outskirts of Brecon. Ascending on to the common, this latter approach passes (½m N from a road fork) the earthworks of the hillfort *Twyn y Gaer*, with, to its E and S, mounds which are probably Bronze Age burial cairns. In another mile, after passing a pond, there is a small standing stone on the left, probably an ancient route marker since a line projected SW from here hits two similar stones at the edge of the common. About 200 yards farther, by another little pond, *Bedd Illtyd*, now no more than two stones in a hollow, is nevertheless by local tradition the grave of St. Illtyd (born 425), founder of the monastery at Llantwit Major. Beyond, a left turn passes now disused *Illtyd Church*, built in 1858 on a site the circular shape of which suggests a very early Celtic foundation, possibly by Illtyd. The *Mountain Centre* (Tel: 0874–3366), ¼m farther and with fine views, offers National Park information, café, picnic facilities etc. Across the W section of the common can be traced a length of the Roman Sarn Helen; and, by contrast, the underground oil pipeline from Milford Haven to the Midlands (1972) crosses the common.

A road from the Mountain Centre drops in rather over 2m to *Libanus* on A470 which, ascending the valley of the Tarell and rounding the W flank of the Beacons, in 3m reaches the nature reserve of *Craig Cerrig-Gleisiad* (Countryside Council for Wales. National Park picnic site), a 698 acre glaciated area of crags, gullies and mountain streams rising from 1200 to 2000ft. Here, more than 300 plant and 60 bird species have been recorded, some of which may be seen from the footpath (permit necessary for other access) which skirts much of the reserve's boundary.—1m. The watershed is at 1440ft, just beyond being the Youth Adventure Centre *Storey Arms*, near which start the Y Gyrn and Pont ar Daf ascents to the Beacons' summits.

A470 now drops with the valley of the Taff, passing plantations and, in succession, Beacons, Cantref and Llwyn-On reservoirs, all providing water for Cardiff. Overlooking the N end of this last reservoir is *Garwnant Visitor Centre* (Tel: 0639–710221), providing information on the forests of the Brecon Beacons and setting the forestry scene within the context of water catchment, farming and the National Park. There is a short forest trail.

In 8m (from the watershed), from a major crossing with A465 (for Merthyr Tydfil, see Rte 31), a small road in 1m reaches a road junction below a limestone crag on top of which are the scanty fragments—traces of two round towers, a vaulted basement and deep pit, this last unfenced and dangerous—of late 13C *Morlais Castle*. The easiest approach to the castle is to follow the Merthyr Tydfil road for about half-a-mile and then walk along the W side of the golf course. The valley minor road continues NE through increasingly wooded scenery (for the nearby Brecon Mountain Railway, see Rte 31, Merthyr Tydfil) to skirt the W length of first *Pontsticill* and then *Pentwyn* reservoirs, in 4m at the N end of the latter bearing right at a fork. Here, however, a short diversion (3m return) should be made to the *Neuadd Reservoirs*, lying in wood and moorland below the Beacons. Above the E side of these two adjacent waters runs the old road, perhaps Roman in origin, until the 19C the main Brecon to Merthyr road and today, leading through The Gap, one of the most popular walkers' routes across the Beacons.

At *Pont Blaen-y-glyn*, less than 2m beyond the road fork at the N end of Pentwyn reservoir, there are Forestry Commission picnic sites marking the starting-points of short waymarked walks, the Waterfall Walk, though the most strenuous, being the most rewarding. The small road continues N, fringing the W side of *Talybont Reservoir*, 2m long and with a dam at its N end. *Danywenallt*, just N of the dam, a National Park study centre with residential courses (Tel: 087487–677), occupies a farmhouse and barn restored (1977) from a derelict condition; the plans were partly the work of architectural students from Kingston Polytechnic, and the local labour was employed under a government job creation scheme.

5m. *Talybont* village, whence Brecon can be reached in 6m by B4558. Alternatively A40 can be joined at *Llansantffraid*, ¾m northeast.

27 Brecon to Aberaeron

A40 to Llanwrda. A482 to Aberaeron. Total distance 51m.—*9m.*
Sennybridge.—*12m.* **Llandovery.**—*4m.* **Llanwrda.**—*7m.*
Pumpsaint.—*7m.* **Lampeter.**—*12m.* **Aberaeron.**

For **Brecon**, see Rte 26A.—*2m. Llanspyddid*, with a 14C church in the
graveyard of which a gravestone is reputed to be that of the local 5C
chieftain Brychan or of Aulach, his father.—*4m. Trallong* where the
church houses an Ogham stone of the 5–6C, though its ringed cross
may be two or so centuries later.—*3m.* **Sennybridge** is a relatively
modern place, dating effectively from the arrival here of the railway
in 1872, though the slight remains of Castell Ddu just W of the town
go back to the 14C and are believed to be on the site of the 11C home
of Sir Reginald Aubrey, friend of Bernard of Newmarch. For Sennybridge to Swansea, see Rte 33.—*3m.* **Trecastle**, with a small
Norman motte-and-bailey, was at its most prosperous during the
coaching years of the 18 and 19C. But, many centuries earlier, both
prehistoric people and, later, the Romans were active around here.
Minor roads wandering SW out of Trecastle in 3m reach the long
wooded *Usk Reservoir*, a sheet of water unknown of course to the
men who erected the massive standing stone, weighing perhaps 20
tons, which can be seen from the road just S of the reservoir's dam at
its E end. The road running S of the reservoir crosses the Usk some
2m below its source, and walkers up the stream's E bank may in
under 1m find a perhaps even remoter prehistoric site comprising a
circle (with seven stones standing, and seven tumbled), a cairn, and
an ellipse with 12 upright and three fallen stones. As to the Romans,
they are represented by traces of a road running NW from Trecastle
(just S of and roughly parallel to A40) to reach in 4m (of which the
first two are motorable) the camps of *Y Pigwn*, earthworks thrown up
in the early years of the Roman occupation, in perhaps 50 to 80, on a
site only a few yards W of already ancient stone circles.

1m. Llywel, where, in the church, the Llywel Stone (a cast of the
original now in the British Museum) is particularly interesting for
bearing carving of three early periods. The Ogham probably dates
from at latest the 5C; the Latin commemorates one Maccutrenus
Salicidunus, believed to have been a local man of c 500; and a small
cross between the two names—possibly carved by some pious
descendant to confer belated Christian respectability and salvation
on a forebear suspected of being a pagan—is probably of the 7C.
Also in this church are another Ogham stone; parts of the 16C rood
screen and loft, the latter, removed in 1869, now forming the
entrance to the vestry; an ancient font; and the stocks of 1798.—At
about 5$^{1}/_{2}$m beyond Llywel, beside the S side of the road, the *Mail
Coach Pillar* gives a dramatic warning from the past against driving
and drinking.—*8m.* (from Llywel) **Llandovery**, see Rte 26.—*4m.* (by
A40) **Llanwrda** where A482 is now taken N while A40 continues S as
Rte 24.

A482 ascends the Dulais to (*4m*) the watershed at *Bwlch Cefn-
Sarth* (759ft), thence descending to (*3m*) **Pumpsaint** (Five Saints), a
village on the site of a Roman settlement busy with the exploitation
and protection of the nearby gold mines. Of the settlement nothing
visible survives—though a bathhouse just S of the village was
excavated and then covered, and Sarn Helen runs N from A482 1m
beyond Pumpsaint—but the Romans' *Dolaucothi Gold Mines* are still
here (NT. Tel: 05585–359, or 605 out of season). The mines—$^{1}/_{2}$m SE

of Pumpsaint village and at the S end of the National Trust's Dolaucothi Estate of 2522 acres, given in 1941–44 by Mr H.T.C. Lloyd-Johnes as a memorial to his family, owners since the time of Henry VII—today include a Visitor Centre and Miners' Way (the latter a self-guided surface trail) which combine to explain the remains of the Roman and other workings which cover some 30 acres.

The complex evidence survives in the form of opencast pits, adits and water courses and is witness to the advanced mining technology of the Romans. The Roman mining remains are, however, overlaid with more recent evidence from the 19 and 20C, this including the 500ft shaft sunk in the early 20C and the foundations of the gold processing plant. In fact the mine saw two major exploitation periods between 1888–1910 (Mitchell Mine) and 1933–38 (Roman Deep Holdings. British Goldfields), but on neither occasion did the returns justify the cost, the mine being closed in 1938, British Goldfields dissolved in 1943 and the machinery and buildings then being scrapped. However, working mining machinery from the 1930s, donated to the National Trust, now helps to provide an insight into the more recent industrial heritage of this ancient site.—The mines are set in oak woodland overlooking the beautiful Cothi valley, served by the small road which passes the mines; later, this road curves E and then SE, descending into the valley of the Towy and, in 11m from Pumpsaint, reaching Llyn Brianne.

At the site there is a boulder showing five depressions, the story being that five (pump) saints—surely the five brothers associated with Llanpumpsaint on Rte 41B—rested here and used this boulder as a pillow.—At *Caio*, 1m SE, a 4C Roman graveslab has been built into the wall of the church.—At *Crugybar*, 2m S on B4302, Felin Newydd is a water-powered corn mill, generally of the 18C but successor to others on this site since perhaps the 14C (Tel: 05585–375).

Beyond Pumpsaint the watershed between the Cothi and the Teifi is crossed at 1025ft, the road then descending to (7m) **Lampeter** on Rte 41B which is crossed here. Leaving Lampeter, A482 rises for 4m before dropping into the rich Vale of Aeron.—*12m*. **Aberaeron**, see Rte 41A.

28 Abergavenny to Skenfrith and Grosmont

B4521 and B4347. Total distance 16m.—*5m*. **White Castle.**—*6m*. **Skenfrith.**—*5m*. **Grosmont.**

After leaving Abergavenny, the principal objectives are the three castles—White, Skenfrith and Grosmont—all in 1201 granted by King John to Hubert de Burgh and becoming known as the Welsh Trilateral. Except for 1205–19, when the castles fell into the hands of William de Braose and his son, the Trilateral continued to be held by Hubert de Burgh until his fall from favour in 1232 when the castles reverted to the Crown. All three castles are probably of early Norman origin, and all have adjacent churches of some interest.

Abergavenny (10,000 inhab. *Inf.* Swan Meadow, Cross Street. Tel: 0873–77588), a place of Roman and Norman origin, is today a busy market centre at the confluence of the Usk and the Gavenny.

History. The town's origins go back to the modest Roman fort of Gobannium, one of those protecting their road up the Usk, but real civic development grew from the settlement which clustered below the Norman stronghold built by Hameline de Balun (1085–1138). This castle later came into the hands of the notorious William de Braose who at Christmas 1176, in revenge for the killing of his uncle by the Welsh, here murdered many of the Welsh lords of Gwent whom he had invited as his guests. The town was sacked by Owen Glendower in 1404, and again by Parliament (by Fairfax) in 1646, but Royalist Jacobite sentiment survived and, in 1688, the town demonstrated in favour of James II and against William III, the result being that its charter (granted 1639) was suspended.

The two principal places of interest, close to one another, are the large Church of St. Mary with its many fine monuments, and the slight remains of the castle, the home today of the town and district museum.

The *Church of St. Mary* was formerly the chapel of a small Benedictine priory, founded by Hameline de Balun as a cell of the abbey of St. Vincent at Le Mans in France. Of this, though, nothing remains, today's church, apart from the mainly modern nave, being largely of the 14C. The choir lost its clerestory and received the present lath-and-plaster groining during early 19C restoration. The *Monuments, spanning from the 13 to the 17C, combine as an outstanding series. First, in the S or Herbert Chapel, there are the recumbent effigies of the Herbert, Cantelupe and Hastings families, in the centre being Sir William ap Thomas (died 1446), father of the 1st Earl of Pembroke of the Herbert line, and of his wife. Here too is what is thought to be a 14C Herbert graveslab, found in 1961 buried in the churchyard. In the nave there is a fine wooden figure of George de Cantelupe, Baron Bergavenny (died 1273), and in the N or Lewis Chapel are effigies of Eva de Braose (died 1246) and of Eva de Cantelupe (died 1257), this latter (sometimes said to be Christina

The fifteenth-century wooden sculpture of Jesse in the Church of St. Mary, Abergavenny

Herbert, died 1307) being a rare example of a figure of a woman with a shield. The monument of Dr David Lewis (died 1584), the first Principal of Jesus College, Oxford, was erected by himself. The large 15C wooden recumbent figure evidently formed the root of a Tree of Jesse, probably once part of the reredos of the high altar.

Noteworthy in the choir are the old stalls, with latticed backs, and the seats for the prior and sub-prior beneath tall tabernacled canopies, mostly probably dating from the late 14C; on the N floor, a small brass to the Stephens (father and son), bearing an intriguing rhyming epitaph; and the font with a Norman bowl and ropework carving.

The slight remains of *Abergavenny Castle* are a short distance south-west. Of Hameline de Balun's early stronghold only the motte and the roughly pentagonal bailey remain, and of the later stonework defences, which were incorporated with the town walls, all that is left is part of the NW curtain wall, with the ruins of the entrance gate and two mural towers. The *Abergavenny and District Museum* (Tel: 0873–4282) is within the castle precincts.

Blorenge (2¹/₂m SW. 1834ft) is capped by mountain limestone and known for its sink or swallow holes. A road leads to close to the summit where there are car parks, one of which, called Foxhunter, was presented by Colonel Llewellyn in memory of his champion horse (died 1959), buried near here. Foxhunter represented Britain 35 times and had 78 international wins.

For *Sugar Loaf*, 2¹/₂m N, see Rte 25A.

For Abergavenny to *Raglan* and *Monmouth*, see Rte 29; to *Newport*, see Rte 30; to *Merthyr Tydfil*, *Neath* and *Swansea*, see Rte 31.

Leaving the town, B4521 runs across the S slopes of *Skirrid Fawr* (1596ft), 205 acres of the summit of which are National Trust property given by Major Jack Herbert in 1939. The notch at the N end of the ridge is locally attributed to an earthquake at the time of the Crucifixion, and the hill is sometimes referred to as Holy Mountain either on account of this or, more probably, because of a chapel which, standing on the summit until the 17C, was long an objective of pilgrimage (some remains survive at the N end of the ridge).

5m (beyond *Llanvetherine*), a small road leads S to the ruins of **White Castle** (WHM. Tel: 0222-465511), of two distinct 12 and 13C periods and once covered by white plaster. The general plan of the castle is a large outer ward to the N; an inner ward protected by a curtain and moat; and to the S a defensive hornwork, also protected by a moat.

History. Earthworks here are evidence of early Norman or other border fortification, but the present stone remains are of a 12 and 13C castle originally known as Llantilio, the title of the local manor, but in the 13C changing its name when its walls were coated with the white plaster, traces of which still survive. In 1201 King John granted White, together with Skenfrith and Grosmont, to Hubert de Burgh, the three then forming what came to be called the Welsh Trilateral (see introduction to this Rte). In c 1263, at the time of the threat from Llewelyn the Last, White Castle, now owned by Henry III, was refortified, a major undertaking which included the transfer of the main entrance from the S to the north. After the subjugation of Wales by Edward I, White sank to become little more than an administrative centre, and already by the 16C it was roofless and abandoned.

The visitor enters the castle through the *Outer Gatehouse*, an addition (on the E side of the outer ward) of the 13C refortification. This structure was essentially a broad rectangular passage with gates at both ends; the portcullis groove can be seen by the outer gate, and the modern bridge crosses the pit formerly covered by the drawbridge. The large *Outer Ward* formed part of the original defences, these surviving today as a bank beyond the ditch (never a real moat and probably always dry) on the N and west. The wall and towers all date from the 13C, the NW tower being rectangular and believed to have served as offices, possibly of the quartermaster. A recess in the W of the wall was a garderobe. The moat is crossed to the *Inner Ward*, the oldest part of the castle, with walls of the late 12C. The gatehouse and towers, however, represent the 13C refortification, the former of standard pattern with towers of four storeys flanking the passage; the portcullis groove can be found. Inside the ward, only the outlines of the rooms survive. The Hall, with its kitchen on the opposite side of the ward, was against the NE wall, the outer foundations representing the original 12C hall (a tall building which probably rose higher than the wall), and the inner foundations the successor hall known to have been built in 1244. South of the hall are the well and the E tower, with, beyond, the Constable's Solar and, S again, the latrine pit. The Chapel occupies the SE corner of the ward, the choir being provided by the SE tower, while the nave projected into the ward. The base course of the S of the ward, the oldest masonry of the castle (early 12C), is all that is left of the original small keep; only the inner part survives, the remainder being cut by a section of 13C wall linking the SE and SW towers. This was the site of the castle's main entrance prior to the refortification, the entrance being protected by the moat and the *Hornwork* beyond. Although a length of 13C wall crosses to the hornwork, it does not seem that this latter was ever given any stonework defences.

The village of **Llantilio Crosseny**, 1½m S, has an ancient and attractive origin. In 556 this was the land of a chief called Ynyr who, when threatened by pagan Saxons, appealed for help to St. Teilo. Teilo responded with prayer, Ynyr set up a large wooden cross and the Saxons were defeated. In gratitude Ynyr gave land to Teilo for the founding of a church, and hence the village's name, meaning Holy Enclosure of Teilo at the Cross of Ynyr.

The *Church* here, successor to several since 556, is mainly of the 12 and 13C. Originally cruciform, the church's N transept was absorbed by a 14C chapel (Cil Llwch, see below) and a clerestory was added in the 15C. The nave was originally considerably lower, as indicated by the low arches at the crossing, and the present structure (Perpendicular in style) is of the 15C. In the N aisle the main windows are modern restoration, but the small window of two lights at the E end, revealed during this restoration, is 16C. It carries the arms of two men thought to have been local manorial lords; a Herbert beheaded after the Battle of Banbury in 1469 during the Wars of the Roses (see also Raglan Castle, Rte 29), and Sir David Gam, killed at Agincourt in 1415 and said to have been the model for Shakespeare's Fluellen ('Davey Gam'). Steps in the wall of the tower, facing the nave, led to the now vanished rood loft. On the W pier of the central crossing arch, will be found a 'Green Man' with foliage coming out of his nostrils, an attractive reminder of the way in which a cautious Christianity adapted what had been a pagan fertility symbol into one of new life and resurrection. In the choir, some of the floor slabs are especially noteworthy, a particularly pleasing one being that of a father, mother, and three sons. There is also (N wall) a marble relief by Flaxman of Mary Ann Bosanquet (died 1819). The Cil Llwch Chapel, the former N transept, derives its name from a medieval manor, now Great Hillborough Farm, 1m south-west. Points of interest are the squints, suggesting that the chapel proper may have been private to the manorial family; and, either side of the altar, stone brackets in the shape of youths' heads, these representing, according to one local tradition, the murdered Princes in the Tower.

6m. **Skenfrith Castle** (NT and WHM) is an unusually small ruined castle, the main feature being a circular tower near the centre of an irregular four-sided ward.

History. There was almost certainly a Norman motte-and-bailey here, but Skenfrith as seen today (one of the Welsh Trilateral, see introduction to this Rte) was largely built by Hubert de Burgh, probably between 1229 and his fall from favour in 1232, and thereafter by the Crown to whom the castle reverted. The W tower seems to have been added in about 1263, at the time when Llewelyn the Last was threatening, but by the 16C Skenfrith was roofless and abandoned. The last Governor of the Trilateral (John Morgan, died 1557) lies in Skenfrith church.

The entrance is through what little remains of the Gatehouse in the N wall. Within the ward, the mound on which the Round Tower (completed by c 1244) stands is not, as might be thought, a survival of an early Norman motte, but a mound built from spoil from the moat and designed to give the tower sufficient height to enable defenders to fire beyond the curtain wall. The tower is of three levels, and it is interesting that there is no communication between ground and first floor, each having its individual entrance, while the second floor and the roof were reached by a stair, partly in the W wall and partly in a turret. The West Range of buildings was revealed by excavation in 1954. The central room here, reached by shallow steps, is divided from the N room by a wall, but it seems probable that the two were originally one; features are a blocked fireplace (perhaps blocked when it was found that flooding made these rooms unusable), and, at the S end, a recess which may represent the site of a stair to a floor above. It seems that virtually no East Range was built, though the kitchens were probably between the Round Tower and the E curtain.

Skenfrith Church. Although there was almost certainly an earlier church on this site, the present one is largely of the 13C, but with aisles which may be up to 200 years later. The church is dedicated to St. Bridget, and the ancient carving of the head of a nun over the porch is reputed to represent her. The tower is semi-defended, with thick walls, this and the upper storeroom suggesting its role as a refuge. In the N aisle is the *Altar-tomb of John Morgan (died 1557), last Governor of the Trilateral, and of his wife (died 1564), with their four sons and his four daughters; the tomb is remarkable for its detail of the dress of the period. The church's stone altar is its original one of 1207; thrown down at the Reformation, it served as floor paving for several years until, comparatively recently, replaced as altar on new supports. The slab bears some small cut consecration crosses (e.g. front left corner). The front of the reading desk in the choir incorporates a part of the medieval rood screen.

The village of **Grosmont**, also with its castle and church, is *5m* NW of Skenfrith and reached by B4347 which branches off B4521 just W of Skenfrith. *Grosmont Castle* (WHM), on a hill as indicated by its Norman name, is the third and northernmost of the Welsh Trilateral (see introduction to this Rte). After reverting to the Crown in 1232, the castle was in the following year besieged by Llewelyn the Great, but saved by the timely approach of Henry III; and in 1402 it was again invested, this time by Owen Glendower who, however, was driven off by the future Henry V. Mostly of the early 13C, but with some 14C additions on the N, Grosmont is a rather fragmentary survival, the most interesting feature, perhaps, being the ruin of the Hall (c 1210), to the right on entering the castle; untypically large, it is also curious for being on the outer side of the later curtain of 1220–40.

In Grosmont *Church*, mostly 13C, noteworthy features are the late Norman arches of the nave, the Norman font, the Early English arcading in the choir, and the Decorated piscina. The church is associated with the enigmatic John Kent (fl. 1400), said to be buried here, also known as John of Kentchurch (Kentchurch Court, 1m NE in England, was the estate of the Scudamores, one of whom married one of Owen Glendower's daughters). A bard—he enjoyed the patronage of the Scudamores who sent him to study at Oxford, afterwards giving him the living of Kentchurch—he became the focus of many stories; that he was a magician, that he lived to be 120, and that (presumably arising from the Scudamore marriage link) he was Owen Glendower in hiding. The large figure in the SE of the nave, long popularly thought to represent this John Kent, in fact seems more likely to be that of a knight.

29 Abergavenny to Raglan and Monmouth

A40. Total distance 16m.—*9m.* **Raglan Castle.**—*7m.* **Monmouth**.

From **Abergavenny** (see Rte 28), A40 briefly descends the valley of the Usk, with the heights of Blorenge to the W, before leaving the river and bearing SE to touch the northern edge of the National Trust estate of *Clytha* (by appointment only. Tel: 0558-822800) with a Classical early 19C mansion and, to the S on a hill, a castle of 1790.

9m. **Raglan Castle** (WHM. Tel: 0222-465511), a stark and striking ruin on a knoll, interestingly combines medieval defensive requirements with the ever pressing demands of manorial elegance and comfort. Built mainly in the 15 and 16C the castle represents the last, though not the least impressive, example of medieval fortification in Britain.

History. The original motte, on which the Great Tower now stands, was raised by William FitzOsbern after the Norman conquest of Gwent in 1067–71. The present castle was started by Sir William ap Thomas, who had been knighted by Henry VI and made Steward of Usk and Caerleon. He built the Great Tower (c 1430–45), and probably also the S gate. His son was William Herbert, Earl of Pembroke, a leading Yorkist who helped to put Edward IV on the throne but was later (1496) defeated in battle and beheaded. It was he who completed the greater part of the present buildings. Later the property passed to the earls of Worcester, the 3rd Earl (William Somerset) between 1548–89 rebuilding the hall and enlarging the Pitched Stone Court to a mainly domestic pattern. In the Civil War Raglan, a principal Royalist centre, was defended for 11 weeks in 1646 against Fairfax by the 5th Earl, aged 84. The castle's fall in August marked the end of the first phase of the Civil War, Raglan later being slighted. At the Restoration the ruins were returned to the 6th Earl.

Approaching the *Gatehouse* the gargoyles above and the heraldic stonework to the left are worth notice. Although this gatehouse was protected by a drawbridge and two portcullises, everything beyond, except for the Great Tower, is residential building in which the fine doorway arches and windows are pleasing features. Beyond the gatehouse the *Pitched Stone Court* is crossed to the *Kitchen* (N corner of castle) containing two large double fireplaces. To the left of the kitchen is the *Pantry*, and the rooms lining the W side of the court are the *Buttery* and the *Great Hall*, the latter with a fine oriel window. From the hall stairs descend to the huge cellars. On the W of the hall are the slight remains of the *Chapel*. The hall and chapel divide the Pitched Stone Court from the *Fountain Court*, occupying the site of the early Norman bailey. In the NW corner the *Grand Staircase* ascended to living apartments, while at the SW corner of the court a gateway leads to the *Bowling Green*, from where steps descend to the *Moat Walk*, with niches (late 16C) which once held statues of Roman emperors. The *Great Tower*, reached from Fountain Court, is a hexagonal detached keep, surrounded by a moat and designed as a self-contained last point of defence. One side was blown up by Fairfax, but the stairway to the top remains.

7m. **Monmouth**, see Rte 34.

30   Abergavenny to Newport

A.   Via Usk and Caerleon

B4598 to Usk. B4596 to Caerleon. B4236 to Newport. Total distance 20m.—*11m.* **Usk**.—*7m.* **Caerleon**.—*2m.* **Newport**.

Running at first SE, then, after crossing A40, due S, B4598 in a little under *7m* for the second time crosses the Usk. At *Bettws Newydd*, 1m NE of this bridge, the church preserves a small but good rood loft, complete with its boarded tympanum, while, just N of the village, the height of *Coed-y-Bwynydd*, also known as Coed Arthur, is a National Trust property of 25 acres (gifted in 1945 by Captain Geoffrey Crawshay in memory of Sergeant Arthur Owen RAF) with a hillfort and affording some good views over the Usk valley.

4m. **Usk** (or Brynbuga. 2000 inhab.), on the E bank of the river of the same name and in part spread over the site of the Roman Burrium, predecessor of Caerleon, is a market town much of which dates from the 18C, though the castle remains and the church span the 12–15C. The small *Castle* (12C; private), belonging to the De Clares and the earls of March, was taken by Simon de Montfort in 1265; the ruins include the keep (1169–76, but altered in the 15C), a round tower on the 13C curtain, and a gatehouse. The parish *Church* was once that of a Benedictine nunnery (refounded by Richard de Clare, son of 'Strongbow', in 1236), the gatehouse of which survives by the churchyard gate. In the church, the nave is early 13C, but the arches of the crossing, the choir and the tower are of the first half of the 12C. The aisle was added during the 13C, but in the 15C rebuilt to a wider scale, its two quite elaborate porches being additions of the same period. Also worth noting are the large circular stair turret that projects into the aisle; the tall 15C rood screen; and a fine brass inscription of c 1400 in an early Welsh dialect.

This district's rural past lives on at the *Gwent Rural Life Museum* at the Malt Barn, New Market Street (Tel:02913–3777 or 2285), a museum which is a great deal better than some of its kind and noteworthy for the detail of the explanations. Housed in a 17 or 18C malt barn and an adjoining Victorian cottage, the material includes wagons, agricultural and craft and trade tools, vintage machinery, and, in the cottage, a kitchen, laundry and dairy.

7m **Caerleon** (7000 inhab.), now to a great extent a dormitory town for Newport and farther afield, is visited for its Roman past, the three principal objectives, all close to one another, being the Amphitheatre, the Baths and the Legionary Museum (parking at Baths for baths and museum).

History. The Roman fortress, dating from c 75, was called Isca from the name of the river Usk, but to the Welsh this became Caerleon, a corruption of Castra Legionis, the Fort of the Legion. The legion was the 2nd Augustan which came here as a permanent garrison after its subjection of the Silures and remained until late in the 4C. The legion's normal strength was 5–6000 men, at first protected by earthworks and timber but soon, by about 100, living behind sound stone walls. Few fortresses such as this continued in isolation, and a civilian settlement beyond the walls soon began to grow into a town, and it is recorded that a Bishop of Caerleon was present in 314 at the Synod of Arles, the first general council of western Christianity. The bishopric seems to have lasted into the 6C when it is said to have been transferred to St. David's by St. David himself, as foretold by Merlin. It was also during this early post-Roman period (though only on the suspect authority of Geoffrey of Monmouth) that Arthur was both crowned and had his capital here, the Roman amphitheatre becoming known as King Arthur's Round Table. Be this as it may, Tennyson came to Caerleon in search of local colour for his 'Idylls of the King'. In 1188 Giraldus passed this way and enthusiastically described the Roman remains.

The Roman fort and town occupied the area immediately SW of today's town, between the town and the Usk, access now being by a road opposite the museum. To the left of this road is the amphitheatre (parking) with, to its left, a length of Roman wall (originally a rectangle of c 540 by 450 yards), virtually all that can be seen of the town. To the right of the approach road, a short way along a path, is the site of the Barracks.

The *Amphitheatre* (WHM. Tel: 0222-465511), dating from 80 to 100 and with seating for the entire legion of 6000, is a hollowed oval area, surrounded by an earth bank and supported by stone walls. There are eight entrances (all originally vaulted so that no seating space was lost), two of these being for performers and six for spectators, those for the performers being the more elaborate ones at the NE and SW, both with traces of a small waiting room and stone benches. At the NW entrance can be seen the drain which ran the length of the amphitheatre.—The *Barracks*. The fort had 64 blocks, originally of wood but of stone from the 2C, these generally arranged in pairs. Of this sytem, the lower course ground plan of four blocks can today be seen.

The *Baths* (WHM. Tel: 0222-465511), by the Museum, were discovered only in 1964. Today, excavated and provided with admirable and imaginative visitor facilities, Caerleon's baths rank as the most complete example of their kind in Britain. Started with the first building of the fort in 75, and in use until about 230, the baths—which may be regarded as forerunners of today's leisure centres, and provided with similar exercise, catering and other facilities,—were eventually a massive stone complex, the three halls (cold, warm, hot) rising to nearly 50ft and the whole on a scale which has been compared to that of a medieval cathedral.

The *Legionary Museum* (Tel: 0633–423134), a branch of the National Museum of Wales, was re-opened in 1987 in a new, modern building, only the classical portico surviving from the museum's original home of 1850. Gone, too, is the dreary Victorian display, succeeded by modern lighting and imaginative presentation which together vividly and instructively bring Roman Isca to life, of perhaps particular note, and a practical help to the imagination in peopling the amphitheatre, barracks and baths, being the lifesize figure of an accoutred legionary. The museum shows also material excavated at Burrium, predecessor of Caerleon and covered now by the town of Usk.—The church adjacent to the museum stands on the site of the legion's headquarters.

It was at the *Hanbury Arms*, a Tudor inn overlooking the river, that Tennyson stayed while in search of colour for his 'Idylls of the King' (1859). Roughly opposite, in private property surrounded by a wall, can be glimpsed an early Norman motte.

2m. **Newport**, see Rte 35.

B. Via Pontypool

A4042. Total distance 16m.—*10m.* **Pontypool**.—*2m.* **Cwmbran**.—*4m.* **Newport**.

The road skirts the E edge of the South Wales mountains and a main industrial area. It also runs just E of the Monmouthshire and Brecon Canal, dating from 1797–1812, closed to commercial traffic in 1932 and now used for recreational purposes (Tel: 0873–831788, British Waterways).

From **Abergavenny** (see Rte 28), A4042 heads S, with Blorenge high on the west.—*10m.* **Pontypool** (39,000 inhab.), today a diversified industrial town, was the home of the Welsh iron industry.

History. The first forge here was in operation as long ago as 1425. The first ironworks followed in 1577, and it is said that the first forge in America (1652) was built by Pontypool emigrants. In 1682 the first rolling mill is thought to have been started here by Thomas Cooke, and in the early 18C Thomas Allgood (died 1716) developed 'Pontypool Japan', a novel and attractive treatment of iron plates by a brilliant and heat-resistant lacquer. In 1829 Pontypool was a Chartist focus, the local leader, William Jones, marching to Newport to help in the assault on the Westgate Hotel; for this he was transported.

One of the town's attractions is Pontypool Park (once the home of the Hanbury family, owners of the local ironworks), the late-Georgian stables of which today house the *Valley Inheritance* (Tel: 04955–52036), where permanent and temporary exhibitions record the social and industrial past of the local Torfaen valley. Canals played a major part in this industrial story, and something of this aspect is well recalled at *Junction Cottage* (Tel: 04955–52036), a canal tollkeeper's cottage of 1814 at the junction of the Monmouthshire and Brecon and Abergavenny canals, roughly within the N angle of A472 and A4042. The exhibition here records the history of the local waterways; there is also a picnic area, and a short walk leads to an aqueduct.

Llandegfedd Reservoir, 2m E of Pontypool, doubles as a water supply for Cardiff and as a recreational area. Picnic sites mark the start of waymarked walks.

2m. **Cwmbran** (44,000 inhab.) is a 'new town' immediately W of A4042. At *Llantarnam*, at the S of the town, a modern abbey stands on the site of a 12C Cistercian predecessor, a gateway of which survives. From near here, B4236 offers an alternative approach to Newport via Caerleon.—*4m.* **Newport**, see Rte 35.

31 Abergavenny to Merthyr Tydfil, Neath and Swansea

A465 to Neath. A474 and A483 to Swansea. Total distance 44m.—
7m. (by A465 Brynmawr.—9m. Merthyr Tydfil.—6m. Hirwaun.—
4m. Glyn Neath.—8m. Aberdulais.—1m. Neath.—9m. Swansea.

Rather bleak, part industrial moorland as far as Glyn Neath is
followed by the part wooded and part industrialised Vale of Neath.

From **Abergavenny** (see Rte 28) there is a choice of roads to
Brynmawr: the direct A465 (7m), or a southerly loop (B4246 and
B4248. 9m) through Blaenavon with its Big Pit mine museum.

DIRECT ROAD TO BRYNMAWR (A465).—*5m Clydach* was the birthplace of Sir Bartle Frere (1815–84), distinguished colonial adminis-
trator and the first High Commissioner of South Africa (1877).
Beyond the village, A465 (known here as the Heads of the Valleys
road, the valleys being Ebbw Fach, Ebbw, Sirhowy and Rhymney, for
all of which see Rte 37), cuts through the *Clydach Gorge*, during the
18 and 19C a focus of great industrial activity, some of the forlorn
relics of which may be spotted from the main and nearby roads. By
contrast the *Cwm Clydach National Nature Reserve*, known primarily, though there is much else, for the beech woodland which has
survived the onslaught during the 18C when charcoal fired the
furnaces and forges, lines the S side of A465 and the Clydach. —*2m.*
Brynmawr (7000 inhab.) developed with the growth of the 19C iron
smelting industry. Although economically a part of the industrial
valleys, geographically the town sprawls over high ground.

VIA BLAENAVON TO BRYNMAWR (B4246 and B4248). Reached in 5m
Blaenavon (8000 inhab.), though associated with heavy industry, is,
surprisingly, set in fine open countryside where, southward, upland
moor meets the pastoral green valley which drops down to Pontypool. This is an area to be visited by anyone with a feel for the
heritage of coal and iron. Ironworks were first established here in
1757—these, a century later, being only one of a string along the N of
the South Wales coalfield—and coalmining started in earnest in c
1782 when it became clear that coal could meet the demands of the
ironworks better than wood, supplies of which were in any case fast
running out. The local ironworks had closed by the 1890s, and Big Pit
coalmine closed in 1980, but both live on as visitor attractions.
Blaenavon Ironworks (Tel: 04955–52036), off the NW edge of
Blaenavon, were built in 1788 and were at their most prosperous in
the 1820s, though it was much later, in 1876, that Gilchrist Thomas
here solved the problem of separating phosphorus from iron. Today,
though forlorn and ruined, the works survive as one of Europe's best
preserved of their kind, and from a viewing platform visitors can
study the remains of blast furnaces, casting houses, a water-balance
lift and even the workers' cottages.—In the town, iron features
interestingly in 18C *St. Peter's Church*, here being an iron font,
memorials to local ironwork pioneers, and, in the churchyard, iron
graveslabs.
Big Pit Mining Museum (Tel: 0495–790311), 1m W of Blaenavon
off B4248, preserves a coalmine which functioned for just a century,
from 1880 to 1980. Today the mine offers both surface interest—an
admirably documented self-guided tour including, for instance, a
geological introduction, winding engine house, blacksmith's yard

Blaenavon Ironworks as they used to be

(a smith is still often at work), pithead baths and suchlike—and an underground tour (not suitable for small children or the disabled). Kitted with helmet and lamp, underground visitors descend 300ft by cage to explore the workings, which include genuine coal faces, workshops, stables and haulage engines. The complex offers also a cafeteria (in the original colliery canteen) and an imaginative gift shop.

On the drive up to the mine, visitors pass the *Big Pit Railway* (Tel: 0873–78518). Originally linking Brynmawr and Pontypool, the line was closed to passengers in 1941 but in part continued to carry coal from Blaenavon to Pontypool until Big Pit was closed in 1980. Today operated by volunteer members of the Pontypool and Blaenavon Railway Company, the line preserves vintage locomotives and rolling stock and provides a moorland ride of up to a mile.

Brynmawr (see above) is reached in 4m from Blaenavon.

Beyond Brynmawr (after some 3m), A465 fringes the northern edge of *Bryn Bach Park*, providing a striking example of how a wasteland resulting from pit and opencast mining can be converted into some 500 acres of grass and plantations. The focus of the park is the Visitor Centre (signed off A465. Tourist Information etc. Tel: 0495–711816), where the story of the ten or so years of reclamation is told, while the adjacent large man-made lake is a focus for the park's many and varied recreational opportunities.

9m (from Brynmawr) **Merthyr Tydfil** (54,000 inhab. *Inf.* 14A Glebeland Street. Tel: 0685–79884), central in the story of Wales's coal, iron and steel (by 1831 Merthyr's population was larger than those of Cardiff, Swansea and Newport combined), and long dependent on these, is today a sprawling mixture of 19C and modern which has largely cleared the scars of a past now replaced by diversified activities which surround the town and tend to be associated with several modern housing estates.

History. The Romans were here first, with a fort on the site of today's Penydarren Park, but the town derives its name from St. Tydfil, a pious daughter of the chieftain Brychan. She was murdered here in the 5C and a settlement grew around her shrine, this settlement developing into a village dependent on Morlais Castle (2m N. See Rte 26B), built in 1275. In the 17C, and by now a sizeable, scattered hill village, Merthyr became a centre for Dissenters, but it was the 18C that brought industry and, with it, explosive change; starting with the opening of John Guest's Dowlais Ironworks in 1759, and followed in smart succession by Crawshay's at Cyfarthfa in 1765, Hill's Plymouth Works in 1767, and Hamfray's Penydarren Works in 1784. The opening in 1795 of the Glamorganshire Canal between Merthyr and Cardiff (substituting water transport for slow and costly packhorses) gave a major boost to the town's prosperity, but soon the many locks between Merthyr and Abercynon proved a deterrent and in 1802 the Penydarren (horse) Tramroad was opened to bypass these (some sections and the tunnels survive). It was along this tramway in 1804 that the earliest steam locomotive, built by Richard Trevithick (1771–1833) was tested. Then, in 1841, Brunel's railway to Cardiff was opened. By now—the largest conurbation in Wales, and with the Dowlais Ironworks, the world's largest, employing 10,000—Merthyr was a commercially prosperous but otherwise grim, smoke-laden complex of ugly iron and coal workings with their associated tips and slagheaps; a place, too, with one of the worst public health records in Britain.

But industrial decline came with the early years of the 20C as the import of cheaper ore from abroad not only killed ironstone mining but also led to the transfer of the steel mills (1928–30) to the coast with its fast-developing ports at which the ore arrived.

Joseph Parry (1841–1903), the composer, was born here; and Merthyr was the home of Lady Charlotte Guest (wife of the owner of the Dowlais Ironworks), translator in 1893 of the 'Mabinogion'. From 1900 the town's Member of Parliament was James Keir Hardie (1856–1915), founder of the Independent Labour Party and the first Labour MP.

The town centre is, for the most part, the area between the railway station and the river, the northern edge being Castle Street. *St. Tydfil's Church*, built in 1809 and said to stand on the site of its patron's murder, is successor to possibly several others including the chapel-shrine around which the early settlement grew; inside the church there are two inscribed stones of the 6–9C. Nearby stands the *Robert and Lucy Thomas Fountain*, a cheerfully ornate cast-iron affair, built, rather curiously, in Glasgow and erected in 1907 in memory of Robert Thomas and his wife who in 1828 pioneered the export of South Wales steam coal, Thomas mining the coal while Lucy, clearly a remarkable woman for her time, developed the markets.

Other sites of interest are outside the immediate town centre. *Joseph Parry's Cottage* (Chapel Row. Tel: 0685–83704), is the 19C ironworks cottage in which the composer was born in 1841. Restored by the Borough Council and leased to Merthyr Tydfil Heritage Trust, the cottage has two exhibition rooms, one devoted to Parry and the other illustrating aspects of Merthyr's past. Outside the cottage, and both restored by British Steel, are a 19C cast-iron bridge (brought here from nearby Rhydycar and erected over an excavated section of the Glamorganshire Canal which once ran here) and a cast iron tram found in the old Dowlais mine workings. Plans for Chapel Row include a craft village, a heritage centre in the (to be rebuilt) ironworkers' chapel of 1788 and the restoration of the cottage to the 1840s' period.

Cyfarthfa Castle (Tel: 0685–723112), in a large hillside park off A470 rather under 1m NW of the station, was built in ostentatious castellated style in 1825, the mansion and its grounds enabling its owner, William Crawshay, to survey the nearby ironworks which carried his family's name and fortunes. Acquired in 1909 by the local authority, Cyfarthfa has long housed Merthyr Tydfil's distinguished museum and art gallery. The former not only tells the town's story, with some emphasis on the social and technical aspects of the industrial past, but also embraces such themes as local archaeology, natural history, geology and even Egyptology; while the art gallery, spanning from the 19C to modern days, includes artists such as Penry Williams (a local watercolour artist patronised by the Crawshay family) as also famous portraitists such as Romney and Lawrence. Additionally there are important collections of silver, china and glass.—*Ynysfach Engine House* (Tel: 0685–721858), across the river a short way W of the town centre, was opened in 1801 (additions in 1836) as an extension of the Crawshay Cyfarthfa ironworks; with two blast furnaces, coke ovens and kilns, it was the first Crawshay furnace to use steam power and soon produced more iron that Cyfarthfa. Closed in 1879, as steel production took over from iron, the site lapsed into ruin until rescued by Merthyr Tydfil Heritage Trust and opened in 1989 as Heritage Centre for the Iron Industry of Merthyr Tydfil and South Wales.

Other Merthyr Tydfil Heritage Trust (Tel: 0685–83704) projects include Pont-ycafnau Bridge of c 1794; the Cyfarthfa furnaces below Cyfarthfa Castle; the mouth of Richard Trevithick's tunnel; the Plymouth Ironworks site; and, as noted above, plans for Chapel Row.
   For *Morlais Castle*, 2m N of the town centre, see Rte 26B.
   For Merthyr Tydfil to *Brecon* (Brecon Beacons. Talybont), see Rte 26.

Railway enthusiasts will make for the *Brecon Mountain Railway*, at Pant Station, Dowlais, 2¹/2m N of Merthyr Tydfil and signed off A465 (Tel: 0685–4854). Running almost entirely on the bed of the Brecon and Merthyr Railway of 1859–1962, this narrow-gauge line drawn by vintage steam locomotives offers a four-mile return ride (50 minutes, with 20 minutes stop at Taf Fechan Reservoir) through the forest and reservoir scenery of the southern part of Brecon Beacons National Park.
   Leaving Merthyr Tydfil, A465 in *6m* reaches **Hirwaun**, a colliery town at the head of the Cynon valley (see Rte 37B). Just beyond, A4061 climbs S in a large loop over Hirwaun Common to descend into the Rhondda valley, see Rte 37A.—*4m.* **Glyn Neath** marks the head of the Vale of Neath.

From Glyn Neath a moorland road (picnic sites and walks) heads N across Fforest Fawr, the section of the Brecon Beacons National Park to the W of the Beacons. The road runs above and to the W of the river Meltte which tumbles in cataracts and falls through a wooded ravine. Car parking, picnic site and start of waterfalls trail at *Porth-yr-Ogof*, 4m from Glyn Neath and 1m short of the upland village of *Ystradfellte*. Beyond Ystradfellte the road ascends the Llia into country known to the Romans, whose Sarn Helen, here a track, comes in from the SW about 2m N of the village. *Maen Madog*, ¹/2m down the track, is a particularly interesting 9ft-high standing stone, presumably erected here around perhaps 2000 BC, and 2500 or more years later, at some date between the 5C and the 9C, given a Latin inscription recording that this is the stone of one Dervacus, son of Justus, who lies here. *Maen Llia*, near the road 2m farther N, is another tall standing stone.

From Glyn Neath, A465 descends the Vale of Neath, a narrow but almost level valley, part afforested, part industrialised and once lovely enough to have been painted by Turner.—*4m.* **Melincourt** (across the valley on B4434) from where a signed path leads to the falls of the same name in a nature reserve owned by Glamorgan Wildlife Trust.—*4m.* **Aberdulais** with four nearby places of interest, the first and nearest being *Aberdulais Falls* (NT. Tel: 0639–636674), a site which, because of the water power readily available, was since the 16C home to a variety of industries; in turn copper works (1584), corn and grist mill (c 1765–1819; painted by Turner), ironworks (c 1819–40) and tin-plate works (c 1840–90), the extant remains being of these last two activities. Today the object of a long-term research, conservation and even ambitious restoration, the site already offers an information centre, industrial archaeology in a fine natural setting, and, of course, the powerful falls.

Two other places will be found within 10m along A4109 (a road leading N off A465 from Aberdulais), the first, reached in 4m, being the *Cefn Coed Colliery Museum* (Tel: 0639–750556), preserving the story of a colliery which once was the world's deepest anthracite mine. Among today's visitor attractions are a massive steam (but now electric) winding engine, with its boiler house and six boilers; a mining gallery; a variety of outdoor exhibits; and an exhibition area with both permanent and temporary displays. *Seven Sisters (Sawmills) Museum* (Tel: 0639–700288), 6m farther N along A4109, a part of a working sawmill, explains the changes in woodworking machinery and techniques which have developed since the 18C. The museum also shows a large collection of mining lamps, and examples of Swansea, Llanelli and Nantgarw pottery and porcelain, while an adventure playground looks after the children.—The fourth attraction close to Aberdulais, 1m N at Cilfrew, is *Penscynor Wildlife Park* (Tel: 0639–642189), with a tropical house, birds of all kinds, deer, marmosets and chimpanzees, an aquarium, and several features for children.

1m. (from Aberdulais) **Neath** (29,000 inhab.), a town with a long industrial background (it was a copper centre, and the first smelter in South Wales was built here in 1584 by copper men from Cornwall), grew around its *Castle* (remains NE of the station) founded by Richard de Granville in c 1130 as successor to a motte-and-bailey which stood on the more vulnerable W bank of the river. Burnt by Llewelyn the Great in 1231, the castle was rebuilt in about 1300 but today survives as little more than the outer face of the gateway with two towers linked by an arch. The basic theme of *Neath Museum*, in Church Place, is all aspects of the local story.

The town is largely on the E bank of its river, but two sites of visitor interest—the 13C abbey and the small remains of Roman Nidum—are on the W side.

The somewhat smoke-begrimed 13C ruins of *Neath Abbey* (WHM. Tel: 0222–465511), beside the W bank of the river just S of the bridge, have the perhaps unique distinction of having in turn served religious, residential and industrial needs.

History. The abbey was founded by Richard de Granville, on land seized from the Welsh, at the same time (c 1130) that he built his castle on the other side of the river. Originally for Sauvigniac monks, the abbey had already become Cistercian by 1147. Quickly achieving prosperity, mainly by trading in wool and hides (in 1291 the inventory is said to have included 5000 sheep), the monks built the present church between 1280 and 1330. Two centuries later, Neath had sunk deep into decline, supporting only eight monks and thus an obvious target for dissolution in 1539. Later in the 16C a part of the abbey was converted into a mansion for Sir John Herbert, a status lost in the 18C when, under the pressure of the accelerating local industrial development, the abbey was used for copper smelting while the Herbert mansion housed the workers.

Beyond the entrance, the Lay Brothers' quarters form the W range of
the site, the chimneys on the E side of these quarters being relics of
the period of industrial use. Moving NE, the site of the main refectory
(with at the N end the washing bays) is crossed to the cloister,
beyond the N side of which is the Church, of which, though, little
remains except the outer walls of the nave and part of the W front. It
once comprised a nave of seven bays and two aisles, with a
presbytery of three bays. The transepts were each of two bays, with
two chapels, and in the S transept can still be seen two altars, a
piscina, and, on the W side, the night-stairs. To the S, beyond the
sacristy, there are traces of the chapter house, beyond this being the
Herbert Mansion standing on the medieval foundations of the
abbot's house. The Dormitory Undercroft, with good medieval vaulting, houses some abbey stones.

The remains of Roman *Nidum*, a fort built in 75–80 on the road
from Caerleon to Carmarthen (Caer Maridunum), were discovered in
1949 during the building of a housing estate. What little there is to be
seen (the lower courses of the E and S gates) can be found by taking
the road signed Pontardawe from the roundabout at the W end of the
river bridge; the remains are then on the right in about ¼m behind
two sets of railings.

9m. **Swansea**, see Rte 38.

32   Hay-on-Wye to Abergavenny

Unclassified through Llanthony to Llanfihangel Crucorney. A465 to
Abergavenny. Total distance 21m.—*11m.* **Llanthony Priory**.—*5m.*
Llanfihangel Crucorney.—*5m.* **Abergavenny**.

From Hay-on-Wye to Llanfihangel Crucorney this Route, running
immediately W of the English border and for much of the way
accompanied by Offa's Dyke, crosses the BLACK MOUNTAINS, a large
district of high moorland just straddling the border but wholly
included within Brecon Beacons National Park and extending southward from Hay-on-Wye to end in the Sugar Loaf above Abergavenny.
On the W—the higher side, with Waun Fach rising to 2660ft—the
mountains are bounded by the Talgarth to Tretower road (Rte 25A),
while to the E the massif, here in England, eases gently down to the
lower ground across which lies the city of Hereford. From the S, from
A465, the mountains are cut by several attractive valleys.

Hay-on-Wye (1500 inhab. *Inf.* Car Park. Tel: 0497–820144), on the
S bank of the Wye, just in Wales, and with both Roman and Norman
roots, is known for two contrasting activities. One is as a market
serving a wide rural community; the huge market area, known as
Smithfield, is home to general, country and sheep markets, this last
mainly for the local Clun and Kerry sheep. The other and more recent
activity is secondhand books, shops for which are scattered around
the town. The Roman association is recalled by the traces of a fort
(½m N across the river), while Hay's Norman roots live on both in its
name ('haie' being Norman French for a hedged or wooded
enclosure) and in its *Castle* (no adm.), originally an early 12C motte-
and-bailey mentioned during the reign of Henry I and standing in the
SW part of today's town but soon, in the reign of King John,
superseded (on today's site) by the stone stronghold of the De Braose
family. This was destroyed in about 1400 by Glendower, but, despite

much rebuilding instigated by Henry IV, little now remains beyond a ruined gatehouse (blown up during the Civil War) and parts of the walls, on to which an Elizabethan or Jacobean manor was grafted. *St. Mary's Church*, restored in 1834, incorporates part of the tower and porch of a church probably contemporary with the original motte-and-bailey.

For Hay-on-Wye to *Brecon* and *Swansea*, see Rte 33.

Leaving Hay-on-Wye the minor road in *2m.* reaches *New Forest*, little more than a fork from which the road to the left, crossing into England, in 2m reaches a farm lane leading NE (^{1}/$_2$m) to the small ruin of *Craswall Priory*, founded by Roger de Lacy in 1222. This Route takes the right fork, soon emerging on to open moor, crossing Offa's Dyke—clearly seen on the E side with Hay Bluff (2219ft) beyond—and, a few yards farther, reaching a stone circle. *Gospel Pass*, between Hay Bluff and Lord Hereford's Knob (2263ft), is next soon reached, the road from here starting its descent of the Honddu and in *5m* reaching *Capel-y-Ffin*, a remote spot which has tended to attract the pious. There are two chapels here, and it was here too in 1870 that the Rev. J.L. Lyne, an Anglican who took the name Father Ignatius, founded a monastery, which, however, did not long survive its founder's death in 1908. Later, in the 1920s, the buildings were for a while used by the sculptor, Eric Gill.

Continuing its descent, for much of the way blind between hedge-topped banks, the road in *4m* reaches **Llanthony Priory**, just before which, on the left beside the road, can be seen the old gatehouse, now forming part of a barn.

History. In 1100, the story goes, the Norman nobleman William de Lacy was hunting in this valley (on land owned by his brother) and sheltered in a ruined chapel dedicated to St. David. So pious was the atmosphere that De Lacy promptly decided to renounce the world and become a contemplative hermit. Three years later he was joined by one Erniseus, a former court chaplain, the two men and their followers then building a church and the community becoming Austin Canons. Soon, however, during the troubled years of Stephen's reign when the Welsh were able to regain much of their land, the De Lacy family lost their estates here and the community had to move first to Hereford and then to Gloucester, returning only in 1175 under the more settled conditions imposed by Henry II and building a new church, the ruins of which are those seen today. But, though initially quite prosperous, the priory constantly suffered the ravages of border warfare and was already in a sorry state (and administratively demoted to being a dependency of Gloucester) when dissolved in 1538.

The usual neglect and decay followed, the two main events of later years being the 18C conversion of the S tower to serve as a shooting lodge, and, in 1807, the purchase of the estate by the poet Walter Savage Landor. But his ambitious plans—embracing a school, 10,000 cedars of Lebanon, and merino sheep—soon put him at loggerheads with his tenants, his neighbours and the local authority, until, bankrupt, he assigned the estate to trustees in 1815.

The best overall view of the ruins—essentially the church, with on the S side some domestic remains—is from the field to the N, this view embracing the long and graceful N arcade of the nave. Of the great church (1175–1220) the W front, with its twin towers, and portions of the nave, transepts, central tower and choir remain, the architecture being a plain and almost severe Transitional combined with some Early English. There was no triforium; doorways rather than arches lead from the aisles to the transepts; and there is generally a sparing use of capitals and correspondingly frequent use of continuous mouldings. The hotel here, originally built as the house of the steward of the 18C hunting lodge, represents the SW tower of the church, various priory domestic buildings (W range) and, in the cellars, something of the remains of the prior's house. The adjacent *Parish Church* dates from the 13C and was probably the priory infirmary and associated chapel.

5m. **Llanfihangel Crucorney**, where A465 is joined and where *Llanfihangel Court* (Tel: 0873–890217) is a Tudor and Stuart manor house remodelled on a medieval predecessor. Among noteworthy features here are the plasterwork ceilings of 1559, oak panelling and a yew staircase.

DIVERSION TO PARTRISHOW CHURCH AND GRWYNE FAWR RESERVOIR. NW, 11m. Minor roads lead first 1m NW to Stanton, then 2m SW through Cwm Coedycerrig, then (at a meeting of five roads) N up the valley of Grwyne Fawr, off which in under a mile is the short lane approach to remote little *Partrishow Church* (or Patricio). The story goes that a holy man named Issui, or Ishow, had a cell near here, probably at the holy well just below the church, the approach to which is marked by a stone cut with a Maltese cross. In the early 11C a chapel was built, tradition says with money left by a pilgrim whom the well had cured of leprosy, and it has been suggested that the chapel (or cell) built on to the W wall of today's church may mark the site of this. Giraldus came here in 1188 and is said to have preached from the cross (in part original) which stands in the churchyard. The church, which was restored in 1908 when in danger of collapse, is of various periods, the earliest parts being the N wall of the chapel and the windows in its W wall, both 13C or earlier. The S wall of the chapel and its roof, and the nave porch, date from the 14C, while the remainder of the church seems to be of the 15C or 16C. Features of note inside the church are the small rood screen and loft (late 15C and probably local work); two very early stone altars in front of the screen, and a third in the chapel; the 15C cradle roof; and a decorated font which may be dated from the inscription round the rim recording in Latin that it was made 'in the time of Genillin', who has been identified as an 11C prince of Powys.

The minor road continues N with Grwyne Fawr to run through Mynydd Du Forest (walks), beyond the forest reaching *Grwyne Fawr Reservoir* in the heart of the Black Mountains.

From Llanfihangel Crucorney, A465 runs below (W) *Sugar Loaf* (1955ft. See Rte 25A) and (E) *Skerrid Fawr* (1596ft. See Rte 28) to reach (*5m*) **Abergavenny,** see Rte 28.

33 Hay-on-Wye to Swansea via Brecon and Sennybridge

B4351 to Clyro. A438 and A470 to Brecon. A40 to Sennybridge. A4067 to Swansea. Total distance 52m.—*1m.* **Clyro.**—*4m.* **Glasbury.**—*1m.* Three Cocks.—*2m.* **Bronllys.**—*8m.* **Brecon.**—*8m.* **Sennybridge.**—*10m.* **Dan-yr-Ogof Caves.**—*3m.* Abercraf.—*8m.* Pontardawe.—*7m.* **Swansea.**

Mixed scenery, including, to Glasbury, the pastoral Wye valley. High, open moorland after Sennybridge; and the largely industrial valley of the Tawe S of Dan-yr-Ogof.

From **Hay-on-Wye**, see Rte 32, this Route for about 5m follows the more interesting N side of the Wye, crossing the river for (*1m*) *Clyro*, once site of a Roman station and with the scanty remains of a motte-and-bailey built by William de Braose. The diarist Francis Kilvert was curate here from 1865–72, living in the 18C house opposite the Baskerville Arms and here writing much of his homely record which describes the village and its surrounding countryside. He is commemorated by a tablet in the church.—*2m. Llowes*, where the church houses a Celtic stone with two faces, the simpler cross dating from the 7C and the wheel from the 11C. Known as the Great Cross of St. Meilig, the stone is thought first to have stood on a nearby height until brought to the churchyard in perhaps the 12C; it was moved into the church in 1956. At *Painscastle*, or Castell Paen, 3m N of Llowes, there is an early Norman motte, first built by Payn FitzJohn (1130) and later, at the close of the 12C and by then rebuilt in stone, in the hands of the notorious William de Braose. The castle is sometimes identified as the 'Garde Doloureuse' of Scott's 'The Betrothed', the siege described in the novel being that by Gwenwynwyn of Powys who (unsuccessfully; the men of Powys were routed) sought to avenge his cousin, a Welsh leader whom De Braose had captured and executed after dragging him to Brecon tied to a horse's tail.

About 1m beyond Llowes a road to the N in $^{1}/_{2}$m reaches *Maesyronen*, a curious Nonconformist chapel of 1696 complete with its contemporary fittings.—*2m.* **Glasbury**, or Clas-ar-Wy, was the site of a Roman station and, in later years, first of a Celtic monastery (the clas on the Wye) and then of a Norman motte-and-bailey. Here the river is crossed for (*1m*) *Three Cocks*, named after a locally well-known coaching inn.—*2m.* **Bronllys**, see Rte 25A which is crossed here.—*2m.* At *Llanfilo*, S of the road, the restored little church has a good 15C rood screen and loft with its original plaster tympanum, box-pews of 1600 and a simple font that may be pre-Norman.—*5m. Llanddew*, just N of A470, preserves some slight remains of a former palace of the bishops of St. David's; the village was also the official home of the archdeacons of Brecon and thus in about 1172 that of Giraldus. The church, of the 12 or 13C, shows the external batter (probably copied from military architecture) typical of many churches in this district, and the transepts, entered by unusually small arches and with very narrow squints, are also of interest.

1m. **Brecon**, see Rte 26A. Rte 25B is crossed here.—For Brecon to (*8m*) **Sennybridge**, see Rte 27.

At Sennybridge this Route turns S on A4067, in $^{3}/_{4}$m reaching *Defynnog* with a church mainly of the 15C but founded as early as c 450. Externally, a curious feature is the 5–6C stone bearing a Latin inscription and traces of decorative work which has been built into the SW angle of the tower, while inside the church the font bears a Runic (ancient Anglo-Saxon) inscription, believed to be the only Runic specimen in Wales. The road now climbs on to upland moor, passing Cray Reservoir and reaching (*7m* from Sennybridge) *Bwlch-y-Rhudd* (1212ft), the pass between, to the NW, Cefn Cul (1844ft) and, to the SE, Fan Gihirych (2381ft). From here the river Tawe is followed all the way down to Swansea.

In a little less than 2m below Bwlch-y-Rhudd, a minor road ascends N up the valley of the Tawe. *Cerrig Duon*, at 1270ft, 2m up the valley and just W of the road and river, is a prehistoric stone oval, a rather rare shape of which there are only some ten examples in Britain. The stones are small, and other curious features are the large standing stone just N of the oval and the rows of small stones starting from near the E side. There is another standing stone 1/2m N on the E of the road.

3m. ***Dan-yr-Ogof Caves** (Tel: 0639–730284) are the main feature of a tourist complex which includes Tourist Information, a small museum , an artificial ski slope, and a Dinosaur Park with a short geological trail. At least two hours should be allowed for a visit to the three show-caves and the Dinosaur Park. Discovered in 1912, explored in the 1930s and opened to the public in the 1960s, the caves comprise Dan-yr-Ogof, the longest show-cave in Britain; Cathedral, with the largest single chamber in any British show-cave; and Bone, perhaps the most interesting of the three, where visitors can learn something about the animals and men who were living here in prehistoric times.—At *Craig-y-Nos*, just S of the caves and in a lovely setting beside the Tawe, the grounds of the mansion have been converted to a country park with over 40 acres of wood, water and open meadow and, in summer, a programme of demonstrations of country skills and pursuits. The mansion, known as Craig-y-Nos Castle, long a geriatric hospital and hopefully to become a music and arts centre, once knew more glittering days. Built in 1842, it was bought in 1878 by the opera singer Adelina Patti as a romantic home for herself and her second husband, the tenor Nicolini. Here, between tours, she arrived by special train, rested in the luxury of a private waiting-room at the station, and then, at Craig-y-Nos, enjoyed her aviary and winter garden (now the Patti Pavilion in Swansea's Victoria Park) and the small theatre (150 seats) which she built in 1891 as a miniature of London's Drury Lane.

Henrhyd Falls (NT), where the Nant Llech plunges over a cliff into the Tawe, are reached by a road leading SE off A4067 (to Coelbren) 1m S of Craig-y-Nos.

Beyond Craig-y-Nos the road starts to enter an industrial area, though there are increasing signs of reclamation.—*11m. Pontardawe*, a colliery centre, *4m* beyond which A4067 crosses the M4 motorway to reach (*3m*) **Swansea**, see Rte 38.

34   Monmouth to Chepstow

A466. Total distance 13m. (Alternative B4293 and B4235. 22m.)—
5m. Bigsweir Bridge.—4m. **Tintern Abbey**.—4m. **Chepstow**.

A466 descends the LOWER WYE VALLEY (for an informative exhibition, visit Tintern Old Station, see below), generally regarded as the stretch between Ross-on-Wye in England and Chepstow, the reach (see 'Blue Guide England') between Ross-on-Wye and Monmouth, a distance of some 15m, being scenically the finest. Over many centuries, from about the 13C until 1900, the valley was industrially important, being the principal iron-producing district in Britain and known for its wire mills. Throughout these centuries, and particularly during the 18 and 19C, the river was a vital waterway (many places building ships), with ships of up to 90 tons ascending to Brockweir (8m below Monmouth), from where goods continued upstream by barge. There was no valley road until the 19C, the road from Monmouth to Chepstow running across the higher ground to the west. The Monmouth to Chepstow railway, opened in 1876, closed in 1959. The forest of the valley was ruthlessly exploited from medieval times until the 1920s when the Forestry Commission took over with the associated aims of improving productivity while at the same time supposedly preserving the scenery and fostering recreational facilities. In 1938 the Wye woodland became a part of the *Dean and Wye Valley Forest Park*. For walkers there is the waymarked Lower Wye Valley Walk (Ross-on-Wye to Chepstow), in part above the valley and in part beside the river, and the Offa's Dyke Path runs with the E bank.

Monmouth (7500 inhab. *Inf.* Church Street. Tel: 0600–3899) is a border town of long history and some character. On the W bank of the Wye immediately N of where it is fed by the Monnow, the town's perhaps best-known feature is its rare 13C fortified bridge gateway.

History. Monmouth was the site of the Roman Blestium. Later, in succession, came Saxon and early Norman forts, the latter built by William FitzOsbern in 1068 and by the 12C succeeded by a stone castle. Typically, a town grew around the castle as also around a Benedictine priory also founded by William FitzOsbern. Among Monmouth's famous sons were (c 1100) the 'historian' Geoffrey of Monmouth, who was perhaps a monk at the priory, and Harry of Monmouth, later Henry V, born in the castle in 1387 and in 1415 the victor of Agincourt, at which battle, according to Shakespeare, Monmouth caps (woollen headgear worn by medieval soldiers) were prominent ('Welshmen did good service ... wearing leeks in their Monmouth caps').

Since Norman times under the jurisdiction of the Lords Marcher, change came in 1535 when Henry VIII created the county of Monmouth, with the town as its capital, a status it has now lost with the formation of the county of Gwent.

Agincourt Square, once the market, is the town centre, with *Shire Hall* (1724) carrying a statue of Henry V placed here in 1792 when the Wye valley was becoming increasingly popular with tourists. It was in this hall that John Frost and other Chartists were tried in 1839, the sentence being death though this was later reduced to transportation. In front of the hall stands a statue (by W. Goscombe John) to the Hon. C.S. Rolls, born at nearby Hendre; one of the founders of Rolls Royce, he was killed in a flying accident in 1910. In the bar of the *King's Head* there is a fine plaster likeness of Charles I, dating from the Restoration. Of the *Castle*, approached by Castle Hill roughly opposite Shire Hall, little survives—it was slighted in 1646—beyond the early 12C keep, or Great Tower. The adjacent *Great Castle House*, now Ministery of Defence property, was built in 1673 (largely with stone from the castle) by the 3rd Marquess of Worcester because, it is said, he wanted the birthplace of his grandson to be as close as possible to that of Henry V.

Priory Street, leading N out of Agincourt Square and constructed in 1837, represents the only significant addition to the town's generally still medieval street plan. Here the Market Hall, a 1969 rebuilding of a Victorian predecessor burnt down in 1963, houses the *Monmouth Museum* (Tel: 0600–3519) with the Local History Centre and the Nelson Collection, this latter consisting largely of material collected by the mother of C.S. Rolls, an admirer of the admiral. Included in the collection are portraits of Nelson and Lady Hamilton, letters and a model of the Battle of Trafalgar. *St. Mary's Church*, a short way NE of the Market Hall and on the site of the church of William FitzOsbern's priory, is mainly a rebuilding of 1881 by G.E. Street, though the tower and spire are older; inside the church there is a cresset stone, probably from an earlier church of c 1102 and thus roughly contemporary with the early priory. In the nearby *Roman Catholic Church* there are relics of John Kemble, a priest executed in Hereford in 1679.

From Agincourt Square Monnow Street leads S to *Monnow Bridge Gateway*, a simple and robust late Norman structure of 1262 and a rare example in Britain (and rare also in Europe) of a fortified gateway on a bridge. Just across the bridge the *Church of St. Thomas*, though much restored, retains its Norman choir arch and a N door (both c 1180) though the porch is mock-Norman of the 19C. To the SW of Monnow Bridge, and with a small medieval bridge, is the *Clawdd Du*, an early earthwork thrown up to defend this outlying part of the town.

For Monmouth to *Abergavenny*, see Rte 29.

This Route now follows A466 down the Wye valley, passing famous Tintern Abbey. However an alternative, perhaps to be chosen by those with an interest in prehistory and some early churches, is offered by B4293, the main road to Chepstow prior to the opening of the valley road in about 1820. This alternative (with several roads linking across to A466) is described immediately below.

TO CHEPSTOW BY B4293 AND B4235. 22m—5m. **Trellech** where the early 14C church is successor to one founded in the 7C or 8C, to which period the base of the preaching cross in the churchyard and the Saxon font may belong. Trellech means Three Stones and these large prehistoric ritual monoliths, inexplicably called the *Harold Stones*, will be found some 250 yards S of the church. Trellech offers two further curiosities, one (SW of the church) being a mound called the *Tump*, probably the surviving trace of a Norman motte-and-bailey, while the other, the *Virtuous Well* (SE, on the road to Tintern), with some medieval stonework and long a place of pilgrimage, probably owes its reputed healing qualities to the iron content of the local water.

Rather less than *4m* farther S, a road bearing generally W in *2m* reaches the *Wolvesnewton Model Farm Folk Museum and Craft Centre* (Tel: 02915–231), set in remote, rolling pastoral scenery. Housed in unique cruciform 18C farm buildings designed by the Duke of Beaufort, the museum comprises the Folklore Collection, the Wagon Shed and the Courtyard with Craft shops. The Folklore Collection—better than many such and of eclectic scope—includes toys; a possibly unique display of 'naughty' seaside postcards; some daunting Victorian pin-ups; a Victorian cottage bedroom; vintage cameras; and some fearsome vintage medical and surgical instruments.

At *Llangwm Uchaf (Pentre)*, 2m W of Wolvesnewton, the church of St. Jerome, at the road's end, is known for its 15C locally carved rood screen and loft, still with tympanum, as also for its three 'green men' at the base of the choir arch, two on the N and one on the S; with oak leaves in their mouths, they cautiously link pagan with Christian tradition.—The road from Llangwm to Chepstow (B4235) in *3m* reaches a junction of six roads, immediately N of which, behind a hedge, is *Caer Llwyd Burial Chamber*, now, however, little more than collapsed stones. For *Wentwood Forest*, SW of here, see Rte 35.—*6m*. **Chepstow**, see below.

TO CHEPSTOW BY A466. 13m.—From Monmouth A466 is followed down the E (English) bank of the Wye to pass in *2m Redbrook*, during the 17C and 18C a copper smelting centre and, from 1771 to 1961, the site of tinplate works.—*3m*. *Bigsweir Bridge*, where the road crosses to the Welsh bank.—*3m*. *Brocksweir Bridge*, during the industrial 18 and 19C the point at which cargoes were transferred from ships to barges. Just beyond, *Tintern Old Station* (Tel: 02918–566), a delightful pastoral and wooded corner, is today a modest visitor complex with tourist information; an exhibition in a railway coach, telling the story both of the Wye Valley Railway as also of the industrial past of the valley; a picnic area; and changing exhibitions in the original station building.

Tintern Abbey from the south-east

1m. ****Tintern Abbey**, beside the Wye below wooded hills, is the loveliest, most impressive and most complete of the abbeys of Wales (WHM. Tel: 0222-465511).

History. The Cistercian abbey was founded here in 1131 by Walter de Clare, the monks coming directly from Normandy, but of this early foundation little remains, today's ruins dating mainly from rebuilding of the 13 to 15C. During this period the 13C saw rebuilding of the refectory and church, the 14C that of the abbot's quarters, while in the 15C it was the turn of the infirmary. Concerned mainly with agriculture, Tintern was at its most prosperous during the 14C, the wealthiest abbey in Wales and a focus of wide power and influence. With the Dissolution, though, came despoiling and neglect—for instance the roofing lead was stripped off, melted and then used at Raglan and Chepstow castles—a process which continued until the then ivy-clad ruins beside the river caught the imagination of the romantically minded travellers of the 18C and 19C.

The principal survival is the great church, but much of the domestic complex can also be seen, though largely only as lower courses or foundations.

Chapel

Infirmary

Abbot's
Lodging

Great

Kitchens

Drain

Abbot's Hall

Infirmary

Cloister

Entrance and
Exhibition

Reredorter

Novices'

Lodging

Day Stairs

Great Drain

Warming
House

Monks'   Refectory

Tintern Abbey

Kitchen

Lay Brothers' Refectory

0   10   20   30 m
0   50   100 ft.

East
Window

Chapter
House

Library

Vestry

North Transept

South Transept

Cloister

Nave

The car park and entrance are on the N of the ruins, immediately beyond the entrance being an introductory exhibition. From here the approach to the church passes on the right the *Reredorter*, with its drain, adjacent (just W) being the *Novices' Lodging*. If this is left by its S door, a right turn passes the Day Stairs and arrives at the N walk of the main cloister. Along this walk are, in turn, the *Warming House*, the *Monks' Refectory*, the *Kitchen* (note the serving hatch) and the *Lay Brothers' Refectory*, this last larger than that of the monks since, with the Cistercian emphasis on agriculture, the lay brothers normally outnumbered the monks.

From the NE corner of the cloister (by the Warming House), the approach to the church is along the E walk, passing on the left the *Parlour*, the *Chapter House*, and then the *Library* and *Vestry*, now, because of the disappearance of the wall between them, a single room. Here the *Church* is entered by the Processional Doorway beside the N transept, the Nave, beyond, being mainly of the late 13C and retaining its clerestory on the S side. Both the W and E ends are magnificent, the former, particularly the fine tracery of the great window of seven lights and the moulded arch enclosing the two trefoil-headed opening of the doorway, best appreciated from the outside. The four large and beautiful arches of the crossing formerly supported a tower, and beyond is the huge and beautifully proportioned *East Window covering almost the whole of the wall.

Returning through the Processional Doorway and along the E walk of the main cloister, a walk along the N side of the Parlour reaches the *Infirmary Cloister*, across which (E) is the *Infirmary*, with, to its N and W, its kitchens. To the N of the kitchens are the *Abbot's Quarters*, with his lodging and adjacent chapel on the E, and his hall to the west.

The abbey made much use of the river as a waterway, and the adjacent Anchor Hotel is on the site of the *Watergate*; a 13C arch leading to a slipway can be seen. Just W of the church, the *Guest House* and other buildings have been partially excavated.

2m. Wyndcliff (800ft) is a well-known lower Wye valley view point, reached either by steps from a car park on the main road or by a path from another car park a short way up the road signed Wyndcliff. *Chepstow Racecourse*, just beyond, the largest and best known in Wales, was first developed in 1926.

2m. **Chepstow** (9000 inhab. *Inf.* The Gatehouse, High Street. Tel: 02912–3772), an ancient walled border town on the W bank of the Wye 2m above where it flows into the Severn, is most visited for its Norman castle, forbiddingly sited high above the river.

History. The town's name, meaning simply Market Town, is Saxon; but to the Romans this was Castell Gwent (in Welsh today, Cas-Gwent) and to the Normans Striguil. From Norman times until the Civil War the town's story was largely that of its castle, under the protection of which, and of a priory of about the same period (1072), it developed not only as a market but also as a port and shipbuilding centre, an activity which was at its most prosperous during the late 18C and early 19C.

*Chepstow Castle (WHM. Tel: 0222-465511), comprising three wards, a keep and a barbican, sprawls strikingly along a precipitous platform of rock washed by a broad reach of the Wye.

History. Within a decade of the Norman Conquest, William FitzOsbern, later Earl of Hereford, thrusting into southern Wales, built a stone keep here, thus leap-frogging the usual timber and earthwork motte-and-bailey stage and making Chepstow the earliest stone Norman castle in Wales, and perhaps also in Britain. As the result of a rebellion FitzOsbern's son soon lost both castle and title, and in 1115 the Marcher lordship of Chepstow was granted to the De Clare family, in 1189 passing to William Marshal (also a De Clare) who, with his five sons, each succeeding in turn, progressively increased their castle's strength. In the 13C Chepstow was held by the Bigods, earls of Norfolk, and in the 15C it passed to William Herbert, Earl of Pembroke, remaining in this family until the present century. During the Civil War, and then owned by that staunch Royalist the Earl of Worcester, Chepstow was twice besieged, falling in 1645 but only after the starving garrison and their gallant commander, Sir Nicholas Kemeys, had fought to the death (memorial plaque in the Lower Ward).

Prisoners in Chepstow included Henry Marten, the regicide, who occupied what is now known as Marten's Tower from 1660 until his death in 1680, and Jeremy Taylor who was here for six months in 1655.

The entrance is through a Gatehouse (1225–45) flanked by towers, beyond being the Lower Ward (mainly 13C), a part of the castle which, overhanging the cliff, offers dizzying glimpses down to the river as also a view upwards to the Great Tower. Marten's Tower is at the NE (see History), recalling an imprisonment which was perhaps not too arduous since Henry Marten managed to survive until the age of 78, during this time publishing his 'Familiar Letters to his Lady of Delight', the lady being his mistress. To the N are the remains of domestic quarters, including a hall and kitchens and, below the former, cellars. The defences dividing the Lower and Middle wards were built by William Marshal (c 1190). The Middle Ward is crossed to the Great Tower, the cellars and lower two storeys of which are survivals of FitzOsbern's original castle of 1067–72, the E door and the S and W wall arcades being the oldest features. Beyond are an Upper Ward and Barbican.

The *Chepstow Museum* (Tel: 0291–625981), across Bridge Street from the castle car park, provides many insights into the local history not only of Chepstow but also of the Wye valley and its once flourishing river trades. At *Stuart Crystal*, in Bridge Street, visitors are offered a factory tour which includes also a museum illustrating half a century of this craft (Tel: 02912–70135).

The 13C *Port Wall*, which enclosed the medieval town (then primarily a port) on the S and W (the N and E were protected by the loop of the Wye), can be traced along much of its course. The W gate, however, though probably more or less reflecting the original 13C design, was rebuilt by the Earl of Worcester in 1524.

As was frequently the Norman practice William FitzOsbern built a priory, in his case Benedictine, as religious complement to his great secular stone keep, and the church of this priory lives on as *St. Mary's Church*, much rebuilt and restored but still with a partly Norman nave. This, though, is of later date than the original church (c 1072), traces of which are thought to survive as pillars and an arch by the W wall of the chapel (all that is left of the original nave aisles demolished in 1841) off the SE end of the nave; in this chapel there is also a font of about the same early period. But St. Mary's is visited largely for two spectacular coloured *Memorial Tombs, restored in what is believed to be the original colouring. One of these, in the S transept, is that of Margaret Cleyton (died 1620) and includes effigies of her two husbands and twelve children; the 'dame' hats worn by two of the girls indicate that at least two of the ten daughters were married off. The other memorial tomb, at the NW of the nave, is that of the 2nd Earl of Worcester (died 1549), shown here with his second wife. The grave of Henry Marten (see Chepstow Castle) is at the church's W entrance; but it is not visible although a wall notice tells about its occupant. Also of interest, in the N transept, is a picture recalling the winning of the Victoria Cross (at Gallipoli in 1915) by Able Seaman

Williams of Chepstow, also remembered by a gun-memorial in the town's Beaufort Square.

For the S coast roads to *Newport, Cardiff, Swansea* and *Carmarthen*, see Rte 35.

35 Severn Bridge to Carmarthen

A48 to Cardiff. A4160 and A4055 to Barry. A4226 and B4265 to St.
Bride's Major. B4524 to Bridgend. A473, then A48 to Penllergaer.
A484 to Carmarthen. Total distance 105m.—*5m.* **Caerwent**.—*9m.*
Newport.—*11m.* **Cardiff**.—*3m.* **Penarth**.—*4m.* **Barry**.—*10m.*
Llantwit Major.—*6m. St. Bride's Major*.—*8m.* **Bridgend**.—*13m.* **Port
Talbot** (for **Cwm Afan**).—*3m.* **Briton Ferry** (for **Swansea**).—*8m.*
Penllergaer.—*6m.* **Llanelli**.—*9m.* **Kidwelly**.—*10m.* **Carmarthen**.

For most of its length this Route runs through industrial South
Wales. Nevertheless industry tends to occur only in pockets, and
there are many stretches which are clear of it, while diversions
either side of the road quickly lead either to an incidental coast or
to scenic valleys slicing up towards often remote moorland.

Wales is entered on the W side of the Severn Bridge. This Route then
leaves the motorway (Exit 22) and continues along A48, reached
either on the outskirts of **Chepstow** (just N. See Rte 34) or by minor
roads to the S through *Mathern* where the church is dedicated to St.
Tewdric, a local chief of the 6C who chose to become a hermit; what
may have been his coffin was reburied in the chancel in 1610.

A left fork off A48, some 3m SW of Chepstow, leads to *Caldicot Castle* (country
park, museum, medieval banquets), built over the 12C to 14C and restored in
the 19C but still with its 14C round keep and the gatehouse. The Country Park
is used for special events, such as jousting, while the Museum, mainly
illustrating local history, also shows costume and includes a section (a tower of
the castle) set aside for exhibitions by local artists and craftsmen. (Tel: 0291–
420241. The Male Voice Choir, Tel: 0291–422894).—*Sudbrook Camp*, on the
shore 1m S of the castle, dates from the early 1C and includes the ruin of a
Norman chapel.

5m (from Chepstow) ***Caerwent** is the site of an extensive Romano-
Welsh town, a place of unusual interest for being essentially civilian
and largely native as compared to most other contemporary Roman
remains which are military.

History. The capital of the native Silures was the hillfort of *Llanmelin*, 1m north.
On occupying new territory it was the Roman custom to transfer the inhabitants
of capital hillforts to new towns, built of course to the Roman pattern, and this
happened to the Silures in c 75. Their new town of Caerwent, or Venta Silurum,
was easily controlled by the Romans whose main London to Caerleon road
(considerably wider than the present road) ran through its centre. The town
would have been at its most prosperous during the 2C, at which time, or a little
later, the original earthwork boundary was strengthened by a stone wall.
Insecurity came with the 4C and in c 340 the town's defences were improved by
the addition of bastions. With the departure of the Romans in c 400 Caerwent,
though partially reoccupied from time to time, began to fall into ruin. Later, the
Normans appeared, building their motte-and-bailey castle in c 1070. Finds from
Caerwent are in Newport Museum and the National Museum of Wales in
Cardiff. Much, however, remains unexcavated below today's village.

Straddling the Roman road, Caerwent is a rectangle covering some
44 acres, divided by streets into 20 regular blocks. The village
Church (13C, but probably successor to an earlier one), roughly

halfway along the E–W (Roman) road, makes a good startingpoint, if only because in the porch there are two exceptionally interesting inscribed stones. One—recording the erection of a statue by the tribal senate of the Silures to Paulinus, successively commander of the 2nd Legion and governor of the Gaul provinces of Narbonensis and Lugdunensis—provides evidence of tribal autonomy combined with some loyalty to Rome, while the other, dedicated to Ocelus Mars, indicates how native and Roman gods become merged into one. Across the road from the church the village war memorial stands on a Roman platform, while a few yards W from here Pound Lane leads N to the remains of a combined shop and house and, just beyond, another house.

Farther W along the Roman road the *West Gate* is reached, a stone stile here giving access to the town walls which can be followed round to the E gate, the most interesting section being the *South Wall* with the remains of the bastions (the addition of c 340) attached to the outer face. From the *South Gate*, contemporary with the 2–3C wall, there is a choice between continuing round the wall, passing at the SE corner the Norman motte; or a lane may be followed due N to its junction with the E–W road, opposite being the excavated *Temple*. The *North Gate* can also be visited.

3m. **Penhow Castle** (Tel: 0633–400800) is a neat fortified manor dating from the 12–16C and first held by the St. Maur family, a name which soon corrupted to Seymour. Later the manor several times changed hands until bought in 1973 and given the major restoration which has made possible today's claim that Penhow is the oldest lived-in castle in Wales. The *Church*, adjacent to the castle, reconstructed in 1914 on its 13C plan, was within the castle's outer ward and thus contributed to defence; note the arrow slits in the tower.

Wentwood Forest, 1¹/₂m N of Penhow, originally belonged to the princes of Gwent, then, after the arrival of the Normans, to the Marcher lordship of Striguil (Chepstow), but at the end of the 15C passed to the 1st Earl of Worcester. By this time tenants' rights had become clearly defined, the law being applied twice yearly at a court held at *Foresters Oaks*, now a road junction just N of Wentwood reservoir. During the 17 and 18C the demand for timber for shipbuilding and for oak bark for tanning led to the enclosure of much of the forest and exploitation continued until well into the present century. Today the forest comprises some 3000 acres, over half of which is managed by the Forestry Commission (several picnic sites, linked by waymarked walks).

The hillfort of *Llanmelin*, ancient capital of the Silures (see Caerwent, above), is 1m SE of Llanvair Discoed, 1m SE of Wentworth reservoir.

A48 crosses M4 and runs through the E suburbs of (*6m*) **Newport** (116,000 inhab. *Inf.* John Frost Square. Tel: 0633–842962). In these suburbs the road splits, the lefthand fork crossing the tidal Usk by George Street Bridge while the righthand fork soon reaches Newport Bridge, just across which are the castle and the city centre. Essentially a busy industrial and commercial centre and port which developed during the 18 and 19C, the town nevertheless has much older roots, evidenced today by its Norman castle and cathedral.

History. Robert FitzHamon built an early Norman motte-and-bailey here, the site of which, near his church on Stow Hill, disappeared when the railway tunnel was dug in the 1840s. This motte-and-bailey was in any event short-lived, in 1191 giving way to a stone castle built that year beside the river, and it was not long before a town and trading centre had developed called Novus Burgus or Castell Newydd (today, in Welsh, Cas Newydd) in distinction to the 'old port' at Caerleon. During the 13C the town was seized by Simon de Montfort, and in 1402 it was sacked by Owen Glendower. Major change came with the industrialisation of South Wales from 1750 onwards, this particularly affecting the docks, hitherto little more than riverside wharfs, and with the opening of the valleys' canals in the 1790s Newport became the principal coal port of the south. But industrialisation also brought unrest, and in 1839 the town was the scene of Chartist riots when John Frost, a distinguished citizen and former mayor, led a large demonstration into the town, only to run into armed soldiery around the Westgate Hotel. The demonstrators broke and fled, leaving many dead, and Frost, at first sentenced to hang, was later transported.

In 1921 Newport was declared an episcopal see (Diocese of Monmouth). **Male Voice Choir**. Tel: 0633–279596.

The stone *Castle* of 1191, at the busy road intersection W of Newport Bridge, was rebuilt in the 14C, burnt by Owen Glendower, much modified in the 15C, slighted after the Civil War, and what survived was in part restored in 1930. What remains is the E side of a former ward rising direct from the tidal mud banks of the Usk, the ruins consisting chiefly of a square central tower (at the top the chapel, and at the bottom the watergate) between two octagonal towers with rectangular bases. Curving away from the bridge, High Street and Commercial Street are two main shopping streets with, near the junction of the two with Bridge Street, the *Westgate Inn*, successor to the hotel which was the scene of the bloody Chartist defeat and with original pillars still showing bullet marks. The bright and well arranged *Museum and Art Gallery* (Tel: 0633–840064), in John Frost Square, a pedestrian area off Commercial Street, has four main themes. The Archaeology displays include a wealth of important discoveries from Caerwent. Local History spans Norman to modern times, some emphasis being given to the industrial development of the 19 and 20C (the port, mining, iron and associated social aspects including the Chartist riots). Natural History covers the flora and fauna of Gwent, while the permanent displays in the Art Gallery include a distinguished collection of 18 and 19C English water-colours; local prints and drawings; a growing selection of Welsh paintings; examples of Welsh Japan ware; and sculpture by such as Rodin, Epstein and Goscombe John.

The *Civic Centre*, a handsome group of buildings 1/2m NW of John Frost Square beyond the railway, is known for its murals (Hans Feibusch, 1961–64), telling the story of Monmouthshire.

St. Woolos Cathedral, until 1921 the parish church, is at the top of Stow Hill, 3/4m SW of John Frost Square.

History. The name is a corruption of Gwynllwy, a local 5C lord who was suddenly converted to Christianity (when his dream that he would find a white ox bearing a black spot came true on this hill) and here built a church. Robert FitzHamon's Norman church followed in about 1171, lasting until the 15C when, after the ravages of Owen Glendower, the N and S aisles were rebuilt and the tower was added. With the creation of the Diocese of Monmouth, the church became a pro-cathedral in 1921 and a full cathedral in 1949. The E end was extended in the 1960s.

On the W exterior is a headless statue, said to be of Jasper Tudor (died 1495), uncle and guardian of the future Henry VII and reputedly builder of part of the tower. The Lady Chapel, immediately E of the tower, is thought to occupy the site of Gwynllwy's first church and is the oldest part of the present one, its E wall being 12C and the others 13C though, it has been suggested, perhaps embodying some pre-Norman material. The Nave (12C, with the 15C aisles rebuilt after the destruction by Owen Glendower) is entered through a particularly fine *Norman arch, the columns of which are thought to be of Roman origin from Caerleon. The nave itself is also typically Norman, with a clerestory of narrow round-headed windows.

Newport's perhaps most conspicuous feature is the curious *Transporter Bridge*, reached by Commercial Street and its extension, Commercial Road. Built in 1906, there are only three others similar, one being at Middlesbrough and the other two in France. A movable platform carries loads up to a total of 120 tons, but, though once very busy, the bridge (no longer open for cars) has now been replaced by the George Street Bridge.—The *Docks* are to the S of the Transporter Bridge.

For Newport to *Caerleon, Usk, Pontypool* and *Abergavenny*, see Rte 30; to the *Ebbw* and *Sirhowy* valleys, see Rte 37E.

The town is left by A48, off which, in 2m, is *Tredegar House and Country Park*, the home of the Morgan family from 1402 until 1951, a school for the next 23 years, and in 1974 acquired by the local authority for restoration and development as a recreation area. The House (Tel: 0633–815880) preserves one stone medieval wing but is otherwise essentially brickwork of the 17C with some 19C additions, mainly service corridors and a servants' wing. The Country Park (90 acres) is open all year from 06.15 to one hour after sunset, but some of the associated attractions (e.g. Craft Workshops, Brewhouse, Donkey rides, Fishing, Boating) have individual seasonal opening times.

A48 now skirts the marshes of the *Wentloog Level*, a fen district bordering the Bristol Channel.—5m. *St. Mellons*, where there is a road fork, the lefthand prong providing the more direct approach to the centre of (*4m*) **Cardiff** (see Rte 36).

In addition to the M4 motorway, there is a choice of three routes between Cardiff and Bridgend. This Route proper takes the more interesting though rather longer sequence of southerly roads through Barry and Llantwit Major. The other two routes—A48 through Cowbridge and a northerly loop via Llantrisant—are described first, immediately below.

CARDIFF TO BRIDGEND VIA COWBRIDGE (A48. 20m.). With the castle on the right, Cardiff is left by Cowbridge Road which in 7m reaches *St. Nicholas*, 1/2m S of which is *Tinkinswood Long Cairn*. Excavated in 1914, this large and quite well preserved burial chamber has, from the grave goods discovered (flint tools, pottery and the bones of some 50 people), been dated to about the middle of the third millennium BC. The weight of the capstone has been estimated as some 50 tons. *Dyffryn House Gardens* (Tel: 0222-593328), just beyond, are spread around some 55 acres and include vast lawns, a rose garden, a pool garden, several formal areas, an arboretum and a children's play area. About 1m farther, beyond the gardens, a left turn almost immediately reaches *St. Lythan Long Cairn*, smaller and not in such good condition as Tinkinswood.

Cowbridge (1500 inhab.), 6m beyond St. Nicholas, is a small town of some character and of Norman origin. A turning (Church Street) S off the long main street leads to the town's 14C walls and gatehouse, with, adjacent, a school founded in 1609 but now housed in 19C buildings. A short way beyond the walls, a right turn at a T junction soon reaches the small ruin of *St. Quentin's Castle* with a 14C gateway; started by Gilbert de Clare, the castle remained unfinished after its owner's death fighting the Scots at Bannockburn in 1314. At *St. Hilary*, 1 1/2m SE of Cowbridge, memorials in the Norman church remember the Basset family, owners of ruined nearby Beaupré Castle, reached by footpath.—A straight stretch of Roman road reaches **Bridgend** (see below) in 7m.

CARDIFF TO BRIDGEND VIA LLANTRISANT (A4119 and A473. 19m). Cardiff is left by Cathedral Road and Llandaff, **Llantrisant** being reached in 10m. Picturesquely sited in a saddle between two steep hills, the town takes its name (Three Saints) from Illtyd, Gwyno and Dyfod, to whom its church (in origin Norman, but rebuilt in the 16 and 19C) is dedicated. Only a fragment of a round tower survives of Richard de Clare's 13C castle, to which, in 1326, Edward II and Hugh Despenser were probably brought after falling into Queen Isabella's hands. The *Royal Mint*, transferred in 1967 from Tower Hill, London, is on a Trading Estate to the NW below the town.—The 13C church at *Coychurch*, 7m W of Llantrisant, has several architectural peculiarities, these including a blank bay before the crossing; lobed quatrefoil windows in diamond frames at the W of each aisle; a cinquefoiled clerestory (S only) in the nave; and unusual buttresses to the choir and N transept. The tower collapsed in 1877 destroying the S transept (rebuilt; both transepts are the only parts of the church not original 13C) and shattering one of the two Celtic crosses of interlaced pattern which then stood in the churchyard. Fragments of the damaged cross, bearing the name Ebisar, and the undamaged cross are now inside the church.—**Bridgend** (see below) is reached in 2m.

Main Route 35 leaves Cardiff by Penarth Road (A4160), in *3m* reaching **Penarth** (23,000 inhab. *Inf.* The Pier. Tel: 0222–708212) sprawling over Penarth Head which at present looks across estuary flats towards Cardiff's docks, a scene which will however change with the progress of the Cardiff Bay Development Project (the approach to Penarth will change, and Penarth Head may receive a coastal harbour village). Leisurely and rather Victorian and Edwardian in character, Penarth is both a respectable suburb of Cardiff and a summer resort, among the attractions being the Esplanade, the 19C pier with its Marina Pavilion, the Italian Gardens and Alexandra Park. *Turner House Art Gallery* (Tel: 0222–708870), in Plymouth Road about ¼m W of the pier, was built in 1888 by James Pyke Thompson as a gallery in which to show selections from his personal collection. Now a branch of the National Museum of Wales, the gallery is used largely for changing exhibitions from the museum's collections. Penarth's Dock, opened in 1865 but now abandoned, is gradually being filled in. *Lavernock Point*, 2¹/₂m S, was the scene in 1897 of Marconi's early experiments in transmitting radio waves across water and of the historic reception of the words 'Are you ready?', transmitted from the island of *Flat Holm*, 3m to the southeast. Over the centuries this island has been a Viking anchorage (in 917; hence the Norse name), a lighthouse, a quarantine hospital and, during the Napoleonic wars, a Bristol Channel defence.

4m. **Barry** (44,500 inhab. *Inf.* The Promenade. Tel: 0446–747171. *Male Voice Choir*, Tel: 0446–737232). The town is named after the 7C St. Baruch said to have been buried here, and owes its modern development (between 1881 and the 1920s the population leapt from about 100 to some 40,000) to its *Docks*, founded between 1884–99 by David Davies, a coal exporter who resented paying the port dues levied by Cardiff. Today, though, the export of coal has dwindled, and, commercially, Barry is perhaps most associated with the import of bananas. To most visitors, though, Barry is a holiday objective, the emphasis being on *Barry Island*, the stubby peninsula projecting between the docks to the N and the shore to the S and largely given over to a large Pleasure Park (Tel: 0446–741250) and a holiday camp. The latter spills southward to Nell's Point, until the 19C known for a holy well much visited for the cure of eye diseases. *The Knap*, to the W, is a quieter and less brash resort area, with a pebble beach, gardens, boating lake, the foundations of a large 1 or 2C Roman building, and parkland. In the N of the area, beside Old Village Road, *Barry Castle*, dating from the 12–13C and the seat of the De Barri family, is known to have already been a ruin by the 16C; all that can be seen today is the ruined S gate and some wall of a fortified manor, restored in 1964. Immediately W of the castle a road descends through *Porthkerry Country Park*, a green and wooded valley running down to the sea (nature trails), while off A4226, some 2m N of Barry Island, there is the *Welsh Hawking Centre* (Tel: 0446–734687), a pleasant and informal place showing over 200 birds of prey (eagles, owls, hawks, falcons, buzzards) from many parts of the world. Breeding, and the care (and, where possible, release) of injured birds are among the centre's activities, and, weather allowing, birds are flown free during the afternoon.

3m. **Rhoose Airport** (Cardiff Airport), with, adjacent, the *Wales Aircraft Museum* (Tel: 0446–710135) showing some 30 different types. Here A4226 becomes A4265. However, a short northward circuit of the airport may be made along minor roads through *Penmarc* where the ruined castle behind the church originally belonged to the Norman Umfravilles; in 1664 it was acquired by that remarkable survivor, the former Parliamentarian Philip Jones.— Although there is nothing now to be seen at *Llancarfan*, 1m farther N, the place is of interest for having been the site of an abbey founded in the 6C by St. Cadoc, a local nobleman who here miraculously survived an attack by a huge bear; the name, though, means Holy Enclosure of the Stags, a reference to another wildlife incident when two stags suddenly appeared and took over some work which had been refused by some lazy monks. Before its destruction by Vikings in 987, the abbey school here is said to have rivalled the one at Llantwit Major, among its famous pupils being the Breton bishop, St. Malo.—From Penmarc, the minor road SW passes *Fonmon Castle* (no adm.), a small late Norman keep with a 17C mansion grafted on its N side; like Penmarc, it was acquired in 1664 by Philip Jones. B4265 can be joined 1m south west.

7m (from Rhoose) **Llantwit Major** (Llanilltyd Fawr. 8500 inhab.), a place of historic importance in the early story of Christianity in Wales and today a town of some character in which the past is represented by a very picturesque 15C town hall (a rebuilding of a predecessor destroyed by Owen Glendower), outside which John Wesley once preached, and, nearby, an exceptionally interesting double church, the **Church of St. Illtyd.*

It was here in c 500 that St. Illtyd, a teacher and craftsman (he invented an improved plough) from Brittany, founded his monastery and school of divinity. An early 7C 'Life of St. Samson' of Dol in Brittany records that Samson was brought by his parents to the school of Illtyd 'the most learned of all the Britons in knowledge of the Scriptures'. Other pupils included Gildas, the historian; St. Paul Aurelian; the bard and seer Taliesin, and even perhaps St. David. The pupils were divided into 24 groups, each responsible for an hour of worship, a system ('laus perennis' or 'continual praise') traditionally also associated with Glastonbury and Old Sarum. The school did not survive the Normans, but the monastery continued until the Dissolution, though only as a cell to Tewkesbury Abbey.

The interesting and curious church is in two parts, and it seems that the Old (or West) Church, in origin c 1100 and probably occupying the site of St. Illtyd's early church, was the parish church, while the New (or East) Church of the late 13C was the monastery church. Of the original Old Church there remain only the lower courses of the crossing (below the tower of c 1200) and the arched S doorway. The transepts disappeared about the middle of the 13C; aisles were added to the original chancel, which then became the nave of the New Church, and to this a new chancel was added on the E, while a chapel was built on the W of the original nave. In the 15C the Old

Church was rebuilt on the original foundations, this becoming at least the third to occupy this site.—The Old Church contains a collection of Celtic stones. A shaft (c 800), once surmounted by a wheel-cross, is known as the Cross of St. Illtyd and bears his name (Iltut) on the back. In front the Latin inscription records that Samson placed this cross here for his soul. The adjacent 6ft high wheel-cross has interlaced carving on both sides and was erected by Howel (Houelt) for the soul of Res his father. Alongside, a cross shaft, without inscription, includes four crosses in its elaborate interlacing. On the N side stands the Samson stone, erected by Abbot Samson for his own soul and for those of Ithael (Iuthahelo) and Arthmael (Artmali), both of whom are recorded 9C chieftains. Also here are the ancient curfew bell, effigies of medieval priests, and the effigies of a lady and her child in Elizabethan costume. The principal features in the New Church are some murals (14–15C; restored in 1950), especially noteworthy being St. Christopher carrying the Christ Child, the carved Tree of Jesse niche (13C) at the E end of the S aisle, and the squints.

The mouth of the little *Afon Colhugh* on which Llantwit stands is said to have once been a port, perhaps the place at which St. Illtyd landed from Brittany. On the cliffs immediately to the E *Castle Ditches* are Iron Age earthworks, while to the W *Tressilian Bay* with its caves has many associations with smuggling. *St. Donat's Castle*, 2m W of Llantwit Major and near the coast, is a restored 14–16C baronial mansion, long owned by the Stradling family, said to have prospered through the use of the castle for smuggling. Bought and restored in the 1930s by the American publisher Randolph Hearst, the castle has since 1962 housed the international Atlantic College. Within the castle grounds St. Donat's Arts Centre (Tel: 04465–4848) offers exhibitions, crafts and theatre in a converted 14C tithe barn.

Leaving Llantwit Major B4265, passing close to several tumuli, heads NW for (6m) *St. Bride's Major* where the church contains, immediately N of the altar, an elaborate 13C graveslab. B4265 provides the direct link to Bridgend, but this Route takes B4524 along the exposed coast and then up the estuary of the Ogmore river to (4m) **Ogmore Castle**, once the heart of the feudal lordship of Ogmore established in early Norman times by William de Londres. In addition to the early earthworks, the site comprises two rectangular wards, each surrounded by a moat, in the larger inner ward, enclosed by an early 13C wall, being an early 12C rectangular keep (probably built by William's son, Maurice), a 13C hall (NE), and a late 12C building (E) of unknown purpose. Ancient stepping stones across the river provide a further pleasant medieval touch.

2m. **Ewenny Priory**, to the E near Corntown on B4524, was founded by Maurice de Londres in 1141 (as a cell of the Benedictine abbey of Gloucester), its church having already been built by Maurice's father, William. The Benedictines, never integrating as successfully as did the Cistercians, were long regarded by the Welsh as no more than Norman intruders, if in religious guise. The monks therefore had always to be ready to repel attack, and, with its early Norman part ecclesiastical and part military character, Ewenny survives as a particularly interesting example of this requirement of those days. The defensive character appears in the crenellation (certainly not merely ornamental at this early period), in the remains of the strong precinct wall (12–13C) and in the gateways (c 1300), in both of which there are loopholes, that on the NW also having a portcullis. At the Dissolution the domestic buildings were bought by Sir Edward Carne (British ambassador to the Vatican until Henry VIII broke off relations) who built a mansion within the walls. The priory Church is in two parts, separated by a 13 or 14C rood screen; the Nave, which is the parish church and was probably always such, and the Chancel (E end) which was for the monks. The Nave, heightened in the late 12C, nevertheless shows much good early Norman work, notably in the arcade and in the arches of the crossing. The Chancel, entered by a separate door (note the adjacent squint) from the churchyard, contains a 14C wooden screen, a double piscina, a leper squint, and, in the surviving transept, the (?13C) graveslab of the priory's founder, bearing the name Morice de Lundres and expressing, in Norman French, the hope that God will reward him for his labours. Outside the church, to the E of the demolished N transept, are traces of a mid-12C chapel.

A pleasant and interesting short diversion (5m) can be made westward from Ewenny, the road crossing the Ewenny river and in under 1m reaching a crossroads, just beyond which the Ogmore river flows below a narrow medieval bridge known as the Dipping Bridge because of the parapets arranged for sheep dipping. From the crossroads a minor road drops into the village of Merthyr Mawr, a period survival of whitewashed and thatched cottages. Beyond the village, the road continues for 1m to a car park and picnic site beside an area of dunes where evidence of Bronze Age, Iron Age and Romano-British occupation has been revealed (crouched burials, brooches, pins, pottery). Candleston Castle, at the car park, is the forlorn ruin of a fortified 15C manor the estate of which succumbed to the dunes although the house remained occupied until the 19C.

2m. (from Ewenny) **Bridgend** (16,000 inhab.) is in Welsh Pen-y-Bont ar Ogwr, or the Crossing of the River Ogmore; a crossing deemed by the Normans to be of sufficient importance to warrant the building of two castles, one on either side of the river. The Old Castle on the E bank has disappeared, recalled only by the fact that the town on this side of the river is known as Oldcastle. Similarly the district on the W bank is known as Newcastle, though here the 12C Castle, with an elaborately decorated Norman gateway, survives high on the hill above. But, for all its Norman origins, modern Bridgend is essentially a diversified industrial development of the 19 and 20C.

The Norman presence is better recalled by the extensive ruins of **Coity Castle**, 1½m NE of Bridgend (WHM. Tel: 0222-465511).

History. Coity was probably first built around the end of the 12C by Sir Gilbert de Turbeville, who, the story goes, accepted and married the beautiful daughter prudently offered to him by the local Welsh chieftain. The castle remained in the family until the line died out during the 14C, subsequent successive owners being Sir Roger Berkerolles and Sir William Gamage, the latter surviving a long siege by Owen Glendower. When the Gamage line became extinct towards the end of the 16C, the estate passed by marriage to the 2nd Earl of Leicester and the castle was abandoned.

The plan is a large, irregular outer ward (14C), on the E of which is a circular inner ward. This latter is entered by the badly ruined Middle Gate, to the left being the keep and to the right against the curtain wall the domestic buildings. The walls of the keep date from the late 12C (and thus represent Gilbert de Turbeville's original construction), but most of what is inside it is 14C, and in Tudor times a four-storey addition was built on the N side. Most of the curtain wall is contemporary with the keep, but, again, the buildings inside it are mainly 14C. In these buildings, the principal rooms, reached by a stairway between the chapel and the hall, were on the first floor above small, vaulted ground floor rooms; the chapel is opposite the Middle Gate, with the hall to its W and then the kitchens. The large rectangular building which occupied much of the N part of the inner ward is of unknown date and purpose.—*Coity Church* (14C, with a 15C tower) contains two small De Turbeville effigies, and a wooden chest with carving of the Passion, possibly a very rare example of a portable Easter Sepulchre (c 1500).

Bridgend is left by A473 which in *2m*, at *Laleston*, merges with A48.

DIVERSION TO PORTHCAWL (A4106. 4m). At *Newton*, reached in 2m, the church (13–15C), E of the road, offers some interesting features; for example, a door high on the E side of the tower, recalling the days when defence was a requirement even for churches; this door gave access to a wooden parapet that could be erected on the corbel immediately below, thus becoming an obvious vantage point for defenders. The S porch is another curiosity, the Norman pillars supporting the outer arch here being upside down, presumably as the result of having been brought from elsewhere. Noteworthy inside the church are the 13C floreated cross on the ledge N of the chancel arch; the E window by Burne-Jones; and, in the chancel, the stone altar, with original base and table, a rare pre-Reformation survival of Edward VI's order that all stone altars should be destroyed.—**Porthcawl** (15,000 inhab. *Inf.* The Old Police Station, John Street. Tel: 065671–6639), in the earlier 19C a busy coal-exporting port (fed first by a horsedrawn tram and then, after 1865, by railway), declined in the face of competition from Barry and Port Talbot, until the dock was closed in 1907 and the inner harbour filled in during the 1920s. However, the decline was foreseen and already by the 1860s the development was under way which soon created what remains today a highly popular seaside resort with all the associated entertainment and facilities. To the NW to Porthcawl, a region of dunes planted with stabilising grass stretches almost to the Margam steelworks on the outskirts of Port Talbot. The area is divided into two by the river Kenfig (or Cynffig), the S part being *Kenfig Burrows* (National Nature Reserve), marked by Kenfig Pool, a small freshwater lake formed in perhaps the 14C. Bronze and Iron Age peoples lived here, and in medieval times (12C) the river mouth boasted a port with, a short way upstream, a castle, a church and a village, all finally overwhelmed by the sands in the early 16C though traces survive about ½m to the N of the pool. The village of *Mawdlam*, off the E side of the Burrows, owes its name to a church of St. Mary Magdalen, originally built in the 13C when old Kenfig's church was threatened by the sands.—The Elizabethan *Sker House*, near the shore, features in R.D. Blackmore's 'Maid of Sker'.

6m (from Laleston) **Margam Country Park** (Tel: 0639–871131 or 881635), to the NE of the main road, originally belonged to Margam Abbey (see below) but at the Dissolution passed to Sir Rice Mansel who in 1537 built a mansion here, succeeded in about 1835 by the Neo-Tudor 'castle' of the local magnate C.R.M. Talbot, a member of the family which acquired the estate during the 18C. Today the park is a large recreational area of some 850 acres offering attractions which include waymarked walks; a deer herd; the Classical 18C Orangery designed by Anthony Keck for the Talbot owner of 1790; a Visitor Centre (in the 'Castle') which includes a Coach House Theatre showing films about Margam; an adventure playground and other amusements for children; a farm trail; a Sculpture Park for contemporary pieces; and the largest maze in Europe. The park also includes (close to a magnificent lace-beech tree) the ruins of the 13C

Margam Abbey, notably the Chapter House which, unlike most Cistercian chapter houses which were rectangular, is 12-sided outside but circular within. It was originally vaulted from a central shafted pillar (the foliated capitals of which survive), which, however, together with the roof, was destroyed in a storm in 1799. From here there is access by a side door to Margam Abbey Church, to which, though, visitors not interested in the park may drive direct by road.

1m. **Margam Abbey Church** (down a minor turn on the right). The abbey was a Cistercian house founded by Robert, Earl of Gloucester (natural son of Henry I), in 1147 near the site of a long vanished Celtic monastery. In 1206 the abbey underwent the possibly unique experience of a violent revolt by its lay brothers, a disturbance it clearly resolved since it went on to become one of the wealthiest houses in Wales. The greater part of the nave of the original abbey church survives in what is today the parish church (in fact the only Cistercian church still in use in Wales). The lower part of the W front (it was much restored in the 19C when the Italianate campaniles were added), the plain and massive arcades, and perhaps the groining of the aisles, date from the 12C. The windows at the W end contain glass by William Morris, and there are a number of Mansel and Talbot tombs. For the Chapter House see Margam Park above.— The adjacent *Abbey and Stones Museum* (Tel: 0656–742678), in a building which was one of the earliest church schools in Britain, shows an important collection of inscribed and sculpted stones spanning from Roman and Celtic through to medieval times. Most were found locally.—*Capel Mair*, a ruined 15C chapel on a spur high above the church, may have been either a private oratory or a place for lay worship.

4m. **Port Talbot** and, adjacent, **Aberavon** (together 50,000 inhab.) are two towns in one, the former a name synonymous with steel, the latter, in total contrast, a popular seaside resort known for its Afan Lido recreation centre. Port Talbot's great (Margam) steelworks sprawl southward towards the dunes, while the town itself, despite a modern shopping centre, retains touches of its Victorian past. The large *Harbour* has grown out of the early riverside wharfs. With the Industrial Revolution and the increase in activity around the mouth of the Afan, it became necessary to provide a dock, so a new cut was made for the river and its former course was converted in 1837 into what is now called the Old Dock. No significant further expansion took place until the 1960s' construction by the British Transport Docks Board, together with the British Steel Corporation, of the modern deep-water harbour with a breakwater a mile long. Opened by H.M. the Queen in 1970, the harbour enables virtually the entire throughput of bulk iron ore for the steel industry, including Llanwern at Newport, to be concentrated here.

CWM AFAN SCENIC ROUTE (A4107) climbs NE out of Port Talbot following a valley which from the 18C until recent times was largely given over to coal mining and industry. The South Wales Mineral Railway came in 1859, linking Briton Ferry with Glyncorrwg (8m up the valley); a passenger rail service was opened in 1885; and A4107 was built in 1930–32 largely as a measure to relieve the unemployment of the depression. Today the railway and the pits have gone, but A4107 has been designated a Scenic Route (with picnic sites and other facilities), an increasingly afforested valley now linking the industrialised coast with the high moorland above Rhondda. The focal point along this Scenic Route is *Afan Argoed Countryside*

Centre (Tel: 0639–850564), 6m above Port Talbot, within Afan Argoed Country Park and offering forest walks, cycle routes, an adventure playground and forest and mountain landrover tours. Here too is the interesting *Welsh Miners Museum* (same Tel.), telling both the technical and the social story of mining in Wales.

3m (from Port Talbot) **Briton Ferry** where viaducts carry A48 across the dock and mouth of the river Neath. For **Swansea**, 5m W, and **Gower** beyond, see Rtes 38 and 39: for **Neath**, 2m N, see Rte 31. A48 heads NW, soon passing (left) *Llandarcy*, with an oil refinery linked by pipelines to Swansea's Queen's Dock, and then rounding the northern and in part industrial outskirts of Swansea to reach (*8m*) *Penllergaer*. Here (close to M4 Exit 47) A48, continuing NW, provides an inland approach to Carmarthen, while this Route bears W on A484 for Gorseinon and (*3m*) **Loughor**, at the head of Burry Inlet where it is entered by the river Loughor. It was at this strategic point that the Romans established their station of Leucarum (1 and 2C), and here too, in c 1110, the Norman Henry de Newburgh built his castle at the SE corner of the Romans' fort. All that is left, the ruin of a 13C square tower, stands on its motte beside the road before it drops down to the river, today crossed by rail and road bridges.

3m. **Llanelli** (28,000 inhab.), essentially industrial with steel, chemical and engineering works, owes its name to the Celtic St. Elli to whom the parish church is dedicated. The *Public Library* (Tel: 0554–773538) shows works by local artists and also receives touring exhibitions, while farther N, in Park Howard off Felinfoel Road (A476: no cars in the park), the *Parc Howard Art Gallery and Museum* (Tel: 0554–773538), also with travelling exhibitions, shows material of local interest, including a good collection of Welsh pottery and works by Welsh artists. The local Male Voice Choir welcomes visitors to rehearsals (Tel: 0554–755985).

Beyond Llanelli, A484 skirts *Burry Inlet*, here some 3m wide and of aviation interest; in June 1928 Amelia Earhart, the first woman to fly the Atlantic, arrived here after a flight of 20 hours and 40 minutes from Trepassy Bay in Newfoundland.

9m. **Kidwelly** (3000 inhab.), at the head of the estuary formed by the confluence of the Gwendraeth Fawr and the Gwendraeth Fach, grew around the castle and priory established here in the early 12C, the latter being Benedictine and founded in c 1130 by Roger, Bishop of Salisbury, as a dependency of Sherborne Abbey in Dorset. The town, which received a charter as early as the reign of Henry I, now lies mainly on the S bank of the latter river, here being the *Church of St. Mary*, successor to the original priory church. The present structure dates principally from c 1320, but was restored in 1884 after the spire, which had already crashed twice, had been struck by lightning. Features of the interior are the unusually broad nave, originally longer and extending west; the squint discovered in the sanctuary wall in 1973; and the mural stair in the vestry leading up to an anchorite's cell, with a loophole to enable him to hear services.

Kidwelly was long associated with tinplate (iron or steel rolled wafer-thin), starting with a forge in 1719 and followed by production in 1737 which lasted until 1941. Today this past lives on as the *Kidwelly Industrial Museum* (Tel: 0554–891078 or 810395), based on the old works to the N of the town on the E bank of the Gwendraeth Fach. Opened in 1988 by the Prince of Wales, the museum includes an exhibition area (with video presentation) occupying the former Sorting and Boxing rooms; the hot rolling mill; the cold rolls engine house; a section devoted to the local coal industry, with colliery pit-head gear; and various steam and diesel locomotives.

From the town the Gwendraeth Fach is crossed by a bridge originally constructed in the 14C; beyond is the site of the original town which lay within the defences of *Kidwelly Castle* (WHM. Tel: 0222-465511). Built by Roger, Bishop of Salisbury, at about the same time as his priory, the castle, sometimes Welsh and sometimes Norman and English, several times changed hands until passing to the Crown during the reign of Henry IV. Of Roger's original castle virtually nothing survives (bar possibly the earthworks to the N and S), the oldest part seen today being the rectangular inner ward dating from c 1275. In plan the castle comprises this inner ward, surrounded by a semicircle of outer ward ending at either end at the river. The wall walk around the outer curtain affords a good general impression.

The Gatehouse (S end of the castle) dates from the 14C and is unusual for being sited on the outer rather than the inner curtain, as also for being a part of the defences of the original town; it contains dungeons, including (NE corner) an oubliette. The outer curtain is also 14C, as are the upper parts of the inner ward's towers, all this, including the gatehouse, being the work of Henry of Lancaster, nephew of Edward I. In the Outer Ward a later period hall of c 1500 lies outside the inner ward between its SW and NW towers, this hall's kitchen being beyond against the outer curtain. At the NE corner of the outer ward, beyond the N gate, are the stables. In the Inner Ward, the oldest part of the castle, the solar and hall (both late 13C or early 14C) are along the E side, beyond being the chapel of the same period occupying the third storey of a tower which projects boldly towards the river. The large kitchen is at the SW corner of the ward.

Tregoning Hill, 4m W on the E headland of the Towy estuary, is a National Trust cliff property of 10 acres offering good views of Carmarthen Bay.

10m. **Carmarthen**, see Rte 40.

36   Cardiff

CARDIFF (Caerdydd. 262,000 inhab.), in 1955 officially confirmed as the capital of Wales, is an exceptionally elegant and progressive city and port which successfully combines such varied roles as national and county capital; home of a historic castle and, at Llandaff, of an equally historic cathedral; cultural and educational focus (University College); and shopping, commercial and industrial centre. The spacious central area of the city is as interesting as it is dignified and striking with its walled and imposing castle, its extensive green riverside parks, its pleasant pedestrian precincts and arcades, and, in Cathays Park, one of Europe's most distinguished groups of public buildings.

Sweeping change will come to the southern areas of the city, and indeed to the whole arc of Cardiff Bay round to Penarth, with the progress (throughout the 1990s and beyond) and eventual completion, in whatever final form, of the bold *Cardiff Bay Development Project*, the key to which is a barrage to link Cardiff's Alexandra Dock with Penarth Head and thus create a large lake to become the focus of high-quality waterside residential and leisure investments.

Visitors to Cardiff and its southern environs as far as Penarth during the 1990s must expect major road layout change.

City Centre, Castle Street–Queen Street–St. David's Centre.

Tourist Information. Bridge Street (S of St. David's Centre). Tel: 0222–227281.—*Tours* Open-top bus tours of city and surrounds.

Airport. Rhoose, 10m west.

Entertainment. *St. David's Hall:* Concerts, including Welsh Promenade Concerts (July) and Welsh Festival of Music (Nov., Dec.). *New Theatre:* Welsh National Opera. Plays. Ballet. *Sherman Theatre* (main and studio): Sherman Company. University and other productions. *Chapter Arts Gallery:* Theatre. Cinemas. Art Gallery.

Choirs. Cardiff Ladies Choir. For rehearsals Tel: 0222–497735. Cardiff Male Choir: For rehearsals Tel: 0222–568593.

History. The Romans are known to have settled here in c 60–90 after their defeat of the Silures, a small civil settlement developing to the S of their fort. Of the period between the Roman withdrawal and the arrival of the Normans virtually nothing is known, through by one tradition Lancelot is said to have fled by sea from here, and there must also have been some association with the chieftain Morgan Mwynfawr (died c 975), from whose name the modern Glamorgan derives. In 1093 Robert FitzHamon arrived, building his primitive fortress on the site of its Roman predecessor, and in 1158 the later castle was successfully stormed by Ifor Bach, ruler of Senghenydd, the district to the N of Cardiff. It was not long before a town began to grow within the castle's protection. By the late 13C there were 2000 inhabitants, already enjoying a charter, confirmed by others in 1340, 1421, 1581, 1600 and 1608, this last continuing until the Municipal Corporations Act of 1835 which brought to an end municipal dependence on the lord of the castle.

Cardiff was overrun by Owen Glendower in 1404, and in 1490 both castle and town came into the hands of Jasper Tudor, uncle of Henry VII. In 1551 Cardiff was presented by Edward VI to Sir William Herbert. During the Civil War the place, with Royalist sympathies, was held alternately for the King and Parliament, but afterwards remained in the possession of the Herberts and their descendants, the marquesses of Bute.

Modern Cardiff was born of the Industrial Revolution, its population increasing from 1000 in 1801 to 30,000 by the middle of the century and over 180,000 in 1911. Important steps were the contruction of the Glamorganshire Canal (Merthyr Tydfil to Cardiff) in 1794; the digging of the first dock, on the initiative and at the personal expense of the 2nd Marquess of Bute, in 1839; the arrival of the railways between about 1848–64; and the opening of another dock in 1860. By the latter part of the 19C Cardiff, largely through being the leading port handling iron and coal, was at the height of its prosperity. At the turn of the century Cathays Park was acquired, the first building, the City Hall, being opened in 1905, the year in which the official status of City was granted. In 1922 the city's boundary was extended to include Llandaff with its cathedral.

After the First World War there was a serious drop in the trade through the docks, and in the last war the city, its docks and Llandaff cathedral were all severely damaged in air raids. The coal trade declined and disappeared and the docks shrank, until, in more recent years, a new prosperity has come with the replanning of the docks for oil, timber and general cargoes and with the diversification into new industries. In 1955 Cardiff was officially confirmed as the capital of Wales; the 1980s have seen the opening of progressive features such as the St. David's Centre and the associated St. David's Hall; and the regeneration of Cardiff Bay should be the chief feature of the 1990s and beyond.

For Cardiff to (E) *Severn Bridge* and (W) *Carmarthen*, see Rte 35: to *The Valleys*, see Rte 37.

A. Cardiff City

*Cardiff Castle (Tel: 0222–822083. Medieval Banquets Tel: 0222–372737). Conveyed to the city in 1948 by the 5th Marquess of Bute, the castle is contained within 19C walls, generally following the line of the Roman enclosure, and architecturally spans from Roman to modern times. The castle's history is essentially that of the town. The principal stages of its construction are c 1093 when Robert FitzHamon threw up the motte, this being followed by the first stone building, probably erected by Robert of Gloucester ('The Consul'), a natural son of Henry I; the building on the motte of the keep in the late 12C; the building by Gilbert de Clare in the later 13C of the Black Tower (today's entrance), the wall linking it to the keep, and the keep gateway, this work dividing the castle into two wards; during the 14 and 15C the move from the keep to more roomy and purely residential apartments along the W wall, this range being extended in Tudor and Stuart times; the removal in the late 18C of the outer buildings of the keep and of the wall dividing the wards; and finally the reconstruction in 1867–75, by William Burges for the 3rd Marquess, of the entire SW part of the castle, this including the addition of a spire to the Octagonal Tower and the erection of the 150ft high Clock Tower in the place of a small turret. At the same time the internal decoration was redesigned throughout in fantastic and colourful style.

The castle is entered by the *Black Tower* where, to the right, a fine length of Roman wall, probably of the 3C, can be visited. From the tower the line of Gilbert de Clare's wall runs across to the *Motte* and *Keep*, this last offering a good view.—The SW buildings can only be visited by conducted tour (45 min.). In the *Clock Tower* the rooms are the Winter Smoking Room (first floor); the Bachelors' Bedroom with, in the adjoining dressingroom, a marble bath of Roman (but not local Roman) origin; and, at the top, the Summer Smoking Room, designed on the theme of the firmament. The *Herbert Tower* (16C) is the southernmost of the projecting towers along the W wall. Here is the Arab Room (1881), with a decorated ceiling in gold leaf and a chimney-piece of white marble and lapis lazuli. Much of the work here is that of imported Arab craftsmen. Beyond is the *Banqueting Hall* of c 1428, with murals depicting the life of Robert of Gloucester. The windows represent the various lords of Cardiff. Next comes the *Octagonal Tower* (early 15C), forming part of the medieval defences. Here the Chaucer Room (decoration 1889) contains windows illustrating the 'Canterbury Tales', the floor is tiled as a maze and there are alphabet tiles in the hearth. A richly decorated staircase leads down to the frescoed *Chapel* (1848), formerly a dressing room but converted after the death of the 2nd Marquess. In the *Bute Tower* the Dining Room has a fine ceiling in gold leaf in Moorish style. At the top of the tower is the Roof Garden (1876), open only May–Sept. The *Library* (early 15C) contains windows inserted by Jasper Tudor, but the room's decorations are 19C. The carved and inlaid bookcases are noteworthy. The *Entrance Hall* has stained glass windows depicting English monarchs who have owned the castle.—The castle also houses two *Regimental Museums*; that of the Welsh Regiment (Tel: 0222–229367), and that of 1st The Queen's Dragoon Guards (Tel: 0222–227611, Ext. 217). The Castle is annually (August) the site of the Cardiff Searchlight Tattoo.

WEST OF THE CASTLE. Castle Street skirts the S side of the castle, to the W crossing the Taff with, to the N, parks and gardens on both sides of the river. On the W bank are, from S to N, *Sophia Gardens*; the *National Sports Centre* (1972); *Glamorgan County Cricket Ground*; and *Pontcanna*, with sports grounds and the municipal caravan site. Cathedral Road, fringing the W of these open spaces, leads to Llandaff (Cathedral) and St. Fagans (Welsh Folk Museum). *Bute Park* stretches along the E side of the river, here, between the castle and the river, being the marked-out foundations of a medieval priory.—Beyond the Taff, Castle Street becomes Cowbridge Road East, off which, in Market Road (³/₄m beyond the river bridge), is the *Chapter Arts Centre* with two cinemas, a theatre, exhibition spaces, studio artists, a restaurant and several workshops.

SOUTH OF THE CASTLE AND WEST OF HIGH STREET. Westgate Street, leading SE from Castle Street, soon passes *Cardiff Arms Park* (named after a former pub), home of Welsh rugby. Beyond, and close to one another, are the bus and central railway stations and the *Empire Swimming Pool*, built in 1958 for the British Empire and Commonwealth Games.

Eastwards Castle Street is prolonged by Duke Street, off which High Street, becoming St. Mary Street (both shopping streets), drops south. Off the E of High Street is the attractive Victorian *Market* (1886–91), farther on, off the same side, being elegant turn-of-the-century arcades.

Queen Street, the eastward extension of Duke Street, is a spacious

pedestrian precinct. *St. John's Church*, just S of the junction of Duke
Street and Queen Street, is the parish church. Restored in 1890–99,
the church dates largely from 1453, although its most ancient part, a
survival from a predecessor, is the 13C S chancel aisle. The tower of
1473 was built by Ann Neville, wife of the future Richard III. Inside,
the church is unusual for having a clerestory in the chancel but not in
the nave, while other noteworthy features are the altarpiece in the S
aisle by Goscombe John and the N (or Herbert) chapel with a
monument to two Herbert brothers (Sir William, died 1609, Keeper of
Cardiff Castle; and Sir John, died 1617, secretary to Queen Elizabeth
and James I).

Queen Street skirts the northern edge of **St. David's Centre**, a large
modern but elegant shopping precinct (1983) which includes *St.
David's Hall*, opened in the same year by the Queen Mother and
accepted as one of Britain's finest concert and conference facilities.

Park Place, leading N out of Queen Street, passes the Edwardian
New Theatre and reaches ***Cathays Park**, Cardiff's distinquished
Civic Centre, a spacious and superbly balanced area of white
Portland stone buildings (most dating from the early years of this
century) set along broad avenues broken by gardens. The *City Hall*,
the central of the three buildings marking the SE flank, was built in
1905 by Lanchester and Rickards in Renaissance style with a dome
surmounted by a Welsh dragon and with a lofty clock tower, 194ft
high. The fountains and the pool in front were completed in 1969 to
commemorate the investiture of Prince Charles as Prince of Wales.
Inside, in the Marble Hall on the first floor, which has pillars of Siena
marble, is a series of eleven statues presented by Lord Rhondda (died
1918) illustrating Welsh history. These include St. David (Goscombe
John), Owen Glendower, Henry Tudor, and Sir Thomas Picton, one
of Wellington's leading commanders. The Council Chamber contains
a collection of city treasures; the Assembly Hall has a rich segmented
ceiling; and in the Lord Mayor's Parlour there is a mosaic of 86,000
marble pieces. The *Law Courts* (1906, Lanchester and Rickards)
stand to the left of City Hall, while to the right is the National
Museum of Wales (see below). To the S of the museum are the
Gorsedd Gardens, with a stone circle commemorating the National
Eisteddfod of 1899. The statues here include David Lloyd George
(Rizzello, 1960), and three others by Goscombe John. The *Welsh
National War Memorial* (J. Ninian Comper, 1928), behind City Hall
in Alexandra Gardens, bears a plaque commemorating also those
who fell in the last war. Museum Avenue runs along the NE side of
Cathays Park, with, beyond the National Museum, various buildings
of the *University College of South Wales*. The W wing (W.D. Caröe)
dates from 1903–09. The N wing (1930s and 1950s) and the S wing
(1960s) are additions in the same style. Founded in 1883, the college
in 1893 became one of the constituent colleges of the University of
Wales, the others being Bangor, Aberystwyth, Swansea and Lampeter. The college's *Sherman Theatre Gallery* receives monthly touring
art exhibitions. To the N of Alexandra Gardens is the *Welsh Office*
(P.K. Hanton, 1938). The University of Wales *Institute of Science and
Technology* stands at the NW corner of the park. From here King
Edward VII Avenue leads SE, with, from N to S, the *Temple of Peace*
(Percy Thomas, 1938), built as a headquarters for Welsh people
fighting war and disease and now housing a variety of organisations
concerned with international affairs and health; another building
(Ivor Jones and Percy Thomas, 1916) of the *Institute of Science and
Technology*; *Mid Glamorgan County Hall* (Vincent Harris and

T. A. Moodie, 1908–10), with a S extension of the 1930s by Ivor Jones and Percy Thomas; and the *University Registry* (Wills and Anderson, 1901–03), extended in 1933 by Alwyn Lloyd. The modern *Cardiff College of Music and Drama* is off the SW side of the park.

From St. David's Hall the southward road sequence The Hayes and Hayes Bridge Road crosses the railway to become the long Bute Street (but the Cardiff Bay Development Project will probably change the geography in this area), at the S end of which (over 1m from St. David's Hall) is the **Welsh Industrial and Maritime Museum** (Tel: 0222–481919), a branch of the National Museum of Wales opened in 1977 to show large and heavy machines. Out of doors there are railway engines and a working replica of Richard Trevithick's steam locomotive (see Rte 31, Merthyr Tydfil). The *Railway Gallery*, a short way N in the restored Bute Street Station and with a rich collection of photographs, models and drawings, traces the story of railways in Wales, while, opposite, a renovated chandlery (126 Bute Street) tells that of Cardiff as a port.

Techniquest (Tel: 0222–460122), opposite the Industrial and Maritime Museum, is a 'hands-on' science and technology project covering an ever-widening field and enabling young and old to make things work and see why and how they do.

From this district there are views across the Taff estuary and towards Penarth, an area to be transformed under the Cardiff Bay Development Project (see opening paragraph of this Rte).

B. **National Museum of Wales

The National Museum (Tel: 0222-397951) of Wales comprises the main building in Cardiff's Cathays Park (the subject of this description) as also several branch museums as outlined below. One of the finest and largest museums in the United Kingdom, the museum here contains important archaeological, art, botanical, geological, industrial and zoological collections. Although the emphasis is on the story of Wales, there is a much broader scope and interest, notably the outstanding collection of modern European art.

Branch Museums. *Welsh Industrial and Maritime Museum*. Cardiff. See Rte 36A above. *Welsh Folk Museum*, St. Fagans, Cardiff. See Rte 36D below. *Turner House*, the art gallery at Penarth, see Rte 35. *Roman Legionary Museum*, Caerleon. See Rte 30A. *Museum of the Welsh Woollen Industry*, Dre-Fach Felindre. See Rte 42. *Segontium Roman Fort Museum*, Caernarfon. See Rte 10. *Welsh Slate Museum*, Llanberis. See Rte 8A. *Museum of the North*, Llanberis. See Rte 8A. *Hen Gapel* (19C religious life), Tre'r-ddol. See Rte 18A.

The Past and the Future. The proposal for a national museum was aired in parliament in 1903, and a Charter of Incorporation was granted by Edward VII in 1907. In 1910 the design by the architects Smith and Brewer was chosen out of 130 entrants in an open competition, but, although the foundation stone was laid by George V in 1912, subsequent work was delayed by the 1914–18 war and it was not until 1922 that the western part of the main hall and the galleries off it were opened to the public, and it was only in 1927 that

George V formally opened the museum. The E and W wings date from later.

The year 1988 saw the start of a major building programme including the refurbishment of existing galleries, the addition of several new ones, the installation of modern air conditioning and lighting, extensions to office and storage areas, and, finally, greatly improved visitor facilities, notably a new bookshop and restaurant. With the completion in about autumn 1993 of the extension building in the rear courtyard (with six new art galleries and an Evolution of Wales feature) the museum complex will be nearly half as large again as in 1988.

Although the Museum remains open throughout the building programme (until 1993), it may from time to time be necessary to close some galleries.

Facilities and Activities include regular temporary exhibitions; a large specialised library; a bookshop selling a wide range of books published by the museum as well as a selection of other titles; a schools service; a lecture programme; free lunchtime concerts; restaurant and snack bar.

The MAIN HALL contains the permanent **Collection of Sculpture**, this including, by *W. Goscombe John:* St. John the Baptist. David Lloyd George. Boy at Play. Lady Goscombe John. Morpheus. The Drummer Boy. By *Peter Lambda*: Aneurin Bevan. By *John Gibson*: Narcissus. Meleager, or The Hunter. Wounded Amazon. Aurora. By *John Evan Thomas*: Death of Tewdric, King of Gwent. George Price Watkins. By *Auguste Rodin*: St. John, the Baptist. The Kiss. The Earth and Moon. Eve. By *Henry Moore*: Upright Motif, No. 8.

During recent years, the museum has received a number of portrait-heads of eminent contemporary Welshmen. The commissions by the Welsh sculptor *Ivor Roberts-Jones* include personalities from the worlds of literature, law, politics and the arts.

SCIENCE GALLERIES. **Discover the Countryside of Wales** presents, with the help of scenic paintings, simulated environments, sound effects and other means, a dramatic and informative picture of the Welsh countryside. Themes include Cwm Idwal; open moorland; bog, with Tregaron as the example; woodland and forest; grassland; lakes and marshes, Llangorse being the example; dunes, cliff and the shore.—The **Animal Kingdom** is a largely specialist exhibition dealing with modern thinking on animal classification.—**Botany in Wales** includes themes such as an introduction to the identification of flowering plants, illustrated by lifelike wax models; the history of plant hunting in Wales; forestry, pollution and reclamation. Recreational facilities such as Nature Trails, Country Parks, Picnic Sites, National Parks etc. are also featured.

ZOOLOGY. Whales and dolphins. The world's largest leatherback turtle. Reptiles. Birds, with dioramas illustrating various environments. A section on the Greak Auk, and a giant egg of the extinct bird, Aepyomis. British mammals. Also, a display of wild animals (including local species of many endangered types) features such as the bison, the snow leopard, impala, wolf, tiger, cheetah and zebra.

There is also a section illustrating concepts interesting modern scientists, e.g., the evolution of animal life, including the role played by inheritance; the relationship between man and animals, with some emphasis on conservation.

INDUSTRY. The museum's main industrial exhibits are now at Cardiff's Welsh Industrial and Maritime Museum.

ARCHAEOLOGY. The archaeological story of Wales is told more or less chronologically. *Prehistory*. Old Stone Age material includes an axe of local quartzite from Cardiff (perhaps 200,000 years old), and stone implements and ivory ornaments from Paviland and other sites. From the New Stone Age are a model of Bryn Celli Ddu, finds from Mynydd Rhiw axe 'factory', and simple grave goods from communal tombs. The Bronze Age is represented by a cist from Brymbo (near Wrexham), with bones; grave goods from other cists and from round cairns, including early metalwork, flint arrowheads, and faience heads, these last probably imported from the Mediterranean around 1400 BC. The increasing wealth and skill of the Bronze Age are well illustrated by gold ornaments, outstanding being neck-rings, bracelets and the *Caergwrle Bowl, with elaborate gold decoration and representing a boat on the waves. From the later Bronze or early Iron Age are a sheet-bronze bucket from Arthog and two cauldrons from Llyn Fawr. It was also at about this time (say 300 BC and later) that the first Celts were arriving in Wales, bringing with them metalwork in the La Tène tradition (La Tène: a site in Switzerland at which were first discovered ornaments and other objects produced by a culture spanning roughly the last 600 years BC), especially noteworthy being shields; a wrought-iron *Firedog from Capel Garmon; and ornaments from Tal-y-Llyn and Llyn Cerrig-Bach. Much other Iron Age material comes from the many hillforts of Wales.

Roman Period military equipment is mainly in the museums of Caerleon and Segontium, though here in Cardiff there is an instructive model of a typical auxiliary fort. Other material includes a 4C mosaic pavement from Caerwent; pottery and tiles from Holt where the 20th Legion had its kilns; and evidence of Roman mining activities.—The *Early Christian Period* is principally represented by the *Gallery of Stone Monuments, a collection of some 23 stones and 14 casts ranging from the earliest inscribed stones of the 5C, through the sculptured high crosses introduced in the 9C, to the locally developed styles which probably survived into the 12C. The stones are arranged in a stepped circular setting, with clusters representing different chronological groups. Each stone is numbered and information boards are provided.—*Medieval Period* material includes rood figures (14–15C); one leaf from an ivory *Diptych (14C, French) from Llandaff; a comparative display of decorated floor tiles (13–16C), and finds from castles, mostly pottery and metalwork reflecting Anglo-Norman influence.

BOTANY. Although the collections have a strong Welsh bias, the department's policy has nevertheless been to take a broad view. Thus plants from all continents are represented, even if the majority come from Britain and Europe. As early as 1920 the department began to commission models, a practice which was continued until 1937 when the first full-time botanical artist was appointed. Since then a large number of plant models have been created out of silk, wire, wax and paper, forming a *Collection of Plant Models acknowledged to be one of the world's finest. At the same time it has always been policy to display both wild and cultivated living speciments.

The collections are in two main parts. One covers the Vascular Plants, these including flowering plants, conifers and ferns and their allies; the other covers the Lower Plants or Cryptograms, with mosses, liverworts, lichens, fungi, slime moulds and algae. There are also collections of Economic Plants, woods, seeds and fruits.

GEOLOGY. The displays in this department are arranged as collections of fossils, minerals and rocks. There is also a collection of maps and manuscripts.

The *Fossil Collection* is arranged stratigraphically and represents all fossil groups throughout the stratigraphical column. The most notable elements (from oldest to youngest) are the very small but also significant set of early Cambrian fossils from The Lleyn; the large collection of brachiopods from the type area of the Ordovician System in Meirionnydd; the small but internationally important collection of the world's earliest vascular plants, from the Upper Ludlow strata of South Wales, and the equally small collection of early plants from the Old Red Sandstone; three major collections from the Coal Measures of South Wales; a small collection of Triassic micro-fossils (the so-called triconodonts), the remains of the earliest mammals, found in fissures in the Vale of Glamorgan; and a group of over 30 ichthyosaurs from the Charles Moore Collection.

The *Minerals Collection* is arranged according to chemical composition. There is a large display of garnets of worldwide provenance, and the representative Welsh specimens include a suite of Welsh gold.—The *Rocks Collection* shows specimens from most Welsh geological formations, these including representative sets of rocks of economic importance.—*Maps and Manuscripts* include several examples of early cartography, both topographical and geological. The collection of manuscripts is made up almost entirely of the letters and diaries of Sir Henry Thomas De la Beche, founder of the Museum of Practical Geology and of the Geological Survey of Great Britain.

FINE ART. The most notable collection is that of the sisters Gwendoline and Margaret Davies of Gregynog (see Rte 18B), bequeathed to the museum in 1952 and 1963. The collection includes Old Masters, works by the Barbizon School, British paintings and drawings, and, above all, French art of the late 19C with particular emphasis on the Impressionists.

Northern Art (c 1500–1650). *Marc Gheeraedts*: Queen Elizabeth. *Anon.*: 2nd Earl of Pembroke. *Lucas Cranach*: Portrait of a man. *Anon.*: Sir Roger Mostyn. *Anon.* (Antwerp): Katheryn Tudor of Berain. *I. Laudin*: Mater Dolorosa (Limoges enamel).

Italian Religious Art (1450–1580). *Giovanni Cima (da Conegliano)*: Madonna and Child (c 1505). *Alessandro Allori*: Virgin and Child, with Saints Francis and Lucy (altarpiece). *Studio of Botticelli*: Virgin and St. John adoring the Child. *After El Greco*: Christ led to Calvary.—Also the *Nynehead Tabernacle (c 1460, Florence) in marble. Originally made for the small church of Santa Maria alla Campora, outside Florence, the tabernacle was brought to England in the 19C and given to the church at Nynehead, Somerset. The door is not the original, but is part of an altarpiece of 1520 by *Francesco Granacci*.

Seventeenth Century. *Jusepe de Ribera*: St. Jerome in the desert. *Frans Hals* and *S. de Bray*: Family group in a landscape. *Nicolas Berchem*: Figures by a well. *Anthony van Dyck*: Portrait of a man. *Aelbert Cuyp*: River landscape with horsemen and peasants. *Benjamin Cuyp*: The blind leading the blind. *Jacob van Ruisdael*: Waterfall, *Jan van Goyen*: River scene. Dunes scene. *Meindert Hobbema*: River scene. *Rembrandt*: Catrina Hooghsaet. *Karel Dujardin*: Travelling musicians. *Andrea Sacchi*: Hagar and Ishmael. *P. P. Rubens* and *Frans Snyders*: The fig. *Gaspard Poussin*: Hilly landscape with classical figures. *Nicholas Poussin*: The body of Phocion carried out of Athens. *Louis* and *Mathieu Le Nain* (?): A tavern quarrel.

But perhaps the most striking as also the most interesting of the works of the 17C are what are now generally known as the *Cardiff

Cartoons, four large tapestry cartoons, first documented in 1650 and bought by the museum in 1979. There is room for opinion as to whether these are by *Rubens* himself of by his School. (*Jan van Boeckhorst*, 1605–68, has been suggested), but so far as the average visitor is concerned this will matter little and he will be content simply to enjoy these bright and sumptuous works.

Eighteenth Century. The emphasis is on the Welsh landscape artist **Richard Wilson*, many of his works showing the influence of Claude Lorrain of a century earlier. Wilson was more concerned with the emotion aroused by a landscape than with detail. Paintings to be seen include Pistyll Cain; Landscape with banditti round a tent; Penn Ponds, Richmond Park; A Maid of Honour; Rome and the Ponte Molle; Landscape with Banditti, the murder; Pembroke town and castle; Caernarfon Castle; Dolbadarn Castle; and View of Dover.— Also in this gallery are Roman ruins, by *Giovanni Panini;* Viscountess Bulkeley as Hebe, by *George Romney;* and Llanthony Priory, by *William Hodges*, a pupil of Richard Wilson. Also porcelain and furniture of the period, and a silver-gilt Rococo toilet service made by *Thomas Heming*, goldsmith to George III, for the marriage of Sir Watkin Williams-Wynn who appears on the left in the portrait group by *Pompeo Batoni*.

Nineteenth Century. *J.M.W. Turner:* Tobias and the Angel. Thames backwater, with Windsor Castle. Fishing boat in a mist. *John Constable:* Landscape near Dedham. *E. Landseer:* Encampment on Loch Avon. The ratcatchers. Landscape with waterfall. *David Cox:* Moorland landscape. *D.G. Rossetti:* Fair Rosamund. *Ford Madox Brown:* King René's honeymoon. *J.-F. Millet:* The Good Samaritan. Faggot gatherers. The shooting stars. The little goose girl. The storm. The peasant's family. *Honoré Daumier:* Head of a man. Workmen in a street. Lunch in the country. A famous case. By the Seine. Don Quixote reading.—The ***Collection of Impressionists.** *Van Gogh:* Rain at Auvers. *Henry Moret:* Village in Clohars. *Pierre Bonnard:* Sunlight at Vernon. *C.-F. Daubigny:* Morning on the Oise. *Eugène Boudin:* The port of Fécamp. River at Bordeaux. Village fair. Venice, jetty at the mouth of the Grand Canal. Beach at Trouville. *J.B.C. Corot:* Fisherman moored to the bank. Distant view of Corbeil, morning. Castel Gandolfo. The pond. *Pierre August Renoir:* Head of a girl. Peasants resting. La Parisienne. *H. Fantin Latour:* Immortality. Larkspurs. *Camille Pissaro:* Pont Neuf, Paris. Sunset at Rouen. *Alfred Sisley:* View in the village of Moret. *Edgar Degas:* Woman putting on a glove. Ballet dancer, aged fourteen (sculpture). Dancer looking at the sole of her foot (sculpture). *Edouard Manet:* Argenteuil, 1874. The rabbit. The church of Petit-Montrouge, Paris. *Auguste Rodin:* The fallen Caryatid (sculpture). *Claude Monet:* Water lilies (1905, 1908, 1906). Rouen Cathedral, sunset. Twilight, Venice. Charing Cross Bridge, London. Palazzo Dario, Venice. San Giorgio Maggiore, Venice. *Paul Cézanne:* Edge of a wood in Provence. Still Life with a teapot. Mountains seen from L'Estaque.

Twentieth Century. Welsh artists are well represented, these including the following. *Augustus John:* Study of a woman's head. A peasant family. Study of a boy. Grace. Aran Islands. La désespérance d'amour. Old Ryan. Dylan Thomas. Madame Suggia. Romany folk. Portrait of Dorelia. *Gwen John:* Dorelia John (drawing). Girl in blue. Girl in profile. Study for 'The brown teapot'. Study of a seated nude. *J.D. Innes:* Pembroke coast. Canigou in snow. *Frank Brangwyn:* Venice, St. Mark's. *David Jones:* Annunciation in a Welsh hill setting.—The major European movements also find a place here.

Pure Cubism is represented by a small bronze of 1912 by *Archipenko,* and its influence can perhaps be traced in the bronze head of Henriette III, by *Matisse* (1929), and the painting Loom + Woman, by *Natalia Goncharova* (1913). German Expressionism is represented by Lake near Moritzburg, by *Erich Heckel* (1909), and Coast scene with red hill, by *Alexei Jawlensky* (1911). Surrealism is seen in The empty mask, by *René Magritte,* and something of abstract art in Three figures with black, by *Willi Baumeister* (1920).—Sculptures in the circular gallery and the small gallery adjoining it include Head of Augustus John by *Jacob Epstein* (1916) and Madame Chia Pi by the same artist (1942).

APPLIED ART is generally shown on the first floor balconies round the main hall. The Welsh china is a particular interest, much of this being Swansea and Nantgarw of the Nance Collection (E. Morton Nance, died 1953, author of 'The Pottery and Porcelain of Swansea and Nant Garw'). Also displayed, British and European glass; the Jackson Collection of Spoons, including a unique Anglo-Saxon spoon, a spoon bearing perhaps the earliest extant example of the London hallmark, and a complete set of 13 Apostle Spoons (Sir Charles Jackson, died 1922, author of 'History of English Plate' and of 'English Goldsmiths and their Marks'); ceramic, japanned wares, ivory and the Investiture Regalia of the Prince of Wales. There is also an exhibition (changed monthly) showing the work of modern artist-craftsmen.

C.   *Llandaff Cathedral

Llandaff Cathedral (12–13C), in the suburb of the same name rather over 2m NW of the city centre, is reached by Cathedral Road or, by walkers, through the parks either side of the Taff.

History. That this was once a pagan site is known from the evidence of pre-Christian probably Romano-British burials discovered under the W part of the cathedral. Tradition connects the founding of the church with St. Teilo (died c 580), appointed Bishop of South Wales by St. Dyfrig (died c 546), and it is known that a pre-Norman church stood here or near here. Another saint, associated with Teilo and Dyfrig, was Euddogwy, the trio being the reason for the three mitres on the present coat-of-arms of the see. The existing church was begun c 1120 by Bishop Urban who, though probably a Welshman, would have been appointed by the Normans. Of this early church the chief remains are the Norman arch dividing the presbytery from the Lady Chapel and some traces of blocked windows in the S wall of the presbytery. It seems that the completion of the nave was delayed by some 50 years, for the N and S doorways (perhaps no longer *in situ*) date from c 1170. Two events of the 12C may be mentioned, one being the death of Geoffrey of Monmouth at Llandaff in 1154, and the other the visit in 1188 by Archbishop Baldwin, accompanied by Giraldus, preaching the Third Crusade (the next visit by an Archbishop of Canterbury would not be until 1972). The present nave and chancel arcades, as well as the W front, which was flanked by EE towers, date from the earlier 13C, and the chapter house was completed in 1250. In 1266 the cathedral was the scene of a great dedication service, which coincided with the enthronement of Bishop William de Braose, during whose time the Lady Chapel was added in Geometrical style. During the 14C the nave walls and aisles, which on the N had apparently begun to lean outwards, were rebuilt, and large windows with pointed heads were inserted. The presbytery was also remodelled by the cutting of arches through Urban's outer walls and windows, and the medieval history of the fabric closed with the rebuilding of the NW tower by Jasper Tudor.

There followed nearly 300 years of neglect. The building was already in dangerous decay by 1575; Cromwell's soldiers used the nave as a tavern and post office, and the font as a pig trough, and burnt the cathedral's books at a formal ceremony at Cardiff Castle; after storms in 1703 and 1723 the SW tower collapsed and the nave roof fell in; and in the 18C 'restoration' took the strange form of an Italian Temple, built within the walls by John Wood, better known for his work at Bath.

Real restoration began in 1835 when Precentor Douglas devoted two years of his stipend to this purpose. Later years saw the removal of Wood's temple (all that remains are two urns outside the NW of the cathedral); the restoration of the Lady Chapel, presbytery, choir, and part of the nave; and the reopening of all these parts for divine service in 1857, Much of the later restoration was under the care of John Prichard, son of a priest of the cathedral and a pupil of Pugin, who rebuilt the SW tower, gave the chapter house its distinctive roof, added the row of sovereigns' heads (S wall; modern heads N wall), and carved four Evangelists on the E face of the tower, It was Prichard's partner, J.B. Seddon, who brought in the Pre-Raphaelite work in glass, carving, and painting. In 1880 Dean Vaughan refounded the Cathedral School (perhaps founded in the 9C), abandoned in the 17C. In January 1941 a German landmine destroyed virtually the whole of the previous century's work, Llandaff being, next to Coventry, the worst damaged of Britain's cathedrals. Restoration, completed in 1960, was largely by George Pace, who added the parabolic concrete arch, the Welch Regiment Memorial Chapel (David Chapel), and the Processional Way.

EXTERIOR. Llandaff is unique among British cathedrals in having no transepts, and the absence of a triforium is also remarkable in so early a building. Externally the most notable feature is the gracefully irregular W front with its 13C centre. The curious pendent tympanum of the doorway (there never was a central shaft) has an original statue (St. Dyfrig or St. Teilo), and in the apex of the gable there is a Majesty. The S doorway of the nave (c 1170) is a rich example of Norman Transitional work. Jasper Tudor's NW tower is of Somerset design, but the elaborately panelled battlement and pinnacles are modern. The SW tower and spire, rebuilt from Prichard's designs of 1869 and bearing figures of saints and clerics, resemble those found in southern Normandy. Prichard and his father are buried in the churchyard near the SE door.

The INTERIOR is at once striking, the dominant feature being Pace's concrete arch, surmounted by a cylindrical organ case (with gilded Pre-Raphaelite figures, formerly in the niches and canopies of the pre-war choir stalls) bearing Jacob Epstein's huge Christus in unpolished aluminium. The effect is to separate nave and choir while not interfering with the lower level vista. The long arcades of the *Nave* and *Choir*, with foliated capitals, are 13C; the flat-panelled ceiling is modern, the hardwood being from Central Africa and Malaya. At the NW corner of the nave is the *Illtyd Chapel*, dedicated to the fallen of the 53rd (Welsh) Infantry Division. The Rossetti Triptych (1846–64) here, forming the reredos of the high altar until 1939, illustrates the Seed of David; Swinburne, Burne-Jones, and William Morris and his wife were the models. The font, at the SW corner of the nave, is by Alan Durst (1952) and depicts Man's fall, Christ's Redemption, and scenes from the lives of SS. Dyfrig and Teilo. Most of the windows in the S aisle are Pre-Raphaelite, but the small panels in the second window are English 17C glass. Above the S door hangs a Madonna and Child, attributed to Murillo. In the *South Presbytery Aisle* a 10C Celtic Cross is the only relic of the pre-Norman church; hidden at the time of the Commonwealth, it was found in 1870 in the garden of the Bishop's Palace. The *Teilo Chapel*, at the E end of the S aisle, contains an albaster figure of Lady Audley (?early 15C).

The *Lady Chapel* (c 1287), finely proportioned and with lovely vaulting, contains in its NE corner the tomb of the builder, Bishop William de Braose. The E window tracery is 19C, and the glass is modern. In the niches of the 15C reredos are bronze panels, each with a wild flower named in Welsh in honour of Our Lady. The richly carved *Urban Arch* dividing the Lady Chapel from the *Presbytery* is a remnant of Bishop Urban's church of c 1120. On the S side of the presbytery, on the site of St. Teilo's shrine, is a 13C effigy of the saint. The silver-gilt shrine, a centre of pilgrimage, stood here until the Reformation when the canons dismantled it rather than have it destroyed, the various pieces soon disappearing. Note the remains of the old Norman window on the S wall. On either side of the altar are heavy Florentine candlesticks (17C), and the windows above the Urban Arch contain stained glass by John Piper and Patrick Reyntiens (who together also did a huge window in Coventry cathedral). In the *Choir* the Bishop's Throne and the stalls are 19C work (restored 1960).

The *Dyfrig Chapel*, the E end of the N aisle, is so called because Urban is said to have buried the saint's bones here in an attempt to boost his cathedral's reputation. It contains the badly broken 14C reredos (originally 3-tiered), removed from its place behind the high altar during the 19C restoration, and, to its S, the tombs of Sir David Mathew, standard bearer to Edward IV at Towton in 1461, and of Sir Christopher Mathew (died 1500). The family had the right to burial in this N aisle until the 18C when they failed to continue to maintain the roof. Six porcelain panels on the W Organ Case were designed by Burne-Jones and are from the Della Robbia pottery at Birkenhead; the model was Elizabeth Siddal, wife of Rossetti and inspiration to the Pre-Raphaelites. West of the organ case is the *Euddogwy Chapel*, commemorating the third saint traditionally associated with the founding of the cathedral and now the memorial chapel of the RAF Auxiliary Squadron. Here, opposite a painting of the Assumption (15C, on board), is the marble monument of Dean Vaughan (died 1897) by Goscombe John. Farther W, on the S side of the N aisle, a modern pulpit commemorates Archbishop John Morgan (died 1957), below it being another Mathew tomb (Sir William and his wife, 1526).

The Norman *Teilo Doorway* leads into Pace's *David Chapel* (1956), the memorial chapel of the Welch Regiment, with furnishings that are gifts from Commonwealth regiments. In the *Processional Way* (also 1956) there hang four medieval gargoyles, rescued from the damage caused by the 1941 landmine.

CATHEDRAL CLOSE. On the green, immediately S of the cathedral, are a restored *Cross* and the remains of a 13C *Bell-Tower*, a ruin since the early 15C; traditionally Exeter cathedral's bell known as 'Great Peter' came from here. Beside the green are the modern Deanery and Canon's Residence, while to the E a pleasant garden (1972) is surrounded by fragments of the former *Bishop's Palace*.

In the village, near the main crossroads, is *St. Michael's Theological College* (1907), with a chapel by George Pace.

Francis Lewis, a signatory of the American Declaration of Independence, was born in Llandaff in 1713.

D. **Welsh Folk Museum

The Welsh Folk Museum (Tel: 0222-569441 or 555105), the largest of the branch museums of the National Museum of Wales, is at St. Fagans, some 4m W of central Cardiff (M4 Junction 33). Long a requirement, a museum on this scale became possible in 1946 when the Earl of Plymouth offered St. Fagan's Castle to the National Museum of Wales, at the same time transferring 80 acres of park on generous terms.

From the main entrance (car park and picnic area) the museum is toured as three individual parts—the Galleries, with exhibitions, shop, restaurant, offices and other facilities; the Outdoor Museum, with its superb range of re-erected buildings; and the Elizabethan St. Fagans Castle.

Working craftsmen may include a woodturner, a cooper and a saddler, and there are additional demonstrations on Saturdays in summer.

The three indoor GALLERIES are devoted to Agriculture, Costume, and Material Culture, this last comprising several small sections illustrating aspects of the domestic, social and cultural life of Wales.

The OUTDOOR MUSEUM, with its fine range of re-erected buildings—cottages, school, chapel, farms, smithy and much else, from many parts of Wales and spanning from the 15C into the early years of the current century—is in two adjacent parts, the Park and the Castle Grounds, linked by a short tunnel. New buildings are added as opportunity offers. Visitors may wander at will (see plan), starting from the rear of the Galleries and ending at St. Fagans Castle. From here it will be necessary to return through the tunnel to regain the car park. For visitors in search of architectural detail, the museum's illustrated guide can be strongly recommended.

ST. FAGAN'S CASTLE is an attractive Elizabethan mansion, built between 1560 and 1590 on the site of a 12C stronghold the 13C curtain wall of which survives. The house has been whitened to restore it to its probable early appearance.

History. The early castle was built by Sir Peter le Surs, on whom Robert FitzHamon, the Norman conqueror of Glamorgan, bestowed the lordship of St. Fagans (Fagan, or Fugatius, may have been a missionary sent to Britain by Pope Eleutherius during the 2C). By the early 16C the castle was already a ruin, but in 1560 a part of the estate came into the possession of Dr John Gibbon, who built the present house, incorporating something of the old N wall. In 1616 Sir Edward Lewis of Caerphilly bought the estate; in 1648 the parish was the scene of a battle in which Parliament under Horton and Jones decisively defeated the Royalists under Poyer and Laugharne; and in 1730 the estate passed by marriage to Other Windsor, 3rd Earl of Plymouth. By the early 19C the place was in serious disrepair, but in the 1860s considerable restoration was carried out, the main staircase was probably inserted, and the tower and servants' hall were built. In 1946 the Earl of Plymouth donated the castle to the National Museum of Wales which in 1981–83 carried out major refurbishment, largely restoring the castle's 17C appearance and period-furnishing the rooms.

The formal **Gardens**, to the N of the house and within their old wall, are generally 18C in landscaping and include topiary, and herb, knot and rose gardens, this last once a part of the village green. There are two bronzes by W. Goscombe John (Joyance and the Elf); and in front of the house (E side) stands a massive lead cistern dating from 1620.

Visitors tour the period-furnished rooms, of particular interest being the Long Gallery with its 17C Mortlake tapestries, and the Kitchen, left largely as it was when first built with its two large open 16C fireplaces. The utensils and furnishings span the 16 to the 18C,

Welsh Folk Museum

particularly noteworthy being the spits (especially the dog-driven one), and the bacon rack and bread crate suspended from the ceiling.

37 The Valleys

The Valleys covered by this Route are Rhondda, Cynon, Taff, Rhymney and Ebbw. The first four are described as from Cardiff; Ebbw, which includes Sirhowy, as from Newport.

Until the second half of the 18C these valleys, a fan of often steep-sided and quite narrow clefts reaching some 20m into the South Wales mountains, were virtually untouched wild countryside. Change came with the Industrial Revolution which in this part of Wales exploded through the combination of high grade coal in the valleys, the plentiful iron ore along their heads and the several ports that could readily be developed at their feet. Communications were at first primitive; by packhorse or mule along atrocious tracks. But soon canals were dug, the Glamorgan Canal between Merthyr Tydfil (and later Aberdare) and Cardiff being opened in 1794, closely followed by the Monmouth Canal in 1796 and the Swansea Canal in 1798. A measure of the speed of industrial development can be judged from the fact that the 50,000 tons carried on the Glamorgan Canal in 1820 had increased to 350,000 tons by 1839. The usefulness of the canals lasted some 50 years, until the railways took over; the Taff Valley railway was authorised in 1836, and the Rhymney dates from 1854–64. By the middle of the 19C the valleys, though untouched on their heights, had below been transformed into disfigured strips along which jostled towns, mines, iron and associated works, canals, roads and railways.

The first step in a long decline came with the invention of improved processes for the large-scale manufacture of steel. These processes demanded better quality iron ore, this in turn meaning either the closure of iron works or their transfer from the heads of the valleys to the coast with its fast-developing ports where foreign ore could be imported and treated. The depression, two wars, the replacement of coal by oil and the need for steelworks to be near the ore ports combined to bring about an accelerating decline, and after the last war it became clear that two related steps demanded urgent attention. The first was the substitution of diversified industry for the mining and heavy industry of the past, an aim now in large part achieved, with modern industrial estates now proliferating and continuing efforts by the Welsh Development Agency (set up in 1976) to attract increasing investment. The second requirement was reclamation, the removal or at least the softening of the scars of the past. This task began to be tackled seriously in the 1960s, although progress was slow and by 1966 only some 99 acres had been treated. The Aberfan tragedy of 1966, when a sliding tip killed 144 people, including 116 children, shocked public opinion and subsequent achievement, now largely the responsibility of the Welsh Development Agency, has been notable with many thousands of acres converting to industrial estates, recreation areas, country parks and suchlike.

The opinion, still widely held, that these valleys are a 'black country' is now far wide of the mark. Admittedly there are some seemingly endless urban areas, some ugly industrial patches and even the occasional colliery, but far commoner features today are the long, low terraces of houses, built in local stone, brightly painted and lining the contours; the clean industrial estates; and the smooth, green landscaped hills that not so long ago were hideous tips. Contrasts can be as frequent as unexpected, and from most places there is quick access on foot or by car to the generally untouched moorland above. Today, the roads ascending the valleys provide convenient, not uninteresting, and often scenic links between the coast and Brecon Beacons National Park.

A.   Rhondda Valley
(Cardiff to Hirwaun)

A470 to Pontypridd. A4058 to Treorchy. A4061 to Hirwaun. Total distance 29m.—*5m.* **Castell Coch.**—*6m.* **Pontypridd.**—*3m.* **Porth.**—*6m.* **Treorchy.**—*9m.* **Hirwaun.**

Comprising the two valleys of Rhondda Fawr and Rhondda Fach, and with a chain of small towns, **Rhondda** is a borough of some 89,000 people. The borough stretches from Pontypridd to Hirwaun Common, is an average of 4m wide and is typical of the general description of The Valleys given above.

With Cathays Park on the E, Cardiff is left by North Road, followed, after crossing the inner bypass (A48), by Northern Avenue. The valley of the Taff is then ascended.—*5m.* ***Castell Coch** (WHM. Tel: 0222-465511), to the E of the main road and romantically perched on a steep wooded slope guarding a glen, is a folly built in 1875–79 by William Burges for the 3rd Marquess of Bute. But, unlike many, this is a folly claiming historical ancestry, for it stands on the massive foundations of a 13C stronghold, recorded as having already been in ruins centuries ago but today still with fragments surviving in the base of the tower nearest to the car park and in its dungeon. The name, too, Red Castle, is that of the early castle which was built of red sandstone. Today's building, a fantasy both in construction and interior decoration, is triangular with at each angle a round tower crowned by a conical roof. Drawbridge and portcullis are working copies of the originals, and the castle's rooms are decorated with romantic murals with scenes from Aesop's fables and Greek mythology, birds, animals and suchlike.—*1m.* *Taff's Well* was at one time noted for its tepid medicinal springs. At *Nantgarw*, just beyond, a porcelain, now greatly valued by collectors, was produced for a short period in the early 19C. Beyond Nantgarw the road passes *Treforest Trading Estate*, founded in 1936 and the first such in Wales.

5m. **Pontypridd** (34,000 inhab.), an industrial town at the confluence of the Taff and the Rhondda, owes its name (meaning Bridge by the Earthen House and coined only in the mid 19C) to a graceful bridge (now disused) over the Taff, built in 1736, in a then wooded rural setting, by one William Edwards, a local stonemason, after two unsuccessful attempts. The bridge, 35ft above the river, has a single span of 140ft forming a segment of a circle 170ft in diameter; a special feature of the design is the lightening of the haunches by three cylindrical tunnels on each side, thus lessening the inward and upward thrust of the masonry and reducing wind resistance. In *Ynysangharad Park*, within the loop of the E bank of the river, statues by W. Goscombe John commemorate Evan and James James (1809–

78 and 1833–92), father and son and author and composer of the Welsh national anthem (1856); down-to-earth mill owners, they stand here looking improbably bardic. For rehearsals by the local Male Voice Choir, Tel: 0443–206440.

Rtes 37B and 37C continue N, while this Route bears NW, now ascending the valley of the lower Rhondda and soon reaching the *Rhondda Heritage Park* (Tel: 0443–682036) where, in refurbished buildings of the Lewis Merthyr colliery (closed 1983), dramatic interpretive presentations tell the story of the men and women and of the 'black gold' of the south Wales valleys and, in particular, of Rhondda, 'the most famous mining valley in the world'. Ambitious plans include more presentations, a village of the 1920s, a country park, a Valleys' chapel and much else.—*3m.* **Porth** was once a miners' town but is today successfully busy in the manufacture of artificial flowers. The name means Gateway, a reminder that Porth is at the junction of the Rhondda Fawr and Rhondda Fach valleys, this Route following the former.

2m. **Tonypandy** was the scene of mining riots in 1910.—*4m.* **Treorchy** is well known for its Royal Male Voice Choir, the oldest in Wales, granted its title by Queen Victoria after a Command Performance at Windsor in 1885 (rehearsals, Tel: 0443–435852).—*2m.* *Treherbert*, beyond which the road, built in 1930–32 by unemployed miners, climbs the NE flank of the head of the valley, crossing Forestry Commission land with several waymarked paths.—*4m.* **Hirwaun Common Pass** (1600ft) affords a sweeping view northwards towards the Brecon Beacons beyond the partly industrialised valley below. Late Bronze and early Iron Age finds at Llyn Fawr (below, NW) are in the National Museum of Wales; and a sign indicates the start of the Coed Morgannwy Way walk to Afan Argoed (13m) and Margam Park (23m), both on Rte 35. Descending in a large loop, the road in *3m* reaches **Hirwaun** on Rte 31.

B.   Cynon Valley (Cardiff to Hirwaun)

A470 to Abercynon. A4059 to Hirwaun. Total distance 25m—*11m.* **Pontypridd.**—*3m.* **Abercynon.**—*2m.* **Aberdare.**—*3m.* **Hirwaun.**

For Cardiff to (*11m*) **Pontypridd**, see Rte 37A.—*3m.* **Abercynon** is, in industrial historical terms, known as the southern end of Richard Trevithick's tramway along which in 1804 he ran his famous steam locomotive (see Rte 31, Merthyr Tydfil).—A470 (Rte 37C) continues N, while this Route bears NW up the valley of the Cynon to reach (*8m*) **Aberdare** (40,000 inhab.), a typical Valleys' town which a century and a half ago was no more than a village although the Abernant Ironworks started up in 1802. But Aberdare's roots reach far back and *St. John's Church* is a centuries-old foundation, surviving parts of which are of the late 12C; the unusual ironwork gates outside the W door were made at the Abernant works. Victoria Square is the town centre, and here stands the blacksmith Griffith Rhys Jones (or Caradog; his first choir was called Cor Caradog), alert with poised baton, a vivid recall of the days (1872 and 1873) when under his leadership the South Wales Choral Union twice won the Crystal Palace Cup. *Dale Valley Country Park* (1972), to the W of the town, has been created on land that formerly was ugly colliery and tips; today this is a valley of trees and waymarked trails touching both natural history and some local industrial archaeology along the Industrial Trail which, starting in the town, for most of its length follows the course of the old Dare Valley Railway (leaflet from Park Warden).—*3m.* **Hirwaun**, see Rte 31.

C.   Taff Valley (Cardiff to Merthyr Tydfil)

A470. Total distance 23m. *14m.* **Abercynon.**—*2m.* **Treharris.**—*2m.* **Aberfan.**—*5m.* **Merthyr Tydfil**.

For Cardiff to (*14m*) **Abercynon**, see Rtes 37A and B.—*2m. Quakers Yard*, at the foot of the Bargoed valley, takes its name from a Quakers' burial ground. It is a part of **Treharris**, a name recalling the principal shareholder in Harris's Navigation Pit (1894). *Llancaiach Fawr* (1m E on B4254. Tel: 0443–412248), a semi-fortified manor of c 1530, today serves as a living history museum of the Civil War.— *2m.* **Aberfan**, the place where in 1966 Pontglas School and a row of houses were engulfed by a sliding coal tip. Of the 144 dead 116 were children, and a memorial garden now softens the site of the school.— The valley becomes more upland in character and at (*2m*) the typical mining village of *Troedyrhiw* it widens considerably.—*3m.* **Merthyr Tydfil**, see Rte 31.

D.   Rhymney Valley (Cardiff to Rhymney)

A469. Total distance 19m.—*5m.* **Thornhill.**—*2m.* **Caerphilly.**—*7m.* **Bargoed.**—*5m.* **Rhymney**.

With Cathays Park on the E, Cardiff is left by North Road, followed, after crossing the inner bypass (A48), by Caerphilly Road, passing through the suburb of *Llanishen* with (E off the main road) a huge complex of government tower-offices.—*5m.* **Thornhill**, 1m to the E of which is *Parc Cefn-Onn* (acquired by the city of Cardiff in 1944), some 200 acres of open country and wooded hillside noted for rhododendrons and azaleas and affording good views. *The Wenallt* (750ft. 140 acres), 1m SW of Thornhill and also belonging to the city, is a rolling expanse of woodland and heath with views across Cardiff to the Bristol Channel.—From the watershed (888ft), ½m N of Thornhill, there is a panoramic view down to Caerphilly and the valleys beyond.

2m. **Caerphilly** (29,000 inhab. *Inf.* Park Lane. Tel: 0222–851378) is an industrial and market town (Carrefour hypermarket) which seems to have started as a Roman station (Caer) and later added the name of St. Fili (6 or 7C), who may have been the son of that St. Cenydd who founded a priory at Llangenydd on Gower. The town was long famed, possibly as long ago as the 13 or 14C, for a bland, white cheese. However the market closed in the early 1900s and the cheese is now made in various other places, notably in Somerset.

For Caerphilly Male Voice Choir rehearsals Tel: 0222–861959.

Caerphilly Castle, the largest in Wales

** *Caerphilly Castle* (WHM. Tel: 0222-465511), the model for the concentric plan adopted by Edward I, is, after Windsor, the largest castle in England and Wales. The castle's defences are notable for their elaboration and ingenuity, and for today's visitor interest is added by working models of some of the medieval siege engines developed to overcome such defences.

History. The earliest fortification here was the Roman fort of c 75, the site of which is now occupied by the Civil War earthwork (the Redoubt) to the NW of the castle. In 1268 Gilbert de Clare, fearful of the threat to Cardiff from Llewelyn the Last, began to build a castle here, but this was destroyed in 1270 by Llewelyn when he invaded the surrounding district of Senghenydd. The following year Gilbert de Clare started again, continuing to build despite a siege by Llewelyn, whom he eventually forced to withdraw. From the Clares Caerphilly passed in 1317 to the Despensers, Edward II finding brief refuge here from Isabella. After this the castle lost its military value and before the middle of the 16C had already fallen into decay. During the Civil War a redoubt for artillery was built beyond the NW of the castle, but later Cromwell drained the lakes and blew up the towers, his attempt on one of which (SE) clearly being only partially successful. Later Caerphilly passed via the earls of Pembroke to the Butes, the 4th Marquess in 1935–37 making careful and extensive restoration before handing the castle over to the Crown.

The castle is a magnificent example of the concentric plan, borrowed, largely through the experience of the Crusades, from Europe and the Near East. It comprises four separate groups of fortification, these being the castle proper, a complex of two concentric wards completely surrounded by a lake; a large barbican system to the E of this, defended by an outer moat; a large hornwork on the W; and, to the NW, the outlying Civil War redoubt. The lake (c 15 acres), created by damming the small Nant-y-Gledr, washed the outer defences on the S and W and was separated only by a narrow bank from the moat (itself filled from the lake) which on the N side flanked the outer ward.

The visitor's approach is across the EAST BARBICAN, a line of embattled curtain wall, in places 60ft high, stretching N and south. This wall, sheltering a raised earthen platform and strengthened by several bastions, also formed a dam for the lake. Approximately in the middle there is a large Gatehouse, which was approached by two drawbridges resting at their ends on the hexagonal stone pier that still survives in the outer moat. The two halves of this barbican could be defended independently, as they were divided by a transverse wall, 20ft high, across the platform. The doorway that connected them was sealed by a portcullis and by a drawbridge over the adjoining overflow channel, which controlled the amount of water in the lake. At the N end of the N platform there is a postern. On the S platform are the remains of a mill, worked by water from the lake, and beyond, at the S end, a large gateway, facing W to prevent the barbican being outflanked and commanding the brook at the point where it was dammed.

The Inner Moat, formerly with a drawbridge, is crossed to the castle proper, the OUTER WARD being reached through the ruins of its E gate. This ward, which surrounds the inner with a wide terrace, was defended by the moat on every side except the south. Its outer boundary was little more than a breastwork above the revetted scarp of the moat, but it was reinforced by wide semicircular bastions at the corners. Just S of the outer ward entrance there are the ruins of what may have been a granary, and, against the wall of the building next to the leaning tower, are the remains of an oven.

The INNER WARD has massive gatehouses on the E and W, both with half-drum-towers to the field. The East Gatehouse is the more impressive and contains on its second floor a hall and (S) an oratory. Of the drum-towers at the angles of the ward, blown up by Cromwell, that on the NE has largely disappeared, while that on the SE survives as a 50ft high segment overhanging its base by 11ft 6ins. The other towers have been restored. The Great Hall is along the S side of the ward. It was probably rebuilt c 1317 by Hugh le Despenser. Note the ball-flower ornament inside. Now restored, the hall is sometimes used for official and charity functions. To the E of the hall are the buttery and a small chapel, together now used as modern kitchen and boiler house; and to the W is a range of state apartments. The Kitchen, very unusually placed, projects S into the outer ward, which, with the adjoining watergate, it effectively blocks on this side. Communication with the fortifications here was by a covered gallery, reached from the ground at the SW corner of the inner ward.

Opposite the W gatehouse of the outer ward, perhaps originally the castle's principal entrance, is the large revetted HORNWORK of c 3 acres, once defended by yet another moat and drawbridge. Beyond, to the NW, is the REDOUBT, the site of the Roman fort, possibly also the site of Gilbert de Clare's first castle, and in the Civil War used for artillery.

B4263 ascends the Nant-y-Aber NW from Caerphilly to (3m) the former mining village of *Senghenydd*. The worst colliery disaster in Britain occurred here in 1913 when 439 miners were killed as the result of an explosion.

4m. **Ystrad Mynach** (meaning, for reasons unknown, the Valley of the Monk) stands at the crossing with A472 leading W to the Taff and Cynon valleys and E to the Sirhowy and Ebbw valleys. *Hengoed Viaduct*, just N, with its lofty curve of 16 arches, dates from 1857; once carrying one of the busiest rail stretches in southern Wales, its line has now long been closed but the viaduct survives as a listed reminder of Victorian energy.—The road now enters an urban strip, skirting *Blackwood* (to the E) and crossing B4254.

GELLIGAER CIRCUIT. An interesting short clockwise round of 4m (to Bargoed) may be made through Gelligaer and across the southern part of Gelligaer Common. *Gelligaer*, reached in 1m, is an upland village of Roman if not prehistoric ancestry with a church of some interest. Selecting this high ground on their road from Cardiff to Brecon's Y Gaer, the Romans built their fort here, probably early in the 2C, and its outlines are still clearly seen behind the church. This church, dating from the 13C but certainly successor to an earlier one and perhaps also standing on a prehistoric ritual site, houses 14C stocks and also the St. Gwladys stone (9–10C), formerly on Gelligaer Common (1m NW along the Romans' Heol Adam) where it stood with *Capel Gwladys* (chapel), founded by this saint (a daughter of Brychan and thus a sister of the martyred Tydfil) in the 6C and still represented by a modest wall and circular enclosure close to the road descending from the common to Bargoed. Along this road, 1m from its leaving Heol Adam, a southerly track leads in a few yards to the earthwork traces of Roman practice camps.

3m (by A469) **Bargoed**, long a valley village, grew rapidly during the 19C and especially after the opening of its colliery in 1897; today the town is notable for its rows of contoured terraces. *Pengam Glassworks* (Stuart Crystal), in Angel Lane, Aberbargoed (A4049, E of Bargoed), offer factory tours enabling many aspects of glass manufacture to be viewed (Tel: 0443–820044 or 831617).—*5m.*

Rhymney was an important iron town—the first works opening here in 1800—but little survives though the past is recalled by pub names such as the Puddlers' Arms and the Blast Furnace. St. David's Church (1843) was endowed by the ironworks company.

Beyond Rhymney, in 1½m, A469 joins Rte 31.

E. Ebbw and Sirhowy Valleys (Newport to Ebbw Vale)

B4591 to Abercarn. A467 to Aberbeeg. A4046 to Ebbw Vale or A467 to Brynmawr. Total distance 17 or 18m—6m. **Sirhowy Valley.**—1m. **Cwmcarn.**—2m. **Newbridge.** 3m. **Aberbeeg.**—5m. **Ebbw Vale** or 6m. **Brynmawr.**

B4591 runs W from Newport's St. Woolos Cathedral (see Rte 35), in 2m reaching **Rogerstone**, with the *Fourteen Locks Canal Interpretation Centre* (Tel: 0633–894802) on the Monmouthshire and Brecon Canal which during the 19C played such an important part in the industrialisation of this part of Wales. Near a complex of locks, tunnels and weirs, the Centre tells the story of the canals of Gwent. The road continues through industrial **Risca** to (4m) **Crosskeys**, at the junction with A4048 which ascends the Sirhowy Valley.

SIRHOWY VALLEY. In 5m A4048 crosses A472 linking (W) Rhymney Valley and (E) Ebbw Valley. Passing *Blackwood*, the road reaches the valley's head at **Tredegar** (14m from Crosskeys), a former iron-working town and colliery centre. *Bedwelty House*, on the southern approach to the town and now Council offices, is a good example of an ironmaster's home of the early 1800s (admission during normal working hours). For the Orpheus Male Voice Choir rehearsals, Tel: 04925–3620. Aneurin Bevan (1897–1960), the Labour politician, was born in Tredegar.

1m. **Cwmcarn** is the starting-point for the Forestry Commission's *Scenic Forest Drive* (Tel: 0633–400205), seven miles of mountain forest with superb views both N towards the Brecon Beacons and S to the Bristol Channel. The woodland here, mostly dating from the 1920s, is successor to the medieval Forest of Machen, destroyed over the centuries by the demands of sheep, tanning, iron smelting and mining. There are several car parks and picnic sites, two of these, in the SE part of the drive, being just below the hillfort of Twmbarlwm (1374ft).

1m. **Abercarn** an industrial town.—1m. **Newbridge** has a fine Roman Catholic church (1939) by P.D. Hepworth. A472, linking Abercynon (W) to Pontypool (E) is crossed at Crumlin, a northwards extension of Newbridge. The large fan-ventilation engine of Crumlin's Navigation Colliery (1907–68) is now in the Welsh Industrial and Maritime Museum, Cardiff, and Penyfan Pond (1½m. NW), once a colliery feeder lake, is now a country park.—3m. **Aberbeeg**, where there is a choice of valleys, the W fork (A4046) being Ebbw Fawr, and the E (A467) being Ebbw Fach.

Along EBBW FAWR the town of **Ebbw Vale** is reached in 5m. A crowded industrial town once dependent on coal and steel, Ebbw Vale was seriously affected by British Steel Corporation's problems during the 1970s and steel making ended in 1978. For the local Male Voice Choir rehearsals, Tel: 0495–305636.

Along EBBW FACH the industrial town of **Abertillery** (40,000 inhab.) is reached in *1m*. A small museum in the Library covers local industrial history and provides a leaflet guide to a Town Trail illustrating the 19C and 20C development of this once rural valley.— *5m*. **Brynmawr**, see Rte 31.

38 Swansea

SWANSEA (Abertawe. 172,500 inhab.)—an industrial, residential and academic city and port, as also the main shopping centre of south-west Wales—sprawls along the NW shore of Swansea Bay, mostly on the right bank of the mouth of the river Tawe. The docks stretch away from the left bank and, with industry confined to the perimeter, the city centre, largely reconstruction after air raid damage during the last war, is spacious and modern. Development has allowed for extensive parks and gardens.

City Centre. The Kingsway—Circus—Princess Way—Oystermouth Road—Westway.

Tourist Information. Singleton Street. Tel: 0792–468321.

Airport. Fairwood Common (5m W).

Entertainment. *Grand Theatre:* Touring productions. *Patti Pavilion:* Variety. Family shows. *Brangwyn Hall:* Concerts. *Dylan Thomas Theatre:* Amateur and professional productions. *Male Voice Choir*, Tel: 0792–206239.

History. The name probably derives from Sweyn's-ey, suggesting that Swansea originated as a Viking settlement, possibly founded by Sweyne Forkbeard who is known to have been active in the Bristol Channel. The castle was first built by the Norman Henry de Newburgh, or Beaumont, who in 1099 led an expedition into Gower, and the town which grew around it received a charter from William de Braose in 1210. Later, the castle was destroyed by Owen Glendower. Shipbuilding and coalmining began in the Swansea district in the 14C, if not before, and trade was early established with Ireland, France, and the Channel Islands. Swansea furnished ships for coast defence for Elizabeth I. In the Civil War the town was Royalist until 1645, when Colonel Philip Jones, a native Parliamentarian, was made governor; the town later received a charter from Cromwell. By 1700 Swansea was the largest port in Wales. Smelters were attracted to the district (many from Cornwall) by the rich coal, and in the 18C numerous copper works were developed (mostly a little inland; the first at Landore), Nelson's ships being sheathed with Swansea copper. In the 19C not only copper, but silver, lead, tin, nickel, zinc, cobalt, and iron ores were imported for smelting and refining on a large scale. For a short time too, in the early 19C, Swansea porcelain was a noted local manufacture. The Swansea Canal, opened in 1798, had a rapid effect on the trade of the port, which increased from 90,000 tons in 1799 to 500,000 tons by 1839, and the first of the enclosed docks (North Dock) was opened in 1852, South Dock following in 1859. Both these docks were on the W bank of the Tawe. As steelmaking developed in the area, and as tinplate and coal became the principal exports, pressure grew for more docks and two were built on the E bank between 1879 (Prince of Wales) and 1909 (New King's). The copper smelting industry began to decline from c 1880, and later, with the rest of South Wales, Swansea suffered from two wars, the depression, and the ousting of coal by oil. This last, however, was turned to good account when in 1918 the first oil refinery in Britain was opened near Swansea, the associated Queen's Dock for tankers following in 1920. During the Second World War (1941), the town centre was so badly damaged by bombing that rebuilding afterwards was to a new plan.

Among eminent natives are Bishop Gower (died 1347), who founded and endowed the original Swansea Hospital; Philip Jones (1618–74), the Parliamentarian; Beau Nash (1674–1762); Count Albert de Bellerocle (1864–1944), the painter, and friend of Manet, Degas, and Lautrec; and Dylan Thomas (1914–53), the poet. Richard Savage, the poet, lived here in 1739–40, on a pension of £50 to which Pope contributed £20.

Swansea

CENTRE. The heart of modern Swansea clusters within a square (each side some 500 yards long) bounded by four streets: Princess Way on the E, Oystermouth road on the S, Westway on the W and The Kingsway along the north. Within this square will be found Tourist Information, the Grand Theatre, the Covered Market (food) and two shopping precincts, the Quadrant Centre and St. David's Square.

NORTH OF THE CENTRE. At its E end The Kingsway runs into The Circus, out of which, on the opposite side, the pedestrian College Street quickly reaches High Street, Swansea's pre-war main street, which leads N to the *Railway Station.*

Belle Vue Way, out of the NW of The Circus, in about 100 yards meets the junction of Grove Place (SW) and Alexandra Road (NE), a short distance along the latter being the **Glyn Vivian Art Gallery** (Tel: 0792–655006). Here the emphasis tends to be on temporary exhibitions and workshop activities, including activities for children, the permanent collection displays depending to a large extent on the space left available. However, pictures by modern Welsh artists, including Augustus John, are likely to be found, while Applied Art will probably include Swansea and Nantgarw porcelain, 17C and 18C glass, and collections of English and Continental paperweights and miniatures.

EAST OF THE CENTRE. On its E side the modern centre is defined by Princess Way, parallel to the E being Castle Street and Wind Street, with, beside the former, the remains of the *Castle.* However, this is not the ruin of Henry de Newburgh's castle, destroyed by Owen Glendower, but of a fortified manor built on the old castle's site in 1330–32 by Bishop Gower. Surviving features are a circular turret, and a tower with the open arcading characteristic of Gower's work. Below the castle is the site of the North Dock of 1852, Swansea's first enclosed dock but now filled in.

SOUTH OF THE CENTRE. Here, immediately S of Victoria Road and its westward extension, Oystermouth Road, there are two museums and the **Leisure Centre** (Tel: 0792–649121). Opened by HM The Queen in 1977 while on her Jubilee tour, the Centre caters for an impressive range of activities, at the heart of the complex being the pool area with waves and a water slide. Behind the Leisure Centre, beside the Marina Main Basin, is the **Maritime and Industrial Museum** (Tel: 0792–470371), also opened in 1977 and a principal feature of Swansea's marina and maritime quarter concept. The museum is devoted to the history of the port of Swansea and of the industry of the city and its environs, together with material on transport and agriculture. Among the exhibits are locomotives, vehicles, the Mumbles tram and ship models. There is also a Woollen Mill, brought here from Neath and still producing, while various boats are moored alongside in what was once the South Dock of 1859 and is now the Marina Main Basin.

The **Royal Institution of South Wales: Swansea Museum** (Tel: 0792–653763), a short way NE, off Victoria Road, is the museum of one of the oldest learned societies in Wales, founded in 1835 and then called the Swansea Philosophical and Literary Institution. The name was changed in 1838 when Queen Victoria consented to became patron. The oldest museum in Wales, and unashamedly old-fashioned, the museum is well worth visiting if only as a museum of a museum; its future, though, is frequently in doubt and seems likely to bring change or even closure. Broadly, the themes of the collections are archaeology, natural history, some geology and Welsh history. Archaeological material includes finds from the Paviland caves; a

Roman milestone from the military road between Nidum (Neath) and
Bovium (Boverton); the Gwindy and Penard Roman coin hoards; a
Roman altar with traces of Ogham inscription; the Gnoll Stone, the
shaft of a Celtic cross of c 1100; and a collection of medieval heraldic
tiles from Neath Abbey. The Natural History section offers several
good dioramas, while within the wide scope of Welsh History may be
mentioned exhibits as diverse as Welsh porcelain; a reproduction of
an early 19C Gower kitchen; a coracle; a horrendous man-trap; a
fascinatingly practical preaching chair; and souvenirs of the
Mumbles tramway.

The *Dylan Thomas Theatre*, just S of the Royal Insititution, stages
both amateur and professional productions, while the *Swansea Arts
Workshop* is opposite the theatre.

WEST OF THE CENTRE most places of interest are strung along
Oystermouth Road and its continuation, Mumbles Road, which run
W close to the shore, the latter reaching Oystermouth (see Rte 39) in
some 4m from the Leisure Centre. The **Guildhall** (Tel: 0792–650821),
built by Sir Percy Thomas in 1934, is set back but nevertheless
conspicuous for its lofty tower. Here the *Brangwyn Hall* (concerts)
shows the British Empire Panels by Sir Frank Brangwyn, originally
painted as a war memorial for the House of Lords, and Brangwyn
sketches also hang in the corridors. *Victoria Park*, immediately W of
the Guildhall, includes the Patti Pavilion, once the opera singer
Adelina Patti's Winter Garden at Craig-y-Nos (Rte 33) and now used
for various forms of entertainment as also for conferences.

The **University College of Wales**, in the large Singleton Park a
mile farther W, includes Singleton Abbey, formerly the seat of Lord
Swansea, and adjacent modern buildings. One of the constituent
colleges of the University of Wales, the college was founded in 1920.
Here the *Taliesin Arts Centre*, with the *Ceri Richards Gallery* (named
after the Swansea artist), is open to the public (Tel: 0792–295438).
The Gallery both shows the College's art collection and also mounts
a programme of special exhibitions of both fine and applied art, while
the Taliesin surrounds show sculpture. Singleton Park, behind the
university, reaches a good 1/2m northwards, towards its NE end being
the Educational Garden with conservatories and rare and subtropical
plants. *Brynmill Park*, immediately E of Singleton, offers ornamental
gardens, a lake and a children's zoo, and *Cwmdonkin Park*, 3/4m
farther NE, was a favourite of the poet Dylan Thomas (memorial).

Mumbles Road, curving S, in rather over 1/2m from University
College reaches Ashleigh Road, or, beyond, Derwen Fawr Road, both
providing approaches to *Clyne Valley Country Park* of over 700
acres.—For **Oystermouth** and **Mumbles**, some 2m farther S, see Rte
39.

For Swansea to *Llandovery, Llandrindod Wells* and *Knighton*, see Rte 24; to
Merthyr Tydfil and *Abergavenny*, see Rte 31; to *Brecon* and *Hay-on-Wye*, see
Rte 33; to (E) *Cardiff, Newport* and the *Severn Bridge*, and to (W) *Carmarthen*,
see Rte 35; for *Gower*, see Rte 39.

39 Gower

Tourist Information. The principal office is Tourist Information, Singleton Street, Swansea. Tel: 0792–468321. Also, but summer only, Oystermouth Square, Mumbles. Tel: 0792–361302.

The **GOWER PENINSULA**, a mass of carboniferous limestone some fifteen miles long by four to eight miles broad projecting from Swansea into the Bristol Channel, is officially designated an Area of Outstanding Natural Beauty, known for its S coast bays, beaches and rocky cliff scenery. The bays, often with limited and expensive parking, can be very crowded in summer. The natural features along the peninsula's spine are, from E to W, Fairwood Common (with Swansea's airport), Cefn Bryn and Rhossili Down, these last two being old red sandstone uplands (over 600ft) affording long vistas. In the W the peninsula ends at the great sandy sweeps of Rhossili and Broughton bays, while the N shore is largely salt marsh. Much of Gower's scenic land, whether cliff, common or marsh, is owned by the National Trust, and there is nearly always footpath access. Indeed, walking is one of the best ways to see many parts of Gower, perhaps the most popular stretches being those between Port Eynon Point and Rhossili, and from Rhossili northward along Rhossili Down to Llangennith and Llanmadoc.

Once Gower was the home of lions, elephants, rhinoceros, hippo-potamus, mammoth, bison, bear and others; animals whose bones have been discovered in the peninsula's many caves. And primitive man was here too, as evidenced by Palaeolithic remains (c 17th millennium BC) found in some caves, notably Paviland. The fact that access to these caves is now often difficult (and even dangerous) and subject to the tide indicates a major change in sea level, or, in some cases, that the carcases of larger animals could have been dragged in by, perhaps, wolves or hyenas. Finds from the caves may be seen in the National Museum of Wales (Cardiff) and at Swansea's Royal Institution.

Also of interest on Gower are prehistoric burial chambers, Iron Age hillforts, ruined medieval castles, nature reserves, and churches (usually basically 13C) notable for their small chancels and battle-mented towers, the latter recalling the days when churches rather than castles were the ordinary person's places of refuge.

In the 12C Henry I planted Flemish colonists in Gower, a source to which some local people still trace their ancestry.

The description that follows starts at Oystermouth-Mumbles, then making a meandering clockwise circuit of, including diversions, some 40 miles to return to Swansea.

Oystermouth is known for its ruined *Castle*, strikingly placed on a green hill above the N end of the town (Tel: 0792–468321).

History. There appear to have been a series of Norman wooden structures here, the first perhaps put up by Henry de Newburgh in c 1099. The first mention of a castle is 1215 when, the lordship having been given to the De Braose family by King John, a castle was burnt by the Welsh. Rebuilt, it was again destroyed by the Welsh in 1256–57 when Llewelyn the Last was in Gower. The keep, the nucleus of today's ruin, probably dates from c 1280 as it is known that Edward I visited here in 1284; the gatehouse and the ward walls are of a few years later. Afterwards the lands passed to the Mowbrays, who during the 14C converted the castle to residential use (the wings to the E and W of the keep dating from this period), and eventually to the Beauforts who presented the castle to Swansea in 1827.

The Gatehouse, originally flanked by two towers, of which traces remain, gives access to a single ward. Immediately on the left is the guardroom, beside which steps lead up to one of the governor's apartments, popularly though for no good reason known as the White Lady's Chamber. The ruins of the barracks are on the right of the ward, and those of kitchens on the left. At the top of the ward is the Keep, the oldest part of the castle, to its left being a three-storey building with a cellar, state rooms, and, on the middle floor, the banqueting hall. To the right is another three-storey building, comprising a basement kitchen (note the roasting-jack holes by the fire), what may have been either a priest's or retainers' room, and, at the top, the chapel, with an aumbrey and a piscina.

Oystermouth *Church*, reputedly built on the site of a Roman villa, has a battlemented 13C tower and an Early English E window. In the churchyard is the tomb of Dr Thomas Bowdler (1754–1825), who by expurgating Shakespeare added his own name to the English language.

Mumbles, the name deriving from the French 'mamelles' meaning 'breasts', strictly refers only to the two islets (accessible at low water) off the promontory beyond Ostermouth, but today the name is generally applied to the whole promontory town, a popular area with a pier. On the outer islet are a lighthouse of 1793 and a fort of 1861, and to the W of Mumbles are popular *Langland Bay* and *Caswell Bay*.—*3m. Bishopston* (on B4436), from where the National Trust's narrow and wooded Bishopston Valley (footpath) winds for nearly 2m down to Pwlldu Bay. Just W of Bishopston is *Pennard* where the 15C church incorporates parts—possibly two lancets in the chancel; a window with moulding in the nave S wall; the font, and the beam supporting the gallery—of an earlier church buried by the dunes to the W near the scanty remains of 13 or 14C *Pennard Castle*, the main surviving features of which are the gate-towers.

Pennard Cliffs is a fine stretch of National Trust land of 248 acres reaching from Pwlldu Head W to Southgate. Below the cliffs are *Bacon Hole* and *Mitchin Hole*, both caves in which ancient animal bones have been found (c 1850), and Mitchin Hole also providing evidence of human occupation during Roman times and the Dark Ages.

From Pennard, B4436 runs briefly N to join A4118, rather over *1m* W along which, from the village of *Parkmill*, a lane leads N to a meadow in which lies prehistoric *Parc le Breose Burial Chamber*, discovered in 1869 and, on excavation, found to contain the scattered bones of some two dozen people within the four chambers off the long passage. The name of the site is of course more modern and recalls the early 13C De Braose owners of Oystermouth Castle. In Cathole, a cave a few hundred yards N of the burial chamber, flint tools found in 1968 suggest human occupation in around 12,000 BC—*1m. Penmaen*, to the S of which are Penmaen Burrows, with traces of a Norman earthwork, an ancient chapel and a prehistoric burial chamber (park beside, or roughly opposite, the post office; then follow path signed Tor Bay for some 500 yards).—*2m. Penrice Park*, within which is Penrice Castle (visits by written application), a ruin of the middle and late 13C (it was built by the Mansel family, of Norman origin) consisting of an irregular single ward with a gatehouse to the N and a round keep to the W, this last being the oldest part of the castle (c 1250). Adjoining the E curtain there is an early

16C dovecot, and the castle stands above a late 18C mansion with a 19C E wing.

From Penrice Park entrance the road dropping S to (*1m*) **Oxwich** crosses a part of *Oxwich National Nature Reserve*, with freshwater marsh on the W and saltmarsh followed by dunes on the east. Of both botanical and ornithological interest, the Reserve also includes, on the N, Crawley Wood and, on the S, Oxwich Wood. Parking is only allowed in the official car park, where there is an information centre; there is no restriction on access to the beach and dunes, but for elsewhere a permit is needed. The small church, a little S above the shore, dates from the 13C and has a tiny chancel which may be a Celtic cell, and tradition holds that the ancient font was brought here by St. Illtyd. The so-called Castle remains are those of a Mansel manor built in c 1541.

From Oxwich, A4118 can be rejoined by following the minor road along the W flank of Penrice Park through (*1m*) the village of *Penrice*, with an early Norman motte or other earthwork and, on the green, the base of a medieval cross. On reaching A4118 a left turn, soon followed by a right turn, leads in about *1m* to **Reynoldston**, whence a road heading E climbs on to **Cefn Bryn**, a ridge (610ft) of open common affording fine views. To the N, and visible from the road, is *Arthur's Stone*, a large burial chamber capstone formed of an erratic block of millstone grit, 14ft by 7ft and weighing around 25 tons. Farther along the road, just S of where it kinks NE, there is a holy well.

1m (from Reynoldston) **Knelston**, where there is a ruined 12C church, and, just beyond, **Llanddewi**, with a church in which the nave and chancel are curiously out of line, presumably due to different building periods. Here too is the *Gower Farm Museum* (Tel: 0792–390130 or 391195), set within original farm buildings, offering a choice of farm trails and showing a variety of animals.

From Llanddewi this Route now travels S to Port Eynon Point and then W to Rhossili and Worms Head. From here walkers may cross Rhossili Down to Llangennith, but motorists must return to Llanddewi to continue the Gower circuit.

3m (from Llanddewi) ***Port Eynon Point** is beyond the village of the same name at the finish of A4118. This limestone headland, affording long coastal views as also across to Somerset and Devon, is a National Trust property above two caves; one, at the point's S tip, was a repository of prehistoric animal bones, while Culver Hole to the W was largely man-made in the 15C as a dovecot. Some of the best cliff walking in Gower, much of it across National Trust land, is between Port Eynon Point and Worms Head.

Returning to (*2m Scurlage*, B4247 is now followed W to (*1m*) *Pilton Green*. From here there is a footpath to (1m) Pilton Cliff, below being *Paviland Caves* (access difficult, and only possible at low water), famous for having been the home of man at around the end of the Ice Age, for it was here, in Goat's Hole in 1823, that Dr Buckland found part of the skeleton of a young man, since scientifically dated to the 17th millennium BC (the bones, stained with ochre, were at first incorrectly identified, their owner becoming known as the Red Lady of Paviland). This man would have been a member of one of the groups of hunters who over centuries moved along this coast as the ice receded, while flints and ornaments also discovered here are evidence that men continued to use these caves over a span of millenia.—*1m*. *Pitton*, less than 1m S of which is *Thurba Head* (200ft), with the remains of an Iron Age hillfort settlement, the head marking the S arm of Mewslade Bay, one of the most scenic of the bays along this coast. Red Chamber, a cave just E of Thurba, is so called from the ochre colouring of its walls.

1m. **Rhossili**, a village at the W end of B4247 (huge parking area; also National Trust visitor centre), lies above the S end of the 5m long great sandy crescent of remote and often windswept Rhossili Bay which marks the W extremity of Gower. One tradition is that the village is named after St. Fili, possibly a son of St. Cenydd (see below). In the church, with a 12C doorway, there is a memorial to Petty Officer Evans, born here, who perished with Scott in the Antarctic in 1912.

The **Gower Coast Nature Reserve** (National Trust and Countryside Council for Wales) includes a Limestone Trail and Worms Head. The *Limestone Trail* (in part dangerous cliff; booklet from Visitor Centre), a 3m anticlockwise circuit starting from and returning to Rhossili car park, passes seven points of interest, the first being a spot from which the remains of a ship, the 'Helvetia', can be seen on the beach where she was wrecked in 1887. 2. Old Castle, on the seaward side of the track, represents the earthwork traces of an Iron Age defended settlement. 3. Rhossili Vile is an open field system of narrow strips dating from Saxon times and largely still in use today. 4. Kitchen Corner, where limestone was quarried in the 18 and 19C and then loaded into boats at the foot of the cliff. 5. Coastguard Lookout, where the southerly slope acts as a suntrap which, with the limestone below, enriches this spot with plant life. 6. Tears Point is a flat-topped headland of bared limestone, the surface of deposits several thousands of feet deep. 7. Fall Bay, with a raised beach of conglomerate shells.—*Worms Head*, deriving its name from the Norse for serpent, consists of two rocky islets connected with the mainland by a natural causeway for about 2½ hours either side of low tide and with each other by a narrow neck of rock. The outer head rises abruptly to a height of 200ft, and ancient animal bones have been found in the cave at its foot, which must in those remote times have been a lot more accessible. The water thrown up by the blowhole near the W extremity can be seen from Rhossili.

Rhossili Down, a National Trust property of over 500 acres and a launch-pad for hang-gliders, stretches for nearly 2m northward from Rhossili village. The *Beacon* (633ft), near the S end, is the highest point in Gower. Farther N, on the E slope, there are two burial chambers known as *Sweyne's Howes*, 'howes' being the ancient word for 'mound' and one tradition being that this is the burial place of Sweyne Forkbeard, said to have given his name to Swansea.

As noted earlier, walkers can cross Rhossili Down to Llangennith, but motorists must return some *6m* to Llanddewi, from where small roads N and then W in rather under *4m* reach **Llangennith** where the church is of interest, if only as an example of continuity. The largest church on Gower, it is a 12C rebuilding of the church of a small priory founded here in the 6C by St. Cenydd and destroyed by Viking raiders in 986. The tower, curiously placed N of the nave, has a saddle-back roof and is a good example of the Gower fortified type, and an ancient graveslab inside the church may be that of St. Cenydd.

Burry Holms, 2m NW (1m walk), an islet marking the N arm of Rhossili Bay, may be accessible for about two hours each side of low water. On the islet there are traces of Iron Age earthworks and the ruins of a medieval monastic chapel, while at low water the remains may be seen of the 'City of Bristol' which ran ashore in Rhossili Bay in 1840; and in this area, too, have been found doubloons and other coins from a Spanish galleon wrecked in the 17C.

2m (backtracking E, then N) **Cheriton**, where the 13C church is one of the most pleasing in Gower, noteworthy features being the S doorway, the good Early English arches and the tower with its saddle-back roof. The church at *Llanmadoc*, ½m W of Cheriton, is said to have been founded by St. Madog, a follower of St. Cenydd; however his simple church has long disappeared and rebuilding of 1865 left little of its 13C successor. The *Bulwark*, belonging to the National Trust, is a large hillfort to the S of the Cheriton to Llanmadoc road.

Whitford Burrows, the peninsula reaching N into Burry Inlet, is a nature reserve of dunes and saltmarsh. Cars must be left at Llanmadoc (Cwm Ivy, just N) and visitors are asked to keep to the paths, one of which (4m) starts from the Warden's house and heads out towards Whitford Point. Visitors are warned that swimming is dangerous and that unexploded shells may be found away from the paths.

Approaching (*1m* from Cheriton) *Landimore* there are fragments of a castle.—*1m.* **Weobley Castle** (WHM. Tel: 0222-465511) is the ruin of a large 13–14C fortified manor well illustrating the era in which comfort was becoming almost as important as security. Owned by the De la Bere family until the 15C and damaged during Owen Glendower's uprising, the property later passed to the Herberts and the Mansels. Beyond the 14C gatehouse there is a single ward with the mid 13C keep, the oldest part of the castle, to the right. The remaining ruins, mostly later 13C, include the chapel, completing the S side, and the kitchens and hall on respectively the E and north. From a more remote era, there is a standing stone in a field behind Windmill Farm, S of the road and roughly opposite the castle approach.—At (*1m*) *Llanrhidian* a stone on the green, possibly the remains of the village cross, seems later to have been used as a pillory, and in the village church porch there is a carved stone bearing human and animal figures and thought to date from the 9C. Note also, on the exterior S wall, the intriguing rhymed epitaph of Robert Hary (died 1646).

B4271 is now followed E for (*5m*) *Fairwood Common* (Swansea airport), whence A4118 reaches central **Swansea** (see Rte 38) in a further *5m*.

40 Carmarthen

CARMARTHEN (14,000 inhab.), in Welsh Caerfyrddin, the county town of Dyfed, rises from the W bank of the Towy some 8m above the river's mouth. Coracles, of a local oval type, may occasionally be seen on the river.

Tourist Information. Lammas Street. Tel: 0267–231557.

History. Carmarthen is the site of the Roman Caer Maridunum, the ruined walls of which were still standing in the time of Giraldus (12–13C) and something of the amphitheatre of which survives today. Later, in popular Dark Ages mythology, Merlin, or Myrddin to give him his native name, was born here, son of a king's daughter and, so she claimed, of a spirit. In c 1096 the Normans established a castle and walled borough here, the former being restored by Edward I c 1313, in which year the town was granted its first charter, soon becoming an important port and centre of the wool trade, exporting to Flanders and elsewhere and in 1353 being declared the staple (monopoly) wool centre of Wales. Prosperity was interrupted in the early 15C, when the town was taken by Owen Glendower in 1403 and 1405, but by 1450 the first festival officially using the name 'eisteddfod' could be held here; metrical rules codified for this occasion are still applied to the Chair Poem of the National Eisteddfod. In 1555 Robert Ferrar, Bishop of St. David's, was burnt at the stake in what is now Nott Square as soon as the heresy laws were reintroduced by Mary I. During the Civil War the castle was held for the King, but soon capitulated (1646) to General Laugharne and was later slighted. Carmarthen continued to prosper as both port and administrative and trading centre; iron smelting and tinplate works were established in the 18C and trade was boosted by the arrival of the railway in 1856. Change and some decline followed the port developments farther E along the coast (the tinplate works closed in 1900), Carmarthen gradually becoming of administrative rather than industrial importance.

Sir William Nott (1782–1845), victor of the First Afghan War; Brindley Richards (1819–65), composer of 'God Bless the Prince of Wales'; Sir Lewis Morris (1833–1907), the poet, and E. W. Tristam (1882–1952), best known for his work in preserving medieval wallpaintings, were natives of the town. Sir Richard Steele, the Irish man of letters, died of a stroke in King Street in 1729.

The **Guildhall**, at the hub of several pedestrian streets, may be regarded as the town centre; rebuilt in 1767, it is successor to one of 1583. Nott Square, just SE, is named for the victor of the First Afghan War (1841–42), while in an earlier context a monument recalls the martyrdom in 1555 of Bishop Ferrar, To the SE, on a bluff above the river, County Hall occupies the site of the *Castle*, the only surviving features of which are a length of curtain wall and a 14C gatehouse.

The more interesting parts of the town are to the NE, King Street leading out of Nott Square and in some 300 yards reaching 12–14C **St. Peter's church**, with a fortified tower. In the S chapel is the altar-tomb, with effigies, of Sir Rhys ap Thomas (died 1525), supporter of Henry Tudor, and of his wife, and here too are memorials to Bishop Ferrar, Sir Richard Steele and General Knott, while Carmarthen's Roman ancestry is represented by a Roman altar in the W porch. Priory Street, leading NE beyond St. Peter's Church, is a name recalling that an Augustinian priory once stood between here and the river; founded in about 1130, and burnt in 1435, this priory was the place at which the 'Black Book of Carmarthen', the oldest manuscript extant in Welsh, was written in the late 12C (now in the National Library, Aberystwyth).

At the junction of Priory Street and Oak Lane (300 yards from the church) stood, until recently, Merlin's Oak, probably planted by a local schoolteacher in 1660 to honour the Restoration of Charles II. Later, however, this oak assumed Merlin mythology (that Merlin had prophesied that should the oak fall, so also would the town), but by the 1980s it had become no more than a dry and withered stump, now removed to the entrance to the Civic Hall (Knott Square) while a short length has found a home in the Carmarthen County Museum. The remains of the *Roman Amphitheatre* are beside the main road about ¼m farther east.

ENVIRONS OF CARMARTHEN. The **Carmarthen County Museum** (Tel: 0267–231691) is at Abergwili on A40 2m E of Carmarthen. In a former palace of the bishops of St. David's, the museum illustrates regional archaeology (with some Ogham/Latin stones), history, natural history and daily life. It was at this palace that Bishop Davies and William Salesbury worked together to produce their Welsh Book of Common Prayer and New Testament (1567).—*Bryn Myrddin*, or *Merlin's Hill*, just N of A40 1m E of Abergwili, claims, as of course do many other places throughout Britain, to be where Merlin sleeps.

A house called Tygwyn, at *Llangunnor* opposite Carmarthen on the E bank of the Towy, was once the property of Mary Scurlock, Sir Richard Steele's second wife and the 'Dearest Prue' of his letters. Steele lived here from 1724 until his death in 1729, and is remembered by a monument in the church.

At **Llansteffan** (or Llanstephan), 7m S of Carmarthen on the W bank of the Towy approaching its mouth, a large ruined *Castle* overlooks the estuary. Built during the 11–13C, but successor to earlier defensive earthworks on this site, the castle's main feature is a fine gatehouse of 1280 which seems to have been converted to a keep and living quarters. *St. Anthony's Well*, ¼m SW of the castle, a wishing well said to have had medicinal properties, has a niche in which the figure of a saint perhaps once stood.

For Carmarthen to *Swansea, Cardiff* and the *Severn Bridge*, see Rte 35; to *Aberystwyth* via *Aberaeron*, see Rte 41A and via *Lampeter* and *Strata Florida*, see Rte 41B; to *Cardigan, Fishguard* and *St. David's*, see Rte 42; to

Haverfordwest and *St. David's* or *Fishguard*, see Rte 43; to *Tenby*, *Pembroke* and *Milford Haven*, see Rte 44.

41   Carmarthen to Aberystwyth

A.   Via Aberaeron

A484 and A486 to Synod Inn. A487 to Aberystwyth. Total distance 47m.—*7m. Cynwyl Elfed.*—*8m.* **Llandyssul.**—*10m. Synod Inn.*—*6m.* **Aberaeron.**—*13m.* **Llanfarian.**—*3m.* **Aberystwyth.**

The first part is scenically pleasant, ascending narrow, winding and wooded valleys and passing a number of wool mills. Later, this Route crosses duller country. For the first 13m, Rte 42 coincides with this one.

Carmarthen, see Rte 40.—*3m. Bronwydd Arms*, starting-point of the Gwili Railway, a private venture (formed 1975) aimed at preserving a stretch of the old Great Western Line between Abergwili and Llanpumpsaint and offering a short ride by steam or diesel (Tel: 0656–732176 or 0267–230666).—A484 ascends the twisting wooded valley of the Gwili, in *4m* reaching *Cynwyl Elfed*, just before which B4333 bears NW offering an upland shortcut to Newcastle Emlyn (Rte 42) while this Route continues N, now ascending the Duad, for (*2m*) *Cwmduad*, where the valley divides into three, A484 choosing the central one.—In a further *3m* a road fork is reached at which Rte 42 bears away NW, soon reaching (in under 2m) the Museum of the Welsh Woollen Industry, a branch of the National Museum of Wales.—The Teifi is crossed before (*3m*) **Llandyssul**, birthplace of Christmas Evans (1766–1838), orphan son of a cobbler who became a Baptist minister because his first choice, the Presbyterians, demanded an academic standard he did not have. Mainly active in Anglesey, he attracted huge crowds to his oratorical and fiery sermons. Llandyssul is a wool centre, with a number of mills, one of which, *Maesllyn*, is a working museum (Tel: 023975–251). And the *Church* here is also of interest for its Norman tower into which a 6C inscribed stone had been built.—*10m. Synod Inn*, where A487 (Rte 46) comes in from the south-west.

The small seaside resort of **New Quay**, 4m N by A486, is built on a steep rocky slope over a sandy bay. From New Quay Head (300ft) there is a view across and around Cardigan Bay to The Lleyn, Snowdonia, Cader Idris and Plynlimon.

6m **Aberaeron** (1500 inhab. *Inf.* The Quay. Tel: 0545–570602) is a small place of some character with a number of Georgian-style houses, notably in Alban Square to the E of the main through road. The small harbour can be crossed by cable car (1988; successor to the Aeron Express of 1885–1932), and on the Quay there is a popular *Aquarium* (Tel: 0545–570142). For Aberaeron to *Dolaucothi* and *Brecon*, see Rte 27.—*1m.* At the church at *Llanddewi Aberarth* there are two incised stones, one a 9C cross and the other hog-backed.—*12m.* **Llanfarian**, where Rte 41B joins from the E just before the river Ystwyth is crossed. About 1½m beyond the river a crossroads is reached whence Rte 23B heads E along A4120 for Devil's Bridge and beyond. This Route here turns NW, passing on the left *Pen Dinas*

(415ft), a ridge between the rivers Ystwyth and Rheidol marked by a monument to the Duke of Wellington and a hillfort, the latter interesting in that there seem originally to have been two separate enclosures, joined into one during the 1C BC.—*3m*. (from Llanfarian) **Aberystwyth**, see Rte 22.

B. Via Lampeter and Strata Florida Abbey

A485 to Lampeter. B4343 to Pontrhydfedigaid. B4340 and B4575 to Llanfarian. A487 to Aberystwyth. Total distance 52m.—*5m. Pont-ar-Sais* (for **Llanpumpsaint**).—*11m*. **Llanybydder**.—*5m*. **Lampeter**.—*4m. Llanfair Clydogau.*—*4m*. **Llandewi Brefi**.—*3m*. **Tregaron**.—*6m. Pontrhydfendigaid* (for **Strata Florida Abbey**).—*11m*. **Llanfarian**.—*3m*. **Aberystwyth**.

Carmarthen, see Rte 40.—A485 heads N, on the outskirts of Carmarthen leaving *Abergwili*, with the Carmarthen County Museum (see Rte 40) 1m to the E along A40.—*5m. Pont-ar-Sais*, 1½m W of which is **Llanpumpsaint**, the Church of the Five Saints. These were Ceitho, Celynen, Gwyn, Gwyno and Grynnaro, brothers (during the 6C) and members of the Cunedda family which, being semi-royal, presumably had little problem in arranging this mass sanctification. In the church the medieval altar-slab bears nine consecration crosses.—Beyond Pont-ar-Sais the road crosses hilly wooded country, with, on the W, several roads to Llandyssul and, on the E, hill roads across to the Cothi valley.—*11m*. **Llanybydder**, a weaving centre on the E bank of the Teifi with a number of mills open to visitors, is also known for its monthly horse fairs.—*1m. Pencarreg*, where the church is worth a visit for its curious ancient font bearing human heads.

4m. **Lampeter** (2000 inhab.), or Llanbedr Pont Steffan, lying below wooded hills on the W side of the Teifi at the crossing of several roads and at one time known for its river ford, has long been the chief centre for the upper Teifi valley. *St. David's College*, the oldest Welsh degree-granting institution, was founded in 1822 by Bishop Burgess of St. David's for Church of England students but in 1971 became a constituent college of the University of Wales. The original buildings, by C.B. Cockerell (1827), are grouped around a quadrangle and lie within pleasant grounds which, contrastingly, contain both an ancient motte and modern university buildings. For Lampeter to (W) *Aberaeron* and (E) *Brecon*, see Rte 27.

A485 provides the fast and direct approach to Tregaron, but this Route chooses the quieter and more interesting B4343 along the E bank of the Teifi, across the river being a succession of hillforts—Castells Olwen, Allt-Goch and Goetre—all, however, minor.—*4m. Llanfair Clydogau*, once the site of Roman silver mines, was on the Roman Sarn Helen. Southward from here this military highway (now modern minor roads) reached the Dolaucothi gold mines; northwards, Sarn Helen crossed the river and in about 4m reached the fort of Bremia (see below).

4m. **Llanddewi Brefi**, where St. David (Dewi) attended a synod in 519, possibly convened to refute the Pelagian heresy but more probably for the enactment of local rules of discipline. The *Church of St. David* stands on a holy mound which, tradition insists, rose under the saint as he preached here; with, it is said, the voice of a trumpet, inspired by the Holy Spirit perched on his shoulder in the form of a dove. Today's church, however, although some 700 years old, is considerably more recent than this theatrical occasion, having been built in around 1287 in association with a college established here by Bishop Beck of St. David's for a precentor and 12 prebendaries. Nevertheless, in keeping with its dramatic past, the church's transepts suddenly collapsed during the 19C. Inside the church there are some venerable stones, one, the tallest, being known as St. David's Staff and another bearing an Ogham inscription. This latter has been sadly mutilated, one suggestion being that it commemorated a heretic of the persuasion which David came here to denounce. But perhaps the most interesting corner of this church is the NW exterior angle of the nave, where, forming part of the fabric of the upper wall, two stones (one of them upside down) bear some fragmentary Latin inscription. Once, certainly in the late 17C, these two stones were a part of a single free-standing memorial in the churchyard and Llanddewi Brefi indeed owes much to a scholar of 1698 who, realising that this memorial dated back to long-lost centuries, recorded the full inscription. It read then: 'hic jacet idnert filivs jacobi qui occisvus fvit propter predam sancti david', or 'Here lies Idnert son of Jacobus who was slain because of the plunder of the Sanctuary of David'. Idnert is generally accepted to have been the murdered Bishop of Llanbadarn Fawr (see Rte 22), but what is important here is not so much Idnert's identity as that this is the earliest known inscription referring to St. David, one carved moreover within a century or so of when he was here. The sad thing is that during the 18 or 19C the nave needed repair and the mason responsible—presumably illiterate, certainly no antiquarian, but quick to spot a useful stone—broke it up and incorporated its pieces in the wall. Today only two separated fifths of the original can be seen, the remainder probably embedded elsewhere in the wall with the inscription tantalisingly buried inwards.

From Llanddewi Brefi Roman enthusiasts may cross the river to meet A485, then turning left to pass the junction with B4578, the arrow-straight modern form of Sarn Helen. Just S of this junction a lane to the left crosses a small humped bridge over a disused railway and arrives at a farm where permission can be asked to visit what remains of the fort of *Bremia*, today no more than seemingly haphazard banks and ditches and a few sorry stones which may represent the baths.

3m. **Tregaron** (4000 inhab.), a small market town and centre for the surrounding hill sheep farms, owes it name to Caron, a local chieftain and self-declared bishop of the 2–3C. Twm Shon Catti (Rte 24) was born here (1530), as was also Henry Richard (1812–88), advocate of international arbitration and founder of the Peace Union, to whom there is a memorial. At *Llangeitho*, 4m W, a centre of Methodism, there is a statue to the Rev. Daniel Rowlands (1713–90), the revivalist, who was born there. For the drover hillroad, across to (18m) *Llanwrtyd Wells*, see Rte 24.

Cors Caron Nature Reserve lies immediately W of B4343 for a distance of 4m N from Tregaron. The reserve, an area of some three square miles either side of the meandering Teifi and of particular interest to botanists and ornithologists, includes three raised peat bogs, the largest being on the W side and the other two on the east. The bogs are 'raised' in that they appear as domes with the centre up to 20ft higher than the edge. This feature has developed over millennia through several stages: briefly, the dropping of glacial moraine forming a dam; the growth of a lake; the silting of the lake, the arrival of vegetation, and the formation of a fen; the vegetation rots, becoming waterlogged, sinking, and under pressure turning to peat; and the shaping of a dome because the peat has formed more easily above the waterlogged centre than above the edges from where the rainfall can seep away. The natural state of the bogs has been damaged by peat cutting (which however ended in 1960), the W bog being the least affected but the other two having only the centres of their domes undisturbed. The reserve can be well viewed from the disused railway embankment below which there are parking areas.

6m (from Tregaron) *Pontrhydfendigaid* means 'Bridge near the ford of the Blessed Virgin'.

*Strata Florida Abbey (WHM. Tel: 0222-465511), 1¹/₂m. SE, was once one of the most celebrated abbeys in Wales.

History. The name is a Latinised form of 'Ystrad Fflur' meaning 'Plain of Flowers'. Although this abbey, a Cistercian house, is known to have been founded in 1164, tradition suggests that there may have been a predecessor, perhaps Cluniac, near Old Abbey Farm, 1¹/₂m S of Pontrhydfendigaid, where in the 19C foundations were excavated and removed. The founder of 1164 was probably Robert FitzStephan, a vassal of the Clares. Two years later his lands were overrun by Rhys ap Gruffydd. Grandson of the founder of the earlier house, and perhaps finding Cistercian ideals of simplicity and poverty akin to local monastic tradition, Rhys refounded the abbey in 1184 and began the existing church, although he died before its dedication in 1201. The greater part of the ruins date from this time, or a few years later (the E extension of the presbytery). The chapter house and the monks' choir are of the 14C, while the cloister is 15C or early 16C. The abbey, wholly Welsh in character, was the political, religious, and educational centre of the country in the 12C and 13C, in 1238 witnessing an assembly of Welsh princes summoned by Llewelyn the Great to swear allegiance to his son Dafydd. Economically the abbey flourished largely from wool, provided by the sheep which grazed on its lands which extended as far as Rhayader. During the Owen Glendower troubles the abbey was abandoned as such, being used as military stables. The building of the stone cloister dates from some time after the return of the monks. After the Dissolution the estates passed through various hands, the Crown assuming responsibility for the ruins in 1931.

Apart from remains of the cloister and the chapter house, the ruins seen today are those of the church. At the entrance there is a small *Exhibition* telling something of the story of the Cistericans and of the abbey. Here too are fragments of sculptured work of a delicacy and richness strangely at variance with the orthodox Cistercian severity of this period.

The CHURCH, in Transitional Norman style, is on the usual Cistercian plan, having an aisled nave of seven bays, transepts (each with three chapels), and an aisleless presbytery. At the W end of the *Nave* the doorway (not quite in its original medieval form) is richly ornamented, with a framing cluster of rolls, continuous from the ground, tied together at intervals by bands ending in crosier-like ornaments. Inside, the arcades were of unique local character, the clustered piers being raised on plain screen walls c 5ft high, an arrangement not known elsewhere in England or Wales though occasionally found in Ireland. The *Crossing* was filled by a monks' choir, with screen walls largely blocking all directions except east. On the E of the choir narrow openings gave access to the *Transepts*, each with three E side chapels, originally vaulted. Remains of altars can be seen, and many of the medieval tiles have been relaid (not *in situ*). The designs on the tiles merit study. In the N transept there is a memorial (1951) to Dafydd ap Gwilym (c 1320–80), described by

Borrow as 'the greatest of his country's songsters'. Born near Aberystwyth, he may be buried either here at Strata Florida or at Talley. The *Presbytery* belongs to two periods, the two W bays being the earlier part and the E bay an addition of c 1250. Later came two more alterations. In the 14C the floor was raised, two steps being placed under the E arch of the crossing; and in the 15C the altar was raised and moved W, leaving space behind for two chapels. Some of the tiles laid during the 15C alteration have been reset. Beyond the S end of the S transept is the *Sacristy*, with doors from both the cloister and the transept.

The CHAPTER HOUSE, immediately S of the sacristy, is in two parts and of two periods (13C and 14C), the oldest masonry being the SE and E wall remains. It seems that the older E part of the building was abandoned, becoming part of the cemetery (note the two graves through the walls). Rhys ap Gruffydd belonged to the princely house of Dynevor, many members of which were buried here. It is thought that the line of tombs outside the angle of the S transept and presbytery represents earlier burials (two of the headstones bear pre-Norman ornamentation). Later burials were in the chapter house, where one slab has been exposed. The CLOISTER, with two doors to the S aisle, had five bays on its N side, each with a window, some of the sills of which survive. The alcove at the centre of the N side was for a lectern. After the Dissolution the W walk was divided into rooms which, with the now ruined W building, formed part of a house.

Teifi Pools, a cluster of small lakes in wild country 2½m NE of the abbey and accessible by a lane and paths, are the source of the Teifi.

B4343, leading N from Pontrhydfendigaid, in 8m reaches *Devil's Bridge* on Rte 23B.

B4340 is now followed NW through *Ystrad Meurig*, where there are traces of a castle of the Clares. Beyond, reaching Ystwyth Forest, the Ystwyth is crossed; there is a FC picnic site ¼m E of the bridge beside the road on the S bank.—*6m* (from Pontrhydfendigaid) *Black Covert, Trawscoed*, near the junction of B4340 and B4575, is another FC picnic site and the start of a forest walk which includes a hillfort and a butterfly reserve.—*5m* (by B4575) *Llanfarian*, where Rte 41A is joined. For Llanfarian to (*3m*) **Aberystwyth**, see Rte 41A.

42   Carmarthen to Cardigan, Fishguard and St. David's

A484 to Cardigan. A487 and B4582 to Nevern. A487 to St. David's. Total distance 60m.—*15m* Henllan—*3m*. **Newcastle Emlyn**.—*3m*. *Cenarth*.—*7m*. **Cardigan**.—*7m*. **Nevern**.—*2m*. **Newport**.—*7m*. **Fishguard**.—*16m*. **St. David's**.

Over the latter part of this Route diversions should be made down side roads in order to enjoy the coastal scenery.

For **Carmarthen** (see Rte 40) to (*12m*) road junction A484/A486, see Rte 41A.—*3m*. *Henllan*, for the Teifi Valley Railway (Tel: 0559–371077) offering a narrow gauge steam or diesel ride above the river (forty minutes; also waterfall visit, woodland walks, picnic and play areas etc.). **Drefach Felindre**, 1m S, was, with many surrounding villages, between 1870 and 1930 the leading woollen manufacturing district of Wales (at the beginning of the century there were 43 mills), an era recalled today by the *Museum of the Welsh Woollen Industry* (Tel: 0559–370929), a branch of the National Museum of Wales. Opened in 1976 and occupying parts of a working mill (Cambrian Mill, built 1911), the museum tells the story of the industry from medieval times onwards; shows a comprehensive collection of machinery and tools; includes an exhibition tracing the progress of wool from sheep to fabric; and offers a variety of demonstrations. The museum is also the start of a Factory Trail around the surviving evidence of the district's once prosperous woollen past.

The road now descends the Teifi, as known today for its salmon as it was in the 12C when Giraldus praised it for abounding with finer salmon than any other river in Wales. However, the beavers, also mentioned by Giraldus, have long disappeared.—*3m.* **Newcastle Emlyn** is a small centre serving the surrounding farming community. Of the original Norman castle, thought to have been on the river's N bank, there is no trace. The 'new' castle was a 16C rebuilding by Sir Rhys ap Thomas of an earlier structure; designed as a fortified manor, it was later held for the King during the Civil War but afterwards slighted, little now remaining above ground other than the gateway to an inner ward. It was in *Adpar*, across the river, that the first printing press in Wales was set up in 1719. *Felin Geri Mill* (Tel: 0239–710810), off B4333 near Cwm Cou 1 1/2m NW of Newcastle Emlyn, is a 17C working water-mill providing stoneground flour.— *3m. Cenarth* is at a point on the Teifi below which, as far as Cilgerran about 7m downstream, coracles may perhaps be seen though these are fast disappearing; and at *Manordeifi*, across the river from (*4m*) *Llechryd*, the old church is known as the Coracle Church.—For *Cilgerran Castle* (1 1/2m W) and *Cardigan Wildlife Park* (2m W), see Rte 46.

3m. **Cardigan** (4000 inhab. *Inf.* Prince Charles Quay. Tel: 0239– 613230) is a pleasant small town on the Teifi some 3m above the river's mouth; hence Cardigan's Welsh name of Aberteifi.

History. A port and the site of primitive fortification in pre-Norman times, the first stone castle here was built in the late 11C or early 12C by Gruffydd ap Rhys. Later, in c 1170, this became a residence of Rhys ap Gruffyd who strengthened the fortifications and in 1176 organised here the first recorded eisteddfod, although this word is not actually used in contemporary chronicles. Town and castle later passed to the Earl of Pembroke who in 1240 rebuilt the latter. Town privileges were granted by Edward I but not confirmed by charter until 1542. In 1645 the castle fell to Parliament, Jeremy Taylor being among the captured garrison. During the 19C the town's prosperity declined with the silting of the estuary.

Cardigan was the home of Mrs Katherine Philips (1631–64), the 'matchless Orinda' who inspired Jeremy Taylor's 'Discourse of Friendship' (1657).

Cardigan's perhaps most attractive feature is the Teifi bridge, of ancient origin and rebuilt in 1726. Immediately to the N is the *Castle* (no adm.), in fact little more than bits of the keep and two ruined towers surviving from the Earl of Pembroke's rebuilding of 1240. From just NW of here High Street and Pendre curve northwards passing the old covered market and, roughly opposite, Priory Street, a name recalling a medieval Benedictine house that once stood here.

Gwbert-on-Sea, 3m N of Cardigan on the E side of the Teifi estuary, is a small resort known for its little bays and cliff walks. Just offshore, E of the estuary mouth, is the cliffbound *Cardigan Island*, home of seals, birds and half-wild Soay sheep (round-the-island boats from Gwbert or St. Dogmaels). *Mwnt*, 1 1/2m E of Cardigan Island, is a coastal National Trust property of nearly 100 acres.

For Cardigan to (N) *Aberaeron* and (S) *Tenby*, see Rte 46. For *Cardigan Wildlife Park* and *Cilgerran Castle* also see Rte 46.

This Route crosses Cardigan Bridge, immediately bearing N along B4546 for, in under 1m, **St. Dogmael's Abbey**, in origin an early Welsh house, sacked by the Vikings and then refounded in 1115 by Robert Martyn, Lord of this district of Cemaes, for monks of the reformed Benedictine Order brought over from Tiron in France. The modest ruins comprise fragments of the refectory and the N and W walls of the nave of the church, the most notable feature being the ball-flower ornament on the moulding of the N door. The site includes a collection of inscribed stones, effigies and suchlike, and also the *Parish Church* (1850) which houses the Sagranus Stone, inscribed in Latin and Ogham and thus (in 1848) providing the key for the interpretation of the Ogham alphabet.

Returning to Cardigan Bridge, this Route heads S, almost immediately forking right along A487 for (*2m*) *Croft*, from where B4582 in *5m* reaches **Nevern**, with, on a hill to the NW, the remains of its *Castle*. Originally a fortress of the local Welsh chieftains of Cemaes, the site was rebuilt as a motte-and-bailey in c 1100 by the Norman Robert Martyn, Marcher Lord of Cemaes. His grandson William, however, moved to Newport before the end of the century, Nevern then being taken over by Rhys ap Gruffyd (his father-in-law) who built a stone castle on the E angle of the ward. The ruins are overgrown, but the motte can be seen together with some fragments of the stone castle. But the most interesting feature of Nevern is its *Church of St. Brynach* (15–16C, but with a Norman tower), dedicated to a 5C Irish holy man whose cell was on Carn Ingli (the Hill of the Angels, 3m SW) and famous for its carved stones. The two inside the church, now forming window sills in the S transept, were found in 1906 embedded in the wall of the passage to the chamber over the chapel. The Maglocunus Stone (?5C) bears both Latin and Ogham inscriptions commemorating Maglocunus (Welsh Maelgwn), son of Clutor. It is of interest that the chieftain who granted land to St. Brynach for his church was called Clether or Clutor and was related to Brynach's wife, but there is no evidence that this Clutor and the one on the stone are the same. The other sill, the Cross Stone (10C), bears a cross of entwined Viking pattern. There are two more stones in the churchyard. The Vitalianus Stone, immediately E of the porch, is inscribed in both Latin and Ogham. The *Great Cross, farther E, is one of the most perfect Celtic crosses in Wales. Dating from the 10C the cross is 13ft high and bears elaborate patterning. Note, on the E and W sides, the examples of the abbreviated writing of the period, that on the W standing for 'dominus', and that on the E possibly for 'Halleluiah!'. There are several other items of interest around the churchyard. To the E of the Great Cross the tombstone epitaph to the infant children of the Rev. D. Griffiths is as amusing as it is touching. Just beyond, a memorial stands to the Rev. John Jones (vicar here 1842–52), who helped Lady Charlotte Guest in translating the 'Mabinogion' into English. A faintly inscribed stone will be found on the N wall of the church (W corner of the sill of the second chancel window); this has been cut to fit its present position and is thought to bear part of a vertical Latin inscription of c 400. On the NE corner of the N transept there is a consecration cross, and by the churchyard entrance there is an 18 or 19C mounting block. A short way W of the church, beyond a stile, the Pilgrim's Cross, cut into the rock, was probably a shrine along the road from Holywell to St. David's.

ENVIRONS OF NEVERN. The burial chamber of ***Pentre Ifan**, 2m S beyond A487, is remotely sited (but accessible by car) on an open hillside, with rocky moorland above and the tumbled summit of Carn Ingli with its Iron Age fort and settlement, once the home of St. Brychan, filling the west. A communal burial place dating from earlier than 2000 BC, the still remarkably intact main structure consists of a long (16ft) capstone supported by massive uprights.

Castell Henllys (Tel: 023979–319), 2m SE of Nevern and to the N of A487, is an Iron Age and Romano-British hillfort, part under excavation and part reconstructed to show huts, crafts, crops and suchlike.

2m. **Newport** (1000 inhab.), once capital of the Marcher lordship of Cemaes, the only such lordship not to have been abolished by Henry VIII, and said to have had a brisk wool trade until in Tudor times the plague diverted the market to Fishguard, is now primarily a holiday place popular for its beaches and sea fishing. The *Castle* (no adm.), dating from the 13C and, for the lords of Cemaes, successor to Nevern, is now incorporated into a modern mansion. For the *Presely Hills*, to the S of Newport, see Rte 46.—*3m* (from Newport) *Dinas* is a village at the base of *Dinas Island*, a 400 acre promontory ending as Dinas Head (463ft). At Cwm-yr-Eglwys, at the promontory's SE base, only the belfry and a wall survive of a church said to have been founded in the 6C and destroyed by a storm in 1839.

4m. **Fishguard** (Abergwaun. 3000 inhab. *Inf.* Town Hall. Tel: 0348–873484) is a pleasant small town perched high above its *Old Harbour*, an inlet at the head of which, at the mouth of the Gwaun, is the quite picturesque Lower Town, the setting for Dylan Thomas's 'Under Milk Wood' filmed here in 1971. Fishguard is associated with the last invasion of Britain, a farcical affair in which on 22 February 1797 three French frigates arrived off Carreg Wastad Point (2m NW. See Pen Caer below) and landed 1400 convicts under the command of the Irish-American General Tate. Local people and militia gathered under the energetic Earl of Cawdor and on 24 February Tate, appreciating that his situation was hopeless (both militarily— tradition insists that he mistook red-cloaked Welsh women for British soldiers—and also because his drunken rabble was threatening to shoot him if he did not sue for peace) signed unconditional surrender at the 'Royal Oak' where relics of the occasion are preserved. At nearby *St. Mary's Church* can be seen the headstone of Jemima Nicholas, 'The Welsh Heroine who boldy marched to meet the French invaders', personally capturing no fewer than 14 Frenchmen. Aged 47, a cobbler by profession and, it is reported, of brawny build and fearsome mien, she was awarded a pension which she enjoyed until her death at the age of eighty-two.

The main road drops sharply to *Goodwick*, once a fishing village but now effectively the base for *Fishguard Harbour*, known for its sea services with Rosslare in Ireland. The harbour (as also that at Rosslare) was built in 1894–1906 by the specially formed Fishguard and Rosslare Railways and Harbours Company, and it was on 30 August 1906 that services, previously running from Neyland (Milford Haven) to Waterford, were transferred to Fishguard and Rosslare. In 1972 Roll on/Roll off facilities were opened, this opening the route to large commercial as well as private vehicles.

A diversion can be made into the broad promontory of **Pen Caer**, the attractions being some prehistoric remnants, cliff scenery and places associated with the invasion of 1797. The principal hamlet is

Llanwnda, best approached by motorists from the W end of Good-wick. Reaching the high ground this road turns right and then left for Llanwnda, near this second turn being a small incised stone set in the bank. (Walkers can climb the lane which starts about ¼m W of the lifeboat station; this passes, on the right, the traces of three burial chambers and joins the motorists' road at the small incised stone). Giraldus was for a while rector at Llanwnda, and, centuries later during the 1797 invasion, the church was attacked by the drunken Franco-Irish rabble and looted of its plate. There is a stone cross cut into the E end of the exterior nave wall, and just S of the church there is a burial chamber, interesting for the labour-saving way in which one end of the capstone rests on the ground and the other on an upright standing in a pit. *Carreg Wastad* (path), ¾m NW, was the landing place of the invaders (eight men were drowned), their leader, Tate, then setting up his headquarters at *Tre-Howel Farm* (1m W of Llanwnda); stocked ready for a wedding, it well suited the soldiery who speedily drank themselves incapable. The small road running W from Tre-Howel in 1m curves S, at which point a smaller road leads 1m N to *Strumble Head* with a lighthouse and fine coastal views. The southward road, passing below *Carn Fawr* (600ft) crowned by a hillfort, continues to *St. Nicholas* where the church has an inscribed stone built into its wall and two Ogham stones in the choir. There is a burial chamber (*Carn Llys*) ½m S of the village, and a standing stone ¾m east. A487 can be joined rather over 1m S of St. Nicholas.

The direct road (A487) between Fishguard and St. David's is of little interest, but there are several side roads down to the coast with its cliff scenery. For *St. Nicholas,*, see above. From *Mathry* (7m from Fishguard) a road angles NW to *Abercastle*, ¼m W of which there is a burial chamber with a long capstone (nearly 16ft) resting on three of its original seven supports.

9m. **St. David's** (Tyddewi). 1500 inhab. *Inf.* City Hall. Tel: 0437–720392), because of its cathedral officially a city (although the smallest such in Britain), is in practice little more than a village straggling across an almost treeless and often either misty or wind-swept plateau above the little river Alun down beside which in Glyn Rhosyn (valley of the little bog) are the Cathedral and Bishop's Palace. Above, the village offers two marine attractions—the *Oceanarium* (Tel: 0437–720453) and the *Marine Life Centre* (Tel: 0437–721665)—while also in the upper village is the partly ruined *Tower Gate*, the main entrance to the cathedral close, a large enclosure, some ¾m in circumference, still in large part surrounded by a wall which though frequently restored is in origin of c 1300. This gate is the last survivor of four, and it and the precinct wall are in the main attributable to Bishop Gower (1328–47) although it has been suggested that the octagonal flanking tower on the N, which is 50 years older than the rest, was originally a detached bell-tower.

The foot approach to the cathedral is by a flight of steps known as the Thirty-nine Articles.

If its city is the smallest such in Britain, ****St. David's Cathedral** is the largest, finest and perhaps most interesting church in Wales.

History. The see was traditionally founded by St. David, patron saint of Wales, in c 550 when he transferred his monastery from Whitesand Bay (1½m NW) to Glyn Rhosyn, but both the church and the monastery he is supposed to have built here have long disappeared. William the Conqueror is known to have paid homage at the saint's shrine, but soon afterwards, in 1088, the Vikings sacked and burnt both the cathedral and its associated settlement. Despite this, St.

David's flourished, kings continuing to make their pilgrimage to a place so remote and sanctified that two pilgrimages here equated with one to Rome.

The present building was begun in 1180 during the episcopate of *Peter de Leia* (1176–98), the third Norman bishop (the first was Bernard, who succeeded the Welshman Wilfred). His nave still stands. Giraldus gives a gossiping account of the see in 1188; he was himself afterwards nominated to the bishopric, but failed to secure it (in spite of three appeals to Rome), partly because of his connection with the Welsh royal line, and partly, no doubt, because he argued for the independence of the Church in Wales. In 1220 the central tower fell, demolishing the choir and transepts; but these, with the lower stage of the tower, were rebuilt practically in the original style by 1250. The successive addition of the chapel of St. Thomas, the ambulatory, and the Lady Chapel (by *Bishop Martyn*, 1296–1328) completed in broad outline the ground plan of the church. *Bishop Gower* (1328–47) raised the height of the nave and chancel, inserting the Decorated windows, and added the middle stage of the central tower. *Bishop Houghton* (1361–88), Lord Chancellor to Edward III, achieved fame by being excommunicated and then himself excommunicating the Pope from the cathedral steps; *Bishop Vaughan* (1508–22) completed the top stage of the tower, and also vaulted the Lady Chapel. Other bishops during the 16C were *Bishop Ferrar* (1548–55), the Marian martyr burnt at Carmarthen, and *Bishop Davies* (1561–68), who procured the first Welsh translation of the Bible.

Archbishop Laud (1621–26) was appointed bishop on relinquishing the presidentship of St. John's College, Oxford, but he never came to St. David's. During the Civil War much of the lead was stripped from the roofs, and the E parts of the cathedral became dilapidated. *Bishop Bull* (1705–10) was known for his strong anti-Catholic preaching during the reign of James II, and *Bishop Thirlwall* (1840–74) as a classical historian and for his addresses relating the attitude of the Church to contemporary political issues.

The W front was rebuilt by John Nash at the end of the 18C. The modern work of restoration, begun in 1846, was afterwards carried on (1862–78) by Sir Gilbert Scott who rebuilt the W front to what is thought to be its original design.

The see now embraces all the modern county of Dyfed.

The Exterior is plain but dignified. Points to note are the lack of high-pitched roofs to the nave and choir; the 125ft high tower; and the huge buttresses on the N side of the nave. The 13–14C building (Chapel of St. Thomas, and library) in the angle between the N transept and the presbytery was originally of three storeys. The S porch is the work of Bishop Gower, except that the parvise was added in c 1515.

The Interior has a total length of 298ft; a width across the nave and aisles of 68ft; and a width across the transepts of 131ft. General features are the softly tinted purple slate and the lavish late-Norman ornament.

The NAVE is of six bays, clerestory, and triforium, with a varied wealth of chevron and other ornament. The flat *Roof of Irish oak, probably erected during the treasurership of Owen Pole (1472–1509), is unique in having a number of arches of fret-like delicacy that apparently carry the ceiling but are in fact pendants of it. The slope of the floor, due to its original construction on ill-drained and ill-prepared ground, is very noticeable; there is a rise of 14ft between the W door and the high altar. Under the second arch from the E of the S arcade is the monument of Bishop John Morgan (1496–1504), with his recumbent effigy and sculptures round the base; including, at the foot, a vigorous panel representing the Resurrection. On the adjacent (W) pier there are traces of murals. At the E end of the S aisle there is a beautiful 13C tomb-niche of a vested priest with a curiously shaped canopy. The elaborate and beautiful *Rood Screen, one of the chief glories of the cathedral, is the work of Bishop Gower, whose tomb, with effigy, occupies the S compartment. To the N of the central opening, which is notable for its unusual skeleton vaulting, is a striking stone reredos.

St. David's Cathedral

The TRANSEPTS, entered from the nave aisles by Norman door-ways instead of by the usual arches, were largely rebuilt after the fall of the tower in 1220; but here, and in the presbytery, the builders, though adopting the Pointed arch, assimilated their new work to the Norman character of the nave. In the *North Transept*, at the back of the choir stalls, is the reputed Shrine of St. Caradoc (died 1124). The two pierced quatrefoils in the base (like those in the shrine of St. David, see below) may have been intended for the insertion of a diseased limb in hope of cure, or for the reception of alms. The great window on the N of the transept was put in Butterfield in 1846. The *Chapel of St. Thomas of Canterbury*, off the E of the N transept, a vestry until 1952, has been restored as a memorial to Bishop Prosser (Archbishop of Wales; died 1949); it contains a beautiful 13C double piscina. The room above, reached by a stair from the N aisle of the presbytery, was originally the chapter house but is now the *Chapter Library*. Originally this was divided into two floors, of which the upper was the Treasury, but this latter has now been converted to a gallery in memory of Bishop Havard (1956). The library cases were restored in 1955 by the Pilgrim Trust. The oldest book is Bishop Lyndewode's 'Provinciale sue Constitutiones Angli' (1505), still today quoted as an authority on Church law. Also in the library are some beautiful fragments of the former organ case (?by Grinling Gibbons), broken up during restoration work. In the *South Transept* there are fragments of two Celtic slabs, one of which commemorates the two sons of Bishop Abraham (1076–78), who was bishop before the present building had been started. In the W wall a doorway gives access to the tower.

East of the nave there follow in succession the Choir, the Presbytery, the Sanctuary, Bishop Vaughan's Chapel, the Ambulatory, and the Lady Chapel.

The CHOIR takes the place of the crossing below the tower, which rests on four fine arches. The circular-headed arch on the W is part of the original wall of Peter de Leia, while the other three are Pointed and date from the rebuilding after 1220. The *Lantern* exhibits the beautiful Decorated work of Bishop Gower. The 28 Choir Stalls date from c 1470, and their design, without the usual tabernacled canopies, is unusual if not unique. Most of the misericords are original and, as always, interesting. The Bishop's Throne, nearly 30ft high and one of the few medieval examples left in Britain, is perhaps from the time of Bishop Morgan, though surrounded by earlier work by Gower. On either side there is a seat for a chaplain. Another rarity (though found in some parish churches) is the Parclose Screen between the choir and presbytery. The Choir Aisles are either side of the presbytery and sanctuary. In the *North Choir Aisle* is the tomb of Rhys Gryg (died 1233), fourth son of Rhys ap Gruffydd; the effigy is, however, of the 14C. The *South Choir Aisle* contains the tomb of Bishop Gervase (Iorwerth; 1215–29) alongside that of Bishop Anselm de la Grace (1231–47), and the recumbent effigy of a knight who may be Rhys ap Gruffydd (died 1197). Another effigy has been suggested as being that of Giraldus, and a slab bears an interesting inscription to Silvester the Physician (?13C).

To the E of the choir is the PRESBYTERY, comprising three and a half bays with chevron and other ornament and originally lighted on the E by two tiers of lancets. The lower row, which formerly looked into the open space now occupied by Bishop Vaughan's Chapel, is now blocked, and enriched with glass mosaics by Salviati. The jambs and arches are decorated with imitation ornament that is richer than any other in the cathedral. The upper tier was reconstructed by Gilbert Scott, from surviving fragments, in place of a poor but genuine window of the 15C. The roof, of 1461, was likewise restored by Scott. On the N of the presbytery is the late 13C *Shrine of St. David* once a magnet for crowds of pilgrims. In the middle is the large altar-tomb (with a handsome modern brass) of Edmund Tudor (died 1456), father of Henry VII, brought here at the Dissolution from the church of the Grey Friars at Carmarthen. On the S, as noted above, is the beautiful recumbent effigy of Bishop Anselm de la Grace (1231–47), alongside that of Bishop Gervase (1215–29).—On the S side of the SANCTUARY is a rare series of wooden sedilia (1460–81), and here the floor is paved with encaustic tiles, many of which are old.

BISHOP VAUGHAN'S CHAPEL, entered from the aisles, is a fine example of late Perpendicular work, with a fan-tracery *Roof (1508–22). Originally this was an open space, bounded by the presbytery and by the three walks of the ambulatory; it was also apparently neglected and dirty, being described as 'vilissimussive sordidissimus locus in tota ecclesia' and the sum of fourpence paid for its cleaning in 1492. The arrangement, unique among British cathedrals, may have been due to the 13C builders' reluctance to block up the three lower lancet windows on the E of the presbytery. An unexplained feature is the recess on the W side, with an opening at the back that looks into the presbytery. This is 12C work of De Leia's time; but of the four crosses (brought from elsewhere) immured around the opening, the one below it, hidden by a coffer, may possibly be a relic of a pre-Norman church. This recess, found walled up by Gilbert Scott, concealed a quantity of bones—possibly those of St. David or St. Justinian, or both—embedded in mortar and probably hidden here at the Reformation; they are now in the coffer just referred to. On the E side of the chapel stands the Altar of the Holy Trinity, made up of old fragments, with a niche and window on either side, an unusual and curious arrangement.

The AMBULATORY contains several 13–14C recumbent effigies. Its E walk is vaulted, while the side walks show evidence of a like but unfulfilled intention at three different periods.—The LADY CHAPEL was the last part of the cathedral to be restored, with a replacement for Bishop Gower's vault which fell in 1775. In addition to fine sedilia, the chapel contains two tomb-niches, probably the work of Gower. The one on the S (restored; no effigy) is thought to be that of Bishop Martyn (1296–1328), the original builder of the chapel. The other (N), perhaps the tomb of Bishop Beck (1280–96; builder of the Bishop's Palace), has been restored as a tomb for Bishop Owen (1897–1926).

On the N side of the nave, and once connected with it by a cloister, are the ruins of ST. MARY'S COLLEGE, founded for secular priests in 1377 by Bishop Houghton and John of Gaunt, fourth son of Edward III. The chief feature is the *Chapel*, above a barrel vault, with a plain tower attached to its SW corner. This originally formed the S range of the quadrangle. During work on the conversion of the buildings into a cathedral hall (1965), a tomb, believed to be that of Bishop Houghton, was discovered.

The remains of the ***Bishop's Palace** (WHM. Tel: 0222-465511) are on the farther side of the Alun rivulet. Started by Bishop Beck and continued by Gower, the palace was mostly built between 1280–1350 and may have had the additional purpose of serving as reception centre for pilgrims to the shrine of St. David. The decay of the palace dates from the time of Bishop Barlow (1536–48), who stripped the lead from the great hall, though perhaps not, as local tradition

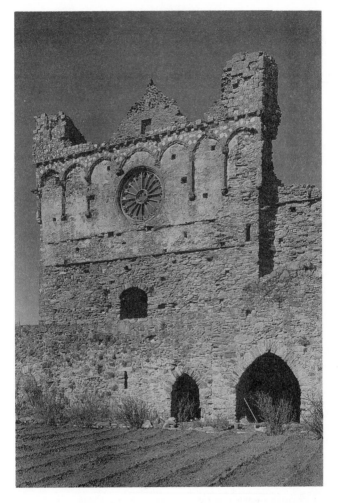

Ruins of the Bishop's Palace, St. David's: the Great Hall

asserts, to portion his five daughters all of whom he married off to bishops.

The palace consists of a single large quadrangle. The open arcade and parapet that run round the top of the whole building on the outer side are typical of Gower's work. The entrance to the quadrangle is by a disproportionately plain gateway at the E end of the N face. Immediately to the left of this is what is supposed to have been the *Private Chapel* (c 1350), raised, like the rest of the palace, on a series of vaults, which provided basement rooms and storage. The *Bishop's Hall* (late 13C; c 60ft by 24ft), on the E side of the quadrangle, has a later entrance porch with a curious doorway exhibiting the semi-octagonal head characteristic of Gower's work. To the S of this hall is the *Kitchen*; to the N, the *Solar*. The *Great Hall* (1327–47; c 120ft by 31ft), on the S side, is noticeably larger than the Bishop's Hall and was doubtless used for public purposes. It is approached by a fine porch at its NE corner, with a striking ogee doorway enriched by canopied niches with now mutilated figures, and has a beautiful rose window at the E end. At its NW corner is the *Chapel* with a piscina and a W bell-turret. The W side of the quadrangle seems to have been occupied by domestic buildings, stables etc.

ENVIRONS OF ST. DAVID'S. The promontory, in the S part of which St. David's lies, is a district known for its cliff scenery, its many bays and its associations with David and other saints. It was described by Giraldus as a remote and infertile corner, but, though the latter term still applies, the district can be crowded in summer. Much of the coastal land is owned or protected by the National Trust, largely as the result of an appeal in 1939 and substantial help from the Pilgrim Trust. Small roads or lanes fan out from St. David's to many of the bays, and the Pembrokeshire Coast National Park's coastal path follows the coast.

Traditionally **St. Non's Bay**, ½m S of St. David's, is where St. David was born, probably early in the 6C. His mother, it seems, was Non (or Nonnita), possibly a nun and daughter of a local chieftain called Brechan, and his father, Sandde, a member of the noble house of Cunedda, though whether Non was seduced, coerced or perhaps married by Sandde is not recorded. Further tradition says that Non later crossed to Brittany, only then becoming a nun; in any event what is claimed to be her tomb is in a chapel at Dirinon not far from Brest. St. David's birthplace is marked by a small ruined chapel of indeterminate age but in origin probably pre-Norman (it lies N to S, and this, together with the primitive masonry at the SW angle, suggests a possibly rare survival of early British church building) and by a nearby holy well. However, again according to tradition, it was not at this well that David was baptised but at a spring beside the Alun at *Porth Clais* (½m W; road from St. David's), an inlet later said to have served as harbour for St. David's monastery beside White-sand Bay and which today is the pretty home of small pleasure craft which cluster below the rough remains of a harbour wall that recalls the prosperous 19C days of coal and limestone.

Porthstinan, 2m W of St. David's, owes its name to St. Justinian, a saint associated with *Ramsey Island* a mile offshore (private; nature reserve and bird sanctuary; seals. Round-the-island boats in summer).

St. Devynog is said to have founded a monastery on the island as early as the 2C, and in the 5C Justinian, a Breton nobleman, became a hermit here. He became also St. David's confessor and friend, a relationship which led him into one particularly black adventure. Told by some sailors that his friend was sick, Justinian accepted their offer to row him across the sound. When halfway, however, Justinian began to have doubts, deciding that the sailors were in fact devils. So he recited Psalm 79, whereupon, doubtless on hearing the words 'Pour out thy wrath upon the heathen', the sailors turned into crows and flew away. Sadly, Justinian's victory was short-lived for the thwarted sailor-devils later returned to the island and took possession of his servants who, on his return from the mainland, attacked and beheaded him. David later transferred his friend's remains to a shrine in his new church.

It is sad that apart from the place's name the only physical reminder at Porthstinan of its doughty saint is a neglected roofless chapel, a charmless relic of the 16C which may or may not be successor to an earlier dedication. For the rest, Porthstinan is a picturesque corner where low green cliffs enclose an intimate bay in which the dominant feature is the lifeboat house perched high above its long slide down to the water.—The rocks to the W of Ramsey Island are known as the *Bishops and Clerks.*

Whitesand Bay (or Porth Mawr), ¹/₂m NW of St. David's and reached by a good road (B4583), is a popular sandy beach. In prehistoric times it was from here that traders sailed to Wicklow in Ireland for copper and gold, and the *Burrows*, the dunes behind the bay, are traditionally the site of the perhaps legendary Roman settlement of Menevia and later of St. David's first monastery.

St. David's Head (no road), a bold promontory with cliffs 100ft high, forms the northern projection of Whitesand Bay. The head is the Octopitarum Promontarium mentioned by Ptolemy. *Clawdd-y-Milwyr*, or Warriors' Dyke, a double rampart of stone across the base of the promontory, is of unknown origin, and, approaching the tip, there are remains of a burial chamber.

Off the approach to Whitesand Bay (4583) there are two farm museums, nearest to St. David's (¹/₂m) being *St. David's Farm Park* (Tel: 0437–721601), essentially a farm animals rare breeds survival centre though there are other attractions such as an adventure playground, picnic area, shop, art gallery and other indoor activities. Among the rare breeds are four-horned Manx Loghtan and Soay sheep, Bagot goats and spotted and red-haired pigs. A short way farther W *Lleithyr Farm Museum* (Tel: 0437–720245) shows agricultural and domestic bygones.

For St. David's to *Haverfordwest* and *Carmarthen*, see Rte 43.

43 Carmarthen to Haverfordwest and St. David's or Fishguard

A40 to Haverfordwest. Either A487 to St. David's or A40 to Fishguard. Total distance 44m.—*9m.* **St. Clears.**—*5m.* **Whitland.**—*8m.* **Canaston Bridge** (for **Llawhaden Castle**).—*3m.* **Picton Castle.**—*4m.* **Haverfordwest**—*15m.* **St. David's** or **Fishguard**.

From **Carmarthen** (see Rte 40) the road skirts the alluvial plain between the mouths of the Towy and Taf to reach (*9m*) **St. Clears** (where Rtes 44A and 44B break away SW and S), a small, generally agricultural centre straggling to the N and S of the main road. In 1406 Owen Glendower was defeated here by the men of Pembroke, and in 1843–44 the village was a focus of the Rebecca Riots. The *Church*, to the S on A4066, has a tower that batters to the top, and preserves also the carved Norman chancel arch of a small Cluniac priory which was attached in 1291 to St. Martin-des-Champs in Paris, while, just beyond, the remains of a motte recall those Norman days.—*5m.* **Whitland** (1500 inhab. *Inf.* Canolfan Hywel Dda. Tel: 0994–240867), on the Taf and another small market town, is historically important as the meeting place of the assembly convened by Hywel Dda in 930 to codify Welsh tribal customs into a single legal system, one so successful that the code lasted until the conquest by Edward I, and indeed in some respects until the Act of Union of 1536. Today Whitland honours this past with a *Memorial* complex comprising a Visitor Centre (Canolfan Hywel Dda. Tel: 0994–240867); a paved area with brickwork representations of the arrival of the delegates to Hywel Dda's assembly; and six small gardens, one for each of the main legal themes, namely Society and Status, Crime and Tort, Women, Contract, the King, and Property. *Whitland Abbey*, today sad and insignificant fragments beside a farm complex 1m NE, was once a great Cistercian house, the 'Alba Domos' of Giraldus, founded by Bernard, the first Norman bishop of St. David's, in 1143. The abbey became mother-house to Cwmhir in the same year and to Strata Florida in 1164.

Beyond the Taf A40 leaves the valley, in *5m* crossing A478 (Rte 46. *Narberth*, 1m S) and in another *2m* reaching *Robeston Wathen* and, *1m* beyond, **Canaston Bridge**, with, close by, places of interest to both the N and the south. To the S, within under 2m, are an early 19C mill and an adventure and leisure complex. The former, *Black Pool Mill* (Tel: 09914–233), beside the Eastern Cleddau river, was built in 1813 for wheat grinding. Originally water-powered with four pairs of millstones, the system was modified in 1901 to turbine power and the mill is considered to be one of the best examples of its kind in Britain. Caverns showing replicas of prehistoric animals are an additional attraction. From Black Pool a walk crosses the bridge, then bears S for 2m to reach the remains of a church of a commandery of the Knights of St. John. Nearby *Slebech Hall* stands on the site of the actual commandery.—*Oakwood*, 1m farther S down A4075, is a family adventure and leisure park with a miniature train, a bobsleigh run, go-kart circuit and suchlike (Tel: 0834–891376).

Llawhaden Castle (WHM. Tel: 0222-465511), 1m N of Canaston Bridge, though now ruined, was once an important residence of the bishops of St. David's.

History. The land around Llawhaden was long a rich possession of the see of St. David's, and in 1115 Bernard, the first Norman bishop, built a circular motte fortification here. However, in 1192 Rhys ap Gruffyd razed this castle (of which all that remains today is the moat) and it was not until the early 13C, by when the bishops had recovered the place, that a stone castle was built. Later, in the early 14C and probably under the direction of Bishop Martyn, Llawhaden was rebuilt and extended as a large fortified mansion. Bishop Barlow is generally supposed to have stripped the roof of its lead and to have left the castle to decay.

Within its circular moat, the castle comprises a single irregular ward round which lie the domestic buildings. The *Gatehouse*, at the SW corner, is largely a late 14C addition. To its W are the *Garrison's Quarters*, today a ruined two-storey building which would probably have been a hall above an undercroft, with, at an angle, the kitchen beyond. Adjoining and immediately NW of the garrison's hall are the foundations of a circular tower, a survival of the early 13C stone castle's curtain wall, which can be traced along the exterior of the garrison's hall. In the *North Range* of buildings, too, the main rooms were on the first floor above vaulted storerooms, but of this upper floor little remains. In the centre the hall extended NW to SE, with on its left the Bakehouse (W) and Kitchen (E), and to its right the Bishop's Private Chamber. The *South Range*, to the E of the gatehouse, comprised two storeys of rooms above undervaults, with beyond, at the castle's SE corner, the Chapel, originally joined to the bishop's chamber. The SE tower contained the chaplain's living quarters.—*Llawhaden Church* dates mainly from the 14C, but has a N tower which is somewhat older.

Continuing W from Canaston Bridge, A40 skirts the northern boundary of Slebech Park and in about *3m* reaches the approach to

(S, 1¹/₂m) **Picton Castle**, with gardens and the Graham Sutherland Gallery. Originally a Norman motte guarding the meeting of the eastern and western Cleddau, the stone castle dates from c 1302 when it was built by Sir John Wogan; a Welshman married to a Norman lady, he was Justiciary of Ireland from 1295–1313. The castle was taken by Owen Glendower in 1405, by the Royalists in 1643 and by Parliament in 1645; a W wing was added in 1800, and in 1954 the castle became the home of the Hon. Hanning Philipps, a descendant of the medieval owners. The *Castle* (Tel: 0437–751296), externally little changed apart from the addition of the W wing, shows an interior essentially of the 18C. The *Gardens* include plants and shrubs from Scotland's famous Lochinch Gardens, the home of Lady Philipps's family. The *Graham Sutherland Gallery* (Tel: 0437–751296), in the castle courtyard, shows works presented by the artist and his wife as a token of the inspiration he drew from Pembrokeshire over many years. There are also temporary exhibitions of works by other artists.

Wiston, 2m N of A40 roughly opposite the turn to Picton Castle, takes its name from Wizo, one of the Flemish colonists planted in this district by Henry I. Something survives of the motte and bean-shaped ward of his castle of c 1120; it was destroyed in 1220 by Llewelyn the Great, and the keep on the motte is probably later 13C rebuilding.

4m. **Haverfordwest** (Hwlffordd. 13,000 inhab. *Inf.* 40 High Street. Tel: 0437–763110) is a solid and busy market town on the Western Cleddau. With some steep streets and several Georgian houses, much of the town has been designated a conservation area.

History. Although the name is a legacy of the days of Viking raids, it was around the Norman castle built here in c 1120 by Gilbert de Clare that the town grew, helped no doubt by Henry I's Flemish settlers. Gruffydd ap Rhys took the town and castle soon afterwards, in 1135, but both were back in Norman hands by 1153 when Henry II visited here. Other kings who came here were John in 1210, Edward I in 1284, Richard II in 1394 and Henry Tudor (before Bosworth, 1485). In 1220 Llewelyn the Great burnt the town, and in 1407 Owen Glendower's French mercenaries did the same, though they failed to take the castle. During the Civil War Haverfordwest changed hands several times. In 1642 it was held for Parliament; in 1643 for the King; in 1644 it was occupied by Parliament's General Laugharne, and in 1645 by the Royalist Sir Charles Gerard; later in 1645 Laugharne returned, and finally the castle was slighted.

During the 18 and 19C Haverfordwest became a prosperous port, trading largely with Bristol and Ireland; and recent years have seen effective conservation measures, such as a wide listing of scheduled buildings and the diversion of traffic away from the centre.

Largely on the W bank of the river, and with Castle Square effectively the town centre, Haverfordwest is a place best appreciated on foot. The remains of the *Castle*, to the NW above Castle Square, represent the shell of the mainly 13C inner ward. By the mid 15C the castle was already a ruin, but in 1779 a gaol was built in the ward against the S wall and today the castle houses the town's *Museum and Art Gallery* (Tel: 0437–763708), concerned mainly with the story of the town and the surrounding district but also regularly receiving touring exhibitions. *St. Martin's Church*, to the W of the castle, is mainly of the 14C.

From Castle Square, High Street, with several Georgian façades, climbs to *St. Mary's Church*, dating originally from c 1250–70 although the N aisle and the clerestories were added during the 15C. The usual entrance is by the N door. The Nave, the W end of which is raised by several steps, has three Early English lancets, somewhat unusually at the W end (the glass forms a war memorial) and, as in the case of the N aisle, a good 15C roof. Also at the raised W end can be seen the mutilated effigy of a pilgrim with scallops on his satchel, almost certainly an indication that he visited the shrine of St. James of Compostella in Spain. At the E of the nave there is an elaborate 15C bench-end (the end of the adjacent pews of the sheriff and mayor) showing St. Michael and the dragon. The *Arches of the chancel, and those of the N arcade, are exceptionally good 13C work, retaining uninjured their capitals of stiff foliage enlivened with masks and small animals.—Barn Street, to the W of St. Mary's, is worth a visit, among the buildings here are the *Tabernacle* of 1774 and a house showing elaborate ironwork.

Quay Street, leading S out of Castle Square, becomes Old Quay which, in about ¼m from Castle Square, passes, beside the river, some remains of a *Priory Church* (under WHM excavation) founded for Augustinian Canons in about 1207 but largely demolished at the Dissolution.

Scolton Manor (Tel: 0437–731328), 5m NE of Haverfordwest by B4329 and dating from c 1840, now houses a good regional museum, among the themes being archaeology (in a special hall), costume, rural trades and vintage agricultural implements. Here too is 'Treddoe', an imaginary Pembroke village with, eventually, a street of shops, school, chapel, surgery, post office, pub and suchlike. The associated Country Park (Tel: 0437–731457) offers a nature trail, an arboretum, a countryside centre, a play area and a butterfly garden.

Llys-y-Fran Reservoir, some 8m NE of Haverfordwest through the village and railway junction of Clarbeston Road, supplies water for the whole area of what was the county of Pembroke. The reservoir and its surrounds are a Country Park providing picnic sites, sailing, fishing etc., and a nature trail which starts at the car parks at either end of the dam and makes the round of the reservoir (7½m).

TO ST. DAVID'S. A487. *6m. Roch Castle* (no adm.), to the E off the main road, takes its name from the outcrop on which it stands, a site said to have been chosen by the Norman Adam de la Roche because of his fear of snakes (the story goes that despite this protection he was killed by the bite of a snake brought in with some firewood). What is seen today is one surviving 13C D-shaped tower with projecting chambers; a block of flats has now been added. The stream just beyond Roch marks the N boundary of what was once English-speaking southern Pembroke, the district colonised in the early 12C by the Flemings.—*2m.* The coast is briefly touched at *Newgale*, a scattered, straggling holiday village with a pebble bank and a long sandy beach. Here, at exceptionally low tide, may be seen the stumps of a submerged forest, known to Giraldus and described by him as a 'grove of ebony'. From here on much of the coast is either owned or protected by the National Trust. The road, though, keeps inland, in *3m* reaching *Solva*, until the 19C a modestly important port but today a picturesque small village and haven at the head of its narrow, winding creek. Solva Nectarium (Tel: 0437–721323), in the grounds of a Georgian house in Lower Solva, offers a stroll amid live butterflies from all over the world, as also galleries of insects including tarantulas, locusts and suchlike.—*4m.* **St. David's,** see Rte 42.

TO FISHGUARD. A40. *3m. Poyston*, 1m E of A40, was the birthplace of Sir Thomas Picton (1758–1815), Governor of Trinidad and distinguished commander during the Peninsular War, who was killed at Waterloo.—In about *2m*, approaching Treffgarne, A40 crosses the Western Cleddau and runs, with the river and the railway, through the wooded **Treffgarne Gorge**, lined with hillforts on either side. Brunel brought his railway as far as here by 1845, only to be defeated by the ancient hard rock, and it was only after another 60 years that the line was completed. *Nant-y-Coy Mill* (Tel: 043787–671), in origin of 1332 or earlier, was rebuilt in 1844 and today offers a variety of attractions such as a cottage showing bygones, many of local provenance, craft workshops and nature walks. Owen Glendower is said to have been born at Little Treffgarne on the E side of the river.—*10m*. **Fishguard**, see Rte 42.

44 Carmarthen to Pembroke and Milford Haven

Two choices are offered; the direct, inland main road, or generally minor roads close to the coast. The two come within a little over a mile of one another at Kilgetty and Saundersfoot, and meet at Pembroke. The coastal choice, longer by some 10m is the more scenic and interesting.

A. Direct

A40 to St. Clears. A477 to Neyland. B4325 to Milford Haven. Total distance 39m.—*9m*. **St. Clears**.—*12m*. **Kilgetty**.—*6m*. **Carew Cheriton** (for **Carew Castle**).—*4m*. **Pembroke**.—*8m*. **Milford Haven**.

Carmarthen, see Rte 40. For Carmarthen to (*9m*) **St. Clears**, see Rte 43.—*2m*. *Llanddowror* where Griffith Jones (1684–1761), a pioneer of Welsh education and organiser of travelling schools, was vicar.—*8m*. From *Killanow*, a hamlet at a crossroads, *Amroth* on Rte 44B is a short distance south.—*2m*. **Kilgetty** and **Begelly**, with important information centres (Wales Tourist Board, AA, RAC, Pembrokeshire Coast National Park). *Avondale Glass*, adjacent, shows glass blowing and manufacture, while, nearby, *Begelly Pottery* is open to visitors (Tel: 0834–811204). For rehearsals of Kilgetty Male Voice Choir, Tel: 0834–860881.

6m. **Carew Cheriton** where the large early 14–15C church, with a mounting block at the entrance, shows various features of interest including tombs of the Carew family, one of these being that of Sir Nicolas (died 1311) who built the earliest stone part of Carew Castle. On the N of the chancel there is an effigy of a vested priest of c 1325, while on the S, and dating from about 1300, rests a very small female figure, either a child or perhaps indicating a heart-burial. The tiles of c 1500 on the chancel floor may at some time have come from Carew Castle, and the detached 14C chantry, or perhaps mortuary chapel, used in 1846 as a school, is a rare survival of an in any case unusual feature.

Just to the N along A4075, in the hamlet of Carew, beside the road and near the castle entrance, stands *Carew Cross*, a magnificent monument nearly 14ft high and with elaborate geometric and intertwined patterns showing both Celtic and Scandianvian influence. Erected in c 1035 to honour Maredudd (killed in battle that year),

The magnificent Carew Cross, set up c 1035

with his brother co-prince of Deheubarth, the cross was made in two parts, the wheel at the top fitted into position by a tenon.

Carew Castle (Tel: 0646–651781. Also for Mill, see below) is an imposing ruin on a low ridge above a tidal creek of the Carew river.

History. The earliest castle, of which nothing survives, is said to have been built by Gerald de Windsor, an Anglo-Norman chieftain, at the close of the 11C. Another tradition is that the estates came to him as the dowry of his wife Nest, daughter of Rhys ap Tewdwr, sister of Gruffydd ap Rhys, and mistress of Henry I. Their son assumed the name of Carew, and their daughter was the mother of Giraldus. The earliest authentic stone structure was the fortified mansion of the Carews, built c 1270–1320. In 1480 Carew was sold to Sir Rhys ap Thomas, who remodelled the place and added the Great Hall. Sir Rhys entertained Henry Tudor after his landing on Milford Haven in 1485, and in 1507 here held a great tournament to celebrate the Garter bestowed on him by Henry, now Henry VII. In 1558 the castle was granted to Sir John Perrot, who rebuilt the whole of the N side in a purely domestic Tudor style. In the Civil War Carew was held for the King in two sieges (1644 and 45), but the damage was apparently such that it was not lived in after 1686.

Architecturally Carew spans the period between the military structures of the 13C (W) to the fortified manors of Tudor times (N). The
plan is roughly rectangular with a three-quarter drum-tower at each
corner, the two on the W being strengthened externally by curious
semi-pyramidal spurs. The entrance on the E, the weakest side, was
specially protected, the whole front being covered by an outer ward
and the actual gateway by a narrow barbican which compelled
approach at right angles; it was also flanked on the S by the drum at
the SE angle, and on the N by a special tower protruding from the
curtain. The original *Carew Manor House* was built inside this E
curtain and included a chapel in the special tower just referred to; it
is representative of the period when defence was moving outwards to
a curtain and away from a keep. The late 15C *Great Hall* built by Sir
Rhys ap Thomas, with its fine entrance tower, is on the W of the ward
(upper storey), while on the N is *Sir John Perrot's Manor* with its
large windows and oriels.—*Carew Tidal Mill*, or French Mill, just W
of the castle and a rare example of a restored mill of this kind, dates
back to 1558 although the four-storey main building is largely
restoration of the early 19C. There is an introductory film, and the
milling process is explained at automatic 'talking points'.

4m (from Carew Cheriton) **Pembroke** (15,000 inhab. *Inf.* Drill Hall,
Castle Terrace. Tel: 0646–682148) is a historic town with a single
Main Street which runs for over ¹/₂m along a narrow ridge above the
Pembroke river. Considerable lengths of the town's 13C walls
survive, particularly on the S, the walls originally being integral with
the castle and served by three gates, West and East gates being at
either end of the Main Street while the North Gate guarded what is
now the bridge across the river. Today there is a lengthy one-way
traffic system, above and below the walls, but with convenient
parking below on the south. There are proposals for a marina and
waterfront development below the castle walls.

The massive and imposing ruins of * * *Pembroke Castle* (Tel: 0646–
681510), occupying the W end of the ridge, sprawl over a promontory
above the river and Monkton Pill.

History. Roman coins have been found on this site, and it may later have been a
Viking stronghold, but the first castle here was built c 1095 by Arnulf de
Montgomery. Described as a 'slender fortress of stakes and turf', it was left in
the hands of Arnulf's steward, Gerald de Windsor (probably builder of Carew),
who withstood a siege by the Welsh in the following year and in 1102, when
Montgomery fell from favour, was granted the castle by Henry I. Three years
later Gerald rebuilt the place. The earldom of Pembroke was created in 1138,
(the first earl was Gilbert de Clare), the title later passing to the Marshals, who
were largely responsible for the castle the remains of which are seen today. The
oldest part is the keep, thought to have been built by William Marshal in c 1210,
and the whole castle seems to have been completed, initially by his five sons in
succession, by the end of the century. In 1452 Henry VI granted Pembroke to
Jasper Tudor, and in 1457 his nephew Henry Tudor, later Henry VII, was born
here. Throughout the Civil War the castle was held for Parliament, but in 1648
the town's military governor John Poyer surprisingly declared for the King.
Cromwell then besieged Pembroke for 48 days, subjecting it to continual
artillery battering until, after capturing the water supply, he was able to compel
surrender. The castle was then slighted and Poyer was shot in London early the
following year. Neglected and used as a quarry for over 200 years, the castle
was restored in 1880, 1928, and later.

The ground-plan is an outer ward to the E, and beyond, above the
curve of the promontory, the smaller and rather older inner ward.
The entrance to the OUTER WARD is across the ditch, now filled in,
which separated the castle from the town, and then by the Gatehouse, noteworthy for its external barbican (restored 1880–85),

Thirteenth-century Pembroke Castle built above the river Pembroke

compelling oblique approach, and for its internal semicircular angle-towers connected by an arch, possibly intended to carry a wooden platform manned by defenders. Within the gatehouse (with a small local museum, open in summer only) there is a maze of rooms and passages. The walls of the ward are strengthened by five circular drum-towers, connected by passages. On the S and W sides the first tower is the Henry VII Tower, confidently stated by Leland (official antiquary to Henry VIII) to be Henry's birthplace. Note the very individual privy in the adjacent wall. Westgate Tower (destroyed 1648, restored 1931) stands at the point where the southern town wall, with the West Gate, joined the castle. The Monkton Tower is different from the others in having separate entrances to its floors. It stands to the S of the Inner Gatehouse, surviving only as foundations, on the inner curtain. This, approached from below by a twisting path, was the original and only entrance to the castle during the period when it consisted of the inner ward only; when, not long afterwards, the outer ward was built, the path was built over and a new and higher Water Gate opened beside Monkton Tower. On the E side of the ward Northgate Tower marks the point where the N town wall joined the castle curtain. Much of the tower's outer wall, destroyed in 1648, is a rebuilding of 1934. To the N the Mill Gate marked the exit to the tidal mill below, the dam of which, with a drawbridge, was the entrance to the town through the North Gate. Mill Gate and the mill were protected by the rectangular St Ann's Bastion (restored 1929).

Just within the INNER WARD stands the circular Great Keep, 75ft high and 24ft in diameter internally at the bottom, with walls 19ft thick at the base. It was possibly built by Gilbert de Clare, but more probably by William Marshal in c 1210. Originally four storeys, it is now open from ground level to the domed stone roof. The chief entrance was on the first floor, up wide steps, the foundations of which were discovered in 1932; the basement entrance was apparently added at an early date. The staircase is a restoration of 1928. At the top, square holes in the outer parapet were probably for the attachment of an archers' platform. The domestic apartments, largely crowded into cramped space NE of the keep, are not on the scale of the rest of the castle. From S to N, beside the inner curtain are the Dungeon Tower; the Oriel, probably a Tudor adaptation of an earlier antechamber; the Norman Hall, the hall being above a basement, and access through either the Oriel or the Northern Hall, again a main floor above a basement. A stairway (dark and often slippery) leads from the Northern Hall down to the Wogan, a large natural cavern, roughly 80ft long and 60ft broad, probably used as a store; the cavern can also be reached by the path around the base of the castle. The Chancery, to the W of the Norman Hall, seems to have been a Tudor addition. In the SW of the inner ward are the scanty remains of the Chapel, alongside the gloomy Western Hall.

Three other places in or near Pembroke repay a visit, two of these being museums in the town. The *National Museum of Gypsy Caravans, Romany Crafts and Lore* (Tel: 0646–681308), in Common Road, shows just what its name promises, while the *Castle Hill Museum* (Tel: 0646–681200), just across the road from the castle, is the home of a wealth of bygones. The third place of interest is *Monkton Priory*, 1/2m W of the castle across Monkton Pill, here dammed to form a mill lake. Founded by Arnulf de Montgomery in 1098 for Benedictine monks as a cell of Sées in Normandy, the priory was given to St. Albans, in 1473. The church has a long, narrow barrel-vaulted nave, and the monastic chancel, though part of the original structure, was re-arranged during the 14C. After lying in ruins for many years, the church was restored in 1878–87. On the exterior the tower is of the local fortified type; in the gable above the E window there is a niche with a headless figure; and, from traces of two small half-blocked windows on the N exterior of the nave, it has been suggested that the masonry incorporated the S wall of a pre-Norman church.

For *Castlemartin Peninsula*, extending S and W from Pembroke, see Rte 45.

A477 (A4139) crosses the river to reach **Pembroke Dock**, a town which, already building wooden warships during the 18C, began to boom after 1814 when the Admiralty Dockyard moved here from Milford Haven; the first ships, 'Valorous' and 'Ariadne', were launched two years later in 1816. Much expanded during the First World War, the government dockyard was in 1930 handed over to the Royal Air Force and Pembroke Dock became well known as a flying boat base playing an important part in the Second World War's Battle of the Atlantic. The 19C town was planned on a generous squared pattern with wide streets, and some confident Victorian architecture survives. In summer there are cruises (from Hobbs Point at the N of the town) in Milford Haven and up Daugleddau (Two Swords), the common estuary of the Western and Eastern Cleddau rivers.

A477 crosses upper Milford Haven by a toll bridge to *Neyland*, the main trading port to southern Ireland until superseded by Fishguard in 1906 and now a recreational area with a large marina.

MILFORD HAVEN is the name both of the huge natural harbour and of the town (see below) on its N shore. The magnificent natural harbour, described by Nelson as the best in the world and with sheltered roadsteads for the largest ships, is some 10m long by ½ to 2m broad, and at its head breaks into several tidal inlets reaching far inland, the longest being the estuaries of the Western and the Eastern Cleddau. Until c 1800, however, the haven served only as temporary refuge. The Norsemen came here (in King Alfred's time one expedition wintered with 23 ships), and both Henry II and John, each with 4–500 ships, set sail from here to conquer Ireland. In 1407, 12,000 French mercenaries landed here to fight for Owen Glendower against Henry IV, and in 1485 Henry Tudor, Earl of Richmond, came ashore at Mill Bay with a small retinue from Brittany to begin the campaign that would end with victory at Bosworth Field and his crowning as Henry VII. In the late 18C Sir William Hamilton (husband of Nelson's Lady Emma) inherited from his first wife the local manors of Pill and Hubberston. He appreciated the potential of the haven but, far away as Envoy Extraordinary to the Court of Naples (a post he held from 1764–1800), there was nothing he could personally do, so he appointed his nephew, the Hon. R. F. Greville, as his agent. In 1790 an Act of Parliament sanctioned the establishment of a town, and at about the same time a naval dockyard was opened, which, however, in 1814 moved to Pembroke Dock. The railway came in 1863, but, although there was some optimistic investment (Milford Haven docks were completed by 1888), large ships failed to use the place. However, the Neyland trawler fleet moved to Milford Haven which by the opening years of the present century had become one of Britain's leading fishing ports. During both wars the Haven was busy with Atlantic convoys, but after 1945 there was a general decline and trawling also began to disappear, although many varieties of fish, including sewin, a sea trout found only in Welsh waters, are still landed at Milford Haven.

New life came with the 1960s as the Haven began to develop into a major oil port, and today it is used by the leading oil companies whose activities have brought huge tankers and a growing spread of oil-related installations. The Haven is under the operational control of the Milford Haven Conservancy Board (1958) whose jurisdiction extends over all tidal waters, which means as far inland as Haverfordwest, Canaston Bridge and Carew. In 1964 the Board's headquarters and signal station at Hubberston Point (W of Milford Haven town) were opened by Princess Marina, Duchess of Kent.

In summer the best way to see the Haven is by cruise boat from Hobbs Point, Pembroke Dock. For the N shore, see Marloes and Dale Peninsula below. For the S shore (Castlemartin Peninsula), see Rte 45.

8m (from Pembroke) **Milford Haven** town (14,000 inhab.) was the creation of R. F. Greville who, empowered by the Act of Parliament of 1790, imported a group of Quaker whalers who had been unsettled by the American War of Independence and contracted a refugee Frenchman, J–L, Barrallier, to lay out the town and dockyard in the squared pattern which survives today. *St. Katherine's Church*, built by Greville over the period 1801–08, was extended in 1907 by the addition of two bays to the E nave and by a new chancel and Lady Chapel. A case shows a Bible and prayer book presented by Nelson, and in the porch are an Egyptian porphyry bowl and a replica of the truck (mast-top disc) of the French battleship 'L'Orient' which blew up at the Battle of the Nile (1798). The bowl had been acquired by Greville, the genuine truck had been presented by Lady Hamilton in honour of Nelson, and Greville had the happy thought to combine the two into a font. However the bishop objected on the grounds that the bowl was pagan and that the truck had been 'polluted ... by blood and carnage'. So the font idea was dropped, the bowl remaining however in the church while the truck is now in the National Maritime Museum at Greenwich. Sir William Hamilton (1730–1803) is buried in the churchyard; his home was Castle Hall at the E of the town. The small remains of *Pill Priory*, built in 1200 by Adam de la Roche, are on the town's N edge, while to the NE, beyond the head of the Pill Inlet, there are slight remains of the medieval *Castle*. *Gellyswick Bay*, to the W of the town, is popular for bathing and sailing.

The indented MARLOES AND DALE peninsula, ending as two promontories, extends nearly 10m westward from Milford Haven. The main road into the peninsula is B4327 from Haverfordwest, the two principal villages, both towards the W end, being Marloes to the N and Dale to the south. The National Park footpath, crossing some National Trust land, follows the coast with its cliff scenery and sandy bays, and there is an Information Centre at Broad Haven at the NE base of the peninsula (Summer only. Tel: 043783–412). To the W there are several islands.

Marloes is an inland village, with *Marloes Sands* around the bay ³/₄m south-west. The W extremity of the bay is marked by *Gateholm Island* (Norse, Goat Island), which is an island only at high tide, on which there are traces of several rectangular huts, survivals of a Dark Ages, possibly monastic, settlement. Albion Sands, immediately W of Gateholm, recall the 'Albion', a paddle-steamer wrecked here in 1840. From *Martin's Haven*, at the road's end 2m W of Marloes, there are sometimes boat trips to the islands.

St. Ishmael's, a village in the S central part of the peninsula, is named after a 6C colleague of St. Teilo. On the N outskirts of the village a motte recalls Norman if not earlier times, while the Long Stone, ½m NW, is the tallest standing stone in the Pembrokeshire Coast National Park. A story attaches to *Mullock Bridge*, on B4327 roughly halfway between St. Ishmael's and Marloes. Sir Rhys ap Thomas of Carew Castle is said to have given his word to Richard III that if Henry Tudor tried to pass through Pembroke it would only be by riding over his body. So when Henry landed at Mill Bay Sir Rhys both satisfied his conscience and ensured his own future by lying under the bridge while Henry rode across; he then hastened to Carew where he welcomed the invader.

Dale, to the S, is a small holiday village and sailing centre (boats to the islands). *Dale Castle* (no adm.), a modern residence, stands on or near the site of a medieval manor first mentioned in 1293 as belonging to one, Robertus de Vale. Around the promontory to the S are Iron Age earthworks across the base of Dale Point; *Dale Fort*, a Victorian fort now a Field Studies Centre; *West Blockhouse Point*, site of coastal defences first erected in about 1580, rebuilt in 1852–57 and in occupation until 1950; and, just beyond, *Mill Bay*, where Henry Tudor landed on 7 August 1485, where, also, on the night of 9 November 1866 six ships were wrecked, and where on 14 March 1964 a ship being towed to Swansea for scrapping broke loose and was driven ashore. At *St. Ann's Head*, accessible by road, there are a coastguard station and lighthouse.

Skomer Island (722 acres) is a National Nature Reserve, known for its seabirds, seals and wild flowers.—Between Skomer and the mainland is *Midland Isle* or *Middleholm* (21 acres).—*Skokholm Island* (242 acres) is also a bird sanctuary, while *Grassholm Island* (23 acres), 7m W of Skomer and famous for gannets, was bought in 1948 by the Royal Society for the Protection of Birds.

B. Via the Coast and Tenby

A40 to St. Clears. A4066 to Pendine. Unclassified to Saundersfoot. A478 to Tenby. A4139 to Pembroke. A477, B4325 to Milford Haven. Total distance 49m.—*9m.* **St. Clears.**—*4m.* **Laugharne**—*5m.* **Pendine.**—*8m.* **Saundersfoot.**—*3m.* **Tenby.**—*6m.* **Manorbier Castle.**—*4m.* **Lamphey Bishop's Palace.**—*2m.* **Pembroke.**—*8m.* **Milford Haven.**

Carmarthen, see Rte 40. For Carmarthen to (*9m*) **St. Clears** (for Rtes 43 and Rte 44A), see Rte 43.

4m. **Laugharne** is a quiet rural town, with Georgian houses, on the W bank of the estuary of the Taf, here over ¹⁄₂m wide and about to broaden further as it meets that of the Towy.

History. For long the history of the town was that of its castle. Founded during the 12C and for a while held by Rhys ap Gruffyd, it was destroyed by Llewelyn the Great in 1215, then rebuilt by the De Brian family. It was Sir Guy de Brian who in 1307 granted a charter by which the town was administered by a portreeve (chief officer) elected every six months by the citizens, a system which in some respects is still honoured today. In Tudor times the castle came to Sir John Perrot who, as he did at Carew, converted the place into a mansion. At the time of the Civil War Laugharne was the home of the general of the same name who held the castle for Parliament in 1647 but later sided with the King. In the 18C Mrs Bridget Bevan (died 1779), associate of Griffith Jones of Llanddowror (see beginning of Rte 44A), lived here, and in more recent years Laugharne was the home of the poet Dylan Thomas (died 1953) who is buried in the churchyard.

The *Castle* (WHM. Tel: 0222-465511), of which little survives, comprises two 12–13C towers and traces of Sir John Perrot's mansion. In the town, the name King Street is an ancient one, commemorating a visit by Henry II, and here it is worth glancing into the tower of the *Town Hall* which contains a curious small prison furnished with a wooden bench with a pillow end. *St. Martin's Church* (14C, modernised 19C) also repays a visit, here being the remains of a Bronze Age man, found during the construction of a local housing estate; a 10C Celtic cross (restored); and a wood carving of St. Martin of Tours, brought from Oberammergau in 1866 and the work of a member of the Lang family, long actively associated with the Passion Play. The poet Dylan Thomas spent the last years of his life in Laugharne (he is buried in the churchyard of St. Martin's), doing much of his writing at what is now known as *Dylan Thomas's Boathouse* (Tel: 0267-234567), some 15 minutes walk from King Street by Victoria Street and narrow Cliff Road (no cars), and as interesting for the estuary views as for the association with the poet.

Llandawke, 1¹⁄₂m W by narrow but motorable lanes, is a lost little hamlet with a very primitive 13C church as simple and evocative as any in Wales. It shelters an ancient stone, inscribed in Ogham and Latin perhaps seven centuries before this church was built, and also the 14C effigy of a lady, perhaps Margaret of Marlos, sister or daughter of Sir Guido de Brian, the local lord. The honorific of Saint which she sometimes enjoys seems to be a purely local canonisation, and if today the lady looks somewhat worn, this is because she spent centuries out in the churchyard before being brought under cover.

5m. **Pendine** is a straggling small resort, today a place of cafés, souvenir shops and caravans but with sands which have an honoured place in motoring and aviation history. Between 1924–27 the world's land speed record was five times attempted here, three times by Malcolm Campbell (1885–1948) and twice by J.G. Parry-Thomas, the latter being killed here in 1927; his car was buried near the beach until dug up in 1969 for restoration. The final speed achieved by Malcolm Campbell was 174.88 mph in 1927, though by 1935 (at Bonneville, Utah) he raised this to over 300. In 1933 Jim and Amy Mollison (Amy Johnson) took off for a non-stop flight to New York, but lack of fuel forced them down only 60m short of their objective. For a fee, modern motorists can drive, but not speed, on the beach. The *Burrows*, stretching E to the Taf estuary, are a Ministry of Defence area (danger zone).—The road climbs inland to (*2m*) *Marros* (450ft), with a quaint 'neolithic' war memorial, before dropping to (*3m*) *Amroth*, an inland and seaside village at the SE extremity of the Pembrokeshire Coast National Park and where the stumps of a now submerged forest may be seen at low tide. *Colby Lodge Garden* (NT; Tel: 0558-822800) is 1m north-west. There are several walks, including one to Amroth.—*2m. Wiseman's Bridge*, where in 1944 Winston Churchhill watched a D Day rehearsal.—*1m.* **Saundersfoot**, today a holiday resort with a harbour crowded with small craft, dates from 1829 when the harbour was built for the export of the anthracite mined a short way inland and brought here by tramway.

3m. **Tenby** (Dynbych-y-Pysgod. 5000 inhab. *Inf.* Guildhall, The Norton. Tel: 0834–2402), an ancient and picturesque walled town and lively resort, sprawls along and spills down an abrupt promontory, narrowing to only a few yards at its SE end. The promontory, separating North Sands and the harbour from South Sands and Castle Sands, ends as the detached spur of St. Catherine's Island.

History. From the evidence of coins found on St. Catherine's Island during the construction of the fort there in the 19C, Tenby may have existed in some form in Roman times, but the first mention of the place is in a poem of c 875 which names the fortress on the promontory as Dynbych-y-Pysgod (Fortlet of the Fishes), the modern word Tenby being a development of Dynbych. This poem praises the court here of the prince, Bleiddudd ap Erbin, a patron of bards. Around 1111 the town, growing to the W of the castle, was settled by Flemish clothworkers, but soon afterwards suffered the usual violence of the times. The castle was taken in 1153 by Rhys ap Gruffydd, in 1187 his son sacked the town, and in 1260 it was taken by Llewelyn the Last. During a part of this time (1172–75) Giraldus was rector here. Although by 1386 the castle was close to ruins, the town, granted a charter by Henry IV, became a flourishing port (importing wines and salt and exporting coal and cloth), a status which lasted well into the 16C. In 1457 the town walls were strengthened by Jasper Tudor, and in 1471, after the Battle of Tewkesbury, Henry Tudor found refuge here before escaping to Brittany. The defences were again strengthened under the threat of the Armada. Although garrisoned for the King during the Civil War, Tenby surrendered in 1644 after a siege of only three days. After decline during the 17C and 18C, the town was rescued in the 19C by Sir William Paxton and others who, helped by the opening of the railway, were able to develop the resort to which Tenby largely owes its present day character.—Robert Recorde, author of 'Ground of Artes', the earliest important mathematical treatise, and inventor of the = sign, was born here in 1510. Augustus John, the artist, was born in 1878 at Belgrave House.

Male Voice Choir. For rehearsals, Tel: 0834–3972.

From the N entrance to the town the street succession The Norton, Crackwell Street and Bridge Street curves generally SE down to Castle Hill, the streets immediately to the right being the main shopping area. Along South Parade, the W edge of this shopping area, runs the surviving length of the *Town Wall*, which, lined roughly across the base of the promontory and with a short return section on the N (now destroyed), was the town's inland defence. First built perhaps in the 13C, strengthened by Jasper Tudor in 1457 and again in 1588 when the Spanish Armada threatened, the wall is some 20ft high with external bastions all of which bar one are cylindrical. South Gate, about halfway along the length of the wall, is protected externally by a semicircular barbican (*Five Arches*), which retains its sole original entrance on the N side, with (a favourite medieval trap for attackers) a right-angled turn. From Five Arches St. George Street leads E, passing on the left below the church an old archway once giving access to the churchyard and prison.

St. Mary's Church is of several periods, the oldest being a 13C rebuilding of an earlier church. But much of today's structure dates from the 15C, with extensive modification during the 19C, these two periods representing Tenby's peaks of prosperity. Features of the exterior are the large South Porch of c 1500, with, above the inner door (refashioned in the 18C), a small window of a 13C chapel; the late 13C Tower, unusual for being to one side of the chancel, with a 15C spire; the 15C West Door, inserted into an older wall and ornamented with moulding and a double-ogee head, all that survives of a large W porch built in 1496 and demolished in 1831; and, to the W, the slight remains of a building erected in conjunction with this porch, probably as a chantry and school. Inside the church, the Nave, basically of the 13C, was much altered in the 15C when the N arcade and a row of arches on the S side were added. The roof was restored in 1966, as was also the pulpit of 1634 with ample ladies around the top. The N aisle is an early 15C addition, while the S aisle results from a throwing together in the late 15C of a number of chapels, its fine roof dating from the same time. The Chancel (13C) was enlarged in about 1470 by the addition on the E of steps and a raised Sanctuary, with a crypt below. The panelled ceiling (restored 1962) has elaborately carved bosses, 75 of which are original. The Chapel of St. Nicholas (N), with the tomb of Bishop Tully of St. David's (1460–82), is an addition of 1480, and St. Thomas's Chapel (S) is also a 15C addition, among the monuments here being two with effigies of Thomas White (died 1482) and his son John (died 1490), both mayors of Tenby, the former at the time of Henry Tudor's escape in 1471.

The *Tudor Merchant's House* (NT. Tel: 0834–2279), on Quay Hill a short way E of St. Mary's, though with furnishing of different periods survives architecturally as a rare example of a prosperous merchant's home of the later 15C. Among notable features are a fine contemporary local-style (Flemish) chimney, contemporary murals, and original fireplaces and chimneys on each of the three storeys.

Bridge Street descends to the *Harbour* (note that several bollards are made from cannons) from where there is a choice of boat trips, the most popular being to Caldey Island while others may include Lydstep, shark or other fishing, or diving. South of the harbour, beyond the narrow neck of the promontory, *St. Catherine's Island*, a detached rock not accessible at high tide, still shows the remains of a small fort built in 1869 but now dismantled. On Castle Hill, the small green extension promontory to the E of the harbour, are a statue to Prince Albert (J.E. Thomas, 1865) and the minor remains of the *Castle*, effectively only a gatehouse, a double tower, and traces of domestic buildings. *Tenby Museum* (Tel: 0834–2809), set up here as long ago as 1878, is both museum and art gallery. The former shows archaeological and historical material relating to Pembrokeshire, and to Tenby in particular, this including a maritime section, while in the art gallery, with a permanent collection and temporary exhibitions, the emphasis is on local interests and local artists, which include Augustus and Gwen John.

CALDEY ISLAND (frequent boat service in summer), 2¼m S of Tenby and owned by Cistercians, is 1½m long (E to W) and ¾m across at its widest point; but the island is so broken by bays and small inlets that the coast is some 9m in length. Features of Caldey are the abbey (the monks of which farm), the flowers (from which the monks distil scent), an Ogham stone and the seabirds. The island's Welsh name of Ynys Pyr probably stems from the name of the Celtic first abbot.

History. Excavations have revealed evidence of early occupation in the form of Stone Age human remains, flint tools and Roman pottery of the 1C. The first monastery seems to have been a Celtic foundation of the late 5C, probably a colony from St. Illtyd's house at Llantwit Major, though some authorities suggest that Caldey may have been the earlier foundation. The most famous abbot of those days was St. Samson of Dol, the patron saint of Caldey, some of whose relics are still preserved. How long this Celtic monastery lasted is not known, but it was presumably still in existence when the Caldey Ogham stone was given its Latin inscription added in the early 9C. Nothing more is heard of the island, except that it became a nest of pirates and fell prey to Norse raids, until 1127 when it was given to the Benedictines of St. Dogmaels who built the priory church and associated monastic quarters. These Benedictines held peaceful possession for over 400 years, until 1534 when their monastery was dissolved and the island given by Henry VIII to secular owners.

Caldey passed through several hands, until 1897 when it was bought by the Rev. W. Done Bushell who did much restoration work. In 1906 it was sold to Aelred Carlyle and became the home of the Anglican community which he founded and which in 1913 was received into the Church of Rome as Benedictine. In 1928 the Benedictines moved to Prinknash Park in Gloucestershire, their place being taken by Cistercians from Chimay in Belgium and their monastery in 1958 being raised to the status of abbey.

On the cliffs, facing Tenby, there is a round Norman tower, now converted to a chapel. The principal building on the island is the *Abbey*, built in 1907–11 (tours for male visitors), the church of which, seriously damaged by fire in 1940, was restored by 1951 and is now typically Cistercian in its austerity. *St. David's Church*, near the abbey, in plan closely resembles the Irish churches of the 8C and 9C and in origin is probably as old if not older. However it was largely rebuilt by the St. Dogmaels Benedictines (note the Norman W door) so that it could serve as the island's parish church, and it was restored at the turn of the current century by W. Done Bushell. To the S is the *Old Priory*, probably on or close to the site of the early Celtic house. Originally built by the St. Dogmaels Benedictines, the structure seen today dates from the 13–14C, with 15C additions, and is of interestingly defensive character. The restored *Church of St. Illtyd,*, with a leaning spire, houses the Caldey Ogham Stone, a slab of sandstone with a cross and a double inscription, one in Ogham (5–6C) and the other in Latin added in the early 9C; the inscription bids those who pass pray for the soul of Catuoconus (Cadogan).

Beyond the Old Priory the track continues to the lighthouse of 1828.—*St. Margaret's Island*, off the NW tip of Caldey, is a nature reserve and bird sanctuary.

From Tenby, scenic walks can be taken N or S along the cliffs, the walk northwards to *Saundersfoot* (some 3m) via Monkstone Point being particularly popular. Southwards, the National Park coastal path leads to *Penally* and *Lydstep*, for both of which see below.

At *Gumfreston*, 1¹/₂m W of Tenby on B4318, there is a small and primitive 12C church (14C tower) with a unique semicircular recess (perhaps a baptistery) on the N of the nave; traces of murals (martyrdom of St. Lawrence); a bronze Sanctus bell; and, in the churchyard, three medicinal springs.—*Manor House Wildlife and Leisure Park* (Tel: 06467–201), a short way farther along B4318, offers exotic birds and animals, an adventure playground, a model railway, a tropical plant house and falcon displays.

For Tenby to *Cardigan* and *Aberaeron*, see Rte 46.

Tenby is left by A4139. Just outside the town there is a road to the right signed Penally, off which, almost immediately, a small road, again to the right, in a few yards reaches a path up to *Hoyle's Mouth* (torch required), a cavern over 50ft deep, containing several chambers and sometimes identified with the Cave of Belarious in Shakespeare's 'Cymbeline'. Excavations during the 19C produced Palaeolithic flint tools, a human jaw and teeth, and bones of extinct animals, some of these finds being in Tenby's museum.—This small road continues for 2m to *St. Florence*, a village which in medieval times was a harbour (today's Ritec stream was a sea inlet) and a centre of Flemish influence. The primitive 13C church of local type has a curious little dark chapel off the S transept.

2m (from Tenby) **Penally**, a village by one tradition both the birth and the burial place of St. Teilo. The 13C church houses a fine wheel-cross of the 10 or 11C and also a fragment of a 9C cross shaft, the work on both, and particularly on the wheel-cross, showing Northumbrian influence. And here too is the graveslab of William and Isemay de Raynoore (1260–90), in dark slate with the alabaster faces let into it in low relief.—*2m. Lydstep Head* (footpath from village), a headland of 54 acres with precipitous limestone cliffs, was in 1936 given to the National Trust by the Pilgrim Trust. Steps descend to the Lydstep Caverns, all, except for Smugglers' Cave, accessible only at low tide.

2m. **Manorbier Castle** (Tel: 0834–871394), to the S off A4139 and in a commanding position above the red sandstone bay of the same name, is perhaps best known as the birthplace of Giraldus.

History. The name may derive from Maenor Pyr (Manor of Pyr), the man thought to have been the first Celtic (5C) abbot of Caldey. The stone castle was probably first built by Odo de Barri in the early 12C, Giraldus being born soon afterwards in about 1146; later, in 1188, he visited here on his journey with Archbishop Baldwin and he is on record as having described Manorbier as 'the pleasantest place in Wales'. Confiscated by Henry IV in 1400, Manorbier was long held by the Crown but returned to private ownership when acquired by a local landowner at the Restoration. Since then the estate has known a variety of owners.

Of Odo de Barri's original building virtually nothing remains, bar, perhaps, the inner side of the gateway, and the buildings seen today—which include the great hall, the chapel, towers and turrets—are essentially of the 13–14C. Life-size figures, including of course Giraldus, 'people' the castle.

Manorbier Church, on the opposite side of the valley, has a mid 12C nave roughly contemporary with Odo de Barri's original Norman structure; but there were successive additions, the church as a result having a somewhat irregular appearance. Features of interest are the 13C tower of local type; the pointed barrel vaults; the primitive arches cut in the walls of the nave; the base of the rood-loft in the N aisle and the gallery by which it is reached; and the 13C recumbent effigy of a de Barri. *King's Quoit*, above the E arm of Manorbier Bay, is a burial chamber the capstone of which at one end rests on two short pillars and at the other on the ground.

3m. Hodgeston where the church chancel preserves a double piscina and a mutilated triple sedilia.

1m. The ruins of ***Lamphey Bishop's Palace** (WHM. Tel: 0222-465511), dating from the early 13C to the late 16C and one of the several manors of the medieval bishops of St. David's, lie just NE of Lamphey village. Despite the troubled early medieval period, and in contrast to the palace at St. David's itself, Lamphey has virtually no defensive features and survived as a country retreat of some elegance and comfort.

History. It is known that Wilfred, the last Welsh bishop before the appointment of the Norman Bernard, was here in 1096. The earliest surviving stonework (early 13C) is parts of the walls of the old hall, to the W end of which the camera (private apartments) was added later in the century. Bishop Gower (1328–47) much extended the palace, adding a new hall (Great Hall), angled away from the SE corner of the earlier one, a battlemented wall enclosing the courtyard, and (NW) the gatehouse. In the 15–16C, largely under the influence of Bishop Vaughan (1509–22), the camera was remodelled and a chapel was added beyond the N side of the old hall. Finally, with the Reformation, Lamphey passed to the Crown, being granted in 1546 to the Devereux, earls of Essex; Robert, the favourite of Elizabeth I, lived here as a boy.

Approaching the palace by road a stream is reached, the marshy hollows on either side of which mark the site of the fishponds, first mentioned in a survey of 1326. At the palace the most notable architectural features are Bishop Gower's typical high battlemented parapets carried on arcades which rise above the roofs, and the circular chimneys above the camera and great hall marking the period of Devereux ownership.

The main range of the palace extends roughly W to E to the S of the *Gatehouse* with its arcades. The *Camera* (c 1250, and 15–16C), at the W end, was a two-storeyed building, the attendants occupying the ground floor and the bishop having his private apartments above, these comprising a main room and, projecting to the S, bedroom and garderobe. Access for the bishop was by either of two stairs at the NE and SE corners. The bedroom and garderobe area was extended in the 15C. Of the fireplace in the centre of the N wall, the lower part is original, but the circular chimney above, as also that at the NW angle of the building, are Devereux insertions. The *Old Hall* (early 13C), extending E from the camera, is a much ruined two-storeyed building in which the actual hall occupied the upper floor. A garderobe juts out to the SW, and it has been suggested that this and the bishop's garderobe were drained by a channel from the stream, though no trace of this has been found. The *Chapel* (early 16C), on the N side of this hall, must have replaced a chapel elsewhere. Also on the upper floor, it has a traceried window of five lights in its E wall, and two other windows, each of three lights, in the N wall. The small projection to the NE was the Sacristy. Bishop Gower's *Great Hall* (1328–47, and 16C), forming the E end of the palace range, is a two-storeyed building with a huge, long vaulted ground floor lit by slits. The hall above was over 70ft long, and from the camera the bishop reached it by crossing the old hall and then using a short passage. The fireplace in the NE corner and the southward projecting garderobe are the main Devereux features. The Gower arcaded parapet is best seen from the N side.

For (*2m*) **Pembroke** and Pembroke to (*8M*) **Milford Haven**, see Rte 44A.

45 Castlemartin Peninsula

Some 9m from E to W and 8m from N to S, the Castlemartin peninsula extends W and SW from Pembroke, its shores being those of Milford Haven and the outer Bristol Channel. The peninsula is best known for its sandy bays and rugged cliff scenery along the S and W coasts (much of it National Trust property) between roughly St. Govan's Head and Angle. The Pembrokeshire Coast National Park footpath follows much of the coast, but is forced inland between St. Govan's Head and Freshwater West by Ministry of Defence ranges, which, when in use, may prevent access to St. Govan's Chapel, the most interesting site on the peninsula, and also to some of the best of the coast (red flags and roadside warnings). The northern part of the peninsula, fringing Milford Haven, is spoilt by oil installations and a large power station.—Castlemartin Black Cattle were one of the two breeds which early in this century were crossed to produce today's Welsh Black. Castlemartin is also associated with the Castlemartin Yeomanry, the force which in 1797 so efficiently dealt with the French landing near Fishguard, thus earning the distinction of the only Battle Honour awarded for action on British soil (Lord Cawdor, commander of the Yeomanry, owned the Stackpole estate; now National Trust, see below).

The clockwise round described below starts from Pembroke and, excluding diversions, covers some 29m, made up of 6m from Pembroke to St. Govan's Chapel; 6m from St. Govan's Chapel to Castlemartin; 7m from Castlemartin to Angle; and 10m from Angle back to Pembroke.

Pembroke is left by B4319 which, after about 2m, reaches a minor road E to *Stackpole* (or *Cheriton*) *Elidor* where the church, with a Norman tower, contains several effigies, these including Richard de Stackpole and his wife (14C) and the coloured kneeling figure of Roger Lort, with his wife and 12 children (17C). The adjacent National Trust Stackpole property of some 2000 acres includes woodland, eight miles of cliffs, two beaches and a hillfort on Green-ala Point (parking at Stackpole Quay and Broadhaven).—After rather over another mile along B4319 another minor road bears S for **Bosherston** with a church (1250–70) interesting for a passage-squint which projects externally in the angle between the S transeptal chapel and the chancel. In the churchyard, what is probably a Preaching Cross (?14C) may have been adapted from an older Crucifixion, the evidence being the differing stone of the shaft and the cross and the relief Christ at the intersection; possibly dismantled at the Reformation, the original shaft seems to have been lost and later replaced by a new stumpy one. Just NE of the village an Iron Age or earlier fort has been tactically sited between two inlets, here too being the *Lily Ponds* (or *Fish Ponds*), the result of silting and at their best in June. A standing stone (the *Harold Stone*), about ½m N of the ponds, shows two cup marks.

Ministry of Defence ranges stretch W from Bosherston and a notice board beside the road states whether or not the approach is clear to *St. Govan's Chapel (1m S), fascinating for its primitiveness, its age (at least 13C and possibly as early as 6C), its legends and for its extraordinary position blocking a narrow cleft in the cliff.

History and Legend. St. Govan, a 6C Irishman from Wexford, was a follower of St. Ailbe (died 527), a native of Solva, near St. David's, who founded the monastery at Dairinis near Wexford. After a visit to Rome, St. Govan entered

Dairinis, of which he eventually became abbot. It was in his old age that he came to Pembroke (presumably because of the link with St. Ailbe), intending to live out his closing years as a contemplative hermit, and it is at this point that legend takes over. Walking along these cliffs, he was attacked by ruffians, whereupon, in response to his prayer for help, the cliff opened, folded gently around him and then opened again as soon as the terrified attackers had fled—a rescue which left any worthy Celtic 'sanctus' with little choice but to build his cell here. St. Govan died here in 586 when, tradition continues, he was buried beneath his chapel's altar.

Descending to the chapel (steps) the visitor enters a world of primitive piety and charming legend. As to the structural age of this place, much if not all the stonework is probably medieval replacement of some much earlier original, but there can surely be little doubt that the rock cell and well are very early Christian. In the tiny chapel there is a stone altar, to the side of which steps lead to a small cell cut in the rock; here there is a fissure, said to be the one which miraculously sheltered St. Govan and which today grants the wishes of anyone able to turn round within it without touching the sides. On the S wall of the chapel are a piscina, an aperture and a window, and in the upper plastering of the W wall there is a circle containing an inscription of unknown age or meaning. Apparently there was once a well in the floor near the door, known for its ability to cure eye and skin complaints, and the well now seen outside the chapel, though now dry, was also effective both for granting wishes and curing. And, to complete the chapel's story, the boulder outside is known as Bell Rock because it hides a silver bell, once in the little bell-tower, stolen by pirates but retrieved by angels and secured within the rock.

When the range is clear, walkers can follow the path W above precipitous cliffs 100 to 160ft high, soon reaching *Huntsman's Leap*, a narrow fissure over which a horseman is said to have leapt—successfully, though soon afterwards dying of fright. Beyond, soon after Huntsman's Leap, and again at the E and W ends of Bullslaughter and Flimston bays, there are remains of clifftop fortifications, the last fort being above the isolated *Elegug Stacks* (roughly 3m from St. Govan's Chapel), massive limestone pillars alive with breeding birds between April and early August ('elegug' is Welsh for guillemot). From here a small road connects to (1½m) B4319 at *Warren*.

From St. Govan's Chapel, motorists must retrace through Bosherston to rejoin B4319, now followed W and in under 2m reaching *Warren*, with the small road S to Elegug Stacks (see above). In *Castlemartin*, a short way farther W, the church contains a Norman font and an organ of 1842 said once to have been owned by Mendelssohn. From here B4319 returns to the coast in 2m at *Freshwater West*, with a beach notoriously dangerous for bathing. Just beyond, in the SE angle where B4319 meets B4320, is the *Devil's Quoit*, a burial chamber with a 12ft capstone. The village of *Angle*, to the W at the end of B4320, stands at the W of Angle Bay which opens into Milford Haven. On *Thorn Island*, 1½m W of Angle, the fort was built in 1852–59.

B4320 is now followed E through somewhat desolate surroundings with oil installations and the Pembroke Power Station to the north. However, the church at *Rhoscrowther*, on the S edge of the oil installations, recalls through its dedication those very different 7C days when St. Decuman was born here, later, it is said, paddling a coracle across to Dunster in Somerset where he was martyred in 706 while at prayer. The church, though basically Norman, was considerably rebuilt in both the 19 and early 20C.—B4320 in another 5m reaches *Monkton* and **Pembroke**, for both of which see Rte 44.

46   Tenby to Cardigan and Aberaeron

A478 to Cardigan. A487 to Aberaeron. Total distance 56m.—*10m.*
Narberth.—*14m.* **Crymych (Presely Hills).**—*7m.* **Cilgerran
Castle.**—*2m.* **Cardigan.**—*23m.* **Aberaeron.**

The first half crosses the Presely Hills, with many prehistoric
archaeological sites and a choice of walks and minor roads.
Between Cardigan and Aberaeron diversions can be made to the
coast with its cliff scenery.

Tenby, see Rte 44B.—*5m. Kilgetty* and *Begelly*, see Rte 44A which is
crossed here.—*3m. Templeton* owes its name to the fact that it once
belonged to the Knights Templar of Slebech who may have had a
hospice here. Traditionally it was near here that a battle was fought
in 1081 which established Gruffydd ap Cynan and Rhys ap Tewdwr
as princes of N and S Wales. *Sentence Castle*, a motte immediately W
of Templeton, is, with nearby Narberth Castle, traditionally the site
of the 'Mabinogion's' legendary court of Pwyll, Prince of Dyfed.
Perhaps Narberth was the site of the court, and perhaps Sentence
was the nearby mound of Gorsedd Arberth to which Pwyll was wont
to withdraw, for the mound had the magical property that if anyone
high-born sat here he could only leave after either receiving a wound
or seeing a wonder. Pwyll was lucky, and met the beautiful
Rhiannon.—*2m.* **Narberth** (1000 inhab), originally Castell yn Arberth
and, as noted above, traditionally associated with the 'Mabinogion',
is today a market town sprawled over a steep hill. The town's origins
may reach back to an early Dark Ages castle, perhaps that of Pwyll,
and it is known that Narberth was burnt by the Norsemen in 994. The
Castle, in the S part of the town, though successor to others,
including an early Norman fortress destroyed by the Welsh in 1115, is
now no more than fragments of the castle built in about 1246 by Sir
Andrew Perrot; later given by Henry VII to Sir Rhys ap Thomas of
Carew, it was dismantled after the Civil War. The *Church*, in origin
13C and with a tower of that date, was rebuilt in 1879.—
Heronsbrook, just SW, is a country park and waterfowl centre, with
several ponds, a woodland walk, picnic areas and some rare farm
breeds (Tel: 0834–860723). A40 (Rte 43) is crossed 1m N of Narberth.
Beyond (*5m*) *Llandissilio* the road climbs the ridge that separates the
Eastern Cleddau valley (W) from that of the Taf. *Penrhos Cottage*
(Tel: 0437–731328), some 2m NW beyond Llanycefn, is preserved as
a traditional Welsh cottage of the early 19C.—*9m* (from Llandissilio)
Crymych, for the Presely Hills.

The PRESELY HILLS (or Mynydd Preseli, or various other spellings),
contained within a fat pouch of the Pembrokeshire Coast National
Park hanging southward between Cardigan and Fishguard, may be
said to be the last southern outriders of the Cambrian Mountains,
that rather vague range running much of the length of Wales which,
though named on many maps, is better known for its parts than for its
whole. An open, wide-shouldered brown moorland picked out with
patches of afforestation and with rocky outcrops similar to the tors of
Dartmoor, the hills lift, in places surprisingly steeply, to 1760ft above

the surrounding pastoral landscape. Flocks of Welsh mountain sheep graze their home areas and mountain ponies are also to be found. But it is the wealth of prehistoric archaeology that is the main interest here. Not only are the hills dotted with cairns, burial chambers, standing stones, stone circles and suchlike, but they also provided, between about 2000–1500 BC, the 'blue stones' for Stonehenge, these (weighing up to four tons) being dragged some 140 miles, part of the way along the ancient trade route from Ireland; a route which, incidentally, explains Geoffrey of Monmouth's belief that the stones in fact came from Ireland. Walkers are warned of the dangers of bogs and mists.

The hills are crossed by A478 (this Route), by B4313 running SE from Fishguard, and by B4329 running SW from Cardigan, these latter two crossing at Greenway (Rosebush). Several minor roads and lanes link these, but not across the main mass of the hills which lies between A478 and B4329, between Crymych on the former and Greenway. Most of this part is accessible only to walkers. Two choices are described below, one for walkers (a basic 6m from A478 near Crymych to B4329 near Greenway) and a motorists' circuit of some 20 miles.

Walkers. What is sometimes called the Bronze Age Track, dating from perhaps 1500 BC, grew out of the movement between the main centre of the Beaker People on Salisbury Plain and Whitesand Bay (NW of St. David's), and thence by boat to Ireland's Wicklow Hills with their copper and gold. From the E the starting-point is *Croesfihangel Tumulus*, 1m SW of Crymych and reached by road, a much eroded burial mound which produced urns and cremated remains dated to c 1000 BC. To the S, off the other side of the road and a bit hard to find in a bank, is a burial chamber of c 2500 BC, today little more than collapsed stones. On *Foeldrygarn* (1200ft), ¹/₂m NW, there is an Iron Age stone-walled hillfort, ramparts here defending the E gate but the S and W gates relying on the steep slopes. Hut sites were excavated here in 1899, finds (some in Tenby's museum) including beads, pottery and a stone lamp. The cairns on the top may be Bronze Age burials. Foeldrygarn provided five volcanic dolerite stones for Stonehenge.

Carn Ferched, beside the track ³/₄m after leaving Croesfihangel, is a small Bronze Age burial mound. To the S of the track after another ³/₄m *Carnmenyn* (Cairn of the Boulders) was the main source of Stonehenge's dolerite stones, while *Carnalw*, 1m N of Carnmenyn, provided four blue rhyolite stones. In another ¹/₂m the track reaches *Bedd Arthur* (Arthur's Grave), an oval of 12 stones, probably Bronze Age and erected perhaps 2000 years before Arthur's time. Next, in ¹/₂m, a branch track S in 1¹/₂m reaches *Cerrig Meibion Arthur* (see Motor Circuit). The main track continues W, in 2m beyond Bedd Arthur reaching a point ¹/₂m N of *Foel Cwmcerwyn* or *Presely Top* (1760ft), the highest point of the hills and with several burial cairns. The view from here can extend from Dunkery Beacon on Exmoor (76m SE) to Snowdonia (85m NNW) and can also include the Irish coast. In legend ('Mabinogion, Culhwch and Olwen') it was on Foel Cwmcerwyn that Arthur and his men had one of their running fights with the giant boar Twrch Trwyth, once a king but punished for his evil ways. Two of Arthur's sons were among the many warriors killed by the boar and are commemorated by Cerrig Meibion Arthur (see Motor Circuit). In another 1¹/₂m the track reaches B4329 at *Bwlch Gwynt* (Windy Pass), here joining the Motor Circuit.

A **Motor Circuit** may start along the minor road which heads W off

A478 immediately S of Crymych, within the first mile passing between the tumulus and burial chamber which mark the start of the Bronze Age Track. Beyond, this very minor road—part through fields, part across moorland, part unfenced—hugs the southern slopes of the hills to reach, in rather over 3m from Crymych, a fork near the junction of several streams. Here the righthand road should be followed, this almost immediately reaching another fork, *Gors-Fawr Stone Circle*, ½m down the lefthand road here, being of the early Bronze Age with 16 stones and two outliers. It has been suggested that it may have been of some ritual significance that the line of sight between these outliers aims directly at Carnmenyn (see above). The righthand small road in 1½m crosses the little Afon Wern at a lonely unfenced spot on the border of the National Park. Here, just N, are the *Cerrig Meibion Arthur*, the Stones of the Sons of Arthur, killed on Foel Cwmcerwyn by the savage boar Twrch Trwyth (see Walkers, above). This road now briefly heads S, almost immediately passing *Maen-y-Parc*, a probably Early Bronze Age standing stone which may have been deliberately shaped. Beyond, in another 2m, B4313 is reached, 1m to the W being two more prehistoric sites; *Dyffryn Circle* is an early Bronze Age burial mound surrounded by stones, and, just to its E, stands the *Budloy Stone*.

B4329 is now followed NE, in rather over 1m N of *Greenway* reaching *Bwlch Gwynt*, or Windy Pass, at the end of the walkers' Bronze Age Track. Here, to the W, rises *Foel Eryr* (Eagle Mountain. 1535ft) with a Bronze Age cairn. The name *Tafarn-y-Bwlch* (Tavern of the Pass), 1m N of Bwlch Gwynt and now a farm, recalls that this was once a coaching and drovers' inn. *Brynberian* is another 1½m farther N along B4329, ½m S being *Bedd-yr-Afanc* (Monster's Grave), thought to be a Neolithic long cairn, or gallery grave, of perhaps 2500 BC and of its kind unique in Wales.

Motorists may now either continue to Cardigan by B4329 and A487, or, at *Crosswell* (1m beyond Brynberian), navigate minor roads E and SE back to Crymych (5m from Crosswell).

Leaving Crymych, A478 continues N, in 7m (but 1m E of the main road) reaching the ruins of **Cilgerran Castle** (WHM and NT. Tel: 0239-614249 or 0222-465511) which, though small compared to some, are theatrically and romantically sprawled across a steep promontory above the Teifi. The ruins have inspired artists such as Richard Wilson and J. M. W. Turner and in the 18C and 19C the boat excursion up from Cardigan was a principal local attraction.

History. An early castle may have been built by Roger de Montgomery c 1093, but it is known that this site was developed by Gerald de Windsor, to whom it was granted by Henry I. It was taken and at least partly destroyed by Rhys ap Gruffydd in 1164; taken by William Marshal, Earl of Pembroke, in 1204; recovered by Llewelyn the Great in 1213; and finally retaken by William Marshal's son, William, in 1233. This last rebuilt the castle, and it is to this period that most of the surviving structure belongs. But Cilgerran was soon neglected, and is recorded as being in ruins by 1326. There were frequent changes of ownership during the Wars of the Roses, and, with the abolition of the Marcher Lordships in 1536, Cilgerran passed to the Vaughans who seem to have lived here until the early 17C. Thereafter the place became no more than romantic ruins. Cilgerran was acquired by the National Trust in 1938, and has since been placed under the guardianship of the Crown.

Occupying a steep promontory above the Teifi and a tributary stream, the castle required little defence on the W and N, but was vulnerable from other directions. The main castle is the inner ward, protected on the E and S by two large round towers and a gatehouse, joined by curtain wall. This inner ward is separated by a ditch from a much larger outer ward to the S, itself defended by a wall and ditch.

The modern entrance is at the SW corner of the OUTER WARD, which represents the bailey of the early Norman motte-and-bailey castle. On the W little defence was necessary. On the S there was a ditch and wall, but though the former can be made out, very little survives of the wall. On the E there was a wall, but this collapsed during slate quarrying in the 19C, and, apart from a short section at the NE corner, the wall seen today is 19C replacement. The most interesting feature of the outer ward is the rock-cut ditch which separates it from the inner ward.—The INNER WARD is entered at its SW corner by the *Gatehouse* (early 13C), which stood beyond a drawbridge over the ditch and was defended by two portcullises. The two round towers and associated curtain wall all date from the early 13C. The *East Tower*, probably the first to be built, was of four storeys and projects outwardly well clear of the curtain wall, this enabling the wall to be covered by fire from the tower. The ground floor is entered directly from the ward. The room on the top floor had a fireplace, and the tower's only outward-facing window. The *West Tower* is generally similar, though one difference was that the entrance was at the first floor, probably by wooden steps, the ground floor being reached by a trap-door from the first (the present doorway into the ground floor is a 14C modification). Other work included the wall dividing the ground floor into two, and the stair on the E side of the new ground floor entrance. The very ruined *North-West Tower* was a rectangular 14C addition. Of the buildings that would have filled the ward only traces survive. The *Kitchens* would have been against the curtain to the S of the North-West Tower, and in the SW corner of the ward something of a 13 or 14C limekiln can be seen. The oldest parts of the castle (12C) are two short sections of wall; one between the kiln and the gatehouse, and the other some remains on the edge of the cliff halfway along the ward's N side.

Cardigan Wildlife Park (Tel: 0239–614449), beside the Teifi and approached from near Cilgerran village, is a 50 acre nature area which includes woodland and river bank among its varied habitats. Among the attractions are nature trails, hides for wildlife observation, relics of slate quarrying, and enclosures showing a range of wild and domestic animals.

2m. **Cardigan**, see Rte 42, crossed here. A487, heading NE, runs at some distance from the sea, but several roads lead to the coast with its cliff scenery (*Aberporth* is an attractive fishing and holiday village. *Penbryn* is a hamlet with a beach and, immediately N, the National Trust Llanborth Farm property. *Llangranog* is a hamlet in a narrow ravine between headlands, and *Lochtyn Farm*, just N of Llangranog, is a National Trust property of 215 acres which include cliffs, an island and two beaches).—*17m. Synod Inn.* For **New Quay**, 4m N by A486, and (*6m*) **Aberaeron**, see Rte 41A.

INDEX

Topographical names are in **bold** print; names of persons in *italics*; other entries in roman print. Where there are several references, the more important are in appropriate cases printed bold.